ATLAS
of the
CIVIL WAR

by

Steven E. Woodworth

and

Kenneth J. Winkle

FOREWORD

by

James M. McPherson

OXFORD
UNIVERSITY PRESS

OXFORD
UNIVERSITY PRESS

Oxford   New York

Auckland   Bangkok   Buenos Aires   Cape Town   Chennai
Dar es Salaam   Delhi   Hong Kong   Istanbul   Karachi   Kolkata
Kuala Lumpur   Madrid   Melbourne   Mexico City   Mumbai   Nairobi
São Paulo   Shanghai   Taipei   Tokyo   Toronto

Oxford is a registered trade mark of Oxford University Press

Published by Oxford University Press, Inc.
198 Madison Avenue, New York, New York 10016
www.oup.com/us

Library of Congress Cataloging-in-Publication Data
Woodworth, Steven E., Atlas of the Civil War / by Steven Woodworth and
Kenneth J. Winkle; Foreword by James M. McPherson

ISBN 0-19-522131-1

1. United States—History—Civil War, 1861–1865.   2. United States—History—
Civil War, 1861–1865—Maps.   3. United States—History—Civil War, 1861–1865—Statistics.
I. Winkle, Kenneth J.   II. Title.

E468.W754 2004
973.7—dc 22

1 2 3 4 5 6 7 8 9 10

Cartography © 2004 Cartographica Limited
Text © Steven E. Woodworth and Kenneth J. Winkle
Foreword © James M. McPherson
All rights reserved

Printed in Singapore

ATLAS
of the
CIVIL WAR

CONTENTS

Men and boys alike met the call to arms.
Here newly-recruited drummer boys
practice their art in Washington D.C.

KEY TO MAPS

TYPE STYLES

A R K A N S A S
State

C l a r k e   C o u n t y
County

SAN ANTONIO DE BEXAR
City

Austin
Town

Fort Belknap
Other / Annotation

Pedernates River
Sharpshooter's Ridge
Blue Ridge Mountains
Physical Feature

ABBREVIATIONS

P.O.	Post Office
C.H.	Court House
R.R.	Railroads
Stn.	Station
Mt.	Mountain

PHYSICAL FEATURES

Stream/Run

River

Major River/Estuary

Canal

Marsh or Swamps

Forest

Agriculture

Hill or Mountain Feature

GENERAL SYMBOLS

Urban Area

Town / Settlement

Farm or Building

Station

Church

Bridge

Pontoon Bridge

Ford

Historical International Border

Modern International Border

Internal Border

Major Road

Minor Road

Small Road / Track

Railroad

GENERAL MILITARY SYMBOLS

Camp Site

Teepee/Indian Settlement

Trading Post

Battle Site

Explosion

Land Mine

Artillery

Artillery Reserve

Fort/Battery/Redoubt

Fortification Lines

Siege Lines

Skirmish Lines

Sail or Sail-steam ship

Gunboat/Ironclad

Ships (various types)

ARMY COLORS

Confederate

Union

Confederate HQ

Union HQ

Advance

Retreat

Movement

ARMY SYMBOLS

LEE MEADE Army Commander

XXX V LONGSTREET Corps

XX STONEY Division

ARMISTEAD Army Units of Varying Strength

BIRNEY Cavalry Units of Varying Strength

XX XX First Position

XX XX Later Position

11

Foreword

The preeminence of the Civil War in America's historical consciousness is no secret. Dozens of national and state Civil War battlefield parks attract millions of visitors every year. Four popular Civil War magazines publish bi-monthly issues with a combined circulation of 250,000. Some four hundred Civil War Round Tables flourish around the country (and several more exist abroad), most of them holding monthly meetings and several of them publishing elaborate newsletters. At least forty thousand reenactors don their replica uniforms and take up their replica weapons to stage scores of mock battles each year. An estimated 50 million viewers in the United States and elsewhere have watched the eleven-hour television documentary on the Civil War produced by Ken Burns. Elaborate preparations are already underway for the bicentennial commemoration of Abraham Lincoln's birth in 2009 and the sesquicentennial observation of the war years from 2011 to 2015. And Civil War books continue to roll off the presses—an average of one per day for the fifty thousand days since the war ended in 1865. What explains this fascination with a war that almost tore the country apart? Asking the question that way suggests part of the answer. The war almost did destroy the United States as one nation. The division of the United States into two countries might have created a precedent for the Balkanization of North America into several nations. But Northern victory resolved two fundamental, festering issues left unresolved by the Revolution of 1776 and the Constitution of 1787 that founded the nation: First, whether this fragile republican experiment called the United States would survive in a world bestrode by kings, queens, emperors, czars, military dictators, and theories of aristocracy which proclaimed that all men are *not* created equal. And second, whether this nation that boasted itself a "beacon of freedom" to all mankind would continue to hold four million human beings in bondage. Both of these questions remained open until 1865. Many Americans had doubted whether the republic would survive; many Europeans had predicted its demise; some Americans advocated the right of secession and periodically threatened to invoke it; eleven states did invoke it in 1860–1861. But since 1865 no state or region has seriously threatened secession. And the war abolished slavery, the institution that had made a mockery of America's self-proclaimed renown as a land of liberty, an institution that Abraham Lincoln had branded in 1854 a "monstrous injustice" that "deprives our republican example of its just influence in the world—enables the enemies of free institutions, with plausibility, to taunt us as hypocrites."

In the process of preserving the Union of 1776 while purging it of slavery, the Civil War also transformed it. Before 1861 the words *United States* were a plural noun: "The United States *are* a large country." Since 1865 United States has been a singular noun. The North went to war to preserve the *Union*; it ended by creating a *nation*. This transformation can be traced in Lincoln's most important wartime speeches and writings. His first inaugural address contained the word *Union* twenty times and the word *nation* not once. In Lincoln's first message to Congress on July 4, 1861, he used *Union* forty-nine times and *nation* only three times. In his famous public letter to Horace Greeley, editor of the *New York Tribune*, of August 22, 1862, concerning slavery and the war, Lincoln spoke of the Union nine times and the nation not at all. But in the Gettysburg Address fifteen months later he did not refer to the Union at all but used the word *nation* five times. And in the second inaugural address, looking back over the past four years, Lincoln spoke of one side's seeking to dissolve the Union in 1861 and the other side's accepting the challenge of war to preserve the nation.

The old decentralized republic, in which the post office was the only agency of national government that touched the average citizen, was transformed by the crucible of war into a centralized polity that taxed people directly and created an internal revenue bureau to collect the taxes, expanded the jurisdiction of federal courts, created a national currency and a federally chartered banking system, drafted men into the army, and created the Freedmen's Bureau as the first national agency for social welfare. Eleven of the first twelve amendments to the Constitution had limited the powers of the national government; six of the next seven, starting with the Thirteenth Amendment in 1865, radically expanded those powers at the expense of the states. The first three of these amendments converted four million slaves into citizens and voters within five years, the most rapid and fundamental social transformation in American history—even if the nation did backslide on part of that commitment for three generations after 1877.

From 1789 to 1861 a southern slaveholder was president of the United States two thirds of the time, and two-thirds of the Speakers of the House and presidents pro tem of the Senate had also been southerners. Twenty of the thirty-five Supreme Court justices appointed during that half century were southerners. The institutions and ideology of a plantation society and a caste system that had dominated half the country before 1861 and sought to dominate more went down with a great crash in 1865 and were replaced by the institutions and ideology of free-labor entrepreneurial capitalism. For better or for worse, the flames of Civil War forged the framework of modern America.

This transformation came at great cost. The 620,000 soldiers who died in the war constituted two percent of the American population at that time. If the United States were to lose two percent of its population in a war fought today, the number of American war dead would be five and one-half million. Why did America experience such a bloodbath? Why did Americans go to war against each other with a ferocity unmatched in the Western world between the end of the Napoleonic Wars in 1815 and the beginning of World War I in 1914?

The origins of the Civil War can be traced to the early years of the republic when slavery was abolished in the states north of Maryland and Kentucky but became more firmly entrenched than ever in the states south of that latitude. Clashes between proponents and opponents of slavery endangered national unity several times during the next half century but were averted by compromises that extended the line between slavery and freedom westward without resolving the fundamental conflict. The annexation of Texas in 1845 and the acquisition of another 700,000 square miles of territory from Mexico in the war of 1846–1848 reopened this running sore. Southerners wanted slavery to be permitted in this new territory; antislavery northerners wanted to keep it out. The North had the votes in the House of Representatives to pass the Wilmot Proviso (a resolution introduced by Congressman David Wilmot of Pennsylvania) stating that slavery should be excluded from all territories acquired from Mexico. Southern senators defeated this resolution when it came before them. Their leader, Senator John C. Calhoun of South Carolina, offered instead a series of resolutions affirming that slaveholders had the constitutional right to take their slave property into any United States territory. These opposing views set the stage for a crisis when gold was discovered in 1848 in California, potentially the richest of the regions acquired from Mexico. Eighty thousand gold seekers poured into California in 1849. To achieve some degree of law and order, they organized a state government and petitioned

Congress for admission as the thirty-first state. This petition met fierce resistance from southerners, for California's constitution prohibited slavery. The crisis intensified when President Zachary Taylor encouraged the huge territory of New Mexico—which included most of the present-day states of New Mexico, Arizona, Utah, Nevada, and Colorado—also to apply for statehood without slavery.

Proslavery southerners vowed to secede from the Union rather than accept this violation of their professed right to have slavery made legal in these territories. "If, by your legislation, you seek to drive us from the territories of California and New Mexico," thundered Robert Toombs of Georgia, "*I am for disunion.*" Senator Albert Gallatin Brown of Mississippi demanded of the North "to give us our rights" in California; "If you refuse, I am for taking them by armed occupation." The controversy in Congress became so heated that Senator Henry S. Foote drew a loaded revolver during a debate and his colleague Jefferson Davis challenged an Illinois congressman to a duel. The American nation seemed to hang together by a thread, with armed conflict between North and South a real possibility in 1850.

But calmer heads prevailed, and the Compromise of 1850 averted a showdown. This series of laws admitted California as a free state but left it to the settlers themselves in the remainder of the Mexican Cession, divided into the territories of New Mexico and Utah, to decide whether to have slavery. (Both territories did legalize slavery during the 1850s but few slaves were taken there.) At the same time, Congress abolished the slave trade in the District of Columbia, ending the shame (in northern eyes) of the buying and selling of human beings within sight of the White House and the Capitol. But the Compromise of 1850 also compensated the South with a new, draconian fugitive slave law that gave federal marshals the power to recover slaves who had escaped into free states and carry them back into slavery.

The Compromise of 1850 did not resolve the sectional crisis; it merely postponed the final break for a decade. During that decade the conflict escalated to larger proportions and a higher pitch of emotional intensity. The Fugitive Slave Law embittered northerners compelled to watch black people—some of whom had lived in their communities for years—being returned by force to slavery. Northern resistance to the law and several spectacular rescues of fugitive slaves angered southerners who denounced Yankee refusal to honor their rights. In an attempt to bring more slave states into the Union, southerners agitated for the purchase of Cuba from Spain and the acquisition of additional territory in Central America. Private armies of "filibusters" composed mainly of southerners even tried to invade Cuba and Nicaragua to overthrow their governments and bring these regions into the United States—with slavery. Nothing did more to polarize slave and free states, however, than the Kansas-Nebraska Act of 1854 and the subsequent guerrilla war between pro- and anti-slavery partisans in Kansas Territory. The region that became the territories of Kansas and Nebraska was part of the Louisiana Purchase acquired by the United States from France in 1803. Three slave states had come into the Union from the Louisiana Purchase—Louisiana, Missouri, and Arkansas—and one free state, Iowa. When Missouri had applied for statehood in 1819, Northern congressmen tried to ban slavery there. This effort precipitated a controversy that was settled in 1820 by the Missouri Compromise, whereby Missouri came in as a slave state (and Maine as a free state) but slavery was banned in the remainder of the Louisiana Purchase north of the latitude of 36° 30'. Regarded by northerners as an inviolable compact, the Missouri Compromise lasted for thirty-four years. But in 1854 southerners broke it by forcing Stephen A. Douglas of Illinois, chairman of the Senate Committee on Territories and leader of the Northern Democrats, to agree to the repeal of the exclusion of slavery from the northern part of the Louisiana Purchase. Douglas caved in to southern pressure even though he knew it would "raise a hell of a storm" in the North. It certainly did. Indeed, the storm was so powerful that it swept away many Northern Democrats and gave rise to the Republican Party, which pledged to keep slavery out of Kansas and all other territories. One of the most eloquent spokesmen for this new party was an Illinois lawyer named Abraham Lincoln. Like many northern people, Lincoln had always considered slavery to be an institution "founded on both injustice and bad policy.... There CAN be no MORAL RIGHT in the enslaving of one man by another." But like most northerners, he recognized the constitutional right of slavery to exist in states where it was legal. Nevertheless, the institution should not be allowed to take root in any new territories. The great "moral wrong and injustice" of the Kansas-Nebraska Act, said Lincoln, was that it opened territory previously closed to slavery, thus putting the institution "on the high road to extension and perpetuity" instead of restricting it as the first step toward persuading the states where it existed to abolish it gradually.

Lincoln and the other members of the new Republican Party, which carried most of the free states in the presidential election of 1856, were convinced that the growing polariziation between free and slave states was an "irrepressible conflict" between social systems based on free labor and slave labor. The United States, said Lincoln in 1858 at the beginning of his famous campaign against Douglas for election to the Senate, was a house divided between slavery and freedom. But "'a house divided against itself cannot stand.' I believe this government cannot endure, permanently half *slave* and half *free*." By preventing further expansion of slavery, Lincoln hoped to "place it where the public mind shall rest in the belief that it is in the course of ultimate extinction."

Douglas won the senatorial election in 1858. But two years later the Democratic Party split into northern and southern halves over the refusal by Northern Democrats to endorse the southern demand for a federal slave code to enforce the right of property in slaves in territories such as Kansas where a majority of residents opposed the institution. The Northern Democrats nominated Douglas for president in 1860 and the Southern Rights Democrats nominated John C. Breckinridge of Kentucky on a slave-code platform. This split ensured the election of the Republican candidate—who turned out to be Abraham Lincoln. Lincoln won the presidency by carrying every Northern state on a platform pledging to restrict the further expansion of slavery. This was the first time in more than a generation that the South had lost effective control of the national government. Charles Francis Adams, the son and grandson of presidents and a founder of the Republican Party, wrote in his diary when he learned the news of Lincoln's election: "The great revolution has actually taken place…. The country has once and for all thrown off the domination of the Slaveholders."

The slaveholders thought so too. In response to the northern revolution that elected Lincoln, they launched their counterrevolution of secession.

James M. McPherson

1861
THE COMING OF WAR

Within days of Lincoln's election, the South Carolina legislature called a convention to take the state out of the Union. By a vote of 169 – 0, the convention dissolved the state's bonds of union with the United States and proclaimed South Carolina an independent nation. One by one, Mississippi, Florida, Alabama, Georgia, Louisiana, and Texas did the same in January and February 1861—they did so because, for the first time in more than a generation, the South had lost effective control of the national government—without a single electoral vote from the slave states, the antislavery Republican Party had won the presidency. Most whites in the seven states of the Lower South feared that the "Black Republicans"—as they contemptuously labeled the party of Lincoln—would enact policies, as Lincoln had forecast in his House Divided speech of 1858, to place slavery in the course of "ultimate extinction." Before Lincoln took office on March 4, delegates from these seven states met in Montgomery, Alabama, and drew up a constitution for the "Confederate States of America." They constituted themselves a provisional Congress and elected Jefferson Davis of Mississippi and Alexander H. Stephens of Georgia as provisional president and vice president. Militia of these states had already seized the national arsenals, mints, forts, and other property within their borders—with the significant exception of Fort Sumter in Charleston harbor.

Secession transformed the principal issue of the sectional conflict from the future of slavery to the survival of the nation itself—when Lincoln took his oath to "preserve, protect, and

defend"—the United States and its Constitution, the "United" States had ceased to exist—Lincoln and most of the northern people refused to accept the legitimacy of secession. "The central idea pervading this struggle," said Lincoln after war had broken out in 1861, "is the necessity that is upon us, of proving that popular government is not an absurdity. We must settle this question now, whether in a free government the minority have the right to break up the government whenever they choose."

Seven states had seceded, but eight slave states had not yet acted when Lincoln became president. Efforts to prevent their secession were clouded by the uncertainty of events at Fort Sumter. Confederate forces ringing Charleston harbor demanded its surrender. Major Robert Anderson and his eighty-odd U.S. soldiers in the fort refused. But Anderson also informed Lincoln that the garrison would be starved out by mid-April unless resupplied. Any attempt by the U.S. Navy to shoot its way into the harbor would place the onus of starting a war on the North and drive the rest of the slave states into secession. But surrender of the fort would legitimize secession and discredit Lincoln in the North. After sleepless nights, the president hit upon an ingenious solution: he would send in unarmed ships with "food for hungry men" and notify Southern leaders in advance of his peaceful intentions. This placed the burden of decision on Jefferson Davis.

Davis did not hesitate; he ordered Confederate artillery to fire on the fort before the relief ships arrived. They did so on April 12, forcing the fort to surrender the following day. The North erupted in patriotic fury at this attack on the American flag, and flocked to recruiting offices in response to Lincoln's call for seventy-five thousand men to suppress the rebellion—this call in turn provoked Virginia, Arkansas, Tennessee, and North Carolina to secede. The shooting war had begun, and before it was over 620,000 Union and Confederate soldiers would be in their graves.

Jefferson Davis, a graduate of West Point who had served as secretary of war under President Franklin Pierce, was inaugurated as president of the Confederacy on February 18, 1861.

Below: This Currier and Ives cartoon shows the southern states seccession early in 1861 as a doomed enterprise.

THE "SECESSION MOVEMENT".

TERRITORIAL EXPANSION, 1783 – 1859

THE PRIMARY HALLMARK OF AMERICAN history from the end of the Revolution to the Civil War was expansion. Territorial expansion provided the foundation for many other kinds of growth—population growth, economic growth, and even the nation's growth as a military power. In 1783, the Treaty of Paris that granted America its independence from Great Britain gave the new nation a vast public domain, stretching between the East Coast and the Mississippi River, that beckoned Americans to move westward and encouraged the nation to expand. The Constitution allowed new states to join the Union on an equal footing with the original thirteen, facilitating a national growth that seemed, to many Americans, imperative and even inevitable.

As president, Thomas Jefferson urged his country to create an expansive empire, which he labeled "An Empire for Liberty," that would allow

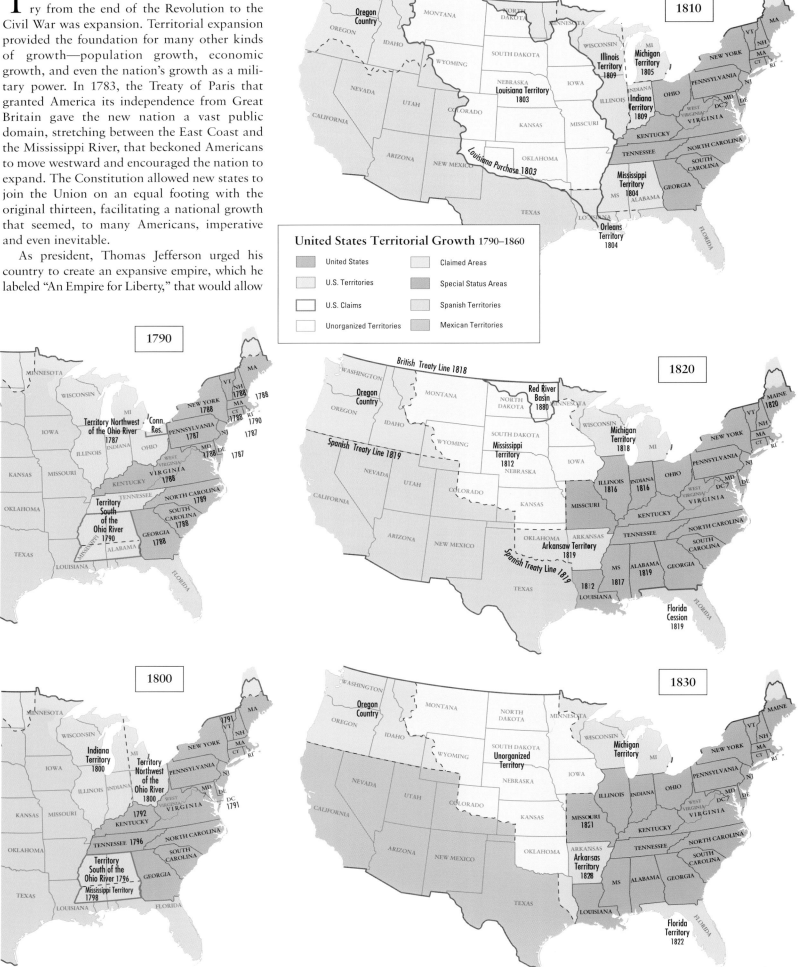

United States Territorial Growth 1790–1860

- United States
- U.S. Territories
- U.S. Claims
- Unorganized Territories
- Claimed Areas
- Special Status Areas
- Spanish Territories
- Mexican Territories

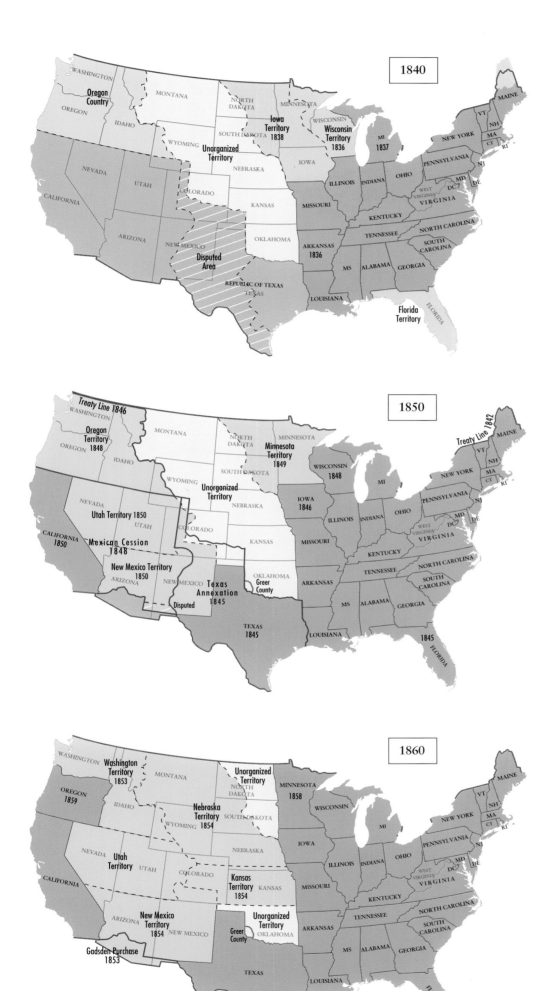

1840

WASHINGTON
Oregon
Country
OREGON
MONTANA
NORTH
DAKOTA
MINNESOTA
MAINE
VT NH
NEW YORK MA
CT RI
IDAHO
Iowa
Territory
1838
WISCONSIN
Territory
1836
MI
1837
WYOMING
SOUTH DAKOTA
Unorganized
Territory
PENNSYLVANIA
NJ
NEVADA
NEBRASKA
IOWA
ILLINOIS INDIANA OHIO
MD
DC
DE
UTAH
COLORADO
KANSAS
MISSOURI
WEST
VIRGINIA
VIRGINIA
CALIFORNIA
KENTUCKY
NORTH CAROLINA
ARIZONA
NEW MEXICO
OKLAHOMA
TENNESSEE
SOUTH
CAROLINA
Disputed
Area
ARKANSAS
1836
MS ALABAMA GEORGIA
REPUBLIC OF TEXAS
TEXAS
LOUISIANA
Florida
Territory
FLORIDA

1850

Treaty Line 1846
WASHINGTON
Oregon
Territory
1848
OREGON
MONTANA
NORTH
DAKOTA
MINNESOTA
Minnesota
Territory
1849
Treaty Line 1842
MAINE
VT
NH
NEW YORK MA
CT RI
IDAHO
WISCONSIN
1848
MI
WYOMING
SOUTH DAKOTA
Unorganized
Territory
PENNSYLVANIA
NJ
DE
NEVADA
Utah Territory 1850
UTAH
NEBRASKA
IOWA
1846
ILLINOIS INDIANA OHIO
MD
WEST
VIRGINIA
VIRGINIA
CALIFORNIA
1850
Mexican Cession
1848
COLORADO
KANSAS
MISSOURI
KENTUCKY
NORTH CAROLINA
New Mexico Territory
1850
ARIZONA
NEW MEXICO
Texas
Annexation
1845
OKLAHOMA
Greer
County
ARKANSAS
TENNESSEE
SOUTH
CAROLINA
Disputed
MS ALABAMA GEORGIA
TEXAS
1845
LOUISIANA
1845
FLORIDA

1860

WASHINGTON
Washington
Territory
1853
MONTANA
Unorganized
Territory
NORTH
DAKOTA
MINNESOTA
1858
MAINE
VT NH
NEW YORK MA
CT RI
OREGON
1859
IDAHO
Nebraska
Territory
1854
SOUTH DAKOTA
WISCONSIN
MI
WYOMING
PENNSYLVANIA
NJ
NEVADA
Utah
Territory
UTAH
NEBRASKA
IOWA
ILLINOIS INDIANA OHIO
MD
DE
CALIFORNIA
COLORADO
Kansas
Territory
1854
KANSAS
MISSOURI
WEST
VIRGINIA
VIRGINIA
KENTUCKY
NORTH CAROLINA
ARIZONA
New Mexico
Territory
1854
NEW MEXICO
Unorganized
Territory
Greer
County
OKLAHOMA
ARKANSAS
TENNESSEE
SOUTH
CAROLINA
Gadsden Purchase
1853
MS ALABAMA GEORGIA
TEXAS
LOUISIANA
FLORIDA

America to spread the advantages of its institutions, including its republican government, across North America. In 1803, Jefferson fulfilled his own dream with the Louisiana Purchase, which nearly doubled the size of the nation, extending its boundary to the Rocky Mountains. The Lewis and Clark Expedition (1804–1806), which Jefferson sent out to explore his purchase, reached those mountains, crossed them, and continued to the Pacific. Jeffersonian expansiveness, of course, required the dispossession of Native Americans—who were forcibly "removed" from their traditional homelands—and the conquest of other nations who stood in America's way. Territorial expansion also aggravated sectional tensions, as southerners sought to extend slavery westward and northerners increasingly tried to stem that movement.

American expansiveness reached its fullest expression during the 1840s. First proposed in 1845, the theory of Manifest Destiny asserted that America had a God-given right, even a duty, to expand—and extend its government, culture, and religion across the continent to the Pacific coast. The election of 1844 proved a major turning point. The Democratic presidential nominee, James K. Polk of Tennessee, embraced expansion and called for the annexation of both Texas and Oregon Territory. Flexing America's growing military muscle, Polk threatened to fight Great Britain to get all of Oregon northward to latitude 54° 40', adopting the slogan "54° 40' or Fight." His Whig opponent, Henry Clay, warned that expansion would indeed bring war, and civil war, as well. Clay urged the nation to slow down its headlong rush to the Pacific.

Polk's narrow victory, however, committed America to Manifest Destiny, bringing war and civil war with it. Under Polk, America annexed Texas (1845) and Oregon (1846), defeated Mexico in the Mexican War (1846–1848), and acquired the Mexican Cession (1848). This series of acquisitions increased the nation's territory by forty percent. In acquiring one-half of Mexico, however, America aggravated its festering sectional wounds. Northerners and southerners competed to settle the new territory, hoping to carve it into free states or slave states thereby gaining political and economic advantages over their sectional rivals. All attempts at compromising this struggle—the Missouri Compromise of 1820, the Compromise of 1850, and the Kansas-Nebraska Act of 1854—could only postpone, rather than prevent, civil war. All told, America's territory more than tripled between 1783 and 1859, and its population increased eight-fold, to 31 million. The original thirteen states grew into thirty-three, fifteen of which maintained slavery. Expansion made the new nation into an economic and military power, but also created a sectional division that soon proved impossible to repair.

EMANCIPATION IN THE NORTH

THE SAME REVOLUTION THAT GRANTED Americans independence from Britain also started the long process that led eventually to the end of slavery. During the Revolutionary War, the British encouraged slaves to flee their American masters, and perhaps twenty thousand crossed over to the enemy, including thirty slaves belonging to Thomas Jefferson. Overall, about five percent of American slaves went over to the British and gained their freedom during the Revolution.

As they struggled for independence, many Revolutionaries concluded that slavery violated the basic rights for which they were fighting. Americans reasoned that true "independence" required self-reliance, while dependence on slavery demeaned both whites and blacks. New ideas about human equality, based on Enlightenment ideals and revolutionary ideology, inspired an abo-

lition movement during the 1770s. In 1787, Congress prohibited slavery in the Old Northwest—modern Ohio, Indiana, Illinois, Michigan, and Wisconsin.

During the generation that followed the Revolution, every other northern state embraced some form of emancipation. Support for emancipation tended to vary inversely with the number of slaves in each state. Two New England states abolished slavery outright—Vermont in its constitution of 1777 and Massachusetts by judicial decree in 1781. Most of the slaves in these states were domestic servants. The other northern states had larger slave populations that worked in agriculture and played a significant economic role. New York, in particular, had as many slaves as the rest of the North combined. Pennsylvania, New Jersey, and New York adopted gradual emancipation pro-

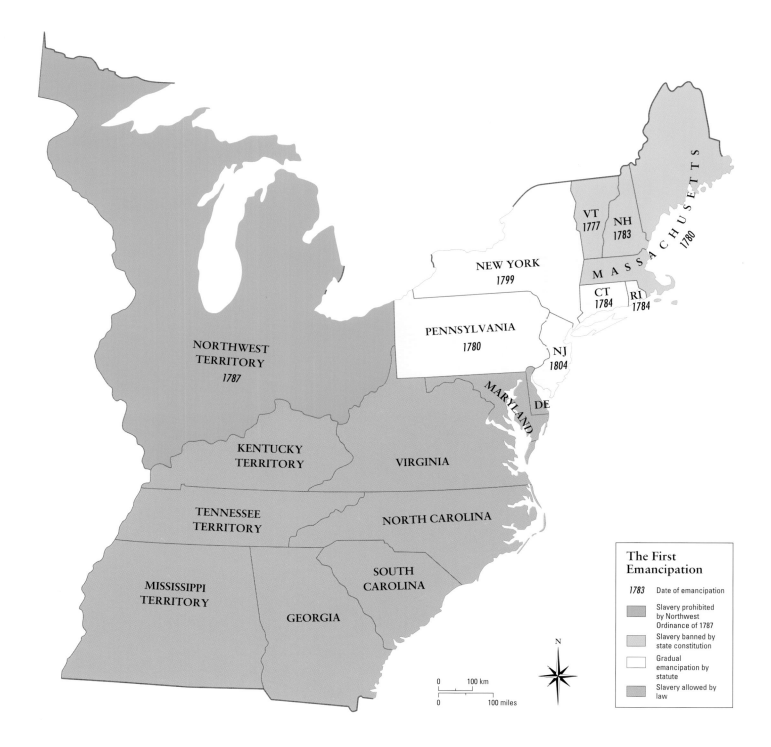

The First
Emancipation

1783   Date of emancipation

   Slavery prohibited by Northwest Ordinance of 1787

   Slavery banned by state constitution

   Gradual emancipation by statute

   Slavery allowed by law

grams that kept all current slaves in bondage for life, while freeing all slaves born in the future at the time they turned twenty-five or twenty-eight. In this way, the Revolutionary generation of the North could guarantee freedom to future generations while keeping their own slaves. By the time New Jersey became the last northern state to adopt an emancipation plan in 1804, America was half slave and half free. A large class of free African Americans arose in the North that eventually numbered a quarter million. By 1810, three-fourths of African Americans in the North were free. By 1840, virtually all of them were. The revolutionary movement toward emancipation culminated in 1808 when Congress banned the importation of slaves into the United States.

The South, with its economy increasingly dependent on slaves, debated the merits of abolishing slavery, but then rejected it. Southerners preferred voluntary programs of emancipation, and the Upper South—Virginia, Maryland, and Delaware—passed laws making it easier for individual masters to free their slaves. A free black population rivaling that of the North grew up in the urban areas of Baltimore, Richmond, and Washington, D.C. Overall, ninety percent of the South's free African Americans lived in the Upper South. Southerners, as well as many northerners, embraced "colonization," a movement to send free blacks to Africa. The colonization movement culminated in the founding of Liberia in 1821. Overall, these initial inroads against slavery led to the division of America into two sections—free states and slaves states—as well as to the creation of a viable population of free African Americans and a growing commitment to stop the spread of slavery.

Free Black Disenfranchisement 1840

- Free blacks barred from voting
- Black suffrage with restrictions
- No restrictions

MAINE

VT

NH

NEW YORK

MA

CT RI

MICHIGAN TERRITORY

PENNSYLVANIA

NJ

ILLINOIS

INDIANA

OHIO

MARYLAND

DE

MISSOURI

KENTUCKY

VIRGINIA

TENNESSEE

NORTH CAROLINA

ARKANSAS

SOUTH CAROLINA

MISSISSIPPI

ALABAMA

GEORGIA

LOUISIANA

FLORIDA

N

0   200 km

0   200 miles

The Webb family toured the northern states promoting African American interests and history, and also gave dramatic readings from Uncle Tom's Cabin, *by Harriet Beecher Stowe.*

25

PREWAR POLITICS

Andrew Jackson, 1767–1845. His superb campaign organization and enormous popularity won him two of the great elections of the nineteenth century.

Presidential Election 1828

- Jacksonian Democrat (Andrew Jackson)
- National Republican (John Quincy Adams)
- (5) Number of voting electors
- Territory not voting

Popular vote
(total: 1,155,350)

508,064 44.0%
647,286 56.0%

Electoral vote
(total : 261)

83 31.8%
178 68.2%

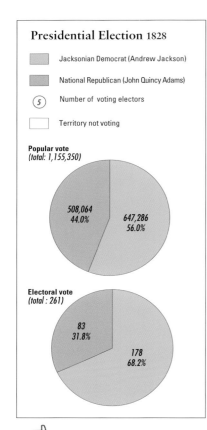

MICHIGAN TERRITORY

UNORGANIZED TERRITORY

MAINE 8 1

7 8

VT 20 16 NH 15

NEW YORK MA CT

RI 4

PENNSYLVANIA 8

28 8 NEW JERSEY 3

ILLINOIS 3 INDIANA 5 OHIO 16 MD 6 DE 5

MISSOURI 3 KENTUCKY 14 VIRGINIA 24

TENNESSEE 11 NORTH CAROLINA 15

ARKANSAS TERRITORY SOUTH CAROLINA 11

MS ALABAMA 5 GEORGIA 9

5 LOUISIANA FLORIDA TERRITORY

Until the 1820s, American government was not particularly democratic. Originally, Americans believed that only the most "virtuous" members of society should exercise a voice in government by voting and holding public office. Most states had property qualifications for voting, requiring voters either to own land or at least pay taxes, assuming that property ownership was a necessary condition of political independence and that only taxpayers should play a role in levying and spending taxes. Some states set up complex systems in which voting and running for different offices required varying amounts of land ownership. A few states, especially in Puritan-dominated New England, had state-run churches and required voters to be church members in good standing. New states that entered the Union questioned these older ideas of restricted suffrage and began a movement toward a more democratic government. Ohio started this process in 1803, allowing landless men to vote and hold office. Most states retained their taxpaying requirement for voting but joined Ohio in dropping the property requirement. Virginia was the first state to abandon religious qualifications for voting, under its Statute of Religious Freedom authored by Thomas Jefferson. The movement toward separation of church and state culminated in the 1830s, when Massachusetts and Connecticut gave up their religious requirements for voting.

As America moved toward universal white male suffrage, political participation surged. As late as 1824, only twenty-seven percent of eligible voters went to the polls. The presidential election of 1828, in which Andrew Jackson ousted John Quincy Adams, was the first presidential election in which more than one-half (fifty-eight percent) of eligible voters cast ballots. Jackson became forever linked with this dramatic surge in democracy, and the term "Jacksonian Democracy" described the new system in which parties courted "the common man." Jackson believed in rotation in office and the spoils system, in which the winning party threw out the losers and reaped the material benefits of victory.

Parties became "political machines" that rewarded voters with patronage—public offices and government contracts—in exchange for their support. Party newspapers printed more propaganda than news, creating strong emotional attachments among lifelong party members. Voter turnout surged even higher—to eighty percent—when another hero from the war, William Henry Harrison, was elected in 1840, and it remained high for the rest of the century. As the Civil War approached, parties adopted a military model of organization. Candidates "campaigned" for office, parties rallied their loyal "troops" for the political "battle" ahead, and voters "marched" to the polls on election day. Mass participation made government more democratic, but many Americans feared that political parties were too responsive, surrendering to the passions of the moment in their quest to attract voters and win elections. Parties increasingly appealed to the emotions and even prejudices of voters in an effort to win at all costs. Ultimately, "Jacksonian Democracy" gave way to "popular sovereignty," a new doctrine in which politicians followed voters rather than leading them. During the 1850s, parties refused to compromise and responded to sectional tensions by breaking apart. Instead of uniting the nation, presidential elections divided it.

After the election of 1852, the Whig Party disappeared, and a new sectional party, the Republicans, took its place. After the election of 1856, the Democratic Party split into two wings. By 1860, the American party system had shattered into four sectional pieces, allowing Abraham Lincoln to win the presidency without a single southern vote. As president, Lincoln asked the South to choose between "ballots or bullets." Refusing to accept the outcome of the presidential election, which they viewed as undemocratic, southerners chose "bullets" and seceded.

William Henry Harrison, 1773–1841. The origins of the modern political campaign are often traced back to 1840. Electioneering involved mass meetings, torchlight parades, and barbecues, and Harrison himself delivered twenty-six speeches in Ohio. The 1840 election provided the highest voter turnout in American history.

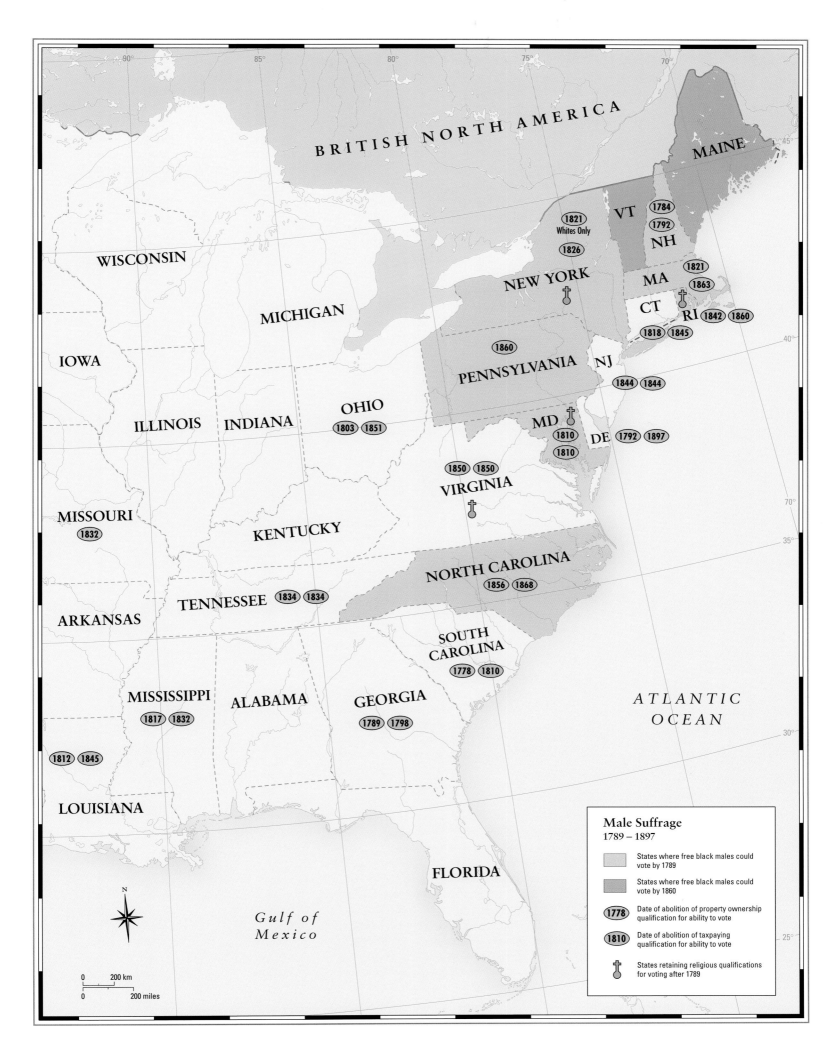

BRITISH NORTH AMERICA

MAINE

WISCONSIN

MICHIGAN

VT
1821
Whites Only
1826

1784
1792

NH

1821
1863

IOWA

NEW YORK

MA

CT

RI

1842 1860

ILLINOIS INDIANA

OHIO
1803 1851

1860

PENNSYLVANIA

1818 1845

NJ
1844 1844

MD
1810
1810

DE
1792 1897

MISSOURI
1832

KENTUCKY

1850 1850

VIRGINIA

ARKANSAS

TENNESSEE
1834 1834

NORTH CAROLINA
1856 1868

SOUTH
CAROLINA
1778 1810

MISSISSIPPI
1817 1832

ALABAMA

GEORGIA
1789 1798

ATLANTIC
OCEAN

1812 1845

LOUISIANA

FLORIDA

N

Gulf of
Mexico

0   200 km
0   200 miles

Male Suffrage
1789 – 1897

States where free black males could
vote by 1789

States where free black males could
vote by 1860

1778 Date of abolition of property ownership
qualification for ability to vote

1810 Date of abolition of taxpaying
qualification for ability to vote

States retaining religious qualifications
for voting after 1789

MISSOURI COMPROMISE OF 1820

WHEN MISSOURI TERRITORY PETITIONED CONGRESS for statehood in 1819, Americans faced a question that they had not thought much about during the preceding generation, but which would occupy the nation for generations to come: Should America allow slavery to expand as the nation moved westward? Congress had prohibited slavery in the Old Northwest in 1789, and all the northern states had ended slavery within their own boundaries by 1809. Now, the westward movement threatened to reverse that trend by allowing southern slavery to expand into the new territories. Many northerners hoped that requiring Missouri to give up slavery as the price of statehood would set the precedent that no new slave states could ever enter the Union.

A northern representative, James Tallmadge, introduced an amendment requiring Missouri to give up its slaves gradually after entering the Union. Missourians could keep their slaves until the slaves turned twenty-five, at which age they would receive their freedom. Southerners vociferously defended what they viewed as their right to take their slaves westward without any restrictions and the prerogative of the people of a territory to decide for themselves whether to become a free state or slave state. Heightening the sectional tension was the equal division of the nation between free states and slave states—eleven apiece at the time. Admitting Missouri would tip the balance of power either toward the slave South or the free North. Congress adjourned in 1819 without making a decision about the admission of Missouri or the status of slavery there. In the following year, however, the Missouri Crisis resumed and produced a deadlock that raised the threat of secession and even civil war.

Under the leadership of Kentucky's Henry Clay, Congress crafted the Missouri Compromise of 1820. Missouri entered the Union as a slave state but, to maintain the national balance of power, Maine would also enter the Union as a free state. In an effort to keep most of the West free from slavery, however, Congress drew the Missouri Compromise Line through the Louisiana Purchase, at 36° 30' of latitude. Any new states joining the Union south of the line, essentially modern Arkansas and Oklahoma, could keep slaves. But the vast region north of the line, encompassing all or parts of ten modern states, would remain free forever.

The South won slavery in Missouri and two other potential states. But they gave up the right to take slaves into most of the western territories and agreed to the precedent that Congress had the power to ban slavery in the territories and even new states. These concessions and the growing hostility of northerners to the spread of slavery prompted the aged Thomas Jefferson to label the compromise "a firebell in the night." Despite the growing tensions, Henry Clay gained the nickname The Great Compromiser, and the Missouri Compromise allowed most Americans to forget about the spread of slavery and the heightening sectional crisis for the next thirty years. Thereafter, slave states and free states entered the Union as pairs to preserve sectional harmony— Arkansas and Michigan, Florida and Iowa, and Texas and Wisconsin. The Mexican War shattered this system by creating new territories that were exempt from the Missouri Compromise.

OREGON COUNTRY
(Joint occupation by Great Britain and United States)

SPANISH POSSESSIONS

Missouri Compromise of 1820
Maine added as free and
Missouri as slave state

Free states and territories

Slave states and territories

Oregon Country

Spanish possessions

U.S. territory

0   150 km
0   150 miles

N

Henry Clay, an outstanding western leader of the 1820s, was elected to the Congress in 1810 and was Speaker of the House from 1811 to 1820, and from 1823 to 1825. He called slavery "the greatest of human evils," although he was, himself, a slave owner.

Free by Missouri
Compromise – 1820

MICHIGAN TERRITORY

MAINE
1820

VT
NH
NEW YORK
MA
CT
RI

PENNSYLVANIA

NEW
JERSEY

ILLINOIS
IN
OHIO
MD
DELAWARE

VIRGINIA

MISSOURI
1821
KENTUCKY

36° 30'

NORTH CAROLINA

TENNESSEE

ARKANSAS TERRITORY

SOUTH
CAROLINA

MS
ALABAMA
GEORGIA

LOUISIANA
FLORIDA

Purchased by U.S.
under Adams–Onís Treaty 1819
Organized as a territory 1822

COMPROMISE OF 1850

I N THE AFTERMATH OF THE MEXICAN WAR, the discovery of gold at Sutter's Mill in California set off a chain of events that propelled America toward civil war. The result was the Compromise of 1850, the last great sectional compromise between the North and the South. During the first year of the gold rush, eighty thousand "forty-niners" rushed to the gold fields, giving the newly acquired California Territory enough residents to apply for statehood. Most of the forty-niners came from the North or from Europe. Opposed to slavery, they petitioned Congress to make California a free state. Admitting California as a free state, however, would have upset the delicate sectional balance that had lasted for thirty years since the Missouri Compromise. (There were fifteen free states and fifteen slave states in 1850.) Led by the eloquent, fire-breathing John C. Calhoun of South Carolina, southerners threatened to secede if Congress admitted California as a free state.

To avoid civil war, Congress hammered out a complex sectional compromise under the leadership of Henry Clay of Kentucky, a Whig, and Stephen Douglas of Illinois, a Democrat. Under the Compromise of 1850, the opponents of slavery won two major concessions. First, California was admitted as a free state, shifting the balance of power in favor of the North. (Congress never again admitted another slave state.) Second, the slave trade was abolished in the nation's capital, the District of Columbia. (Slavery continued in the district, but slaves could no longer be bought and sold there.) In exchange, southerners won two major concessions. First, New Mexico and Utah territories adopted the principle of "popular sovereignty," meaning that the people of those territories—not Congress—could decide if they would become slave or free states. This was a major victory for the South, making this large region—modern New Mexico, Arizona, Utah, Nevada, and one-half of Colorado—eligible to adopt slavery. Second, Congress passed a new and stronger Fugitive Slave Law.

Thousands of fugitive slaves from the South were living openly in the North without fear of recapture and re-enslavement. The Fugitive Slave Law, which Ralph Waldo Emerson justifiably labeled "a filthy law," required federal marshals to hunt down runaway slaves in the North and return them to their owners in the South. The law set up special courts to try fugitive slaves without juries, legal representation, or the right of appeal. The law was retroactive, so fugitives who had lived freely in the North for decades were subject to re-enslavement. Northerners reacted to the Fugitive Slave Law with disgust. Every free state passed laws weakening or invalidating its provisions. The Underground Railroad emerged to help runaway slaves slip past the federal marshals, dubbed "slave catchers," and reach Canada. Northern mobs rescued runaways from slave catchers and set them free. As a result of the Fugitive Slave Law, more northerners than ever grew to hate slavery and resent the power of southern slave owners. Instead of relieving sectional tensions, as it was designed to do, the Compromise of 1850 aggravated them and pushed America ever closer to civil war.

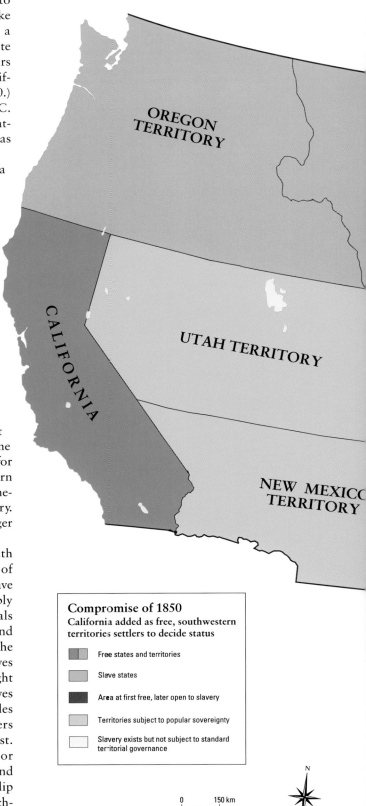

Compromise of 1850
California added as free, southwestern territories settlers to decide status

Free states and territories

Slave states

Area at first free, later open to slavery

Territories subject to popular sovereignty

Slavery exists but not subject to standard territorial governance

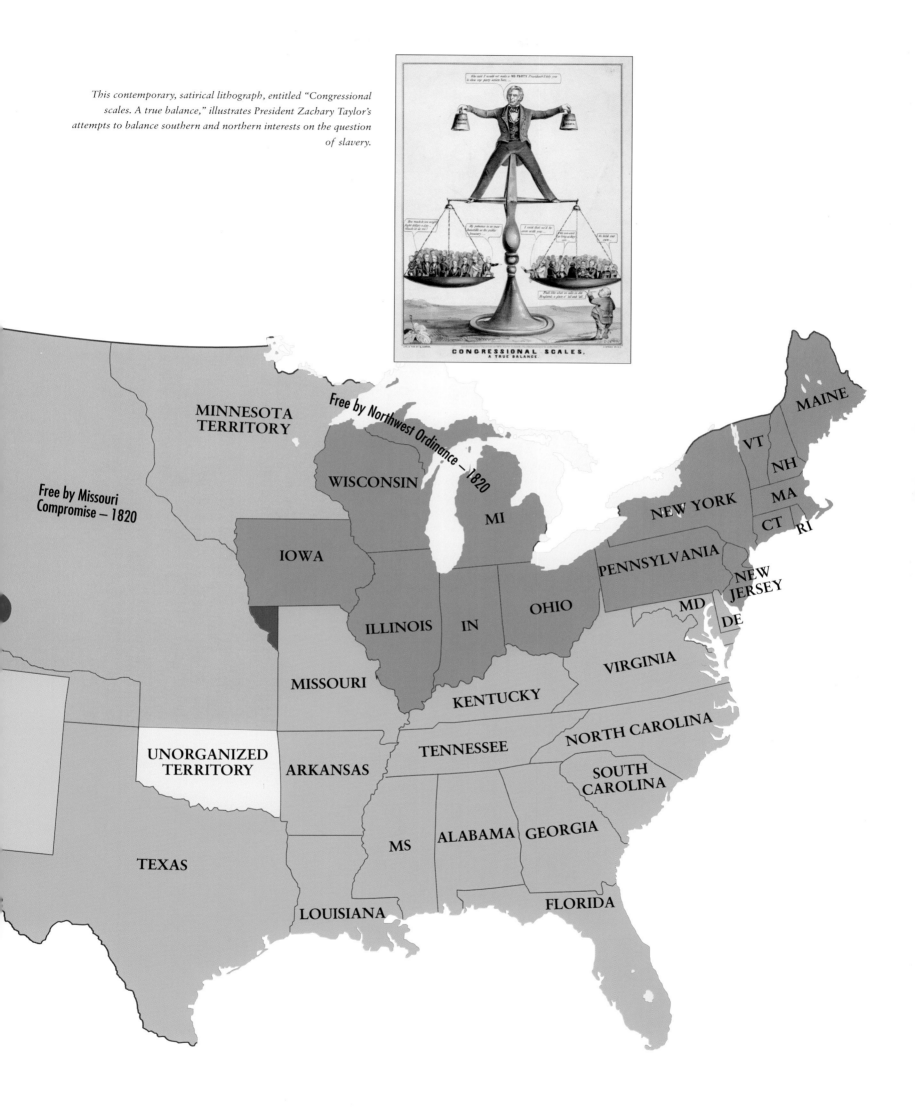

This contemporary, satirical lithograph, entitled "Congressional scales. A true balance," illustrates President Zachary Taylor's attempts to balance southern and northern interests on the question of slavery.

MINNESOTA TERRITORY

Free by Northwest Ordinance — 1820

MAINE

VT

NH

Free by Missouri Compromise — 1820

WISCONSIN

MI

NEW YORK

MA

CT

RI

IOWA

PENNSYLVANIA

NEW JERSEY

ILLINOIS

IN

OHIO

MD

DE

MISSOURI

KENTUCKY

VIRGINIA

UNORGANIZED TERRITORY

ARKANSAS

TENNESSEE

NORTH CAROLINA

SOUTH CAROLINA

TEXAS

MS

ALABAMA

GEORGIA

LOUISIANA

FLORIDA

KANSAS–NEBRASKA ACT

During the 1850s, Americans dreamed of constructing a transcontinental railroad that would connect the East Coast with the Pacific Ocean. The sectional controversy delayed construction, however, because both the North and the South wanted a route that would favor their region. A northern route would boost Chicago and feed western commerce through the Great Lakes. A southern route would boost the fortunes of St. Louis, Memphis, and New Orleans on the Mississippi River. Senator Stephen Douglas of Illinois supported the northern route.

As chairman of the Senate Committee on Territories, Douglas introduced a bill that organized the remaining parts of the Louisiana Purchase into a single territory called Nebraska. Once the territory had a government, Congress could charter a railroad through it along a northern route. Because the Missouri Compromise of 1820 prohibited slavery within the Louisiana Purchase north of 36° 30' latitude, Douglas's bill prohibited slavery in Nebraska Territory. Southerners refused to support the bill in an effort to block a northern railroad route and to readmit slavery into Nebraska. Douglas placated southern Democrats by submitting a new Nebraska Bill that divided the region into two territories, Nebraska and Kansas, and instituted popular sovereignty, which allowed the people in those territories to choose slavery or freedom. His bill went a step further and explicitly repealed the Missouri Compromise.

Under Democratic control, Congress passed the bill, and President Franklin Pierce signed the Kansas-Nebraska Act in May 1854. Even Douglas knew that this law went too far in favoring the South and predicted that "it will raise a hell of a storm." He was right. Northerners of all parties reacted with outrage, portraying the repeal of the Missouri Compromise as a southern conspiracy to reopen the West to slavery. They condemned Douglas as a self-serving politician who violated a sacred trust to build a railroad, attract southern votes, and win the presidency in 1856. "Anti-Nebraska" parties arose overnight, gathering former Whigs; Free-Soilers, who wanted to prevent the spread of slavery into new territories; and even anti-Douglas Democrats into a coalition that swept the North like a political whirlwind.

In the fall of 1854, Democrats lost their majority in Congress under an Anti-Nebraska landslide. Southerners gained firmer control of the Democratic Party, and a new Republican Party began to emerge in the North. The repeal of the Missouri Compromise convinced many northerners, including Abraham Lincoln, that a "slave power conspiracy" was using the Democratic Party to take over the country, subvert democratic government, and make slavery a national institution with no limits or restraints. The Kansas-Nebraska Act provoked a civil war in Kansas, where settlers argued over the future of the territory. Southern settlers created a "slave state" government at Lecompten, Kansas, while northerners created their own "free state" government at Topeka. The resulting bloodshed lent the nickname Bleeding Kansas to the region and provided a preview of the violence that would soon erupt on a national scale.

OREGON TERRITORY

UTAH TERRITORY

CALIFORNIA

Compromise Line of 1820

NEW MEXICO TERRITORY

Gadsden Purchase 1853

Kansas-Nebraska Act 1854
Settlers to decide in Kansas and Nebraska territories

- Free states and territories
- Slave states
- Slave or free, to be decided by popular sovereignty, Kansas-Nebraska Act
- Slave or free to be decided by popular sovereignty, Compromise of 1850
- Slavery exists but not subject to standard territorial governance

0   150 km

0   150 miles

This illustration demonstrates a popular indictment of the Democratic administration's responsibility for the bloodshed and violence as a result of the Kansas-Nebraska Act of 1854.

NEBRASKA TERRITORY

Free by Missouri Compromise — 1820

Open to Slavery by Kansas-Nebraska Act — 1854

KANSAS TERRITORY 1854

Topeka • • Lecompton

MINNESOTA TERRITORY

Free by Northwest Ordinance — 1820

WISCONSIN

IOWA

MI

ILLINOIS IN OHIO

MISSOURI

KENTUCKY

MAINE 1820

VT NH

NEW YORK MA

CT RI

PENNSYLVANIA

NEW JERSEY

MD DELAWARE

VIRGINIA

UNORGANIZED TERRITORY

ARKANSAS

TENNESSEE

NORTH CAROLINA

SOUTH CAROLINA

MS ALABAMA GEORGIA

TEXAS

LOUISIANA

FLORIDA

ELECTIONS OF 1852 AND 1856

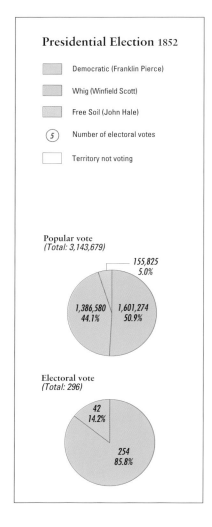

Presidential Election 1852

- Democratic (Franklin Pierce)
- Whig (Winfield Scott)
- Free Soil (John Hale)
- (5) Number of electoral votes
- Territory not voting

Popular vote
(Total: 3,143,679)

155,825
5.0%

1,386,580
44.1%

1,601,274
50.9%

Electoral vote
(Total: 296)

42
14.2%

254
85.8%

President Franklin Pierce 1804–1869. By signing the Kansas-Nebraska Act in 1854, Pierce did irreparable political damage to himself, and two years later he failed to win renomination from his party.

B ETWEEN 1852 AND 1856, the Whig Party disintegrated under the pressure of sectional tensions, and a new party, the Republican Party, took its place. The Compromise of 1850 satisfied no one. Northerners resented the parts that favored the South—popular sovereignty in New Mexico and Utah territories and the strengthened Fugitive Slave Law. Southerners resented the parts that favored the North—admission of California as a free state and the end of the slave trade in the nation's capital. Meanwhile, the compromise divided both parties. Northern Democrats supported the compromise, but southern Democrats opposed it. Northern Whigs opposed it, but southern Whigs supported it. To unify their parties, in 1852, both the Democratic and Whig conventions offered lukewarm support for the Compromise of 1850. Many voters concluded that the two major parties were avoiding the slavery issue and could see no real difference between them.

Voters' growing cynicism hurt the Whig Party. Winfield Scott, the Whig nominee, was a general in the Mexican War. Politically inexperienced, he ran as a war hero—a symbol of national unity—and avoided taking stands on important issues, including slavery. In fact, the Whig Party was badly split over slavery. "Cotton Whigs," who lived in the South or invested in cotton mills in the North, supported the expansion of slavery. "Conscience Whigs" opposed slavery as immoral and tried to restrict it. In the election of 1852, the

2222

2222222

Whigs carried only two free states and two slave states. The Democratic nominee, Franklin Pierce, won the election, and the Whigs were never nationally competitive again. Several parties attempted to replace the Whigs, but when Congress passed the Kansas-Nebraska Act in 1854, northerners' outrage at the repeal of the Missouri Compromise boosted the Republican Party. Republicans advocated keeping slavery out of the West and restricting it to the South, where it already existed. They reasoned that limiting the spread of slavery would undermine the institution, representing the first step in its eventual extinction. The Republicans were openly sectional, hoping to win the presidency on northern votes alone.

In 1856, three candidates ran for president. The Democrats nominated James Buchanan of Pennsylvania, who tried to stay neutral on the slavery issue. Millard Fillmore, a former Whig president, represented the American or Know-Nothing Party. Abandoning its antislavery emphasis but retaining its anti-immigrant and anti-Catholic platform, the American Party attracted many former Whig voters in the South. The Republicans nominated a popular military hero, John C. Frémont of California. Frémont was a famed army officer who had blazed the Oregon Trail and seized California during the Mexican War. Republicans knew that they could not win the election of 1856 but hoped to capture a majority of votes in the North. Frémont accomplished

that mission, coming in second and winning eleven of the sixteen free states. He was particularly popular in the Upper North—New England, New York, Michigan, and Wisconsin. Republicans reasoned that if they could carry more states in the Lower North, including Pennsylvania, Indiana, and Illinois, they could win the election of 1860. The election of 1856 proved that the Republicans could compete for the presidency and had a good chance of winning the election of 1860.

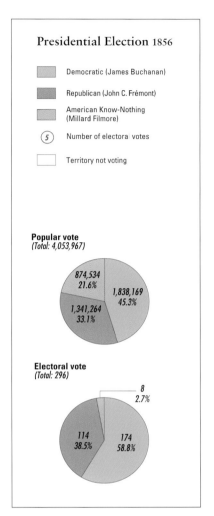

Presidential Election 1856

Democratic (James Buchanan)

Republican (John C. Frémont)

American Know-Nothing (Millard Filmore)

⑤ Number of electoral votes

Territory not voting

Popular vote (Total: 4,053,967)

874,534 21.6%
1,838,169 45.3%
1,341,264 33.1%

Electoral vote (Total: 296)

8 2.7%
114 38.5%
174 58.8%

President James Buchanan 1791–1868. Buchanan, who pledged to serve only one term, did little to halt the country's drift toward civil war. By 1860 he was relieved that his presidency was ending, and supported Vice President John Breckinridge as his successor.

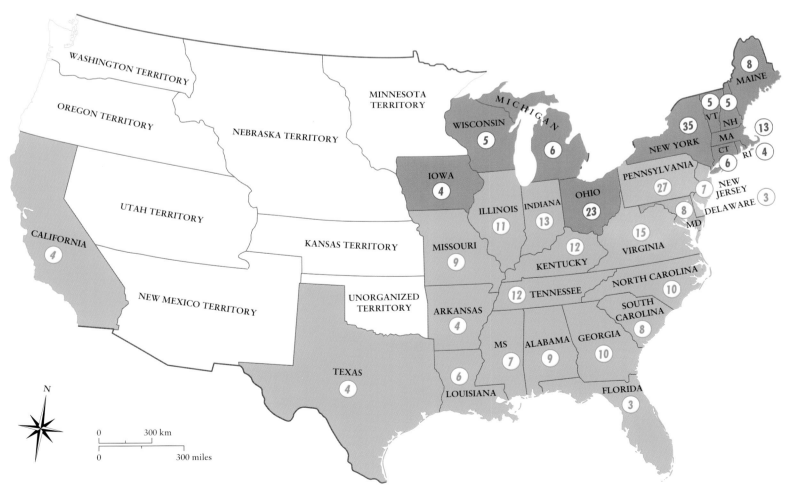

SPREAD OF SLAVERY, 1800 – 1860

This 1862 photograph depicts five generations of a slave family on a South Carolina plantation, illustrating a highly complex network of kin relationships. Despite the horrors of separation and sale, some black families survived slavery.

cal developments encouraged the spread of slavery westward across the Gulf Coast, created a region of intensive cotton production known as the Black Belt, and introduced slavery into new rice- and sugar-growing regions. Eli Whitney's cotton gin increased the efficiency of harvesting cotton by fifty times and established the profitability of "short-staple" cotton, which could grow all across the South. Soon, a new cotton region emerged in South Carolina and Georgia, which became dependent on slave labor.

After the War of 1812, cotton prices rose, and cotton plantations moved westward into Alabama and Mississippi. Planters near Rodney, Mississippi, developed a new variety of cotton that was easier to pick, and "Rodney" cotton quickly spread westward across the Gulf Coast. Meanwhile, rice production boomed along the lower Atlantic coast, and sugar plantations dominated the area around New Orleans, which replaced Charleston, South Carolina, as the largest city in the South. The spread of plantation culture required a massive shift of slaves from the East to the West, more than one million had already moved west by 1820. In the early years, most slaves moved with their owners as they relocated their plantations from the Upper South to the Gulf Coast, and they were often able to maintain stable family relationships as they moved.

After 1815, however, the vast majority of slaves were sold to professional slave traders. Separated from their families forever, they were forced to walk on a two-month trek to the auction houses of the new center of the slave trade, New Orleans. Many planters in the older regions earned more money selling slaves than growing crops, and southerners began to view any threat to the interstate slave trade as an attack on their entire way of life. The slave trade broke up one-third of slave marriages and sent one-third of all slave children "down the river" to New Orleans. Slavery in the new states of the Southwest was notoriously brutal. With a 7:3 male-to-female ratio, families had a hard time forming and surviving, and slaveowners drove their slaves relentlessly as cotton prices boomed throughout the 1850s.

A⊤ THE TIME OF THE AMERICAN REVOLUTION, slavery was concentrated along the Atlantic coast and was more prevalent in the tobacco-growing region around Chesapeake Bay than in the cotton country farther south. Beginning in the 1790s, however, several economic and politi-

The rice- and sugar-growing regions along the Atlantic coast and the Gulf States exhibited an entirely different kind of enslavement. Slaves needed more skills to tend rice and sugar, and they therefore enjoyed more autonomy and authority in regulating their own labor. Absentee owners sometimes left their slaves to run entire plantations by themselves. The rice and sugar regions also adopted communal living arrangements that resembled the traditional structure of extended families in Africa, and more components of African culture could survive.

Significant Plantations in the Antebellum South
- Plantation
- Skilled labor, mixed agriculture
- Lowland task labor
- Gang labor

0   100 km
0   100 miles

This illustration, from the London Illustrated News *in 1856, shows a slave market at Richmond, Virginia, where an African American woman is being sold. The strain on slave families could be intense when individual members were sold.*

As slavery spread westward, the institution adapted to new circumstances and took on new dimensions while exacting a hideous toll from slave families and individuals. Still, the core of slavery remained the cotton culture of the Black Belt, where the five largest cotton-growing states had nearly one-half of all their wealth invested in slaves. In this expanding Cotton Kingdom, an aggressive defense of slavery became second nature.

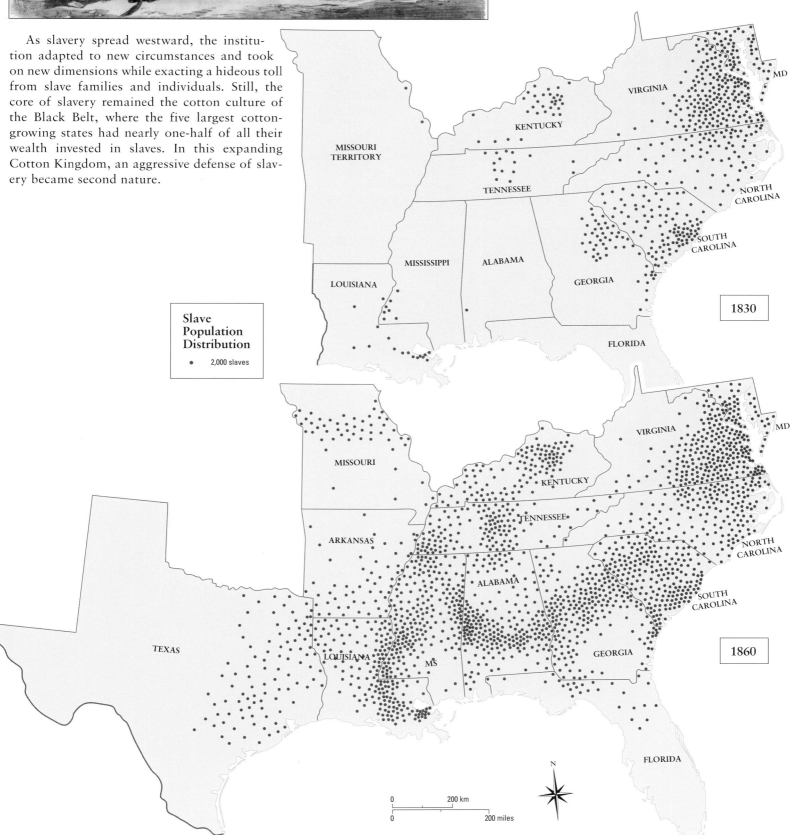

Slave Population Distribution

• 2,000 slaves

1830

1860

0   200 km

0   200 miles

SLAVERY IN 1860

AMERICA WAS DIVIDED INTO TWO sections, slave and free, in 1860. In many ways, the South was itself divided into two distinct societies. Attesting that there were "two Souths" before the Civil War, a northerner who traveled through the region wrote, "for every rich man's house, I am sure I passed a dozen shabby and half-furnished cottages and at least a hundred cabins—mere hovels, such as none but a poor farmer would house his cattle in at the North." Superficially, the South seemed wealthy in 1860. Plantation slavery was extremely efficient and profitable. The South's per capita economic growth rate was the highest in the nation and one of the highest in the world. Cotton production—"King Cotton"—accounted for one-half of all exports from the United States and was a vital source of foreign capital.

The price of cotton rose steadily, from five cents per pound during the 1840s to an average of eleven cents per pound during the 1850s. In the decade before the Civil War, the average price of slaves doubled, the overall value of slave plantations tripled, and the per acre value of cotton land quadrupled. The total value of slaves peaked in 1860 at $3 billion, during a time when the gross national product was just $4 billion. Southern slavery looked like a booming success that was vital to the American economy. But the South's fabled wealth was superficial, benefitting a relative handful of the region's wealthiest planters at the expense of African American slaves and poor whites. A planter aristocracy—just ten percent of white southerners—owned sixty percent of all of the region's wealth. Despite their arrogance and power, slave owners had good reason to feel beleaguered. The South's other commercial crops—tobacco, sugar, rice, and hemp—were less lucrative than cotton, so planters gambled their futures on growing ever more of this single crop.

In order to expand cotton production, planters were required to move their operations westward onto cheaper but more productive land. In fact, many southerners believed that cotton production had to expand westward or the institution of slavery would die. As a result, any threat to slavery in the territories seemed like a direct assault against the South. Planters aggressively defended the westward movement of slavery into the territories at all costs.

This westward movement depended on the sale of slaves from the East to the West, and many planters in the older regions made more money from selling slaves than from agriculture. They therefore defended the interstate slave trade as not only a right but also an economic necessity for the South. Many northerners agreed that keeping slavery from expanding westward would destroy the institution. They therefore mounted a "free soil" campaign to contain slavery in the South and keep it from spreading, which they were convinced would place slavery "in the course of ultimate extinction," as Abraham Lincoln put it.

Above all, many Americans' growing conviction that slavery was not only economically and socially backward but fundamentally immoral rallied northerners to the antislavery cause with growing religious zeal. Led by the new Republican Party, northerners mounted an ever more determined campaign to keep slavery from expanding westward. With an equally intense commitment, southerners defended their institution. As the Civil War approached, the future of the South—and the nation—rested on the outcome.

Eli Whitney's cotton gin (engine) transformed cotton production in the southern states. Its simple construction allowed many southern farmers to build their own gins. Between 1820 and 1860 cotton production rose from 400,000 bales to around 3,750,000 bales, while the number of slaves rose from 1,500,000 to 4,000,000.

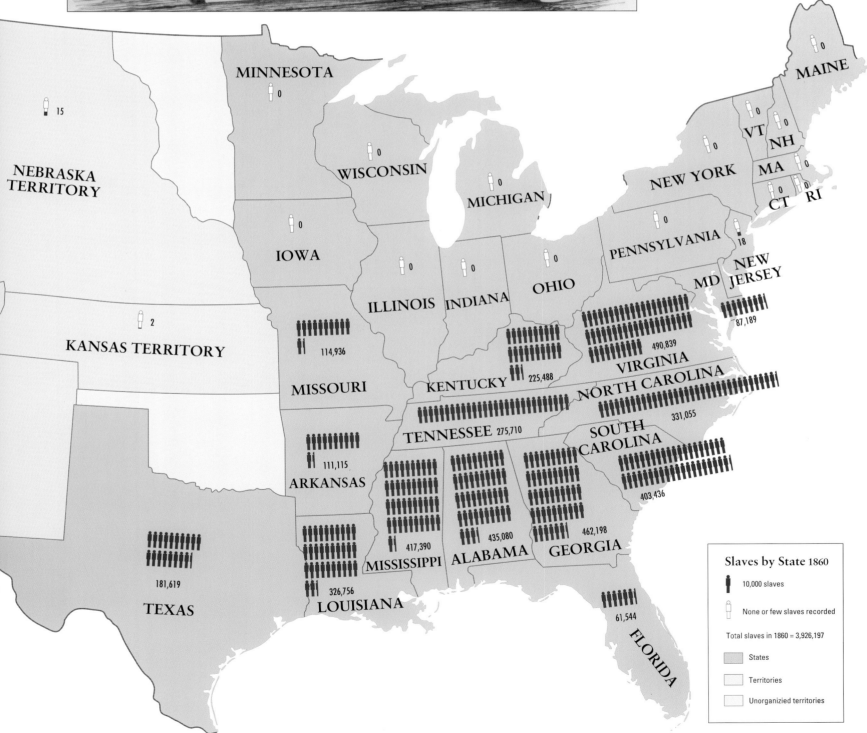

NEBRASKA TERRITORY

15

MINNESOTA 0

WISCONSIN 0

MICHIGAN 0

MAINE 0

VT 0   NH 0

NEW YORK   MA 0

CT 0   RI 0

IOWA 0

PENNSYLVANIA 0

KANSAS TERRITORY 2

ILLINOIS 0   INDIANA 0   OHIO 0

MD 18   NEW JERSEY 87,189

MISSOURI 114,936

KENTUCKY 225,488

VIRGINIA 490,839

NORTH CAROLINA 331,055

TENNESSEE 275,710

SOUTH CAROLINA 403,436

ARKANSAS 111,115

TEXAS 181,619

MISSISSIPPI 417,390

ALABAMA 435,080

GEORGIA 462,198

LOUISIANA 326,756

FLORIDA 61,544

Slaves by State 1860

10,000 slaves

None or few slaves recorded

Total slaves in 1860 = 3,926,197

States

Territories

Unorganizied territories

FREE BLACKS BEFORE THE CIVIL WAR

WHEN THE CIVIL WAR BEGAN, one-tenth of African Americans living in the United States—more than 400,000—were free. While better off than the South's four million slaves, free blacks suffered legal, political, and social discrimination that relegated them to a status somewhere between slavery and freedom. One-half of all free blacks lived in northern states, all of which had adopted emancipation plans by 1804. Most lived in cities, such as Boston, New York, and Philadelphia; performed unskilled labor; and lived in segregated neighborhoods. Discrimination tended to vary inversely with the number of African Americans. Most states in New England, the states with the fewest African Americans, allowed free blacks to vote. Massachusetts was the only state in the Union that included them in juries. The Lower North, especially the new western states of Ohio, Indiana, and Illinois, attracted fugitives and former slaves from the South and

Born a slave in New York, Isabella Baumfree took the name Sojourner Truth in 1843 and became a prominent itinerant preacher, abolitionist, and feminist. In a famous speech in 1851, Truth attacked both racism and sexism by asking "Ain't I a woman?"

imposed severe legal discrimination on them. Their "black laws" systematically denied the right to vote, testify in court, and practice some occupations. Several states required free blacks to post bonds to guarantee that they would not become public charges, and three states—Indiana, Illinois, and Oregon—banned the settlement of African Americans inside their borders. Beyond this legal discrimination, whites routinely harassed free blacks and even launched race riots targeting their communities for destruction. In Cincinnati, a free city bordering the slave state Kentucky, for example, whites drove one-half of all the free blacks out of the city and attacked a school that dared to admit African Americans.

Life was even bleaker for free blacks who lived in the South. They enjoyed more economic opportunities than their northern counterparts, because whites not only allowed but expected them to perform skilled crafts. Segregation was less severe than in the North, because whites distrusted and feared black communities. Free blacks hired themselves out, mingled with their white employers, and lived in alleyways behind palatial homes. Legal discrimination, however, was much more

African American Newspapers and Periodicals, 1820–1860

- ● City with five or more African American newspapers and/or periodicals
- • City with one to four African American newspapers and/or periodicals

0   200 km

0   200 miles

N

severe in the South. Basic human rights, including freedom of speech and assembly, seemed unthinkable. With re-enslavement a constant menace, African Americans carried "freedom papers." They also needed "passes" to travel freely. The Upper South claimed four-fifths of the region's free blacks.

Fearing massive slave rebellions, the Deep South discouraged and even outlawed emancipation. In some instances, free blacks had thirty days to leave the state or face re-enslavement. Most free black communities in the Deep South originated during French or Spanish colonial days in the 1790s, and many had roots in the French Caribbean. These Creoles—native-born African

Americans of French or Spanish ancestry—created flourishing communities in New Orleans and Charleston and enjoyed educational and economic opportunities of which most African Americans never dreamed. This black middle class supported schools, businesses, newspapers, and theaters. Mixing more freely with white Americans than most free blacks, these urban Creoles laid the cultural and political foundations for the post–Civil War South. Wherever they lived, free blacks suffered entrenched discrimination before the Civil War. But the two geographical extremes—New England to the North and New Orleans to the South—offered some glimpses of freedom and the promise of equality to come.

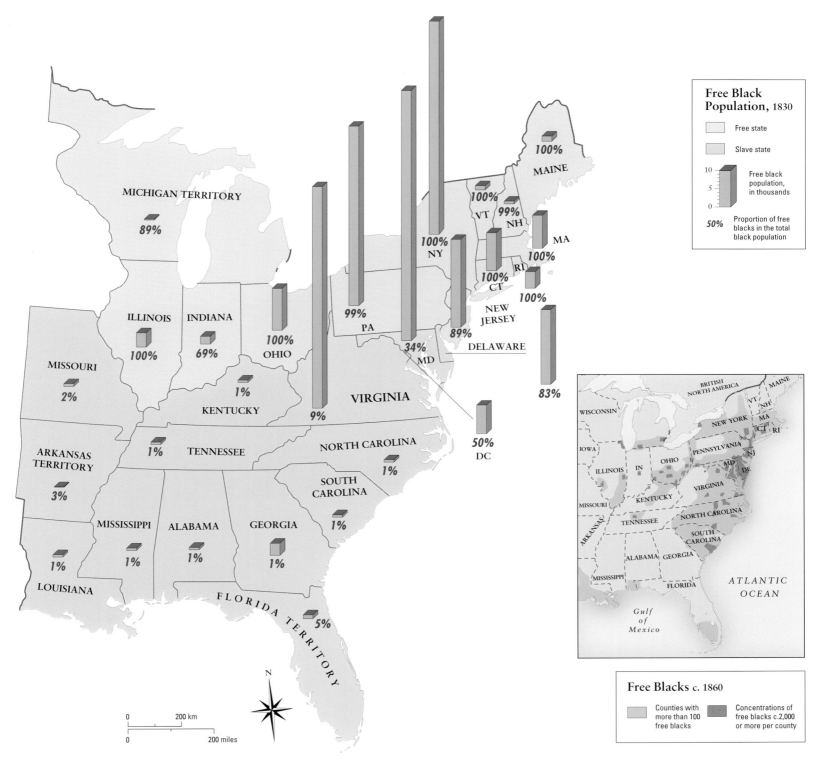

GROWTH OF POPULATION, 1800 – 1860

As AMERICA STOOD AT THE BRINK of civil war in 1860, its single most important resource—population—clearly favored the North. When the Constitution was adopted, the nation's population was evenly divided between the North and the South, so the two regions enjoyed a fairly equal balance of power. Quickly, however, the South's population began lagging behind the North's, and that gap grew steadily with each passing year. By 1860, the South could claim only slightly more than one-third of America's people. The most visible reason for this shifting population balance was the North's rapid urbanization, fueled by the Industrial Revolution, advances in transportation, and the mechanization of agriculture. By 1860, when the North was one-fourth urban, only ten percent of southerners lived in towns and cities. Remaining fundamentally rural in its culture and outlook, the South had few large cities and only one-fifth of America's urban population.

On the eve of the Civil War, in fact, only one of America's ten largest cities—New Orleans—was southern. Immigration gave another major boost to the North's population that widened the gap between the two regions. Proverbially a nation of immigrants, the United States welcomed four million of them between 1820 and 1860, but only one-in-ten settled in the South. Attracted by the economic opportunities of the North's booming cities and family-oriented farms, immigrants were equally repelled by slavery, which degraded labor, depressed wages, and stifled opportunity. By 1860, only three percent of southerners were immigrants, compared to 14 percent of northerners.

The westward movement also hurt the South. In 1800, only one-tenth of all Americans lived west of the Appalachian Mountains. By 1860, one-half were westerners. Both southerners and northerners moved west, but the westward movement favored the North. Roughly 200,000 southerners left slave states to move westward into the free states of the Midwest, primarily Ohio, Indiana, Illinois, and Iowa. Relatively few northerners moved into the slave states before the Civil War. Between 1845 and 1860, five new western states—Iowa, Wisconsin, California, Minnesota, and Oregon—entered the Union. All of them were free states. Not a single slave state entered the Union during that same fifteen-year period, severely shifting the national balance of power against the South and slavery

Overall, the three greatest population trends of the nineteenth century—urbanization, immigration, and the westward movement—all favored the North at the expense of the South. Politically, the South lost electoral votes in presidential elections and representation in Congress as its population lagged behind. Aggravating this growing minority status, the Constitution's "three-fifths clause" counted slaves as only three-fifths of a person for purposes of representation. With nearly four million slaves in 1860, this partial accounting of slaves cost the South about one-seventh of its potential electoral vote and its seats in the House of Representatives. The steady shift of political power to the rapidly expanding free states was a major cause of secession.

The South's disadvantage in population also proved a decisive factor in its military defeat. Only eleven of the nation's thirty-three states joined the Confederacy, and nearly two-fifths of its people were slaves. Overall, the Confederacy included only one-third of the states and only one-fourth of America's white population. Lagging behind the North socially, economically, and politically, but above all in population, the Confederacy seemed hopelessly outnumbered from its very inception.

This painting by Samuel B. Waugh shows Irish immigrants arriving at the Battery in New York harbor, 1848.

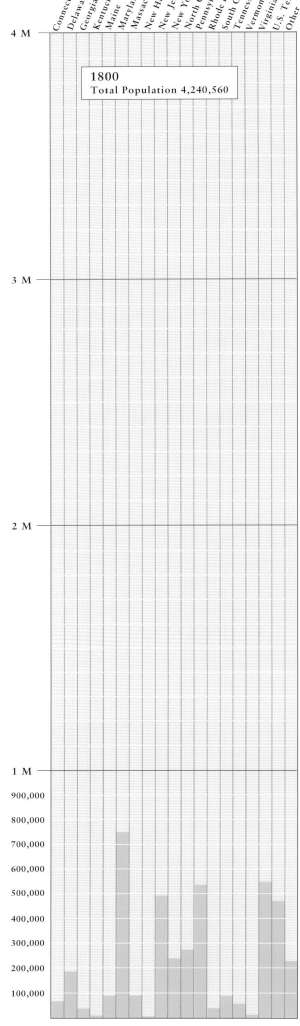

1830
Total Population 16,956,528

1860
Total Population 31,173,924

Left chart state labels: Alabama, Arkansas, Connecticut, Delaware, Florida, Georgia, Illinois, Indiana, Kentucky, Louisiana, Maine, Maryland, Massachusetts, Mississippi, Missouri, New Hampshire, New Jersey, New York, North Carolina, Ohio, Pennsylvania, Rhode Island, South Carolina, Tennessee, Vermont, Virginia, U.S. Territories

Right chart state labels: Alabama, Arkansas, California, Connecticut, Delaware, Florida, Georgia, Illinois, Indiana, Iowa, Kentucky, Louisiana, Maine, Maryland, Massachusetts, Michigan, Minnesota, Mississippi, Missouri, New Hampshire, New Jersey, New York, North Carolina, Ohio, Oregon, Pennsylvania, Rhode Island, South Carolina, Tennessee, Texas, Vermont, Virginia, Wisconsin, U.S. Territories

CITIES IN 1860

A birds-eye view of New York City in the 1860's looking north from Governor's island across Manhattan and the busy waterway of the East River.

UNTIL THE TWENTIETH CENTURY, AMERICA was a predominantly rural nation. When the Constitution was adopted, only one-in-twenty Americans lived in a town or city of two thousand five hundred or more people. There were only twenty-four cities of that size in the entire country, and only twelve had five thousand or more people. As America expanded, agricultural productivity rose, immigration increased, and industry gained momentum, the number of cities began doubling every twenty years. By 1860, one-fifth of the American population was urban. Still, by modern standards, American cities were small. Only nine of them had more than 100,000 people, and the nation's largest city—New York—had only slightly more than 800,000. Urbanization was concentrated in the North, which gave the Union a tremendous economic and military advantage. Of the fifty largest cities, three-fourths (thirty-eight) were northern, and only eight belonged to the future Confederacy. New York State alone equaled that number of large cities in 1860. In fact, among the one hundred largest American cities in 1860, only twelve ended up in the Confederacy. Five of those were in Virginia, which helps to explain the economic, strategic, military, and political value of that single state to the Confederate cause throughout the Civil War.

Northern cities proliferated while the South failed to urbanize for many reasons. The North invested in a dense transportation network, founded on railroads and canals, that concentrated population at key points and produced cities. The South depended on natural waterways—rivers—that were slower, less efficient, and unsuited to an industrial economy. Dramatic increases in northern agricultural productivity, accomplished largely through the mechanization of agriculture, created a surplus population of farm boys and farmers' daughters who moved to the growing cities. Another important factor in northern urbanization was immigration. More than three million European immigrants arrived in the two decades before 1860. Avoiding the South, where they had to compete with slave labor, nine-tenths of all immigrants settled in the North, primarily in cities.

The South was slow to industrialize. Instead of investing their profits in building factories, slave owners preferred to buy more slaves. Slavery did not support the kind of skilled, educated, and literate work force that industrialization demanded, so southerners sent their raw cotton to northern cities to be manufactured into cloth. Fundamentally, an industrial economy can support more cities than an agricultural society, so urban growth was concentrated in the industrial states of New York and Massachusetts. With fewer cities, the South's population lagged behind the North, its congressional representation fell, and its political power faded. The region's lack of cities and industry proved a devastating weakness in wartime, as well. Never economically self-sufficient, the Confederacy struggled to arm, clothe, and even feed its soldiers during the Civil War.

Northern cities, meanwhile, churned out armaments and matériel, while providing an abundant supply of soldiers to support the Union war effort. The southern way of life, built upon slavery, cotton, and tradition, motivated the Confederacy to fight but also proved its greatest weakness.

OREGO

San Francisco ⊙

CALIFORNI

POPULATION OF CITIES 1860

Northern Cities	State	Population
New York	NY	805,651
Philadelphia	PA	585,529
Brooklyn	NY	266,661
Boston	MA	177,812
Cincinnati	OH	161,044
St. Louis	MO	160,773
Chicago	IL	109,260
Buffalo	NY	81,129
Newark	NJ	71,914
Albany	NY	62,367
San Francisco	CA	56,802
Providence	RI	50,666
Pittsburgh	PA	49,217
Rochester	NY	48,204
Detroit	MI	45,619
Milwaukee	WI	45,246
Cleveland	OH	42,417
New Haven	CT	39,267
Troy	NY	39,232
Lowell	MA	36,827
Jersey City	NJ	29,226
Hartford	CT	29,154
Allegheny	PA	28,702
Syracuse	NY	28,119
Portland	ME	26,341
Cambridge	MA	26,060
Roxbury	MA	25,137
Worcester	MA	24,960
Reading	PA	23,161
Utica	NY	22,529
Salem	MA	22,252
Manchester	NH	20,109
Dayton	OH	20,081
Baltimore	MD	212,418
Louisville	KY	68,033
Washington	DC	61,121
Wilmington	DE	21,508
Confederate Cities		
New Orleans	LA	168,675
Charleston	SC	40,578
Richmond	VA	37,910
Mobile	AL	29,258
Memphis	TN	22,623
Savannah	GA	22,292
Montgomery	AL	8,843

Cities in 1860

- Free state
- Slave state
- Territory theoretically open to slavery after the Dred Scott decision of 1857
- Less than 25,000
- 25,000–50,000
- 50,000–100,000
- 100,000–500,000
- More than 500,000

0   150 km

0   150 miles

IMMIGRATION, 1783 – 1860

Uncle Sam beckons the dispossessed, desperate, and adventurous of Europe.

FOR A HALF-CENTURY AFTER THE American Revolution, most immigrants to America came from Britain. Historians call them "invisible immigrants," because they spoke English, shared a common heritage with Americans, practiced Protestantism, and therefore blended relatively quickly into their new country. Around 1845, the first great influx of non-English and non-Protestant immigrants in American history began. During one decade, from 1845 to 1854, three million Irish and German immigrants reached America. Ireland's potato blight, which broke out in 1846, devastated the island's agriculture, produced the famous Irish potato famine, and drew four million Irish immigrants to America by the end of the nineteenth century.

Irish immigrants, who were generally poor, arrived in America with few belongings and skills and found work performing menial labor. Arriving without relatives or resources, most Irish immigrants settled near their ports of entry—Boston, New York City, and Philadelphia—in what became America's first urban ghettos. Generally Catholic, the Irish suffered religious discrimination that intensified their plight at the bottom of America's economic ladder. Even more German immigrants—five million—settled in

America during the nineteenth century. Many of them were the "48ers," political reformers who led unsuccessful revolutions in Europe in 1848 and then fled to America. German immigrants tended to be better educated and better off than the Irish. They usually booked passage further inland from the East Coast, settling in the growing Midwestern cities of Cincinnati, Cleveland, Chicago, Milwaukee, and St. Louis. Representing Lutheran Protestants and Catholics in roughly equal numbers, the German immigrants suffered less religious discrimination than the Irish Catholics but faced a language barrier that tended to slow their assimilation.

America experienced its greatest rate of immigration, as a percentage of population, during the 1850s. The arrival of so many non-English and non-Protestant immigrants created a reaction known as nativism. Nativists tried to restrict immigration, delay naturalization for up to twenty-one years, prevent immigrants from voting, and introduce Protestant religious instruction into public schools. The Order of the Star Spangled Banner, a secret society with an anti-immigrant and anti-Catholic agenda, arose in New York City in 1850. When asked about their activities, its members answered "I know nothing." Thus, the Know-Nothing Party was born. Also called the American Party, the Know-Nothings became the largest nativist political party in American history. During the 1850s, the Know-Nothings attracted millions of antislavery voters who viewed both slavery and unchecked immigration as threats to the American republic. The American Party soon broke into northern and southern wings and faded away as the new Republican Party emerged. Ninety percent of the Irish and German immigrants settled in the North, where they created an increasingly heterogeneous culture and society, substantially boosted the region's population, provided a growing industrial labor force, and played an active role in political life on the eve of the Civil War.

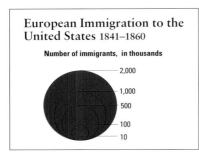

European Immigration to the United States 1841–1860

Number of immigrants, in thousands

- 2,000
- 1,000
- 500
- 100
- 10

1841–1850

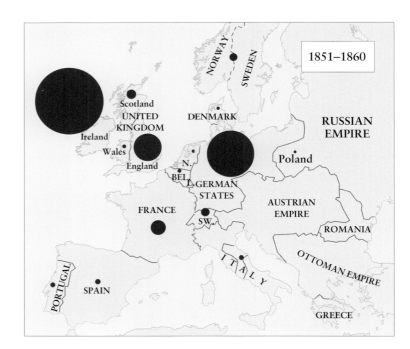

1851–1860

Emigration to the United States from Northwestern Europe
1815–1860

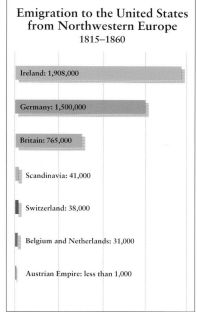

Ireland: 1,908,000

Germany: 1,500,000

Britain: 765,000

Scandinavia: 41,000

Switzerland: 38,000

Belgium and Netherlands: 31,000

Austrian Empire: less than 1,000

Throughout the famine years in Ireland, landlords continued to evict their tenants. It is estimated that between 1845 and 1848, thirty thousand families were dispossessed.

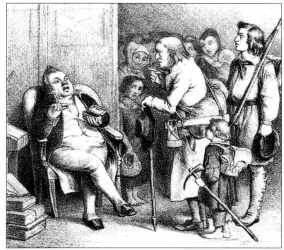

Although the revolutionary upheavals of 1848 prompted many people to emigrate from Germany, daily oppression by petty officialdom was probably a stronger motive, as this 1849 cartoon points out. "My dear people," the official asks, "Is there no way to keep you here?" "Sure, sir," the old peasant replies. "If you would leave, we would stay."

The migrations of this period involved entire families, although fathers, and later both parents, first traveled to the United States to earn enough money for their immediate families and later extended families, to join them in their new land. These migrants almost never came from the poorest sections of society. They had to be prosperous enough to pay their fares and survive long enough to buy land or find jobs.

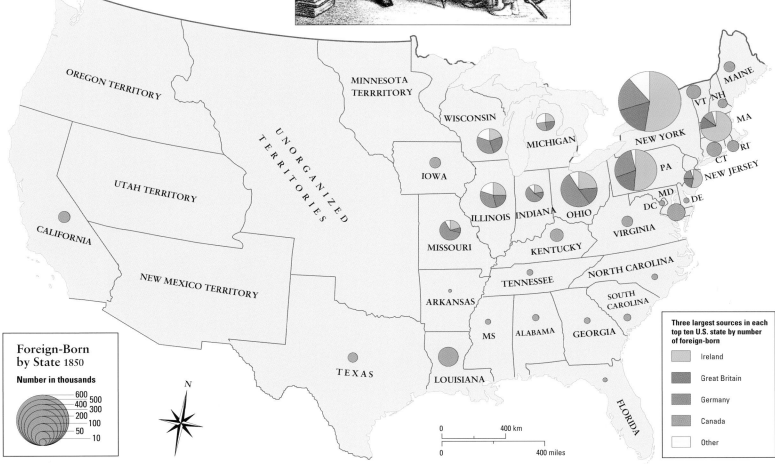

Foreign-Born by State 1850

Number in thousands

600 500
400 300
200
100
50
10

N

Three largest sources in each top ten U.S. state by number of foreign-born

- Ireland
- Great Britain
- Germany
- Canada
- Other

0   400 km

0   400 miles

FARMLAND BY VALUE

BEFORE THE CIVIL WAR, southern agriculture was extremely profitable. The average southern farmer was six times wealthier than the average northern farmer. In part, this difference reflected the size of southern plantations. The average farm in the South was five-and-a-half times larger than the typical farm in the North.

The real difference, however, was slavery. Southern agriculture, whether devoted to "King Cotton," tobacco, sugar, or rice, was almost entirely dependent on slaves. In the South, slaves were as important as land as a form of property, accounting for almost one-half of the wealth of the five leading cotton-growing states. But the benefits of slavery were unevenly distributed, and most free southerners were considerably less wealthy than even the average northerner. Three-fourths of southern families owned no slaves at all. They labored with their families to feed and clothe themselves, and entire regions of the South—especially the uplands of the Cumberland Mountains and the Ozarks—were neutral or even hostile toward slavery

Even among slave owners, there was a wide disparity in wealth. One-half of southern slave owners had five or fewer slaves. These farmers lived mostly in the Upper South or the uplands and specialized in tobacco. A planter aristocracy of ten thousand southern families owned fifty or more slaves, and a mere three thousand of the South's wealthiest elites owned one hundred or more. A tiny minority in the South, these great planters exercised overwhelming economic and political power by virtue of their tremendous wealth. Owning most of the slaves, they set the economic agenda and political tone for the entire region.

The largest plantations were clustered on the best cotton-growing land, because cotton was the most lucrative crop grown in the world at the time. Most slaves lived and worked in the cotton-growing states of the Lower South, stretching from South Carolina westward along the Gulf coast into eastern Texas. The per acre value of these cotton plantations was more than three times greater than that of the South's nonslave farms. While most southerners did not own slaves, they benefitted indirectly from the institution and certainly knew that the region's entire economy depended on it. They therefore felt an interest in defending it.

Northern farmers, unlike the wealthy southern planters, relied on their families rather than slaves or even hired hands for most of their labor, and owned relatively small tracts of land. Typical farms ranged from eighty acres in the Northeast to one hundred and sixty acres (a quarter-mile section) in the West, but a farm family could rarely cultivate more than sixty acres by themselves. As a result, wealth was much more evenly distributed in the North than in the South.

The North developed a more egalitarian spirit of opportunity, in which anyone could work hard and succeed, and there was no entrenched aristocracy to impede economic development or control politics. Without slave labor, northerners had an incentive to mechanize their agriculture and improve their land, which increased productivity and freed the next generation to leave their farms. By 1860, only forty percent of northerners were engaged in agriculture as opposed to eighty percent in the South. The North diversified, both economically and culturally. To preserve its ostentatious but superficial wealth, the South clung to its traditional ways and stagnated. To most northerners, the superiority of free labor seemed obvious, while the South's dependence on slave labor increasingly seemed a curse.

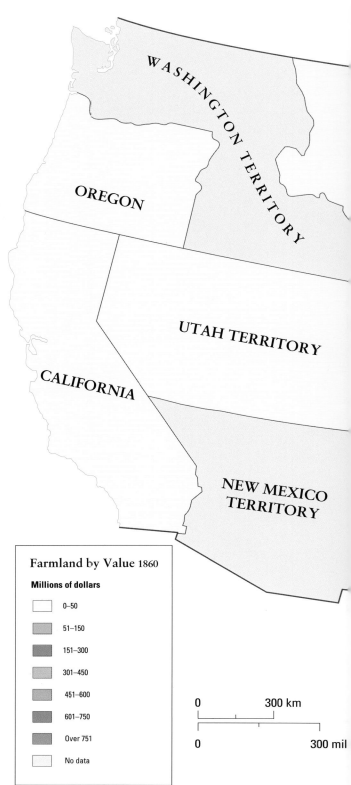

Farmland by Value 1860

Millions of dollars

- 0–50
- 51–150
- 151–300
- 301–450
- 451–600
- 601–750
- Over 751
- No data

0   300 km

0   300 mil

In the North a free work force, seen here celebrating a full harvest, carved out a prosperous life, organizing, mechanizing, and improving their farms. Once established, the second generation of these families could, if they chose, head off for life in the cities to face new risks and opportunities in expanding industries.

AGRICULTURE, 1820 – 1860

THE NORTH UNDERWENT AN "agricultural revolution" before the Civil War. In 1820, most northern farmers practiced subsistence agriculture, growing enough food and fiber to feed and clothe their families and little more. They farmed with their families, who provided most of the labor they needed. Their sons learned how to farm and settled nearby on farms of their own when they came of age. Priding themselves on their independence and self-reliance, farmers diversified and grew most of the crops that they and their neighbors needed. As the North industrialized and cities emerged, however, demand for food grew and farmers began growing cash crops for sale on a national market. Transportation routes—originally canals and later railroads—allowed farmers to ship their produce over long distances.

The mechanization of agriculture increased productivity, allowed farmers to expand their operations, and encouraged their sons and daughters to leave agriculture entirely and move to cities. Northern farmers specialized in grain, which was durable and easy to harvest with machines. As farmers moved west, a wheat belt stretched from Pennsylvania through the Midwest into Minnesota. Railroad centers, such as Chicago and Minneapolis, milled the wheat into flour before shipping it eastward. Farther south, the Corn Belt stretched from the Ohio Valley through Iowa and into Kansas. Farmers fed wheat to cattle and corn to hogs, and a meatpacking industry arose in the major cities of the Midwest. Northern agriculture supported the growth of cities, which processed and transported their crops, manufactured farm machinery, and ate the finished product. As agriculture moved westward onto new lands, northeastern farmers began to specialize. Farmers in New York State turned to dairying, and a dairy belt stretching westward into Michigan and

As the frontier moved west, northern farmers settled down to a comfortable existence. With industrialization the cities of the north demanded an increasing food supply, to meet this requirement northern farmers mechanized, sending cash crops to the newly developing markets.

Growth in Total Acreage, 1850 – 1860

State	Total Acreage 1850	Total Acreage 1860	Change by percent	Average Acreage 1850	Average Acreage 1860	Change by percent
Alabama	12,137,681	19,104,545	57.40	289	346	19.72
Arkansas	2,598,214	9,573,706	268.47	146	245	67.81
California	3,893,985	8,730,034	124.19	—	466	—
Connecticut	2,383,879	2,504,264	5.05	106	99	−6.60
Delaware	956,144	1,004,295	5.04	158	151	−4.43
Florida	1,595,144	2,520,228	57.99	371	444	19.68
Georgia	22,821,379	26,650,490	16.78	441	430	−2.49
Illinois	12,037,412	20,911,898	73.72	158	146	−7.59
Iowa	2,736,064	10,069,907	268.04	185	165	−10.81
Kansas	N/A	N/A	1,778,400	N/A	N/A	171
Kentucky	16,949,748	19,163,261	13.06	227	211	−7.05
Louisiana	4,989,043	9,298,576	86.38	372	536	44.09
Maine	4,555,393	5,727,671	25.73	97	103	6.19
Maryland	4,634,350	4,835,571	4.34	212	190	−10.38
Massachusetts	3,356,012	3,338,724	−0.52	99	94	−5.05
Michigan	4,383,890	7,030,834	60.38	129	113	−12.40
Minnesota	28,881	2,711,968	9,290.15	184	149	−19.02
Mississippi	10,490,419	15,839,684	50.99	309	370	19.74
Missouri	9,732,670	19,984,810	105.34	179	215	20.11
New Hampshire	3,392,414	3,744,625	10.38	116	123	6.03
New Jersey	2,752,946	1,983,525	−27.95	115	108	−6.09
New York	19,119,084	20,974,958	9.71	112	106	−5.36
North Carolina	20,996,983	23,762,969	13.17	369	316	−14.36
Ohio	17,997,493	20,472,141	13.75	125	114	−8.80
Pennsylvania	14,923,347	17,012,149	14.00	117	109	−6.84
Rhode Island	553,938	521,224	−5.91	96	103	7.29
South Carolina	16,217,700	16,195,919	−0.13	541	488	−9.80
Tennessee	18,984,022	20,669,265	8.88	261	251	−3.83
Texas	11,496,334	25,344,028	120.45	942	591	−37.26
Vermont	4,125,822	4,274,414	3.60	139	135	−2.88
Virginia	26,152,311	31,117,036	18.98	340	324	−4.71
Wisconsin	2,976,658	7,893,587	165.18	148	114	−22.97

Wisconsin produced milk, butter, and cheese. Farmers near big cities specialized in growing perishable foods, such as vegetables, and orchard fruits for an urban market.

Southern agriculture was less innovative, growing by leaps and bounds in output but resisting change. Cotton production dominated the southern economy, rising eight-fold between 1820 and 1850 and doubling yet again by 1860. In contrast to northern farmers' independence and self-reliance, however, southern agriculture was mired in slavery. Planters exported most of their cotton to England and later New England, where it was processed into cloth, so cotton production did not stimulate industrialization or urban growth in the South. In fact, the first ready-made clothing that came out of the New England textile mills was shipped south to clothe the slaves who grew the cotton. Preferring to devote slave labor to producing cotton rather than food, the South could not feed itself and imported food from the North. By 1860, slaves represented one-third of the South's twelve million people. Underfed and poorly clothed, however, they did not stimulate economic growth as consumers. Southern planters saw little reason to diversify their agriculture when they could simply move entire plantations westward onto new lands. Driving their slaves ruthlessly, they did not bother to mechanize their agricultural operations. A tobacco region in the Upper South, rice culture along the Atlantic coast, and sugar production along the Gulf coast represented important exceptions to the domination of King Cotton. But they, too, depended on slave labor and failed to stimulate economic diversification, industry, and urban growth. The northern economy was dynamic, innovative, and independent even in its agricultural sector, in marked contrast to the lucrative but traditional farming practices, mired in slavery, of the agricultural South.

MECHANIZATION OF AGRICULTURE

THE GENUINE MOLINE PLOW.

John Deere, agricultural innovator, introduced the heavy steel plow that enabled western settlers to break up and plow "new ground."

Midwest to eastern cities, and commercial agriculture spread westward. Mechanization freed farmers' sons to move to the cities, providing economic opportunities unheard of in the South. By 1860, only forty percent of the northern labor force worked in agriculture, compared to eighty-one percent of southerners. Northern farmers invested twice as much per acre in farming implements. These investments paid off, because their land was valued at two-and-a-half times as much per acre as southern land in the census of 1860.

ONE OF THE NORTH'S GREATEST advantages in its competition with the South was its stunning agricultural productivity. Because the North gave up slavery after the American Revolution, its agriculture was founded on family farms. Southern planters could increase production by buying more land and more slaves, but northern farmers were limited to the amount of land that their family members could plant and harvest. The primary northern crop, wheat, had to be harvested within a ten-day period. As a result, most farmers could plant no more than fifteen acres, and farms in the North tended to be small, usually forty acres. Unlike wheat, cotton was durable, so there was no rush to harvest it, and plantations could encompass thousands of acres. A farm laborer could harvest two acres of wheat per day with a scythe, so the only way that northern farmers could plant more grain was to mechanize.

Northern inventors contributed many innovations to planting and harvesting. John Deere introduced a steel plow that could break thick prairie sod and allowed cultivation of the prairies and eventually the Great Plains. The McCormick reaper harnessed horses to harvest grain more efficiently. By hand, one bushel of wheat took two hours and forty minutes to harvest. By machine, the same task took four minutes. A succession of farm machines—grain drills, wheat threshers, hay mowers, reapers, and binders—mechanized the process of planting and reaping and used horse-power to boost overall efficiency five-fold.

Wheat production shot up seventy-two percent during the 1850s alone, thanks to the sale of seventy thousand reapers during the decade. Railroads carried farm surpluses from the

Mechanized agriculture provided a decisive military advantage. During the Civil War, the North could enlist more men without diminishing agricultural productivity, providing a crucial edge in manpower. Despite the enlistment of two million men in the Union army, northern agricultural production set new records, and the Union army was the best fed up to that time in American history.

Southern agriculture, however, suffered major wartime disruptions. The South had imported most of its food from the North, so cotton planters had to convert to food crops. The Confederacy drafted half a million farmers, and planters' wives soon found themselves pushing plows

Chronic food shortages led to bread riots, consistently weakened Confederate armies, and undermined civilian morale. The mechanized agriculture of the North promoted economic development and opportunity, which were absent in the South, and gave the Union a crucial advantage over the Confederacy in both manpower and matériel.

Mechanical reapers pulled by horses or oxen, could harvest grain with great efficiency. Whereas one bushel of wheat took almost three hours to reap by hand, with the introduction of mechanical harvesting, the same task took a mere four minutes. Along with other manufacturers like McCormick, shown on the poster right dating from 1864, R. Hoffhein of Pennsylvania offers its latest design to Northern farmers. Although around two million men joined the Union Army, the North's agricultural output, thanks to mechanization, showed no reduction in its productivity. In fact, Northern soldiers were the best fed in American history up to that time.

R. HOFFHEIN'S

IMPROVED SELF-RAKING

MOWER AND REAPER!

MANUFACTURED BY

R. HOFFHEIN'S,

DOVER, YORK COUNTY, PENN'A.

SELF-RAKE.

THE cut herewith presented represents the Combined Machine with the most perfect Self-Rake known. The production of a perfect Self-Rake has engaged the attention of the most ingenious inventors for a long time, and with only partial success, until the one now applied to the Hoffhein's Machine was put into practical use. It was tested by over one hundred farmers during the past season, and in every instance, gave entire satisfaction. By this device the cut grain can be delivered from the platform more perfectly than by hand, with the saving of one man's labor.

For the benefit of those wishing to purchase a good REAPER AND MOWER, we will describe briefly the *Points of Excellence* we claim for this Machine:—1st. The carriage is mounted on *two* driving wheels: in connection with each of these is a spur wheel and pinion, making the Machine, stronger and more durable than any single geared Machine can be.

2nd. The relation between these two driving wheels, is such that they operate conjointly or seperately, as circumstances may require. The result of this is, that when the Machine is mowing on a curve, either to the right or left, the usual speed of the knife is retained, clogging avoided and turning and backing made easy.

3d. The weight of the Machine being all upon *two* driving wheels, instead of one, the machine is not so liable to sink on soft ground, having a bearing of surface of ten inches instead of six.

4th. The weight of the carriage as well as that of the raker and driver is thrown directly upon the driving wheels, by which the following advantages are gained: 1st. The wheels do not slip on the ground and clog the knives. 2nd. A powerful stroke to the knife is produced, enabling the machine to cut the most difficult grain or grass without clogging. 3rd. Side draft is thereby avoided.

5th. The machine both as a *REAPER & MOWER*, has a flexible cutter-bar, which adapts itself to the uneven surface of the ground.

SEP. 10, 1864.

Oliver Stuck, Printer, "Democratic Press" office, Centre Hall Centre Square, York, Penn'a.

KING COTTON, 1830 – 1860

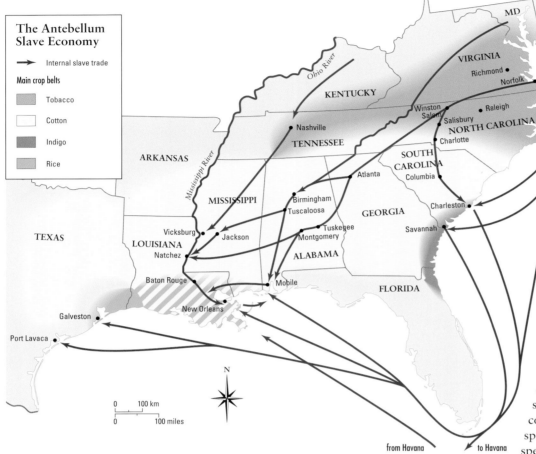

The Antebellum
Slave Economy

→ Internal slave trade

Main crop belts

Tobacco
Cotton
Indigo
Rice

*Slaves working the fields on Pope's
Plantation near Hilton Head, South
Carolina, shortly before the Civil War.*

A T THE END OF THE AMERICAN Revolution, slavery seemed on the decline. Northern states began eliminating slavery through gradual emancipation. Congress prohibited slavery in the Northwest Territory in 1787 and outlawed the importation of slaves into the United States in 1808. In the eighteenth century most southern slaves worked on tobacco plantations around the Chesapeake Bay. Cotton was not a major crop, because long-staple, or sea island, cotton could only be grown in the humid climate of the low-lying South Carolina and Georgia coast. With its

long, silky fibers, sea island cotton could be efficiently processed by hand, because the seeds easily pulled away from the fibers. The coastal regions, however, could produce a meager three thousand bales of long-staple cotton per year. Technological innovations, however, lowered the cost of production and gave rise to an increased demand for cotton.

In 1793, Eli Whitney patented his cotton gin, a machine that made the production of short-staple cotton commercially viable for the first time. The cotton gin pulled the seeds out of short-staple cotton bolls fifty times faster than the work could be done by hand. Now, southern planters could market short-staple cotton, which could be grown throughout the South. At the same time, the mechanization of spinning and weaving in England—and soon New England—dramatically increased the demand for cotton. Water-powered and later steam-powered textile mills gobbled up raw cotton, and their spinning jennies (multiple-spindle spinning machines) and power looms spewed out thread and cloth. To feed this insatiable appetite, cotton planters locked their economy into dependence on slave labor.

The southern climate allowed three growing seasons per year, so there was little slack time when slaves were idle and any investment in slaves paid off handsomely. Rather than buying—let alone inventing—labor-saving farm machinery, cotton planters simply bought more slaves. Instead of rotating cotton with crops that produced less profit, planters overfarmed their land, abandoned it when it wore out, and moved westward onto fresh land. This slave-dependent plantation culture spread westward along the Cotton Belt that stretched across Georgia, Alabama, and Mississippi. During the 1850s, the cotton frontier reached Arkansas and Texas. Planters moved 800,000 slaves into the Southwest, where they were driven ruthlessly in pursuit of profit. Slaves came to dread sale "down the river" to New Orleans, which became America's paramount market for field hands.

Cotton production—King Cotton—dominated the southern economy and eventually three-fourths of southern farmers grew cotton. From 1790 to 1860, cotton production jumped from three thousand bales to 4,500,000 bales per year. To buy more slaves—and live their lavish lifestyles—cotton planters went into debt, often to northern creditors. So cotton production actually drained wealth out of the South rather than enriching the region. The Cotton Belt became known as the "Black Belt," because African Americans often outnumbered white slave owners. Their dependence on slavery and their fear of rebellion drove southerners into an increasingly virulent defense of the institution, and planters kept a firm grip on politics and government. Although three-fourths of southerners did not own any slaves, they felt dependent on both slavery and the cotton economy as the foundations of their way of life. Any threat to slavery—real or imagined—could trigger an overreaction and propel the South relentlessly toward secession and civil war.

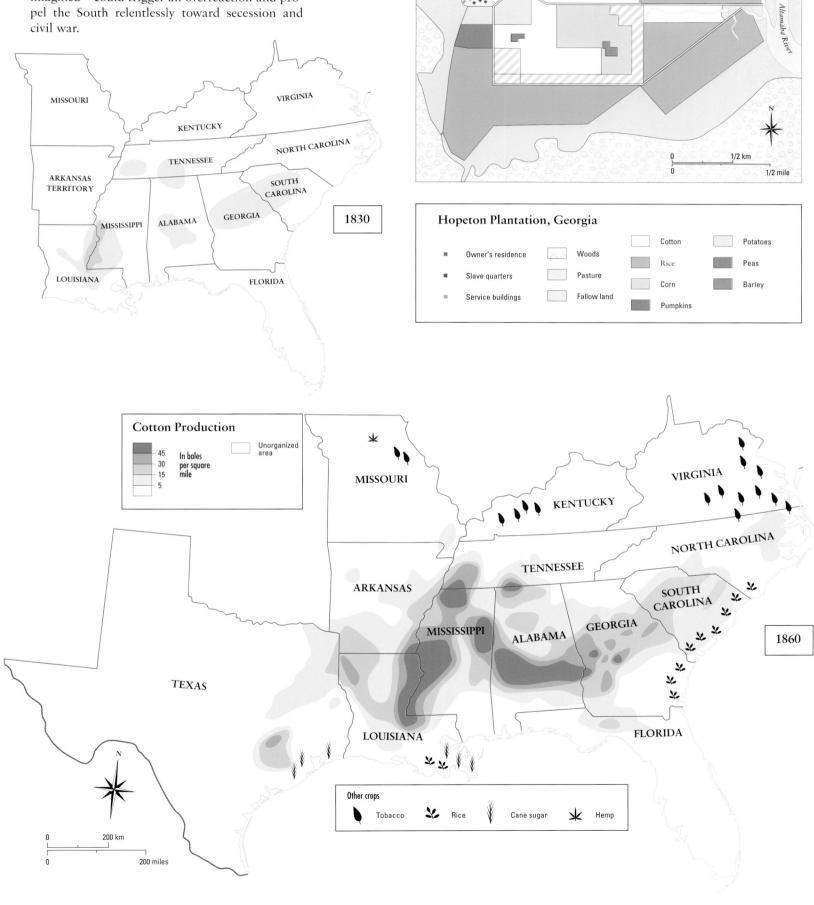

Hopeton Plantation, Georgia

- ■ Owner's residence
- ■ Slave quarters
- ■ Service buildings

- Woods
- Pasture
- Fallow land

- Cotton
- Rice
- Corn
- Pumpkins

- Potatoes
- Peas
- Barley

1830

Cotton Production

45
30
15
5
In bales per square mile

Unorganized area

1860

Other crops

- Tobacco
- Rice
- Cane sugar
- Hemp

INDUSTRY 1820 – 1860

INDUSTRY WAS ONE OF THE PRIMARY sectional differences that divided the North and the South. The North enjoyed tremendous advantages in industrialization, while the South had strong incentives to remain agricultural, mostly because of its commitment to slavery. Geographically, the North's steep-banked, narrow, and fast-moving rivers provided abundant water-power to drive the wheels of the textile mills that were the nation's first factories. The wide, flat, slow-moving rivers of the South were excellent transportation routes but were difficult to harness as water-power sites.

Economically, the wage system of the North encouraged manufacturers to keep their labor costs as low as possible by mechanizing production. Southern slave owners saw little incentive to save labor, because they could drive their slaves ruthlessly year-round without incurring additional labor costs.

The North's educational system, which provided free, compulsory education in public schools, produced a skilled labor force to design, build, and run machines and factories. Southern states were slow in funding schools for an agricultural society that perpetuated traditional practices and rejected economic and cultural innovations. Above all, the North's free society encouraged individuals to invest in industry as a way to profit from innovation and enterprise. Southerners invested most of their profits in more land and more slaves instead of devising new ways of making money. Ironically, the North's first factories processed the cotton that the South grew with slave labor.

During the 1780s, Moses Brown, a merchant in Providence, Rhode Island, opened the Old Pawtucket Mill, which adopted English textile technology to spin cotton and wool into thread. Women and girls across New England put away their spinning wheels and bought thread from the new mills. Soon, a group of investors, the Boston Associates, began hiring those girls to weave thread into cloth on power looms at Lowell and Lawrence, Massachusetts. The textile industry boomed and set the pattern of centralized production on water-powered machines using the surplus labor, mostly girls, from the North's mechanized agricultural economy. Above all, factory owners re-invested their profits by designing and building more machinery and factories.

This "American System" of manufacturing emphasized division of labor, efficiency, self-discipline, standardization, and eventually the assembly line and mass marketing. The system soon spread to other industries, including shoemaking, meatpacking, watchmaking, and railroads. This innovative, industrial mentality infused northern society, fueling a transportation revolution that culminated in the transcontinental railroads, concentrating people and economic activities in growing cities throughout the North, rewarding literacy and education, and promoting self-improvement.

By the Civil War, the North had eighty-four percent of all industrial capital in America. Only forty percent of northerners practiced agriculture, as opposed to eighty percent of southerners. One-

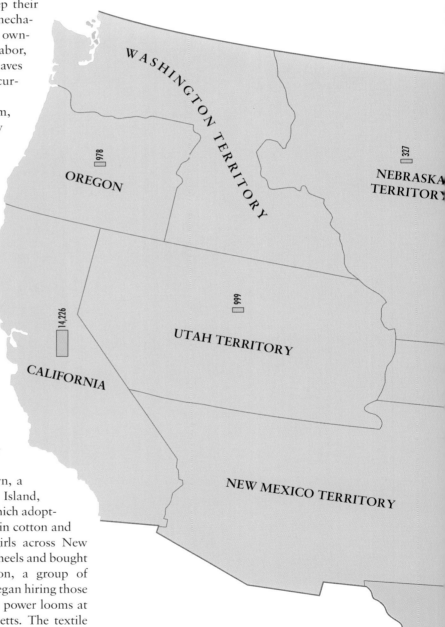

fourth of northerners lived in cities, as opposed to one-tenth of southerners. Twice as many northern children were enrolled in school, and one-third more were literate than the children in the south. By 1860, America had the fourth-largest industrial economy on Earth, trailing only Britain, Germany, and France. The Civil War and the economic boom that followed it would soon propel the nation above those rivals to become the world's largest industrial power.

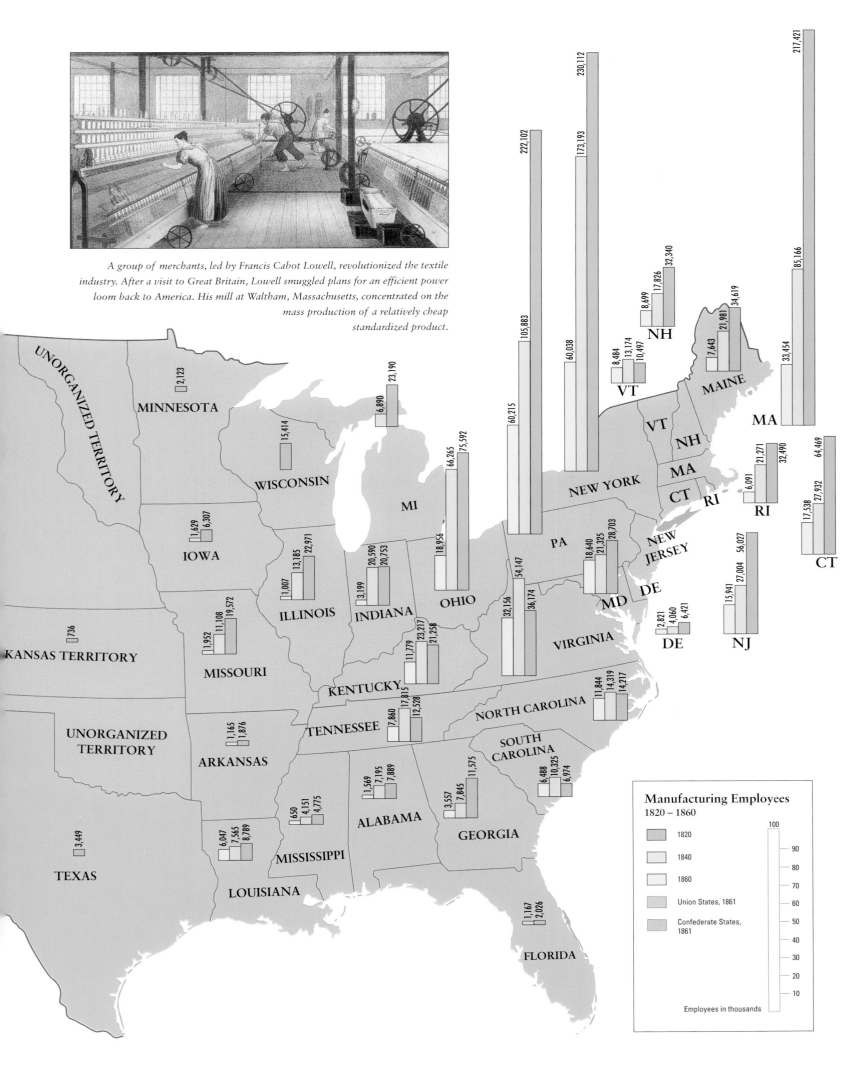

A group of merchants, led by Francis Cabot Lowell, revolutionized the textile industry. After a visit to Great Britain, Lowell smuggled plans for an efficient power loom back to America. His mill at Waltham, Massachusetts, concentrated on the mass production of a relatively cheap standardized product.

MINNESOTA — 2,123

WISCONSIN — 6,890 / 23,190

MI — 15,414

IOWA — 1,629 / 6,307

ILLINOIS — 1,007 / 13,185 / 22,971

INDIANA — 3,199 / 20,590 / 20,753

OHIO — 18,956 / 66,265 / 75,592

NEW YORK — 60,215 / 105,883 / 222,102

VT — 8,484 / 13,174 / 10,497

NH — 8,699 / 17,826 / 32,340

MAINE — 7,643 / 21,981 / 34,619

MA — 33,454 / 85,166 / 217,421

RI — 6,091 / 21,271 / 32,490

CT — 17,538 / 27,932 / 64,469

PA — 60,038 / 173,193 / 230,112

NEW JERSEY — 15,941 / 27,004 / 56,027

DE — 2,821 / 4,060 / 6,421

MD — 18,640 / 21,325 / 28,703

MISSOURI — 1,952 / 11,108 / 19,572

KANSAS TERRITORY — 736

KENTUCKY — 11,779 / 23,217 / 21,258

TENNESSEE — 7,860 / 17,815 / 12,528

VIRGINIA — 32,156 / 54,147 / 36,174

NORTH CAROLINA — 11,844 / 14,319 / 14,217

SOUTH CAROLINA — 6,488 / 10,325 / 6,974

ARKANSAS — 1,165 / 1,876

ALABAMA — 1,569 / 7,195 / 7,889

GEORGIA — 3,557 / 7,845 / 11,575

MISSISSIPPI — 650 / 4,151 / 4,775

LOUISIANA — 6,047 / 7,565 / 8,789

TEXAS — 3,449

FLORIDA — 1,167 / 2,026

Manufacturing Employees
1820 – 1860

- 1820
- 1840
- 1860
- Union States, 1861
- Confederate States, 1861

100
90
80
70
60
50
40
30
20
10

Employees in thousands

RAILROAD CONSTRUCTION, 1840 – 1860

AS AMERICANS MOVED WESTWARD, they needed transportation routes to send their agricultural products to the East Coast and to carry manufactured goods from the booming factory towns of New York and New England. The nation's first great regional transportation route was the Erie Canal. Completed in 1825, this technological marvel ran three hundred and sixty-three miles from Albany on the Hudson River to Buffalo on Lake Erie, connecting America's agricultural heartland with the East for the first time. Canals, however, proved expensive to maintain and were seasonal transportation routes, freezing in the winter and flooding in the summer. Railroads were much faster and ran year-round, creating efficient connections between eastern cities and factories and the farms of the Midwest. Railroads could be built anywhere, and could run in any season, day or night.

State governments had invested in canals, many of which went bankrupt. So the federal government and the states let private investors build the railroads. This new industry caught the popular imagination, propelled the New York

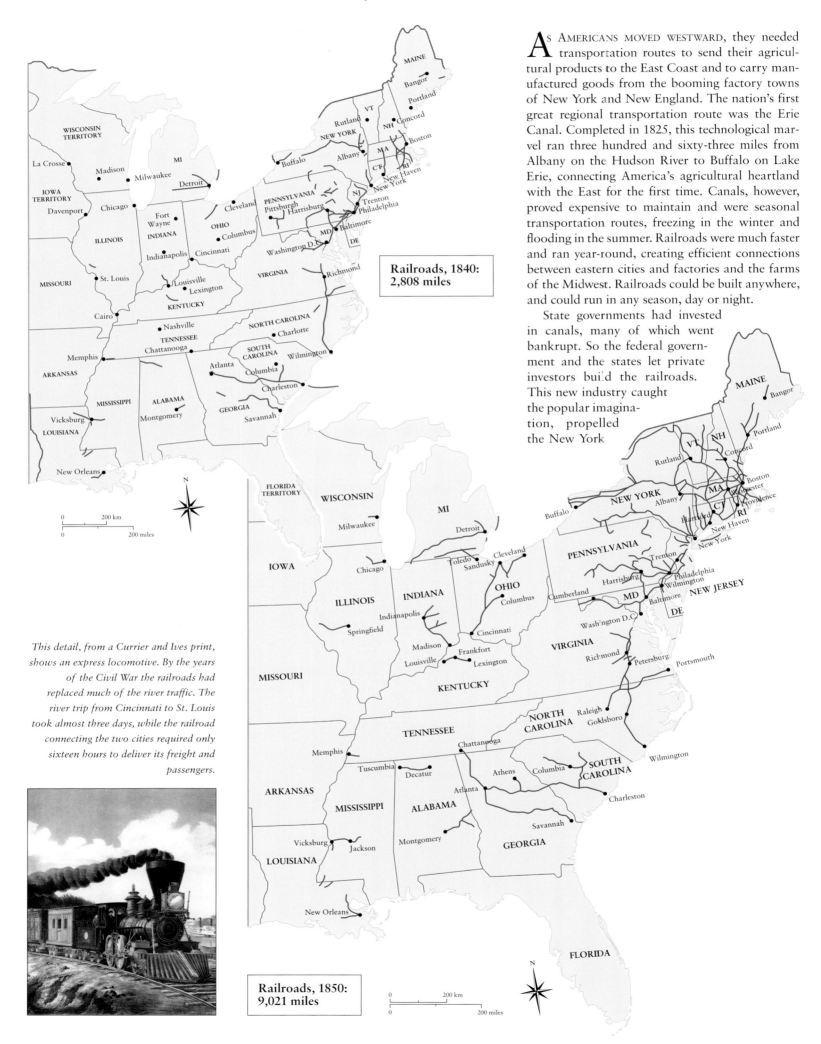

Railroads, 1840:
2,808 miles

This detail, from a Currier and Ives print, shows an express locomotive. By the years of the Civil War the railroads had replaced much of the river traffic. The river trip from Cincinnati to St. Louis took almost three days, while the railroad connecting the two cities required only sixteen hours to deliver its freight and passengers.

Railroads, 1850:
9,021 miles

Stock Exchange into a national and eventually global institution, and attracted capital from England, France, and Germany. The first major railroads ran parallel to the Erie Canal, connecting the great eastern cities—New York, Boston, Philadelphia, and Baltimore—with the booming cities of the new Midwest, especially Chicago. By 1840, America had almost three thousand miles of railroads. By 1860, there were thirty thousand miles, half of all the railroad mileage on Earth.

Railroads dramatically increased the speed and efficiency of the North's industrial and agricultural economies. A trip from Cincinnati to New York City took forty or fifty days by wagon, eighteen days by canal, but only eight days by railroad. Technological innovation followed the railroad wherever it went. Close ties between the railroad and the new telegraph, the steel industry, electrical utilities, agriculture, manufacturing, and mining stimulated economic development throughout the North. The great north-eastern railroads—the Erie, the

Pennsylvania, the Baltimore & Ohio, and the New York Central—linked the Midwest with the East Coast, creating a formidable economic and, later, political alliance.

Overall, the railroads created a national economic network that increasingly isolated the South. Slower to build railroads, the South had only one-third of the nation's mileage in 1860. Southern railroads used a narrower gauge (the distance between the tracks) and connected with the northern railroad network at only three points, threatening to isolate the South from the nation's vibrant industrial economy. Efforts to build a transcontinental railroad to the Pacific also inflamed the sectional crisis, putting the North and South in competition for a route that would boost their own economic interests. When the South seceded, Congress funded a central route through huge land grants to the Union Pacific and Central Pacific railroads. The Union's dense railroad network also proved a decisive military advantage during the Civil War, speeding the mobilization of troops and matériel and binding the North together behind a unified war effort.

**Railroads and
Track Gauges, 1860**

4'8½'	5'4"
4'10"	5'6"
5'	6'

THE U.S. ARMY 1800 – 1860

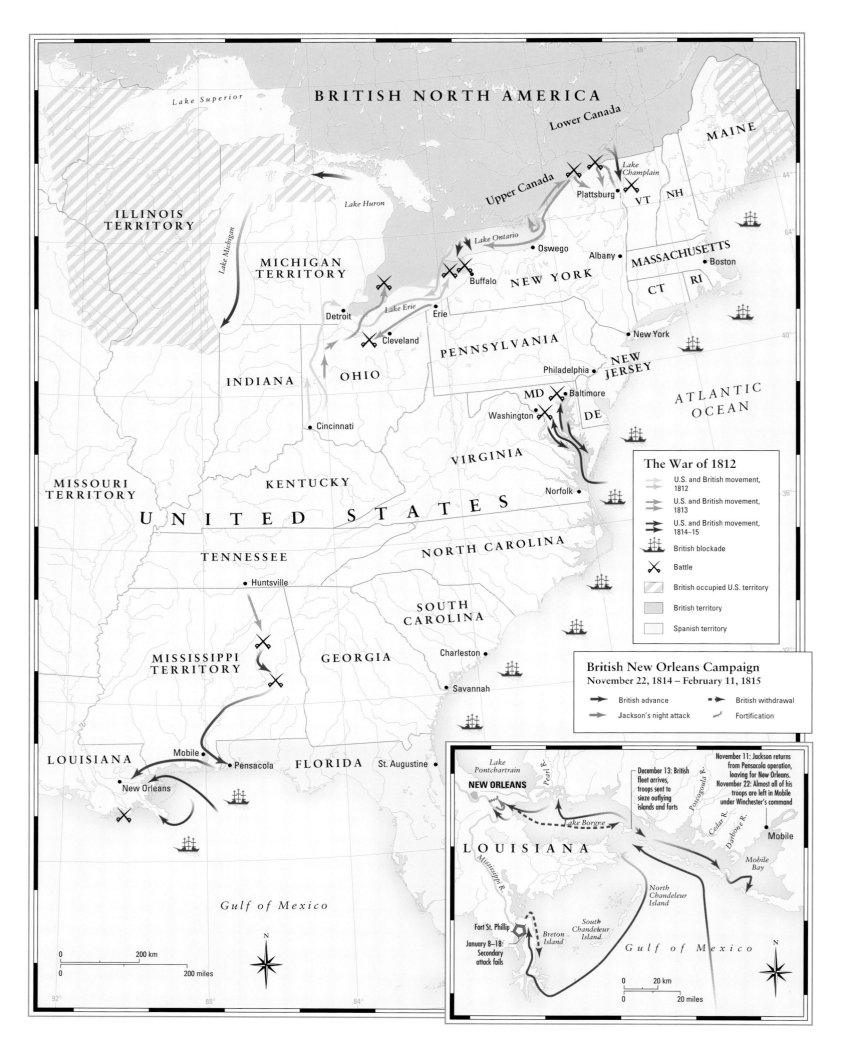

BRITISH NORTH AMERICA

Lake Superior

Lower Canada

MAINE

Upper Canada

Plattsburg

Lake Champlain

VT   NH

ILLINOIS
TERRITORY

Lake Huron

Lake Michigan

Lake Ontario

• Oswego

Albany •

MASSACHUSETTS

MICHIGAN
TERRITORY

Buffalo

NEW YORK

• Boston

CT   RI

Detroit •

Lake Erie

Erie •

Cleveland •

• New York

INDIANA

OHIO

PENNSYLVANIA

Philadelphia •

NEW
JERSEY

ATLANTIC
OCEAN

• Cincinnati

MD

• Baltimore

Washington •

DE

MISSOURI
TERRITORY

KENTUCKY

VIRGINIA

U N I T E D   S T A T E S

Norfolk •

NORTH CAROLINA

The War of 1812

TENNESSEE

• Huntsville

SOUTH
CAROLINA

Charleston •

U.S. and British movement, 1812

U.S. and British movement, 1813

U.S. and British movement, 1814–15

British blockade

Battle

British occupied U.S. territory

British territory

Spanish territory

MISSISSIPPI
TERRITORY

GEORGIA

Savannah •

British New Orleans Campaign
November 22, 1814 – February 11, 1815

British advance

British withdrawal

Jackson's night attack

Fortification

LOUISIANA

Mobile •

• Pensacola

FLORIDA

St. Augustine •

New Orleans •

Gulf of Mexico

N

0 ___ 200 km

0 ___ 200 miles

Lake
Pontchartrain

Pearl R.

NEW ORLEANS

Pascagoula R.

December 13: British fleet arrives, troops sent to sieze outlying islands and forts

November 11: Jackson returns from Pensacola operation, leaving for New Orleans. November 22: Almost all of his troops are left in Mobile under Winchester's command

Lake Borgne

Cedar R.

Darbone R.

Mobile •

L O U I S I A N A

Mississippi R.

Mobile
Bay

North
Chandeleur
Island

Fort St. Phillip

January 8–18: Secondary attack fails

Breton
Island

South
Chandeleur
Island

Gulf of Mexico

N

0 ___ 20 km

0 ___ 20 miles

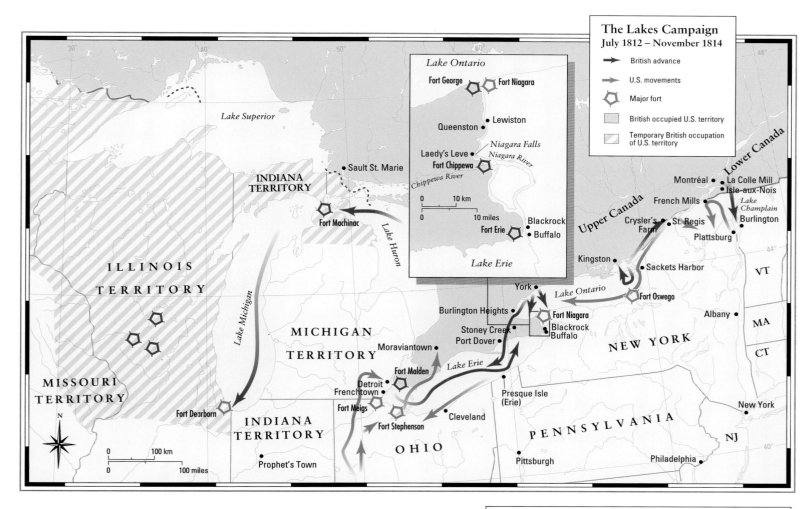

The Lakes Campaign
July 1812 – November 1814

→ British advance
→ U.S. movements
⬠ Major fort
British occupied U.S. territory
Temporary British occupation of U.S. territory

PRIOR TO THE CIVIL WAR THE U.S. Army had been a small force that had served primarily as a frontier constabulary and in two wars with foreign enemies. It had, however, developed a corps of professionally trained officers who played vital roles on both sides in the Civil War. In 1802 the United States Military Academy opened at West Point, New York. The academy at once became a focal point of political controversy and continued as such throughout the antebellum period. Opponents of the academy claimed that it was elitist and that it produced would-be aristocrats who were in fact no better at fighting the republic's wars than any man with natural leadership capacity.

In the War of 1812 the U.S. Army fought against highly trained and disciplined British regulars as well as untrained but extremely fierce Indians. The regular U.S. Army, though small, performed well, showing itself the equal of the British regulars in training and discipline. West Point-trained officers, who at this time filled many of the army's junior officer positions, more than proved their value by providing superb leadership at the small-unit level, in camp, on the march, and in battle. Yet, the bulk of U.S. soldiers who served during the War of 1812 were militiamen, who often proved appallingly undisciplined and spectacularly unsuccessful in combat. The September 1814 Battle of Bladensburg, near Washington, D.C., was only the most notable of the militia's many dismal performances. There, American citizen soldiers fled from the field so precipitately that the battle was sometimes derisively referred to as the "Bladensburg Races."

Yet the War of 1812 did not serve to prove conclusively in the minds of the American people or their politicians the superiority of well-disciplined regular troops on the need for a professional officer corps. That it did not was largely a result of the U.S. victory at the January 1815 Battle of New Orleans. There Andrew Jackson led an army composed mostly of American militia to a lopsided victory over a powerful British army. Jackson had had no formal military training but considerable experience. He was also a man of exceptional natural abilities for leadership and planning. Although few of his troops were regulars, his militia included a sizable contingent of frontiersmen, who possessed impressive personal fighting prowess as well as more than a years experience serving under Jackson's command against hostile Indian tribes. The unusual nature of Jackson and his army, as well as the special circumstances of the battlefield at Chalmette

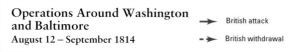

Operations Around Washington and Baltimore
August 12 – September 1814

→ British attack
-→ British withdrawal

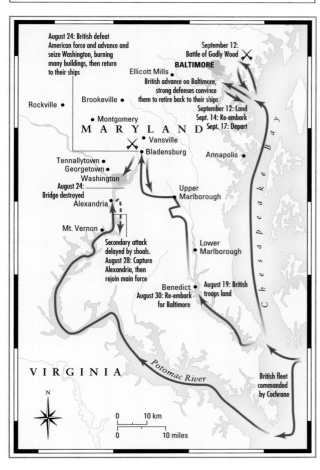

In this earliest-known war photograph, an 1846 daguerreotype, General John E. Wool, front left, is seen with his staff in Saltillo, Mexico.

Plantation, led to a dramatic American victory at New Orleans. Celebrated for years afterward, the Battle of New Orleans convinced many Americans and their political leaders that untrained citizen soldiers led by untrained officers were all the fighting force a republic needed for its defense.

Between 1815 and 1846 the U.S. Army's frontier constabulary duties were punctuated by the Blackhawk War and the first and second Seminole Wars. The Blackhawk War provided little challenge for the U.S. military though additional opportunities for untrained militia to show their inadequacy in battle and indiscipline in camp. The Seminole Wars, on the other hand, were exercises in futility for both regulars and militia, as the wily Indians waged mostly successful guerrilla warfare in the swamps of their native Florida.

The Mexican War proved to be a training ground for many junior officers who would later become generals in the Civil War. The chief U.S. generals of the war, Zachary Taylor and Winfield Scott, though not West Point graduates, were nevertheless veterans of long service who provided examples of professionalism to the younger officers in their armies. Captain Robert E. Lee served ably as an engineer officer on Scott's staff and in that capacity helped plan and execute all of that general's brilliant victories leading to the capture of Mexico City. Lieutenant Ulysses S. Grant gained vital experience in logistics as a regimental quartermaster. Like Lee and Grant, dozens of future Civil War generals gained combat experience in the Mexican War.

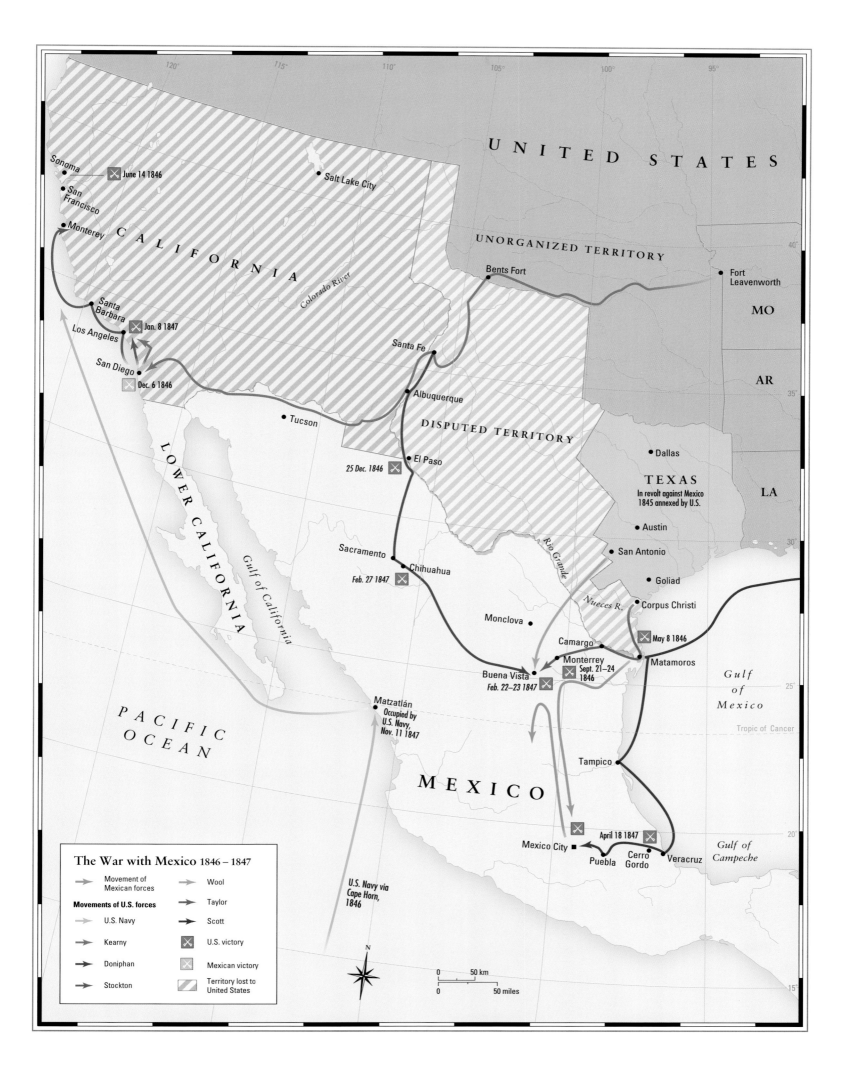

UNITED STATES

UNORGANIZED TERRITORY

Sonoma
☒ June 14 1846
San Francisco
Monterey
CALIFORNIA
Salt Lake City

Santa Barbara
Los Angeles
☒ Jan. 8 1847
San Diego
☒ Dec. 6 1846

Colorado River

Bents Fort

Fort Leavenworth

MO

AR

Tucson

Santa Fe

Albuquerque

DISPUTED TERRITORY

El Paso
25 Dec. 1846 ☒

Dallas

TEXAS
In revolt against Mexico
1845 annexed by U.S.

LA

Austin

LOWER CALIFORNIA

Gulf of California

Sacramento

Chihuahua
Feb. 27 1847 ☒

Monclova

Rio Grande

San Antonio

Goliad

Nueces R.
Corpus Christi

Camargo
Monterrey
Sept. 21–24
1846

May 8 1846 ☒
Matamoros

Gulf
of
Mexico

PACIFIC
OCEAN

Matzatlán
Occupied by
U.S. Navy,
Nov. 11 1847

Buena Vista
Feb. 22–23 1847 ☒

Tropic of Cancer

MEXICO

Tampico

U.S. Navy via
Cape Horn,
1846

Mexico City ■
Puebla
April 18 1847 ☒
Cerro Gordo
Veracruz

Gulf of
Campeche

The War with Mexico 1846–1847

→ Movement of Mexican forces
→ Wool

Movements of U.S. forces
→ U.S. Navy
→ Taylor
→ Kearny
→ Scott
→ Doniphan
☒ U.S. victory
→ Stockton
☒ Mexican victory
▨ Territory lost to United States

N

0 — 50 km
0 — 50 miles

THE ELECTION OF 1860

BY 1860, THE SLAVERY ISSUE and sectional tensions had fragmented America's political parties. Five nominees competed for the presidency, and each proposed a dramatically different solution to the crisis over slavery. The Republican Party stood united behind Abraham Lincoln, who championed the idea of free soil, preventing the spread of slavery westward in hopes of leading to the institution's "ultimate extinction." The Democratic Party split in two. Southern Democrats called for a "federal slave code," designed to protect slave owners' right to bring their slaves into the western territories. Northern Democrats, led by Senator Stephen Douglas of Illinois, championed "popular sovereignty," the right of the people of each territory to decide for themselves whether to support slavery or freedom. Meeting in Charleston, South Carolina, the Democratic Convention adopted a platform that endorsed popular sovereignty. Southern Democrats walked out of the convention in disgust and later nominated Vice President John Breckinridge of Kentucky, who supported a federal slave code. Northern Democrats reassembled in Baltimore and nominated Douglas for president on a platform of popular sovereignty. A fourth political party, the Constitutional Union Party, advocated a constitutional compromise to solve the sectional crisis, such as extending the Missouri Compromise Line all the way to the Pacific Ocean, dividing the West permanently between slavery

and freedom. Popular in the Upper South, the Constitutional Unionists nominated John Bell of Kentucky. Finally, the Abolition Party, which advocated the immediate emancipation of all southern slaves, campaigned in New England and the Upper Midwest, nominating Gerrit Smith of New York, an abolitionist.

Republicans knew that they could win the election with only northern votes. They did not campaign in the South, and Lincoln's name was not on the ballot in most of the slave states. The key to Lincoln's victory was winning the states of the Lower North—New Jersey, Indiana, Illinois, and especially Pennsylvania. He therefore took a moderate stand on the slavery issue, assuring the South that he would never attack slavery directly, that he would enforce the Fugitive Slave Law, and that he would not interfere with the interstate slave trade. But he made clear that he would do everything in his power to prevent the spread of slavery into the western territories. That seemed threatening enough, and many southerners declared that if Lincoln won the election they would secede.

In November, Lincoln won less than forty percent of the popular vote, the smallest winning total in American history. But he carried every state in the North, capturing every northern electoral vote except for three in New Jersey. The Southern Democrat, Breckinridge, won the entire Deep South and came in second. Bell won three

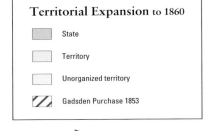

Territorial Expansion to 1860

- State
- Territory
- Unorganized territory
- Gadsden Purchase 1853

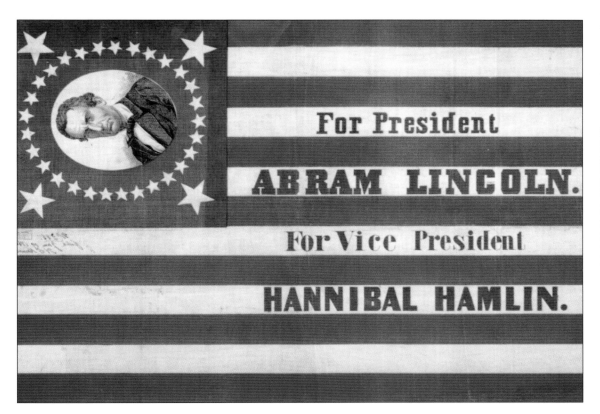

For President
ABRAM LINCOLN.
For Vice President
HANNIBAL HAMLIN.

A large campaign banner for the 1860 Republican presidential candidate Abraham Lincoln—represented here as Abram—and his running mate Hannibal Hamlin.

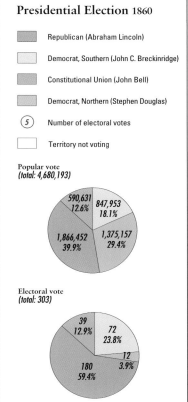

Presidential Election 1860

- Republican (Abraham Lincoln)
- Democrat, Southern (John C. Breckinridge)
- Constitutional Union (John Bell)
- Democrat, Northern (Stephen Douglas)
- (5) Number of electoral votes
- Territory not voting

Popular vote
(total: 4,680,193)

590,631 12.6%
847,953 18.1%
1,866,452 39.9%
1,375,157 29.4%

Electoral vote
(total: 303)

39 12.9%
72 23.8%
12 3.9%
180 59.4%

states in the Upper South, and Douglas took only one state, Missouri. The Abolition Party attracted less than 1 percent of the popular vote. True to their word, seven slave states in the Deep South—led by South Carolina—seceded from the Union even before Lincoln became president. When Lincoln took the oath of office in March 1861, the nation he led was already divided, and a rival government, the Confederate States of America, was underway.

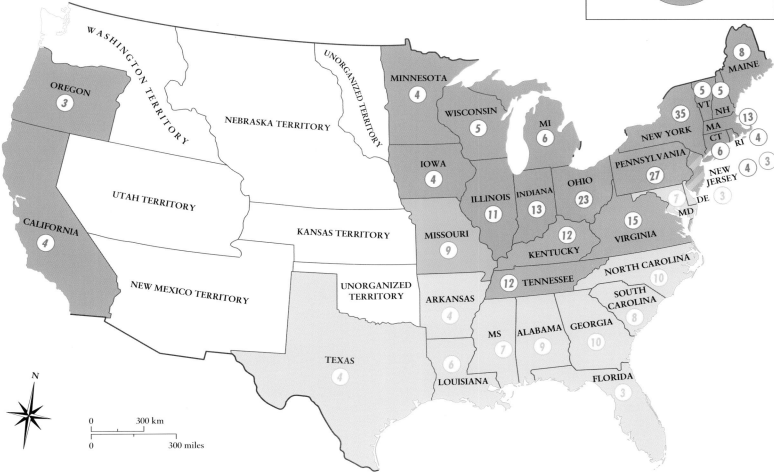

SECESSION

During the election of 1860, Abraham Lincoln promised the South that he would not attack slavery directly or interfere with the interstate slave trade. Lincoln's assurances provoked three distinct responses within the South. "Immediate Secessionists," who predominated in the Deep South, did not trust Lincoln and viewed his pledge to stop the spread of slavery as an indirect assault on the South designed to abolish slavery eventually. They swore that they would leave the Union immediately upon Lincoln's election without giving him a chance to act moderately or even waiting to see what he would do. The "Conditional Unionists" of the Upper South gave Lincoln the benefit of the doubt. They pledged to stay in the Union as long as he acted moderately, did not attack the South, and tolerated the slave trade. They hoped that cooperation and compromise could ward off civil war. The "Unconditional Unionists" of the Border States considered the Union more important than slavery. They vowed to stay in the Union no matter what Lincoln did.

True to their word, the Immediate Secessionists left the Union as soon as Lincoln was elected. On December 20, 1860, South Carolina seceded and created the Palmetto Republic, an independent nation. The new government sent commissioners to all the other slave states to persuade them to secede. Their work bore fruit, and a wave of secession drew the Deep South—Mississippi, Florida, Alabama, Georgia, Louisiana, and Texas—out of the Union. These seven states created the Confederacy on February 9, 1861, in Montgomery, Alabama, choos-

ing Jefferson Davis of Mississippi as president and Alexander Stephens of Georgia as vice president. Confederates seized federal forts and armories across the Deep South in an effort to prepare for war. All eyes focused on Lincoln. True to his word—and his instincts—Lincoln acted moderately.

In his inaugural address, Lincoln tried desperately to keep the remaining eight slave states in the Union, appealing to the Conditional Unionists and Unconditional Unionists in the Upper South and Border States. He pledged not to interfere with slavery in the South, promised to enforce the Fugitive Slave Law, and supported a constitutional amendment guaranteeing southern states the right to keep their slaves. Lincoln even promised not to attempt to recapture the federal forts or even enforce federal law in the Confederacy. His moderation might have paid off, except that Fort Sumter, sitting squarely in Charleston harbor but still under Union control, was running low on supplies. Refusing to surrender another federal fort, Lincoln sent supplies on unarmed ships.

On the morning of April 12, 1861, Confederate cannons opened fire on Fort Sumter. When Lincoln declared the Confederacy in rebellion and called for volunteers to defend the Union, the Conditional Unionists decided to secede. Four states in the Upper South—Virginia, North Carolina, Tennessee, and Arkansas—launched a second wave of secession in April 1861. All told, eleven slave states—one-third of the Union's thirty-three states—seceded. The four Border States—Maryland, Kentucky, Missouri, and Delaware—stayed in the Union, as they had pledged to do. The Civil War had begun.

The United States January 1861

- Free state
- Slave state
- Territory theoretically open to slavery after the Dred Scott decision of 1857

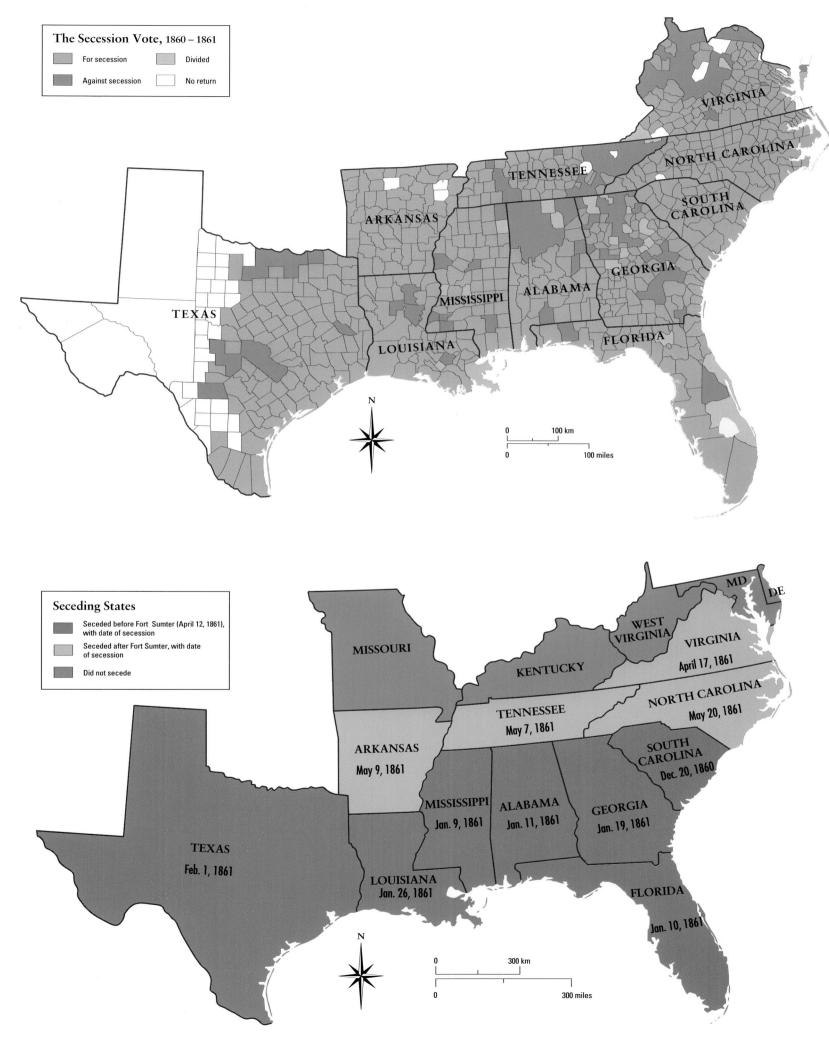

The Secession Vote, 1860 – 1861

- For secession
- Against secession
- Divided
- No return

VIRGINIA

TENNESSEE

NORTH CAROLINA

ARKANSAS

SOUTH CAROLINA

MISSISSIPPI

ALABAMA

GEORGIA

TEXAS

LOUISIANA

FLORIDA

N

0   100 km

0   100 miles

Seceding States

- Seceded before Fort Sumter (April 12, 1861), with date of secession
- Seceded after Fort Sumter, with date of secession
- Did not secede

MD

DE

MISSOURI

WEST VIRGINIA

KENTUCKY

VIRGINIA
April 17, 1861

TENNESSEE
May 7, 1861

NORTH CAROLINA
May 20, 1861

ARKANSAS
May 9, 1861

SOUTH CAROLINA
Dec. 20, 1860

MISSISSIPPI
Jan. 9, 1861

ALABAMA
Jan. 11, 1861

GEORGIA
Jan. 19, 1861

TEXAS
Feb. 1, 1861

LOUISIANA
Jan. 26, 1861

FLORIDA
Jan. 10, 1861

N

0   300 km

0   300 miles

FEDERAL AND CONFEDERATE FINANCES

THE UNION BEGAN THE CIVIL WAR in a much stronger financial position than the Confederacy. The North possessed nine-tenths of America's industrial capacity, three-fourths of its improved farmland, two-thirds of its railroad mileage, and three-fourths of its wealth overall. The Union could devote fewer of its resources to the war simply because it had so much more to begin with. The Confederacy was hampered by its lack of capital, which was invested mostly in land and slaves and was therefore difficult to mobilize. Exploiting its more meager resources and supporting an uphill war effort required the South to tax more heavily and impose more stringent financial measures than the North. The Confederacy began the war by borrowing money from its own citizens, in the form of government bonds, and absorbed all available capital within the first year.

The Confederate Congress quickly authorized treasury notes—the infamous Confederate money—to pay for most of its war effort (sixty percent). The Confederate notes, which could be redeemed for gold or silver two years after the war ended, depreciated immediately. Skyrocketing food prices undermined morale and ignited bread riots.

With counterfeiting rife and inflation eventually exceeding nine thousand percent, southerners abandoned the paper money and resorted to barter. The Confederate Congress turned reluctantly to heavy taxation, imposing an eight percent sales tax, a ten percent profits tax, and an income tax that ranged up to fifteen percent. Draining the Confederate economy and breeding popular discontent, the taxes provided only five percent of the Confederacy's revenue. In a desperate attempt to supply its armies, the South eventually adopted a tax-in-kind, which required farmers to turn over ten percent of their crops, beyond bare subsistence, to the government. Confederate armies eventually confiscated materiel in war zones, paying a fraction of the market price for the goods. These draconian economic measures provoked bitter resentment and fueled opposition to the war, especially in the uplands where there were few slaves

The Union, with its larger tax base, could keep tax rates lower while still raising more money than the Confederacy could. Taxes, including the nation's first income tax, supported more than one-fifth of the Union war effort. The Union could also borrow more money at lower interest rates than the South, because lenders had more faith in its ability to win the war.

The famous greenbacks—paper money that bore the likeness of Secretary of the Treasury Salmon Chase—were backed by gold and silver and therefore tended to hold their value. They provided thirteen percent of the Union's revenue and produced just eighty percent inflation during the entire war. Nearly a million ordinary northerners bought government bonds, displaying support for the war effort and investing in their nation's future. Congress not only exploited the northern economy to finance the war but also enacted reforms that strengthened the nation's economic structure over the long run. The National Bank Act created a system of federally chartered banks that issued stable bank notes and represented the backbone of the American economy into the twentieth century. Overall, its thriving economy provided an overwhelming military advantage for the Union. The Civil War, in turn, boosted the northern economy while dealing a long-term setback to the aspirations of the beleaguered South.

The likeness of Salmon Chase appeared on the original U.S. dollar bill—the famous "greenbacks." Backed by reserves of gold and silver, the currency held its value.

Confederate treasury notes were not backed by gold or silver until two years after the war's "successful" outcome. Although the Confederate government managed to finance a large part of its war effort via the issue of these notes, the population soon lost confidence in them, and by 1865 commerce in the South was largely reduced to bartering.

ARMS PRODUCTION—UNION AND CONFEDERATE

WHEN THE CIVIL WAR BEGAN, the United States had twenty-two armories and arsenals. (By definition, armories produced weapons, while arsenals stored them, but the two terms were used interchangeably.) After seceding, the Confederate states seized the armories and arsenals within their limits to prepare for war. Thirteen of these facilities ended up in the Union, nine in the Confederacy. Despite these formidable arms production facilities, the Confederacy began the war with about one-half as many small arms as the Union. The South was also hampered in its arms production by severe shortages of raw materials, particularly gunpowder and lead, as well as skilled labor.

Central Laboratory in Macon, Georgia, with duplicating the famous British Enfield rifle.

By the end of 1862, however, severe shortages of raw materials led Southerners to scavenge copper from whiskey stills and lead from window weights and water pipes. The South's armories were also inviting military targets. Union troops burned the workshops at Harpers Ferry, which thereafter functioned only as an arsenal. General William T. Sherman targeted Gorgas's armories as his men marched through Georgia. Despite the South's inability to produce arms rivaling the Union's Springfield rifle in quality, Confederate armies were relatively well armed throughout the war, as the devastation they continually inflicted

Company H of the Sixth Vermont Infantry in drill practice at Camp Griffin, Virginia. Its men would see action on many battlefields of the war and though well fed and supplied, some forty percent of them would not return.

One of the benefits of attracting Virginia into the Confederacy in April 1861 was the acquisition of the Tredegar Iron Works in Richmond and the federal armory and arsenal at Harpers Ferry. The Tredegar Works, the primary foundry in the South, cast the largest guns that were available to Confederate artillery units. The day after Virginia seceded, the state militia captured Harpers Ferry, seizing four thousand firearms and components for ten thousand more. Harpers Ferry's superb rifle-making machinery was relocated to Richmond, Virginia, and Fayetteville, North Carolina, for the duration of the war. The Confederacy's chief of ordnance, Colonel Josiah Gorgas, advocated a crash program of importing arms from Europe before the Union could mount a blockade. Overruled by President Jefferson Davis, Gorgas focused instead on arms production, centralizing control over arms and concentrating production in Georgia. He turned the Augusta Armory into an important powder mill, as well as founding new arsenals in Atlanta and Columbus. He charged the Confederate States

upon the Union army attests.

Meanwhile, the South's blockade-runners were charged with the task of importing small arms, managing to smuggle 600,000 of them past the Union frigates. In fact, two-thirds of the Confederacy's small arms were imported from Europe. By every measure, the Union far surpassed the Confederacy in arms production. Still, northern armories were seriously unprepared for a war of this magnitude. During the first year of war, the federal government imported hundreds of thousands of arms from Europe. By the end of 1862, domestic armories were meeting the War Department's needs, led by the Springfield Armory in Massachusetts, which produced one-half of all the Union's rifles. Samuel Colt's armory in Hartford, Connecticut, manufactured most of the Union's pistols, at the rate of thirty-five thousand per year. All told, Northern armories supplied nearly 1.5 million small arms to Union soldiers. The North's overwhelming industrial power translated into an equally imposing battlefield advantage.

Right: Cannons, mortars, and ammunition are concentrated at Ship Point near Yorktown. This seemingly endless supply was intended to be deployed by McClellan's army on the peninsula.

Northern Industry was able to keep the army, navy and railroads supplied with all their required materials. To the right a yard full of stored rails stand ready for use by U.S. military railroads in Alexandria, Virginia.

Far Right: The Tredagar Ironworks in Richmond, from 1861 to 1865 was dedicated to meeting the ordnance needs of the Confederacy and could do little to support the railroad infrastructure of the south.

Strategic Railroads and the Civil War

————— 4'8½" or 4'10" gauge railroad

————— 5' gauge railroad

——▶ Northern route

——▶ Southern route

1 September 1863: Longstreet's First Corp of the Army of North Virginia moved from Richmond to Northern Georgia

2 October 1863: Twenty five thousand men moved from Washington to Tennessee in ten days.

CONFEDERATE ARMY, ORGANIZATION, AND RECRUITMENT

UNLIKE THE UNION, THE CONFEDERACY had no long-standing regular army in 1861. It did, however, have certain characteristics that gave it a head start over the North in raising the large armies that would be needed in the Civil War. The South had long prided itself as being a uniquely militant society. Partially this was simply a matter of self-image, but it was also partially based on reality. Historians still argue about the relative prevalence of military schools and volunteer companies in the North and in the South, but it seems clear at least that the South had a far larger number of such institutions in proportion to its smaller population.

Military colleges such as Virginia Military Institute (V.M.I.), in Lexington, Virginia, and the Citadel, in Charleston, South Carolina, were only the most famous of the many schools in the South that trained young men to be army officers as well as educated members of society. By a curious irony, even while some southerners, such as Tennessee senator Andrew Johnson, were among

Much of the Confederate war effort was almost a cottage industry. The illustration above shows ladies making uniforms for the army.

the foremost critics of West Point and of military education in general, others, such as Mississippi senator (soon to be Confederate president) Jefferson Davis, were among the staunchest defenders of the national military academy and of the many smaller public and private institutions across the south that were largely patterned after West Point. Schools such as V.M.I. and the Citadel were important in providing a cadre of trained officers for the Confederate armies (along with the several hundred West Point-trained U.S. Army officers who resigned to side with the Confederacy), particularly the Army of Northern Virginia. Among the most famous V.M.I. graduates to rise to high rank was Major General Robert E. Rodes, one of Lee's finest division commanders. Major General Micah Jenkins, another of the Army of Northern Virginia's premier division commanders, was a graduate of the Citadel.

Another element of the South's military culture

was the volunteer company. Although ordinary militia organization in most states had almost completely lapsed by the time of the Civil War, the active element of the militia was kept up in the form of volunteer companies. Volunteer companies exited in both the North and the South, though per capita they may have been more common in the South. Volunteer companies such as the Rome Light Guards, of Rome, Georgia, or the Oglethorpe Light Infantry, of Savannah, Georgia, or hundreds of others throughout the country, organized themselves, elected officers, bought their own fancy dress uniforms, and generally functioned more as social clubs than as military organizations. One did not enlist in such organizations; one applied.

Even in the militant South, however, most of the recruits of 1861 joined new volunteer companies that had not existed before secession. When in April 1861 Confederate president Jefferson Davis called for 100,000 volunteers to serve for one year, hundreds of volunteer companies sprang up almost overnight all over the South. Most of them had names, originally, though many made none of the pretensions of high social status that the prewar volunteer companies had done. The company that the lawyer (later General) John B. Gordon raised in the area where the states of Tennessee, Georgia, and Alabama came together called itself the Raccoon Roughs.

As the Confederate war department called upon state governors to provide their quotas of troops, the governors in turn sent orders to the various volunteer companies—new or old—that had offered their services to the state. As each volunteer company received its orders from the governor it traveled to the designated place of organization near the fighting front. This might be Richmond, for troops earmarked for the Virginia theater, or various other cities for troops who would be serving elsewhere. Only once the companies arrived their were they organized into regimental armies. Thus, both the Rome Light Guards and the Oglethorpe Light Infantry traveled separately to a camp outside Richmond, and there, along with eight other independent Georgia companies, were organized into the Eighth Georgia Infantry Regiment. At that point the old names fell away, and the Rome Light Guards and the Oglethorpe Light Infantry became, respectively, companies A and B. So it went with all of the volunteer companies.

Right: Entitled "Our National Confederate Anthem," this rare illustrated sheet music cover was issued in the Confederacy. Published by the composer in Richmond, the cover features a Confederate soldier holding a flag with the motto "God Save the South." Few illustrated music sheets were issued in the South due to the relatively undeveloped lithography industry.

FORT SUMTER

As THE SEVEN DEEP SOUTH states announced their secession between December 20, 1860, and February 1, 1861, rebellious militia in each state, acting on behalf of the secessionist state governments, seized all the U.S. government facilities in those states, including arsenals, shipyards, and forts. Only two federal installations in the rebellious states escaped this fate. One was Fort Pickens off the coast of Pensacola, Florida. The other was Fort Sumter, located on a mud bar inside the harbor of Charleston, South Carolina.

Although Fort Pickens remained insignificant, Fort Sumter was a different matter entirely. South Carolina was the first state to secede and Charleston was the hotbed of secessionist agitation in the state. South Carolinians were extremely eager to seize the federal forts in their state as a symbolic statement of their independence.

The commander of U.S. Army forces in the Charleston area was Major Robert Anderson. On December 20, 1860, when South Carolina declared itself no longer part of the United States, Anderson's command of less than one hundred men was located at Fort Moultrie on Sullivan's Island adjacent to Charleston harbor. An obsolete and dilapidated fort, Moultrie was almost without defenses on its landward side, leaving Anderson and his troops vulnerable to the Charleston mob or the large number of state militia that had begun to assemble in the Charleston area. In order to avoid a confrontation and to find a more secure position for his men, Anderson on the night of December 26 quietly transported his command to Fort Sumter, a not-quite-completed brick fort in the middle of the harbor.

South Carolinians were outraged, charging that Anderson had acted in bad faith by making it more difficult for them to attack him. They seized the remaining—now empty—forts around Charleston, as well as the post office, arsenal, and customs house—part of the process of seizures that would soon be sweeping the Deep South.

On January 9, 1861, the unarmed merchant steamer *Star of the West* arrived at Charleston from Brooklyn, carrying supplies and reinforcements for Fort Sumter. When *Star of the West* attempted to enter the harbor, however, the South Carolina batteries around the harbor opened fire, forcing the ship to turn back. Anderson's men stood to their guns in Fort Sumter, but as Anderson had no instructions from his superiors as to what to do in such a case, he did not give the order to fire.

There President James Buchanan let the matter of Fort Sumter rest for the remaining two months of his presidency. Meanwhile representatives of the seven seceding states convened in Montgomery, Alabama, organized themselves as the Confederate States of America, and selected Jefferson Davis, a recently resigned U.S. senator from Mississippi, as their president. The Confederacy adopted the militia around Charleston as part of the new Confederate army, and Davis sent Pierre Gustave Toutant Beauregard, a graduate of West Point from Louisiana, to take command there.

In his inaugural address, Lincoln stated that he would not attack the South but would maintain the Union. Specifically, he would continue to hold the remaining federal installations in the South, now reduced to forts Pickens and Sumter. Only a few hours later, however, a letter from Anderson informed him that the major would have to surrender the fort if not re-provisioned within six weeks. Against the advice of army general in chief Winfield Scott and several members of his cabinet, including Secretary of State William Seward, Lincoln remained determined to hold Fort Sumter. In early April, with time and provisions running out for the fort, Lincoln adopted a plan to send supplies. He would notify the governor of South Carolina that an expedition was

The interior of Fort Sumter after a bombardment by forty-seven howitzers and mortars, cheered on by local citizens. Anderson's Union garrison offered what was not much more than token resistance, eventually agreeing to terms offered by the besieging Confederate forces.

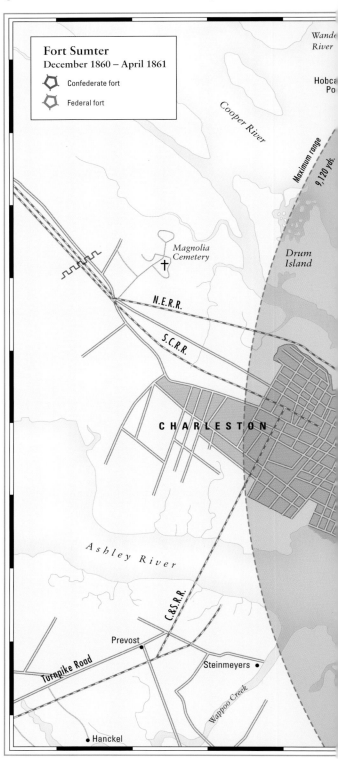

Fort Sumter
December 1860 – April 1861

⬡ Confederate fort

⬡ Federal fort

on the way to bring the garrison supplies only—not weapons or reinforcements—and that is exactly what the expedition would do, unless the Rebels fired on it. In the latter case, warships accompanying the expedition would shoot their way into the harbor to get the supplies to the fort.

This already desperate plan became even more so when Secretary of State Seward—who had been holding secret, indirect communications with Confederate emissaries and had promised them, unbeknownst to Lincoln, that Sumter would be abandoned—diverted the most powerful warship attached to the expedition. This effectively removed the option of forcible re-supply.

On receiving Lincoln's notice, South Carolina

governor Francis Pickens immediately sent word to Jefferson Davis, who was at the Confederate capital in Montgomery, Alabama. Davis ordered Beauregard to take the fort. In the predawn hours of April 12, 1861, after receiving Anderson's refusal to surrender, Beauregard's staff officers gave the order for the bombardment to commence. Thirty-four hours later, Anderson surrendered. Ironically, the opening action of what was to become America's bloodiest war resulted in not a single fatality. However, when under the terms of his surrender agreement Anderson was permitted to fire a salute to the U.S. flag before evacuating the fort, one of the cannons misfired, killing one artillerist and mortally wounding another.

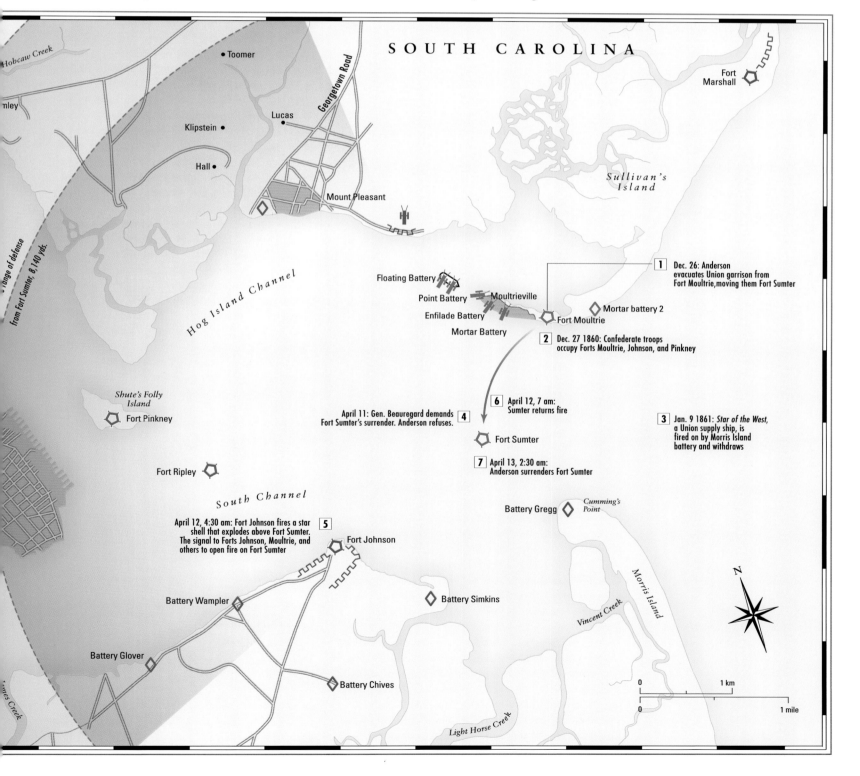

WESTERN VIRGINIA

THE NORTHWESTERN COUNTIES OF VIRGINIA contained few slaves and therefore had little reason to sympathize with the South's slaveholding Confederacy. The region strongly opposed secession, and in June 1861 representatives of twenty-six northwestern counties met in Wheeling to begin the process that would lead, in 1863, to the creation of the new state of West Virginia.

During the summer of 1861 western Virginia was the scene of several small clashes that were disproportionate both in the attention they received at the time and in their effect on the ultimate separation of West Virginia from Virginia. Union forces in the region, some twenty thousand men, belonged to the Department of the Ohio commanded by Major General George B. McClellan. Confederate forces under the command of Brigadier General Robert S. Garnett numbered four thousand five hundred. On June 3, a column of several thousand Union troops under Brigadier General Thomas A. Morris routed seven hundred and seventy-five Confederates under Colonel George A. Porterfield at Philippi, a skirmish so one-sided that Unionists came to call it "the Philippi Races." Union casualties totaled two, and Confederate about fifteen.

Garnett withdrew his forces to Rich Mountain, and McClellan followed. By July 7, advanced elements of the two forces were skirmishing. McClellan's subordinate Brigadier General William S. Rosecrans devised a plan to flank a one thousand two hundred-man detachment of Garnett's force under Lieutenant Colonel John Pegram that was guarding Buckhannon Pass and the town of Beverly. McClellan agreed to threaten Garnett in front, then attack when he heard Rosecrans begin his flank attack. On July 11, Rosecrans attacked and routed Pegram, but most of the Confederate troops were

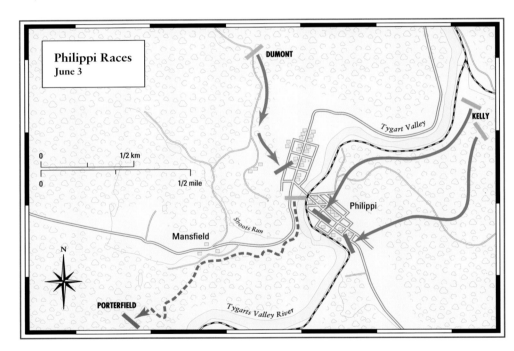

able to escape because McClellan never attacked. Union casualties at Rich Mountain numbered seventy-four, and Confederate eighty-eight. With his position on Rich Mountain turned, Garnett once again retreated. After a two-day chase, on July 13 Union forces under Morris succeeded in overtaking Garnett at Carrick's Ford. Among the Confederate casualties at this skirmish was Garnett, who was mortally wounded. Trapped, Pegram surrendered some five hundred and fifty men.

McClellan's role in the victories in western Virginia had been minimal. Rosecrans and Morris had done all the fighting while their commander remained well to the rear. Nevertheless, McClellan got the credit, and, when after the July 21 debacle at Bull Run the country was urgently in the market for a winning general, it seized eagerly on McClellan, a clear case of mistaken identity.

Command in western Virginia passed to Rosecrans, and a brief lull followed in the region.

In August, the Confederate government began to dream of recovering lost ground in western Virginia and dispatched forces for that purpose. To supervise the new effort, Jefferson Davis sent one of the Confederacy's highest-ranking generals, Robert E. Lee. In early September, one of Lee's subordinates, Brigadier General John B. Floyd, a former Virginia governor and U.S. secretary of war, led a column down the Kanawha River valley. He crossed the Gauley River, a tributary of the Kanawha, at Carnifex Ferry, threatening several small Union garrisons in the area, while Lee made plans to attack the Federals at Cheat Mountain.

Rosecrans advanced with seven thousand men against Floyd, threatening his communications. Floyd fell back to Carnifex Ferry, and Rosecrans attacked him there on September 10 but could not break his lines. Another Confederate force under Brigadier General Henry A. Wise was not far away at the time, but Wise and Floyd were nursing a personal feud—neither would aid or cooperate with the other. Floyd had to fall back across the Gauley River after a day of inconclusive fighting. Union casualties at Carnifex Ferry totaled about one hundred and fifty, and Confederate only twenty.

September 10 was the first day of Lee's first Civil War battle, a complicated offensive against two thousand Union troops under Brigadier General Joseph J. Reynolds at Cheat Mountain. Lee divided his fifteen thousand men into five columns that were to follow a close timetable coordinating their operations. This proved completely unrealistic amid the rough terrain and incessant autumn rains. Lee's march was delayed and the offensive postponed to the following day. When that day came, the commander of the column that was to open Lee's attack failed to do so. In halting and confused maneuvering, Lee's forces fumbled away the element of surprise. By September 15, Lee realized that the situation was hopeless and withdrew his forces, leaving northwestern Virginia solidly in Union control for the remainder of the war.

Western Virginia

1 May 30: Union troops under the command of Col. B.F. Kelly occupied Grafton, Virginia, in order to protect the Baltimore & Ohio Railroad.

2 June 2: Despite inclement weather Brig. Gen. T.A. Morris's Union force made a night march in two columns through rough country toward Philippi.

3 June 3: Before dawn Morris's Unionist surprised and routed Col. G.A. Porterfield's Confederates in "the Philippi Races."

4 July 7–10: Maj. Gen. George B. McClellan's forces advanced and confronted Brig. Gen. Robert S. Garnett's strong defensive position at Rich Mountain.

5 July 11: Brig. Gen. William S. Rosecrans's brigade attacked and defeated Col. John Pegram's Confederate detachment, forcing Garnett to abandon his line along Rich Mountain and retreat to the northeast.

6 July 13: Pursuing Union troops caught up with the Confederates at Carrick's Ford, where Garnett is mortally wounded in a rear-guard skirmish. Pegram surrenders.

7 July 11–29: Union troops under the command of Brig. Gen. Jacob D. Cox advanced and occupied the Kanawha River valley as far as the Gauley River.

8 August 26: Confederate troops, under the command of Brig. Gen. John B. Floyd, advanced down the Kanawha to Carnifex Ferry on the Gauley River, threatening Cox's command.

9 Sept. 2–10: Rosecrans marched from Clarksburg and attacked Floyd at Carnifex Ferry with inconclusive results. Floyd retreats.

10 Sept. 9–12: Gen. Robert E. Lee, having taken command of Confederate forces in western Virginia, attempted a complicated attack in multiple columns against greatly outnumbered Union forces on Cheat Mountain; it fails miserably.

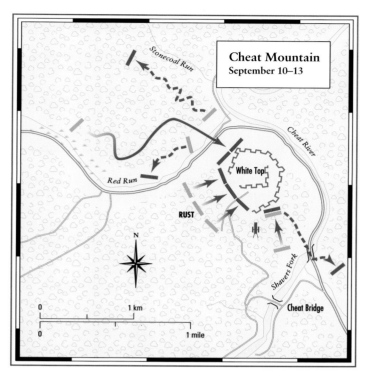

Cheat Mountain
September 10–13

Stonecoal Run

Cheat River

Red Run

White Top!

RUST

N

Shavers Fork

Cheat Bridge

0   1 km

0   1 mile

The telegraph brought about a revolution in military communications, linking units in the field directly to high command. Grant would later write "In each brigade a mule would be led to the rear unwinding a coil of wire, thus in a few moments we would be linked to the Army headquarters."

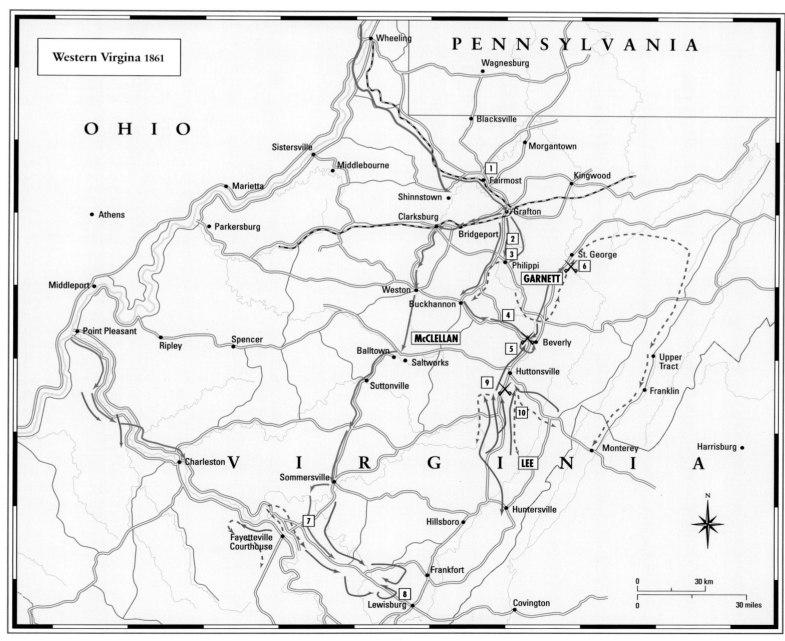

Western Virgina 1861

PENNSYLVANIA

Wheeling

Wagnesburg

OHIO

Blacksville

Sistersville

Morgantown

Middlebourne

Kingwood

1   Fairmost

Shinnstown

Marietta

Grafton

Clarksburg

Athens

Bridgeport

Parkersburg

2

3   St. George

Philippi

GARNETT   6

Middleport

Weston

Buckhannon

McCLELLAN

4

Point Pleasant

Balltown

5   Beverly

Ripley

Spencer

Saltworks

Upper Tract

Suttonville

Huttonsville

Franklin

9

10

Charleston   V   I   R   G   I   N   LEE   I   A

Monterey

Harrisburg

Sommersville

Huntersville

Hillsboro

7

Fayetteville Courthouse

Frankfort

8

Lewisburg

Covington

N

0   30 km

0   30 miles

VIRGINIA

IN EARLY SUMMER 1861, NORTHERN newspapers clamored for quick and decisive action in Virginia. Horace Greeley's *New York Tribune* was particularly shrill in its calls for an immediate advance. Greeley placed the words *On to Richmond* on his paper's masthead and demanded in its columns that the Confederate capital be taken before the Confederate congress could assemble there for the first time, an event scheduled for July 20. Additional impetus for an early advance sprang from the fact that the first seventy-five thousand Union volunteers had been enlisted for only ninety days and their terms of service were about to expire. Recruitment of three-year volunteers had begun, but Union authorities still faced pressure to use the army before the ninety-day recruits went home.

Lincoln responded by applying pressure to Brigadier General Irvin McDowell, who commanded U.S. forces around Washington, D.C., and on July 16 McDowell responded by marching his woefully untrained army of thirty-five thousand men toward Richmond. In his path waited Confederate General Pierre G. T. Beauregard with twenty-two thousand men just south of a stream called "Bull Run." Beauregard received notice of the advance the night before from the Washington socialite and Confederate spy Rose Greenhow, and he read about it in the Washington newspapers that morning. Immediately he sent word to Jefferson Davis in Richmond, and Davis in turn

sent orders to General Joseph E. Johnston—who commanded thirteen thousand Confederate troops in the Shenandoah Valley near Winchester, Virginia—to march to Beauregard's aid. Johnston was able to move his troops because Major General Robert Patterson, in command of the Union troops in the valley, remained idle.

McDowell's inexperienced army moved slowly, reaching Bull Run on July 18 and skirmishing inconclusively with Beauregard's forces at Blackburn's Ford. By the time McDowell was ready to launch his major attack on July 21, Johnston's troops had joined Beauregard and numbers were about equal on both sides. The attack almost succeeded, but when the Confederates managed to hold the key Henry House Hill, forcing McDowell to retreat, his untrained troops became confused and disorganized, and many of them fled in panic all the way back to Washington. The equally disorganized Confederate army was unable to pursue.

The defeat at Bull Run convinced Northerners that a much greater effort would be required in order to win the war. Lincoln called for 500,000 three-year volunteers, and recruits flocked to answer the summons. In place of the discredited McDowell, Lincoln appointed Major General George B. McClellan, who had won several minor victories in the western part of Virginia, to command Union forces around Washington. McClellan proved an excellent organizer and trainer of troops. However, as months went by and the ideal campaigning weather of fall passed without any significant movement by McClellan's superbly organized and equipped Army of the Potomac, Northern public opinion, and particularly the Republican majority in Congress, became dissatisfied.

The Army of the Potomac's only movement during the fall months served to intensify that feeling. McClellan planned a reconnaissance by elements of his army and ordered Brigadier General Charles P. Stone's division to make a demonstration against Confederate forces near Leesburg, Virginia. Stone, an experienced regular-army officer, led a column across the Potomac at Edward's Ferry, while he sent another column under the command of Colonel Edward D. Baker to cross the river several miles away at Ball's Bluff.

A prominent Republican politician and close personal friend of Lincoln, Baker, like many others at the time, had grandiose military ambitions and no concept at all of how to conduct warfare. He led his force into a defeat that cost the Confederates only one hundred and fifty-five casualties but lost the Union some nine hundred and twenty-one men, including Baker himself. Though by military standards a minor skirmish, the affair at Ball's Bluff was significant for its political repercussions. The Congressional Republicans made a martyr of Baker and imprisoned the hapless Stone. Most significant, they established the Joint Committee on the Conduct of the War, which hounded Lincoln and, occasionally, Union commanders, especially in Virginia, throughout the rest of the conflict.

Battle of Ball's Bluff
October 21

SHANKS

Ravine

Ravine

Field

BAKER

Flood Plain

Potomac River

Harrison's Island

Although the Confederacy had been spectacularly successful in the year's two most prominent clashes in Virginia, animosity was also rife in the Confederate high command. Johnston, senior Confederate field commander in Virginia, complained bitterly that his rank was not high enough. Beauregard alleged that Davis had prevented him from winning the war that summer by not allowing him to pursue grandiose offensive operations, and all three men remained morbidly sensitive to suggestions that they had missed an opportunity after the victory at Bull Run. That October they discussed, but could not agree on, plans for a Confederate offensive in the fall.

A French Creole from Louisiana, P. G. T. Beauregard resigned from his U.S. Army commission on February 20, 1861, and was given the rank of brigadier general by the Confederacy. Ironically, Beauregard had received his artillery training at the hands of Sumter's defender, Robert Anderson.

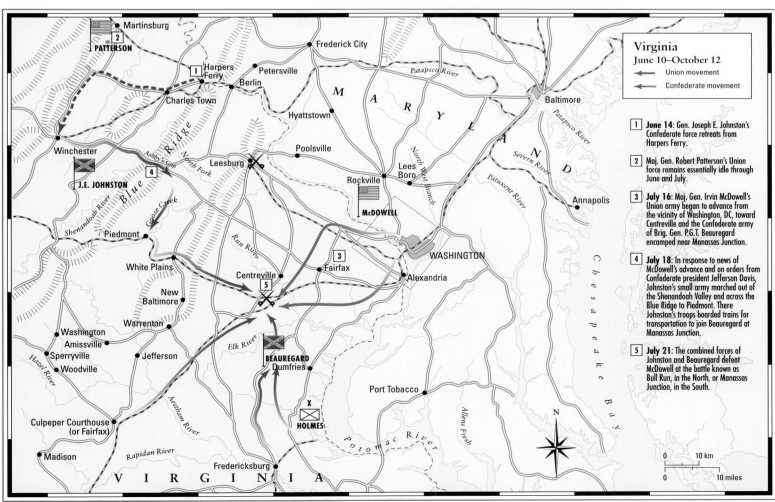

Virginia
June 10–October 12

← Union movement
← Confederate movement

1 **June 14**: Gen. Joseph E. Johnston's Confederate force retreats from Harpers Ferry.

2 **Maj. Gen. Robert Patterson's** Union force remains essentially idle through June and July.

3 **July 16**: Maj. Gen. Irvin McDowell's Union army began to advance from the vicinity of Washington, DC, toward Centreville and the Confederate army of Brig. Gen. P.G.T. Beauregard encamped near Manassas Junction.

4 **July 18**: In response to news of McDowell's advance and on orders from Confederate president Jefferson Davis, Johnston's small army marched out of the Shenandoah Valley and across the Blue Ridge to Piedmont. There Johnston's troops boarded trains for transportation to join Beauregard at Manassas Junction.

5 **July 21**: The combined forces of Johnston and Beauregard defeat McDowell at the battle known as Bull Run, in the North, or Manassas Junction, in the South.

FIRST BATTLE OF MANASSAS (BULL RUN)

Irvin McDowell had studied in France and had observed French staff procedures. It was this education that recommended him to Lincoln; but he had no experience as a field commander.

AS THE UNION ARMY OF BRIGADIER General Irwin McDowell faced the Confederate army of Brigadier General Pierre G. T. Beauregard across Bull Run, each general made plans to attack the other on the morning of July 21 by attacking the other's right flank. It was McDowell who moved first, however, and Beauregard never got the chance to implement his own scheme. The key to McDowell's plan was a flanking column that would march a number of miles to the northwest during the predawn hours, cross Bull Run at Sudley's Ford, and then turn southeastward to descend on the left flank of Beauregard's army. As the flanking column advanced, rolling up the

Confederate line and uncovering additional crossings of Bull Run, more Union troops would cross the creek and join in the battle.

The initial stages of the battle went well for McDowell. The flanking column reached its assigned position and began its attack. Confederate Colonel Nathan G. Evans, whose small brigade was assigned to cover the Stone Bridge on the Warrenton Turnpike, was the first Confederate officer to perceive the threat and he led his command aggressively to meet it. The time he gained allowed Beauregard to begin repositioning his units to meet the attacking Union army.

Some of the first troops Beauregard dispatched

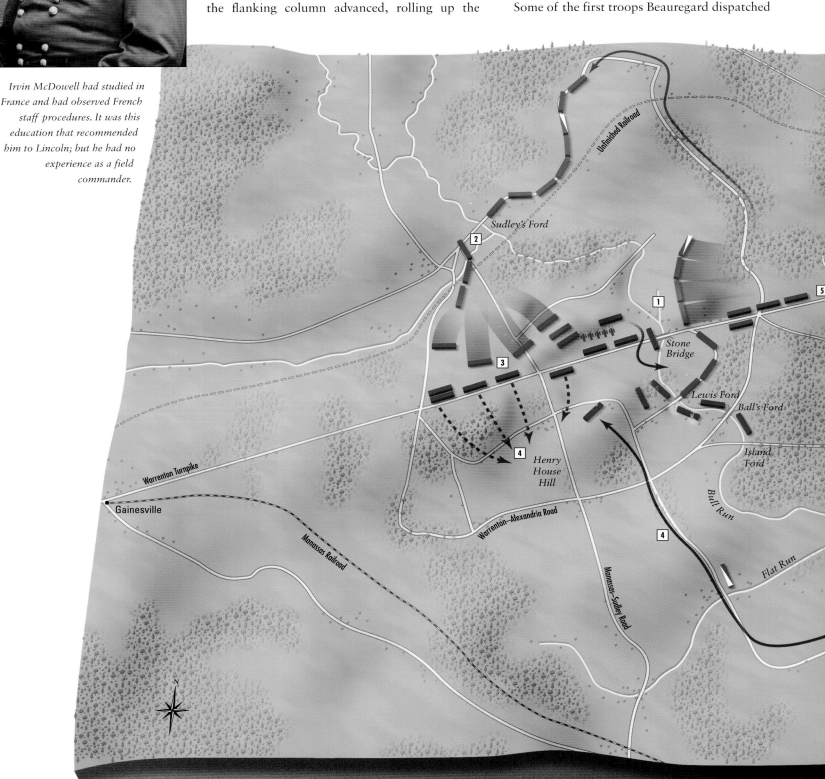

to reinforce Evans were a brigade of Georgians under Colonel Francis Bartow and a brigade of South Carolinians under Brigadier General Barnard Bee, who as senior officer took command of the Confederate forces on that part of the field. Bee continued Evans's aggressive tactics, throwing his troops forward in an effort to blunt the Union advance. The two sides fought ferociously on Matthews Hill, northwest of the turnpike, where McDowell's troops succeeded in overwhelming the Confederates and driving them back in disorder across the turnpike toward Henry House Hill.

While Bartow and Bee fought their losing battle on Matthews Hill, Beauregard was able to send

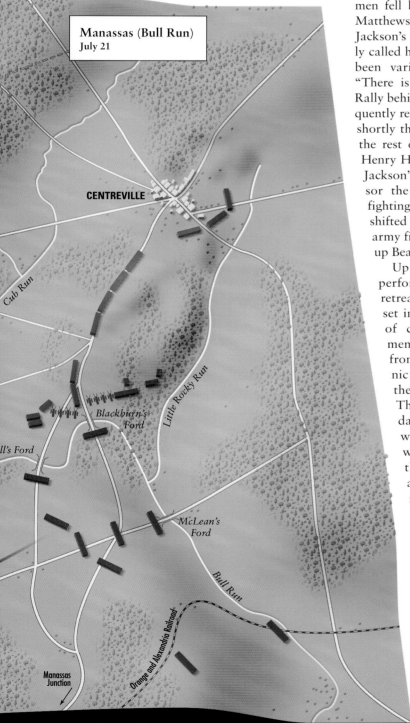

several more brigades to his endangered left flank. Helping Beauregard to shift his troops was General Joseph E. Johnston, who had arrived from the Shenandoah Valley with reinforcements the day before. Although Johnston ranked Beauregard, he allowed his subordinate, who was familiar with the area, to direct the battle. While Beauregard galloped toward Henry House Hill, Johnston remained at headquarters forwarding additional troops to the scene of the fighting.

Among the defenders of Henry House Hill was a brigade of Virginians commanded by the former U.S. Army officer and Virginia Military Institute instructor Brigadier General Thomas J. Jackson. Jackson and his men were part of Johnston's force that had only recently arrived. As General Bee's men fell back in disorder after their retreat on Matthews Hill, Bee noticed the steady line of Jackson's brigade on Henry House Hill and loudly called his men's attention to it. His words have been variously reported, most frequently as "There is Jackson, standing like a stone wall! Rally behind the Virginians!" Bee could not subsequently report his own words because he fell dead shortly thereafter. His men, however, along with the rest of the Confederate army, did rally on Henry House Hill, behind and on either side of Jackson's sturdy line, winning the former professor the nickname "Stonewall." More fierce fighting took place, but the tide of battle had shifted in the Confederates' favor. The Union army finally had to abandon its attempt to roll up Beauregard's line and pull back.

Up to this point, McDowell's troops had performed well, but during the difficult retreat they became confused. Panic quickly set in. Making matters worse were crowds of civilian sightseers, including several members of Congress, who had come out from Washington with carriages and picnic baskets to enjoy a pleasant outing in the country and watch a major battle. They had hovered in the army's rear all day and now they were squarely in the way of its retreat clogging the roads with their carriages and transmitting their abject terror to McDowell's already badly shaken soldiers. For many of the troops the retreat quickly became a stampede that ended only when they reached Washington the next day. McDowell had reserves, however, that remained steady and covered the retreat.

The Confederate army was in no condition to pursue anyway, and when Jefferson Davis arrived from Richmond that evening, he ordered only a small probe to follow the Federals a short distance. Heavy rain set in about midnight, transforming Virginia's dirt roads into quagmires and ruling out any further aggressive operations.

[1] Brigadier General Tyler's Union division approaches the Stone Bridge over Bull Run in order to divert the attention of Colonel Nathan G. Evans and his Confederate brigade guarding the bridge.

[2] The divisions of Colonel David Hunter's and Colonel Samuel P. Heintzelman's divisions make a flanking march and cross Bull Run at Sudley's Ford.

[3] The Union flanking column advances until met first by Evans's brigade and then by the brigades of Brigadier General Barnard Bee and Colonel Francis Bartow on Matthews Hill.

[4] The Union drive the Confederates back to Henry House Hill, where they rally on the brigade of Brigadier General Thomas J. "Stonewall" Jackson and other fresh troops and repulse the Union attack.

[5] The Union retreat becomes a rout.

MISSOURI DIVIDED

MISSOURI, THE NORTHERNMOST SLAVE STATE, was sharply divided on the question of secession. The majority of its people favored remaining loyal to the Union, but Governor Claiborne Jackson and a large and vocal minority stridently favored secession. When Confederate forces inaugurated the war at Fort Sumter and Lincoln responded by calling militia into federal service, Jackson indignantly refused to allow Missouri's militia to defend the Union.

On May 6, 1861, the state's secessionist-dominated militia assembled ominously at Camp Jackson, just outside the city of St. Louis. Captain Nathaniel Lyon, commander of the St. Louis arsenal, and pro-Union politician Frank Blair received information that they believed indicated the secessionist militia was preparing to seize the arsenal. To preempt this, Lyon, leading a force composed of a few regulars and a large contingent of pro-Union German American home guards, surrounded Camp Jackson and secured the surrender of the secessionist militia. As the militiamen were being marched through the streets of St. Louis on their way to captivity, pro-secession civilians rioted, attacking the regulars and home guards. A number of civilians were killed and injured.

The capture of Camp Jackson and the St. Louis riot marked the beginning of bitter hostility in Missouri. Pro-secession Missourians were outraged. Eleven days later pro-Southern U.S. Army general William S. Harney made an agreement with General Sterling Price of the pro-secession militia. By their agreement, Harney would keep U.S. troops out of Missouri and allow the secessionists to run the state as long as they kept order and committed no overt attack on the U.S. government. Lyon, Blair, and the rest of Missouri's pro-Union faction were shocked at this surrender,

and the authorities in Washington were suspicious. Lincoln gave Blair authority to remove Harney from command, and on May 31 Blair replaced him with Lyon, who in the meantime had been promoted to brigadier general. On June 11, Lyon and Blair met with Price and Jackson in the Planter House Hotel in St. Louis to discuss a continuation of Harney's truce. Lyon, with Blair's backing, refused to allow the secessionists to dictate where, when, and whether U.S. troops could move through the state, and so the talks broke down.

Thereafter a state of war existed between the Union and the Missouri secessionists. The next day Governor Jackson called for the enlistment of fifty thousand Missouri Rebels, but on June 14 he had to evacuate the state capital at Jefferson City in the face of Lyon's advancing army. Lyon entered the capital the next day, while Jackson and company set up shop in Boonville, fifty miles to the northwest. On June 17, Lyon and his force, traveling by boat up the Missouri River, arrived at Boonville and after a brief skirmish chased off Jackson's Rebels. The secessionist government took refuge in the southeastern corner of the state.

In July, a Unionist state convention declared the office of governor vacant, elected Hamilton R. Gamble as governor, and moved the state capital to St. Louis. Now Missouri had rival pro-Union and pro-Confederate governments each claiming to be legitimate. In August, the Confederacy formally "admitted" Missouri—by which it meant Jackson's rump government—as one of its states.

Meanwhile, Lyon had continued to advance and now occupied Springfield. In early August, however, a Confederate army under Brigadier General Ben McCulloch joined Price's small army of Missouri Rebels. After a bit of squabbling, Price agreed to allow McCulloch to command the combined force, which now numbered some eleven thousand men to Lyon's five thousand four hundred. McCulloch's force advanced toward Springfield. Realizing that his case was desperate, Lyon chose audacity and advanced to attack the Rebels. He struck them at Wilson's Creek early on the morning of August 10. Brigadier General Franz Sigel, commanding one thousand two hundred of Lyon's men, failed miserably and his troops fled, but Lyon and the rest of the army fought on. Lyon was killed around mid-morning, but his army continued to fend off all Confederate attacks for another two hours. Despite the army's successful defense of Oak Hills, or Bloody Ridge, Major Samuel Sturgis, who had succeeded to command, led the Union army back in retreat, through Springfield and ultimately all the way to Rolla, more than one hundred miles to the northeast. Union casualties totaled one thousand three hundred and seventeen, and Confederate, one thousand two hundred and twenty-two.

Price followed up the Confederate victory at Wilson's Creek by advancing with seven thousand men to Lexington, more than one hundred and fifty miles north of Springfield. There he besieged a force of three thousand five hundred Federals under Colonel James A. Mulligan from September 13 to 20. Price successfully fought off a small relief column led by Sturgis and finally compelled Mulligan to surrender, a severe blow to the Union cause in Missouri.

Battle of Wilson's Creek
August 10

1 August 10, 5:30 a.m.: Lyon's two thousand Union troops, attacks approximately three thousand two hundred Confererates under Price.

2 McCulloch's brigade attack across the cornfield but is later driven back by Union artillery.

3 Sigel's artillery opens fire on Price's line, Greer withdraws from his position along the river.

4 McCulloch launches counterattack.

5 McCulloch routs Union artillery, Sigel withdraws. Pearce's brigade advances to support Price.

6 10:30 a.m.: Lyon is killed, the outnumbered Union force withdraws.

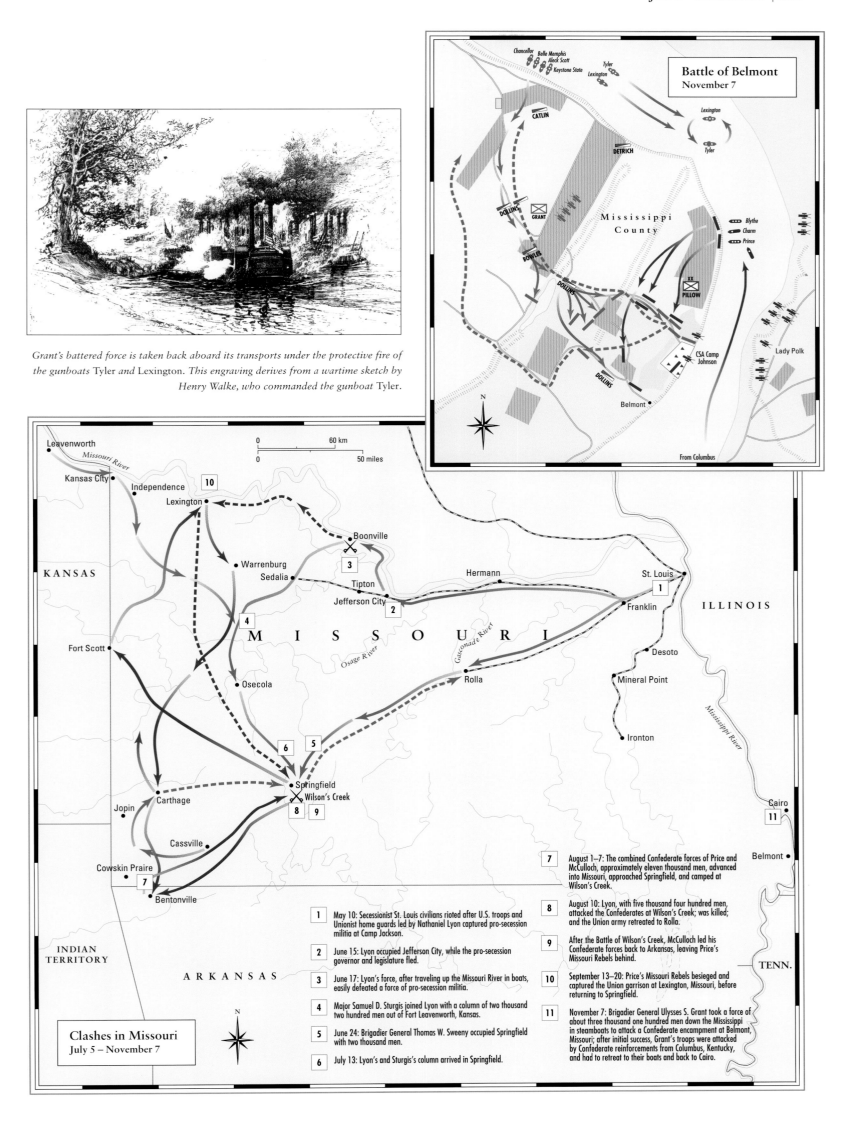

Grant's battered force is taken back aboard its transports under the protective fire of the gunboats Tyler and Lexington. This engraving derives from a wartime sketch by Henry Walke, who commanded the gunboat Tyler.

Battle of Belmont
November 7

Clashes in Missouri
July 5 – November 7

1 May 10: Secessionist St. Louis civilians rioted after U.S. troops and Unionist home guards led by Nathaniel Lyon captured pro-secession militia at Camp Jackson.

2 June 15: Lyon occupied Jefferson City, while the pro-secession governor and legislature fled.

3 June 17: Lyon's force, after traveling up the Missouri River in boats, easily defeated a force of pro-secession militia.

4 Major Samuel D. Sturgis joined Lyon with a column of two thousand two hundred men out of Fort Leavenworth, Kansas.

5 June 24: Brigadier General Thomas W. Sweeny occupied Springfield with two thousand men.

6 July 13: Lyon's and Sturgis's column arrived in Springfield.

7 August 1–7: The combined Confederate forces of Price and McCulloch, approximately eleven thousand men, advanced into Missouri, approached Springfield, and camped at Wilson's Creek.

8 August 10: Lyon, with five thousand four hundred men, attacked the Confederates at Wilson's Creek; was killed; and the Union army retreated to Rolla.

9 After the Battle of Wilson's Creek, McCulloch led his Confederate forces back to Arkansas, leaving Price's Missouri Rebels behind.

10 September 13–20: Price's Missouri Rebels besieged and captured the Union garrison at Lexington, Missouri, before returning to Springfield.

11 November 7: Brigadier General Ulysses S. Grant took a force of about three thousand one hundred men down the Mississippi in steamboats to attack a Confederate encampment at Belmont, Missouri; after initial success, Grant's troops were attacked by Confederate reinforcements from Columbus, Kentucky, and had to retreat to their boats and back to Cairo.

NEW ORLEANS

NEW ORLEANS WAS THE LARGEST CITY in the seceding states, and was an important financial and industrial center as well as the port city at the mouth of the Mississippi River, the most important water-borne trade route on the North American continent. Union authorities began planning for the capture of New Orleans late in 1861. The springboard for the operation was Ship Island in Mississippi Sound off the coast of Mississippi. Ship Island was unique among the islands of the Gulf coast in that it offered a deep-water anchorage sufficient for the expedition's numerous warships and transports and thus could serve as a staging area less than one hundred miles

Once beyond the forts the Rebels could only harass Farragut's fleet, as the snipers in Allen Redwood's contemporary sketch are doing.

from the mouth of the Mississippi.

In mid-April an expedition under Flag Officer David G. Farragut entered the mouth of the Mississippi River and proceeded twelve miles upstream to approach Confederate forts Jackson and St. Philip. Confederate president Jefferson Davis had concentrated his downstream defense of New Orleans in these two forts, transferring troops and naval vessels freely away from the crescent city to other areas he deemed more seriously threatened. For the reduction of the forts, Union authorities were relying on a flotilla of nineteen mortar schooners attached to Farragut's expedition and under the immediate command of Lieutenant David D. Porter. Porter hoped his mortar schooners could lob shells into the forts until they would be forced to surrender. Farragut had his doubts.

Porter began the bombardment on April 18, but after almost a week of round-the-clock shelling, the forts seemed no closer to surrender. Meanwhile, Farragut had decided on a different approach, and he began preparations even as the bombardment continued. On the night of April 20 he sent several ships to clear obstructions Confederates had placed across the river below the forts. By April 23, he had determined to run his fleet of seventeen warships past the forts, defying their 110 guns.

He put his plan into action in the predawn hours of April 24, leading his fleet up the river in his flagship, U.S.S. *Hartford*. The result was a

spectacular battle that lasted for several hours. While battling the forts' big guns, Farragut's fleet also had to contend with the vessels of the Confederate River Defense Fleet, a collection of twelve armed riverboats, as well as the diminutive ironclad *Manassas*, and numerous blazing fire rafts, pushed toward his ships by steam tugs. Moored alongside Fort St. Philip was the large but unfinished ironclad *Louisiana*, a powerful vessel that did not yet have engines but did have guns and armor. All but three of Farragut's warships passed the forts successfully and then completely defeated the Confederate River Defense Fleet.

The successful running of the forts left

Farragut alone, cut off, and low on both coal and ammunition, but with admirable audacity he steamed upriver to New Orleans, arriving there around noon on April 24. The city had no effective defenses against a force such as Farragut's. The Confederate commander, Major General Mansfield Lovell, quickly evacuated his small forces, and when Farragut boldly demanded the surrender of the city the mayor meekly complied. A small army force that had accompanied Farragut under the command of Major General Benjamin Butler occupied New Orleans. With the mouth of the river in Union hands, the forts Farragut had by-passed had no means of obtain-

ing fresh supplies. Several days later, their garrisons mutinied and surrendered.

The Union capture of New Orleans was a devastating blow to the Confederacy. The loss of financial and manufacturing resources, communications, and trade was matched by the heavy impact on both Confederate morale and overseas diplomatic negotiations. The disaster made foreign countries such as Britain and France less likely to recognize the southern states' claim to independence. With New Orleans in Union hands, Farragut was free to take his fleet up the Mississippi, capturing Baton Rouge and threatening Vicksburg, Mississippi, later that spring.

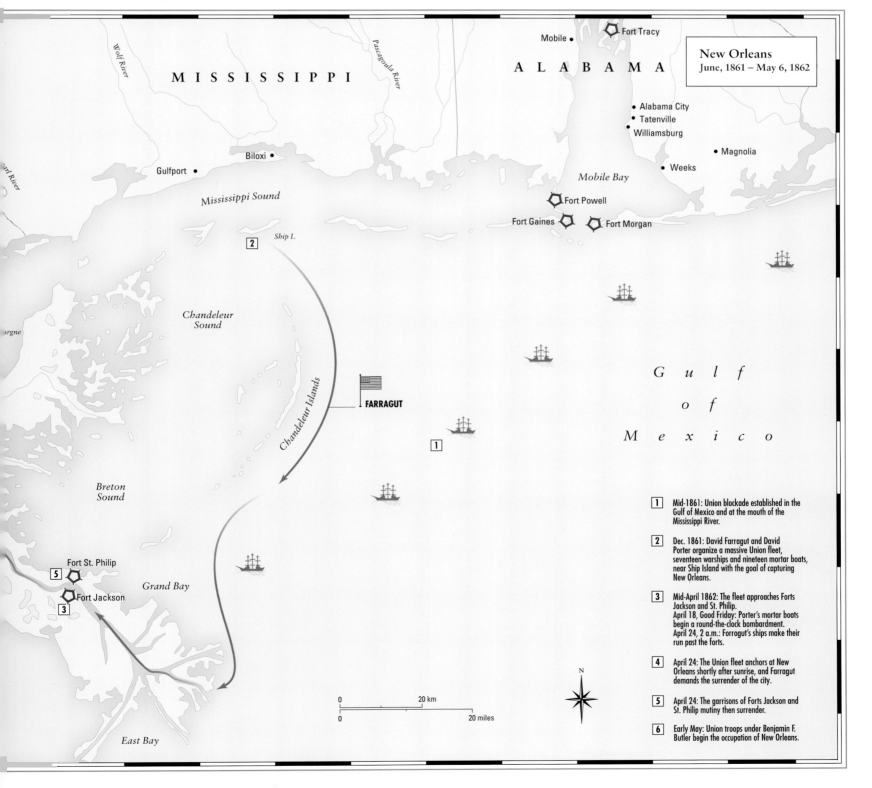

New Orleans
June, 1861 – May 6, 1862

1 Mid-1861: Union blockade established in the Gulf of Mexico and at the mouth of the Mississippi River.

2 Dec. 1861: David Farragut and David Porter organize a massive Union fleet, seventeen warships and nineteen mortar boats, near Ship Island with the goal of capturing New Orleans.

3 Mid-April 1862: The fleet approaches Forts Jackson and St. Philip.
April 18, Good Friday: Porter's mortar boats begin a round-the-clock bombardment.
April 24, 2 a.m.: Farragut's ships make their run past the forts.

4 April 24: The Union fleet anchors at New Orleans shortly after sunrise, and Farragut demands the surrender of the city.

5 April 24: The garrisons of Forts Jackson and St. Philip mutiny then surrender.

6 Early May: Union troops under Benjamin F. Butler begin the occupation of New Orleans.

SOUTH ATLANTIC COAST

Brigadier General Thomas West Sherman commanded the land forces at Port Royal Sound; the operation was a notable success. Sherman also managed careful cooperation between the army and the navy—notable because joint operations were notorious for their rivalry.

AFTER LINCOLN DECLARED ON APRIL 19, 1861, a blockade of the rebellious states, the U.S. Navy began drawing in its scattered vessels and building and acquiring new ones in order to implement the blockade. In July 1861, the navy organized the North and South Atlantic blockading squadrons. The North Atlantic Squadron blockaded the coasts of Virginia and North Carolina, while the South Atlantic Squadron blockaded the coasts of South Carolina, Georgia, and Florida (on the Atlantic side). In order to maintain the blockade, it became desirable to seize certain points along the coast. The South Atlantic Squadron, in particular, was badly in need of coaling and supply stations near its patrol areas. In both sectors control of key inlets among coastal islands was necessary in order to close off as many blockade-runners as possible.

The latter was the purpose of the first Union coastal incursion, which occurred in August 1861.

Hatteras Inlet, on the Outer Banks of North Carolina, was valuable to Confederate blockade-runners, who used the waterway to slip past U.S. warships. The Confederates built two forts to protect the inlet, Fort Clark and Fort Hatteras. On August 26, 1861, a force of eight ships under Flag Officer Silas H. Stringham and nine hundred troops under Major General Benjamin Butler set out from the Union base at Hampton Roads, Virginia. The following day they arrived off Hatteras Inlet. The warships exchanged fire with the Rebel forts while troops landed, experiencing much difficulty in the heavy surf. Their presence, however, forced the Confederates to abandon Fort Clark and draw all their forces into Fort Hatteras. The Union troops occupied Fort Clark without opposition. On August 28, after much additional naval bombardment, Fort Hatteras surrendered with six hundred and seventy men and thirty-five cannons. The success was an important boost to Union morale.

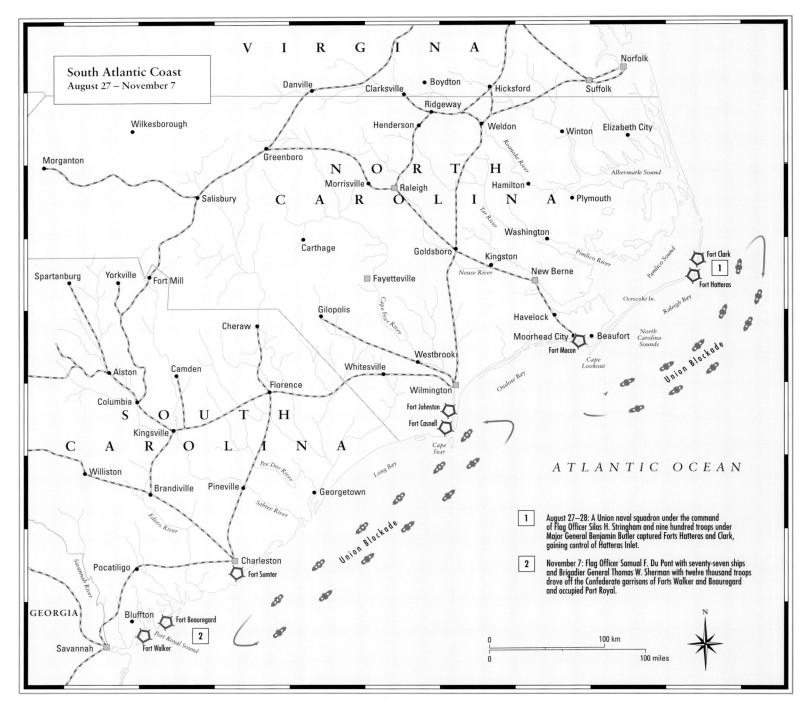

South Atlantic Coast
August 27 – November 7

1 August 27–28: A Union naval squadron under the command of Flag Officer Silas H. Stringham and nine hundred troops under Major General Benjamin Butler captured Forts Hatteras and Clark, gaining control of Hatteras Inlet.

2 November 7: Flag Officer Samuel F. Du Pont with seventy-seven ships and Brigadier General Thomas W. Sherman with twelve thousand troops drove off the Confederate garrisons of Forts Walker and Beauregard and occupied Port Royal.

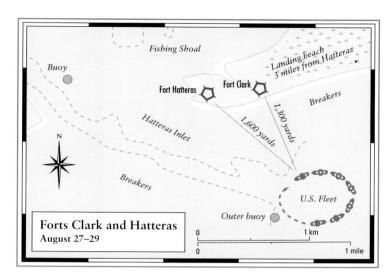

Forts Clark and Hatteras
August 27–29

The Union fleet arrived off Hilton Head on November 7 and attacked at once. The Confederate gunboats were helpless in the face of the heavy Union warships. To attack the forts, Du Pont utilized an innovative tactic. He had his warships steam in a continuous circle in the body of water between the two forts. This allowed them to bombard both positions simultaneously and presented Rebel gunners with constantly moving targets. By afternoon, Fort Walker ran out of ammunition, and its garrison fled. Ninety minutes later the garrison of Fort Beauregard followed them, and Sherman's troops easily took possession of Port Royal. Total Union casualties for the operation numbered thirty one, while the Confederates lost sixty six men. None of the Union warships received major damage. On November 9, Union forces advanced about five miles inland from Port Royal and occupied the valuable city of Beaufort, South Carolina, without opposition.

The large steam frigate U.S.S. Wabash, *the Union flagship.*

The need for a coaling and supply base for the South Atlantic Blockading Squadron prompted the next Union descent on the southern coast. Port Royal, South Carolina, was selected as the most promising location for such a base. In order to take it, the Union put together a major operation, including seventy-seven ships under Flag Officer Samuel F. Du Pont and twelve thousand troops under Brigadier General Thomas W. Sherman. The defenses of Port Royal Sound were two flanking forts, Fort Beauregard on St. Helena Island and Fort Walker on adjacent Hilton Head Island. Between them they boasted a combined total of forty-one guns. A Rebel naval flotilla consisting of four small vessels was also present.

The Union enclave on the South Carolina coast became important in several ways. It at once fulfilled its purpose as a naval base, allowing the vessels of the South Atlantic Squadron to spend much more time on station, patrolling for blockade-runners. It also posed a severe threat to rest of the Confederacy's southern coastline. Robert E. Lee, then commanding in that region, wrote to the Richmond authorities that there was great potential for the Union to further exploit its naval strength along the southern coast. Throughout the war, substantial numbers of Confederate troops continued to garrison the coast, despite the Confederacy's sore need of that manpower elsewhere. Finally, Port Royal and Beaufort were situated in one of the most heavily slave-populated areas in the country. Escaping slaves flocked to Union lines, even before official government policy mandated their emancipation. Thus it was in the Port Royal enclave that the government first had to confront the issue of how to accommodate the former slaves.

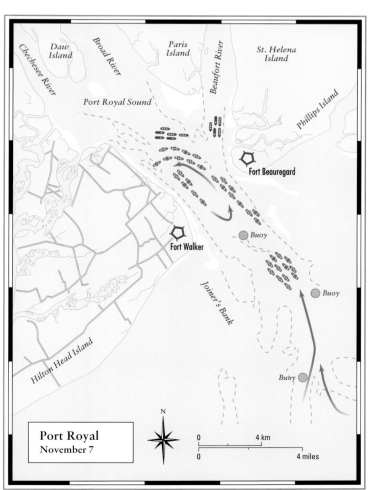

Port Royal
November 7

Fort Macon, a sturdy masonry work near Morehead City that dominated the southern approaches to Pamlico Sound. After ten hours of pounding, the fort surrendered.

1862
THE STRUGGLE FOR UNION

The year 1862 opened on a gloomy note in Washington. Union finances were in disarray. Northern banks had suspended specie payments. The Union navy's capture of Port Royal in November did not offset Confederate military victories at Manassas, Wilson's Creek, and Ball's Bluff during preceding months. Union armies in Kentucky and Virginia seemed to be doing nothing, and General McClellan had typhoid fever. On the back of a letter from one of his commanders who had written to explain why he could not advance, Lincoln wrote in January: "It is exceedingly discouraging. As everywhere else, nothing can be done."

But these days in January turned out to be the darkness before dawn for the Union cause—though darkness would come again all too soon. Nevertheless, starting with a small Northern victory at Logan's Crossroads in Kentucky on January 19, Union arms won a stunning series of victories during the next four and one-half months that seemed likely to win the war by the Fourth of July. In February a combined force of army troops and river gunboats under General Ulysses S. Grant and Captain Andrew H. Foote captured Forts Henry and Donelson on the Tennessee and Cumberland rivers, enabling Union gunboats to range southward to Florence, Alabama, and resulting in the capture of Nashville. In early March, Yankee soldiers won the Battle of Pea Ridge and gained control of northern Arkansas. Another army-navy task force drove down the Mississippi and captured the Confederate stronghold at Island No. 10. Meanwhile, in the largest bloodbath of the war so far, a Confederate counteroffensive against Grant's army camped at

Band of the Eighth New York State Militia.

Pittsburg Landing on the Tennessee River just north of the Mississippi border was beaten back in the two-day Battle of Shiloh April 6–7. Three weeks later the Union navy won a spectacular success by capturing the Confederacy's largest city and port, New Orleans. Two naval forces moving upriver from New Orleans and downriver from Island No. 10 besieged the Confederate "Gibraltar of the West" at Vicksburg after capturing Memphis. Meanwhile, other army–navy task forces gained control of several forts and cities and estuaries in coastal North Carolina, Georgia, and Florida. By mid-May, McClellan's Army of the Potomac had advanced to within five miles of Richmond. The Confederacy's days seemed numbered.

But then the Northern war machine went into reverse, while new leadership invigorated the Confederate cause. General "Stonewall" Jackson's small army routed Union forces in Virginia's Shenandoah Valley in May and early June. After General Joseph E. Johnston was wounded in the Battle of Seven Pines just east of Richmond on May 31, Robert E. Lee took command of the Army of Northern Virginia. On June 26 he launched a counteroffensive that drove McClellan away from Richmond in the Seven Days' Battles. Lee shifted his army to northern Virginia and inflicted a humiliating defeat on the forces under General John Pope in the second Battle of Manassas (Bull Run) August 29–30.

Meanwhile, Confederate armies in Tennessee invaded Kentucky while Lee decided to move north into Maryland looking for a knockout victory over the Army of the Potomac. Northern forces blunted these invasions in the Battle of Antietam September 17 and the Battle of Perryville October 8. But the pursuit of retreating Confederates after these battles was so sluggish that Lincoln relieved the two Union commanders— McClellan and General Don Carlos Buell—of their commands.

Battles in December at Fredericksburg, Virginia, and at Vicksburg, resulting in two more Union defeats, and in the same month a battle at Murfreesboro, Tennessee, ended in a draw. The year 1862 closed on almost as gloomy a note in the North as it had begun.

Next to these military campaigns and battles, the most notable development in 1862 was Lincoln's decision to issue an Emancipation Proclamation. From the war's beginning, many Northern Republicans had clamored for a policy of emancipation. A war begun by the South in defense of slavery, they insisted, could only be won by attacking slavery and freeing the slaves whose labor sustained the Confederate economy and logistics. Lincoln resisted this argument until July 1862 because he feared that any move against slavery would alienate Border-State Unionists and Northern Democrats from his war effort. But in that month he decided that "we must free the slaves or be ourselves subdued." Secretary of State William H. Seward persuaded Lincoln to withhold the Emancipation Proclamation until a victory by Union arms could give it legitimacy and impetus. The equivocal victory at Antietam gave Lincoln his opportunity. Five days later he issued a warning proclamation declaring that in all states or portions of states still in rebellion on January 1, 1863, he would invoke his war powers as Commander in Chief to seize enemy property being used to wage war against the United States and declare slaves, who were property, in those areas "forever free." On New Year's Day 1863 Lincoln fulfilled that promise.

President Abraham Lincoln meets with General George B. McClellan and his staff officers near Antietam, towards the end of September 1862.

THE CAMPAIGNS OF 1861 – 1862

THE FIRST MAJOR CAMPAIGNS of the war took place in the summer of 1861 and involved untrained forces on both sides. Brigadier General Irvin McDowell led a Union army from Washington, D.C., toward the new Confederate capital at Richmond, Virginia, but was defeated in a rout at the First Battle of Bull Run on July 21, 1861. The following month Brigadier General Nathaniel Lyon led a Union army to defeat at the Battle of Wilson's Creek, near Springfield, Missouri. Lyon himself was among the slain.

A six-month hiatus of major battles followed, as both sides exerted themselves to raise, train, and equip much larger armies. Lincoln gave command of the Army of the Potomac, the main Union army operating in Virginia, to Major General George B. McClellan, but McClellan made no significant

The Awkward Squad is a graphic example of the challenge faced by Civil War drill sergeants. To reveal the mysteries of close-order drill to totally untrained farm boys, officers had each one tie a tuft of hay to his left foot and straw to his right, and chants of "Hay-foot, Straw-foot!" echoed across the parade grounds. "Straw-foot" soon became the slang for any new recruit.

advance against the enemy until well into 1862. This lack of action—along with the small but wretchedly mismanaged affair at Ball's Bluff on October 21, 1861, where Confederates trapped several Union regiments on the south bank of the Potomac—led the increasingly restive Congress to step up the political pressure on McClellan to produce significant progress in the war.

In the western theater of the war, Brigadier General Ulysses S. Grant, commanding at Cairo, Illinois, secured the reluctant permission of his immediate superior, Major General Henry W. Halleck, to advance up the Tennessee River. Grant, with naval cooperation, captured the strategic Fort Henry, in Tennessee just south of the Kentucky line, on February 6. A few days later he crossed over the fifteen-mile-wide neck of land to the Cumberland River and, after a fierce battle, captured the equally important Fort Donelson on February 16. Grant's twin victories at Forts Henry and Donelson were by far the most significant military events of 1862. Fifteen thousand badly needed Confederate troops were taken prisoner. These victories also opened the way to the interior of the southern heartland and led directly to the Union occupation of the western two-thirds of Tennessee.

At Halleck's order, Grant halted along the Tennessee River to await the arrival of additional Union forces. While he was waiting, on April 6 and 7, a Confederate army under General Albert Sidney Johnston attacked him in what became known as the Battle of Shiloh, after a church on the battlefield. Grant narrowly avoided defeat in what was the bloodiest battle in U.S. history up to that time. Subsequently, Halleck took command of Grant's greatly reinforced army and advanced to take the rail junction of Corinth, Mississippi, on May 30. Elsewhere in the western theater, Union forces made dramatic advances, taking New Orleans on April 24 and Memphis on June 7.

In the East, McClellan finally moved that spring, transporting his army by water to the peninsula between the James and York rivers in Virginia and then proceeding up the peninsula toward Richmond. He had reached the outskirts of the Confederate capital when on May 31 his opposing commander, Confederate general Joseph E. Johnston, was wounded during inconclusive fighting. Johnston's replacement, Robert E. Lee, was far more aggressive and skillful than his predecessor. Lee attacked McClellan on June 25, sparking a week of bloody fighting known as the Seven Days' Battles. The battles themselves were inconclusive, but they persuaded McClellan to retreat back down the peninsula.

Disgusted with McClellan, Lincoln entrusted Major General John Pope with another Union army in northern Virginia, but Lee, ably seconded by Major General Thomas J. "Stonewall" Jackson, trounced Pope at the Second Battle of Bull Run before audaciously crossing the Potomac. In desperation, Lincoln turned back to McClellan, whose army he combined with Pope's and placed under the McClellan's command. McClellan met Lee along Antietam Creek in Maryland, on September 17, 1863. Once again the fighting was inconclusive, but this time Lee was forced to retreat, returning to Virginia. When McClellan proved slow to pursue, Lincoln replaced him with Major General Ambrose Burnside, who led the Army of the Potomac to lopsided defeat at the Battle of Fredericksburg in Virginia on December 13.

In the West, the final campaigns of 1862 brought mixed results. Confederate offensives in Mississippi and Kentucky failed during September and August. In December, however, Confederates stopped Grant's two-pronged offensive against Vicksburg, Mississippi, with defeats at Holly Springs and Chickasaw Bayou. A short Union offensive in Middle Tennessee resulted in a bloody and indecisive Union victory at Stone's River.

Defeats such as Holly Springs, Chickasaw Bayou, and especially Fredericksburg cast a pall over popular morale in the North during the winter of 1862–1863. Yet the cumulative result of the 1862 campaigns was that the Union had gained vast territories in Tennessee and the strategic Mississippi Valley while the Confederacy had sustained manpower losses it could ill afford.

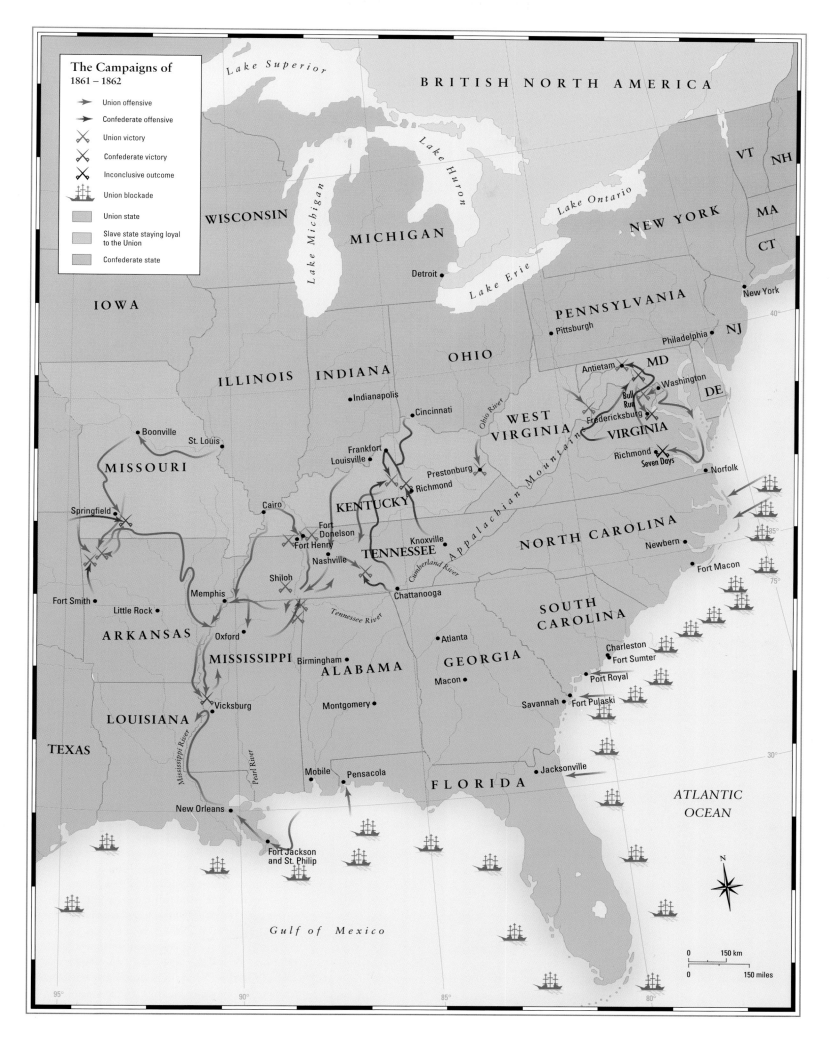

The Campaigns of
1861 – 1862

→ Union offensive
→ Confederate offensive
⚔ Union victory
⚔ Confederate victory
⚔ Inconclusive outcome
⛵ Union blockade
▨ Union state
▨ Slave state staying loyal
to the Union
▨ Confederate state

NEW MEXICO CAMPAIGN

Brigadier General Henry Hopkins Sibley, a graduate of West Point, had considerable experience in the southwestern theater before the war. He later exclaimed "Except for its geographical position, the territory of New Mexico is not worth a quarter of the blood and the treasure expended on its conquest."

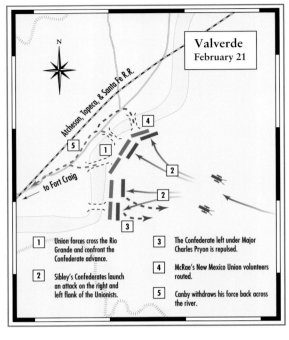

Valverde
February 21

1. Union forces cross the Rio Grande and confront the Confederate advance.
2. Sibley's Confederates launch an attack on the right and left flank of the Unionists.
3. The Confederate left under Major Charles Pryon is repulsed.
4. McRae's New Mexico Union volunteers routed.
5. Canby withdraws his force back across the river.

TEXANS HAD LAID CLAIM TO New Mexico east of the Rio Grande ever since the founding of the Republic of Texas back in 1836. A couple of Texan expeditions in that direction had come to grief at Mexican hands before the United States annexed Texas. In 1850, Texas's claim to the lands east of the Rio Grande had been a major issue of contention in debates in the U.S. Congress, which had finally assigned the disputed territory to New Mexico. So when the Civil War broke out, Texans were eager to take New Mexico. Henry Hopkins Sibley resigned from the U.S. Army and became a brigadier general in the service of the Confederacy. With authorization from Richmond he raised a brigade of three thousand five hundred Texas horsemen for the express purpose of conquering New Mexico.

On February 7, 1862, Sibley's force marched north out of El Paso following the road that paralleled the west bank of the Rio Grande. By February 16 they were approaching Fort Craig—where Sibley learned his opposing commander, Colonel Edward R. S. Canby, had some three thousand eight hundred

men. In fact, most of Canby's troops were untrained, ill-equipped, and unreliable territorial militia. Nevertheless, Sibley determined to bypass Fort Craig by crossing to the east bank of the Rio Grande, where another road led through hills out of sight of the fort. Canby refused to allow the Confederates to pass unchallenged. On February 21 he sent part of his force across the river to attack the Confederates. In the resulting Battle of Valverde, the Confederates forced Canby to pull his force back to the west side of the river, leaving Sibley free to continue his northward march and Canby cut off from the rest of the Union forces in New Mexico. On March 2, Union forces evacuated Albuquerque and Sibley's men marched in. Continuing northward up the Rio Grande they took Santa Fe two days later.

Meanwhile Union authorities had recruited some one thousand three hundred volunteers in the mining camps of Colorado. Under the command of Colonel John P. Slough this force, along with a few U.S. Army regulars, marched southward to secure vital Fort Union in north central New Mexico. Arriving there on March 11, Slough paused for eleven days before marching on toward Santa Fe. The Confederates learned of Slough's approach and a detachment of four hundred men under Colonel William R. Scurry moved out to intercept him. On March 26, Scurry's force encountered Slough's advance guard under Major John M. Chivington in Apache Canyon. The two forces were about equal in numbers, and the Colorado volunteers got the better of the Confederates. That evening, however, Chivington fell back to join Slough at Pigeon's Ranch, near Glorieta.

On March 28, Scurry, now heavily reinforced from Sibley's forces in Santa Fe, advanced through Glorieta Pass and attacked Slough's force at Pigeon's Ranch. In several hours of tough fighting, they drove the outnumbered Federals back until Slough withdrew his command to Kozlowski's Ranch. It would have been a fairly successful day for the Confederates had it not been for Chivington and his four hundred men. Crossing difficult mountain terrain, Chivington's detachment got behind the Confederate position and destroyed eighty supply wagons at Johnson's Ranch.

The loss of their wagon train transformed the Confederate's supply situation from bad to desperate. First Scurry and then Sibley had to retreat. They abandoned Santa Fe on April 12 and started a long, hard retreat down the Rio Grande valley. Terrain and weather made travel difficult, and food was scarce. To avoid Canby's force still lurking at Fort Craig, Sibley this time made a lengthy detour to the west, successfully dodging Canby but adding greatly to the Texans' suffering. After a pause at Mesilla, the expedition continued its retreat to El Paso and then eastward across Texas, reaching San Antonio in July.

Sibley had not managed the expedition well, and in San Antonio one of his officers brought court-martial charges against him for drunkenness, cowardice, misappropriation of government property, and mistreatment of the sick and wounded. The case never came to trial, as Sibley convinced President Davis to dismiss the charges. In any case, the Confederacy never made another bid for the Far West.

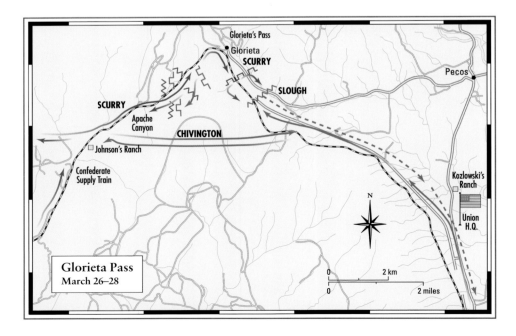

Glorieta Pass
March 26–28

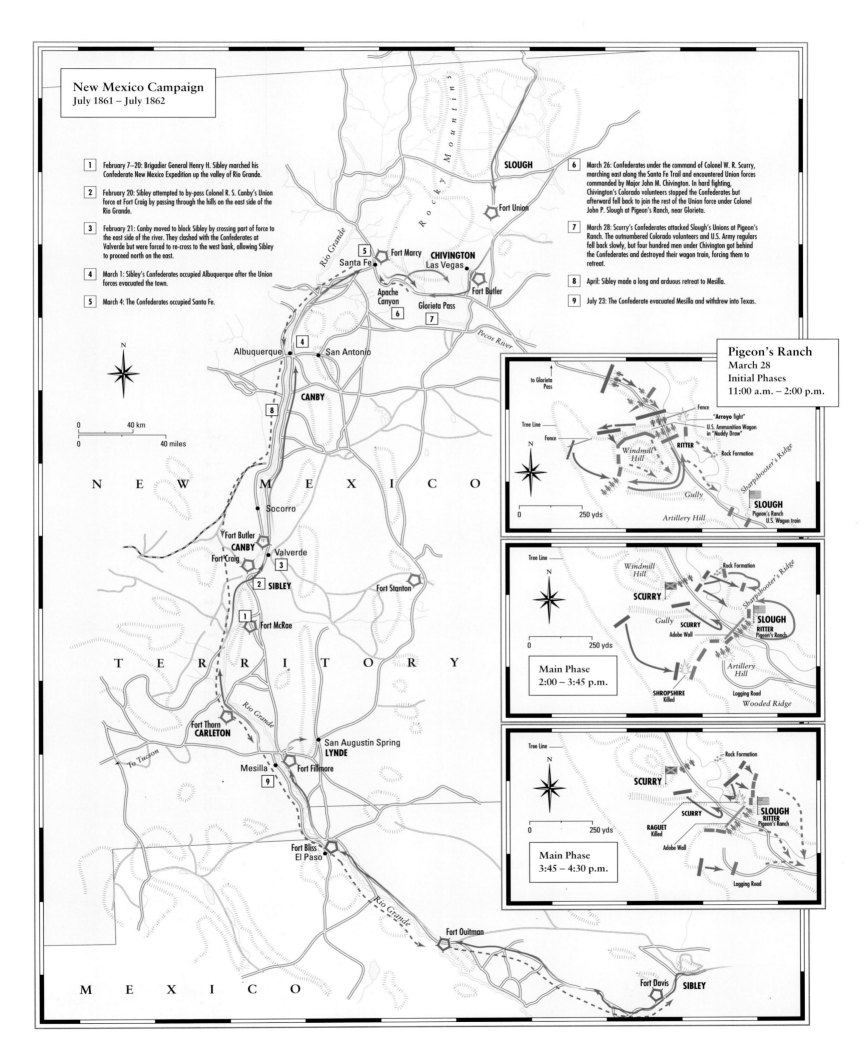

New Mexico Campaign
July 1861 – July 1862

1 February 7–20: Brigadier General Henry H. Sibley marched his Confederate New Mexico Expedition up the valley of Rio Grande.

2 February 20: Sibley attempted to by-pass Colonel R. S. Canby's Union force at Fort Craig by passing through the hills on the east side of the Rio Grande.

3 February 21: Canby moved to block Sibley by crossing part of force to the east side of the river. They clashed with the Confederates at Valverde but were forced to re-cross to the west bank, allowing Sibley to proceed north on the east.

4 March 1: Sibley's Confederates occupied Albuquerque after the Union forces evacuated the town.

5 March 4: The Confederates occupied Santa Fe.

6 March 26: Confederates under the command of Colonel W. R. Scurry, marching east along the Santa Fe Trail and encountered Union forces commanded by Major John M. Chivington. In hard fighting, Chivington's Colorado volunteers stopped the Confederates but afterward fell back to join the rest of the Union force under Colonel John P. Slough at Pigeon's Ranch, near Glorieta.

7 March 28: Scurry's Confederates attacked Slough's Unions at Pigeon's Ranch. The outnumbered Colorado volunteers and U.S. Army regulars fell back slowly, but four hundred men under Chivington got behind the Confederates and destroyed their wagon train, forcing them to retreat.

8 April: Sibley made a long and arduous retreat to Mesilla.

9 July 23: The Confederate evacuated Mesilla and withdrew into Texas.

Pigeon's Ranch
March 28
Initial Phases
11:00 a.m. – 2:00 p.m.

Main Phase
2:00 – 3:45 p.m.

Main Phase
3:45 – 4:30 p.m.

EASTERN KENTUCKY AND TENNESSEE

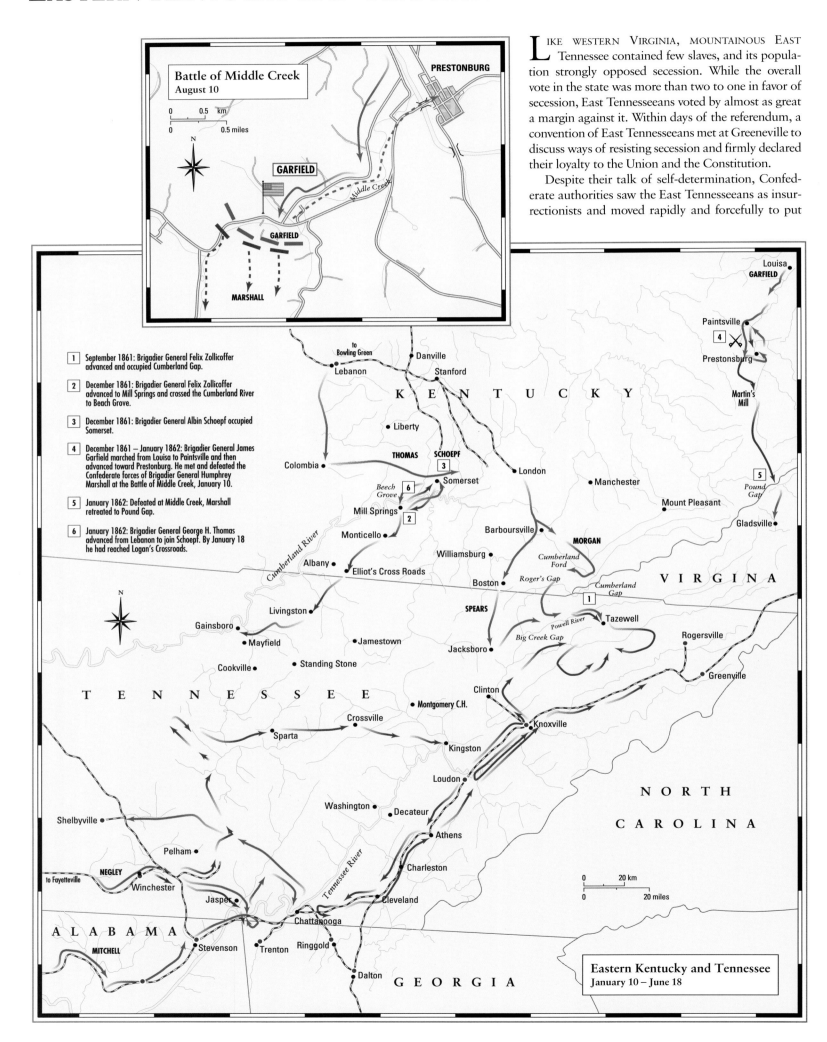

Battle of Middle Creek
August 10

0   0.5   km
0   0.5 miles

PRESTONBURG

GARFIELD

GARFIELD

Middle Creek

MARSHALL

LIKE WESTERN VIRGINIA, MOUNTAINOUS EAST Tennessee contained few slaves, and its population strongly opposed secession. While the overall vote in the state was more than two to one in favor of secession, East Tennesseeans voted by almost as great a margin against it. Within days of the referendum, a convention of East Tennesseeans met at Greeneville to discuss ways of resisting secession and firmly declared their loyalty to the Union and the Constitution.

Despite their talk of self-determination, Confederate authorities saw the East Tennesseeans as insurrectionists and moved rapidly and forcefully to put

1 September 1861: Brigadier General Felix Zollicoffer advanced and occupied Cumberland Gap.

2 December 1861: Brigadier General Felix Zollicoffer advanced to Mill Springs and crossed the Cumberland River to Beach Grove.

3 December 1861: Brigadier General Albin Schoepf occupied Somerset.

4 December 1861 – January 1862: Brigadier General James Garfield marched from Louisa to Paintsville and then advanced toward Prestonburg. He met and defeated the Confederate forces of Brigadier General Humphrey Marshall at the Battle of Middle Creek, January 10.

5 January 1862: Defeated at Middle Creek, Marshall retreated to Pound Gap.

6 January 1862: Brigadier General George H. Thomas advanced from Lebanon to join Schoepf. By January 18 he had reached Logan's Crossroads.

to Bowling Green

Danville

Lebanon

Stanford

K E N T U C K Y

Liberty

Louisa

GARFIELD

Paintsville

4

Prestonsburg

Martin's Mill

THOMAS   SCHOEPF
3

Colombia

Beech Grove   **6**   Somerset

London

Manchester

Mount Pleasant

5

Pound Gap

Mill Springs   **2**

Monticello

Barboursville

MORGAN

Gladsville

Williamsburg

Cumberland Ford

V I R G I N I A

Albany

Cumberland River

Elliot's Cross Roads

Boston   Roger's Gap

Cumberland Gap   **1**

Livingston

Gainsboro

Mayfield

Jamestown

SPEARS

Powell River   Tazewell

Big Creek Gap

Rogersville

Cookville

Standing Stone

Jacksboro

Greenville

T E N N E S S E E

Clinton

Montgomery C.H.

Crossville

Knoxville

Sparta

Kingston

Loudon

N O R T H

Washington

Decatur

C A R O L I N A

Shelbyville

Athens

Pelham

Charleston

NEGLEY

to Fayetteville

Winchester

Tennessee River

Cleveland

0   20   km
0   20 miles

Jasper

Chattanooga

A L A B A M A

MITCHELL

Stevenson

Trenton

Ringgold

Eastern Kentucky and Tennessee
January 10 – June 18

Dalton

G E O R G I A

them down by sending troops into the region. To command those troops Jefferson Davis appointed former Nashville newspaper editor Felix K. Zollicoffer. Beyond a year's stint as a militia lieutenant during the Second Seminole War, Zollicoffer had no military background, but he was prominent in Whig Party politics and as such had originally mildly opposed secession. He seemed an ideal choice to suppress and perhaps win over the antisecessionists of East Tennessee. As Kentucky was neutral and would not permit transit of troops from either side, it appeared Zollicoffer would face nothing more than poorly trained and disorganized insurrectionists.

That changed when in early September Kentucky's neutrality ceased, and the entire northern boundary of Tennessee became exposed to possible invasion. Zollifcoffer promptly advanced his forces to Cumberland Gap, in the southeastern corner of Kentucky. Several weeks later he advanced to Mill Springs, on the southeastern bank of the upper Cumberland River about one hundred miles west-northwest of Cumberland Gap. There he established a number of outposts along the river. Using ferryboats, he also established a foothold and large garrison at Beech Grove, on the northwest bank of the Cumberland River opposite Mill Springs, in early December. Too late to prevent the move, Zollicoffer's department commander, General Albert Sidney Johnston, advised against crossing to the north bank of the Cumberland.

Meanwhile, Lincoln was eager to support any southern Unionists, whom he mistakenly thought formed the true majority in the South. In October he began urging his generals to advance toward Cumberland Gap and East Tennessee, not only to aid the Unionists there but also to take possession of the strategic Virginia & Tennessee Railroad. Doing so, however, was extremely difficult, as the terrain was rough, the roads few and poor, and the problems of supplying an advancing army almost insurmountable. The task fell to Brigadier General Don Carlos Buell, commander of the Union Department of the Ohio, headquartered in Louisville, Kentucky.

While Buell, never a fast mover, worried about the practical difficulties of getting troops to East Tennessee, the East Tennesseans ran out of patience. On November 8 they began an uprising against Rebel rule, burning important bridges and skirmishing with Confederate troops. Confederate authorities eventually succeeded in suppressing the uprising and hanged a number of its participants as rebels.

Meanwhile Buell's troops were finally on the move. A brigade under Brigadier General Albin Schoepf advanced southeastward through Kentucky and by early December occupied Somerset, a town twenty-five miles northwest of Mill Springs, and began skirmishing with Zollicoffer's patrols. At about the same time another brigade, commanded by Colonel James Garfield, moved farther east than Schoepf's troops and in early January routed a Confederate brigade under Brigadier General Humphrey Marshall at the Battle of Middle Creek near Prestonburg, Kentucky. Buell ordered an additional brigade under Brigadier General George H. Thomas to join Schoepf and attack Zollicoffer at Beech Grove.

More or less simultaneously, Confederate Major General George B. Crittenden arrived at Mill Springs, dispatched by Jefferson Davis to supervise Zollicoffer. He realized that Zollicoffer's position was extremely hazardous, as most of his forces were at Beech Grove and could not retreat back across the Cumberland River except by the long and laborious process of crossing on small ferryboats. With superior Union forces approaching, Crittenden decided that their only hope was to advance and catch Thomas's force before it could unite with Schoepf's. On the rainy night of January 18, 1862, Crittenden and Zollicoffer marched their troops northward six miles to Thomas's position at Logan's Crossroads.

The Rebels attacked on the morning of January 19. Recovering from their initial surprise, Thomas's troops rallied and dramatically routed the small Confederate army. Becoming confused in the mist and rain, Zollicoffer blundered into Union lines and was shot dead. The Confederates abandoned much of their equipment in getting back across the river at Mill Springs. The battle, known by various names but most often as Mill Springs, involved about four thousand men on each side. Union casualties totaled two hundred and sixty-one men and Confederate, five hundred and thirty-three. Union morale in uncertain Kentucky got an important boost, and Crittenden's army was temporarily rendered all but completely incapable of further combat. The constraints of supply, however, prevented the Union from following up its victory with a direct advance into East Tennessee.

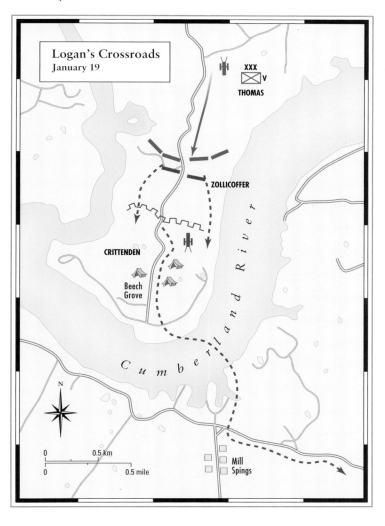

NORTHWESTERN ARKANSAS

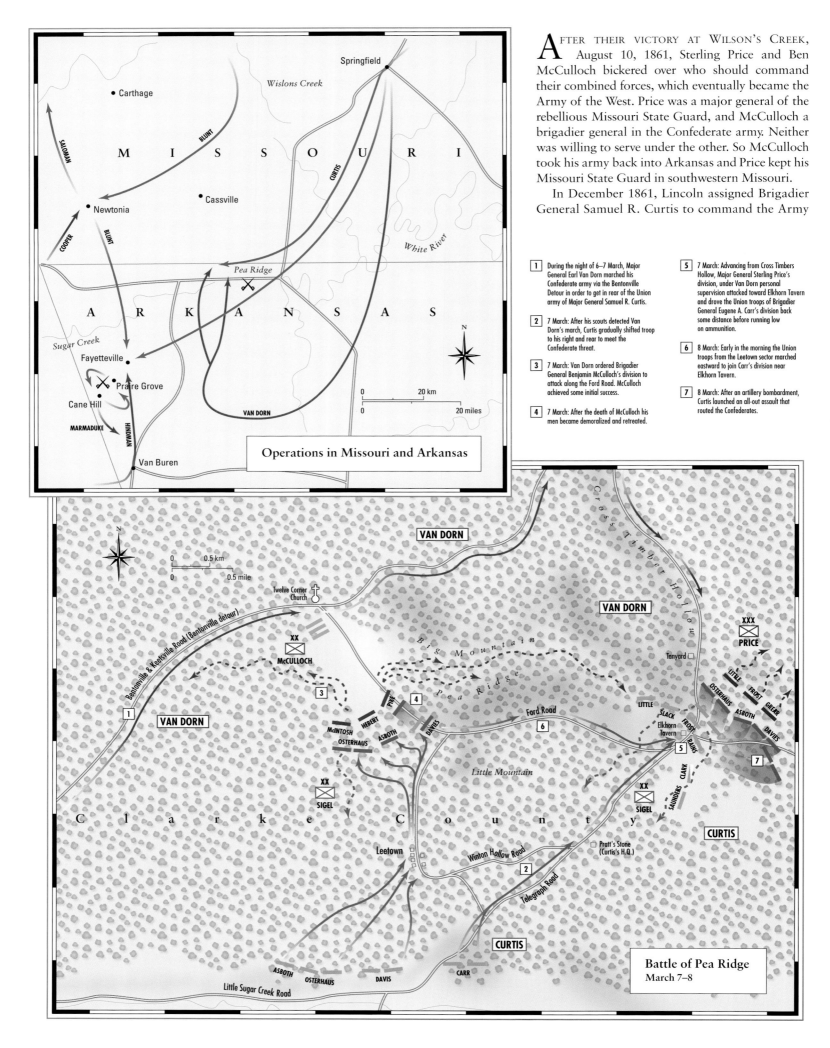

Operations in Missouri and Arkansas

A FTER THEIR VICTORY AT WILSON'S CREEK, August 10, 1861, Sterling Price and Ben McCulloch bickered over who should command their combined forces, which eventually became the Army of the West. Price was a major general of the rebellious Missouri State Guard, and McCulloch a brigadier general in the Confederate army. Neither was willing to serve under the other. So McCulloch took his army back into Arkansas and Price kept his Missouri State Guard in southwestern Missouri.

In December 1861, Lincoln assigned Brigadier General Samuel R. Curtis to command the Army

1 During the night of 6–7 March, Major General Earl Van Dorn marched his Confederate army via the Bentonville Detour in order to get in rear of the Union army of Major General Samuel R. Curtis.

2 7 March: After his scouts detected Van Dorn's march, Curtis gradually shifted troop to his right and rear to meet the Confederate threat.

3 7 March: Van Dorn ordered Brigadier General Benjamin McCulloch's division to attack along the Ford Road. McCulloch achieved some initial success.

4 7 March: After the death of McCulloch his men became demoralized and retreated.

5 7 March: Advancing from Cross Timbers Hollow, Major General Sterling Price's division, under Van Dorn personal supervision attacked toward Elkhorn Tavern and drove the Union troops of Brigadier General Eugene A. Carr's division back some distance before running low on ammunition.

6 8 March: Early in the morning the Union troops from the Leetown sector marched eastward to join Carr's division near Elkhorn Tavern.

7 8 March: After an artillery bombardment, Curtis launched an all-out assault that routed the Confederates.

Battle of Pea Ridge
March 7–8

of Southwest Missouri in the Department of the Missouri. Curtis outnumbered Price significantly, and as he advanced Price retreated deep into Arkansas. On February 23, Union troops occupied Fayetteville, Arkansas. Fortunes soon shifted, however, as Confederate major general Earl Van Dorn arrived in early March to take command of the Confederacy's Trans-Mississippi District. Van Dorn re-unified the forces of Price and McCulloch, and faced with this combined force it was now Curtis who had to fall back. The Union commander took up a strong defensive position behind Sugar Creek in the extreme north of Arkansas only a few miles from the Missouri line.

Van Dorn dreamed of the conquest of Missouri. "I must have St. Louis," he wrote to his wife, "then huzzah!" The first step was to defeat Curtis. Van Dorn advanced until his army faced Curtis's across Sugar Creek and the armies skirmished lightly on March 6. Then, leaving his campfires burning to deceive the enemy, Van Dorn led his army on a night march around the Union flank, intending to get in rear of Curtis and attack him from the north on the morning of March 7. Price's division led the march, but McCulloch's fell behind. Unwilling to delay the attack, Van Dorn ordered both divisions to attack from where they were, Price's from north of the Union position and McCulloch's from the northwest. The resulting battle, known as Pea Ridge or Elkhorn Tavern, thus consisted of two separate fights some two miles apart, as McCulloch's column attempted to advance near Leetown, west of Pea Ridge, and Price's attacked near Elkhorn Tavern, at the eastern end of Pea Ridge.

The Union forces detected Van Dorn's approach from their rear and responded quickly. McCulloch's column met the Union divisions of brigadier generals Peter J. Osterhaus and Jefferson C. Davis. At first McCulloch's troops drove back the Federals and captured a Union battery. Conspicuous in the successful Confederate charge was a regiment of Confederate Cherokees under the command of Stand Watie. Union troops later claimed that Watie's men scalped dead and wounded Union soldiers on the battlefield.

After his initial success, McCulloch's advance ran into stiffer Union resistance. Going forward to make a personal reconnaissance, McCulloch was shot in the chest. He died almost instantly. Command of the division passed to Brigadier General James McIntosh, but he was killed only a few minutes after McCulloch. With that, the division became disorganized and its attack stalled completely. Meanwhile, Van Dorn and Price led the latter's wing of the army against Brigadier General Eugene A. Carr's Union division near Elkhorn Tavern. In a full day of intense fighting Price's men succeeded in taking the tavern and driving Carr about a mile to the south.

The next morning, March 8, both Van Dorn and Curtis massed all their forces not far from Elkhorn Tavern, Curtis's army just south of Pea Ridge and Van Dorn's on its lower southern slopes. Curtis had his artillery bombard the Rebels for several hours before ordering the divisions of Carr and Brigadier

General Franz Sigel to attack. Van Dorn's army, exhausted and low on supplies, including ammunition, crumbled under the Union assault and fled in several directions. It could not be reassembled for several days. In all, the Battle of Pea Ridge saw some eleven thousand Federals engaging about fourteen thousand Confederates. Union casualties totaled one thousand three hundred and eighty-four, and Confederate probably about two thousand. Never again would the Confederacy be able to mount a truly significant threat to Missouri.

Troops on the offensive became prodigious marchers, particularly in the western theater. In one of Private Alfred Mathews's sketches Union troops cross a Kentucky river.

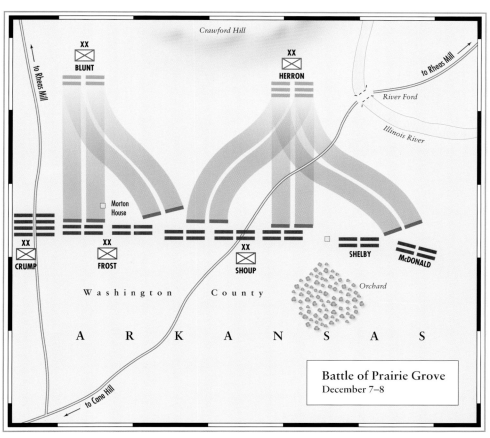

Battle of Prairie Grove
December 7–8

GRANT'S FIRST VICKSBURG CAMPAIGN

In this watercolor by Frederick B. Schell the large armored steamer Blackhawk *patrols the Mississippi.*

Sherman's column marched out of Memphis as planned on November 26. The following day, Hovey's division landed at Friar's Point, Mississippi, and began its eastward march. Having given the flanking columns a few days' start, Grant's column began its advance down the Mississippi Central. By December 1 it had reached the Tallahatchie, only to find that Pemberton had retreated, concerned about the threats to both his flank and his supply line. Sherman's and Grant's columns both crossed the Tallahatchie unopposed and linked up with each other on December 2.

The first two phases of Grant's offensive had succeeded completely. His forces had moved out of Tennessee and advanced more than fifty miles into Mississippi. His problem was that the farther he advanced along this line the more tenuous his supply line became. With Pemberton's army still intact and falling back in front of him, this was a serious problem. Fighting Pemberton somewhere between Holly Springs and Oxford was one thing. Fighting him somewhere deep in the interior of Mississippi, while dangling at the end of an extremely vulnerable supply line, was quite another.

On advice from Henry Halleck in Washington, Grant and Sherman decided to alter their plan.

IN THE FALL OF 1862 GRANT planned an offensive against Confederate forces in Mississippi with the ultimate goal of capturing Vicksburg. He initially planned to approach the Confederate stronghold from the interior of Mississippi. On November 2, he sent thirty-one thousand men in two columns marching toward the important rail nexus of Grand Junction, Tennessee, from which the Mississippi Central Railroad provided an avenue to potentially advance deep into the state. The Confederate commander in this region, Lieutenant General John C. Pemberton, made no effort to halt Grant's advance, and Union troops occupied Grand Junction after only minor skirmishing.

Grant paused there and prepared for the next stage of his offensive, aimed at Pemberton's army, which was holding the south bank of the Tallahatchie River. Again, Grant planned to use multiple columns. While his thirty-one thousand men, now united, advanced straight southward from Grand Junction along the Mississippi Central Railroad, William T. Sherman, with another fifteen thousand men, would advance southeastward from Memphis, threatening Pemberton's flank. A third column, consisting of a single division under Brigadier General Alvin P. Hovey, would cross into Mississippi from Arkansas and march eastward toward Grenada, Mississippi, threatening Pemberton's communications.

The plan worked well—almost too well, for instead of defeating Pemberton, it prompted his immediate retreat deeper into Mississippi.

Under the new scheme, Grant would continue to advance down the Mississippi Central, fast enough to keep pressure on Pemberton and keep the Rebel field army occupied along this line. Sherman would take one division, return to Memphis, join additional forces there, and with an expedition of thirty-two thousand men travel down the Mississippi River in steamboats to Vicksburg. There he would land his troops and—as only a small garrison, in theory, would be holding the town—easily take the Vicksburg. If Pemberton rushed south to defend Vicksburg,

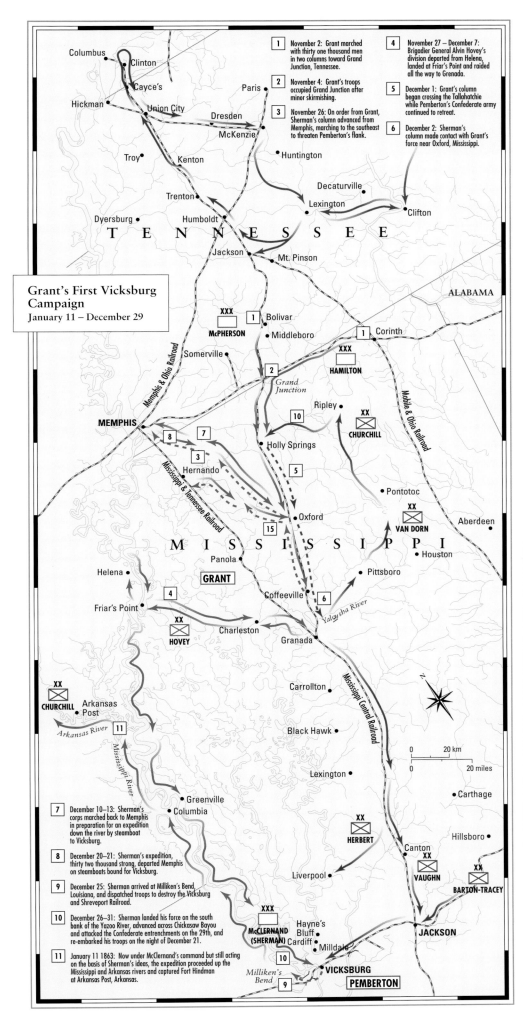

Grant's First Vicksburg Campaign
January 11 – December 29

1 November 2: Grant marched in two columns with thirty one thousand men toward Grand Junction, Tennessee.

2 November 4: Grant's troops occupied Grand Junction after minor skirmishing.

3 November 26: On order from Grant, Sherman's column advanced from Memphis, marching to the southeast to threaten Pemberton's flank.

4 November 27 – December 7: Brigadier General Alvin Hovey's division departed from Helena, landed at Friar's Point and raided all the way to Grenada.

5 December 1: Grant's column began crossing the Tallahatchie while Pemberton's Confederate army continued to retreat.

6 December 2: Sherman's column made contact with Grant's force near Oxford, Mississippi.

7 December 10–13: Sherman's corps marched back to Memphis in preparation for an expedition down the river by steamboat to Vicksburg.

8 December 20–21: Sherman's expedition, thirty two thousand strong, departed Memphis on steamboats bound for Vicksburg.

9 December 25: Sherman arrived at Milliken's Bend, Louisiana, and dispatched troops to destroy the Vicksburg and Shreveport Railroad.

10 December 26–31: Sherman landed his force on the south bank of the Yazoo River, advanced across Chickasaw Bayou and attacked the Confederate entrenchments on the 29th, and re-embarked his troops on the night of December 21.

11 January 11 1863: Now under McClernand's command but still acting on the basis of Sherman's ideas, the expedition proceeded up the Mississippi and Arkansas rivers and captured Fort Hindman at Arkansas Post, Arkansas.

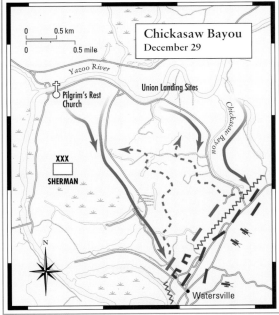

Chickasaw Bayou
December 29

Grant would be on his heels.

Sherman reached Memphis on December 13 and spent the next week gathering the necessary number of steamboats. Just before he set out, he received word that Rebel cavalry had raided Grant's supply depot at Holly Springs. Assuming that Grant would deal with the problem, Sherman proceeded on his way, arriving in the vicinity of Vicksburg on Christmas Day. In fact, the Holly Springs raid had been much more serious than Sherman realized. Major General Earl Van Dorn's Confederate cavalry had completely destroyed the depot, rendering Grant's supply situation impossible and leaving him no choice but to retreat. By the time Sherman reached Vicksburg, Grant was already well on his march back to Tennessee, and reinforcements from Pemberton's army were pouring into Vicksburg.

Sherman first landed on the Louisiana shore of the Mississippi and destroyed the railroad that approached Vicksburg from the west. Next he took his expedition a few miles up the Yazoo River, which flowed into the Mississippi a few miles above Vicksburg. After landing on the south bank of the Yazoo, all Sherman's troops had to do was march southward a few miles right into the town. Their way was barred, however, first by the bottomlands of Chickasaw Bayou, a tributary of the Yazoo with multiple winding channels, and then by the Chickasaw Bluffs, or Walnut Hills, which were surmounted by a powerful Confederate defensive line. From

December 26 to 29, Sherman attempted to find an advantageous way of attacking the Confederate line, but there was none. So on December 29, Sherman attacked at a severe disadvantage, losing one thousand seven hundred and seventy-six men to Confederate losses of less than four hundred. On the last day of 1862, Sherman re-embarked his expedition and withdrew from the Yazoo River.

FORTS HENRY AND DONELSON

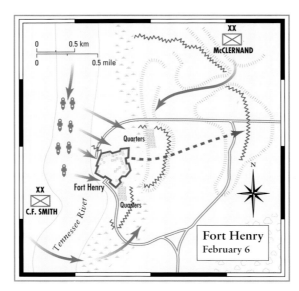

Fort Henry
February 6

WHEN IN JANUARY 1862 a reconnaissance in western Kentucky revealed that Fort Henry, guarding the Tennessee River, was weak and could probably be taken, Union brigadier general Ulysses S. Grant requested permission to attack it. His department commander, Major General Henry W. Halleck, had rejected Grant's previous offensive plans. Now, however, Lincoln was urging aggressive action, and a false report had it that Confederate troops were about to be transferred from Virginia to Tennessee. To please the president and forestall the Confederate reinforcement, Halleck turned Grant loose.

Using steamboats, Grant moved his army up the Tennessee River from his bases at Cairo, Illinois, and Paducah, Kentucky, accompanied by a naval squadron under the command of Flag Officer Andrew H. Foote. Grant's troops landed several miles north of Fort Henry, beyond the range of its guns, and began a difficult march over roads muddy from recent heavy rains. Not waiting for the army to get into position, Foote attacked with his ironclad gunboats. At the cost of serious damage to one gunboat, he battered the fort into surrender in less than an hour. Most of Fort Henry's garrison fled to Fort Donelson, thirteen miles to the east, escaping capture. Union casualties, all naval, totaled forty-seven. The Confederates lost five men and surrendered another ninety-four.

Grant almost nonchalantly telegraphed Halleck that he would march his army across the ten-mile-wide neck of land separating the Tennessee and Cumberland rivers and take Fort Donelson, on the Cumberland, in a day or two. He

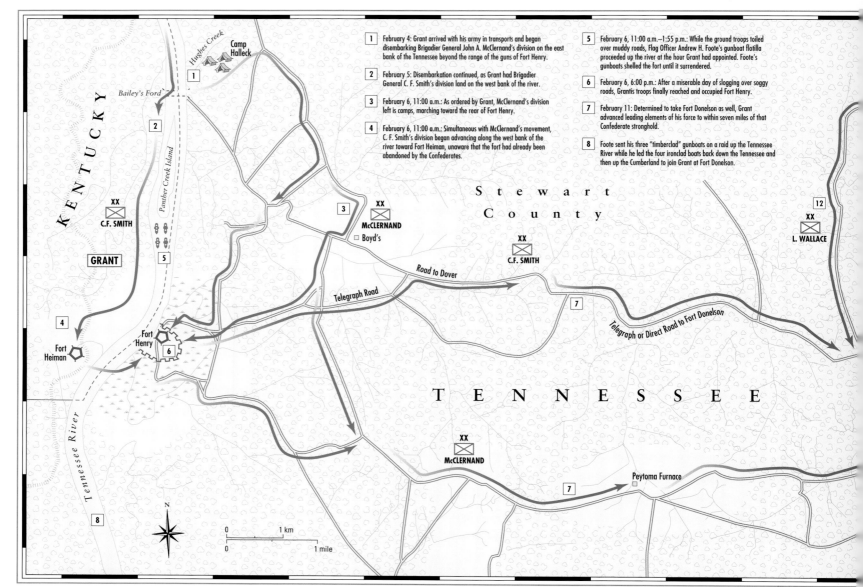

1 February 4: Grant arrived with his army in transports and began disembarking Brigadier General John A. McClernand's division on the east bank of the Tennessee beyond the range of the guns of Fort Henry.

2 February 5: Disembarkation continued, as Grant had Brigadier General C. F. Smith's division land on the west bank of the river.

3 February 6, 11:00 a.m.: As ordered by Grant, McClernand's division left is camps, marching toward the rear of Fort Henry.

4 February 6, 11:00 a.m.: Simultaneous with McClernand's movement, C. F. Smith's division began advancing along the west bank of the river toward Fort Heiman, unaware that the fort had already been abandoned by the Confederates.

5 February 6, 11:00 a.m.–1:55 p.m.: While the ground troops toiled over muddy roads, Flag Officer Andrew H. Foote's gunboat flotilla proceeded up the river at the hour Grant had appointed. Foote's gunboats shelled the fort until it surrendered.

6 February 6, 6:00 p.m.: After a miserable day of slogging over soggy roads, Grant's troops finally reached and occupied Fort Henry.

7 February 11: Determined to take Fort Donelson as well, Grant advanced leading elements of his force to within seven miles of that Confederate stronghold.

8 Foote sent his three "timberclad" gunboats on a raid up the Tennessee River while he led the four ironclad boats back down the Tennessee and then up the Cumberland to join Grant at Fort Donelson.

started as planned, but the job proved more difficult than anticipated.

The news of Fort Henry's fall caused consternation in the Confederate high command, among whom the ironclads were assumed to be unstoppable. Albert Sidney Johnston, meeting with several subordinates including Pierre G. T. Beauregard, concluded that nothing more than delaying actions was possible along the Cumberland River and the Mississippi north of Memphis. Delay was vital on the Cumberland as Johnston's main army at Bowling Green, Kentucky, would be trapped if the Cumberland River came under Union control before the troops could reach its south bank. That delay would have to occur at Fort Donelson. Johnston had no heavy artillery to send and no time to do so if he had, but he sent infantry so that the garrison would be strong enough to cut its way out of any Union encirclement once the gunboats made the position untenable. The reinforcements raised the garrison to perhaps twenty-one thousand men.

Grant's troops began arriving around Fort Donelson on February 12, but not until the 14th did he actually possess numbers equal to those inside the fort. On that day the gunboats made their assault. To everyone's surprise the shore batteries knocked out all four ironclads. Before dawn the next morning, Foote, who had been wounded, sent Grant a request to meet him at the river landing, several miles from the army. Foote wanted to inform Grant that the gunboats would be returning to Cairo for repairs. While Grant was gone, however, the Confederate garrison launched a breakout attempt. Throughout the morning most of the Confederate troops concentrated on the right of Grant's encircling line, driving back the division of Brigadier General John A. McClernand while Grant's other two divisions remained idle, obeying the orders he had left before going to see Foote.

By midday the Rebels had succeeded in opening an escape route that would allow them to march to Nashville. Then, however, the Confederate commander, Brigadier General John B. Floyd, allowed his second-in-command, Brigadier General Gideon Pillow, to talk him into pulling his troops back into the fort, apparently believing Grant's army had been completely routed. Grant returned to the battlefield at about that time and at once ordered an attack all along the line. By nightfall, Union troops under Brigadier General Lew Wallace had retaken the ground the Confederates had gained that morning, closing off most avenues of escape, while Federals under Brigadier General Charles F. Smith had captured key positions that rendered the fort untenable.

Floyd and Pillow escaped just before the fort capitulated, leaving the next ranking officer, Brigadier General Simon B. Buckner, to surrender to Grant on the morning of February 16. Grant demanded unconditional surrender. Possibly as many as six thousand Confederates made off in the confusion during and after the surrender. About fifteen thousand remained as prisoners. Grant's casualties totaled two thousand eight hundred and thirty-two. The loss of the forts was one of the greatest single blows the Confederacy suffered. Johnston could ill-afford the loss of the captured troops, and Grant's victory gave the Union control of more than half of Tennessee.

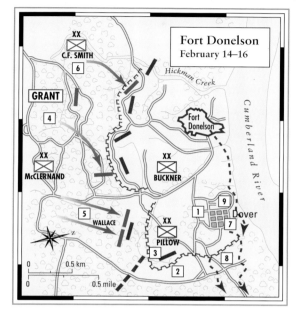

Fort Donelson
February 14–16

1. February 14–15 : Confederate commander, Brigadier General John B. Floyd, decided the time had come to break out with the garrison and escape to Nashville.

2. February 15, dawn–noon: At Floyd's order, Brigadier General Simon B. Buckner and Brigadier General Gideon J. Pillow massed their troops against the Union right, held by McClernand's division. In several hours of fierce fighting they succeeded in driving the Union troops back.

3. February 15, noon: In a major blunder, Floyd ordered his troops back into the fort.

4. February 15, 1:00 p.m.: Grant returned to the battlefield and ordered a counterattack.

5. February 15, 1:00–5:00 p.m.: Wallace's division retook some of the positions McClernand had lost in the morning's fighting.

6. February 15, 1:00–5:00 p.m.: Smith's division attacked and captured key Confederate entrenchments.

7. February 15–16, night: The top three Confederate commanders met and decided to surrender. Floyd and Pillow fled, leaving Buckner to capitulate.

8. February 16, pre-dawn: Colonel Nathan Bedford Forrest led his cavalry out of the fort by wading a flooded backwater.

9. February 16, dawn: Grant rode to Dover to accept the unconditional surrender of the fort and remaining garrison.

General Ulysses S. Grant watches the battle unfold as his men doggedly advance toward Fort Donelson.

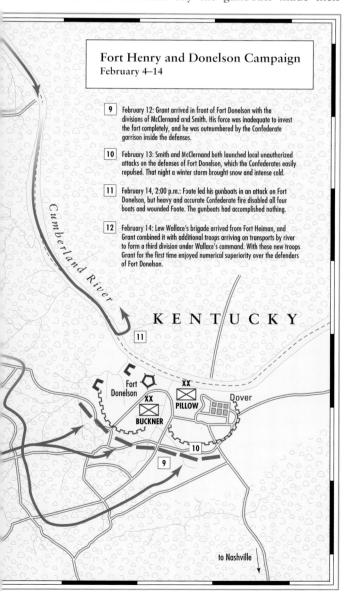

Fort Henry and Donelson Campaign
February 4–14

9. February 12: Grant arrived in front of Fort Donelson with the divisions of McClernand and Smith. His force was inadequate to invest the fort completely, and he was outnumbered by the Confederate garrison inside the defenses.

10. February 13: Smith and McClernand both launched local unauthorized attacks on the defenses of Fort Donelson, which the Confederates easily repulsed. That night a winter storm brought snow and intense cold.

11. February 14, 2:00 p.m.: Foote led his gunboats in an attack on Fort Donelson, but heavy and accurate Confederate fire disabled all four boats and wounded Foote. The gunboats had accomplished nothing.

12. February 14: Lew Wallace's brigade arrived from Fort Heiman, and Grant combined it with additional troops arriving on transports by river to form a third division under Wallace's command. With these new troops Grant for the first time enjoyed numerical superiority over the defenders of Fort Donelson.

KENTUCKY

NORTH CAROLINA CAMPAIGN

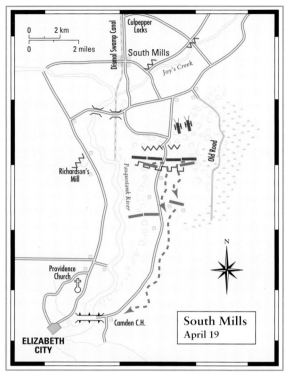

South Mills
April 19

EARLY IN 1862 THE UNION high command moved to follow up on the advantages it had gained through combined coastal operations the previous year. On January 2, Union Flag Officer Louis M. Goldsborough set sail from Fort Monroe, Virginia, with twenty-six warships and eighty transports carrying fifteen thousand troops commanded by Brigadier General Ambrose Burnside. They were bound for Hatteras Inlet, North Carolina, and the access it offered to the sheltered waters of the North Carolina sounds. With their many inlets and islands, the sounds provided innumerable havens for blockade-runners as well as possibilities for naval coaling stations. The presence of a Union fleet in the sounds would also pose a serious coastal threat to the Confederacy.

The fleet arrived off the Hatteras Inlet on January 13 and immediately encountered some of the Carolina sounds' difficulties. The sounds were shallow, and an even shallower bar spanned the inlet. Among the many vessels of Goldsborough's enormous fleet, there were not enough of shallow-draft for the expedition to advance immediately into the sounds. The fleet was delayed while suitable vessels were obtained and then delayed again while the smaller vessels slowly shuttled the army to shore and the shallow-draft warships laboriously warped their way over the bar.

By February 7, Goldsborough had a fleet inside the sounds. His warships easily scattered the handful of Confederate armed vessels he found there and then steamed northward through Pamlico Sound to the expedition's first target, Roanoke Island. There, Burnside's troops began going ashore on the south end of the island. By the following morning, Burnside had seven thousand five hundred of his men on Roanoke and they advanced up the island toward the Rebel camp. Confederate brigadier general Henry A. Wise met him with two thousand men, but Burnside overwhelmed his small force and drove it to the north end of the island, where Wise had no choice but surrender.

After the capture of Roanoke Island, the Union campaign proceeded with a rapid succession of small victories. On February 10, Goldsborough's fleet steamed to Elizabeth City, annihilated what remained of the Confederate coastal flotilla, and once again set Burnside and his troops on the sandy North Carolina soil, where the blue-coats quickly secured the town. Two days later, Union forces went ashore at Edenton, North Carolina, and by February 18 they had proceeded up Curratuck Sound to occupy the town of Winton, North Carolina.

On March 12, Goldborough's and Burnside's forces rendezvoused at Roanoke Island and set out for New Bern, North Carolina. By the following afternoon, Burnside went ashore on the southwest bank of the Neuse River below New Bern with eleven thousand men and immediately marched toward the town. To counter their advance the Confederacy had only four thousand men under the command of Brigadier General Lawrence O'Bryan Branch, and these proved far too few. On the morning of March 14, Burnside easily defeated Branch and a few hours later another Carolina coastal town was in Union hands.

The next Union target was Carolina City on Beaufort Inlet. On March 23, Brigadier General John G. Parke marched from New Bern to Carolina City and demanded the surrender of Fort Macon, which guarded Beaufort Inlet. The Confederate commander, Colonel Moses J. White, refused, so Parke settled down to lay siege to the fort. Over the next month, while the siege went on, Burnside saw to it that Parke received a steady stream of reinforcements. Finally, on April 25, Union forces unleashed a powerful bombardment on Fort Macon, both from the fleet and from Parke's batteries on shore. With the reduction of the fort now but a matter of time, and not very much time, Colonel White surrendered the fort and its four-hundred-man garrison.

The Union successes in the Carolina sounds during the first four months of 1862 made blockading easier for the U.S. Navy and blockade-running more difficult for the Rebels. It also caused consternation in the Confederacy's coastal areas, leading to the diversion of many troops to guard a coast that could never really be adequately protected. Amphibious operations such as those conducted by Goldsborough and Burnside in 1862 showed much promise for further Union successes—promise that some historians believe the government in Washington never fully seized upon. Finally, the season of success on the Carolina coast elevated Ambrose Burnside to national prominence as a successful general and planted in some minds, notably Lincoln's, the idea that he might be a prospect for even higher command in the future.

Fort Macon
April 25

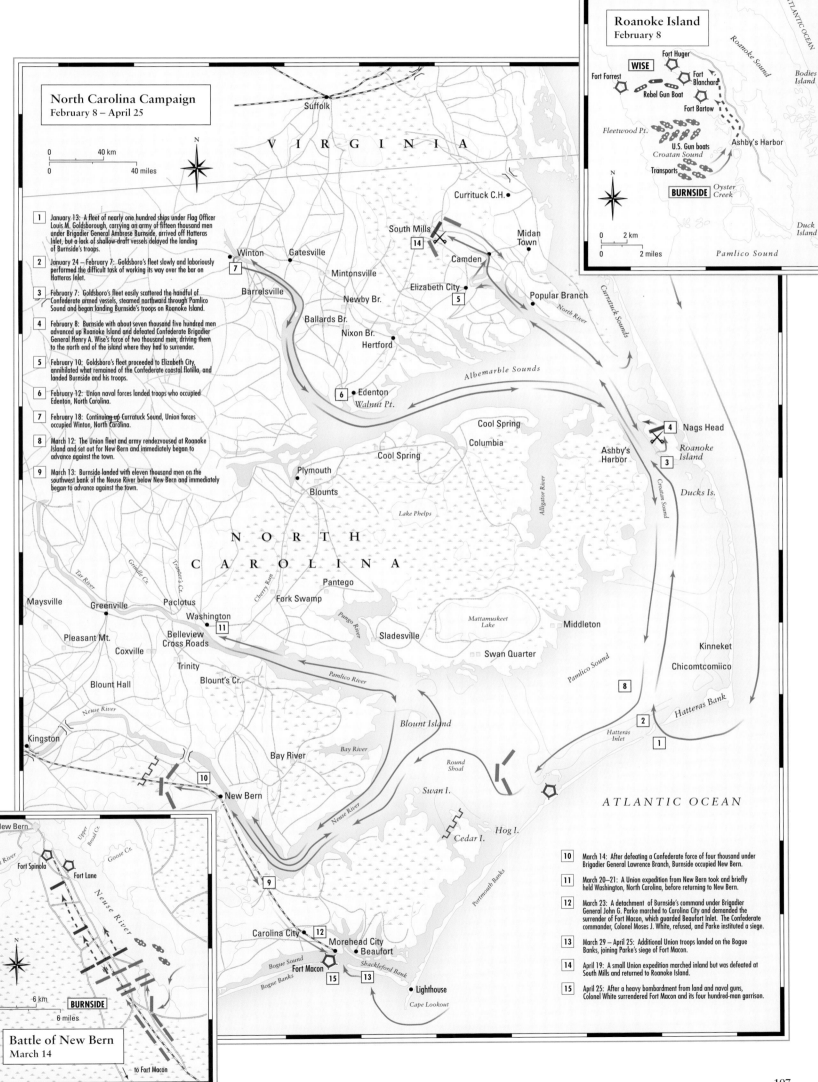

Roanoke Island
February 8

WISE

Fort Huger
Fort Forrest
Fort Blanchard
Rebel Gun Boat
Fort Bartow
U.S. Gun boats
Ashby's Harbor
Fleetwood Pt.
Croatan Sound
Transports
BURNSIDE
Oyster Creek

Roanoke Sound
ATLANTIC OCEAN
Bodies Island
Duck Island
Pamlico Sound

0   2 km
0   2 miles

North Carolina Campaign
February 8 – April 25

0   40 km
0   40 miles
N

1 January 13: A fleet of nearly one hundred ships under Flag Officer Louis M. Goldsborough, carrying an army of fifteen thousand men under Brigadier General Ambrose Burnside, arrived off Hatteras Inlet, but a lack of shallow-draft vessels delayed the landing of Burnside's troops.

2 January 24 – February 7: Goldsboro's fleet slowly and laboriously performed the difficult task of working its way over the bar on Hatteras Inlet.

3 February 7: Goldsboro's fleet easily scattered the handful of Confederate armed vessels, steamed northward through Pamlico Sound and began landing Burnside's troops on Roanoke Island.

4 February 8: Burnside with about seven thousand five hundred men advanced up Roanoke Island and defeated Confederate Brigadier General Henry A. Wise's force of two thousand men; driving them to the north end of the island where they had to surrender.

5 February 10: Goldsboro's fleet proceeded to Elizabeth City, annihilated what remained of the Confederate coastal flotilla, and landed Burnside and his troops.

6 February 12: Union naval forces landed troops who occupied Edenton, North Carolina.

7 February 18: Continuing up Currituck Sound, Union forces occupied Winton, North Carolina.

8 March 12: The Union fleet and army rendezvoused at Roanoke Island and set out for New Bern and immediately began to advance against the town.

9 March 13: Burnside landed with eleven thousand men on the southwest bank of the Neuse River below New Bern and immediately began to advance against the town.

10 March 14: After defeating a Confederate force of four thousand under Brigadier General Lawrence Branch, Burnside occupied New Bern.

11 March 20–21: A Union expedition from New Bern took and briefly held Washington, North Carolina, before returning to New Bern.

12 March 23: A detachment of Burnside's command under Brigadier General John G. Parke marched to Carolina City and demanded the surrender of Fort Macon, which guarded Beaufort Inlet. The Confederate commander, Colonel Moses J. White, refused, and Parke instituted a siege.

13 March 29 – April 25: Additional Union troops landed on the Bogue Banks, joining Parke's siege of Fort Macon.

14 April 19: A small Union expedition marched inland but was defeated at South Mills and returned to Roanoke Island.

15 April 25: After a heavy bombardment from land and naval guns, Colonel White surrendered Fort Macon and its four hundred-man garrison.

VIRGINIA
Suffolk
Currituck C.H.
South Mills
Midan Town
Camden
Winton
Gatesville
Mintonsville
Newby Br.
Elizabeth City
Popular Branch
Barrelsville
Ballards Br.
Nixon Br.
Hertford
North River
Currituck Sounds
Edenton
Walnut Pt.
Albemarle Sounds
Cool Spring
Columbia
Cool Spring
Nags Head
Ashby's Harbor
Roanoke Island
Plymouth
Blounts
Alligator River
Lake Phelps
Croatan Sound
Ducks Is.
NORTH CAROLINA
Maysville
Greenville
Paclotus
Washington
Cherry Run
Pantego
Fork Swamp
Mattamuskeet Lake
Middleton
Kinneket
Chicomtcomiico
Pleasant Mt.
Belleview Cross Roads
Coxville
Pungo River
Sladesville
Swan Quarter
Pamlico Sound
Trinity
Blount's Cr.
Pamlico River
Blount Hall
Neuse River
Kingston
Blount Island
Bay River
Bay River
Hatteras Bank
New Bern
Round Shoal
Swan I.
Hatteras Inlet
ATLANTIC OCEAN
Neuse River
Cedar I.
Hog I.
Carolina City
Morehead City
Beaufort
Bogue Sound
Fort Macon
Shackleford Bank
Bogue Banks
Lighthouse
Cape Lookout
Portsmouth Banks

Battle of New Bern
March 14

New Bern
Fort Spinola
Fort Lane
Treat River
Upper Broad Cr.
Goose Cr.
Neuse River
BURNSIDE
0   6 km
0   6 miles
to Fort Macon

UPPER MISSISSIPPI VALLEY

Military and Naval Movements
March – June

1. March: After the fall of Fort Henry forced the Confederates to abandon their fortifications at Columbus, Halleck dispatched Brigadier General John Pope overland to attack New Madrid while the navy's gunboats, commanded by Flag Officer Andrew H. Foote proceeded down the river.

2. March 13 – April 17: Foote and Pope cooperated in besieging New Madrid, Island No. 10, and their associated fortifications, compelling their surrender with seven thousand men.

3. April 29 – May 30: Halleck's massive army advanced ponderously toward the key rail junction at Corinth, which the Confederates finally evacuated on May 30.

4. April 14: The Union mortar fleet began bombarding Fort Pillow.

5. May 10: The Confederate River Defense Fleet under command of Captain James E. Montgomery attacked the Union gunboats at Plum Run Bend north of Fort Pillow, sinking two but sustaining significant damage. Montgomery's vessels then return to Memphis.

6. June 7: The Union fleet under Flag Officer Charles H. Davis decisively defeated Montgomery's River Defense Fleet. Memphis surrendered.

1. March 13: Pope's artillery began bombarding New Madrid.

2. April 4: During a heavy night-time storm, the gunboat *Carondelet* successfully passed the Confederate batteries at Island No. 10.

3. April 6–7: Pope's troops moved down the west bank of the Mississippi and crossed the river below Island No. 10.

4. April 7: Pope's troops got into position behind Island No. 10, cutting off the garrison's escape.

5. Bombarded by the gunboats and trapped by Pope, seven thousand Confederates surrendered.

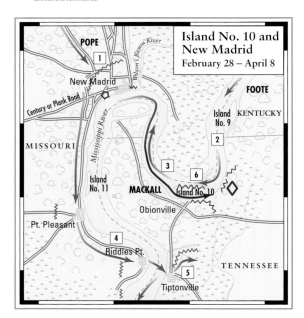

Island No. 10 and New Madrid
February 28 – April 8

BOTH SIDES IMMEDIATELY RECOGNIZED THE importance of the Mississippi River as an artery of commerce and a potential avenue for invasion. The first Union base in the Mississippi Valley was Cairo, Illinois, located at the extreme southern tip of the state at the confluence of the Mississippi and Ohio rivers. In geologic terms, the Mississippi Delta begins at Cairo, and from there to the Gulf of Mexico the river meanders broadly across a wide, swampy flood plain on which the highest ground is found on the natural levees, formed from sediment deposited by the river itself.

As the flood plain offered few viable defensive positions against vessels steaming down the river, great importance was concentrated on those places where the river's meanders brought it close to the high bluffs at one of the edges of the flood plain. These bluffs offered a high, strong defensive position overlooking the river.

The first such position taken up by the Confederates was at Columbus, Kentucky, where bluffs called the "Chalk Banks" and "Iron Bluffs" rise on the east bank of the river. Troops under Major General Leonidas Polk occupied Columbus in early September 1861, and in doing so broke Kentucky's neutrality and drove many of the state's citizens to side with the Union. Polk massively fortified Columbus, emplacing one hundred and forty guns there, but its strength was never tested. When Union forces took control of the Tennessee River in February 1862, Polk was compelled to abandon Columbus without firing a shot to avoid certain encirclement, siege, and capture.

The Confederacy's next defensive position on the river was at Island No. 10 and the adjacent town, New Madrid, Missouri. The island offered no bluffs but there was a sharp bend of the river around which vessels would have to steam. Passing vessels were vulnerable to fire from both the Missouri and Tennessee shores and the island, where most of the guns from the Columbus fortifications were relocated. Union troops under Brigadier General John Pope advanced down the Missouri side of the river and approached New Madrid in early March 1862. On March 13, Pope's artillery bombarded New Madrid, and the following day his troops advanced to find that the Confederates had evacuated during the night, fleeing to Island No. 10. Pope continued to operate against the island. Then on the night of April 4, the Union ironclad gunboat *Carondelet* ran past the island's batteries. With a Union gunboat in the river below them, the Confederates on the island were in a desperate situation. After the gunboat *Pittsburg* joined *Carondelet* on April 7, the garrisons on the island and on the Tennessee shore, some seven thousand men, surrendered.

The next Confederate position on the river was Fort Pillow, located on the bluffs on the Tennessee side. On April 14, just one week after the fall of Island No. 10, the Union fleet, commanded by Captain Charles H. Davis, arrived near Fort Pillow and mortar boats began bombarding the fort. On May 10, Confederate naval captain James E. Montgomery led a squadron of eight armed riverboats known as the River Defense Fleet in attacking the mortar boats and their seven escorting gunboats near Plum Run Bend, a few miles above Memphis. Two Union ironclads were sunk in shallow water but subsequently raised, and four of Montgomery's riverboats were disabled. Union forces continued to operate against Fort Pillow, but progress was slow because Halleck had drawn off most of the land forces associated with the expedition in order to strengthen his own vast army advancing on Corinth, Mississippi. When Corinth fell on May 30, Fort Pillow became untenable, and the Confederates evacuated it by June 5.

Early the next morning Davis's fleet approached Memphis. Memphis had bluffs, but they were not fortified. Instead, the hilltops were lined with Memphis citizens who turned out to see their River Defense Fleet attempt to fight off the Union gunboats and rams. Nine Union vessels engaged eight Confederate boats. Two of the Union vessels suffered damage, but three of the Confederate boats were destroyed and four others captured. Only one escaped. The battle was over by about 7:30 a.m., and at 11:00 a.m. the mayor formally surrendered the city.

An Ohio regiment building breastworks near Corinth.

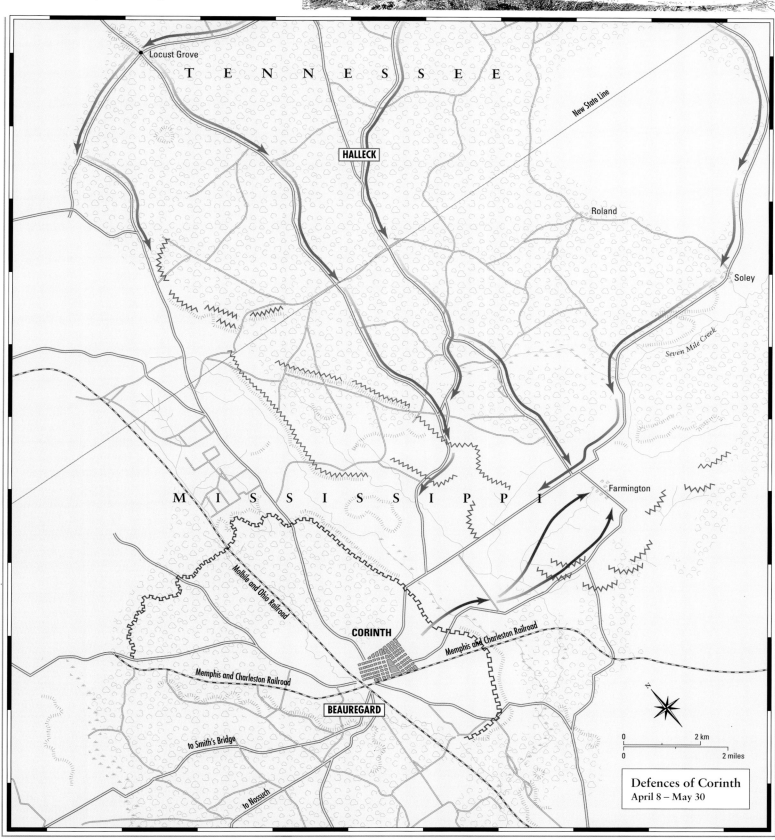

Defences of Corinth
April 8 – May 30

HAMPTON ROADS

U.S. officers examine the battle damage to U.S.S. Monitor. *Despite several hours of close engagement, the resulting damage to the ironclad was slight.*

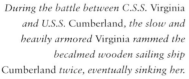

During the battle between C.S.S. Virginia *and U.S.S.* Cumberland, *the slow and heavily armored* Virginia *rammed the becalmed wooden sailing ship* Cumberland *twice, eventually sinking her.*

WHEN IN APRIL 1861 VIRGINIA joined the rebellion, U.S. forces evacuated the Gosport Navy Yard in Norfolk, where the large steam frigate U.S.S. *Merrimac* was laid up for engine repairs. Unable to remove her, they set her afire, and she burned to the waterline and sank. No sooner were the Confederates in control of the navy yard than they went to work to raise and rebuild *Merrimac*, not as the stately frigate she had once been but rather as an ungainly ironclad. They cut her down to the berth deck, three feet above the waterline and gave her a flat deck that stretched two hundred and sixty-three feet from stem to stern. Atop this they built a casemate one hundred and seventy-eight feet long and twenty-four feet high, with sides that sloped thirty-six degrees and were composed of four inches of oak and twenty-four inches of pine, topped with four inches of iron. Inside the casemate they placed twelve guns and on her bow an iron ram below the waterline. The finished product, re-christened C.S.S. *Virginia*, was a slow, unmaneuverable, but very powerful vessel.

After getting wind of the Confederates' secret weapon, the U.S. government entertained various plans for ironclad warships and adopted several. The smallest and least conventional of the lot was U.S.S. *Monitor*, designed by the brilliant but eccentric Swedish American inventor John Ericsson. *Monitor*'s one hundred and seventy-two-foot-long deck cleared the surface by only eighteen inches and was perfectly flat save for a three-foot-tall pilot house and a single turret, nine feet tall and twenty feet in diameter, mounting two large guns. *Monitor* was much smaller than *Virginia*, and many feared she would be no match for the Confederate ironclad.

At 1:00 p.m. on March 8, 1862, *Virginia*, commanded by Captain Franklin Buchanan and accompanied by several small unarmored gunboats, steamed down the Elizabeth River and into Hampton Roads, the body of water at the mouth of the James and Elizabeth rivers. She first attacked the frigate U.S.S. *Cumberland*, a sailing vessel that lay becalmed and was thus unable to flee or maneuver. During *Virginia*'s long, slow approach, *Cumberland* fired broadside after broadside, but her shot simply glanced off *Virginia*'s armored casemate without inflicting damage. *Virginia*'s fire, on the other hand, proved devastating to the wooden *Cumberland*, strewing her decks with the mangled bodies of her crew. Inexorably

Virginia crept closer, driven by her decrepit engines, until she finally succeeded in ramming *Cumberland*, tearing a hole seven feet wide. It took *Virginia* some thirty minutes to back clear of her victim, during which time it appeared that the sinking *Cumberland* might take the ironclad to the bottom with her. *Cumberland*'s sailors stood to their guns until their ship sank under them. Then many took refuge in her rigging, which remained above the shallow waters of Hampton Roads after her hull settled on the bottom.

Buchanan then turned *Virginia* against the similarly helpless sailing frigate U.S.S. *Congress*. The latter ship's captain had a tug tow his vessel into shallow waters close to shore, where the deep-draft *Virginia* could not follow. Unable to ram, *Virginia* took up a position toward which none of *Congress*'s guns would bear and from which she could shell the wooden vessel at a range of two hundred yards. This continued until, with blood running from the wooden ship's scuppers and her captain dead, the senior surviving officer ordered her colors struck. Buchanan sent over a boat to take possession of *Congress* but several Confederate sailors and officers were struck by rifle fire from Union troops on shore. Enraged, Buchanan had his gunners fire red-hot shot into *Congress*, setting her afire, while he himself stood on the open deck with a rifle, shooting at the Union soldiers until one of them shot him in the leg.

The steam frigates U.S.S. *Minnesota* and *Roanoke* had attempted to come to the aid of their consorts but had run aground in the treacherous shallows of the roads. *Virginia* turned ominously toward *Minnesota* but before the slow, clumsy ironclad could close in on the frigate darkness fell, and *Virginia* returned to the Elizabeth River and anchored under the protection of Confederate shore batteries for the night.

During the night the blazing *Congress* exploded, and *Monitor*, having survived a storm-imperiled voyage from New York City, arrived at Hampton Roads and anchored near *Minnesota*. Shortly after sunrise on March 9, *Virginia* stood down the Elizabeth River again and headed for *Minnesota*. *Monitor* got underway and intercepted *Virginia*. By 8:45 a.m. the two ironclads came to close quarters and there they spent most of the next three and a half hours hammering at each other's armor while inflicting only minor damage. Then *Virginia* withdrew, ending the first battle between ironclads. Two months later, without engaging in another action, *Virginia* was scuttled to avoid capture when Union land forces captured her home port.

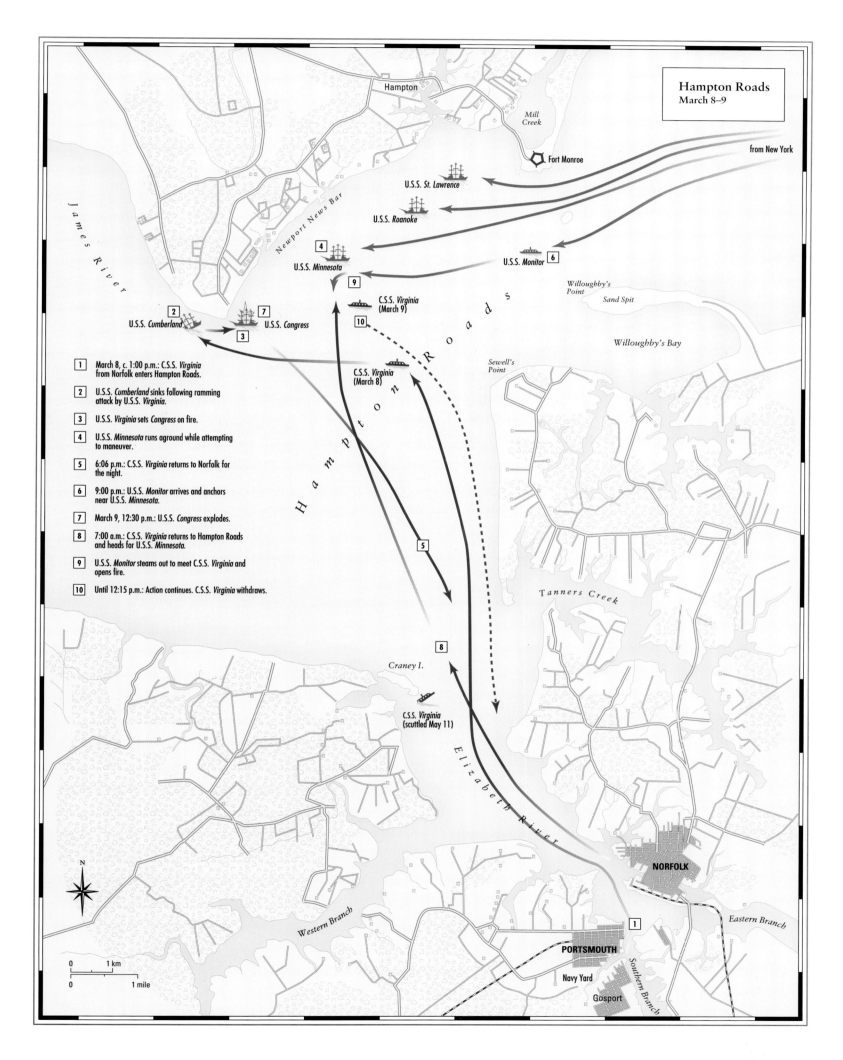

Hampton Roads
March 8–9

1   March 8, c. 1:00 p.m.: C.S.S. *Virginia* from Norfolk enters Hampton Roads.

2   U.S.S. *Cumberland* sinks following ramming attack by U.S.S. *Virginia*.

3   U.S.S. *Virginia* sets *Congress* on fire.

4   U.S.S. *Minnesota* runs aground while attempting to maneuver.

5   6:06 p.m.: C.S.S. *Virginia* returns to Norfolk for the night.

6   9:00 p.m.: U.S.S. *Monitor* arrives and anchors near U.S.S. *Minnesota*.

7   March 9, 12:30 p.m.: U.S.S. *Congress* explodes.

8   7:00 a.m.: C.S.S. *Virginia* returns to Hampton Roads and heads for U.S.S. *Minnesota*.

9   U.S.S. *Monitor* steams out to meet C.S.S. *Virginia* and opens fire.

10   Until 12:15 p.m.: Action continues. C.S.S. *Virginia* withdraws.

JACKSON'S SHENANDOAH VALLEY CAMPAIGN, PHASE I

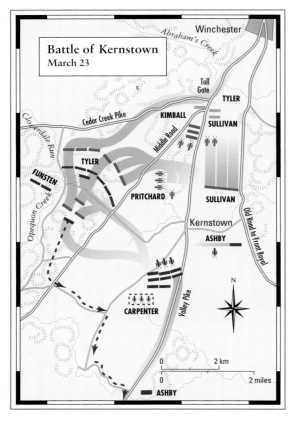

Battle of Kernstown
March 23

STONEWALL JACKSON HAD ORDERS FROM Richmond to prevent the Federals from drawing their forces out of the Shenandoah Valley to support George B. McClellan's campaign against Richmond. In mid-March 1862, Jackson received information that precisely such a movement was happening. The information was generally correct, but exaggerated and premature. Acting on the basis of it, Jackson attacked Kernstown on March 23, thinking only a weak Union force would be present. What he encountered was in fact the Union division of Brigadier General James Shields. Jackson's army was soundly repulsed and had to beat a hasty retreat. Still, Jackson's rash attack served to accomplish his strategic purpose. The Union high command was convinced that he was still dangerous and that a sizable force ought to be left in the Shenandoah rather than transferred to McClellan's aid.

By late April, McClellan's army posed a dire threat to Richmond. General Joseph E. Johnston, commanding the Confederate army defending Richmond, was inclined to summon Jackson's force to join him unless he could tie up larger numbers of Federals in the Shenandoah Valley. Jackson believed he could; Robert E. Lee, general in chief of Confederate armies under the direction of President Davis, agreed. Acting with the audacity that was to characterize his conduct of the war, Lee sent Jackson reinforcements in the form of Major General Richard S. Ewell's division, which joined Jackson at Conrad's Store on April 30.

Jackson planned a whirlwind campaign in which much would depend on the element of surprise. He therefore opened it by marching his army out of the Shenandoah Valley and then immediately shipping them back in by train, in hopes of confusing any spies who might be observing the army's movements. Back in the valley, Jackson's first order of business was to unite his force with the small army of Brigadier General Edward Johnson and defeat the Union army of Major General John C. Frémont, which was advancing through the mountains of western Virginia. Leaving Ewell to watch the Union forces in the valley, Jackson joined Johnson on May 6 at Staunton, ninety-five miles southwest of Winchester. Two days later their combined forces, about nine thousand men, encountered Frémont's advance guard of about six thousand men under Brigadier General Robert Milroy at the Battle of McDowell. The fighting was intense and Jackson suffered five hundred casualties to Milroy's two hundred and fifty-six, but Frémont's forces retreated. After chasing Frémont in a four-day march to the north, Jackson returned to the valley intent on his next objective.

That objective was the Union army of

Major General Nathaniel P. Banks, a Massachusetts politician who had wangled himself a general's commission and hoped for military glory. Hearing of Jackson's renewed activities, Banks left Harrisonburg, twenty-five miles northeast of Staunton, on May 6 and had retreated all the way to Strasburg, another fifty miles to the northeast, by May 13. By May 15, Jackson was back in the valley after his excursion to McDowell, and marching straight for Banks. Five days later, however, at New Market, Jackson veered off the direct route down the valley and crossed over to the Luray Valley, an arm of the Shenandoah Valley separated from the main valley by the long, high ridge of Massanutten Mountain. Screened by the great bulk of Massanutten, Jackson marched rapidly down the Luray Valley to emerge on May 23 at Front Royal, at the confluence of the north and south forks of the Shenandoah River, fourteen miles east of Strasburg, where his troops easily routed the small garrison Banks had left to guard the place.

In Front Royal, Jackson posed a serious threat to Banks's line of supply and retreat, and the Union general began a rapid retreat down the valley to Winchester. Jackson caught up with him there and lost no time in attacking. The resulting First Battle of Winchester was a Confederate victory. Jackson lost 400 casualties out of his army of sixteen thousand men, while Banks, who had only eight thousand men in the battle, lost two thousand and nineteen—one thousand seven hundred and fourteen of them captured or missing. What was left of Banks's army fled once more and even faster, with Jackson pursuing as rapidly as his army could, given the fatigue and growing disorganization created by one of the most remarkable lightning campaigns in military history. It was a feeble pursuit, but by May 29 Jackson's troops were threatening Harpers Ferry on the Potomac, though Banks was safely north of that river.

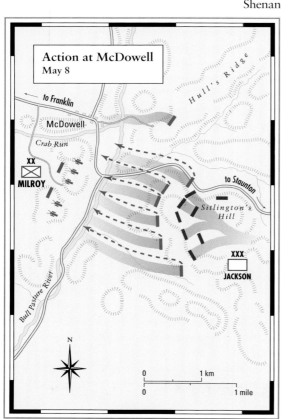

Action at McDowell
May 8

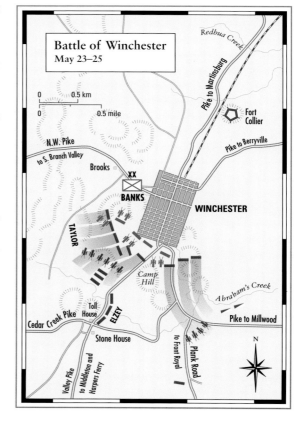

Battle of Winchester
May 23–25

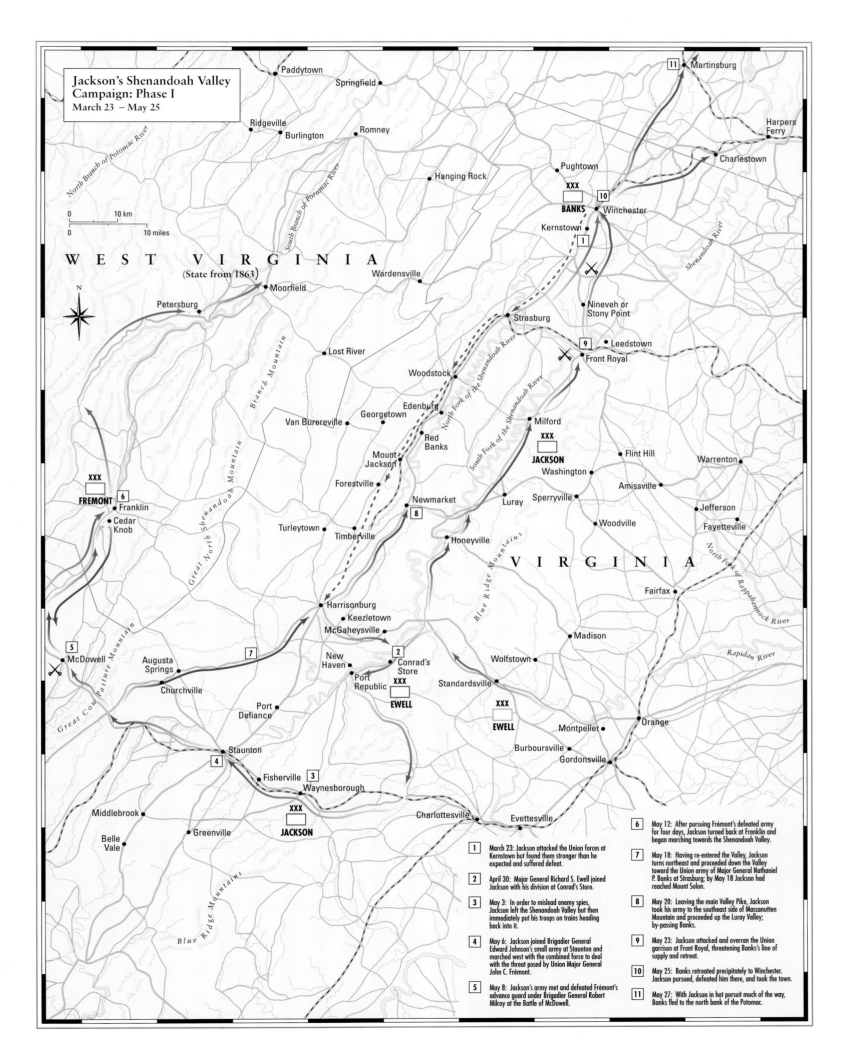

Jackson's Shenandoah Valley Campaign: Phase I
March 23 – May 25

WEST VIRGINIA
(State from 1863)

VIRGINIA

0   10 km
0   10 miles

N

Paddytown
Springfield
Ridgeville
Burlington
Romney
Hanging Rock
Pughtown
Martinsburg
Harpers Ferry
Charlestown
XXX BANKS
10 Winchester
Kernstown
North Branch of Potomac River
South Branch of Potomac River
Moorfield
Petersburg
Wardensville
1
Nineveh or Stony Point
Lost River
Strasburg
9 Leedstown
Front Royal
Woodstock
Edenburg
Van Burereville
Georgetown
Red Banks
Milford
Flint Hill
Warrenton
XXX JACKSON
Mount Jackson
Washington
Amissville
Forestville
Newmarket
8
Luray
Sperryville
Jefferson
Fayetteville
Woodville
Branch Mountain
Great North Shenandoah Mountain
North Fork of the Shenandoah River
South Fork of the Shenandoah River
XXX FREMONT
6 Franklin
Cedar Knob
Turleytown
Timberville
Honeyville
Blue Ridge Mountains
Fairfax
North Fork of Rappahannock River
Harrisonburg
Keezletown
McGaheysville
Madison
Wolfstown
Rapidan River
5 McDowell
Augusta Springs
Churchville
New Haven
7
2 Conrad's Store
XXX EWELL
Standardsville
Woodstown
Great Cow Pasture Mountain
Port Republic
Port Defiance
XXX EWELL
Montpelier
Orange
Staunton
4
Fisherville
3 Waynesborough
XXX JACKSON
Middlebrook
Belle Vale
Greenville
Charlottesville
Evettesville
Burboursville
Gordonsville
Blue Ridge Mountains

1 March 23: Jackson attacked the Union forces at Kernstown but found them stronger than he expected and suffered defeat.

2 April 30: Major General Richard S. Ewell joined Jackson with his division at Conrad's Store.

3 May 3: In order to mislead enemy spies, Jackson left the Shenandoah Valley but then immediately put his troops on trains heading back into it.

4 May 6: Jackson joined Brigadier General Edward Johnson's small army at Staunton and marched west with the combined force to deal with the threat posed by Union Major General John C. Frémont.

5 May 8: Jackson's army met and defeated Frémont's advance guard under Brigadier General Robert Milroy at the Battle of McDowell.

6 May 12: After pursuing Frémont's defeated army for four days, Jackson turned back at Franklin and began marching towards the Shenandoah Valley.

7 May 18: Having re-entered the Valley, Jackson turns northeast and proceeded down the Valley toward the Union army of Major General Nathaniel P. Banks at Strasburg; by May 18 Jackson had reached Mount Solon.

8 May 20: Leaving the main Valley Pike, Jackson took his army to the southeast side of Massanutten Mountain and proceeded up the Luray Valley; by-passing Banks.

9 May 23: Jackson attacked and overran the Union garrison at Front Royal, threatening Banks's line of supply and retreat.

10 May 25: Banks retreated precipitately to Winchester. Jackson pursued, defeated him there, and took the town.

11 May 27: With Jackson in hot pursuit much of the way, Banks fled to the north bank of the Potomac.

McClellan's Peninsula Campaign

IN DECEMBER 1861, ARMY OF the Potomac commander George B. McClellan conceived the idea of reaching Richmond without a large battle by transporting his army through Chesapeake Bay and up one of its many broad estuaries to land behind the Confederate position. In the plan's first form McClellan envisioned landing at Urbanna, Virginia, on the south bank of the Rappahannock River, fifty-six miles east of Richmond. McClellan did not inform Lincoln of his plan because he thought military operations were none of the president's business.

However, in late January 1862, Lincoln, becoming increasingly impatient for action, issued his President's General War Orders Number 1, ordering that all Union armies should advance on February 22. McClellan was not ready to implement the Urbanna plan by that deadline, and he was unwilling to attack Joseph E. Johnston's Confederates in their defenses near Manassas Junction. So, in order to buy time he let the commander in chief in on the secret of his Urbanna plan. Lincoln had his doubts about its wisdom, pointing out that by avoiding the direct approach to Richmond it also allowed the Confederates a direct approach to Washington. After long discussions and agreeing, very reluctantly, to leave substantial forces in northern Virginia to cover the capital, McClellan secured Lincoln's approval.

Then on March 9, Johnston, who knew nothing of McClellan's plans, nevertheless ruined the Urbanna scheme by pulling his Confederate army back from Manassas Junction to the south bank of the Rappahannock, where it was well positioned to block any advance from Urbanna to Richmond. Getting to the Confederate capital without major fighting would now require a new plan, and McClellan quickly produced one. In his new scheme, the army would land at Fort Monroe, Virginia, on the tip of the peninsula between the York and the James rivers about seventy five miles southeast of Richmond. The army would then advance up the peninsula with its flanks and supply lines, at least at first, secured by the rivers. With some misgivings, Lincoln gave his consent.

McClellan began transporting his army to the peninsula on March 17, and by April 4 he had about 100,000 troops there. Barring his path to Richmond was Confederate Major General John B. Magruder with a force of seventeen thousand men entrenched across the peninsula from the James River to Yorktown on the York River. Much of Magruder's line ran along a small stream called the Warwick River. McClellan could have crushed Magruder's small force, but, unable to sort through mistaken intelligence reports, he concluded that he was outnumbered and settled down to besiege Yorktown. The siege began on April 5 and lasted until the Confederates evacuated Yorktown and the Warwick River line on May 3. During that time, General Joseph E. Johnston's army marched south to Richmond and east to join the defenders of the peninsula, raising Confederate numbers there to about sixty thousand.

As the Confederates, under Johnston's overall command, retreated from the Warwick River line, McClellan's army pursued and clashed inconclusively with the Confederate rear guard at Williamsburg on May 5. In damp and muddy conditions, forty thousand Federals engaged about thirty-one thousand Confederates. Union casualties totaled two thousand two hundred and thirty-nine and Confederate, one thousand seven hundred and three.

The Confederate retreat continued, resulting in the loss of Norfolk, Virginia, on May 9. Norfolk was the home port of the ironclad C.S.S. *Virginia* (formerly U.S.S. *Merrimac*). Not fit for the open sea but too deep of draft to retreat up the James River, *Virginia* was destroyed by her crew on May 11. Freed of the large ironclad's threat, the Union navy proceeded up the James but was stopped by river obstructions and Confederate batteries at Drewry's Bluff on May 15.

By late May, Johnston's retreat had taken him to the outskirts of Richmond. McClellan had followed cautiously, avoiding further clashes with the Confederates. Confederate president Jefferson Davis was very dissatisfied with Johnston's failure to challenge McClellan's advance and demanded that he fight rather than give up Richmond. On May 31, Johnston attacked. McClellan's army straddled the Chickahominy River, a small stream that flowed through broad, swampy bottomland now flooded by recent heavy rains. Johnston aimed his attack at the smaller portion of McClellan's army, which was south of the Chickahominy, hoping to destroy it before the rest of the Union army could cross the difficult flooded swamps.

Johnston and his chief subordinate, Major General James Longstreet, sadly mismanaged the battle, however, and produced inconclusive results. Late in the day, Johnston was wounded and temporarily replaced by his second-in-command, Major General Gustavus W. Smith. Equally indecisive fighting concluded the battle, known as Fair Oaks in the North and Seven Pines in the South, on June 1. Each side had about forty-two thousand men engaged. Union casualties totaled five thousand and thirty-one and Confederate, six thousand one hundred and thirty-four. Later on June 1, Robert E. Lee took over command of the Confederate army outside Richmond.

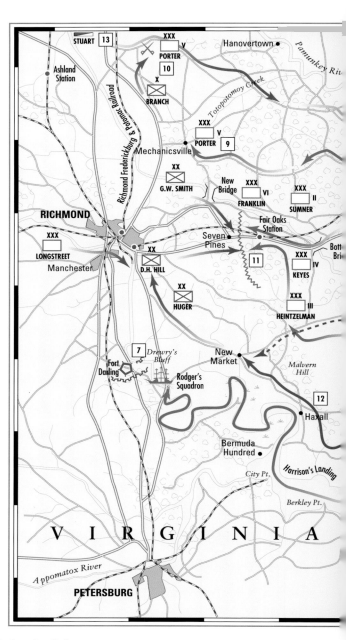

Union troops entering Yorktown on May 4 march past the commanding general's headquarters. "The success is brilliant." wrote McClellan.

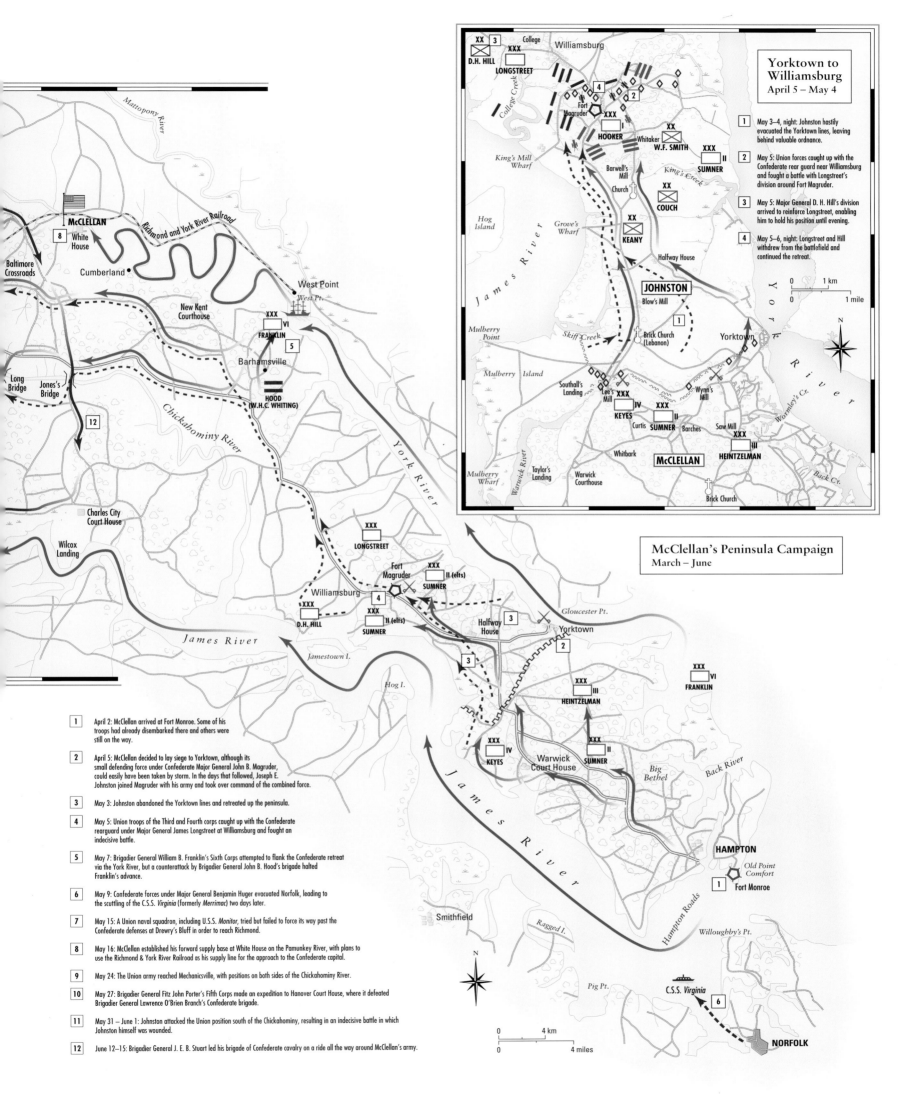

Yorktown to Williamsburg
April 5 – May 4

1. May 3–4, night: Johnston hastily evacuated the Yorktown lines, leaving behind valuable ordnance.

2. May 5: Union forces caught up with the Confederate rear guard near Williamsburg and fought a battle with Longstreet's division around Fort Magruder.

3. May 5: Major General D. H. Hill's division arrived to reinforce Longstreet, enabling him to hold his position until evening.

4. May 5–6, night: Longstreet and Hill withdrew from the battlefield and continued the retreat.

McClellan's Peninsula Campaign
March – June

1. April 2: McClellan arrived at Fort Monroe. Some of his troops had already disembarked there and others were still on the way.

2. April 5: McClellan decided to lay siege to Yorktown, although its small defending force under Confederate Major General John B. Magruder, could easily have been taken by storm. In the days that followed, Joseph E. Johnston joined Magruder with his army and took over command of the combined force.

3. May 3: Johnston abandoned the Yorktown lines and retreated up the peninsula.

4. May 5: Union troops of the Third and Fourth corps caught up with the Confederate rearguard under Major General James Longstreet at Williamsburg and fought an indecisive battle.

5. May 7: Brigadier General William B. Franklin's Sixth Corps attempted to flank the Confederate retreat via the York River, but a counterattack by Brigadier General John B. Hood's brigade halted Franklin's advance.

6. May 9: Confederate forces under Major General Benjamin Huger evacuated Norfolk, leading to the scuttling of the C.S.S. Virginia (formerly Merrimac) two days later.

7. May 15: A Union naval squadron, including U.S.S. Monitor, tried but failed to force its way past the Confederate defenses at Drewry's Bluff in order to reach Richmond.

8. May 16: McClellan established his forward supply base at White House on the Pamunkey River, with plans to use the Richmond & York River Railroad as his supply line for the approach to the Confederate capital.

9. May 24: The Union army reached Mechanicsville, with positions on both sides of the Chickahominy River.

10. May 27: Brigadier General Fitz John Porter's Fifth Corps made an expedition to Hanover Court House, where it defeated Brigadier General Lawrence O'Brien Branch's Confederate brigade.

11. May 31 – June 1: Johnston attacked the Union position south of the Chickahominy, resulting in an indecisive battle in which Johnston himself was wounded.

12. June 12–15: Brigadier General J. E. B. Stuart led his brigade of Confederate cavalry on a ride all the way around McClellan's army.

SHILOH, APRIL 6

AFTER THE DISASTERS AT FORTS Henry and Donelson, Albert Sidney Johnston drew his Confederate troops back from their advanced positions at Bowling Green and Columbus, Kentucky, and ordered them to concentrate at the key rail junction town of Corinth, Mississippi. Simultaneously, Jefferson Davis directed reinforcements from New Orleans and Pensacola to join Johnston there, boosting his army to about forty thousand men.

That the Confederates had time for such maneuvers was not Grant's doing but that of his department commander, Halleck. Jealous of Grant's success at Henry and Donelson, Halleck briefly removed Grant from command from March 4 to 13. On March 1, Halleck ordered Grant's army to go southward, up the Tennessee River to the vicinity of Savannah, Tennessee. There, the army was to await the arrival of Halleck himself, as well as additional Union forces including the army of Brigadier General Don Carlos Buell, which was marching overland from Nashville. Brigadier General Charles F. Smith,

who commanded the army in Grant's absence, encamped most of the troops at Pittsburg Landing, on the west bank of the Tennessee, where a road led directly to Corinth, twenty miles away. By early April, constant reinforcements had increased the army to about forty-two thousand men in six divisions. Five divisions were encamped at Pittsburg Landing and the sixth at Crump's Landing, six miles downstream.

Johnston knew he must attack Grant before Buell arrived. When scouts brought word that Buell was only a few days away, on April 2 Johnston ordered his army to march to Pittsburg Landing and attack at dawn on April 4. Heavy rains, along with the inexperience of the Confederate troops and officers, slowed the march, however, so the attack had to be postponed first to April 5 and then to April 6. By the evening of the 5th, Johnston's chief subordinates, particularly his second-in-command, Pierre G. T. Beauregard, claimed that the element of surprise was lost and that the Federals would be heavily entrenched. They begged Johnston to march the army back to Corinth without giving battle. Johnston remained steadfast.

In fact, despite abundant information from scouts and numerous small clashes with Rebel forces just beyond Union lines on April 4 and 5, Brigadier General William T. Sherman, senior officer of the Pittsburg Landing encampment in command one of Grant's divisions, suspected nothing. Convinced that the Rebels would make no stand nearer than Corinth, he interpreted all data to fit that assumption. Grant—from his headquarters at Savannah, Tennessee, ten miles down the river— did the same. Thus by the morning of April 6 the five divisions at Pittsburg Landing were not entrenched nor even deployed in a continuous line of battle but rather in scattered camps sited primarily for the availability of wood and water.

Before dawn the Confederate army deployed for battle with each of its three corps stretched clear across the battlefield, one behind the other, a clumsy arrangement ordered by Beauregard. Before it could be changed, fighting broke out. Union brigade and regimental commanders in outlying camps by no means shared Sherman's complacency, and one of them dispatched an early morning patrol that collided with the Confederate line and opened the battle. Combat soon became intense as Johnston's army began its drive toward the Tennessee River.

Rough and wooded terrain, as well as Beauregard's ill-conceived arrangement of corps, tended to disorganize the Confederate army. So too did the effects of heavy fighting. As Johnston's men drove the Federals back and captured several divisional encampments, many Confederate soldiers fell out of ranks to plunder. Johnston's original plan of striking the Union left, rolling it up, and pushing Grant's army into a pocket formed by the swamps of Snake and Owl creeks, quickly became impossible. He did, however, have a chance of pushing Grant's army into the Tennessee River and came close to doing so.

Shiloh Campaign
April 6

MISSOURI

KENTUCKY

Smithland

Paducah

Cairo

Columbus

Hope

New Madrid

Fort Henry

Clarksville

Union City

Fort Heiman

Fort Donelson

Dover

Paris

XX

CHEATHAM

Charlot

Danville

Fort Pillow

AR

Humbolt

GRANT

Fort Randolph

Jackson

TENNEESSE

BUELL

1

MEMPHIS

XX

RUGGLES

Purdy

Waynesboro

Bethel

XXX

4

Crump's Landings

HARDEE

Pittsburg Landing

Grand Junction

3

XXX

RES

BRECKINRIDGE

Corinth

2

Eastport

Burnsville

Iuka

Florence

JOHNSTON

XXX

Tuscumbia

BRAGG

MISSISSIPPI

Tupelo

0   30 km

0   30 miles

1 March 1: Grant and his fifty six thousand-strong Army of the Tennessee move into Tennessee arriving at Pittsburg Landing on April 3 to await the arrival of Buell's army.

2 March 1: Johnston with fifty five thousand Confederates concentrate in Corinth.

3 April 3: Bad weather delays Johnston's advance to Pittsburg Landing.

4 April 6: Johnston launches surprise attack on Grant before Buell could reinforce Grant's army.

In mid-afternoon Johnston was killed leading a charge against stubborn Federals in the Peach Orchard. Later, Confederates cut off and surrounded a pocket of Union resistance known as the Hornet's Nest, forcing Brigadier General Benjamin Prentiss and about two thousand Federals to surrender. Throughout the day, Grant, who had hastened to the battlefield as soon as the fighting started, had expected the arrival of Major General Lew Wallace's division from Crump's Landing as well as the leading elements of Buell's army, which had been in Savannah that morning. As sunset approached, the first of Buell's reg-

iments arrived opposite Pittsburg Landing and began crossing the river on steamboats, but Wallace was nowhere to be seen. Grant had his army, reduced to an effective strength about eighteen thousand, drawn up in a strong position covering the landing awaiting the final Confederate attack of the day. It never came, however, as Beauregard ordered his troops to pull back and spend the night in the captured Union camps.

Private Sampson Altman Jr., Company C 29th Regiment Georgian Volunteers, fought at Shiloh, and later died of disease April 23, 1863.

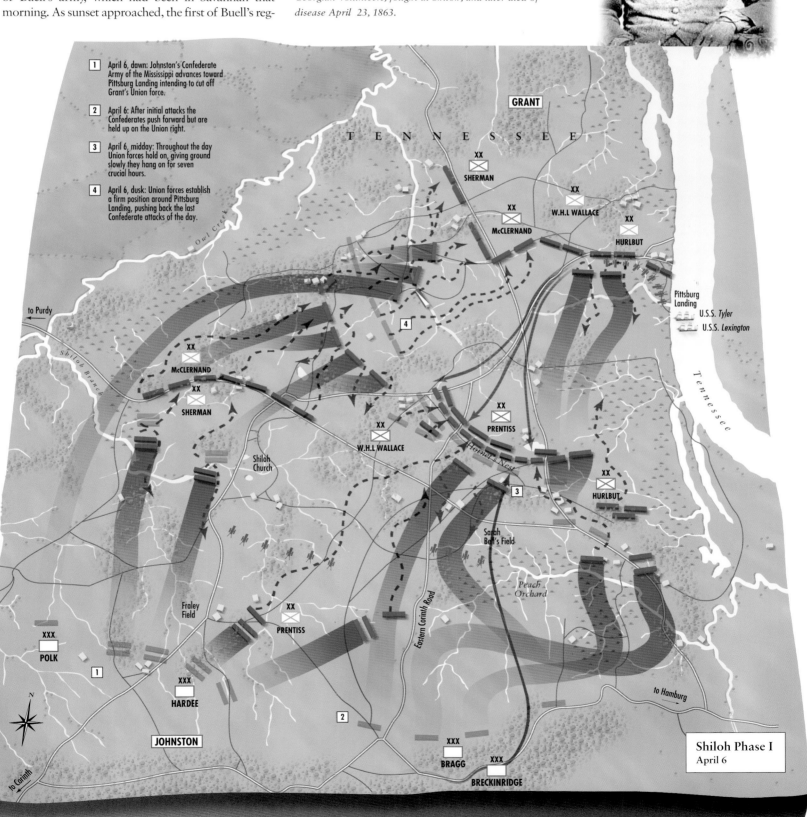

1 April 6, dawn: Johnston's Confederate Army of the Mississippi advances toward Pittsburg Landing intending to cut off Grant's Union force.

2 April 6: After initial attacks the Confederates push forward but are held up on the Union right.

3 April 6, midday: Throughout the day Union forces hold on, giving ground slowly they hang on for seven crucial hours.

4 April 6, dusk: Union forces establish a firm position around Pittsburg Landing, pushing back the last Confederate attacks of the day.

Shiloh Phase I
April 6

SHILOH, APRIL 7

AFTER THE CLOSE OF FIGHTING on the evening of April 6, significant numbers of Buell's troops began crossing the Tennessee River, and Wallace's division finally arrived. Heavy rain began to fall about midnight, making the night miserable for the Union troops and horrible for the thousands of wounded still lying on the battlefield. Union gunboats in the river kept up an all-night harassing fire in the direction of the Confederate army. Grant, who outranked Buell and thus would command the combined Union forces, remained confident and determined. With the seven thousand fresh

before the Federals gained solid control of the sector and pushed on with their advance. On the Union right, Grant's own battered army, spearheaded by Wallace's fresh division, drove the Rebels out of one position after another and fought off Confederate counterattacks. Confederates under the command of Major General Braxton Bragg made a particularly stubborn stand at the important intersection of the Corinth and Hamburg–Purdy roads, near the center of the battlefield. Both Buell's and Grant's troops attacked the position repeatedly, crossing a shallow sheet of water called "Water Oaks Pond."

The so-called Sunken Road meandered through the area that became known as the "Hornet's Nest." Union troops, supported by a few artillery pieces, held the line along the road. John Marmaduke's Confederate soldiers advance from the right of this view.

troops of Wallace's division and perhaps twenty thousand more from Buell, he planned to attack the next morning and drive the Rebels back.

Early on the morning of April 7, Grant's reinforced army began its advance. For the first mile or so they encountered little resistance, as the Confederates had pulled back that distance the evening before. Once Grant's line made contact with the main Rebel forces, heavy fighting broke out. Men who experienced both the first and the second day at Shiloh wrote that at certain times and places on the battlefield the fighting on the second day became as intense as any on the first. However, overall the second day did not feature the same sustained ferocity, hour after hour, that soldiers had experienced on April 6.

Buell's troops, advancing on the Union left, pushed the Confederates back beyond the Peach Orchard but the Rebels counterattacked, driving them back for a time. Intense fighting raged back and forth several times across the Davis wheat field

Gunfire in the woods just beyond Water Oaks Pond became so intense that Sherman said it was the heaviest he had ever heard.

Early in the afternoon, with his army nearing the point of collapse, Beauregard finally ordered a retreat back to Corinth. Grant's forces were too exhausted to mount a major pursuit, but he ordered Sherman to pursue for a short distance with his badly depleted division. At a field containing a number of downed trees and known as Fallen Timbers, Sherman's men ran into a Confederate cavalry force under Brigadier General Nathan Bedford Forrest, covering the Rebel retreat. The action there was among the first of those that would eventually build Forrest's reputation as one of the most remarkable natural fighters and leaders of the war. The Confederate cavalry charged headlong toward the front of Sherman's column, briefly throwing it into confusion. In close-quarters fighting with pistols, sabers, and bayonets, Forrest suffered a serious wound but succeeded in halting the Union pursuit.

A few days after the battle, Halleck arrived and took command at Pittsburg Landing. Once the army of Major General John Pope joined him there, he advanced toward Corinth with the three combined armies of Grant, Buell, and Pope—more than 100,000 men. Beauregard had also received reinforcements, the army of Major General Earl Van Dorn from the Trans-Mississippi District, but his total strength barely topped sixty thousand. Determined not to allow himself to be surprised and dedicated to a scientific, mathematical style of warfare, Halleck had his troops advance an average of one thousand two hundred yards per day and then build elaborate entrenchments. He took six weeks to cover the twenty miles from Pittsburg Landing to Corinth, which Beauregard had evacuated on May 30.

Many on both sides felt dissatisfied with the campaign. Northerners were disappointed because the Rebel army had escaped to fight somewhere else, prolonging the war. Confederates, including Jefferson Davis, were vexed because Beauregard had abandoned the vital transportation nexus at Corinth without a fight.

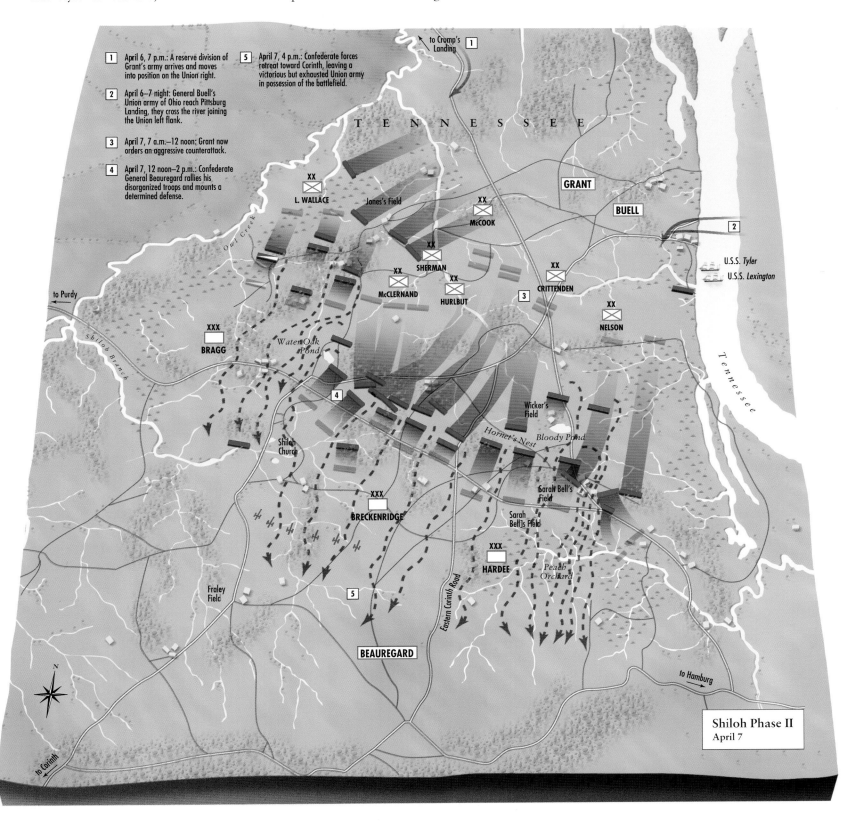

1   April 6, 7 p.m.: A reserve division of Grant's army arrives and moves into position on the Union right.

2   April 6–7 night: General Buell's Union army of Ohio reach Pittsburg Landing, they cross the river joining the Union left flank.

3   April 7, 7 a.m.–12 noon: Grant now orders an aggressive counterattack.

4   April 7, 12 noon–2 p.m.: Confederate General Beauregard rallies his disorganized troops and mounts a determined defense.

5   April 7, 4 p.m.: Confederate forces retreat toward Corinth, leaving a victorious but exhausted Union army in possession of the battlefield.

Shiloh Phase II
April 7

LOWER MISSISSIPPI VALLEY

AFTER THE SURRENDER OF NEW ORLEANS on April 25, 1862, Flag Officer David G. Farragut proceeded up the Mississippi River with his seagoing fleet, past Louisiana's capital city at Baton Rouge and on to Natchez, Mississippi. The mayor of Natchez surrendered on May 12 and Farragut briefly occupied the city. Six days later Farragut's fleet arrived off Vicksburg, Mississippi, and he demanded the city's surrender. Confederate brigadier general Martin Luther Smith, however, refused. As Farragut had no appreciable land force with him, and the city occupied a strong position on high bluffs, he could do nothing.

A month later, New Orleans Union army commander Major General Benjamin Butler sent three thousand men under command of Brigadier General Thomas Williams to cooperate with Farragut against Vicksburg. Meanwhile, Confederate defenses had increased, both in men and guns, and the Rebels were now commanded by Major General Earl Van Dorn. Williams's force was too small to assault Vicksburg, so he set his men to digging a canal across De Soto Point, the spit of land on the Louisiana shore opposite Vicksburg. As Vicksburg lay on the outside of a sharp eastward

Farragut's fleet steamed passed Vicksburg twice, escaping serious damage while passing the land batteries, but the action made it clear that Vicksburg could not be captured by a river-borne fleet unaided by land-based troops.

bend of the river, the canal through De Soto Point would cut off that bend and allow river traffic to bypass the Confederate stronghold. The project went slowly, as the men dug laboriously through the swampy, mosquito-infested terrain and succumbed in alarming numbers to the various diseases endemic to the lower Mississippi Valley. After a few weeks, Williams and his men withdrew to Baton Rouge.

Early on the morning of June 28, Farragut ran his fleet past the Vicksburg batteries, suffering forty-five personnel casualties and minor damage to ships, but, despite the powerful broadsides of Farragut's ships, the Vicksburg defenses remained virtually undamaged. Cruising above Vicksburg, Farragut on July 1 met Flag Officer Charles H. Davis's gunboat squadron coming down the river after having captured Memphis on June 7. Yet aside from occasional ineffective bombardments, there was nothing the combined fleet could do about Vicksburg.

Since October 1861 the Confederates had been working on an ironclad of their own, building it in a cornfield alongside the Yazoo River, a tributary that joins the Mississippi just above Vicksburg. Although deficient in many ways and equipped with unreliable engines, C.S.S. *Arkansas* was nevertheless a powerful ironclad carrying ten guns and a crew of two hundred men. On July 15, Confederate Commander Isaac N. Brown took her down the Yazoo and into the Mississippi, attacking the combined squadrons of Farragut and Davis as she steamed through them. *Arkansas* reached the Vicksburg waterfront where she tied up under the protection of the Confederate guns, battered but still battle worthy. Three Union vessels suffered severe damage in the fight. That evening in an attempt to destroy *Arkansas*, Farragut ran his seagoing squadron past Vicksburg again, this time going downstream. As each Union ship passed, it blasted a broadside into the Confederate ironclad, but inflicted only moderate damage.

On July 24, with the river level dropping toward dangerously shallow depths for his large ships and needing to get back to his blockade duties in the Gulf of Mexico, Farragut turned his squadron back down the Mississippi toward New Orleans. He left five gunboats to guard the stretch of river between Vicksburg and Baton Rouge.

Believing the time had come to take the initiative in the lower Mississippi Valley, the Confederates determined to retake Baton Rouge. Major General John C. Breckinridge led a force of two thousand six hundred men against Williams and some two thousand five hundred Federals who held the city. Breckinridge was to be supported by the seemingly invincible *Arkansas*. On August 5, Breckinridge arrived at Baton Rouge, but *Arkansas*, hindered by engine trouble, did not. In a fight that lasted several hours, the Federals drove off their attackers. Union casualties totaled three hundred and eighty-three, including Williams, who was killed. Confederate casualties came to four hundred and fifty-six. Breckinridge withdrew about twenty-five miles upstream and began to fortify a strong position on the east bank of the river at Port Hudson, Louisiana.

The next day, *Arkansas* belatedly arrived near Baton Rouge. Five Union vessels, including the ironclad *Essex*, immediately attacked. In the midst of the fight, *Arkansas*'s cranky engines broke down again. With their vessel helpless, *Arkansas*'s crew scuttled her. This marked a disappointing end to Confederate hopes of retaking Baton Rouge. However, the establishment of a fortified outpost at Port Hudson gave the Confederacy at least the potential for exercising control of the Mississippi River between there and Vicksburg.

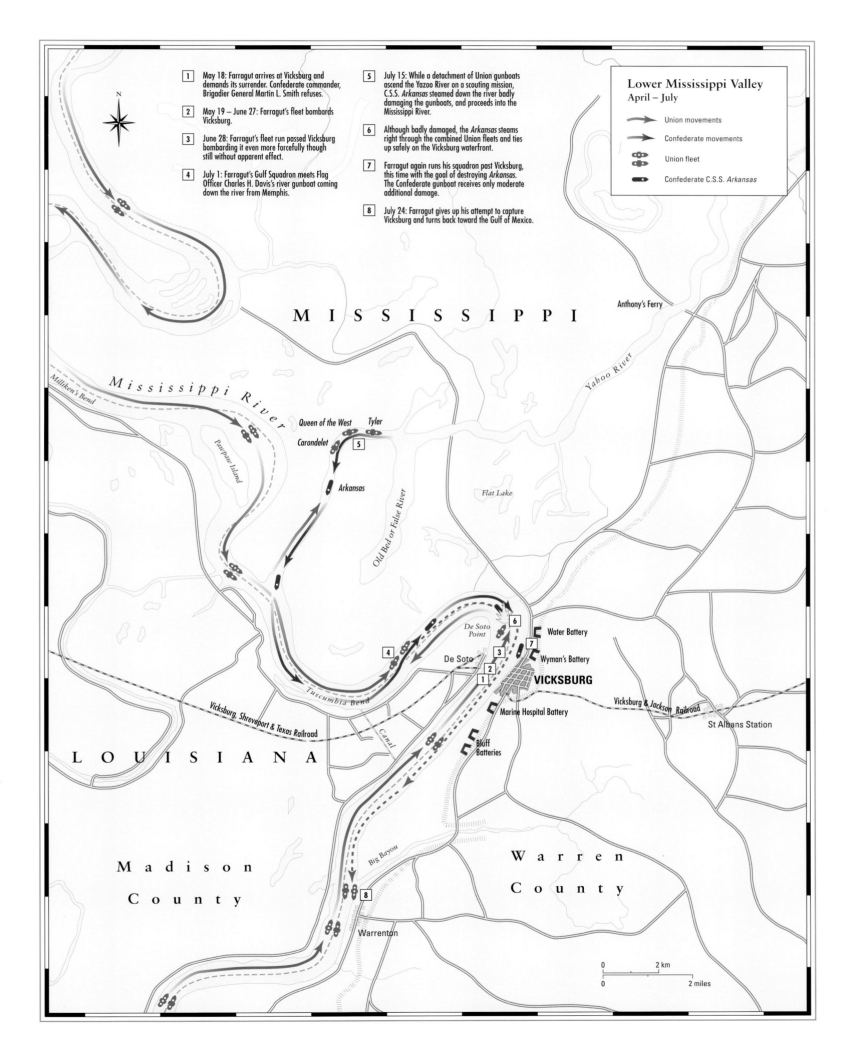

1 May 18: Farragut arrives at Vicksburg and demands its surrender. Confederate commander, Brigadier General Martin L. Smith refuses.

2 May 19 – June 27: Farragut's fleet bombards Vicksburg.

3 June 28: Farragut's fleet run passed Vicksburg bombarding it even more forcefully though still without apparent effect.

4 July 1: Farragut's Gulf Squadron meets Flag Officer Charles H. Davis's river gunboat coming down the river from Memphis.

5 July 15: While a detachment of Union gunboats ascend the Yazoo River on a scouting mission, C.S.S. Arkansas steamed down the river badly damaging the gunboats, and proceeds into the Mississippi River.

6 Although badly damaged, the Arkansas steams right through the combined Union fleets and ties up safely on the Vicksburg waterfront.

7 Farragut again runs his squadron past Vicksburg, this time with the goal of destroying Arkansas. The Confederate gunboat receives only moderate additional damage.

8 July 24: Farragut gives up his attempt to capture Vicksburg and turns back toward the Gulf of Mexico.

Lower Mississippi Valley
April – July

→ Union movements
→ Confederate movements
Union fleet
Confederate C.S.S. Arkansas

MISSISSIPPI

Anthony's Ferry

Milliken's Bend

Mississippi River

Paw paw Island

Yahoo River

Queen of the West   Tyler
Carondelet
5

Arkansas

Old Bed or False River

Flat Lake

De Soto Point
6
Water Battery
De Soto
3
7
4   2   Wyman's Battery
1
VICKSBURG

Tuscumbia Bend

Vicksburg, Shreveport & Texas Railroad

Canal

Marine Hospital Battery

Vicksburg & Jackson Railroad

St Albans Station

LOUISIANA

Bluff Batteries

Big Bayou

MADISON County

WARREN County

8

Warrenton

0   2 km
0   2 miles

JACKSON'S SHENANDOAH VALLEY CAMPAIGN, PHASE II

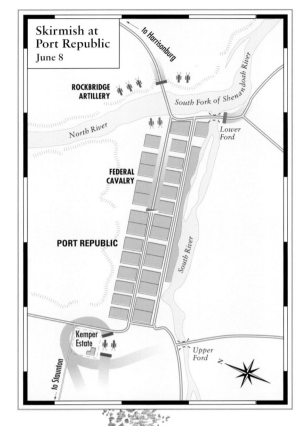

Skirmish at Port Republic
June 8

to Harrisonburg

ROCKBRIDGE ARTILLERY

South Fork of Shenandoah River

North River

Lower Ford

FEDERAL CAVALRY

PORT REPUBLIC

South River

to Staunton

Kemper Estate

Upper Ford

N

Keeping troops on campaign required an enormous supply of healthy and well-shod horses. Above, in a drawing by Walton Taber, blacksmiths at a mobile army forge are shown at their work.

O N THE DAY OF JACKSON'S VICTORY at Winchester, May 28, Lincoln directed the movement of Union armies to trap Jackson. Lincoln directed Major General Irvin McDowell's corps to march westward from Fredericksburg, Virginia, and Frémont to turn and march back to the east from his position in the mountains of western Virginia. Between them, Lincoln believed the two forces would be able to catch Jackson in deadly pincers.

By May 30, Frémont had reached Wardensville, thirty miles west of Winchester, and was closing in on Jackson's line of retreat. That same day McDowell's advance guard under Brigadier General James Shields reached Front Royal, further threatening Jackson's retreat and skirmishing with some of his forces. Most of Jackson's army was still up in the vicinity of Harpers Ferry that morning, but Jackson discovered the danger he was in and put his troops to another grueling march, this time bound southwestward, up the valley, to escape the rapidly closing Union trap. By the narrowest of margins, Jackson succeeded in sliding between the jaws of the trap. On June 1 he was at Strasburg, directly between the two Union forces, and the next day he was south of them. Frémont's army followed in close pursuit, skirmishing frequently all the way to Harrisonburg as Jackson's army hurried along the Valley Pike. Just south of Harrisonburg, Colonel Turner Ashby, Jackson's undisciplined but flamboyant and charismatic chief of cavalry, was killed in one of the many rearguard skirmishes.

Meanwhile, McDowell's corps turned into the Luray Valley, paralleling Jackson's march and threatened to do to him what he had done to Banks only a few days before. A few miles south of Harrisonburg, Jackson's army turned at bay. On June 8, Jackson assigned Ewell's division to cover the important road junction at Cross Keys, which Frémont would have to pass in his pursuit of Jackson's army. Ewell's six thousand and five hundred men successfully fended off the ten thousand five hundred-man vanguard of

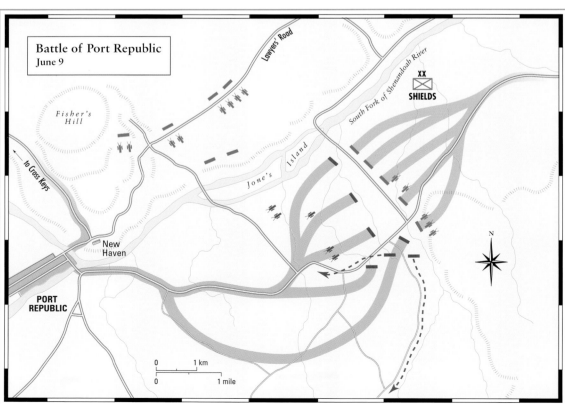

Battle of Port Republic
June 9

Lowyer's Road

South Fork of Shenandoah River

XX
SHIELDS

Fisher's Hill

to Cross Keys

Jone's Island

New Haven

PORT REPUBLIC

N

0   1 km

0   1 mile

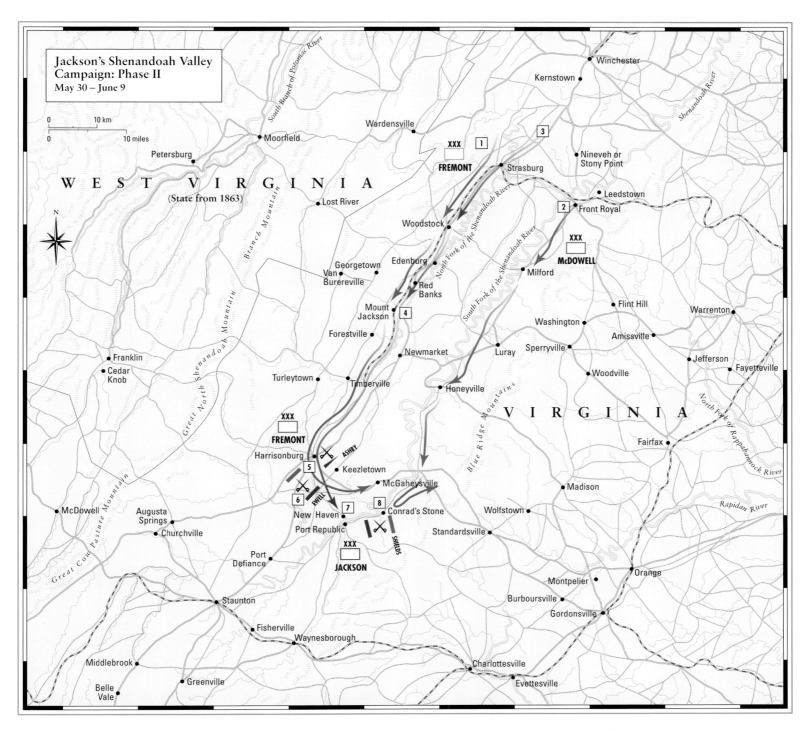

Jackson's Shenandoah Valley
Campaign: Phase II
May 30 – June 9

0   10 km
0   10 miles

WEST VIRGINIA
(State from 1863)

VIRGINIA

Frémont's army. Union casualties for the Battle of Cross Keys totaled six hundred and eighty-four, while Ewell lost only two hundred and eighty-eight men. Jackson meanwhile was in Port Republic, several miles away, and that day just missed an encounter with a party of Union cavalry that briefly rode into the town.

The following day, June 9, Jackson left only a small force near Cross Keys to watch Frémont. He drew in the rest of Ewell's troops to join him at Port Republic, where he turned and struck viciously at the lead unit of McDowell's pursuers coming out of the Luray Valley, the brigade of Brigadier General Erastus B. Tyler. The Battle of Port Republic was the hardest fought contest of the campaign. Jackson's advantage in numbers, five thousand nine hundred Confederates to only three thousand Federals, ultimately proved decisive. After several hours of fighting, Tyler withdrew, and Jackson made little attempt at pursuit. Union casualties totaled

one thousand and eighteen, including five hundred and fifty-eight missing or captured. Total Confederate losses were eight hundred and four.

The Battle of Port Republic marked the end of Jackson's Shenandoah Valley campaign. In a little more than five weeks since returning to the valley after its brief absence in early May, Jackson's army had won five battles and marched several hundred miles. Though the Union forces deployed against him always greatly exceeded the total strength of his own army, Jackson usually managed to have more men on the battlefield. For rapid and brilliant maneuvering the campaign rivals Grant's 1863 Vicksburg campaign as one of the most remarkable of the war. Jackson occupied thousands of Union troops who would otherwise have reinforced McClellan's drive on Richmond. He also won for himself an unrivaled reputation for military genius within the Confederacy and beyond.

1 May 30: Frémont closed in from the northwest in an effort to cut off Jackson's retreat.

2 May 30: Major General Irvin McDowell's advance guard under Brigadier General James Shields reached Front Royal, further threatening Jackson's retreat and skirmishing with some of his forces.

3 May 30: Jackson pulled his army back from its positions near Harpers Ferry and began a rapid march southwestward, up the Valley Pike, narrowly avoiding being cut off by the converging Union columns.

4 June 3: Jackson's rear guard skirmished with Frémont's advance guard as the latter pursued Jackson's army southwestward up the Valley.

5 June 6: In another rear guard skirmish, Jackson's cavalry leader, Colonel Turner Ashby was killed.

6 June 8: Ewell's division held off the attack of Frémont's Unionists.

7 June 8: While Ewell fought at Cross Keys, a party of Union cavalry galloped into the town of Port Republic and almost captured Jackson himself.

8 June 9: Jackson massed his force against the leading elements of McDowell's column and defeated them at the Battle of Port Republic.

SEVEN DAYS' BATTLES, JUNE 25–28

Throughout June General Robert E. Lee fortified Ricmond and made plans to attack McClellan's army. During these preparations J.E.B. Stuart's cavalry was able to keep Lee informed about the exact deployment of the Union army in a daring ride around the enemy positions.

ON TAKING COMMAND OF THE Confederate army outside Richmond on June 1, 1862, General Robert E. Lee began planning an offensive that would not only relieve the threat to the Confederate capital but also trap and annihilate Major General George B. McClellan's Army of the Potomac. His plan was a daring one. While a thin screen of troops maintained the Confederate lines between Richmond and the bulk of McClellan's army, Lee would mass the greater part of his own army against a single Union corps, Major General Fitz John Porter's Fifth Corps, north of the Chickahominy River near the village of Mechanicsville. To insure Porter's destruction and avoid the high casualties expected in a pure frontal assault, Lee directed Major General Thomas J. "Stonewall" Jackson to march his three divisions on a roundabout route to strike the Union right flank.

Porter occupied his precarious position, in isolation from the rest of the army, because McClellan wanted to protect his supply line along the Richmond & York River Railroad leading to the depot at White House Landing on the Pamunkey River. McClellan also wanted Porter north of the Chickahominy River in order to link up with additional Union troops he hoped would soon be marching south from Washington. The Fifth Corps held good defensive ground fronting a swampy creek bottom.

Lee scheduled his attack for June 26, on assurance from Jackson that he would be able to position his force by that time. On June 25, although he did not suspect Lee's plans or the weakened lines in front of Richmond, McClellan ordered a minor probe of the

Confederate line by troops of the Third Corps commanded by Major General Samuel Heintzelman. The result of the probe was five hundred and sixteen Union casualties, three hundred and sixteen Confederate, no change in the battle lines, and no glimmering of a suspicion in McClellan's mind.

On June 26, Confederate president Jefferson Davis rode out from Richmond to see the opening of the great offensive, scheduled to begin with Jackson's attack on the Union right flank that morning. Much to Lee's chagrin, no attack occurred in the morning or any other time that day. Highly uncharacteristically and for reasons never satisfactorily explained, Jackson seems to have experienced great difficulty all week getting his troops into position on time. While the army waited for Jackson, Major General Ambrose Powell Hill—commanding the left division in Lee's lines, exhausted his never very abundant patience and decided to launch his division in a headlong assault. Thinking it was Jackson's arrival that had prompted Hill's advance, the rest of the army joined in the attack. The result was a bloody repulse for Lee. Some fourteen thousand of his troops attacked about fifteen thousand Union defenders. Confederate losses totaled one thousand four hundred and eighty-four, with Union losses of three hundred and sixty-one.

That night, worried about Jackson's flank march and the possible threat to his supply line, McClellan decided to retreat and to shift his base of supplies from the Pamunkey to the James River. He ordered Porter to pull his Fifth Corps back to a strong defensive position behind Boatswain's Creek, just south of Gaine's Mill. There, Porter was to make a delaying

Captain John C. Turnbull and his staff, serving at Mechanicsville, contributed to the severe Confederate casualties.

stand before crossing to the south bank of the Chickahominy and joining the rest of the army in its retreat toward Harrison's Landing on the James River.

Lee's army followed the retreating Federals, and Lee planned for an attack on June 27 much like the one he intended for the day before. What happened, at least initially, was more like what had in fact occurred on June 26. Once again Jackson failed to launch his flank attack, so that Lee's army was left to fight another battle as a pure frontal assault. This time, however, by massing greatly superior numbers

against the isolated Fifth Corps and through the exceptional valor of Brigadier General John Bell Hood and his Texas Brigade, Lee was able to break the Union line, forcing Porter's retreat. The Union general, however, had sufficient reserves to cover his withdrawal to the south bank of the Chickahominy. The day's fighting had seen fifty-seven thousand Confederates attacking thirty-six thousand Federals. Casualties totaled approximately eight thousand seven hundred and fifty for the former and six thousand eight hundred and thirty-seven for the latter.

1 June 25: Unaware of Lee's planned offensive, McClellan launched a probe of Confederate lines south of the Chickahominy by Major General Samuel Heintzelman's Third Corps.

2 June 26: Lee's forces attacked Brigadier General Fitz John Porter's Fifth Corps north of the Chickahominy but suffered a bloody repulse.

3 June 26: Although he failed to get his wing of the army into the battle, Jackson approached Porter's right flank late in the day, posing a serious threat.

4 June 26–27: With his right flank threatened McClellan decided on retreat and ordered Porter to withdraw during the night to a position behind Boatswain's Creek.

5 June 27: With Jackson again failing to get into position, Lee launched another frontal assault against Porter and this time succeeded in breaking his lines and driving him back across the river.

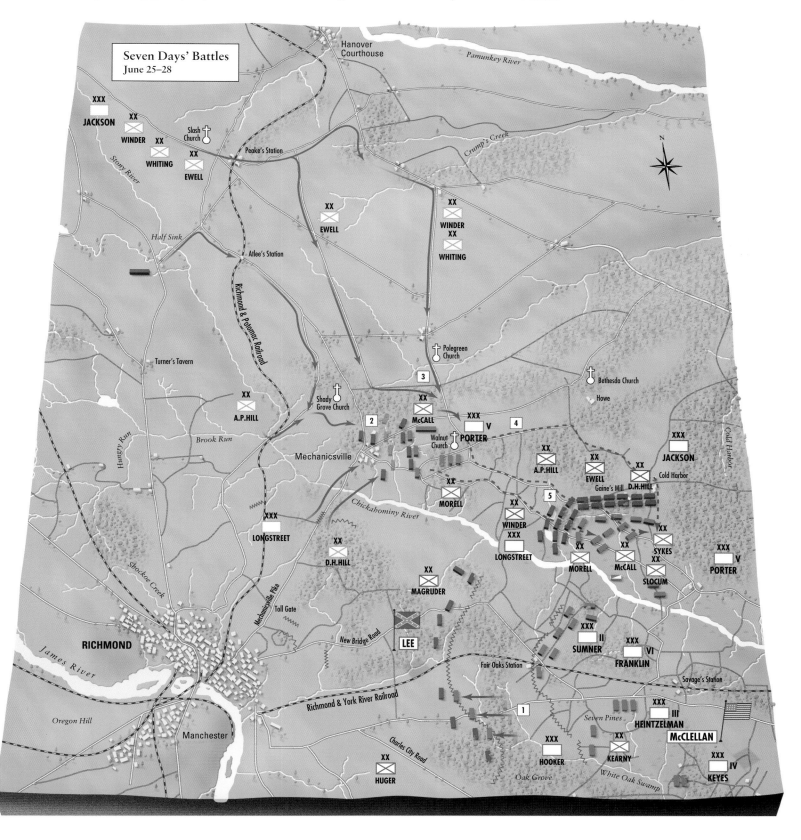

Seven Days' Battles
June 25–28

SEVEN DAYS' BATTLES, JUNE 29 – JULY 1

Above: Professor Thaddeus S. C. Lowe's aerial reconnaissance squadron launches one of the professor's two hydrogen balloons, one of which soars aloft near McClellan's headquarters. As the shellbursts suggest, the Rebels tried hard to shoot down the spies, bringing up one of their accurate English Whitworth rifled guns, but they scored no hits; anti-aircraft gunnery was too new an art.

A LULL IN THE FIGHTING OCCURRED on June 28, as McClellan's army shifted its large train of supplies toward the James River and destroyed and abandoned its depot at White House Landing on the Pamunkey. Lee spent the day determining that McClellan had indeed abandoned the north bank of the Chickahominy and preparing his army to follow. Lee still hoped to cut McClellan off from his line of communication and destroy his army.

The next day, Lee's forces crossed to the south bank of the Chickahominy and gave chase. They collided with McClellan's rear guard, Major General Edwin Vose Sumner's Second Corps at Savage's Station. Lee's lack of an efficient staff during this campaign led to confusion and disorganization among the major units of his army. This, combined with another puzzling lapse by Jackson, weakened the Confederate army's drive, and Sumner was able to hold his position. Nevertheless, McClellan ordered that the retreat continue, requiring the Union troops to abandon their large field hospital in the rear of Savage's Station leaving behind two thousand five hundred sick and wounded Federals.

Lee's final and perhaps best chance to trap and destroy the Army of the Potomac came on June 30. If his army could seize the vital crossroads at the village of Glendale, he could cut McClellan's army in two and trap a large part of it. Jackson was to attack from the north across White Oak Swamp while most of the rest of Lee's army attacked from the west. Once again Jackson did not perform as expected, and his attack failed to materialize. Desperate fighting raged around the Glendale crossroads, however, as Longstreet's and General Daniel Harvey Hill's troops pressed their attacks. The Federals, directed by several corps commanders in the absence of McClellan, who had hurried to the rear, managed to hang on to the crossroads long enough for the balance of the

Army of the Potomac to continue its retreat toward Harrison's Landing on the James.

This battle—which is variously known by the names Glendale, Frayser's Farm, and White Oak Swamp, as well as five other names—was the most decisive of the Seven Days' Battles. Once the Army of the Potomac successfully passed the crossroads at Glendale, Lee no longer had any chance of cutting it off from its new base of supplies on the James River. Loose work by Lee's small and inexperienced staff, along with the strange lethargy of Stonewall Jackson had combined with staunch fighting by the Federals to blunt Lee's offensive thrust.

Lee, however, was not ready to give up and, on July 1, he determined to pursue and attack the retreating Army of the Potomac. McClellan had arranged his army in a strong defensive position on Malvern Hill. Although the side of the hill from which the Confederate army would be approaching was a gentle, almost imperceptible, slope, it presented a splendid field of fire for the massed Union artillery. Lee and Jackson spent several hours that morning seeking good positions for their own artillery, with which they hoped to beat down the Union guns making possible a successful infantry assault. The attempt proved a dismal failure, however. The Union guns were larger, more numerous, better served, better sited, and supplied with better ammunition. They demolished the Confederate batteries almost before the latter could get into position and unlimber.

The infantry assault that followed was an even greater fiasco for the Confederates. The Union guns shredded the advancing Confederate lines so that few attackers even came close to the Union line. The Battle of Malvern Hill was one of the few Civil War battles in which most of the casualties were inflicted by artillery. Confederate general Daniel Harvey Hill, whose troops participated in the deba-

In this drawing by Alfred Waud, who covered the Peninsula Campaign on behalf of Harper's, Confederate troops are retreating through Mechanicsville.

cle, wrote in a post-war magazine article about the battle, "It was not war; it was murder." Despite the opportunity offered by Lee's defeat, McClellan declined to assume the offensive and instead continued his retreat to Harrison's Landing.

With the Battle of Malvern Hill, the Seven Days' Battles came to an end. Lee started the campaign with the largest army he would ever command, some ninety-seven thousand men. The initial strength of the Union, 103,000, meant that the campaign was one of only two during the course of the war in which Lee enjoyed near parity in numbers. Total casualties came to fifteen thousand eight hundred and forty-nine for the Union, and a staggering twenty thousand one hundred and forty-one for the Confederacy—a ratio the less populace South could not afford. Lee had moved the scene of the fighting fifteen or twenty miles farther away from Richmond than at the start of the battle but had failed to destroy the Army of the Potomac as he had hoped. He had, however, raised Confederate spirits and correspondingly lowered those in the North.

1 June 29: Confederate troops marched in pursuit of McClellan's retreating army south of the Chickahominy.

2 June 29: Confederate and Union forces clashed indecisively at Savage's Station. The Unionists withdrew, abandoning the Army of the Potomac's general hospital with two thousand five hundred sick and wounded soldiers.

3 June 30: Major General James Longstreet's Confederate division, supported by several others, struck at Brigadier General McCall's Union division at the crossroads of Glendale, or Frayser's Farm. The fighting was extremely intense, but the Union troops managed to hold the crossroads long enough to prevent Lee from cutting off any part of the retreating Army of the Potomac.

4 July 1: Lee pursued McClellan on July 1 and found him in a very strong position on Malvern Hill, where Lee launched a series of bloody and futile attacks.

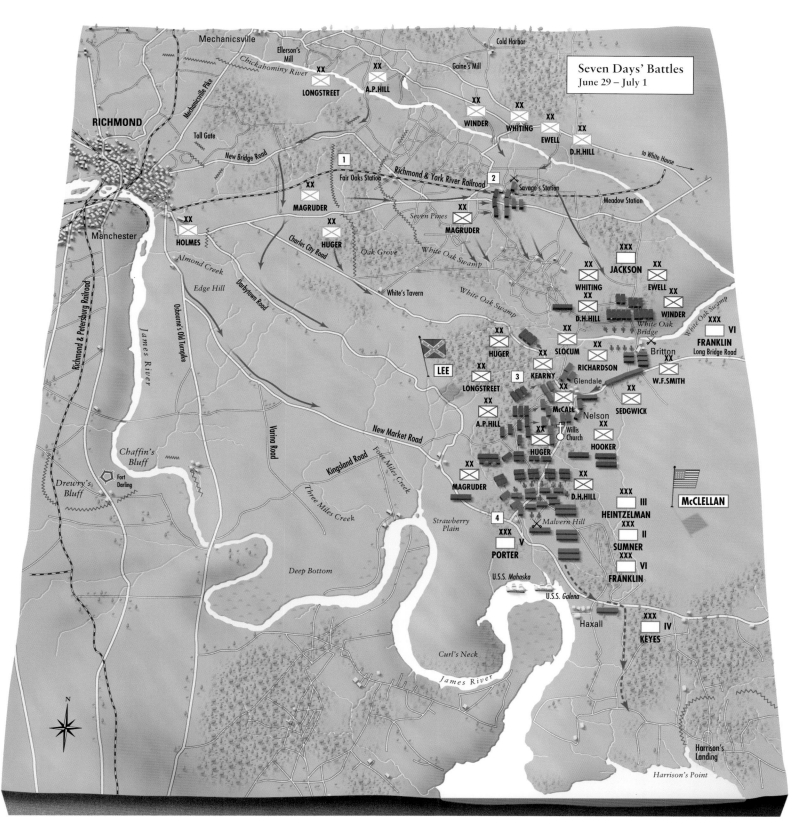

CONFEDERATE CAVALRY RAIDS IN KENTUCKY AND TENNESSEE

COLONEL JOHN HUNT MORGAN WAS born in Alabama in 1825 but moved to Kentucky as a child with his family. In 1857, he organized a militia company, the Kentucky Rifles, of which he was captain. In July 1861, he led his company into Confederate service. Later he transferred to the Confederate cavalry and became known for his exploits as a raider. In February 1862 he was promoted to colonel and in April given command of the Second Kentucky Cavalry (Confederate).

On July 4, Morgan set out from Knoxville, Tennessee, on his first Kentucky raid, leading a small brigade of cavalry that numbered about nine hundred men. Five days later Morgan routed four companies of the Ninth Pennsylvania Cavalry and captured Tompkinsville, Kentucky. The next day Morgan issued a proclamation calling on Kentuckians to "rise and arm, and drive the Hessian invaders from their soil." One of Morgan's men was a telegraph operator who frequently tapped into the wires and kept Morgan informed of Union troop movements aimed at catching him. As he moved through Kentucky, Morgan burned bridges and warehouses, tore up railroads, and captured horses and mules. In some towns in the Bluegrass region, there was strong pro-Confederate sentiment, and Morgan's men were received as heroes. Some of the enthusiasm, however, stemmed more from Morgan's celebrity status as a daring raider than from true devotion to the Confederate cause.

On July 12, Morgan took Lebanon, Kentucky, after a brief fight with a small Union detachment there. The next day some of his men had a slight skirmish with local home guards at Mackville, Kentucky. Alarmed citizens of Cincinnati, Frankfort, Lexington, and Louisville feared that their own cities might be Morgan's next target. However, Morgan concentrated his efforts on smaller towns. By July 14 Morgan and his men turned up in the vicinity of Cynthiana, Kentucky, and on July 17 they captured the town after a fierce fight with about three hundred and forty Union defenders, most of them home guards and untrained recruits. Two days later Morgan's command skirmished with Federals near Paris, Kentucky.

By this time sizable Union forces were in pursuit of Morgan. Retiring to Crab Orchard, Kentucky, he again employed his telegraph operator and portable telegraph device to tap into the lines and send messages to various Union commanders countermanding the orders for his pursuit. On July 22, Morgan's raiders arrived safely at Livingston, Tennessee, having completed their first Kentucky raid. Morgan lost about ninety casualties during the raid but garnered so many new Kentucky recruits that his command numbered one thousand two hundred when he reached Livingston.

Simultaneously with Morgan's first Kentucky raid, Colonel Nathan Bedford Forrest, a former slave trader, led another Confederate raid into Middle Tennessee. He set out from Chattanooga on July 9 with two regiments of cavalry and rendezvoused on July 11 with another regiment and several independent companies, bringing his total force to one thousand four hundred men. The next day Forrest rode

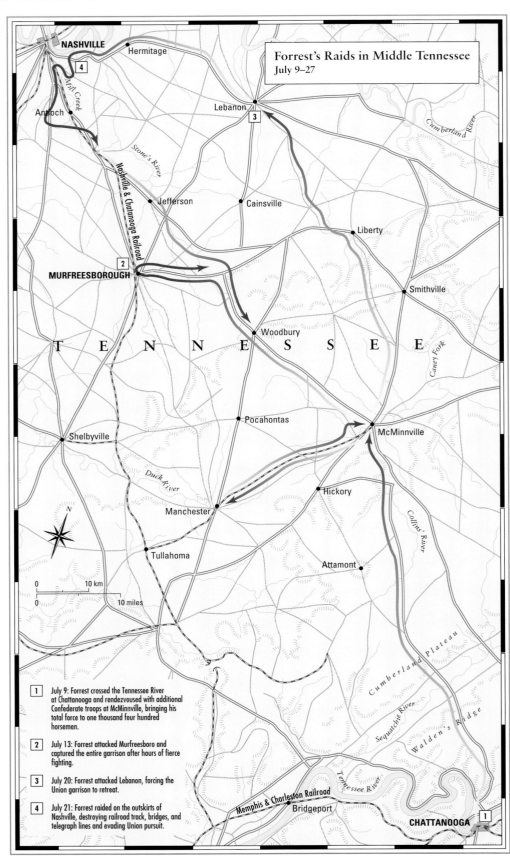

Forrest's Raids in Middle Tennessee
July 9–27

1 July 9: Forrest crossed the Tennessee River at Chattanooga and rendezvoused with additional Confederate troops at McMinnville, bringing his total force to one thousand four hundred horsemen.

2 July 13: Forrest attacked Murfreesboro and captured the entire garrison after hours of fierce fighting.

3 July 20: Forrest attacked Lebanon, forcing the Union garrison to retreat.

4 July 21: Forrest raided on the outskirts of Nashville, destroying railroad track, bridges, and telegraph lines and evading Union pursuit.

with his command for Murfreesboro, Tennessee, where he arrived on July 13 at 4:30 a.m. and immediately attacked the Union troops in and around the town. The Federals were divided in several different camps and in the surprise of Forrest's sudden attack were unable to unite their forces. After five or six hours of fierce fighting, the surviving Union troops surrendered. Forrest destroyed bridges and tore up railroad track in the vicinity, cut telegraph wires, and burned large stocks of supplies and equipment before retreating.

The two mid-summer raids disrupted Union efforts in Tennessee and Kentucky and raised Confederate morale. Morgan's raid, in particular, raised the prospect in many minds that with the appearance of a significant Rebel force Kentuckians might be willing to rise en masse in the Confederate cause.

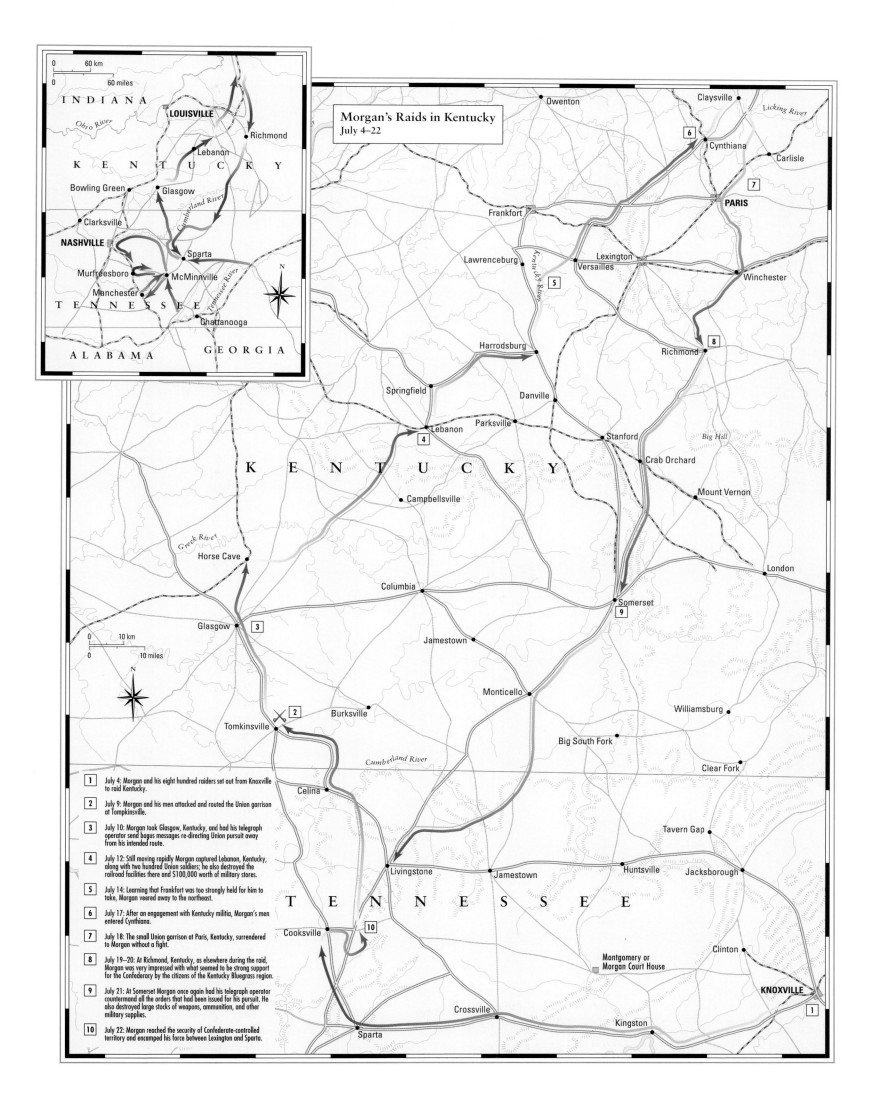

Morgan's Raids in Kentucky
July 4–22

1 July 4: Morgan and his eight hundred raiders set out from Knoxville to raid Kentucky.

2 July 9: Morgan and his men attacked and routed the Union garrison at Tompkinsville.

3 July 10: Morgan took Glasgow, Kentucky, and had his telegraph operator send bogus messages re-directing Union pursuit away from his intended route.

4 July 12: Still moving rapidly Morgan captured Lebanon, Kentucky, along with two hundred Union soldiers; he also destroyed the railroad facilities there and $100,000 worth of military stores.

5 July 14: Learning that Frankfort was too strongly held for him to take, Morgan veered away to the northeast.

6 July 17: After an engagement with Kentucky militia, Morgan's men entered Cynthiana.

7 July 18: The small Union garrison at Paris, Kentucky, surrendered to Morgan without a fight.

8 July 19–20: At Richmond, Kentucky, as elsewhere during the raid, Morgan was very impressed with what seemed to be strong support for the Confederacy by the citizens of the Kentucky Bluegrass region.

9 July 21: At Somerset Morgan once again had his telegraph operator countermand all the orders that had been issued for his pursuit. He also destroyed large stocks of weapons, ammunition, and other military supplies.

10 July 22: Morgan reached the security of Confederate-controlled territory and encamped his force between Lexington and Sparta.

CONFEDERATE INVASION OF KENTUCKY

Confederate Invasion of Kentucky August 14 – October 8

1 August 14: Kirby Smith marched north out of Knoxville, by-passing Cumberland Gap.

2 August 14: Bragg's army marched north from Chattanooga, crossing Walden's Ridge.

3 August 30: Kirby Smith's troops routed a small force of mostly untrained Union troops at Richmond, Kentucky.

4 September 5: With his position turned by Bragg's advance and his communications threatened, Buell retreated to Murfreesboro, Tennessee.

5 September 14: Bragg's army reached Glasgow, Kentucky, and marched on toward Munfordville.

6 September 14: Buell's army reached Bowling Green, Kentucky.

7 September 17: Colonel John T. Wilder surrendered the garrison of Munfordville to Bragg.

8 September 28: Buell's forces reach Louisville.

9 September 30: Bragg arrives in Bardstown.

10 October 1: Reinforced and resupplied, Buell's army advanced from Louisville in several columns.

11 October 4: Bragg inaugurated Richard Hawes as Kentucky's Confederate governor.

12 October 8: Bragg's and Buell's forces fought an inconclusive battle at Perryville.

B Y MID-SUMMER 1862 OPERATIONS in the western theater were at a standstill. This was partially the result of a severe drought that made it difficult for marching armies to find water for man and beast. It also stemmed from decisions made by the Union's western theater commander Henry W. Halleck. Halleck dispersed his troops in garrisons rather than keep his army concentrated for aggressive operations. He also dispatched Brigadier General Don Carlos Buell with a medium-sized army to march east from Corinth, Mississippi, to repair the Memphis & Charleston Railroad all the way to strategically significant Chattanooga, Tennessee. With this pedestrian strategy, Halleck surrendered the initiative. Even after Halleck was transferred to Washington, the summer lull in the West continued.

Braxton Bragg, commanding the major Confederate army in the West, had been reluctant to attack into the teeth of Halleck's defenses in Mississippi. But, when Major General Edmund Kirby Smith, commanding the Confederate department of East Tennessee, pled with him for help against Buell's slow progress toward Chattanooga, Bragg saw an opportunity. Buell was slow to move at best, and this time Confederate guerrillas bedeviled his army, destroying the railroad faster than the Federals could repair it. Bragg sent his cavalry and artillery eastward across Alabama and shipped his infantry by rail via Mobile to Chattanooga. Both arrived well ahead of Buell. Bragg was poised to march north-westward from Chattanooga. He planned to turn Buell, forcing him to retreat and give battle on terms favorable to the combined armies of Bragg and Kirby Smith, perhaps somewhere in Middle Tennessee. Bragg's use of rail transport was the most significant and innovative yet seen in military history and its result was a dramatic reversal of fortunes in the West, with both Bragg's and Buell's armies soon marching rapidly northward.

Yet Bragg's plans soon went awry. Notwithstanding his promises of cooperation, Kirby Smith was lured by rumors of vast, latent pro-Confederate sentiment in the Kentucky Bluegrass region, and he led his army on a rapid march to that territory, hoping to gain many recruits for his army and spark a popular uprising against the Union. Bragg was left to handle Buell's more numerous forces by himself. Though he outranked Kirby Smith, Bragg could command him only when their two armies actually combined, something Kirby Smith carefully avoided. Kirby Smith's irresponsible movement forced Bragg to follow him into Kentucky, lest Buell get between the two Confederate forces and destroy both. Henceforth the campaign's only real hope was a mass rising by pro-Confederate Kentuckians. To arm them, Bragg's wagon train carried thousands of extra rifles.

Kirby Smith's army won a minor victory over raw Union recruits at Richmond, Kentucky, on August 30, and went on to occupy Lexington, the heart of the Bluegrass. Then he dispersed his army to gather supplies. Bragg succeeded in capturing a Union brigade at Munfordville, Kentucky, on September 17. He was now between Buell and his base of supplies at Louisville, but Buell stubbornly refused to attack. Kirby Smith just as stubbornly refused to send either troops or supplies to support Bragg. Running out of supplies and without sufficient force to attack Buell, Bragg had to give up his advantageous position and march to the Bluegrass. There he obtained food and, at last, direct command of Kirby Smith. Buell, in turn, reached Louisville and obtained both supplies and massive reinforcements.

As Buell's large army advanced from Louisville in several columns, Bragg desperately played his last card. The Kentuckians had not volunteered. Perhaps they feared losing their property if Union forces should regain control of the state. Bragg therefore opted to install a Confederate governor in the state's capital of Frankfort, thus enabling him to implement the Confederacy's conscription law. Kentuckians would be pulled into Confederate ranks one way or another, and they could now plead compulsion if Union authorities threatened to confiscate their land.

Buell's advance guard approached Frankfort almost before the new governor finished his inaugural address. Bragg had ordered one wing of his army to strike Buell's advancing column in flank while his

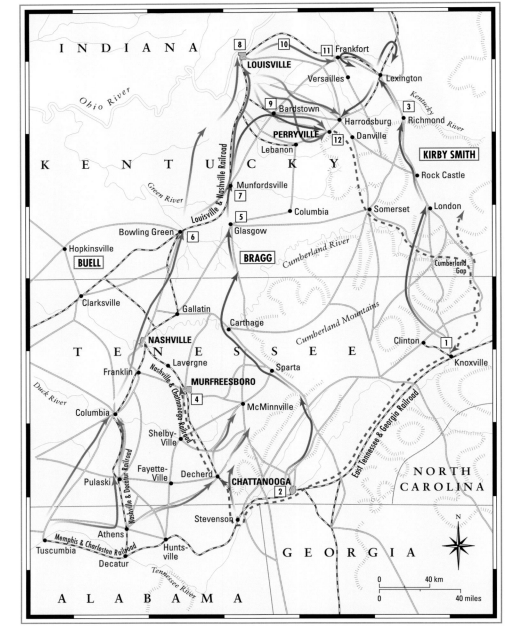

other forces attacked in front. The commander of the flanking force, Major General Leonidas Polk, disobeyed, and Bragg had no choice but to retreat and abandon Frankfort. With that, all hope of enlisting Kentuckians—and thus waging a successful campaign—vanished.

Still unwilling to concede defeat, Bragg hoped to defeat Buell's separate columns. A Union column had been squabbling with Polk's wing of Bragg's army over some pools of stagnant water in the nearly dry bed of Doctor's Creek, near Perryville, Kentucky. Bragg ordered Polk to attack, but Polk balked again, and the attack did not begin until Bragg arrived in person. When the attack began, Bragg's troops crushed the Union left flank and there was a brief hope that the whole Union force might unravel. Then Federal resistance stiffened. That night Bragg discovered that the column with which he had been contending was in fact Buell's main army, which greatly outnumbered his own. Simultaneously, Buell learned that there had been a battle that day. A mile or so to the rear, he had not heard the firing, and no one had thought to tell him.

Finally convinced that nothing more could be accomplished in Kentucky, Bragg withdrew his army. Both commanding generals received heavy criticism after the campaign. In Bragg's case, the critics were led by Polk and Kirby Smith, who claimed that he had made wrong decisions at almost every turn of the campaign, despite the fact that it was their own mistakes and disobedience that had made the largest contribution to its failure. Union authorities, including Lincoln, were displeased with Buell because of the slow, hesitant way in which he had conducted the campaign, finally allowing Bragg to escape.

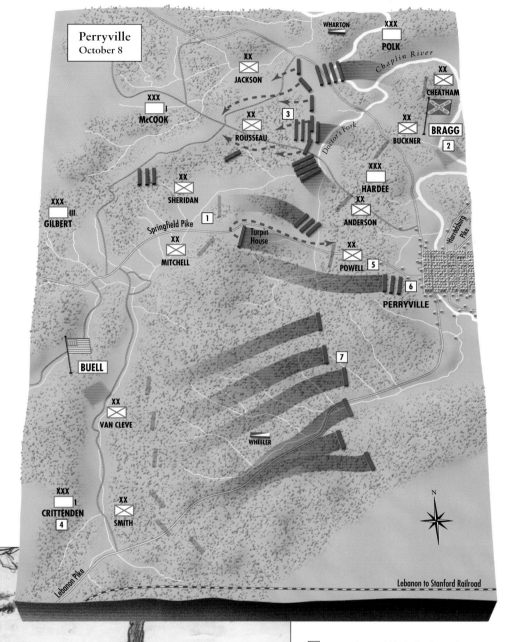

Perryville
October 8

1. Dawn: Brigadier General Philip Sheridan's division, advancing eastward along the Springfield Pike, encountered Brigadier General St. John R. Liddell's Confederate division and drove it back beyond Doctor's Creek.

2. 11:00 a.m.: Bragg arrived and ordered Polk to attack the Union left.

3. 2:00 p.m.: The Confederate divisions of Major General Benjamin F. Cheatham and Major General Simon B. Buckner attacked McCook's corps and drove it back in fierce fighting.

4. Distracted by Major General Joseph Wheeler's Confederate cavalry, Major General Thomas L. Crittenden's corps remained idle throughout the battle.

5. 4:15 p.m.: The Confederate brigade of Brigadier General Samuel Powell attacked Sheridan but was repulsed.

6. Some of Sheridan's troops then counterattacked and drove the Confederates through Perryville.

7. Night: Buell, who had learned of the battle only when it was almost over, now moved the rest of his forces up to the battlefield. Bragg, realizing that he was badly outnumbered, ordered a retreat.

After the Battle of Perryville the Confederates pulled their main forces out of Kentucky raiding and skirmishing as they withdrew. One such action was fought along the banks of the Cumberland River as shown in Walter Fenn's watercolor the Defense of Cage's Forge.

SECOND BATTLE OF MANASSAS (BULL RUN), CAMPAIGN

AS THE PENINSULA CAMPAIGN NEARED its culmination in the Seven Days' Battles, in June 1862, Lincoln appointed Major General John Pope to command the newly created Army of Virginia, consolidating Union troops that had already been operating in the northern part of that state. Pope's mission was to protect Washington, D.C., and to present a threat from the north to the Confederate forces currently opposing McClellan east of Richmond. After the Seven Days' Battles, while the armies of Lee and McClellan continued to confront each other near Harrison's Landing, Pope began a slow advance.

The war was entering a new phase during the summer of 1862. Stubborn Confederate resistance and Southern white civilians' bitter hostility toward the Union and their willingness to support Confederate guerrillas convinced Union authorities that firmer measures were necessary. Lincoln decided that month to issue his Emancipation Proclamation, though he did not announce it until September. Congress passed a second Confiscation Act—which, like the first, passed several months before, was aimed at confiscating the slaves of rebellious southerners—the same day Pope took Gordonsville. And, in the various theaters of the war, Union soldiers, from privates to generals, were coming to realize that Southern whites should no longer be treated as friendly civilians but rather as enemy civilians would be treated in an ordinary war. Pope was in the forefront of this transition, and his proximity to the rival capitals brought his new measures much publicity.

On July 18, Pope issued orders that his army would subsist off the countryside and hold local civilians financially responsible for the guerrillas' destruction of railroads, bridges, and telegraph lines. He followed up five days later with an order that any adult males in Union territory who would not take the oath of allegiance be sent beyond Union lines.

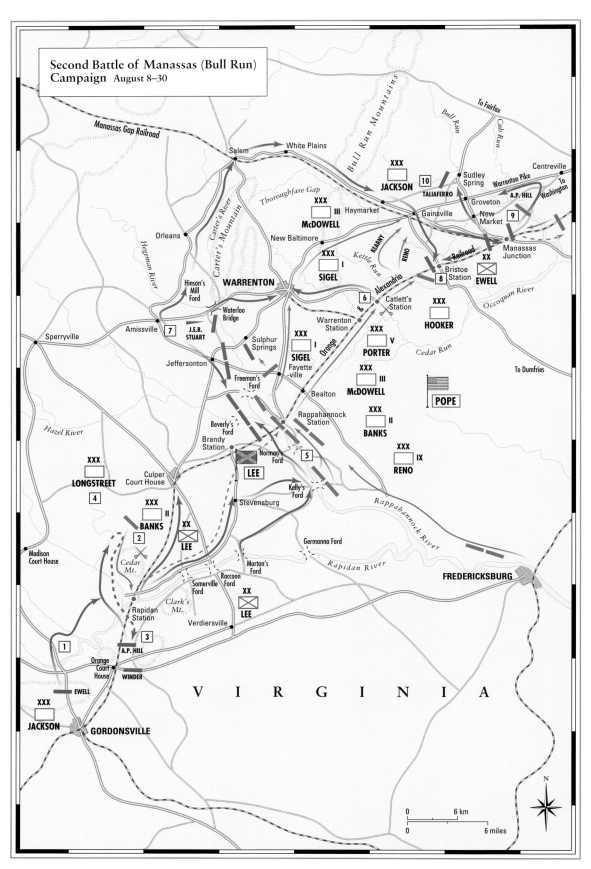

Second Battle of Manassas (Bull Run) Campaign August 8–30

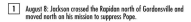

1 August 8: Jackson crossed the Rapidan north of Gordonsville and moved north on his mission to suppress Pope.

2 August 9: The lead corps of Pope's army under Major General Nathaniel P. Banks, attacked Jackson and scored some initial success before Jackson's troops rallied and drove it back.

3 August 11: Learning that additional Union troops were approaching, Jackson retreated back across the Rapidan.

4 August 13: Lee issued orders for the other wing of his army, commanded by Major General James Longstreet, to move from the peninsula to the vicinity of Gordonsville, preparatory to joining the campaign.

5 August 18: Pressed by Lee's combined forces, Pope withdrew to the north bank of the Rappahannock.

6 August 22: Jeb Stuart's Confederate cavalry raided all the way to Catlett's Station, directly in the rear of Pope's army, capturing Pope's headquarters wagons and papers.

7 August 25: Jackson began a long flanking march around Pope's army.

8 August 27: Having reached the rear of Pope's army, Jackson posted Ewell's division at Bristoe Station to block or delay the approach of Pope's troops.

9 August 27: With the rest of his force Jackson captured the major Union supply depot at Manassas Junction, easily defeating a single Union brigade that attempted to re-take it. Jackson's men reveled in unaccustomed abundance before destroying what they could not use or carry away.

10 August 27–28, night: Jackson drew his corps together and deployed it in an unfinished railroad cut paralleling the Warrenton Turnpike just west of the old Bull Run battlefield.

Confederate officials were outraged at these measures. Jefferson Davis announced that henceforth any commissioned officers of Pope's army who were captured would be treated not as prisoners of war but as felons.

As Pope advanced southward to Culpeper, Virginia, Lee detached Stonewall Jackson's corps of his army to proceed northwest from Richmond and confront Pope. Jackson's force collided with the leading corps of Pope's army at Cedar Mountain, near Culpeper, on August 9. Commanding the eight thousand Union troops on the battlefield was Major General Nathaniel P. Banks, a politician in uniform who Jack-son had defeated in the Shenandoah Valley that spring. Banks performed with his usual incompetence, but Jackson, who brought sixteen thousand eight hundred troops to Cedar Mountain, got off to a bad start. Banks's men got the better of the fight with Jackson's two leading divisions, and only with the arrival Jackson's third and last division, under Major General Ambrose Powell Hill, did the tide of battle turn in favor of the Confederates. Banks retreated. Union casualties totaled two thousand three hundred and eighty-one, and Confederate, one thousand three hundred and forty-one.

Meanwhile on August 3, Union authorities in Washington, D.C., ordered McClellan to withdraw his army from the Peninsula and return to Aquia Creek, just north of Fredericksburg, whence it could march to aid Pope. McClellan, who bitterly opposed the movement, proceeded very slowly. Within a week, Lee had learned of the order and on August 13 began shifting his own troops away from Richmond, which McClellan no longer even appeared to threaten, and up into northern Virginia to join Jackson in confronting Pope. The first of McClellan's troops did not arrive at Aquia Creek, fifty miles north-northeast of Culpeper, until August 14.

Threatened by the approach of Lee's army, on August 18, Pope retreated to the north bank of the Rappahannock River and endeavored to hold the crossings of that stream against Lee's advance. The armies skirmished along the Rappahannock for the next week. Then, on August 25, Lee dispatched Jackson's corps to move west and then north in a wide turning maneuver that would take him around Pope's right flank into the Union rear all the way to the rail nexus and supply depot at Manassas Junction, Virginia. Jackson's troops began arriving at Manassas Junction August 26 and got to work destroying railroads, telegraph lines, and supplies. The following day Pope realized that his position had been turned and began to move his army north toward Manassas, hoping to trap Jackson. Lee with the larger of his two corps, commanded by Longstreet, took up the march along the path Jackson had taken, looking to reunite his army near Manassas Junction.

[1] Immediately upon detecting the approaching of Jackson's corps, Banks launched his own corps in a headlong assault.

[2] The Union attack routed the division of Brigadier General Charles S. Winder, who was killed early in the fight.

[3] Jackson personally helped rally the retreating troops.

[4] A. P. Hill's division arrived and turned the tide of battle, driving Banks's badly outnumbered army off the field of battle.

Cedar Mountain
August 9

SECOND BATTLE OF MANASSAS (BULL RUN)

1 August 28: Jackson attacked the lone brigade of Brigadier General John Gibbon as it passed on the Warrenton Turnpike, but Gibbon's tough Wisconsin and Indiana soldiers held their own and wounded Confederate generals William B. Taliaferro and Richard S. Ewell.

2 August 29: Pope came up with the rest of his army and throughout the day hurled his troops in determined but unsuccessful attacks against Jackson's line.

3 August 29: Unaware that Lee was on hand with Longstreet's wing of the Confederate army, Pope ordered Porter's Fifth Corps to shift closer to the rest of the army. Unbeknownst to Pope, he was thus removing the Fifth Corps from a position on Lee's right flank to a position where Lee would be able to strike the Fifth Corps in its left flank.

4 August 30, 3:00–3:30 p.m.: Porter's Fifth Corps assaulted Jackson's lines but was repulsed with heavy losses.

5 August 30, 3:30 p.m.: Longstreet attacked the exposed left flank of the Union line, which crumbled. As the Union troops began to fall back, Jackson joined the attack.

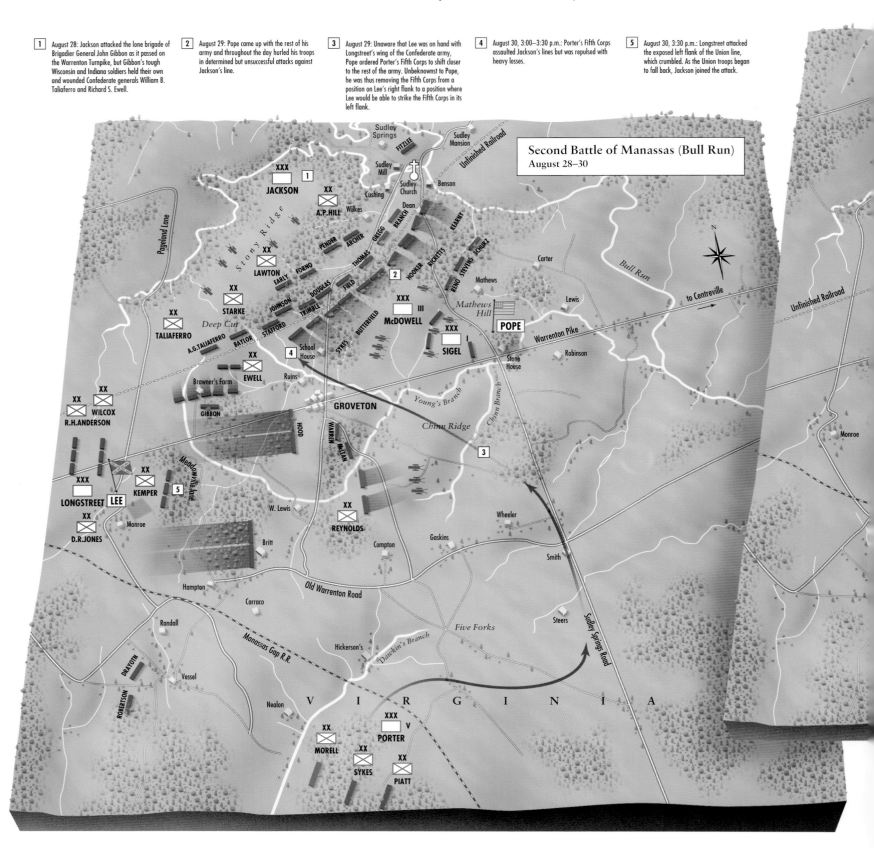

Second Battle of Manassas (Bull Run)
August 28–30

By AUGUST 28, LEE AND JACKSON had outmaneuvered Pope, but Pope did not yet realize it. Still believing he was about to trap Jackson at Manassas Junction, Pope arrived there on the afternoon of August 28, only to find that Jackson had withdrawn the night before. Pope could get no clear reports as to Jackson's present whereabouts and so gave orders to his army to concentrate at Centreville, Virginia.

In obedience to that order, Brigadier General Rufus King's division was marching northeast along the Warrenton Turnpike at about 5:30 that afternoon when it was suddenly and unexpectedly attacked by Confederates near the town of Groveton. In fact, Jackson had withdrawn not to the north, as Pope supposed, but rather to the west, taking up a position on Brawner's Farm near the Warrenton Turnpike concealed by woods. Jackson's attack on King's division sparked an evening battle at Groveton that lasted for several

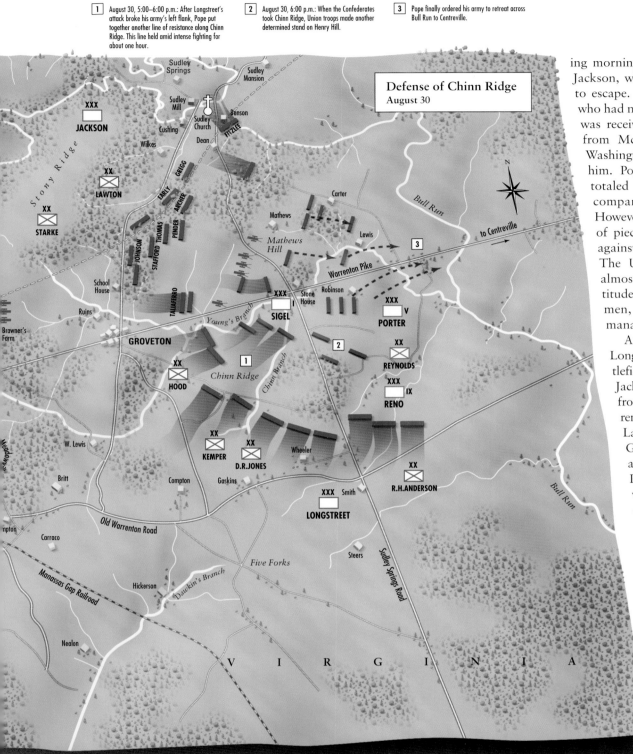

1 August 30, 5:00–6:00 p.m.: After Longstreet's attack broke his army's left flank, Pope put together another line of resistance along Chinn Ridge. This line held amid intense fighting for about one hour.

2 August 30, 6:00 p.m.: When the Confederates took Chinn Ridge, Union troops made another determined stand on Henry Hill.

3 Pope finally ordered his army to retreat across Bull Run to Centreville.

Defense of Chinn Ridge
August 30

ing morning, August 29, Pope advanced against Jackson, who he mistakenly thought was trying to escape. He soon "caught up" with Jackson, who had no thought of fleeing. By this time Pope was receiving a steady flow of reinforcements from McClellan's troops, who had reached Washington and were marching out to join him. Pope's numbers on the field this day totaled about sixty-two thousand men, as compared to Jackson's twenty thousand. However, Pope launched his troops in a series of piecemeal, uncoordinated frontal attacks against Jackson's strong defensive position. The Union troops fought heroically and almost broke Jackson's line despite the ineptitude of their commander, but Jackson's men, fighting with equal stubbornness, managed to hang on. Casualties were heavy.

Around noon that day, Lee and Longstreet arrived at the old Bull Run battlefield. Lee placed Longstreet's corps on Jackson's right, angling sharply forward from Jackson's line. Longstreet's troops remained generally concealed by woods. Late in the day, Pope ordered Major General Fitz John Porter's recently arrived Fifth Corps of the Army of the Potomac to attack Jackson's right. This was impossible because of the presence of Longstreet's corps, but Pope, despite repeated warnings of Longstreet's approach, refused to believe his corps was present. He later had Porter court-martialed for failing to make the attack as ordered.

During the night the Confederates made some slight adjustments in their line, which the next morning Pope interpreted as a retreat and ordered his army to pursue. After perhaps the shortest pursuit in military history, Pope's troops once again encountered Jackson's solid lines along the railroad grade, and Pope again resorted to frontal attacks. Again, the courage of his men nearly overcame what was lack-

hours and was extremely bloody for its duration and the number of troops engaged. Major General Richard S. Ewell, among the Confederate casualties, lost a leg in the fight.

On learning of the Battle of Groveton, Pope concluded that Jackson was retreating to the west and ordered his army to pursue. That same day Lee, accompanying Longstreet's corps of the Army of Northern Virginia on its way to join Jackson, arrived at Thoroughfare Gap in the Bull Run Mountains and found the pass held by Brigadier General James B. Ricketts's Union division. After some skirmishing Lee succeeded in outflanking Ricketts by getting his troops onto the high ground on either side of the gap. Lee also dispatched Major General Cadmus M. Wilcox's division to take Hopewell Gap, to the north of Thoroughfare. Ricketts abandoned the gap and retreated toward Manassas Junction, and Lee and Longstreet's Confederates continued their own march in the same direction.

That night Jackson moved his corps a slight distance to the grade of an unfinished railroad on the old Bull Run battlefield. The follow-

ing in his tactics, as they almost broke through the Confederate line. With Jackson's troops running out of ammunition and resorting to throwing stones at their attackers, Lee ordered Longstreet to join the fight. Longstreet refused, however, saying the time was not ripe. With the help of well-positioned Confederate artillery, Jackson was able to hang on. Late that afternoon, Longstreet finally launched his attack, crushing Pope's left flank and driving his army back across the old Bull Run battlefield. Pope's troops rallied several times and made determined stands, but Pope ultimately had to retreat toward Washington. Union casualties totaled thirteen thousand eight hundred and twenty-six, and Confederate, eight thousand three hundred and fifty-three.

Two days later on September 1, Jackson attempted to cut off Pope's retreat and clashed with Federal forces at Chantilly, Virginia. In a fierce battle during a raging thunderstorm, the Union divisions of Major General Isaac I. Stevens and Major General Philip Kearny succeeded in stopping Jackson, though both division commanders, among the best in the Army of the Potomac, were killed in the fight.

THE ANTIETAM CAMPAIGN

AFTER HIS VICTORY IN THE Second Battle of Bull Run, Lee decided to invade the northern states. On September 4 the Army of Northern Virginia began crossing the Potomac into Maryland at Leesburg, Virginia. The Confederates had expected the citizens of Maryland, a slave state, to rally to their cause, but most of the slaves in Maryland were in the eastern part of the state. Here in western Maryland the overwhelmingly non-slaveholding populace was also overwhelmingly pro-Union. Meanwhile, on September 2, Lincoln restored McClellan to command of Union forces in Virginia. While Lee marched to

The abrupt surrender of the Union garrison at Harpers Ferry aided Lee in the re-concentration of his army.

Frederick, Maryland, McClellan re-organized the Army of the Potomac within the fortifications of Washington, D.C. Then, on September 7, McClellan's army began to move slowly northward, so as to cover both Washington and Baltimore from Lee's advance.

Lee's plan of invasion called for his army to establish a supply line through the Shenandoah Valley, but this was not possible as long as Union forces maintained a garrison at Harpers Ferry. Lee had assumed that once he reached Frederick, cutting the line of communication between Harpers Ferry and Washington, its garrison would retreat. But, the Federals at Harpers Ferry, some ten thousand of them, did not react as Lee had anticipated.

Taking Harpers Ferry and forcing the garrison to surrender would be simple once the high ground around it was taken, and Lee had troops enough to do it. However, this action would entail dividing his army into several columns, and sending those columns on roundabout routes through the mountains to reach the heights around Harpers Ferry. It was a risky move, but Lee decided to count on the well-known slowness and caution of McClellan and on what he hoped was the demoralized state of the Union army. On September 9 he issued Special

Orders Number 191, spelling out how the army was to move in the coming days as it maneuvered to capture Harpers Ferry. Over the next few days Lee's army split up and moved west.

Still slowly advancing, McClellan's army entered Frederick on September 12. The next morning, two Union soldiers found a paper wrapped around three cigars, lying on the ground. The paper was a copy of Lee's Special Orders Number 191, which had somehow been lost. It was soon in McClellan's hands, and with it he had the exact details of where he could find and destroy the vulnerable separate columns of Lee's army.

Armed with this information, McClellan moved somewhat faster, but not fast enough. Lee got word of the information leak and began desperate efforts to concentrate his army and to hold McClellan back until he could do so. On September 14, detachments of the Army of Northern Virginia attempted to hold the passes of South Mountain against McClellan. They succeeded in delaying McClellan several hours before the numerically superior Army of the Potomac pushed them out of their strong position and continued its advance. Now it was Lee's turn to encounter a stroke of luck; on September 15, the Union commander of Harpers Ferry, Colonel Dixon Miles, surrendered so abruptly as to raise serious questions about his loyalty. Ironically, one of the last Confederate shots, fired after the surrender had been agreed to, killed Miles. The premature surrender of Harpers Ferry was an enormous help to Lee in speeding the re-concentration of his army.

By September 16, Lee had gathered much of his army on the west bank of Antietam Creek. His decision to turn at bay here—with his back to the Potomac, which could be crossed only at a single ford—was the height of audacity. Lee continued to count on the poor generalship of McClellan and what he hoped would be the broken spirit of the Union soldiers. McClellan approached Lee's army that afternoon and sparred gingerly but did not attack Lee's still incomplete force. By the following morning when McClellan finally advanced, all but a single division of Lee's army was on hand. The Union general badly mismanaged the battle, but his troops belied Lee's expectation by fighting with superb élan. Several times during the day Lee came within a hair's breadth of disaster. On the final occasion only the timely arrival of the Army of Northern Virginia's last division saved it from destruction.

With an audacity that bordered on madness, Lee kept his battered army on the battlefield the following day, daring McClellan to do his worst and actually seeking an opportunity for a counterstroke. Neither general saw a chance to attack on September 18, however, and Antietam remained a one-day battle, the bloodiest in American history. Union casualties totaled twelve thousand four hundred and sixty-nine and Confederate, thirteen thousand and seven hundred and twenty-four. On the night of 18–19 September, Lee withdrew into Virginia, effectively ending the campaign.

McClellan's battle plan called for Hooker's corps to ford Antietam Creek in preparation for striking Lee's flank.

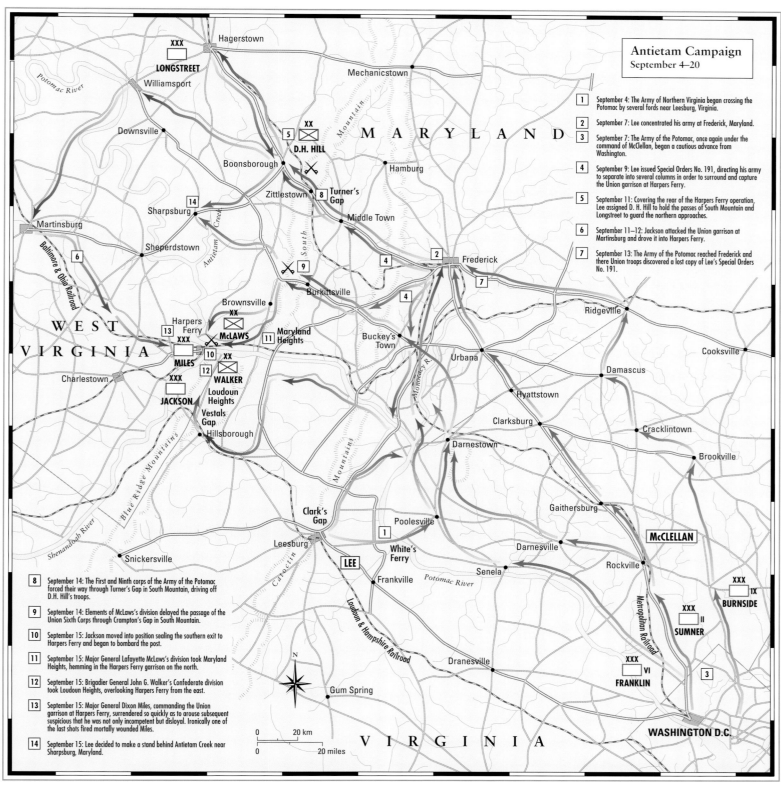

Antietam Campaign
September 4–20

[1] September 4: The Army of Northern Virginia began crossing the Potomac by several fords near Leesburg, Virginia.

[2] September 7: Lee concentrated his army at Frederick, Maryland.

[3] September 7: The Army of the Potomac, once again under the command of McClellan, began a cautious advance from Washington.

[4] September 9: Lee issued Special Orders No. 191, directing his army to separate into several columns in order to surround and capture the Union garrison at Harpers Ferry.

[5] September 11: Covering the rear of the Harpers Ferry operation, Lee assigned D. H. Hill to hold the passes of South Mountain and Longstreet to guard the northern approaches.

[6] September 11–12: Jackson attacked the Union garrison at Martinsburg and drove it into Harpers Ferry.

[7] September 13: The Army of the Potomac reached Frederick and there Union troops discovered a lost copy of Lee's Special Orders No. 191.

[8] September 14: The First and Ninth corps of the Army of the Potomac forced their way through Turner's Gap in South Mountain, driving off D.H. Hill's troops.

[9] September 14: Elements of McLaws's division delayed the passage of the Union Sixth Corps through Crampton's Gap in South Mountain.

[10] September 15: Jackson moved into position sealing the southern exit to Harpers Ferry and began to bombard the post.

[11] September 15: Major General Lafayette McLaws's division took Maryland Heights, hemming in the Harpers Ferry garrison on the north.

[12] September 15: Brigadier General John G. Walker's Confederate division took Loudoun Heights, overlooking Harpers Ferry from the east.

[13] September 15: Major General Dixon Miles, commanding the Union garrison at Harpers Ferry, surrendered so quickly as to arouse subsequent suspicion that he was not only incompetent but disloyal. Ironically one of the last shots fired mortally wounded Miles.

[14] September 15: Lee decided to make a stand behind Antietam Creek near Sharpsburg, Maryland.

137

BATTLE OF ANTIETAM, PHASE I

THE NATURE OF LEE'S FALL 1862 campaign in Maryland changed abruptly when a copy of his Special Orders Number 191 fell into Union hands, revealing that Lee had divided the Army of Northern Virginia in order to attack Harpers Ferry. McClellan advanced toward Lee, who hurriedly reunited his army and turned at bay behind Antietam Creek with the Potomac River, crossable only at a single ford, at his back. If the coming battle should result unfavorably for him, most of his forty thousand troops would be unable to retreat via that ford in time to escape capture, effectively ending the Army of Northern Virginia.

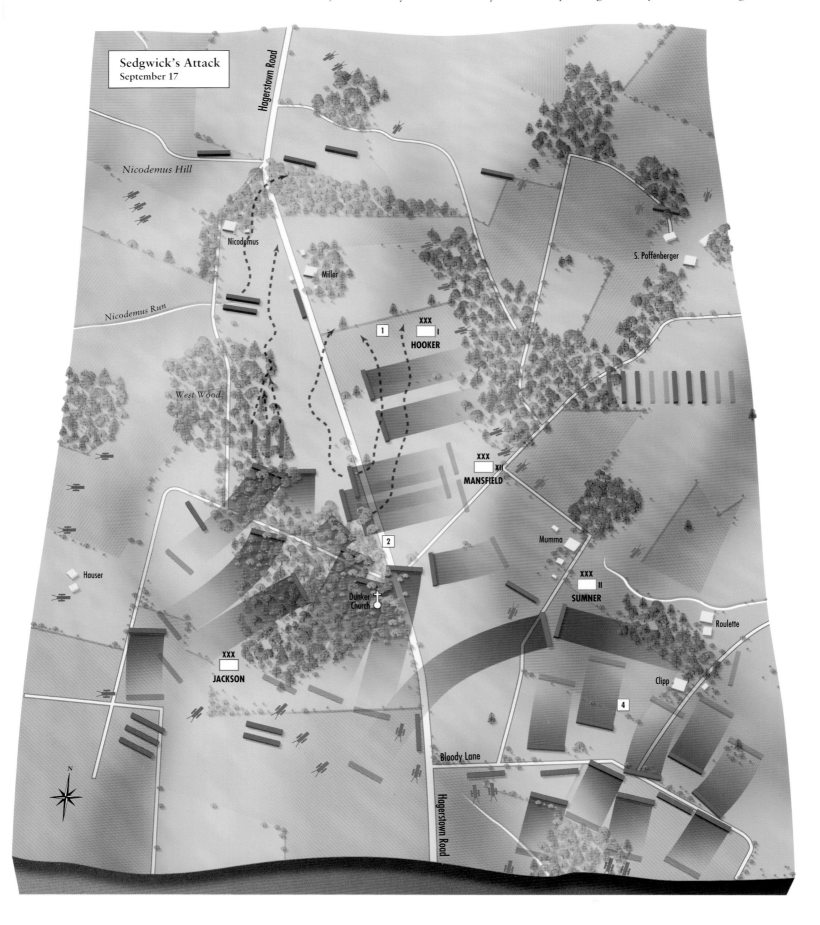

Right: *Confederate dead along the Hagerstown Pike at Antietam.*

1 Major General Joseph Hooker's First Corps attacked the Confederate left. After some initial success amid heavy fighting in the Cornfield and the West Woods, First Corps had to fall back under Confederate counterattack. Hooker was wounded and replaced by Brigadier General George G. Meade.

2 After Hooker's repulse, Major General Joseph K. F. Mansfield's Twelfth Corps attacked the Confederate left. More heavy fighting followed in the East Woods, Cornfield, and West Woods. Mansfield was killed and Confederate reinforcements drove the Twelfth Corps back.

3 Next, Major General William V. Sumner led his Second Corps to the attack but allowed its three divisions to become widely separated. Sumner personally led Major General John Sedgwick's division all the way to the West Woods, where it was flanked and driven back with heavy casualties.

4 Sumner's other two divisions, those of Major General Israel B. Richardson and Brigadier General William H. French, veered southwest and struck the Confederate line along a slightly sunken farm lane that came to be called Bloody Lane. Timely Confederate reinforcements narrowly averted a decisive Union breakthrough in this sector.

Below: *Burnside's Bridge at Antietam was captured by elements of his Ninth Corps after a bloody struggle, allowing his men to cross Antietam Creek and attack the Confederate left.*

BATTLE OF ANTIETAM, PHASE II

1 After hours of delay, Major General Ambrose Burnside finally launched elements of his Ninth Corps in an assault that captured the bridge that has since borne his name.

2 Brigadier General Rodman's division of the Ninth Corps crossed Antietam Creek via Snavely's Ford and provided cover for the rest of the corps as it crossed the bridge and deployed on the west side of the creek.

3 Burnside's Ninth Corps mounted an assault toward Sharpsburg, driving the Confederate defenders to the outskirts of the town.

4 Ambrose Powell Hill's Confederate division arrived after a day-long forced march from Harpers Ferry, just in time to flank and drive back Burnside's attackers.

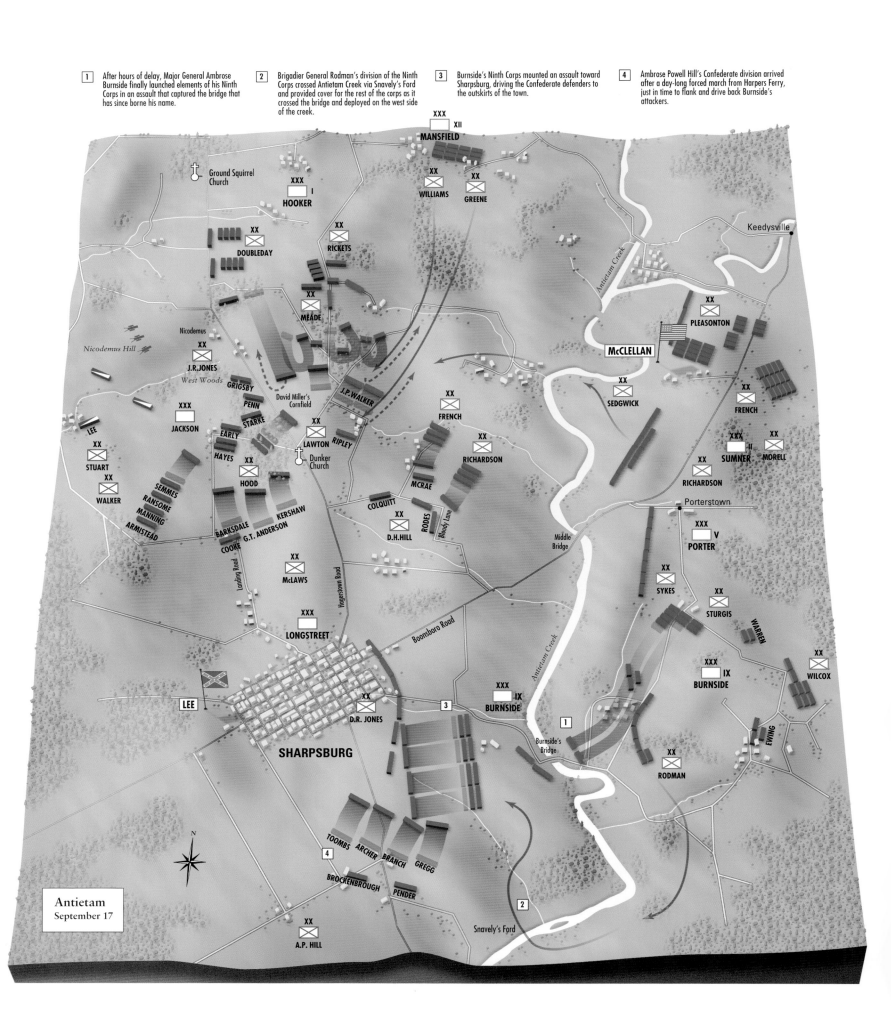

Antietam
September 17

McClellan, almost pathologically convinced that he faced a Confederate host of 200,000 men, arrived with his own seventy-five thousand-man Army of the Potomac on September 16. Early on the morning of September 17, McClellan ordered the First Corps, commanded by Major General Joseph Hooker, to attack the Confederate left flank, commanded by Major General Thomas J. "Stonewall" Jackson. Hooker's men succeeded in taking the East Woods and the Cornfield, threatening to roll up Lee's flank. A counterattack led by Brigadier General John B. Hood succeeded in blunting the Federal advance and retaking the Cornfield. The Confederate left flank held, though by the narrowest of margins. Hooker was wounded and carried off the field, and his corps rested.

The vortex of the battle shifted to the advance of Brigadier General Joseph K. F. Mansfield's Twelfth Corps, which moved through the East Woods toward the Dunker Church. Many of the same Confederate troops that had fought off Hooker's attack now turned to repulse the Twelfth Corps. Mansfield was killed early in the action, and his troops finally came to a standstill short of the Dunker Church.

McClellan continued to insert his army piecemeal into the battle, and following Mansfield's advance he sent forward Major General Edwin Vose Sumner's Second Corps. Sumner rode with his lead division, which was commanded by Major General John Sedgwick as it advanced all the way past the Dunker Church and into the West Wood only to be flanked by a Confederate counterattack and routed.

The two trailing divisions of the Second Corps diverged from Sedgwick's course and struck the center of the Confederate line. Here, the fighting focused on a section of sunken road, eroded below the surrounding surface, which the Confederates used as a ready-made trench in a strong defilade position. After hours of appalling slaughter on both sides, Union troops succeeded in capturing the sunken road, which by then was almost filled with Confederate dead and was henceforth called "Bloody Lane." This Union breakthrough could well have been fatal for Lee's army. However, by desperately stripping other sectors in order to obtain reinforcements and because the Union troops were confused and exhausted, Lee was able to contain the breakthrough.

Lee was able to concentrate almost all his reserves against each successive Union thrust thanks to McClellan's persistence in dribbling his troops into the battle one corps at a time, each of which was defeated before the next got into the fight. In the final phase of the battle, McClellan's mismanagement was exacerbated by the incompetence of his friend, Ninth Corps commander Major General Ambrose Burnside. Assigned to take his corps across the Lower, or Rohrbach, Bridge (since known as Burnside's Bridge), Burnside spent hours in ineffective efforts to take the bridge by the most unimaginative methods, despite the fact that only a handful of Confederates held the far bank. After his men finally succeeded in taking the bridge in the mid-afternoon, Burnside led his corps across and attacked. The weak Confederate forces in front of the town of Sharpsburg crumbled. It appeared anni-

hilation was at hand for the Army of Northern Virginia. Then, at the most opportune moment, Major General Ambrose Powell Hill's Confederate division arrived from Harpers Ferry after a day's forced march. Hill's weary troops struck the Ninth Corps flank, halting its attack and securing, for the moment at least, the survival of the Army of Northern Virginia.

Of McClellan's seventy-five thousand men, probably no more than forty-six thousand had gone into action. He had more fresh troops waiting in reserve when Hill's troops arrived than Lee had unwounded soldiers left in his army, but he chose to do nothing. Throughout the remainder of September 17 and all of the 18th, the armies watched each other quietly. Lee retreated across the Potomac during the night of September 18–19.

Union casualties amounted to twelve thousand four hundred and sixty-nine and Confederate to thirteen thousand seven hundred and twenty-four. Tactically, the outcome was a draw, but strategically it left Lee with no choice but to withdraw into Virginia. His army was too severely weakened to continue the campaign in Maryland in the face of McClellan's active opposition. This gave Lincoln, who had been waiting for a Union victory, the opportunity, on September 22, to announce his Preliminary Emancipation Proclamation, declaring that all slaves in areas still in rebellion against U.S. authority as of January 1, 1863, would be forever free.

After a bitter struggle, two divisions of the Second Corps finally overran the Confederates occupying a sunken lane used as a ready-made trench in the center of their line. Almost filled with Confederate dead it was thereafter known as "Bloody Lane."

THE CORINTH AND IUKA CAMPAIGNS

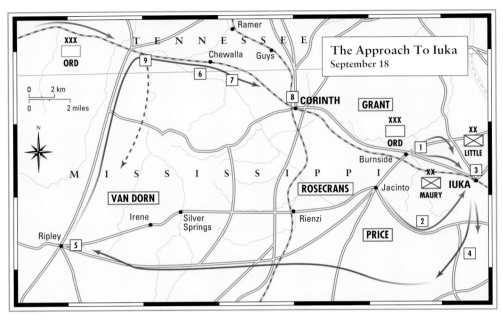

The Approach To Iuka
September 18

1. September 18–19: Accompanied by Grant, Ord's wing of the army slowly approached Iuka from the northwest, waiting for Rosecrans to get into position.

2. September 19: Delayed by muddy roads, Rosecrans finally approached Iuka from the south but failed to block all possible Confederate routes of escape on that side.

3. September 19, 4:00–9:00 p.m.: Price attacked the head of Rosecrans's column and a sharp but inconclusive battle raged for several hours.

4. September 20: Price escaped Grant's trap, and his rear guard ambushed the pursuing Union cavalry.

5. September 28: Price and Van Dorn joined forces at Ripley, and Van Dorn, now in command, began planning an attack on Corinth.

6. October 2: Hoping to surprise the Union defenders of Corinth by attacking from the rear, Van Dorn led his force on a roundabout approach that brought him to Chewalla, Tennessee, about ten miles from Corinth.

7. October 3, dawn to 10:00 a.m.: Van Dorn advanced toward Corinth, skirmishing with a single brigade of Union infantry that Rosecrans had sent out to delay and report his march.

8. October 3–4: Van Dorn hurled his army at the Union defenders of Corinth in a series of bloody and unsuccessful assaults.

9. Union troops under Ord, sent by Grant to block Van Dorn's escape, seized Davis Bridge in a fight known as the Battle of the Hatchie. With no pursuit by Rosecrans, however, Van Dorn was able to cross the Hatchie farther upstream and made good his escape.

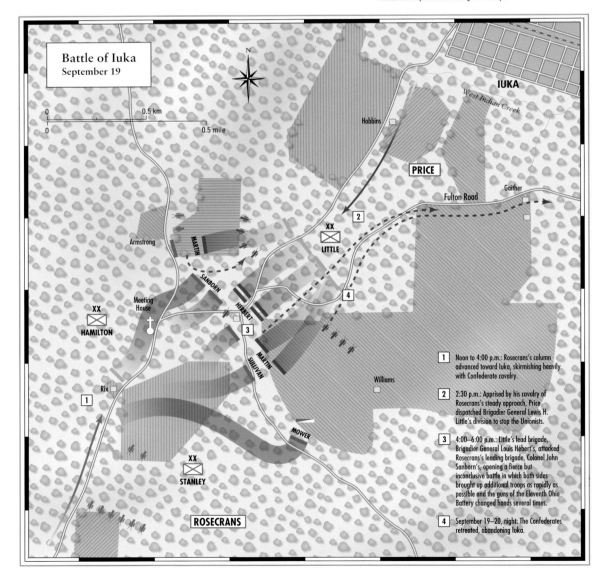

Battle of Iuka
September 19

1. Noon to 4:00 p.m.: Rosecrans's column advanced toward Iuka, skirmishing heavily with Confederate cavalry.

2. 2:30 p.m.: Apprised by his cavalry of Rosecrans's steady approach, Price dispatched Brigadier General Lewis H. Little's division to stop the Unionists.

3. 4:00–6:00 p.m.: Little's lead brigade, Brigadier General Louis Hébert's, attacked Rosecrans's leading brigade, Colonel John Sanborn's, opening a fierce but inconclusive battle in which both sides brought up additional troops as rapidly as possible and the guns of the Eleventh Ohio Battery changed hands several times.

4. September 19–20, night: The Confederates retreated, abandoning Iuka.

WHEN GENERAL BRAXTON BRAGG TOOK the bulk of his army from Tupelo, Mississippi, to Chattanooga to launch his offensive into Kentucky in the late summer of 1862, he left two separate Confederate forces in Mississippi. Guarding Vicksburg against the Union threat via the Mississippi River was a force of about sixteen thousand men under Major General Earl Van Dorn. Another force of about equal size under Major General Sterling Price confronted the Federals in northern Mississippi. Bragg left orders for Price to prevent Grant from detaching troops in Mississippi and West Tennessee to reinforce Union troops in Kentucky. If Grant did detach troops, and perhaps even if he did not, Price would press into Middle Tennessee, to join Bragg for the showdown in Kentucky. Once the threat to Vicksburg ended—which it did at this time—Van Dorn was to act on the same orders as Price.

Price and Van Dorn refused to cooperate with each other. Van Dorn ranked Price, but would not be able to give him orders until the two forces were actually united, an event that for some time seemed unlikely as each general followed his own agenda. Price thought they ought to obey Bragg's orders, move northwest, threaten Grant, and see if they could get into Middle Tennessee. Van Dorn had various unrealistic ideas about taking Memphis.

With the two Confederate columns still maneuvering separately, Price advanced toward the town of Iuka, Mississippi. Iuka was a small Union supply depot, the eastern most point on the Memphis & Charleston Railroad held by Grant's troops. A few miles west of the Tennessee River, Iuka was twenty-two miles east of the main rail junction and Union base at Corinth. Price's advance guard arrived in Iuka on the morning of September 13. The Union commander, Colonel Robert Murphy, put up a half-hearted defense and then promptly withdrew his force toward Corinth, allowing the valuable supplies to fall into Price's hands.

Although he was displeased with Murphy's performance, Grant nevertheless saw an opportunity to destroy Price's small army and marched toward Iuka with seventeen thousand men. Grant's subordinate Brigadier General William S. Rosecrans persuaded Grant to allow him to take nine thousand men from Grant's force and march around to the south side of Iuka, so that the Rebels would be caught between two converging Union forces. This questionable tactic went astray almost immediately as Rosecrans's column got bogged down on muddy roads and failed to get into place on time. Grant directed his column not to attack until they heard Rosecrans's guns.

Then, as Rosecrans's column approached within several miles of

Iuka on the evening of September 19, Price attacked savagely. While a meteorological phenomenon known as an acoustic shadow prevented anyone in Grant's column from hearing the sound of gunfire only a few miles away, Rosecrans's force fought a small but extremely intense battle involving about four thousand five hundred of Rosecrans's men and three thousand two hundred of Price's. The fight was inconclusive. Rosecrans, who was supposed to know the area's roads well, had left one key route open, and Price's Confederates were able to escape before Grant's troops got word that a fight had taken place. Union casualties for the Battle of Iuka totaled seven hundred and ninety and Confederate, one thousand five hundred and sixteen.

Having escaped from Grant's trap, Price finally united with Van Dorn, who had adopted a more cooperative attitude by this time. They agreed that their next step should be an attack on Corinth. Their forces arrived near the Union base on October 3. Rosecrans defended the town with a force that Grant had by then reinforced to

some twenty-three thousand men. Van Dorn, with about thirty thousand, hoped to surprise Rosecrans by marching northwest of Corinth and then turning to attack the town from that direction. However, this strategy accomplished little beyond making Van Dorn's army vulnerable to being trapped by Grant's troops, which were closing in rapidly from several directions.

Throughout October 3 and 4, Van Dorn hurled his troops at Rosecrans's defenders. Rosecrans unwisely had many of his troops fight outside of their breastworks, and when Confederate troops briefly broke through his lines and actually reached the streets of Corinth the Union general panicked. Nevertheless the stubborn fighting quality of this troops, along with Van Dorn's unimaginative tactics, saved him. After the battle, Rosecrans's failure to pursue saved Van Dorn, who was able to escape the other forces Grant had dispatched to trap him. Total Union casualties for the Battle of Corinth were two thousand five hundred and twenty and Confederate, four thousand two hundred and thirty-three.

1 October 3, 7:30 a.m.: Van Dorn began his advance toward Corinth, skirmishing with the detached brigade of Colonel John M. Oliver.

2 October 3, 10:00 a.m.: By Rosecrans's order, the Union divisions of Brigadier General Thomas J. McKean and Brigadier General Thomas A. Davies deployed along a line of weakly constructed former Confederate breastworks about two and a half miles from Corinth. They were soon joined by the retreating Oliver, but still had far too few men to cover the extensive breastworks.

3 October 3, 11:00 a.m.: Brigadier General Dabney Maury's division attacked the thin Union line and drove it back. McKean's and Davies's men made a fighting retreat to the College Hill line, a more compact and defensible position closer to Corinth and anchored by Battery Robinett.

4 October 3, Noon: Major General Mansfield Lovell's division attacked but McKean's division stubbornly held the left of the College Hill line.

5 October 3–4, night: Rosecrans rearranged his troops, placing Stanley's division in the center, near Battery Robinett, between the tired divisions of McKean and Davies.

6 October 4, 4:00–7:00 a.m.: Van Dorn ordered an artillery bombardment by fourteen of his guns in order to soften up the Union lines. Union artillery responded at dawn and quickly silenced the Confederate guns.

7 October 4, 10:00 a.m.–1:00 p.m.: At Van Dorn's order, Hébert's division, commanded by Brigadier General Martin E. Green in place of the ailing Hébert, attacked Davies's exhausted and over-extended division and broke through its thin lines, penetrating into the streets of Corinth before Davies's men rallied and drove them back.

8 Green's simultaneous attack against Hamilton's division scored only minor gains.

9 October 4, noon–1:00 p.m.: Maury's division mounted an assault on Battery Robinett, ending in bloody repulse.

10 October 4, 1:00 p.m.: Van Dorn's army withdrew.

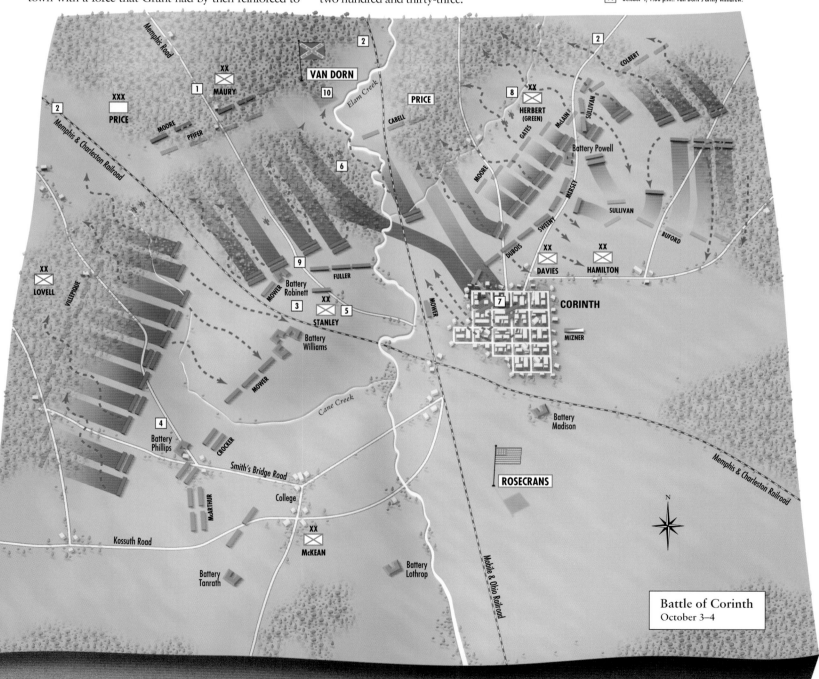

Battle of Corinth
October 3–4

EMANCIPATION PROCLAMATION

WHEN THE CIVIL WAR BEGAN, President Lincoln argued that his primary goal was to save the Union, not to free the slaves. He feared that transforming the war into a crusade against slavery would discourage northern Democrats and border-state Unionists from supporting the war effort. Lincoln even hoped that southern slave owners would return to the Union if they believed that they could keep their slaves. He also believed that, as president, he had no constitutional authority to free slaves in southern states even if he wanted to. During the first year of the war, he ignored critics who ridiculed the idea of the North fighting and winning the war only to allow the South to keep its slaves. He overruled and even relieved Union

A Federal agent, standing on the right, explains the Emancipation Proclamation to a group of ex-slaves.

generals who tried to use their military powers to undermine slavery. When Congress took the first tentative steps toward emancipation through the "confiscation" of southern slaves, Lincoln resisted.

During the summer of 1862, however, Lincoln decided to issue an emancipation proclamation as an "act of justice" and a military measure that was necessary to win the war. As the war dragged on and casualties mounted, Lincoln felt that emancipation would add a popular, moral dimension to the conflict that would encourage a deeper national commitment to victory. He also hoped that adopting emancipation as a new war aim would generate international support for the Union and

deny the Confederacy potential allies, such as England. Emancipation would also strike a blow against the heart of the southern economy, undermining the Confederate war effort and weakening the rebel armies. Lincoln also expected many free blacks and former slaves to join the Union army, creating a new source of manpower for the Northern military.

Lincoln read the proclamation to his cabinet in July 1862 but wanted to issue it after the Union won a battle. He waited until September, when the Battle of Antietam, the bloodiest battle of the war, gave him that opportunity. On September 22, 1862, Lincoln issued the Preliminary Emancipation Proclamation. He was careful to justify emancipation on narrow military grounds, as an action "warranted by the Constitution upon military necessity" and carried out under his powers as commander in chief. To that end, Lincoln believed that he could free slaves only in areas that were currently in rebellion and therefore under martial law. When he issued his Final Emancipation Proclamation on January 1, 1863, he listed those rebellious areas by state and county to ensure that any slave owners who remained loyal to the Union could keep their slaves. The four Border States, West Virginia, Tennessee, and large areas of Virginia and Louisiana that were occupied by the Union army were exempt. The rebellious areas contained 3,083,614 slaves in 1860. The loyal areas that Lincoln exempted contained 838,817 slaves, so twenty-one percent of all slaves were excluded from the emancipation order.

Throughout his presidency, Lincoln believed that he had the power only to free slaves under military necessity, in areas of rebellion, and only temporarily. For these reasons, he supported a constitutional amendment to free slaves throughout the nation, even in the loyal areas. Congress approved the Thirteenth Amendment, freeing all four million slaves, one month before Lincoln died. Throughout his presidency, Lincoln believed that the best way to free the slaves was to win the war and save the Union.

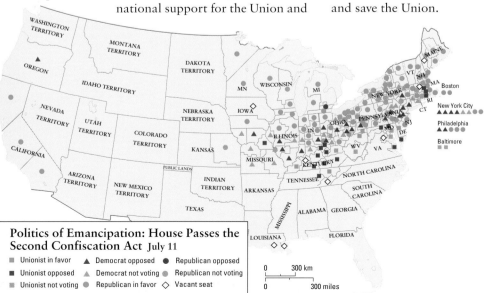

Politics of Emancipation: House Passes the Second Confiscation Act July 11

- ■ Unionist in favor
- ▲ Democrat opposed
- ● Republican opposed
- ■ Unionist opposed
- ▲ Democrat not voting
- ● Republican not voting
- ■ Unionist not voting
- ● Republican in favor
- ◇ Vacant seat

0   300 km
0   300 miles

Slaves per County
c. July 1862

ALABAMA

County	Slaves
Jackson	3,405
De Kalb	848
Madison	14,573
Limestone	8,085
Lauderdale	6,737
Lawrence	6,788
Franklin	8,495
Morgan/Cotaco	3,706
Marshall	1,821
Cherokee	3,002
Blount	666
Winston/Hancock	122
Marion	1,283
Calhoun/Benton	4,342
St Clair	1,768
Walker	519
Jefferson	2,649
Fayette	1,703
Talladega	8,865
Randolph	1,904
Tuscaloosa	10,145
Shelby	3,622
Pickens	12,191
Chambers	11,849
Bibb	3,842
Tallapoosa	6,672
Coosa	5,212
Perry	18,206
Greene	23,598
Russell	15,638
Autauga	9,607
Sumter	18,091
Macon	18,176
Dallas	25,760
Marengo	24,409
Montgomery	23,710
Lowndes	19,340
Wilcox	17,797
Barbour	16,150
Choctaw	7,094
Pike	8,785
Butler	6,818
Henry	4,433
Clarke	7,436
Dale	1,809
Monroe	8,705
Conecuh	4,882
Coffee	1,417
Covington	821
Washington	2,494
Baldwin	3,714
Mobile	11,376

ARKANSAS

County	Slaves
Greene	189
Randolph	359
Lawrence	494
Fulton	88
Marion	261
Carroll	330
Madison	296
Benton	384
Izard	382
Washington	1,493
Searcy	93
Independence	1,337
Mississippi	1,461
Newton	24
Craighead	87
Jackson	2,535
Poinsett	1,086
Van Buren	200
Crawford	858
Pope	978
Johnson	973
Franklin	962
White	1,432
Crittenden	2,347
St Francis	2,621
Conway	802
Sebastian	680
Yell	998
Perry	303
Scott	215
Prairie	2,839
Pulaski	3,505
Phillips	8,941
Monroe	2,226
Saline	749
Montgomery	92
Polk	172
Arkansas	4,921
Hot Spring	613
Jefferson	7,146
Pike	227
Clark	2,214
Desha	3,784
Sevier	3,366
Dallas	3,494
Hempstead	5,398
Bradley	2,690
Ouachita	4,478
Chicot	7,512
Drew	3,497
Calhoun	981
Lafayette	4,311
Columbia	3,599
Ashley	3,761
Union	6,331

DELAWARE

County	Slaves
New Castle	254
Kent	203
Sussex	1,341

FLORIDA

County	Slaves
Nassau	1,612
Jackson	4,902
Duval	1,987
Holmes	112
Columbia	2,063
Walton	441
Bradford/ New River	744
Santa Rosa	1,371
Hamilton	1,397
Escambia	1,961
Madison	4,249
Jefferson	6,374
Leon	9,089
Washington	474
Gadsden	5,409
St Johns	1,003
Suwannee	835
Calhoun	524
Liberty	521
Clay	519
Taylor	125
Lafayette	577
Wakulla	1,167
Putnam	1,047
Alachua	4,457
Franklin	520
Volusia	297
Marion	5,314
Levy	450
Orange/Mosquito	163
Hernando/Benton	?
Sumter	549
Hillsborough	564
Brevard/St Lucie	21
Manatee	253
Monroe-Dade	453

GEORGIA

Rabun	206
Towns	108
Union	116
Fannin	143
Murray	1,442
Whitfield	1,732
Catoosa	710
Walker	1,535
Dade	300
Habersham	787
White	263
Lumpkin	432
Gilmer	167
Franklin	1,313
Hart	1,528
Gordon	2,106
Dawson	326
Banks	1,086
Hall	1,261
Chattooga	2,014
Pickens	246
Elbert	5,711
Jackson	3,329
Madison	1,992
Cherokee	1,199
Bartow/Cass	4,282
Floyd	5,913
Forsyth	890
Milton	617
Wilkes	7,953
Lincoln	3,768
Gwinnett	2,551
Oglethorpe	7,514
Clarke	5,660
Cobb	3,819
Paulding	572
Polk	2,440
Fulton	2,955
Walton	4,621
De Kalb	2,000
Columbia	8,293
Richmond	8,389
Morgan	7,006
Greene	8,398
Taliaferro	2,849
Newton	6,458
Haralson	229
Warren	5,379
Campbell	2,004
Carroll	1,862
Henry	4,515
Clayton	1,226
Hancock	8,137
Fayette	2,019
Burke	12,052
Putnam	7,138
Jasper	6,954
Jefferson	6,045
Glascock	758
Coweta	7,248
Butts	3,067
Washington	6,532
Screven	4,530
Spalding	3,819
Baldwin	4,929
Heard	2,811
Jones	5,989
Monroe	10,177
Pike	4,722
Meriwether	8,748
Troup	10,002
Emanuel	1,294
Wilkinson	3,887
Bibb	6,790
Effingham	2,165
Upson	4,888
Twiggs	5,318
Johnson	849
Bulloch	2,162
Crawford	4,270
Taylor	2,397
Laurens	3,269
Harris	7,736
Houston	10,755
Talbot	8,603
Pulaski	4,106
Macon	4,865
Chatham	14,807
Tattnall	1,157
Montgomery	977
Bryan	2,379
Muscogee	7,445
Liberty	6,083
Marion	3,529
Schley	2,348
Chattahoochee	2,758
Dooly	4,070
Sumter	4,890
Telfair	836
Wilcox	421
Stewart	7,884
Appling	745
Webster	2,287
McIntosh	4,063
Coffee	663
Wayne	621
Irwin	246
Lee	4,947
Worth	632
Randolph	4,467
Terrell	2,888
Quitman	1,625
Glynn	2,839
Pierce	233
Ware	377
Clay	2,253
Dougherty	6,079
Calhoun	2,731
Colquitt	110
Berrien	432
Camden	4,143
Charlton	557
Mitchell	1,589

Baker	3,492
Early	4,057
Clinch	449
Miller	640
Lowndes	2,399
Brooks	3,282
Thomas	6,244
Decatur	5,924
Echols	314

KENTUCKY

Rowan	142
Boone	1,745
Campbell	116
Kenton	567
Greenup	363
Lewis	230
Gallatin	708
Bracken	750
Grant	696
Mason	3,772
Pendleton	424
Carroll	1,045
Boyd	156
Owen	1,660
Carter	309
Trimble	831
Fleming	2,018
Nicholas	1,614
Harrison	3,289
Henry	3,311
Scott	5,744
Lawrence	146
Oldham	2,431
Shelby	6,634
Jefferson	10,304
Montgomery	2,752
Bourbon	6,767
Bath	2,500
Franklin	3,384
Morgan	170
Fayette	10,015
Woodford	5,829
Johnson	27
Clark	4,762
Anderson	1,357
Meade	1,932
Powell	125
Spencer	2,205
Floyd	147
Magoffin	71
Pike	97
Bullitt	1,458
Hardin	2,530
Jessamine	3,698
Madison	6,034
Estill	507
Mercer	3,274
Nelson	5,530
Washington	2,822
Garrard	3,578
Breathitt	190
Breckinridge	2,340
Hancock	818
Livingston	1,222
Henderson	5,767
Knox	489
Russell	559
Caldwell	2,406
Metcalfe	781
Barren	4,078
Owsley	112
Whitley	183
Warren	5,318
Boyle	3,279
Wayne	987
Daviess	3,515
Christian	9,951
Ballard	1,718
Lyon	1,094
McCracken	1,738
Larue	900
Logan	6,356
Marion	3,479
Cumberland	1,413
Jackson	7
Todd	4,849
Perry	73
Clinton	258
Monroe	922
Allen	1,522
Lincoln	3,430
Union	3,105
Rockcastle	357
Trigg	3,448
Ohio	1,292
Simpson	2,307
Marshall	351
Graves	2,845
Grayson	351
Letcher	108
Casey	666
McLean	888
Calloway	1,492
Clay	349
Hickman	1,249
Webster	1,083
Taylor	1,597
Green	2,372
Laurel	186
Hart	1,395
Fulton	1,078
Pulaski	1,330
Hopkins	2,009
Butler	770
Muhlenberg	1,584
Adair	1,607
Crittenden	939
Harlan	127
Edmonson	273

LOUISIANA

Carroll	13,908
Morehouse	6,569
Union	3,745
Claiborne	7,848
Bossier	8,000
Caddo	7,338
Ouachita	2,840
Jackson	4,098
Madison	12,477
Bienville	???
Franklin	3,402
De Soto	8,507
Caldwell	1,945
Tensas	14,592
Winn	1,354
Natchitoches	9,434
Catahoula	6,113
Sabine	1,713
Concordia	12,542
Rapides	15,358
Avoyelles	7,185
Washington	1,690
Pointe Coupee	12,903
St Helena	3,711
East Feliciana	10,593
West Feliciana	9,571
St Landry	11,436
Calcasieu	1,171
St Tammany	1,871
E. Baton Rouge	8,570
Livingston	1,311
W. Baton Rouge	5,340
Iberville	10,680
St Martin	7,358
Ascension	7,376
Lafayette	4,463
St John The Bap.	4,594
St Bernard	2,240
Orleans	14,484
St James	8,090
St Charles	4,182
Vermillion	1,316
Jefferson	5,120
Assumption	8,096
Plaquemines	5,385
Lafourche	6,395
St Mary	13,057
Terrebonne	6,785

MARYLAND

Cecil	950
Harford	1,800
Baltimore	3,182
Carroll	783
Frederick	3,243
Washington	1,435
St Marys	6,549
Kent	2,509
Allegany	666
Queen Annes	4,174
Baltimore City	2,218
Howard	2,862
Anne Arundel	7,332
Montgomery	5,421
Caroline	739
Prince Georges	12,479
Talbot	3,725
Dorchester	4,123
Calvert	4,609
Worcester	3,648
Somerset	5,089
Charles	9,653

MISSISSIPPI

Tishomingo	4,981
Tippah	6,331
Marshall	17,439
De Soto	13,987
Tunica	3,483
Lafayette	7,129
Panola	8,557
Itawamba	3,528
Pontotoc	7,596
Coahoma	5,085
Calhoun	1,823
Yalobusha	9,531
Monroe	12,729
Tallahatchie	5,054
Chickasaw	9,087
Bolivar	9,078
Sunflower	???
Lowndes	16,730
Choctaw	4,197
Oktibbeha	7,631
Carroll	13,808
Washington	???
Noxubee	15,496
Winston	4,223
Holmes	11,975
Attala	5,015
Yazoo	16,716
Kemper	5,741
Neshoba	2,212
Leake	3,056
Issaquena	7,244
Madison	18,113
Lauderdale	5,083
Rankin	7,103
Scott	2,959
Newton	3,379
Warren	13,763
Hinds	22,363
Clarke	5,076
Jasper	4,549
Smith	2,195
Claiborne	12,296
Simpson	2,324
Copiah	7,965
Wayne	1,947
Jones	407
Covington	1,563
Jefferson	12,356
Lawrence	3,656
Adams	14,292
Franklin	4,752
Greene	705
Perry	738
Marion	2,185
Pike	4,935
Amite	7,900
Wilkinson	13,132
Jackson	1,087
Harrison	1,015
Hancock	???

MISSOURI

Scotland	131
Schuyler	39
Putnam	31
Mercer	24
Harrison	25
Gentry	118
Clark	455
Sullivan	102
Adair	86
Knox	284
Lewis	1,279
Grundy	285
Daviess	358
Macon	660
Linn	577
Marion	3,017
Shelby	724
Nodaway	127
Atchison	59
De Kalb	137
Holt	309
Andrew	880
Livingston	605
Clinton	1,144
Ralls	1,791
Caldwell	222
Buchanan	2,011
Chariton	2,839
Monroe	3,021
Pike	4,055
Carroll	1,068
Randolph	2,619
Ray	2,047
Platte	3,313
Saline	4,876
Clay	3,455
Audrain	1,166
Howard	5,886
Lincoln	2,845
Boone	5,034
Lafayette	6,374
Jackson	3,944
Montgomery	1,647
Warren	1,034
St Charles	2,181
Callaway	4,523
Cooper	3,800
St Louis	4,346
Pettis	1,882
Johnson	1,896
Cole	987
Moniteau	745
Morgan	649
Franklin	1,601
Osage	256
Gasconade	76
Cass/Van Buren	1,010
Jefferson	564
Henry/Rives	1,245
Benton	599
Miller	238
Bates	442
Maries	64
Washington	1,028
Crawford	182
Camden	206
Texas	56
Barton	21
Ste Genevieve	617
Phelps	84
Dade	346
St Clair	574
Wright	66
Webster	220
Scott	503
Shannon	13
Greene	1,668
St Francois	877
Jasper	335
Wayne	261
Lawrence	284
Mississippi	1,010
Stoddard	215
Perry	739
Hickory	195
Carter	20
Pulaski	56
Christian	229
Howell	36
Douglas	0
Vernon	136
Newton	426
Butler	52
New Madrid	1,777
Stone	16
Dallas	114
Taney	82
Oregon	26
Barry	247
Laclede	305
Ripley	78
Cedar	211
Dent	156
Ozark	43
Iron	313
Dunklin	171
McDonald	72
Madison	467
Bollinger	245
Cape Girardeau	1,533
Polk	512
Pemiscot	268
Reynolds	38

NORTH CAROLINA

Currituck	2,523
Camden	2,127
Gates	3,901
Hertford	4,445
Pasquotank	2,983
Northampton	6,804
Perquimans	3,558
Warren	10,401
Chowan	3,713
Halifax	10,349
Granville	11,086
Caswell	9,355
Bertie	8,185
Person	5,195
Rockingham	6,318
Stokes	2,469
Tyrrell	1,597
Hyde	2,791
Franklin	7,076
Edgecombe	10,108
Nash	4,680
Surry	1,246
Washington	2,461
Martin	4,309
Alleghany	206
Ashe	391
Orange	5,108
Wilkes	1,208
Alamance	3,445
Wake	10,733
Guilford	3,625
Beaufort	5,878
Yadkin	1,436
Forsyth	1,764
Pitt	8,473
Wilson	3,496
Watauga	104
Davidson	3,076
Chatham	6,246
Johnston	4,916
Davie	2,392
Alexander	611
Randolph	1,645
Greene	3,947
Iredell	4,177
Yancey	362
Caldwell	1,088
Wayne	5,451
Craven	6,189
Rowan	3,930
Lenoir	5,140
Burke	2,371
Madison	213
Harnett	2,584
Catawba	1,664
McDowell	1,305
Moore	2,518
Carteret	1,969
Jones	3,413
Montgomery	1,823
Sampson	7,028
Buncombe	1,933
Duplin	7,124
Cumberland	5,830
Stanly	1,169
Cabarrus	3,040
Lincoln	2,115
Haywood	313
Mecklenburg	6,541
Cleveland	2,131
Rutherford	2,391
Jackson	268
Onslow	3,499
Gaston	2,199
Macon	519
Henderson	1,382
Anson	6,951
Richmond	5,453
Union	2,246
Polk	620
Robeson	5,455
New Hanover	7,103
Lillington	3,228
Cherokee	519
Bladen	5,327
Columbus	2,463
Brunswick	3,631

SOUTH CAROLINA

York	9,984
Spartanburg	8,270
Lancaster	5,650
Union	10,801
Marlboro	6,893
Greenville	7,049
Chesterfield	4,348
Chester	10,868
Pickens	4,195
Marion	9,951
Kershaw	7,841
Darlington	11,877
Anderson	8,425
Laurens	13,200
Horry	2,359
Fairfield	15,534
Newberry	13,695
Sumter	16,682
Lexington	6,202
Abbeville	20,502
Williamsburg	10,259
Richland	11,005
Clarendon	8,566
Edgefield	24,060
Georgetown	18,109
Orangeburg	16,583
Barnwell	17,401
Charleston	37,290
Colleton	32,307
Beaufort	32,530

TENNESSEE

Johnson	233
Sullivan	1,074
Hawkins	1,925
Hancock	246
Carter	374
Claiborne	743
Washington	952
Campbell	366
Scott	59
Fentress	187
Greene	1,297
Overton	1,087
Jackson	1,212
Macon	929
Grainger	1,065
Sumner	7,700
Jefferson	2,096
Robertson	4,861
Union	182
Montgomery	9,554
Stewart	2,406
Anderson	583
Morgan	120
Smith	4,228
Cocke	849
Henry	5,530
Benton	534
Knox	2,370
Cheatham	1,882
Weakley	4,213
Davidson	14,790
Putnam	682
Obion	2,399
Wilson	7,964
Sevier	538
Dickson	2,201
Cumberland	121
Roane	1,748
Humphreys	1,463
De Kalb	1,025
White	1,145
Blount	1,363
Rutherford	12,984
Van Buren	239
Dyer	2,641
Gibson	6,141
Carroll	4,064
Cannon	974
Williamson	12,367
Rhea	615
Monroe	1,600
Warren	2,320
Hickman	1,753
Bledsoe	689
Meigs	638
McMinn	1,909
Maury	14,654
Lauderdale	2,854
Perry	548
Decatur	784
Coffee	1,529
Haywood	11,026
Henderson	3,283
Marshall	4,480
Bedford	6,744
Lewis	247
Madison	10,012
Grundy	266
Hamilton	1,419
Sequatchie	201
Bradley	1,173
Polk	434
Tipton	5,288
Wayne	1,259
Giles	10,848
Marion	678
Lawrence	1,160
Franklin	3,551
Lincoln	6,847
Hardin	1,623
McNairy	1,900
Hardeman	7,236
Fayette	15,473
Shelby	16,953

TEXAS

Van Zandt	322
Fort Bend	4,127
Young	92
Hardeman	0
Clay	0
Montague	35
Baylor	0
Knox	0
Cooke	369
Grayson	1,292
Fannin	1,721
Throckmorton	0
Haskell	0
Wise	128
Jack	50
Denton	251
Collin	1,047
Hunt	577
Cass/Davis	3,476
Jones	0
Tarrant	???
Palo Pinto	130
Shackelford	9
Parker	222
Stephens/Buchanan	32
Dallas	1,074
Kaufman	533
Marion	2,017
Harrison	8,784
Callahan	0
Taylor	0
Bexar	1,395
Eastland	0
Erath	118
Johnson	513
El Paso	15
Ellis	1,104
Panola	3,048
Henderson	1,116
Navarro	1,890
Bosque	293
Comanche	61
Hill	650
Coleman	0
Runnels	0
Brown	0
Hamilton	26
Freestone	3,613
Shelby	1,476
McLennan	2,395
Limestone	1,072
Coryell	306
Presidio	4
Concho	0
San Augustine	1,717
Sabine	1,150
San Saba	89
McCulloch	0
Lampasas	153
Falls	1,716
Robertson	2,258
Bell	1,005
Menora	0
Jasper	1,611
Newton	1,013
Milam	1,542
Tyler	1,148
Llano	54
Mason	18
Burnet	235
Brazos	1,063
Williamson	891
Kimble	0
Burleson	2,003
Travis	3,136
Gillespie	33
Hardin	191
Blanco	???
Kerr	49
Edwards	0
Bastrop	2,591
Washington	7,951
Hays	797
Orange	392
Jefferson	309
Fayette	3,786
Comal	193
Caldwell	1,610
Bandera	12
Colorado	3,559
Guadalupe	1,748
Dawson	0
Uvalde	27
Medina	106
Gonzales	3,168
Kinney	0
Lavaca	1,707
Wharton	2,734
De Witt	1,643
Atascosa	107
Zavala	0
Matagorda	2,107
Karnes	327
Jackson	1,194
Maverick	1
Frio	2
Victoria	1,413
Red River	3,039
Lamar	2,833
Goliad	843
Dimmit	0
Live Oak	85
Bee	79
McMullen	0
La Salle	0
Calhoun	414
Bowie	2,651
Webb	0
Duval	0
San Patricio	95
Encinal	0
Nueces	216
Refugio	234
Hopkins	990
Titus	2,438
Zapata	0
Starr	6
Hidalgo	1
Cameron	7
Upshur	3,794
Wood	1,005
Smith	4,982
Rusk	6,132
Cherokee	3,246
Anderson	3,668
Nacogdoches	2,359
Leon	2,620
Houston	2,819
Angelina	686
Trinity	959
Madison	675
Walker	4,135
Polk	4,198
Grimes	5,468
Montgomery	2,811
Liberty	1,079
Austin	3,914
Harris	2,053
Chambers	513
Brazoria	5,110
Galveston	1,520

VIRGINIA

Wood	176
Hancock	2
Brooke	18
Ohio	100
Rockingham	2,387
Wirt	23
Stafford	3,314
Marshall	29
Morgan	94
Berkeley	1,650
Culpeper	6,675
Hampshire	1,213
Calhoun	9
Jefferson	3,960
Preston	67
Monongalia	101
Madison	4,397
Wetzel	10
King George	3,673
Braxton	104
Frederick	2,259
Loudoun	5,501
Marion	63
Accomack	4,507
Spotsylvania	7,786
Webster	3
Orange	6,111
Clarke	3,375
Tyler	18
Taylor	112
Westmoreland	3,704
Hardy	1,073
Fairfax	3,116
Harrison	582
Greene	1,984
Doddridge	34
Pocahontas	252
Arlington/Alexand	1,386
Pleasants	15
Shenandoah	753
Barbour	95
Tucker	20
Caroline	10,672
Warren	1,575
Highland	402
Fauquier	10,455
Prince William	2,356
Ritchie	38
Essex	6,696
Augusta	5,616
Richmond	2,466
Randolph	183
Clay	21
Rappahannock	3,520
Lewis	230
Upshur	212
Northumberland	3,439
Pendleton	244
Gilmer	52
Page	850
Nicholas	154
Albemarle	13,916
Jackson	55
Louisa	10,194
Mason	376
Roane	72
King And Queen	6,139
Lancaster	2,869
Bath	946
Hanover	9,483
King William	5,525
Putnam	580
Middlesex	2,375
Fluvanna	4,994
Kanawha	2,184
Cabell	305
Gloucester	5,736
Greenbrier	1,525
Northampton	3,872
Goochland	6,139
Nelson	6,238
Fayette	271
Rockbridge	3,985
Henrico	20,041
Wayne	143
New Kent	3,374
Mathews	3,008
Cumberland	6,705
Buckingham	8,811
Amherst	6,278
Chesterfield	8,354
Boone	158
Logan	148
Alleghany	990
Powhatan	5,403
Charles City	2,947
James City	2,586
Botetourt	2,769
York	1,925
Amelia	7,655
Raleigh	57
Appomattox	4,600
Warwick	1,019
Bedford	10,176
Prince George	4,997
Monroe	1,114
Surry	2,515
Craig	420
Elizabeth City	2,417
Mercer	362
Prince Edward	7,341
Dinwiddie	12,774
Campbell	11,580
Isle Of Wight	3,570
Nottoway	6,468
Sussex	6,384
Princess Anne	3,186
Norfolk	9,004
Giles	778
Southampton	5,408
Charlotte	9,238
Nansemond	5,481
Roanoke	2,643
Wyoming	64
Lunenburg	7,305
Montgomery	2,219
Brunswick	9,146
Franklin	6,351
Greensville	4,167
Halifax	14,897
Pittsylvania	14,340
Pulaski	1,589
Tazewell	1,202
Floyd	475
Mecklenburg	12,420
Wythe	2,162
Henry	5,018
Patrick	2,070
Carroll	262
Smyth	1,037
McDowell	0
Grayson	547
Lee	824
Buchanan	30
Wise	66
Russell	1,099
Scott	490
Washington	2,547

FREDERICKSBURG

Upon relieving McClellan of command of the Army of the Potomac, Lincoln appointed Ambrose Burnside in his place. Burnside protested that he did not feel competent for the task, but Lincoln assumed Burnside was merely being modest. Indeed modesty was among the general's many good qualities. He was also loyal, honest, brave, and competent within his limits. Unfortunately, commanding an army lay outside those limits. Burnside knew that Lincoln expected prompt action; so on November 15 he put the army in motion toward Fredericksburg, Virginia. Burnside's plan was to move quickly, cross the Rappahannock River at Fredericksburg before Lee's army could arrive there, then press southward and get between Lee and Richmond.

The left wing of the Army of the Potomac crossed the Rappahannock River on the twin pontoon spans, shown above, built under fire by Burnside's engineers.

By November 17 about one-third of Burnside's army was at Falmouth, Virginia, on the north bank of the Rappahannock opposite Fredericksburg. Lee's troops were not yet present in force, and a river crossing was quite feasible. However, the Army of the Potomac's pontoon train had lagged behind. So while the Army of Northern Virginia marched rapidly toward Fredericksburg, the growing strength of the Army of the Potomac sat down and waited on Stafford Heights above Falmouth, north of Fredericksburg.

Lieutenant General James Longstreet's corps of Lee's army arrived at Fredericksburg on November 19 and took up positions on the hills south of the town. Lee arrived the next day, surveyed the situation, and sent orders for Jackson's corps to leave its camps around Winchester, Virginia, in the Shenandoah Valley, and march at once to Fredericksburg. While Jackson's men marched, operations around Fredericksburg continued to unfold with almost surreal slowness. On November 21, Burnside summoned the mayor of Fredericksburg to surrender the town. The mayor refused. Burnside warned that he would bombard Fredericksburg and gave sixteen hours

to evacuate the women and children. The mayor asked for more time, and the Federals agreed. The long line of guns on Stafford Heights remained silent throughout the closing days of November. Burnside conferred with Lincoln during those days but rejected the president's suggestion of a turning movement, preferring instead a head-on assault at Fredericksburg.

All the troops of both armies were on hand, and had been for some days, when on December 11 Burnside finally launched his grand offensive. His engineers attempted to lay a pontoon bridge across the Rappahannock but were repeatedly driven off by rifle fire from a Confederate brigade inside Fredericksburg itself. The Union batteries finally opened, battering the historic town but failing to dislodge the Rebels. Union infantry then made a cross-river assault in pontoon boats and succeeded in driving off the defenders, who fell back to join the rest of Lee's army on the heights south of town. The engineers then laid their pontoon bridges without hindrance and Burnside's army began crossing. All that day and the next, troops marched across the swaying bridges.

On December 13, Burnside sent his troops forward to drive Lee off the heights. On the Union left troops under Major General George G. Meade found a flaw in Jackson's lines and briefly broke through. Intense fighting raged as Jackson's men rallied and drove the Federals back out of their lines. Meade might have been able to win the battle there, if he had been reinforced.

Instead, Burnside concentrated his effort on the Union right, across a broad, gently sloping plain that led from the town to the foot of a ridge known as Marye's Heights. It was a splendid field of fire, every inch of it amply covered by Confederate artillery on the heights as well as infantry dug in behind a stone wall in a sunken lane at the foot of the heights. A drainage ditch crossed the field in such a way as to allow the advance of only one Union brigade at a time and then only directly toward the strongest part of the Confederate defenses. All day long Burnside hurled his troops forward in charges that did not have the remotest chance of success. Brigade after brigade performed prodigies of valor only to be slaughtered in front of the stone wall.

That night Burnside considered continuing the butchery the next day, but his generals dissuaded him. Lee had hoped he would do so, planning then to follow up with an attack of his own against the bloodied Army of the Potomac, trapping it with its back to the river. Instead, the Federals withdrew to the north bank of the Rappahannock on the night of December 14–15. Union casualties for the Battle of Fredericksburg came to twelve thousand six hundred and fifty-three out of its total strength of 114,000. The Army of Northern Virginia, with a strength of seventy-two thousand five hundred men, lost five thousand three hundred and nine. Union morale plunged to new depths.

1. December 11, 7:00 a.m.: Brigadier General William Barksdale's Confederate brigade took shelter in the houses of Fredericksburg and fired on Union engineers attempting to construct pontoon bridges over the Rappahannock.

2. December 11: Union artillery on Stafford Heights bombarded Fredericksburg, attempting to drive Barksdale's men out of the town.

3. December 11: Union troops finally succeeded in a cross-river assault in pontoon boats and drove out Barksdale's men in house-to-house fighting, allowing the engineers to finish their bridges.

4. December 13: Using two guns until one of them was disabled Major John Pelham frequently changed positions and held up the Union advance on the southern flank until he ran out of ammunition.

5. December 13, noon–2:30 p.m.: The Union left wing attacked and briefly broke through the defenders' line before a Confederate counterattack drove them back.

6. December 13, 10:00 a.m.–5:00 p.m.: The Union right wing made twelve different frontal assaults across an open field toward an impregnable Confederate position, suffering massive casualties, inflicting few, and failing to accomplish anything.

Battle of Fredericksburg
December 11–13

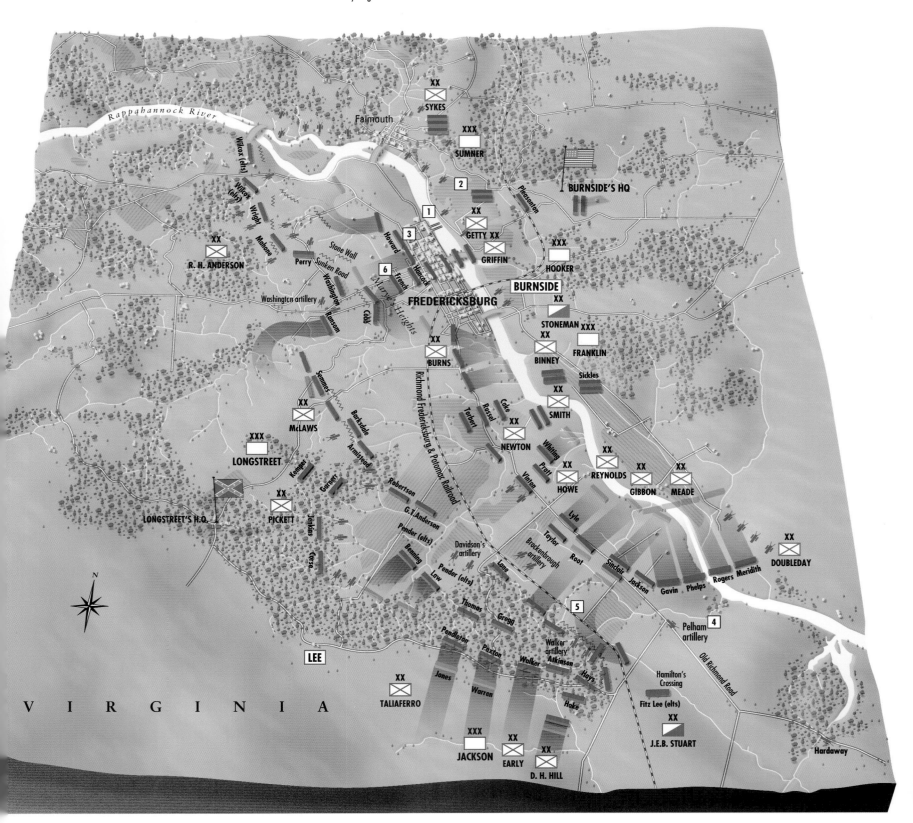

MURFREESBORO (STONE'S RIVER)

IN THE LATE FALL OF 1862, the Lincoln administration was impatient to see significant progress on the fighting fronts. Like the other newly assigned generals that fall, William S. Rosecrans, commanding the Army of the Cumberland, knew the president expected an early and vigorous advance from his base at Nashville, Tennessee.

General Braxton Bragg, commanding the Confederate Army of Tennessee, had his own problems with presidential authority. In December 1862, Confederate president Jefferson Davis made an inspection tour of his western armies, including Bragg's base at Murfreesboro, Tennessee. Deeply concerned about the threat to his home state of Mississippi, Davis ordered Bragg to detach ten thousand infantry (about one-fourth of his total), and send them to reinforce Lieutenant General John C. Pemberton in the Magnolia State. The Chattanooga *Daily Rebel*—with the lax security of information typical of the day—promptly reported the movement.

known as Stone's River angled across the prospective battlefield in broad meanders, passing through the right-center of the Confederate line and around the left flank of the Union line. About a quarter of the Confederate battle line lay on the east side of the river, the remainder on the west. Ironically, each general planned to attack the other's right on the morning of December 31 and massed his army accordingly. Bragg's army was afoot earlier and struck first, flanking and crumpling the thinly held Union right, the corps of Major General Alexander McCook.

Throughout the morning, Rosecrans attempted to adjust to the unexpected attack while his army fought desperately to stay the Confederate onslaught. The division of Major General Philip H. Sheridan put up a stout fight, winning valuable time before it was finally overwhelmed and forced back. By afternoon Bragg's troops had bent the Union right wing backward ninety degrees. The Army of the Cumberland's right was

The scene above comes from Private Mathews's sketches and shows Union reinforcements arriving on the line.

Among the most interested readers of the *Daily Rebel* was Rosecrans, who saw in Bragg's movement an opportunity to make the advance Lincoln expected. On December 26, his Army of the Cumberland marched out of Nashville heading toward Murfreesboro, about thirty miles away. After several days of skirmishing, on December 30, the Army of the Cumberland arrived in front of the Army of Tennessee's lines just northwest of Nashville.

Rosecrans's line of advance and supply was the Nashville Pike, which ran perpendicularly through the center of both armies on its course from Nashville to Murfreesboro. A shallow stream

now composed of survivors of the earlier debacle, pioneer troops, and units drawn off from the proposed attack on the left. This ad hoc collection of units formed a line running parallel and just in front of the vital Nashville Pike. Yet here, only a few scores yards short of cutting Rosecrans's line of communication, the Confederate attack had finally spent itself. Exhausted, overextended, and thinned by casualties, the Confederates were unable to break this last line. Intense fighting raged around a patch of woods known as the Round Forest, at the angle of the Union line, but the Federal position held.

Bragg desperately needed reinforcements, but the only uncommitted troops he had left belonged to the division of Major General John C. Breckinridge, on the east side of Stone's River. When Bragg ordered him to bring his division across the river and join the attack, Breckinridge was in a state of confusion about false reports of Union troops somewhere out beyond his right flank. None were there, but Breckinridge was so anxious about the imaginary threat that he long delayed obeying Bragg's order. When he did obey, he sent his brigades piecemeal, one or two at a time. On this short winter afternoon, it was by then too late to send the fresh brigades all the way around the battlefield to attack along the Nashville Pike, so, as fast as the brigades arrived, Bragg committed them to attacks on the Round Forest—without success.

On January 1, 1863, the armies remained in position without any major fighting. The following day,

Union forces occupied a hill on the east bank of Stone's River that gave them a significant tactical advantage, and Bragg ordered Breckinridge to take it from them. Breckinridge's division charged and took the hill but became disorganized and overpursued, advancing to a position near the river in which they were exposed to devastating Union artillery fire. Driven back with heavy losses, they were unable to hold the hill against a Union counterattack.

Late that night, Bragg's generals came to him demanding that the Army of Tennessee retreat. Bragg at first demurred, but his generals were insistent, and he finally gave in. The Confederates marched southeast and within a few days took up a position at Tullahoma about thirty-five miles from Murfreesboro. Total casualties for the Battle of Stone's River were twelve thousand nine hundred and six Union and eleven thousand nine hundred and thirty-nine Confederate.

Murfreesboro (Stone's River)
December 31 – January 2

[1] December 31, a.m.: Hardee slams into McCook's corps and routs Johnson, but Union resistance stiffens, slowing Hardee's attack. Bragg orders Polk to reinforce Hardee.

[2] 6:10 a.m.: Van Cleve's Union division crosses the river, but frantic pleas from McCook for help forces Rosecrans to redeploy entire army to meet massive Confederate attack.

[3] 10:00 a.m.–12 noon: Hardee and Polk force McCook back to pike. Sheridan holds Nashville Pike and Federals rally. Unionist corps of Thomas and Crittenden check Confederate advance.

[4] January 2: Bragg switches assault to strike Union left but is beaten back by overwhelming firepower at river crossing.

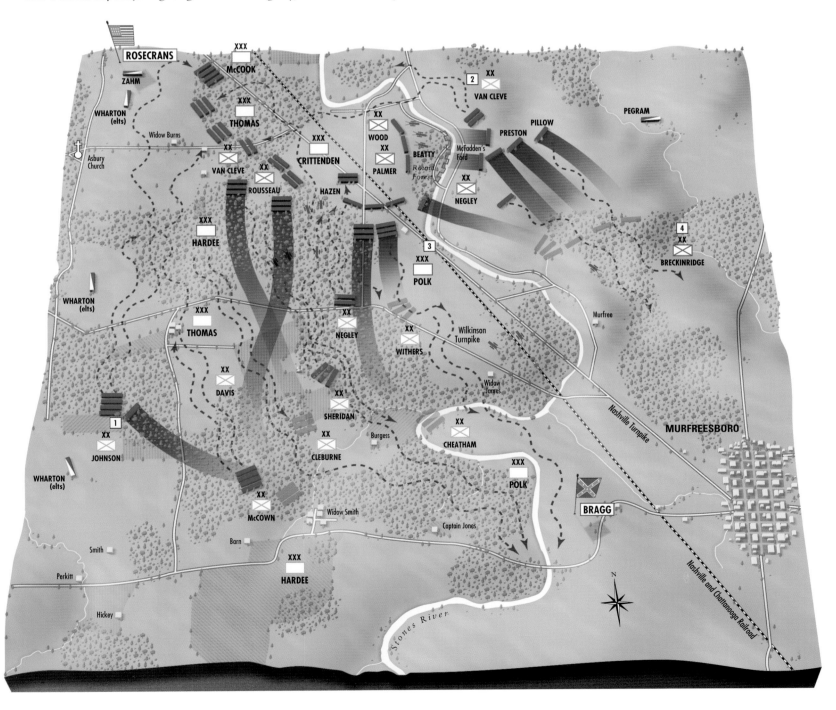

TACTICS, STRATEGY, AND ENGINEERS

To bring a battery of six 12-pounder cannon into action would require the efforts of around 170 men. The 12-pounder was the mainstay of both the Union and the Confederate armies.

MILITARY TACTICS WERE IN A STATE of transition during the Civil War. In the days of Napoleon and before, troops had stood in lines or columns in the open and had marched in these "close order" formations to within very close range of their enemies, often charging them with the bayonet. Such tactics were make more difficult in the Civil War because of a technological advance in the 1850s. Captain Claude Minié of the French Garde Nationale invented a new type of bullet, called the "Minié ball," which allowed accurate, long-range rifles to be loaded as quickly and easily as inaccurate, short-range muskets. With the use of the Minié ball, the effective range of infantry fire increased from one hundred to approximately three hundred and fifty yards, and the fire became much more deadly within that range.

Civil War field artillery was fired by "direct laying," pointing the gun precisely at the target.

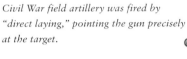

By 1863, most Civil War soldiers on both sides were carrying Minié-type rifles. This drastically strengthened the defender and increased the cost of the old tactics. Closing with the enemy in elbow-to-elbow line sometimes came to seem almost suicidal. The effect was multiplied when defending troops built breastworks or dug trenches for protection, as they did almost constantly after about the middle of 1863. The problem of the more deadly battlefield was obvious, but how to change tactics to cope with it was not. In 1864, Union Colonel Emory Upton responded with what amounted to a tactical throwback, having his troops charge in a dense column and rely on their bayonets. Other officers from time to time experimented with having their soldiers fight from a prone position and in "open" or skirmish order, in which individual soldiers were several yards apart.

Cannons firing case shot into advancing enemy infantry could have a devastating effect as long as the gun crews' nerve held against incoming gunfire.

Because the tactical problem was never completely solved during the Civil War, generals had to rely on skillful use of operations to compensate for tactical futility. On the operational level, generals maneuvered units of several thousand men each across an area larger than an individual battlefield—for example, the Shenandoah Valley in Virginia or the part of the state of Mississippi between Vicksburg and Jackson. Important concepts in the operational art of the Civil War were: 1) massing an overwhelming force against a portion of the enemy's army, 2) occupying geographic positions of great strength, 3) threatening the enemy's lines of supply, communications, and retreat, preferably without exposing one's own, and 4) striking the enemy's linear formations in the flank, where they were weakest.

At the highest level of command, generals and

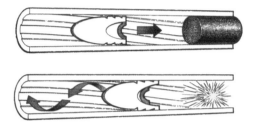

The Minié Principle: the bullet is rammed back to the charge. On firing the bullet is sent spiraling down the barrel, expanding and gripping the grooves in an air-tight fit propelling the bullet with increased accuracy.

their respective commanders-in-chief practiced strategy, attempting to use the accomplishments of operations and tactics to achieve the nation's goals in the larger war. Strategic questions faced by the two sides might have included: What invasion routes offer the best access to the southern heartland? Is quick victory more likely east of the Appalachian Mountains, or west of them? Can any decisive results be achieved west of the Mississippi River?

One of the most important strategic concepts of the Civil War was the idea of interior lines. The side that had interior lines was the side that had the more centralized, compact position, with its enemy spread out around it in exterior lines. This was exactly the South's situation, and during the first two years of the war Confederate leaders made use of interior lines to shift troops rapidly from one threatened point to another before Union commanders, operating on longer exterior lines, could respond in kind. A good example of this would be the transfer of about ten thousand troops from the Army of Northern Virginia to the Army of Tennessee in the late summer of 1863. The Union eventually overcame this difficulty by means of its superior rail lines, thus allowing more rapid transport even over longer distances, and by coordinating simultaneous offenses on every front, thus leaving the Confederates no unengaged troops to transfer.

Cadets at West Point during the decades before the Civil War received relatively little instruction in tactics, operations, and strategy but a great deal in the area of military engineering. Partially this was because the leading military thinker of the area,

Under the cover of darkness these troops begin to dig zigzag trenches toward the enemy positions. Ahead of them they push a "sap-roller" to protect themselves from enemy fire until the trench, or sap, was deep enough to give the necessary cover.

Swiss author Antoine Henri de Jomini, tended to see warfare was an exercise in geometry. In its forms most practical for the waging of war, military engineering taught officers how to assess terrain and how it would affect their operations, how to identify a strong position, and how best to attack it if the enemy held the desirable terrain. At the heart of Civil War era, military engineering was siegecraft, the art of taking a strongly fortified enemy position by "regular approaches." Following a well-defined system, the attacking general and his engineer officers had their troops dig zigzag trenches closer and closer to the fortifications, using purpose-built "sap-rollers" to protect them from defensive fire. They used gabions (elongated wicker baskets packed with earth or other dense substances) to build up their new positions.

Given enough time and strength, regular approaches offered a general the nearest thing to absolute certainty that he was ever likely to get in war. Eventually, the approach trenches would lead to the construction of close-range gun emplacements, which would allow the besieger to batter the fortifications to pieces and easily take the position by storm. Defenders never waited for that final blow to fall but surrendered first. With its certainty and mathematical precision, siegecraft appealed to unaggressive generals such as George B. McClellan who unnecessarily utilized it at Yorktown in 1862. The most successful siege of the war, however, was carried out by its most aggressive general, Ulysses S. Grant, at Vicksburg in 1863.

A detailed drawing of Fort Sedgwick, a Union strong point, at Petersburg, known to the troops as Fort Hell. It sat opposite the Confederate Fort Mahone, nicknamed Fort Damnation. One of Meade's staff officers described how such forts were built: "The mass throw up earth; the engineer soldiers do the 'revetting,' that is the interior facing of logs. The engineer sergeants run about with tapes and stakes, measuring busily; and the engineer officers look as wise as possible and superintend."

THE STATE OF THE CONFEDERACY, THE NATION, AND ITS ARMY

FACING SO MANY DEFICIENCIES in resources—manpower, arms, materiel, transport, and even food—the Confederacy's top priority was mobilization. During its first year, the Confederate government exploited its few advantages brilliantly to mount a surprisingly effective defensive war.

To start off, the southern cause attracted an outstanding corps of military leaders—about thirty percent of the U.S. Army's officers. The War Office dispatched them to locally based departments to mobilize and lead volunteers throughout the Confederacy. The South's mobilization rate, in fact, ran nearly double that of the Union but still could not offset the North's three-to-one advantage in manpower. Supplementing the regular army, guerrilla bands operated throughout the Border States and Upper South early in the war and ranged behind enemy lines as the Union advanced southward. These military advantages produced initial victories that ushered in a long war, which favored the South strategically but eventually demanded an even greater mobilization of resources. In fact, many of the South's early military victories were Pyrrhic costing the Confederacy more casualties than they inflicted on the Union.

In February 1862, President Jefferson Davis handed a tall order to the Confederate Congress. To fight the Union indefinitely, the Confederacy had to double the size of its army, procure 750,000 more small arms and five thousand more artillery pieces, and build fifty ironclad ships. Answering this challenge, Congress passed a conscription law that drafted able-bodied men aged eighteen to thirty-five into the Confederate Army for three years. Balancing the need for soldiers against demands for materiel, Congress exempted workers in crucial war industries, such as mining, steel, and transportation. Congress also recognized slavery as essential to the Confederate war effort and passed the "twenty-slave law" that exempted from the draft the owner or overseer on any plantation with twenty or more slaves. Encouraging and coordinating guerrilla activities, Congress incorporated ranger companies as official units in the Confederate Army. The South also launched its first ironclad attack in March when the *Virginia* met the *Monitor* off Norfolk, Virginia.

Despite the *Virginia*'s failure, the Confederacy went on to build a total of thirty-seven armored warships. Even more important were the blockade-runners that smuggled arms into the Confederacy with a ninety percent success rate during the first year of the war. Arms production fell to Colonel Josiah Gorgas, chief of the Ordnance Bureau. Gorgas reorganized the bureau in the spring of 1862 to provide greater government oversight of war industries, set up a system of armories and arsenals, and managed to double arms production during the next year, before shortages set in. Of course, the Confederacy had to pay for all these initiatives. The Confederate Congress tried to avoid taxes and, with its small tax base, could meet only five percent of its revenue needs through taxation, in any event. Instead, about thirty-five percent of Confederate revenues came from loans and sixty percent from paper money. These Confederate dollars depreciated immediately, producing a modest inflation of thirty-five percent during the first year of the war but five hundred percent by the end of 1862.

This initial burst of morale and mobilization, the legislation that cut deeply into the South's ever scarcer resources, and initial victories in the eastern theater temporarily masked the Confederacy's long-term strategic disadvantages. In the spring of 1862, as General Robert E. Lee made plans to lead his army northward toward the Potomac, the long war of attrition that would favor the North and wear down the South was only beginning.

A Confederate artillery unit photographed near Charleston, South Carolina. Despite the efforts of Colonel Josiah Gorgas, chief of the Ordnance Bureau, in stepping up and organizing armaments production, the Confederate Army continued to be bedevilled by shortages.

Below: C.S.S. Merrimack engages U.S.S. Monitor. Although the Merrimack was unsuccessful the Confederacy went on to build thirty-seven armored warships.

THE STATE OF THE NORTH, THE NATION, AND ITS ARMY

THE SPRING OF 1862 WAS THE low point for the Union. In the eastern theater, the Peninsular campaign, designed to strike a fatal blow against the Confederacy through the capture of Richmond, had failed. General George McClellan's Army of the Potomac had approached within five miles of the Confederate capital but withdrew after the brutal Battle of Seven Pines—known as the Battle of Fair Oaks in the North. More ominous, the Confederate commander, General Joseph E. Johnston, was wounded at Seven Pines, and General Robert E. Lee assumed command of the Army of Northern Virginia. Lee launched a series of characteristically aggressive counter-strikes against McClellan's army as it retreated, producing the horrible bloodletting of the Seven Days' Battles. The thirty-six thousand casualties heralded a long and brutal war. Lee was now poised to move northward toward Bull Run, for the second time, and Antietam.

The western theater provided the only ray of hope for the beleaguered Union military during the spring of 1862. The Union was making inroads into West Tennessee, under the forceful leadership of General Ulysses S. Grant, and Louisiana, preparing a campaign to control and capture the Mississippi River and cut the Confederacy in two. With casualties mounting and the Confederacy clearly in command of the eastern theater, however, northern morale reached a wartime low. When President Abraham Lincoln called for 300,000 more men to replenish the ranks, the response was disappointing, and the U.S. Congress instituted a draft to meet enlistment quotas. Cities, states, and eventually the federal government began paying "bounties" to encourage men to volunteer.

Meanwhile, critics of the war effort assailed Lincoln from opposite directions. The Democratic Party split into two wings, with War Democrats supporting a vigorous prosecution of the war and Peace Democrats opposed. Dubbed "Copperheads," the Peace Democrats favored negotiation and compromise to end the war, restore the Union, and keep slavery intact. At the other extreme, a growing minority of Radical Republicans, in both Congress and the Union Army, supported emancipation as a new war aim. They argued that freeing the South's slaves would undermine the Confederate war effort while adding a new moral urgency to the war

Lincoln, however, insisted on the Union as his paramount war aim and continued to deny that he had the constitutional authority to free any slaves. Meanwhile, African Americans by the thousands freed themselves and poured across Union lines. Defined legally as "contraband of war," these fugitive slaves or "Contrabands" went to work for the Union Army and forced a decision about their status. Republicans in Congress sent a clear signal in March 1862 by prohibiting U.A. Army officers from returning fugitive slaves to their owners, under penalty of court martial. A month later, Congress abolished slavery in the District of Columbia and gave African Americans basic civil rights.

When Union generals began emancipating slaves, however, Lincoln drew the line. Standing on the principle of Union as his war aim, Lincoln rescinded the emancipation orders. Congress responded by passing a Confiscation Act declaring all fugitive slaves "forever free." By the spring of 1862, however, Lincoln himself agreed that slavery must end and that emancipation would speed Union victory. His initial plan proposed gradual, voluntary emancipation in the Border States as a way to pave the way toward freedom. When Border State representatives rejected his plan, however, Lincoln decided to issue an emancipation proclamation. As Lee's army moved northward, he began to draft his announcement, which he considered "an act of justice, warranted by the Constitution, upon military necessity," but decided to wait for a victory before issuing it. Through the long summer, Lincoln—and the nation—waited.

Freed slaves or "contrabands" liberated by the Union Army. This particular group, clad partly in old Union uniforms, was organized as teamsters in the Union chain of supply.

A 12-pounder howitzer gun captured by Butterfield's brigade near Hanover Court House on May 27, 1862.

THE COST OF WAR

B Y THE END OF 1862, BOTH the Union and the Confederacy were heavily mobilized for war. The illusions of a brief and relatively bloodless war had disappeared in the confusion of the First Battle of Bull Run and were utterly shattered by the demoralizing Union retreat during the Peninsula campaign. Both sides had spent the first six months of the war mobilizing and organizing their armies and struggling to take control of the Border States.

The Union Army grew more than ten times in size from a peacetime force of sixteen thousand men to 186,000 by mid-1861. The high enlistments of volunteers that characterized 1861 fell off after the bloodletting of the Seven Days' Battle, so Congress passed the Militia Act, the first draft in U.S. history, in July 1862. President Lincoln called for a total of 600,000 troops to serve for nine months, and the army more than tripled in size during 1862.

The Confederate Army grew from scratch to about 112,000 men by the middle of 1861. When the initial round of one-year volunteers ran out in the spring of 1862, the Confederate Congress instituted the South's first draft. The Confederacy had fewer men to mobilize than the Union, so their draftees had to serve for three years. The one hundred and fifty-six battles that took place dur-

ing 1861 represented only seven percent of the war's total engagements but gave the Union crucial control over Missouri, Kentucky, Maryland, and western Virginia. The number of engagements in 1862 mushroomed to five hundred and sixty-four, an average of 1.5 per day. Already by the end of 1862, the North and South had fought one-third of the entire war's engagements. During these first two years of war, sixty percent of all the engagements took place in the Upper South.

During 1861 and 1862, about one-fifth of all the battles occurred in Missouri alone, where the Union Army fought to keep the state in the Union and quell guerrilla campaigns. Tennessee, Kentucky, and Virginia each hosted about one-tenth of all the engagements. As the scale of war escalated, forty major battles inflicted more than 300,000 casualties (killed, missing, or wounded), even before the commencement of the "total" or "hard" war of later years. Despite having fewer men at arms, the Confederacy suffered more casualties than the Union during these initial years, a situation that held true until the North began its last, big push to end the war early in 1864.

The Battle of Antietam in September 1862 exemplified these patterns of engagement and casualties

Above: *This small group of slaves, photographed at Hilton Head, South Carolina in May 1862, together with all other slaves in the South, would see their lives transformed when Lincoln issued his Preliminary Emancipation Proclamation declaring that all slaves in areas still in rebellion against U.S. authority, as of January 1, 1863, would be forever free.*

Left: *Men whose names would appear on the terrible casualty list at Antietam lie dead near the Dunker Church. More Americans died in this engagement than on any other single day in American military history.*

during the first two years of war. Like most of the battles during this early period, Antietam took place in the Upper South. Fought in Union territory—Maryland—Antietam was the culmination of one of General Robert E. Lee's most important offensive campaigns against the North. Pitting Lee's Army of Northern Virginia against General George McClellan's Army of the Potomac, the battle inflicted more casualties than any other engagement in the Civil War. Indeed, more Americans died in the battle than on any other single day in the nation's military history. Confederate casualties were nearly double the Union losses, but Lee's army slipped back across the Potomac, resulting in a draw. Lincoln, however, seized on this opportunity to issue his Preliminary Emancipation Proclamation, transforming the war into a campaign for liberation and raising the stakes for both sides.

Overall, 1861 and 1862 introduced the nation to the kinds of hideous losses that this war could inflict, focused on the Upper South as both sides maneuvered for strategic advantage, initiated conscription into both armies, provoked a new war aim, and hurt the Confederacy worse than the Union.

1863
THE TURNING OF THE TIDE

Morale in Union armies and on the home front reached a new low in the early months of 1863. Desertion rates rose, and many soldiers believed the war was no longer worth the cost in lives and resources. "All think Virginia is not worth such a loss of life," wrote one soldier in the Army of the Potomac. "Why not confess we are worsted, and some to an agreement?" The staunch pro-war editor of the *Chicago Tribune* Joseph Medill, wrote glumly that "an armistice is bound to come during the year '63. The rebs can't be conquered by the present machinery." Some soldiers growled that the Emancipation Proclamation had changed the purpose of the war from restoring the Union to abolishing slavery—a goal for which they were not willing to risk their lives. In the Army of the Potomac, according to a New York captain, men "say it has turned into a 'nigger war' and all are anxious to return to their homes for it was to preserve the Union that they volunteered."

Things got worse for the North before they got better. The enactment of conscription in March provoked anti-draft riots in several communities—most notably in New York City in July,

when mobs controlled the city for several days before being put down by police and soldiers with a loss of at least 120 lives. In the Mississippi Valley thousands of Union soldiers fell sick and hundreds died in the Louisiana swamps as Grant seemed to be floundering in his campaign against Vicksburg. Lincoln had to fight off pressure to remove Grant from command as a drunkard and a failure. In Virginia, General Joseph Hooker replaced Ambrose Burnside as commander of the Army of the Potomac. Hooker revived morale and at the end of April launched a campaign against the Army of Northern Virginia along the Rappahannock River that initially promised success. But Lee stopped a befuddled Hooker in his tracks and then drove the Yankees back across the river in another humiliating defeat. "My God, My God!" said Lincoln when he heard the news. "What will the country say?" It said plenty, all bad. The anti-war Peace Democrats in the North (stigmatized as "Copperheads" by the Republicans) stepped up their campaign to bring about a cease-fire. Lee decided to use his victory at Chancellorsville as a springboard to invade the North again,

The eighth U.S. Infantry Provost Guard at the headquarters of the Army of the Potomac, June 1863.

hoping to complete a one-two punch by another victory to knock the North out of the war.

But in early July came two virtually simultaneous events that turned the war around full circle. At the crossroads town of Gettysburg in Pennsylvania on July 1–3 the Army of the Potomac finally bested its enemy in a battle that sent the crippled Army of Northern Virginia limping back to its namesake state after suffering at least twenty-five thousand casualties. In Mississippi, Grant accepted the surrender of thirty thousand Confederate soldiers at Vicksburg on the Fourth of July. During the rest of the summer, Union forces in Louisiana, Arkansas, and Tennessee also advanced. After a

An illustration of the gallant charge made by two companies of the Sixth Michigan rearguard on the Confederates near Falling Water, where part of the Army of the Northern Virginia had withdrawn on July 12, after the Battle of Gettysburg.

setback at the bloody Battle of Chickamauga in northern Georgia on September 19–20, Union troops routed the enemy at Chattanooga two months later and sent them in pell-mell retreat. Republicans won decisive victories in off-year state elections that constituted an endorsement of Lincoln's war policies including emancipation. The year 1863, in contrast to the two previous years, ended with high hopes in the North and gloom in the South. "The crisis which threatened the friends of the Union is past," said Lincoln in his message to Congress on December 8, and a Confederate official wrote in his diary: "I have never actually despaired of the cause, but now steadfastness is yielding to a sense of hopelessness."

THE CAMPAIGNS OF 1863

The Battle of Stone's River was fought during the last days of 1862 and the first days of 1863. In the illustration above, General James S. Negley's division attacks across Stone's River.

THE YEAR 1863 OPENED WITH Sherman's army, now commanded by Major General John A. McClernand, recouping its Chickasaw Bayou setback by capturing, on January 11, the small but important Confederate Fort Hindman at Arkansas Post. This movement rendered Union communication on the Mississippi River much more secure.

The problem of taking Vicksburg remained and seemed almost insoluble. Grant, the Union department commander, came down from Memphis and took personal command of Sherman's and McClernand's forces. He encamped them along the Louisiana shore of the Mississippi just north of Vicksburg and focused his efforts on finding a way to approach Vicksburg other than via the obvious death trap of Chickasaw Bayou. After a winter of unsuccessful attempts via swamps and bayous, Grant adopted an audacious plan that ultimately led to the siege of Vicksburg and its capitulation on July 4. This led directly to the surrender of Port Hudson, Louisiana, five days later, and with that, Lincoln could state with satisfaction, "The Father of Waters again goes unvexed to the sea."

While Grant maneuvered toward Vicksburg, Major General Joseph Hooker opened a new campaign against Lee, Jackson, and the hitherto all but invincible Army of Northern Virginia. Hooker, however, was full of confidence, even swagger—until his army actually made contact with Lee's. Then he seemed to shrink away, drawing his army back into a defensive position that left both the initiative and all the advantages of terrain in the hands of Lee and Jackson. They capitalized, and the resulting Battle of Chancellorsville became their most dramatic victory. Jackson, however, was wounded by friendly-fire, and died May 10.

On July 2, 1863, Jubal Early's Confederates attack Union positions around the elaborate entrance gate to Gettysburg's town cemetery.

Lee followed up his success at Chancellorsville with an invasion of the North, somewhat reluctantly agreed to by Jefferson Davis and the Confederate cabinet. Lee disengaged from Hooker along the Rappahannock River, moved west into the Shenandoah Valley, and then northeastward, down the valley, across the Potomac, and into Pennsylvania. The Confederates ranged almost to Harrisburg, destroying factories, warehouses, bridges, and railroads; plundering civilians of food, clothing, and shoes; and capturing blacks for enslavement in the South. Hooker pursued haltingly, until Major General George G. Meade replaced him on June 28. Meade's and Lee's forces collided unexpectedly at Gettysburg, where three days of Confederate attacks ended in Lee's first clear-cut defeat. Yet Meade did not pursue aggressively, and Lee escaped back into Virginia with his army intact, albeit much reduced.

As events in Pennsylvania and Mississippi were nearing their respective climaxes, Major General William S. Rosecrans, after months of insistent urging from Washington, finally put his army in motion southeastward from his base at Murfreesboro, Tennessee. In the space of nine days from June 26 to July 4, Rosecrans succeeded in maneuvering Bragg out of Middle Tennessee and all the way back to Chattanooga without a major battle. Rosecrans halted sixty miles short of Chattanooga, on the other side of the Cumberland Plateau, having failed to trap Bragg's army.

Rosecrans's advance and a simultaneous advance by a Union army under the command of Major General Ambrose Burnside, moving from Kentucky toward Knoxville, persuaded the Confederate high command to transfer troops from Lee's army westward for the only time during the war. Some ten thousand men under the command of Lieutenant General James Longstreet traveled by rail on a roundabout route made necessary by Burnside's occupation of Knoxville. By the time they reached Georgia, Rosecrans was on the move again and had maneuvered Bragg out of Chattanooga, but with Longstreet's and other reinforcements Bragg turned on Rosecrans and defeated him at Chickamauga Creek.

Rosecrans retreated into Chattanooga, abandoning the surrounding heights. From that high ground Bragg was able to prevent almost any supplies from reaching Rosecrans. Washington appointed Grant to take over command in the entire western theater. Grant repaired in person to Chattanooga, promptly opened a viable supply line, and from November 23 to 25 resoundingly defeated Bragg, driving his army from apparently impregnable positions on Lookout Mountain and Missionary Ridge.

Meanwhile, Longstreet's force, which Bragg had detached at Davis's urging, was laying half-hearted siege to Burnside at Knoxville. A November 29 assault by Longstreet's troops ended in bloody failure. On December 6, Longstreet vacated the area upon learning of the approach of a relieving force under Sherman, whom Grant had dispatched to Burnside's aid.

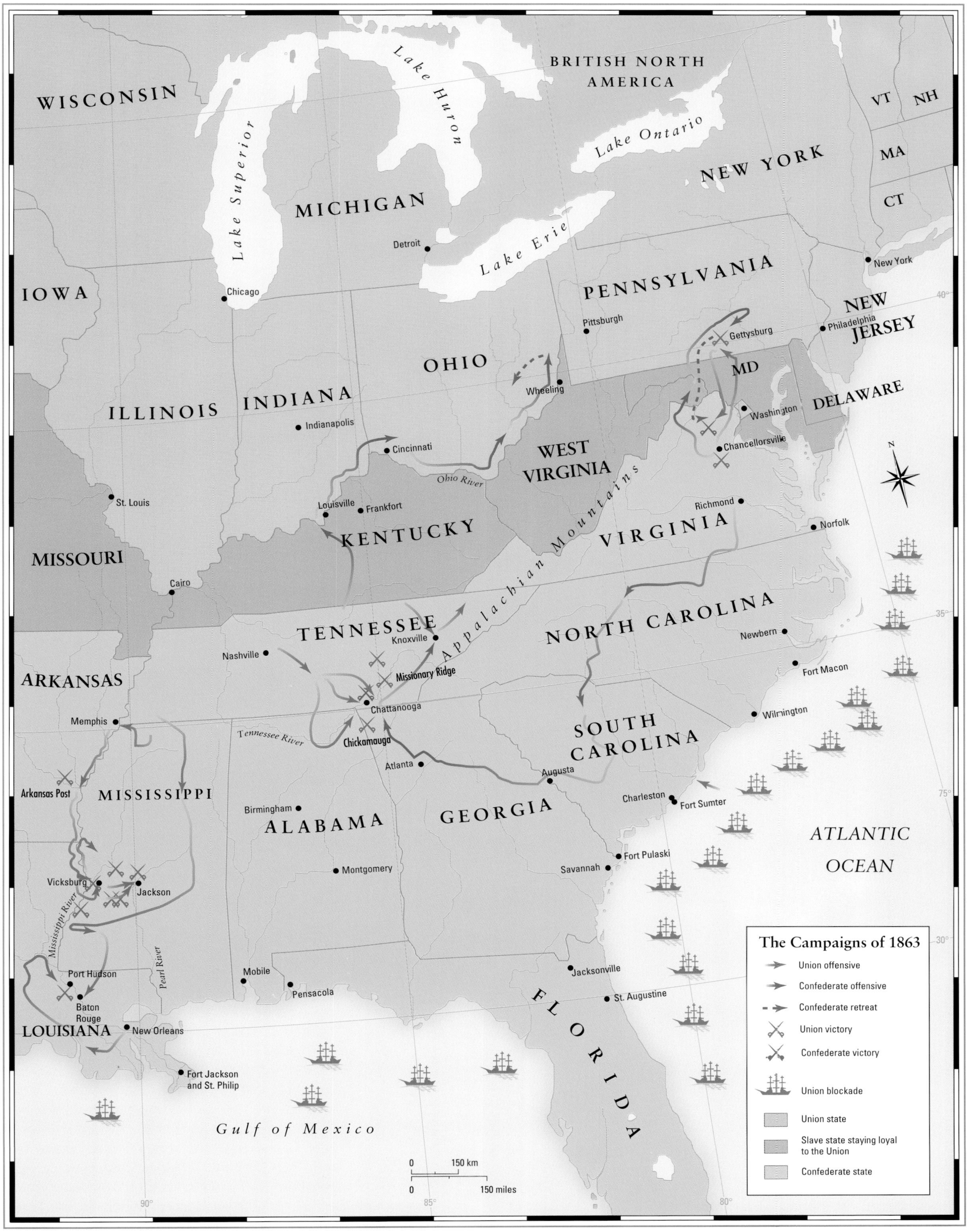
BRITISH NORTH AMERICA
WISCONSIN
Lake Superior
Lake Huron
Lake Ontario
Lake Erie
MICHIGAN
NEW YORK
VT
NH
MA
CT
IOWA
ILLINOIS
INDIANA
OHIO
PENNSYLVANIA
NEW JERSEY
MD
DELAWARE
WEST VIRGINIA
VIRGINIA
KENTUCKY
MISSOURI
TENNESSEE
NORTH CAROLINA
SOUTH CAROLINA
ARKANSAS
MISSISSIPPI
ALABAMA
GEORGIA
LOUISIANA
FLORIDA
ATLANTIC OCEAN
Gulf of Mexico
Appalachian Mountains
Ohio River
Tennessee River
Mississippi River
Pearl River
Detroit
Chicago
New York
Philadelphia
Pittsburgh
Gettysburg
Wheeling
Washington
Chancellorsville
Indianapolis
Cincinnati
St. Louis
Louisville
Frankfort
Richmond
Norfolk
Cairo
Knoxville
Nashville
Missionary Ridge
Chattanooga
Chickamauga
Newbern
Fort Macon
Wilmington
Memphis
Atlanta
Augusta
Charleston
Fort Sumter
Arkansas Post
Birmingham
Vicksburg
Jackson
Montgomery
Fort Pulaski
Savannah
Port Hudson
Baton Rouge
Mobile
Pensacola
Jacksonville
St. Augustine
New Orleans
Fort Jackson and St. Philip
The Campaigns of 1863
Union offensive
Confederate offensive
Confederate retreat
Union victory
Confederate victory
Union blockade
Union state
Slave state staying loyal to the Union
Confederate state
0 150 km
0 150 miles
N
40°
35°
30°
75°
80°
85°
90°

GRANT'S SECOND VICKSBURG CAMPAIGN, PHASE I

Milliken's Bend to Port Gibson
January 30 – May 1

1 January 24 – March 29: Sherman's attempt to cut a canal across De Soto Point fails.

2 January 30: Grant establishes his headquarters at Milliken's Bend.

3 March 31 – April 28: McClernand's corps and elements of McPherson's corps, move from Milliken's Bend to Hard Times Landing.

4 April 29 – May 1: Grant cancels landing operations at Grand Gulf. Meanwhile Porter's ships run the Grand Gulf gauntlet. Grant, with two corps, crosses the Mississippi at Bruinsburg.

5 May 1: Union victory near Port Gibson secures bridgehead, Confederate forces retreat across the Bayou Pierre.

A FTER THE FAILURE OF HIS FIRST campaign against Vicksburg in November and December of 1862, Grant determined to try again but along much different lines. This time he would operate entirely from the Mississippi River with no inland column. His reasons for this decision were both strategic and political. Strategically, as the Holly Springs raid had demonstrated, an overland supply line of the necessary length was extremely vulnerable.

Politically, Grant faced a situation in which prominent Illinois politician-turned-general John A. McClernand had persuaded Lincoln to issue orders vaguely empowering him to lead an expedition down the Mississippi—within the military department of which Grant was commander. McClernand had taken over command of Sherman's Mississippi River expedition just after the repulse at Chickasaw Bayou. The Illinois politician had some talent for command but not nearly as much as he imagined, and he was an obnoxious glory-hog with one eye fixed intently on future elections.

Sherman and his naval counterpart Rear Admiral David D. Porter shuddered to think of him continuing in command of the Mississippi River expedition and pressed their views on Grant. The only way to avoid that situation was for Grant to make the river expedition the single offensive thrust of his department and to join it himself. Then he, as department commander, would outrank McClernand. Thus in mid-January, with Grant in command and a furious McClernand leading only a single corps within it, the Union Army of the Tennessee encamped at Young's Point and Milliken's Bend on the Louisiana shore of the Mississippi River just above Vicksburg.

There, Grant faced a seemingly impossible task. Vicksburg could be approached from four directions, two of them were impossible to assault and the other two impossible to reach. An approach from the north led across the Chickasaw bottoms, and no Federal was eager to try that again. An approach from the west meant a direct amphibious assault on the Vicksburg waterfront, under the muzzles of numerous heavy cannons. That looked suicidal. The town might be approached successfully from the south or east, but reaching those positions from the Mississippi River above Vicksburg seemed impossible. To get onto dry land south of Vicksburg, the gunboats and transports had to reach that stretch of river, but the powerful Vicksburg batteries barred the way. The countryside east of Vicksburg might be reached from the Yazoo River, but Confederate batteries at Hayne's Bluff forbade Union vessels from penetrating any farther up the Yazoo than they had at the time of Sherman's disastrous Chickasaw Bayou effort. With that, the problem had come full circle back to a known impossibility.

Grant would not give up. With Porter's enthusiastic cooperation he tried a series of schemes aimed at introducing the fleet, transports, and army into either the Yazoo River above Hayne's Bluff or the Mississippi River below Vicksburg. First, Grant set his men to digging a canal across De Soto Point, a peninsula enclosed by a bend of the Mississippi River opposite Vicksburg. In theory, the waters of the river would flow through the canal, enlarging it sufficiently to allow passage of the fleet. Perversely, the main flow of the river, which routinely cut off bends in this manner, spurned the proffered channel, and the scheme failed.

Next, Grant tried a route that could, with some digging, be made to lead through Lake Providence in Louisiana above Vicksburg, through various bayous and into the Red River, which empties into the Mississippi below Vicksburg. When that proved impractical, he sent another expedition to cut the levee on the Mississippi at a place called Yazoo Pass, letting the flooded river flow into the headwaters of the Yazoo. Gunboats and transports then followed the new waterway into the Yazoo proper. Because of the new stream's difficult conditions, the Confederates were able to stop the Union gunboats with a flimsy earthwork mounting only two guns. Another bid to reach the Yazoo via Deer Creek and Sunflower Bayou, east of the Mississippi in the Delta country north of Vicksburg also failed.

Throughout January, February, and March 1863, while detachments of the Union army pursued these ill-fated schemes, the troops of the Army of the Tennessee suffered through miserable living conditions in camps that were muddy and sometimes flooded. Disease took a steady toll in lives, and the army's dead had to be buried along the levee, which was the only place within reach dry enough for burials.

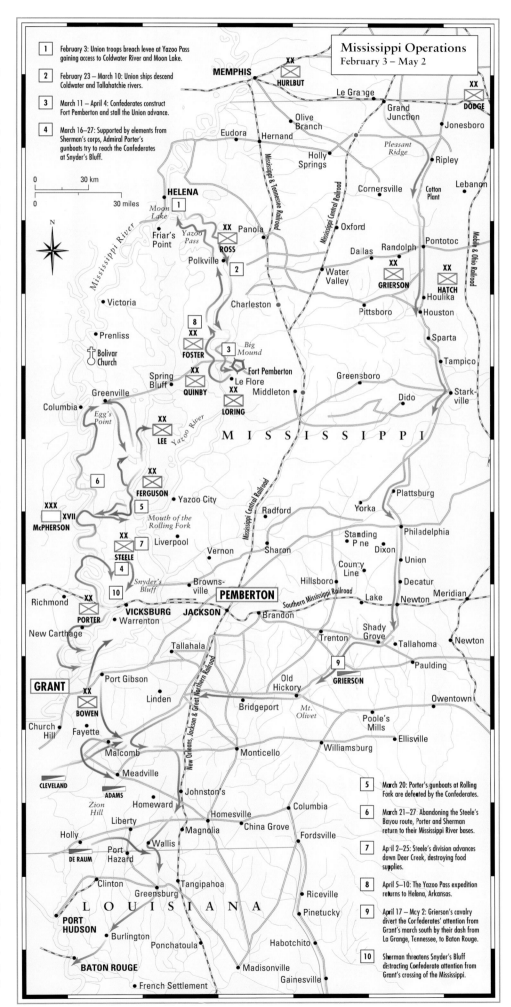

Mississippi Operations
February 3 – May 2

1 February 3: Union troops breach levee at Yazoo Pass gaining access to Coldwater River and Moon Lake.

2 February 23 – March 10: Union ships descend Coldwater and Tallahatchie rivers.

3 March 11 – April 4: Confederates construct Fort Pemberton and stall the Union advance.

4 March 16–27: Supported by elements from Sherman's corps, Admiral Porter's gunboats try to reach the Confederates at Snyder's Bluff.

5 March 20: Porter's gunboats at Rolling Fork are defeated by the Confederates.

6 March 21–27: Abandoning the Steele's Bayou route, Porter and Sherman return to their Mississippi River bases.

7 April 2–25: Steele's division advances down Deer Creek, destroying food supplies.

8 April 5–10: The Yazoo Pass expedition returns to Helena, Arkansas.

9 April 17 – May 2: Grierson's cavalry divert the Confederates' attention from Grant's march south by their dash from La Grange, Tennessee, to Baton Rouge.

10 Sherman threatens Snyder's Bluff distracting Confederate attention from Grant's crossing of the Mississippi.

GRANT'S SECOND VICKSBURG CAMPAIGN, PHASE II

AS ONE AFTER ANOTHER OF his various schemes for getting the gunboats and transports past Vicksburg failed, Grant's thoughts moved steadily toward a final desperate solution. He asked Porter to run the fleet directly past the Vicksburg batteries, betting that enough vessels could get through to serve his purposes in the river below Vicksburg. Porter was willing, but warned Grant that the move would be irreversible. The gunboats might attempt to run the batteries going downstream with the current adding to their speed, but it would be madness to attempt the same feat going upstream. Grant was undeterred, and Porter made plans to run the batteries on the night of April 16.

1 March 30: Grant ordered McClernand to take his Thirteenth Corps and begin finding a feasible route through the swamps and bayous down the west bank of the Mississippi. The rest of the army would follow.

2 April 16: At Grant's request, Rear Admiral David D. Porter led seven ironclads, one armed ram, three army transports, and a tug past Vicksburg batteries.

3 April 29: Leading elements of the Thirteenth Corps reached Hard Times Landing.

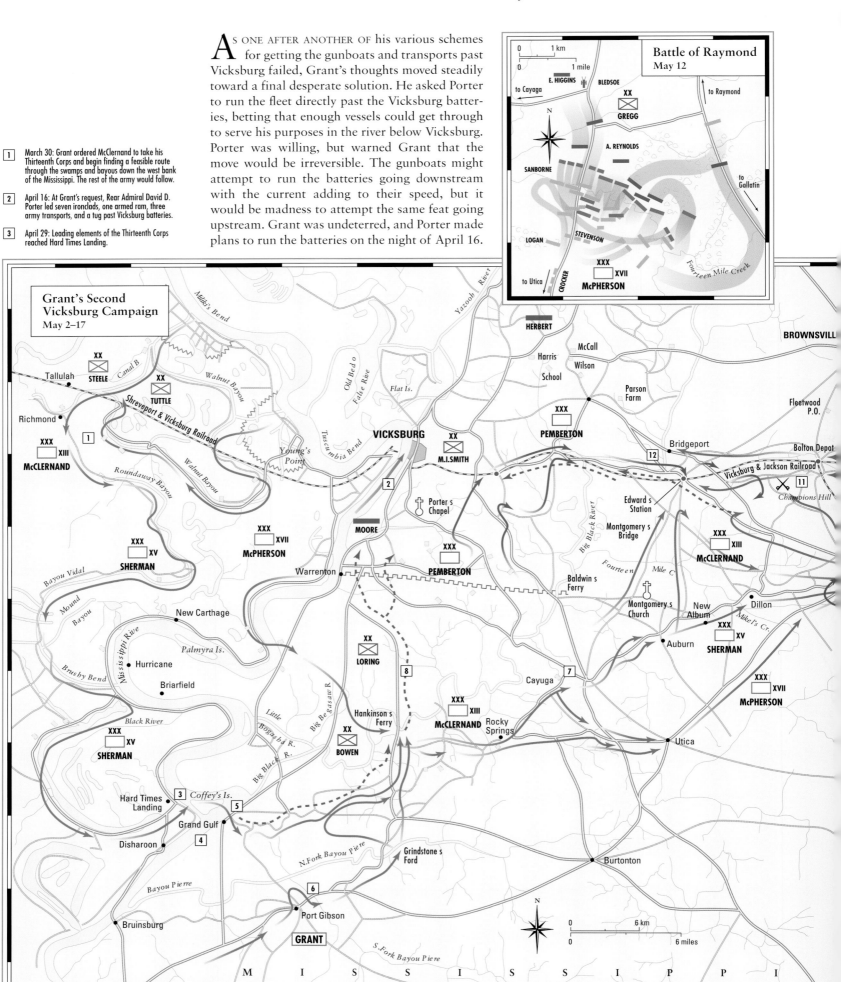

Battle of Raymond
May 12

Grant's Second
Vicksburg Campaign
May 2–17

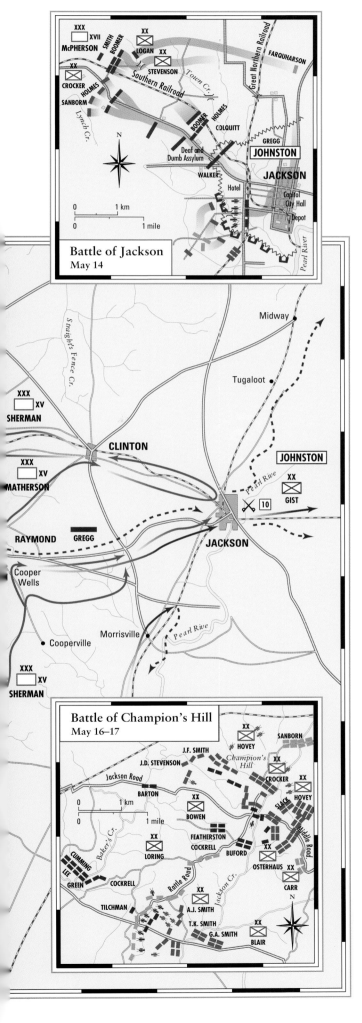

Battle of Jackson
May 14

Battle of Champion's Hill
May 16–17

At the same time Grant had one corps of his army begin exploring a possible route down the west bank of the river. This was no simple task, as the terrain was a maze of flooded swamps and sinuous islands where the natural levees projected above the level of the spring high water. McClernand's Thirteenth Corps was encamped closest to the route and got the job. By the time the navy attempted to run the batteries, McClernand's troops were on the west bank below Vicksburg and ready to cooperate.

The running of the batteries went off as scheduled on the night of April 16, with the loss of only a single transport. Several more transports attempted to make the run six nights later, suffering higher losses, but Grant's purpose had been achieved: both fleet and transports were in the river below Vicksburg, ready to support the army in a cross-river assault. At first Grant hoped to land his troops at Grand Gulf, on the east side of the Mississippi about thirty miles below Vicksburg, but when an hours-long bombardment by Union gunboats failed to suppress the Confederate defenses there, he had to shift his target downstream to Bruinsburg, Mississippi. His troops landed there on April 30, unopposed, marched across the river bottoms, and gained the bluffs on the far side.

Eager to push inland, Grant ordered a night march, but shortly after midnight his troops encountered a detachment of Pemberton's army under Major General John Bowen not far from the town of Port Gibson, Mississippi, about seven miles southeast of Grand Gulf. After skirmishing through the rest of the night, Grant's forces

attacked at daybreak on May 1. Fighting was difficult in the rugged terrain, which was cut by many deep ravines, but Grant's greater numbers held at last and Bowen had to flee. Grant's troops continued their advance the next day, crossing Bayou Pierre and reaching the Big Black River. Rather than move directly north to Vicksburg, over terrain as difficult as that of the Port Hudson battlefield, however, Grant decided instead to swing farther to the northeast before turning westward toward Vicksburg.

By May 12, Grant's army was closing in on Pemberton's Confederate army near Edwards Station, Mississippi. On that day, however, a single Confederate brigade operating out of Jackson, Mississippi, attacked Grant's left-flank column, Major General James B. McPherson's Seventeenth Corps. McPherson defeated the Rebel attackers at the Battle of Raymond, but the attack convinced Grant that Jackson, Mississippi, was a potential threat that could not be left on his flank and rear without being neutralized. Leaving one corps to threaten Pemberton, Grant sent the other two corps, Sherman's and McPherson's to take Jackson and destroy its military facilities. This they did on May 14. Then, while Sherman completed the destruction, McPherson's corps joined McClernand's for the advance against Pemberton.

The Union corps met Pemberton on May 16 at Champion's Hill, just east of Edwards Station. In this hard-fought battle, the actual numbers engaged were about the same on each side, roughly 15,500 for Grant and perhaps a few more for Pemberton. Grant had another 17,500 men on hand under McClernand, but that officer misconstrued his orders and sat idle only a few hundred yards away throughout the entire battle. Nevertheless, Champion's Hill was a great victory for Grant, and Pemberton's defeated army retreated in disorder. Union casualties were 2,441 and Confederate, 3,851.

The next day a portion of Pemberton's force attempted to make a stand in an entrenched bridgehead at Big Black Bridge but collapsed immediately under a Union assault. Total Union casualties for the battle were only 279, but more than 1,700 Confederate were captured, along with a number of cannons. Again Pemberton's battered army fled westward, with Grant in pursuit, this time all the way into the Vicksburg lines. By May 18, Grant's army was taking up positions to surround the Vicksburg defenses. Grant's army had also opened up a supply line to Union gunboats on the Yazoo River above Vicksburg, where the Confederates had been compelled to abandon their fortifications. The siege of Vicksburg was on.

4   April 29, 7:00 a.m.: Porter's gunboats attacked the batteries at Grand Gulf but were unable to silence them so that Grant's troops could land there. Grant had the Thirteenth Corps march to Disharoon's Plantation that night while the gunboats and transports ran past the Grand Gulf batteries.

5   April 30: Grant had the Thirteenth Corps loaded onto the steamboats and carried across the river, accompanying them himself. While the Thirteenth Corps pressed inland, the boats continued shuttling the rest of the army across the river.

6   May 1: Grant's troops met Major General John Bowen's Confederate command outside the town of Port Gibson. Despite difficult terrain, the Union troops drove off the Confederates and occupied the town.

7   May 3: Major General John A. Logan's division of the Seventeenth Corps took Hankinson's Ferry, but Grant opted to move farther to the northeast before turning toward Vicksburg, thus allowing his army to approach over more favorable terrain.

8   May 3: Bowen's Confederate evacuated Grand Gulf and retreated toward Vicksburg.

9   May 12: The Confederate garrison of Jackson attempted to strike the flank of Grant's column at Raymond but instead struck Logan's division head-on and were repulsed. Grant decided to take Jackson before turning toward Vicksburg.

10   May 14: Major General William T. Sherman's Fifteenth Corps and Major General James B. McPherson's Seventeenth Corps captured Jackson. The Confederate garrison, now commanded by General Joseph E. Johnston, withdrew to the northeast.

11   May 16: Grant's and Pemberton's armies clashed in the major battle of the campaign at Champion's Hill. In a hard-fought, day-long battle, Grant was victorious. Pemberton's defeated forces fled west.

12   May 17: Grant caught up with the Confederates at Big Black Bridge, attacked and overran a Confederate division in a fortified bridgehead. Pemberton's battered army fled into the Vicksburg fortifications.

THE CAMPAIGN AGAINST CHARLESTON

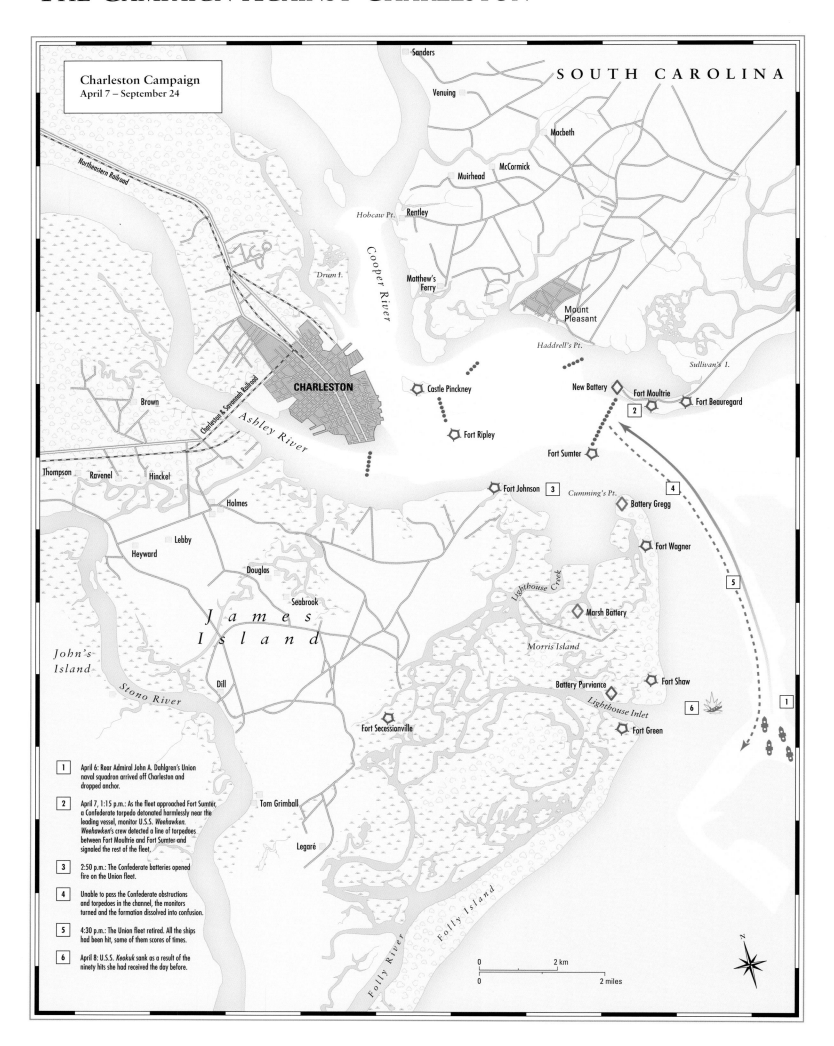

Charleston Campaign
April 7 – September 24

SOUTH CAROLINA

Sanders

Venuing

Macbeth

McCormick

Muirhead

Northeastern Railroad

Rentley

Hobcaw Pt.

Drum I.

Matthew's
Ferry

Mount
Pleasant

Cooper River

Haddrell's Pt.

Sullivan's I.

Castle Pinckney

New Battery

Fort Moultrie

CHARLESTON

2

Fort Beauregard

Charleston & Savannah Railroad

Brown

Fort Ripley

Ashley River

Fort Sumter

Thompson   Ravenel   Hinckel

Fort Johnson   3

Cumming's Pt.

4

Battery Gregg

Holmes

Fort Wagner

Lebby

Heyward

Douglas

Lighthouse Creek

Seabrook

Marsh Battery

5

*James
Island*

Morris Island

*John's
Island*

Dill

Battery Purviance

Fort Shaw

Stono River

Lighthouse Inlet

6

Fort Secessionville

Fort Green

1

Tom Grimball

Legaré

1   April 6: Rear Admiral John A. Dahlgren's Union
    naval squadron arrived off Charleston and
    dropped anchor.

2   April 7, 1:15 p.m.: As the fleet approached Fort Sumter,
    a Confederate torpedo detonated harmlessly near the
    leading vessel, monitor U.S.S. *Weehawken*.
    Weehawken's crew detected a line of torpedoes
    between Fort Moultrie and Fort Sumter and
    signaled the rest of the fleet.

3   2:50 p.m.: The Confederate batteries opened
    fire on the Union fleet.

4   Unable to pass the Confederate obstructions
    and torpedoes in the channel, the monitors
    turned and the formation dissolved into confusion.

5   4:30 p.m.: The Union fleet retired. All the ships
    had been hit, some of them scores of times.

6   April 8: U.S.S. *Keokuk* sank as a result of the
    ninety hits she had received the day before.

Folly River   *Folly Island*

0   2 km

0   2 miles

N

O N APRIL 7, FLAG OFFICER Samuel F. Du Pont's fleet steamed into Charleston harbor to attack Fort Sumter. Among the fleet's nine ironclads were the frigate *New Ironsides*, seven monitors, and *Keokuk*, a small ironclad of an untried design. During the course of the fight, the Confederate guns in Fort Sumter and Fort Moultrie fired a total of 2,209 times and scored a large number of hits, chiefly on the monitors and *Keokuk*, which because of their shallow drafts were able to approach more closely. Some of these vessels were temporarily disabled. *Keokuk* wallowed lower and lower in the Atlantic swells until it sank the next morning.

The fleet was not able to generate much firepower in response to the Confederate bombardment it received. *New Ironsides*, because of its deep draft, had to remain at long range. *Keokuk* and the monitors mounted two guns each, which had very slow rates of fire in the constricted space of the monitors' revolving turrets and *Keokuk*'s small casemates. During the whole fight, the ironclads got off a combined total of only 154 shots. These did minimal damage to the walls of Fort Sumter, which was soon repaired. Clearly, even the most powerful ironclads available in 1863 were not going to be able to pound the Charleston defenses into submission by themselves. Lincoln ordered Du Pont to maintain his position inside the bar of Charleston harbor, but that was all Du Pont could do.

Thus matters stood until July, when Secretary of the Navy Gideon Welles, displeased with Du Pont for the failure of the attack, replaced him with Rear Admiral John A. Dahlgren with the understanding that Dahlgren would push operations against Charleston more aggressively than had been the case under Du Pont. For these new operations, Dahlgren was to have the active cooperation of army forces under the command of Major General Quincy A. Gillmore, a highly regarded military engineer. On July 10, Gillmore's troops landed on the southern end of Morris Island, which lay on the south side of Charleston harbor, under cover of a heavy naval bombardment that turned into another fierce battle between ships and shore. Gillmore's plan was to advance up the island and take Battery Wagner, a sturdy, sand-and-palmetto-log fortification at the north end of the island. Wagner was an important part of the Charleston defenses, and from its position Union batteries could bombard Fort Sumter at relatively close range. Moving quickly, Gillmore assaulted Battery Wagner the next day. Advancing with great determination, Union troops pressed forward all the way to the top of Wagner's parapet but could go no further and soon had to fall back under deadly Rebel fire.

One week later, on July 18, after steady

Nicknamed "the Swamp Angel", the Union Marsh battery, designed and constructed by Colonel Sewell of the New York Engineers, fired thirty-five rounds into the city of Charleston. On firing the thirty-sixth round, the gun exploded.

bombardment by the guns of the Union fleet and some thirty-six pieces of artillery on Morris Island, the Federals charged again, but once again the attack was a bloody failure. Among the several Union regiments that suffered heavy casualties in the assault was the Fifty-fourth Massachusetts Colored Infantry, whose colonel, the abolitionist Robert Gould Shaw, was among the slain. Union casualties totaled 1,515 and Confederate 174.

Thereafter, Gillmore and his troops settled down for a lengthy siege. Over the weeks that followed, Union naval guns continued to pound Fort Sumter and Battery Wagner while the Federal soldiers planted batteries of heavy guns on land and dug their approach trenches closer and closer to Battery Wagner. They brought in a massive two-hundred-pounder Parrott gun, nicknamed the Swamp Angel, as well as additional pieces of artillery. By August 11 the new Union batteries were ready and began practice bombardments, lofting their shells over Battery Wagner and slamming them against the brick walls of Fort Sumter. The "practice" firing continued for five days. Masses of brickwork crumbled on Fort Sumter, but the Rebel garrison worked hard, shoring up their defenses with sand-filled gabions.

Then on August 17 Gillmore's and Dahlgren's guns unleashed the first great bombardment of Fort Sumter, which continued through the firing of 5,009 artillery rounds over the course of the next week. The rain of heavy shells reduced the fort's brick walls to shapeless heaps of sand and rubble, but these, it turned out, were better protection against incoming fire than the brick walls had been. Fort Sumter was reduced to four serviceable guns, but it still held out. The Swamp Angel, on the other hand, burst on the firing of its thirty-sixth round. The Confederates attempted to strike back by sending a small steam torpedo boat to attack *New Ironsides*, but the effort proved unsuccessful. On the night of September 6–7, Confederate troops evacuated Battery Wagner and nearby Battery Gregg. The Federals occupied both on the morning of the 7th, but Fort Sumter, now a pile of rubble, still seemed as far from surrendering as ever.

7 July 10: The fleet and land batteries mounted a day-long bombardment of Confederate positions on Morris Island, concentrating especially on Battery Wagner.

8 July 11: Union infantry assaulted Battery Wagner but met a bloody repulse.

9 July 18: Dahlgren and Union ground commander Major General Quincy Gillmore tried again, but the second bombardment and land assault met the same fate as the first.

10 July 19 – September 5: Gillmore's and Dahlgren's guns continued to bombard the fort while sappers dug regular approaches.

11 September 6: The Confederates evacuated Battery Wagner under cover of darkness.

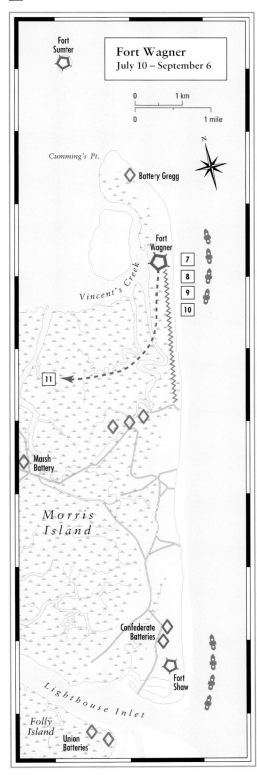

Fort Sumter

Fort Wagner
July 10 – September 6

0   1 km
0   1 mile

N

Cumming's Pt.

Battery Gregg

Fort Wagner

Vincent's Creek

Marsh Battery

Morris Island

Confederate Batteries

Fort Shaw

Lighthouse Inlet

Folly Island

Union Batteries

CHANCELLORSVILLE, PHASE I

This contemporary watercolor by Edwin Forbes depicts the reading of General Order Number 47 to the troops, part of which read "the operations of the last three days have determined that our enemy must either ingloriously fly, or come out from behind their defenses and give us battle on our own ground, where certain destruction awaits him."

AFTER THE DEBACLE AT FREDERICKSBURG and a subsequent fiasco in which an attempted January campaign had to be halted not far from the army's camps on the north bank of the Rappahannock River due to heavy rains and muddy roads—an almost farcical episode that the soldiers referred to as "the Mud March"—morale in the Army of the Potomac sank alarmingly. Some of the army's generals became almost mutinous in their efforts to lobby the administration for the removal of the army's commander Major General Ambrose Burnside. Several traveled to Washington to urge a patient but increasingly displeased Lincoln to remove the army commander he had appointed scarcely two months before. Particularly active in this effort was Major General Joseph "Fighting Joe" Hooker. Lincoln was in a difficult situation. Burnside was unquestionably loyal, earnest, and dedicated, but he had blundered miserably at Fredericksburg. Lincoln rightly suspected a considerable degree of self-interest in at least some of Burnside's critics among the generals, especially Hooker, who combined extreme ambition with shocking political views and loathsome personal habits. Still, the skillful and aggressive Fighting Joe appeared to be

the man most likely to lead the Army of the Potomac to victory, which Lincoln and the country badly needed.

The president decided that Burnside had to go and that Hooker would replace him. On appointing Hooker, Lincoln sent the general a sage letter. "There are some things in regard to which, I am not quite satisfied with you," the president frankly wrote:

"I believe you to be a brave and skillful soldier, which, of course, I like. I also believe you do not mix politics with your profession, in which you are right. You have confidence in yourself, which is a valuable, if not an indispensable quality. You are ambitious, which, within reasonable bounds, does good rather than harm. But I think that during General Burnside's command of the Army, you have taken counsel of your ambition, and thwarted him as much as you could, in which you did a great wrong to the country, and to a most meritorious and honorable brother officer. I have heard, in such way as to believe it, of your recently saying that both the Army and the Government needed a Dictator. Of course it was not for this, but

1. April 27: The Army of the Potomac began moving out of its camps around Falmouth, Virginia, moving up the north bank of the Rappahannock to turn Lee's left flank.

2. April 28: Union troops began crossing the Rappahannock at United States Ford and Kelly's Ford.

3. April 29: The bulk of the Army of the Potomac completed its crossing and proceeded into an area of dense thickets and second-growth timber known as the Wilderness.

4. April 29: Major General John Sedgwick, commanding his own Sixth Corps as well as Major General John Reynolds's First Corps, made movements threatening an attack at Fredericksburg in order to divert Confederate attention away from the movement of the rest of the Army of the Potomac.

5. April 30: The main body of the Army of the Potomac, accompanied by Hooker, encamped near Chancellorsville.

6. May 1: Leaving Major General Jubal Early with ten thousand men to cover Fredericksburg, Lee marched the rest of his army to confront Hooker in the Wilderness.

7. May 1: After beginning to advance out of the Wilderness, Hooker inexplicably ordered his troops to fall back into that area, where his army's advantage in numbers was of minimal value.

in spite of it, that I have given you the command. Only those generals who gain successes, can set up dictators. What I now ask of you is military success, and I will risk the dictatorship."

Hooker was very impressed with Lincoln's wisdom and kindness and went to work to restore the Army of the Potomac to fighting trim. Over the months that followed he proved to be a superb organizer and administrator as well as a genius in raising morale. Among numerous other reforms, he instituted the wearing of patches on the soldiers' uniforms, identifying their corps and division affiliation. This fostered unit pride as well facilitating the provost guards' efforts to control straggling. By April, the Army of the Potomac was bigger and better equipped than ever before. Hooker called it "the finest army on the planet." Hooker adopted a new plan of campaign suggested to him by the quartermaster general of the U.S. Army, Brigadier General Montgomery C. Meigs.

The plan called for one corps of the Army of the Potomac to fake a crossing of the Rappahannock at Fredericksburg. Meanwhile, the remainder of the army would march west and turn Lee's left flank, crossing the Rappahannock and

Rapidan rivers in rapid succession, and then pass through an area of dense woods and thickets known as the Wilderness. Upon emerging from the Wilderness, the army would, in theory, be between Lee and Richmond and able to force battle on terms favorable for a Union victory. To enhance the effect of his turning maneuver, Hooker would send all his cavalry, under Major General George Stoneman, on a raid far behind Confederate lines. Contemplating his planned offensive, Hooker exuded confidence, even cockiness, boasting, "May God have mercy on Bobby Lee, for I shall have none."

On April 27, 1863, the Army of the Potomac marched out of its camps around Falmouth, Virginia, and headed west, toward the upper fords of the Rappahannock River. The next day the army began crossing the Rappahannock.

Major General Joseph "Fighting Joe" Hooker, appointed by President Lincoln to replace Major General Burnside.

On May 2 Lee sent half of his army, under Stonewall Jackson, on a long flanking march. In the evening of the same day, Jackson attacked and demolished the exposed Union right wing. In the scene below, also by Edwin Forbes, Union artillery attempt to stem the attack along Old Orange Turnpike.

CHANCELLORSVILLE, PHASE II

1. May 2, morning: Near the beginning of their long flank march, Jackson's men skirmished with Union troops probing forward beyond Catherine's Furnace.

2. May 2: Jackson's column spent most of the day reaching a position on the Union flank.

3. May 2, 6:00 p.m.: Jackson finally launched his flanking attack, crumpling the Union Eleventh Corps.

4. May 2, 9:00 p.m.: Returning from a reconnaissance with his staff after the day's fighting had ended, Jackson was caught in the middle of a flare up of picket firing and wounded slightly in the right hand and severely in the left arm. Command of his corps passed to Jeb Stuart.

5. May 3, morning: Confederate artillery occupied a commanding position at Hazel Grove and continued to pound Chancellorsville throughout the day.

6. May 3: Both Lee and Stuart mounted costly frontal assaults against Hooker's lines, pushing them back into a tighter perimeter and linking the two halves of the Confederate army.

7. May 5: Hooker withdrew his forces across the Rappahannock.

ON MAY 1, LEE REACTED TO Hooker's threatening move around his left. Leaving the division of Major General Jubal Early to watch Fredericksburg, he took the rest of the Army of Northern Virginia on a rapid march to the west to confront Hooker before the Army of the Potomac could exit the Wilderness. A battle in that area would negate the large Union advantage in artillery and minimize the impact of Hooker's greater numbers. Hooker could easily have pushed forward to the open country beyond those dark woods, and it would have been much to his advantage to do so. It

therefore came as a shock to all concerned when after brief and inconsequential skirmishing, Hooker that afternoon withdrew his army into the heart of the Wilderness, abandoned the initiative, and assumed a passive defensive position.

That night Lee and Jackson, acting on excellent intelligence from cavalry commander Major General Jeb Stuart, decided on a movement of sublime audacity. Though facing an enemy force in the Wilderness of some seventy thousand men, Lee would divide his own forty-seven thousand, sending twenty-six thousand of them under

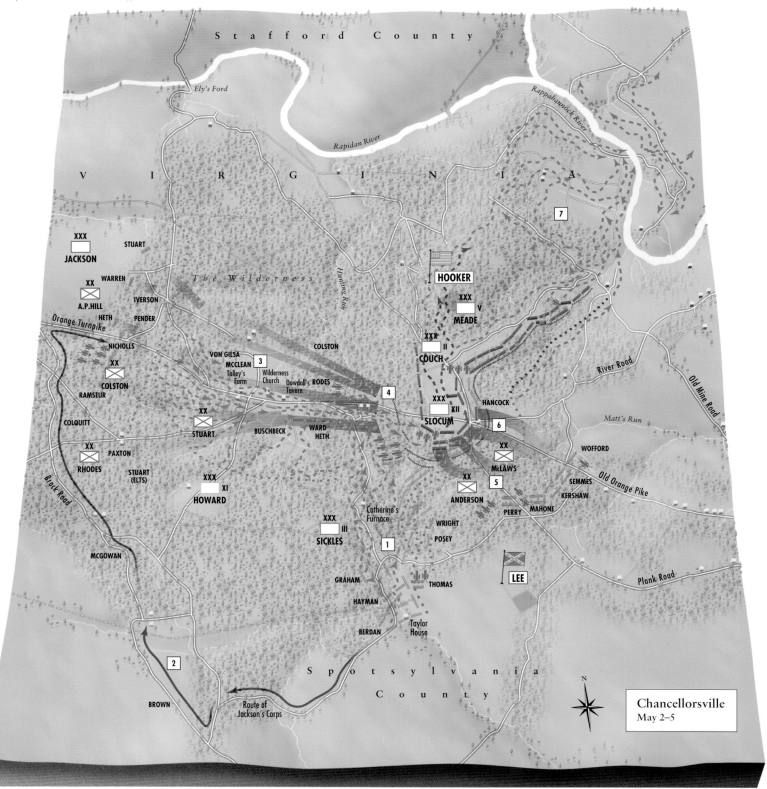

Jackson's command on a roundabout march via back roads to strike Hooker's right flank. With his remaining force, Lee would endeavor to keep Hooker's attention focused on his center, while Jackson's column made its day-long march.

Jackson started early on May 2. While passing the vicinity of Catherine Furnace, where iron had once been smelted before the local ore deposits gave out a number of years before the war, his column attracted the attention of Union troops of the Third Corps. Their commander—Tammany Hall politician and Hooker's good friend and fellow rake, Major General Daniel E. Sickles—interpreted the sighting as evidence of a Confederate retreat. With Hooker's agreement he pushed forward and skirmished briefly with Jackson's rear guard, with only minor results.

By late afternoon Jackson had his corps positioned astride the Union right flank. The Federals there belonged to the Sixth Corps, whose commander, Major General Oliver O. Howard, was leading a corps in battle for the first time. Confused by a day of conflicting dispatches from Hooker bidding him to prepare both for desperate defense and for headlong pursuit of a fleeing enemy, Howard had failed to secure his corps's flank. Jackson attacked and rolled up the Sixth Corps. Despite brave stands by many of its units, by nightfall the corps had been routed, and Jackson's troops had advanced some three miles. As darkness gathered, Jackson, accompanied by his staff, rode forward to reconnoiter the right flank of the new line the Federals were throwing together just west of the Wilderness crossroads known as Chancellorsville. As he approached Confederate lines on his return, firing flared up, as it frequently did between armies at night. Two shots from Confederate lines struck Jackson, and several more struck members of his staff. Jackson was carried off the battlefield for amputation of his left arm. Command of his corps passed to Jeb Stuart.

With superior numbers positioned between the two severed halves of Lee's army, Hooker's situation on May 3 offered opportunities, but Hooker remained passive. When Sickles pulled back into a tight perimeter around Chancellorsville the night before, he abandoned the high ground around Hazel Grove, which the Confederates then turned into an excellent artillery position for pounding Chancellorsville. One shell struck a porch column of the Chancellor House—more or less the only building in Chancellorsville—while Hooker was leaning on it, stunning but, unfortunately for Lee, not killing the Union commander. Hooker remained semicoherent for the rest of the day, which seemed to make little difference in his conduct of the battle. He ordered his army to pull back to a strong perimeter with both flanks anchored solidly, the right on the Rapidan and the left on the Rappahannock. His generals considered but rejected the idea of removing him as no longer fit to command.

Meanwhile, Major General John Sedgwick had advanced from Fredericksburg in response to Hooker's cries for help. After several unsuccessful

attempts, his troops took Marye's Heights from Jubal Early's men and pressed on toward Chancellorsville. While Hooker did nothing, Lee turned much of his force against Sedgwick, nearly surrounding him. With difficulty, Sedgwick was able to escape to the north bank of the Rappahannock. Lee then made plans to attack Hooker's strong defensive position, but before he could do so, the Union commander ordered his army back across the rivers in retreat. The Battle of Chancellorsville is considered the greatest victory of the Lee-Jackson team. It was also the last, as Jackson died on May 10. Union casualties totaled 17,287, and Confederate 12,764.

Major General Joseph Hooker made his headquarters at the Chancellor House, the only substantial structure for miles around. The picture above is believed to have been drawn by Robert Sneden of the 40th New York Regiment.

1 May 4: Brigadier General Cadmus Wilcox's brigade, fighting a delaying action against Sedgwick's advance, made a stubborn stand at Salem Church.

2 The four brigades of Major General Lafayette McLaws's division, moved into line on either side of Wilcox.

3 Major General Richard H. Anderson's division arrived and confronted Sedgwick from the south.

4 Major General Jubal Early's command, rallied after its defeat at Fredericksburg the day before, moved up behind Sedgwick, threatening him from the east.

5 Sedgwick's troops staunchly fought off the Confederate attacks before withdrawing across the Rappahannock under cover of darkness.

Salem Church
May 4

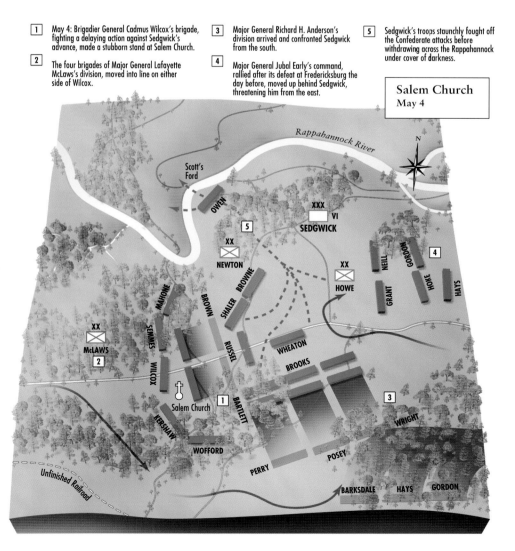

PORT HUDSON CAMPAIGN

During the Confederacy's late-summer and early-fall offensives in 1862, Confederate troops under the command of Major General John C. Breckinridge tried unsuccessfully to retake Baton Rouge, Louisiana, from the Union garrison there. After the failure of that attempt, Breckinridge withdrew several miles to the north and began to fortify the bluffs on the east bank of the Mississippi at Port Hudson, Louisiana. As long as the Confederacy could hold fortresses at Vicksburg and Port Hudson, it could not only keep the Mississippi closed to northern commerce, but also, at least in theory, keep U.S. Navy warships out of the segment of river between them. That would allow the Confederacy to move large troop formations and major amounts of supplies across the Mississippi, something that would be highly problematic if not impossible if Union vessels could patrol the entire length of the river.

Taking Port Hudson therefore became an important object to the Union forces in the lower Mississippi Valley, headquartered at New Orleans.

This 1863 hand-colored lithograph by Currier and Ives, shows Admiral Farragut's fleet bombarding Port Hudson and its defenses. The unfortunate U.S.S Mississippi is depicted in flames.

On March 7, 1863, those forces, under the command of Major General Nathaniel P. Banks, began an advance toward Port Hudson. One week later, as Banks's forces approached Port Hudson and began to threaten the bastion's landward defenses, the cooperating naval squadron of David G. Farragut steamed up the river to run past the batteries of Port Hudson. Confederate gunnery proved surprisingly effective. The sloop-of-war U.S.S. *Hartford*, Farragut's flagship, and the gunboat U.S.S. *Albatross* successfully passed the batteries, but U.S.S. *Richmond* and U.S.S. *Monongahela* had to drop back down the river with severe damage. U.S.S. *Mississipp*i ran aground under the deadly fire of the guns, which pounded her until she caught fire. *Mississippi*'s crew went over the side, and the vessel burned until she exploded in mid-stream. The destruction of *Mississippi* was one of the most serious naval losses of the war on inland waters. Nevertheless, Farragut, with *Hartford* and

Albatross, was now in the stretch of water that had for the preceding seven months been free of patrolling Union warships.

Finding he could make no headway against Port Hudson for the time, Banks withdrew from the vicinity and turned to deal with a small Confederate army under Lieutenant General Richard Taylor on the west side of the Mississippi in the area of Bayou Teche. Between March 25 and May 7, Banks campaigned in that region, chasing Taylor away, cutting off the flow of Confederate supplies through Bayou Teche to Port Hudson, and, on May 7, occupying Alexandria, Louisiana, shortly after U.S. Navy gunboats had taken possession of the town. With his rear thus secured against harassment by Taylor, Banks could once again turn his attention to Port Hudson.

On May 14, Banks turned down the Red River with three divisions toward Port Hudson, while two more Union divisions advanced from Baton Rouge toward the same goal. On May 21, the Confederate commander at Port Hudson, Major General Franklin Gardner, with a garrison of seven thousand men, made a brief foray to Plains Store, Louisiana, in hopes of forestalling a junction of the two Union columns. Failing, he retreated back into the Port Hudson entrenchments and presently found himself surrounded by a combined force of some thirty thousand Federals on land and Farragut's warships in the river.

The prospect of a prolonged siege in the heat of a Louisiana summer, with its attendant disease, was a strong motivation for Banks to attempt to finish Port Hudson quickly. So he ordered an assault for May 27. The effort proved to be a bloody failure. The terrain was difficult, and Banks was no great commander. His assault was uncoordinated and piecemeal, allowing Gardner to shift his troops and overcome Banks's large superiority in numbers. The only bright spot for the Federals was the fact that two regiments of black troops, the First and Third Louisiana Native Guards, fought just as well and suffered casualties as high as their white counterparts. This was encouraging because it was the first major combat for black troops, and it began to dispel the prejudice that black troops would not fight. Still, the May 27 assault was, on the whole, a disaster for Banks. Union casualties were 1,995 and Confederate, 235.

After a fortnight of siege, Banks called on Gardner to surrender, but the Confederate refused. So on June 14, Banks launched another assault, which was more disastrous for his forces than the first. Union casualties totaled 1,792, and Confederate 47. The siege went on until July 7, when Gardner received news that Vicksburg had surrendered to Grant on the 4th. The next day he agreed to surrender to Banks, and the following day, July 9, formal surrender ceremonies took place.

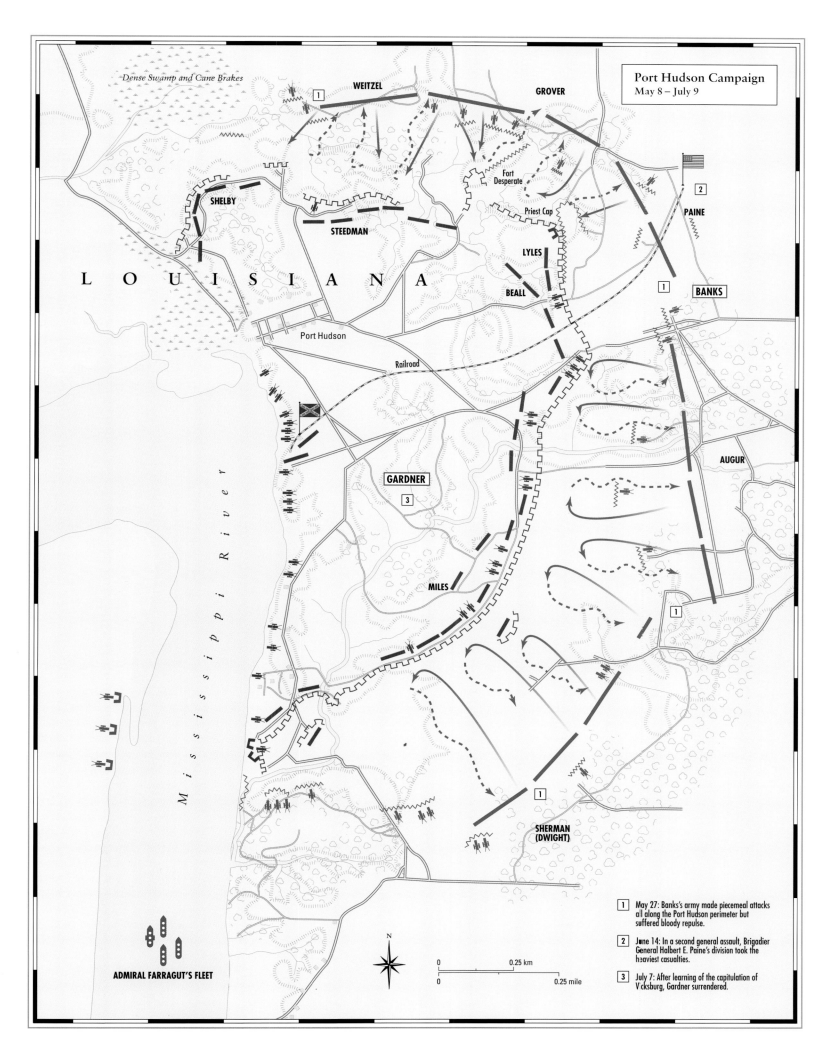

Dense Swamp and Cane Brakes

WEITZEL

GROVER

1

Fort
Desperate

Priest Cap

2

SHELBY

STEEDMAN

PAINE

LYLES

L O U I S I A N A

BEALL

1

BANKS

Port Hudson

Railroad

AUGUR

GARDNER

3

MILES

1

Mississippi River

SHERMAN
(DWIGHT)

ADMIRAL FARRAGUT'S FLEET

N

Port Hudson Campaign
May 8 – July 9

0   0.25 km

0   0.25 mile

1   May 27: Banks's army made piecemeal attacks
     all along the Port Hudson perimeter but
     suffered bloody repulse.

2   June 14: In a second general assault, Brigadier
     General Halbert E. Paine's division took the
     heaviest casualties.

3   July 7: After learning of the capitulation of
     Vicksburg, Gardner surrendered.

SIEGE AND CAPTURE OF VICKSBURG

AFTER BEING DEFEATED AT THE Battle of Big Black Bridge, May 17, 1863, Confederate Major General John C. Pemberton retreated westward into the fortifications of Vicksburg. Grant followed, as soon as new bridges could be laid across the Big Black River, and arrived outside Vicksburg the next day. He believed, not without reason, that Pemberton's army was badly demoralized after the series of defeats it had sustained, culminating in the battles of Champion's Hill and Big Black Bridge. This demoralization, Grant thought, might allow his army to break into Vicksburg in one bold assault; so on May 19, he sent his troops forward.

The result was failure. Two of the five Confederate divisions inside Vicksburg had remained in garrison throughout the campaign and had not been subject to the recent defeats. The other Confederate troops had quickly recovered their fighting spirit inside the extremely strong defensive works around Vicksburg. The terrain—characterized by steep, narrow ridges and deep ravines filled with jungle-like foliage—was so favorable to the defenders that most units of

With the failure of the grand assault on May 22, Grant accepted the inevitability of a prolonged siege. His men began the operations from the positions to which they had retreated after the assault, steadily digging their way closer and closer to the Confederate lines. Union troops continued artillery bombardment and sharpshooting more or less without interruption. The defenders made little reply to the constant Union fire, both because their supply of ammunition was limited and because opening a gun port or peering over the parapet invited a Union sniper's bullet. Some of Grant's troops tunneled under one of the Confederate forts and detonated a large mine, blowing the fort and its defenders skyward. Union troops attempted to advance through the gap created, but the Confederates were able to beat back the attack and restore their lines.

While siege operations continued against Vicksburg, Grant prepared for the possibility of a Confederate attempt to raise the siege. He detached part of his army and placed it under the command of his most trusted subordinate, Major General William T. Sherman, with orders to move eastward to the Big

In late June a detachment of Yankee ex-coal miners dug a tunnel under the principal Confederate redoubt, mined it with over a ton of gunpowder, and on June 25 detonated the explosives. The White House shown on the edge of the Union position in Fenn's drawing was later photographed in July, when Union dugouts hastily improvised on the reverse slope to exploit shade as well as protection from enemy fire could still be seen.

Grant's army were not even able to reach their assigned attacking positions before the day ended.

Grant was loath to settle down to a siege. It would tie up needed Union forces for an indefinite period; would expose his troops to the hazards of disease in the Mississippi Valley during the hot summer months; and carried the added danger that a Confederate relieving army, then forming under General Joseph E. Johnston north of Jackson, Mississippi, might attempt to intervene. Grant therefore spent the next two days getting troops and artillery into position and then on May 22 ordered a coordinated assault all along the line. For hours Union artillery and naval vessels bombarded the defenses and then at 10:00 a.m. Grant's infantry charged. With extreme valor Union soldiers advanced in many cases all the way to the outer ditch of the fortifications, and a dozen brave men actually fought their way into one of the many forts. The Confederate line held, however, and forced the attackers to pull back several hundred yards. Union casualties for the assault totaled approximately 3,200 while Confederate losses were less than 500.

Black River and guard the army's rear against the possibility of an advance by Johnston. As the siege went on, the Union high command in Washington saw to it that Grant received ample reinforcements, and he sent most of these troops to bolster Sherman's force. Johnston made no move to attack, but instead complained constantly to the Richmond authorities that he did not have enough men.

By early July food had grown very scarce in Vicksburg. The Union siege lines had approached in some places to within ten yards of the Confederate parapet, and the morale of Pemberton's soldiers was low. On July 3, Pemberton opened negotiations with Grant and the next day surrendered Vicksburg. Grant paroled the thirty-thousand-man garrison. Five days later, the subsidiary Confederate stronghold of Port Hudson, Louisiana, surrendered to a smaller Union besieging force. The capture of the Confederacy's last two fortresses on the Mississippi River allowed Lincoln to announce, "The Father of Waters again goes unvexed to the sea."

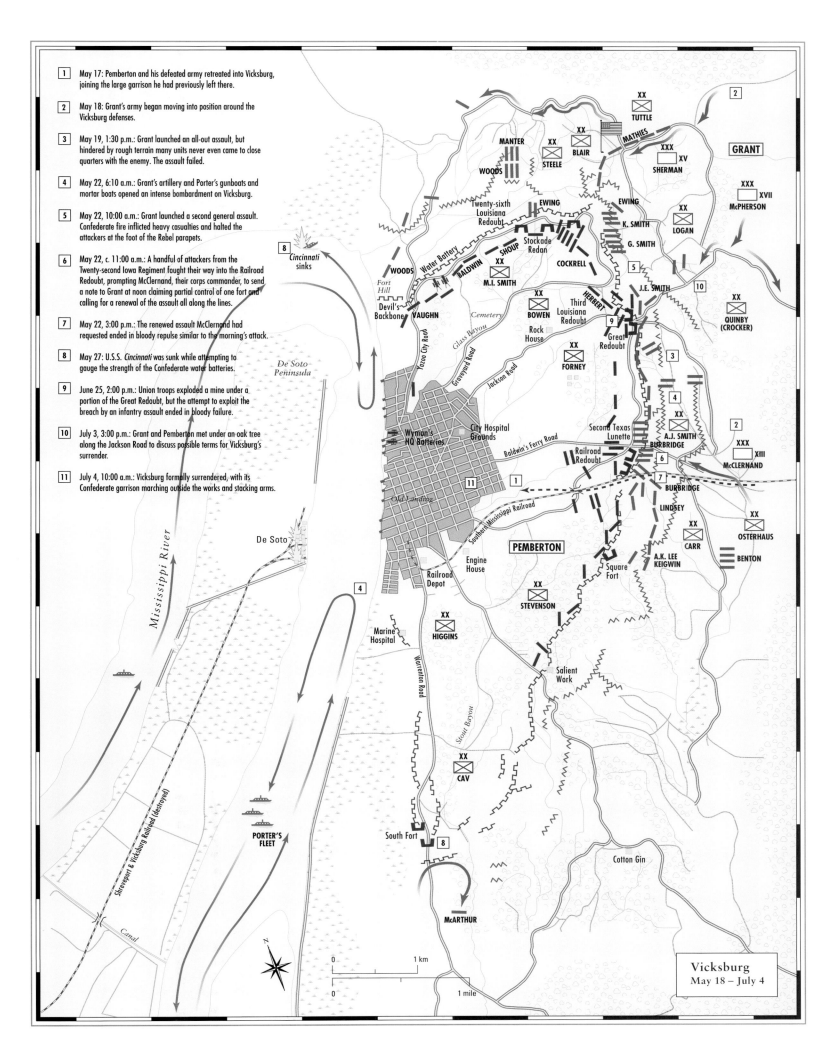

1 May 17: Pemberton and his defeated army retreated into Vicksburg, joining the large garrison he had previously left there.

2 May 18: Grant's army began moving into position around the Vicksburg defenses.

3 May 19, 1:30 p.m.: Grant launched an all-out assault, but hindered by rough terrain many units never even came to close quarters with the enemy. The assault failed.

4 May 22, 6:10 a.m.: Grant's artillery and Porter's gunboats and mortar boats opened an intense bombardment on Vicksburg.

5 May 22, 10:00 a.m.: Grant launched a second general assault. Confederate fire inflicted heavy casualties and halted the attackers at the foot of the Rebel parapets.

6 May 22, c. 11:00 a.m.: A handful of attackers from the Twenty-second Iowa Regiment fought their way into the Railroad Redoubt, prompting McClernand, their corps commander, to send a note to Grant at noon claiming partial control of one fort and calling for a renewal of the assault all along the lines.

7 May 22, 3:00 p.m.: The renewed assault McClernand had requested ended in bloody repulse similar to the morning's attack.

8 May 27: U.S.S. Cincinnati was sunk while attempting to gauge the strength of the Confederate water batteries.

9 June 25, 2:00 p.m.: Union troops exploded a mine under a portion of the Great Redoubt, but the attempt to exploit the breach by an infantry assault ended in bloody failure.

10 July 3, 3:00 p.m.: Grant and Pemberton met under an oak tree along the Jackson Road to discuss possible terms for Vicksburg's surrender.

11 July 4, 10:00 a.m.: Vicksburg formally surrendered, with its Confederate garrison marching outside the works and stacking arms.

Vicksburg
May 18 – July 4

GETTYSBURG CAMPAIGN—THE INVASION OF THE NORTH

URING THE EARLY MONTHS OF 1863, Lee and Jackson contemplated an offensive into the North. Such a movement, they believed, might force the Army of the Potomac into battle on terms favorable to the Confederates, and it was possible to hope that a great Confederate victory won on Northern soil might damage Union morale to the point of accepting Confederate independence. Such an offensive would have to wait until spring, when the roads had dried out and the grass had grown enough to strengthen the army's draft animals. In late April, before Lee was ready to launch his offensive, Major General Joseph Hooker launched one of his own, resulting in the Battle of Chancellorsville in early May. Considered the pinnacle of Lee and Jackson's cooperation, the Confederate victory at Chancellorsville also resulted in the wounding and death, eight days later, of Jackson.

1 June 9: Union cavalry surprises J.E.B. Stuart's Confederate cavalry at Brandy Station. This turns into the largest cavalry battle of the war.

2 June 13: Hooker retreats northward from Fredericksburg.

3 June 14: Ewell's corps routs Major General Milroy's Union force at Winchester.

4 June 15: Lee's army crosses the Potomac River.

5 June 25: J.E.B. Stuart leads his cavalry force away from the main army intending to reunite with Lee at York.

6 June 28: Hooker is relieved as command and Meade becomes his successor.

7 June 30: Cavalry skirmish at Hanover Junction.

8 June 30: Reynolds receives orders from Meade to occupy Gettysburg.

9 July 2: J.E.B. Stuart's cavalry finally rejoins Lee's army on the second day of the Battle of Gettysburg.

Invasion of the North
June 1 – July 2

→ Confederate Infantry movements

⇢ Confederate Cavalry movements

→ Union Infantry movements

⇢ Union Cavalry movements

Convinced more than ever of the need to seize the initiative rather than wait for another dangerous Union offensive, Lee sought permission from Jefferson Davis to lead the Army of Northern Virginia across the Potomac. As always, Davis liked the idea of offensive action, but he hesitated at assuming the large risks involved. In two days of discussions during mid-May, Lee convinced both Davis and the Confederate cabinet that the army should invade the North. In making his case, Lee stressed the more modest goals of his planned offensive—disrupting Union offensive plans, drawing the Army of the Potomac out of Virginia, and allowing the Army of Northern Virginia to feed itself by plundering Northern civilians.

With the approval of president and cabinet, Lee's army on June 3 began to move westward from the vicinity of Fredericksburg, Virginia. Over the next several days Lee's troops marched up the south bank of the Rappahannock, then over the passes of the Blue Ridge before turning northeastward, down the Shenandoah Valley.

A suspicious Hooker ordered his cavalry corps, commanded by Major General Alfred Pleasonton, to probe south of the Rappahannock. Pleasonton did so on June 9 at Brandy Station, Virginia, precipitating the largest cavalry engagement of the war. Catching Jeb Stuart by surprise, Pleasonton's men gave the Confederate cavalry a hard fight before the latter rallied, with the help of Confederate infantry, and drove the Federals back to the north bank of the Rappahannock. From the information gained in the attack, Hooker came to the conclusion that the Rebels were planning a large cavalry raid, possibly supported by infantry. Hooker suggested to the authorities in Washington that he ought to take Richmond while Lee was away, but Lincoln suggested that Lee's army ought to be Hooker's chief target.

On June 14, Lieutenant General Richard S. Ewell's Second Corps of the Army of Northern Virginia, leading Lee's advance, approached Winchester, Virginia, and skirmished with the Union garrison of the town commanded by Major General Robert Milroy. That night as Milroy attempted to withdraw, Ewell routed his smaller force, taking four thousand Union prisoners and capturing twenty-three cannons. Meanwhile other troops of Ewell's corps captured Martinsburg, Virginia, along with more guns and prisoners, and began crossing the Potomac.

By June 24, Lieutenant General James Longstreet's First Corps, now bringing up the rear of Lee's long column, was crossing the Potomac, and Ewell's forces were already ranging far up the Cumberland Valley in Pennsylvania and beginning to pose a threat to Harrisburg. Lee had given an order that his men should not engage in individual plundering, but rather that Confederate commissary officers should, in an orderly manner, confiscate all the food, fodder, and livestock they encountered in Pennsylvania. This they did, but Confederate soldiers also helped themselves, in wholesale violation of Lee's order. The Confederate army also destroyed bridges, depots, warehouses, and an iron factory belonging to Congressman Thaddeus

Stevens. White Pennsylvanians were generally safe in their persons, but the Confederates followed a policy of kidnapping any blacks they encountered for enslavement in the South.

Hooker's army got a late start but pursued Lee by hard marches. When General-in-Chief Henry Halleck would not endorse some of his plans, Hooker asked to be relieved of command. His replacement, George Meade, took command on June 27. Meade continued the army's northward movement so as to cover

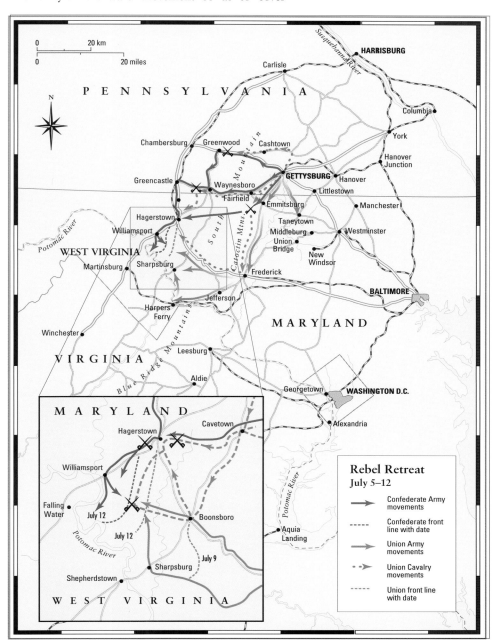

Washington and Baltimore and relieve the Confederate threat to Harrisburg. By June 30 the leading elements of the Army of the Potomac, the First and Eleventh corps, under the command of Major General John Reynolds, were a few miles south of Gettysburg, Pennsylvania. Until June 28, Lee, due to a failure of Jeb Stuart's cavalry, was unaware that the Army of the Potomac was north of its namesake river. Apprised by a scout of the enemy's proximity, Lee gave orders for his own army to concentrate at Cashtown, Pennsylvania, on the east slope of South Mountain, nine miles northwest of Gettysburg.

GETTYSBURG, PHASE I

1. July 1, 1:00 p.m.: Having rallied from its earlier repulse, Rodes's division renewed its attack and this time succeeded in driving in the right flank of the First Corps.

2. Heth's division also renewed its assault on McPherson's Ridge and finally succeeded in driving back the First Corps after ferocious fighting in which some regiments suffered eighty percent casualties.

3. Early's division attacked almost simultaneously from the north and northeast, crumbling the line of Eleventh Corps north of Gettysburg.

4. Elements of the First Corps made a stand on Seminary Ridge and inflicted ruinous casualties on two brigades of Major General William Dorsey Pender's division before being driven back toward the town.

5. C. 4:00 p.m.: The fugitives of the First and Eleventh corps streamed through Gettysburg in retreat. Some were captured by pursuing Confederates.

6. C. 6:00 p.m.: Major General Oliver O. Howard and newly arrived Major General Winfield S. Hancock rallied the First and Eleventh corps on Cemetery Hill, where Howard had posted a reserve brigade.

7. Hancock dispatched elements of the First Corps to hold vital Culp's Hill nearby.

WHEN GENERAL ROBERT E. LEE learned on June 28 that the Army of the Potomac was north of its namesake river, he ordered his Army of Northern Virginia to assemble at Cashtown, Pennsylvania. From west, north, and northeast, Confederate columns began marching in that direction. Lieutenant General Ambrose Powell Hill's Confederate Third Corps was the first to concentrate at Cashtown, and one of Hill's division commanders, Major General Henry Heth, requested permission of Hill and Lee to take his division and probe toward Gettysburg, six miles to the southeast, on July 1.

Major General George G. Meade had picked out a defensive position along Pipe Creek in Maryland, toward which he hoped to lure Lee. His forces were spread across a wide swath of Maryland and southern Pennsylvania in order to guard against any possible Confederate lunge toward Washington or Baltimore. On June 30 he sent his corps commanders orders to prepare to draw back and assemble along Pipe Creek. Major General John Reynolds, who was in command of the advanced wing of the Army of the Potomac, had not received the Pipe Creek order when he decided to proceed to Gettysburg on July 1. His aim was to secure the Union hold on Gettysburg, as it was an important hub for numerous roads in south central Pennsylvania.

Early on the morning of July 1, Heth's troops encountered Union cavalrymen, under the command of Brigadier General John Buford, who were holding Gettysburg and nearby roads. In several hours of skirmishing, they slowly drove the dismounted cavalrymen back toward the town until Buford's men made a determined stand along McPherson's Ridge. Just as Heth was finally launching a full-scale assault with two brigades, Union troops of the First Corps arrived on the field, led personally by Reynolds. They caught the attacking Confederates by surprise and routed them, capturing Confederate Brigadier General James J. Archer. Reynolds, however, was killed in the opening volley. Command of Union troops on the battlefield passed to Major General Abner Doubleday, and then, with the arrival of the Eleventh Corps, to its commander, Major General Oliver O. Howard.

Howard faced an impossible situation. With only the small First and Eleventh corps, he lacked the manpower to cover the northern and western approaches to Gettysburg. Yet Reynolds, his late superior, had before his death committed this wing of the army to holding Gettysburg. Unknown to Howard, two-thirds of the Army of Northern Virginia was approaching Gettysburg from north and west, as Confederate commanders on their way to Cashtown wisely marched toward the sound of the guns. Howard, like Reynolds, had not received the Pipe Creek order and so assumed that other nearby corps of the Army of the Potomac, especially the Third and Twelfth corps, would hasten to his aid if he stood and fought.

Stand and fight he did, and met disaster. Lee arrived that afternoon and reluctantly approved an all-out assault. Lee would rather have waited until his whole army was assembled, but this opportunity seemed too good to miss. Lee's troops broke the lines of the Eleventh Corps north of Gettysburg and the First Corps west of it. The defeated troops fled through the town, where the pursuing Confederates captured many of them. The rest sought refuge on Cemetery Hill, south of Gettysburg. Howard had noticed this commanding hill early in the day and placed a reserve brigade there. Now his foresight paid off, as the reserve brigade formed a nucleus around which the broken troops could rally.

Also on Cemetery Hill by that time was Major General Winfield Scott Hancock, commander of the Second Corps. Meade, still at Taneytown, Maryland, had dispatched Hancock to the battlefield that afternoon instead of going himself. In doing so Meade authorized Hancock to take command of the battlefield even though Howard was senior to him in rank. Hancock's corps was still some miles away, but Hancock was on hand to take command and help Howard in rallying troops on Cemetery Hill and neighboring Culp's Hill. Hancock and Howard prepared the troops to meet the Confederate attack that all expected.

No attack came that evening. Lee, who by this time had made his headquarters where the Chambersburg Pike crosses Seminary Ridge just west of Gettysburg, had significant fresh forces of the Confederate Third Corps available either on Seminary Ridge or within easy reach behind it.

However, because of the continued absence of Major General James Ewell Brown "Jeb" Stuart, commanding the Confederate cavalry, Lee lacked information about the location of the rest of the Union army, the five corps his troops had not encountered yet that day. This made him reluctant to commit his reserves. He therefore sent an order to Lieutenant General Richard S. Ewell, commander of the Confederate Second Corps, directing him to advance and take Cemetery Hill if he thought he could do so without bringing on a general engagement. With tired troops, an enemy presenting a resolute front, and a very cryptic order from Lee, Ewell decided to halt. The day's fighting was over.

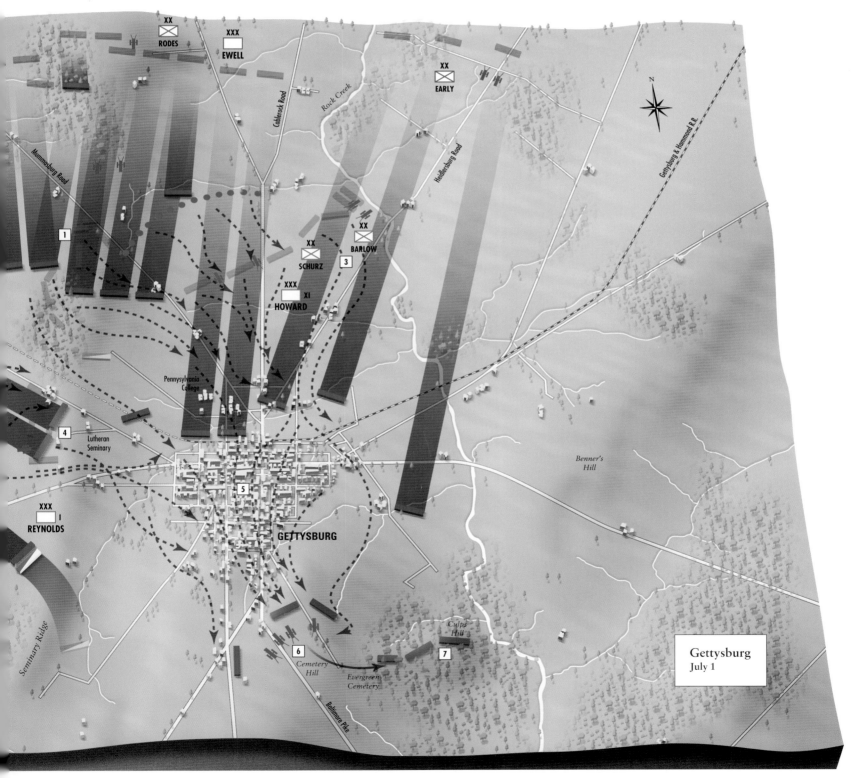

Gettysburg
July 1

GETTYSBURG, PHASE II

BY THE MORNING OF JULY 1, most units of both armies had arrived near Gettysburg. Meade, with perhaps sixty thousand troops available for action, was still awaiting the arrival of the fifteen-thousand-man Sixth Corps. As his army arrived he deployed it in a position shaped like a fishhook with

Confederate dead lay scattered around the lower slopes of Little Round Top. They were killed during the July 2 assault and this photograph was probably taken on July 4.

its barb at Culp's Hill, the curve at Cemetery Hill, and a long, straight shank running south along the low Cemetery Ridge to the eye of the hook at a high, conical hill called "Little Round Top." In this strong position, he awaited Lee's attack.

Lee was determined to deliver that attack, believing he had an opportunity to defeat the Army of the Potomac by following up the success of the previous day. He had somewhat more than sixty thousand men available for action this day, with only Stuart's cavalry and Major General George E. Pickett's division of infantry still on the way. Lee ordered his most experienced corps commander, Lieutenant General James Longstreet of the Confederate First Corps, to take the divisions of major generals John B. Hood and LaFayette McLaws of his own corps plus Major General Richard H. Anderson's division detached from the Confederate Third Corps and attack the Union left flank. Lee hoped the attack would be a repetition

of Stonewall Jackson's success at Chancellorsville.

Faulty reconnaissance led Lee to believe that the Union line extended along the Emmitsburg Road, rather than Cemetery Ridge, and that it simply stopped a mile or two southwest of Gettysburg. He ordered Longstreet to take a position athwart the road beyond the Union flank, and roll up the Army of the Potomac. Longstreet did not wish to attack, and protested these orders repeatedly. Controversy persists as to whether he obeyed them with appropriate vigor.

While Longstreet prepared to attack, the position of the Union line changed. The untrained Major General Daniel E. Sickles, a politician in uniform commanding the Third Corps, took a disliking to the position Meade had assigned him on lower Cemetery Ridge and Little Round Top. In blatant violation of orders, he decided to stretch his corps along the Emmitsburg Road and through the Peach Orchard, the Wheat Field, and a large pile of boulders called "Devil's Den." Thus deployed, they were spread far too thin for effective defense. By the time Meade discovered Sickles's blunder, it was too late to withdraw the Third Corps before Longstreet's attack struck at 4:00 p.m.

As Longstreet's troops advanced, Meade's chief engineer, Major General Gouverneur K. Warren, noticed that Sickles had left Little Round Top undefended. He hastily brought up a brigade of the Fifth Corps to hold this key terrain, which it did in several hours of heroic fighting. Meade sent the rest of the Fifth Corps and a division of the Second Corps to reinforce the hard-pressed Union left. Sickles lost a leg to a cannon ball and his corps was all but destroyed in Longstreet's attack. It was a near-run thing, but the Federal line finally stabilized and held roughly along the line of Cemetery Ridge and Little Round Top, where Meade had originally ordered Sickles to place his corps. Shortly before nightfall, Major General John Sedgwick's Sixth Corps arrived after a day's forced march, ending Confederate hopes of a breakthrough on the Union left.

The day's fighting was not over, however. Lee had directed Ewell to make demonstrations against Culp's and Cemetery hills and to be prepared to turn those demonstrations into real attacks if an opportunity appeared. Ewell's corps had managed nothing more than an ineffective artillery bombardment that afternoon, but as light began to fade Major General Edward Johnson's division of Ewell's Second Corps advanced against Culp's Hill. Some time before, Meade had ordered the defenders of the hill, Major General Henry W. Slocum's Twelfth Corps, to march to the aid of the hard-pressed left. Slocum wisely remonstrated, and Meade allowed him to leave one brigade. By dint of hard fighting, that brigade was able to hold on to the higher of the two summits of Culp's Hill before darkness closed the fighting there. In almost complete darkness, Major General Jubal Early's division of Ewell's Second Corps then attacked Cemetery Hill and briefly reached the Federal guns there before being repulsed, ending the second day's fighting.

1. July 2, 4:00 p.m.: Major General John B. Hood's division led off Longstreet's attack, crushing the poorly deployed troops of Major General Daniel E. Sickles's Third Corps on the extreme Union left.

2. 5:00 p.m.: Colonel Strong Vincent's brigade of the Fifth Corps arrived just in time to hold Little Round Top.

3. Brigadier General George T. Anderson's brigade of Hood's division waged a long and intense struggle for the Wheat Field, which changed hands four times before nightfall.

4. Major General Lafayette McLaws's division joined the assault and drove Union troops out of the Peach Orchard.

5. Brigadier General William Barksdale's brigade of McLaws's division broke through the Union line and penetrated deeply before being stopped by Union reinforcements.

6. Major General Richard H. Anderson's division joined the attack and penetrated almost all the way to Cemetery Ridge before being stopped by a Union counterattack.

7. Meade ordered Major General Henry W. Slocum to take the entire Twenty-first Corps off of Culp's Hill and march to the support of the Union's left. Slocum protested, and Meade allowed him to leave a single brigade.

8. Major General John Sedgwick's Sixth Corps arrived after a forced march, provided Meade with much needed reserves.

9. Confederate troops of Major General Edward Johnson's division attacked and took some of the abandoned Twelfth Corps positions on Culp's Hill but were prevented from taking the summit by the well-entrenched brigade of Brigadier General George S. Greene.

10. In the gathering darkness, Early's division assaulted Cemetery Hill and got among some of the cannons there before Union infantry drove them back.

11. Major General Geary's division of the Twelfth went astray, marching down the Baltimore Pike for some distance before turning and marching back. None of the Twelfth Corps units became engaged on the left and all returned late in the night to find their former positions held by Johnson's Confederates.

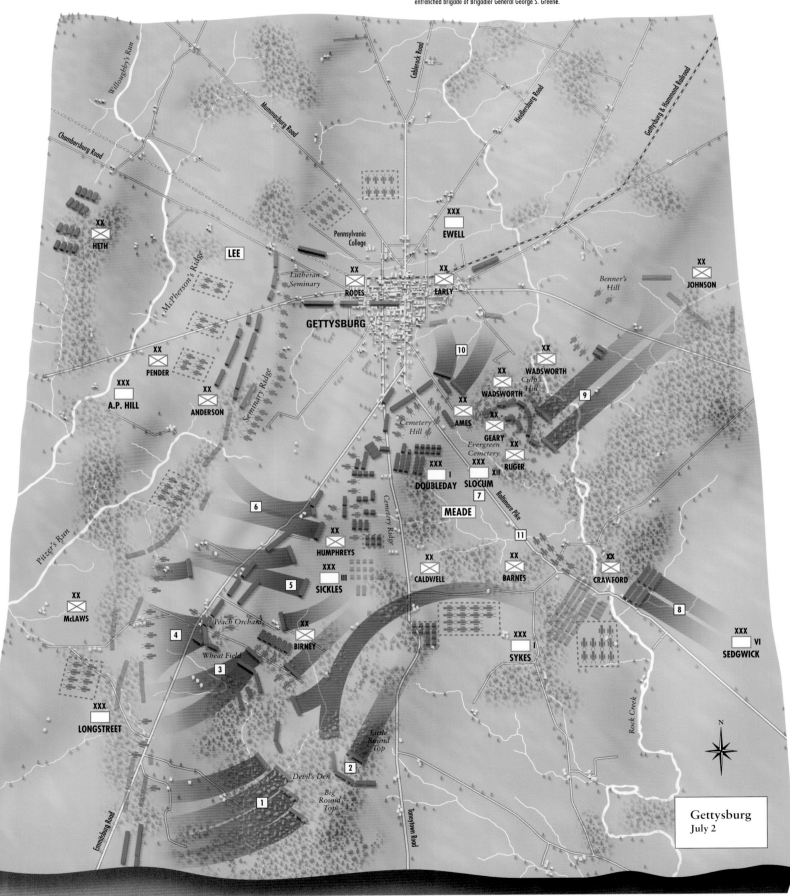

Gettysburg
July 2

GETTYSBURG, PHASE III

During the night, the Twelfth Corps, minus the one brigade that had held the summit of Culp's Hill, returned from its unnecessary march toward the Union left to find that its positions on the southeastern shoulder of Culp's Hill had been occupied by Confederates of Johnson's division. The Union officers determined to drive them off at dawn. Meanwhile, Johnson made plans to continue his advance of the evening before. At 4:30 a.m. Union artillery opened a preparatory bombardment, but fifteen minutes later it was not the Union but the Confederate infantry that charged. For the next five hours Johnson's Confederates attempted to drive the Federals from Culp's Hill but were stopped by heavy Union fire.

Lee hoped that Ewell's continued attack on Culp's Hill would serve as a diversion for an early morning attack by Longstreet's corps against the Union left or center. With the arrival of Pickett's division the previous day, Longstreet's First Corps was complete, and Lee designated it to make his primary assault. Longstreet again proved unwilling and this time definitely uncooperative. He failed to get his troops into position for a morning assault, and he complained that Hood's and McLaws's divisions were unfit for action after their fighting the evening before. Lee agreed to provide Longstreet with other troops to take the place of Hood's and McLaws's. These proved to be Heth's division and two brigades of Major General William Dorsey Pender's, both very roughly used on July 1. As both Heth and Pender were injured, Brigadier General James J. Pettigrew now commanded Heth's division and Major General Isaac Trimble commanded Pender's two brigades.

Lee hoped that a heavy artillery bombardment would knock out the Union cannons in the center of the line, on Cemetery Ridge, and weaken the Union infantry in that sector. For this purpose he massed some 164 pieces of artillery under the direction of First Corps artillery commander Colonel E. Porter Alexander. Longstreet tried to shift responsibility to Alexander by ordering him to decide whether the bombardment would be sufficiently effective to justify an infantry advance. Alexander knew, however, that the army had only enough artillery ammunition for a single bombardment. Once the guns opened, the scheduled attack would be the army's only remaining option.

At 1:07 p.m. Alexander's guns opened, and what followed for approximately the next forty-five minutes was the heaviest artillery bombardment ever heard on the North American continent. Many of the Union guns waited for as long as fifteen minutes before returning fire, in order to conserve ammunition. Eventually, eighty or more Union cannons answered the bombardment. Superior ammunition and training rendered the Union return fire more deadly to the waiting Confederate infantry than the Confederate bombardment was to the Union soldiers defending Cemetery Ridge. All the while, Union chief of artillery Brigadier General Henry J. Hunt was holding numerous additional batteries in reserve, ready to use them against the infantry attack that everyone knew would follow the bombardment.

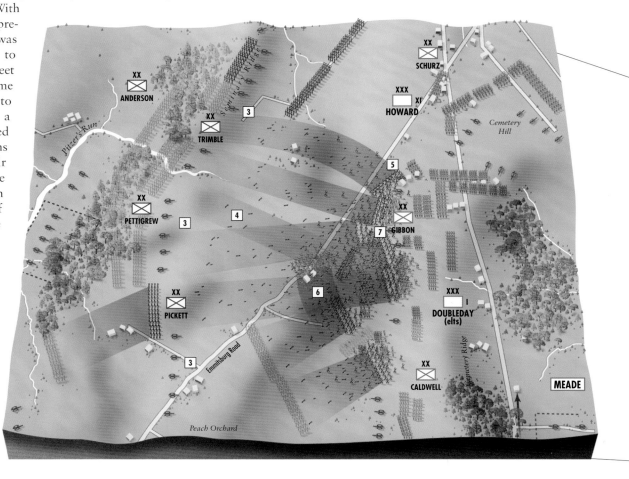

After his guns had been in action about thirty minutes, Hunt ordered them to cease firing, battery by battery, hoping the diminishing volume of return fire would convince the Confederates to launch their attack while Union guns still had ammunition. In fact, Alexander's guns were even then firing their last shells. Noting the reduced Union fire, Alexander sent word to Pickett that the time had come for the infantry to advance. Seeing Pickett's division begin to move forward, Pettigrew and Trimble advanced as well.

The attackers, about thirteen thousand men, had to cross 1,200 yards of open ground to reach Union lines. As they began their advance, friend and foe alike were impressed with their magnificent formation. All three divisions were visible at the same time, and from a distance their lines appeared as neat as if they were on parade. During the first nine hundred yards of the advance, Union long-range artillery on both flanks inflicted moderate casualties, but the guns in the sector directly in front of the attackers were out of long-range ammunition, and therefore remained silent and waiting, loaded with deadly short-range canister. Between two hundred and four hundred yards from the Union line, the Emmitsburg Road angled across the attackers' path, with, in some places, stout rail fences that the Confederates had to climb. Many of the troops were doing just that when the Union infantry and short-range artillery opened fire with devastating effect. Many of Pickett's troops and perhaps a few of Pettigrew's succeeded in pushing forward all the way to the low stone fence that fronted the Union position, briefly driving back the defenders. Then, however, Union troops rallied, and the assault ended in failure with the attackers having lost nearly half their number.

Later that day a Union cavalry division made a foolish and unauthorized foray against the Confederate right flank. With that, the major fighting of the Battle of Gettysburg was over.

1 | July 3, 4:30 a.m.: The Twelfth Corps's artillery opened a barrage in preparation for an attack to retake the positions Johnson's Confederates had seized the night before in the corps's absence.

2 | 4:45 a.m.: As Twelfth Corps infantry prepared to advance, Johnson's Confederates pre-empted them with an attack of their own. The Union troops went over to the defensive and beat off repeated Confederate attacks until at 10:00 a.m. Johnson gave up the attempt to take the rest of Culp's Hill.

3 | 1:07 p.m.: Confederate artillery opened a massed barrage on Union lines with one hundred and sixty-four guns.

4 | 2:30 p.m.: Pickett's and Pettigrews's divisions, along with two brigades of Major General Isaac Trimble's advance toward the Union center, all under the command of Longstreet.

5 | 3:00 p.m.: The Eighth Ohio Regiment attacked the left flank of the advancing Confederate line.

6 | 3:15 p.m.: Brigadier General George Stannard's Vermont brigade attacked to the right flank of Pickett's division.

7 | 3:15 p.m.: The Confederate attackers reached Union lines and a few of them briefly got in amongst a battery of guns before being driven back with heavy losses.

8 | 5:30 p.m.: Brigadier General Judson Kilpatrick, without orders from Meade, launched an ill-conceived cavalry attack on the extreme right flank of the confederate line, which accomplished nothing beyond getting some of his men shot.

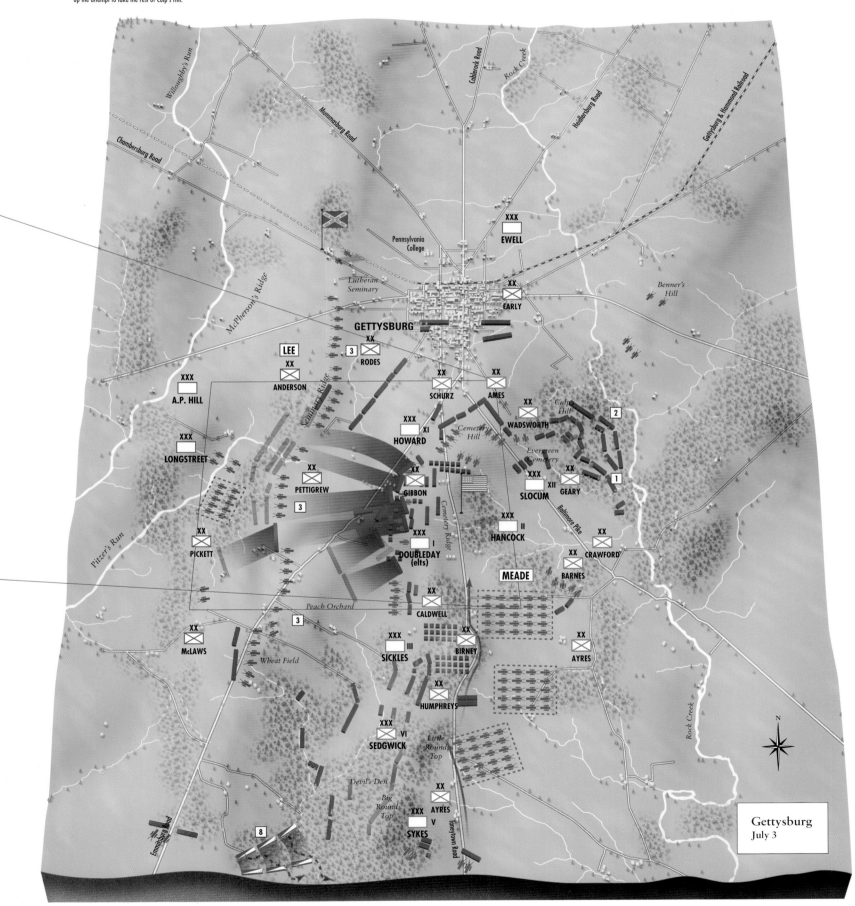

Gettysburg
July 3

TULLAHOMA CAMPAIGN AND ADVANCE ON CHATTANOOGA

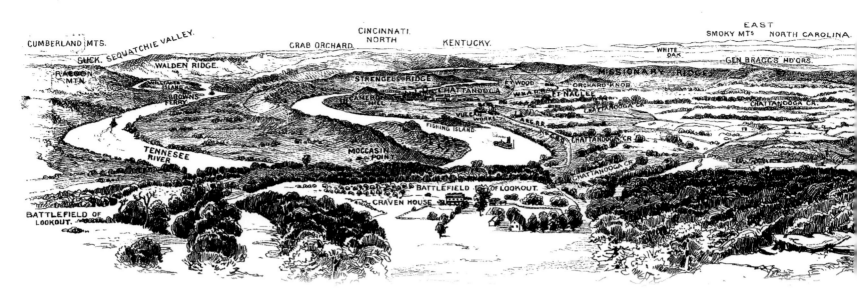

This panorama of the high ground west, south, and east of the city was drawn from a position on Lookout Mountain. Confederate guns controlled the loop in the Tenneese River cutting rail and river supply routes into the city.

FOR SIX MONTHS AFTER THE Battle of Stone's River at the close of 1862, Major General William S. Rosecrans's Army of the Cumberland remained idle while major campaigns took place in other theaters of the war. Grant carried out his lightning campaign of maneuver against Vicksburg and trapped Lieutenant General John C. Pemberton inside the city. The Confederate Army of Tennessee, facing Rosecrans, was able to detach five thousand troops for the relief of Vicksburg, and yet Rosecrans still did nothing. The general insisted that every aspect of supply and equipment within his army must be brought to a state of perfection before he would move. Lincoln, Secretary of War Edwin M. Stanton, and Halleck prodded, coaxed, scolded, and threatened but could not get their reluctant general to advance.

Finally, on June 24, 1863, the Army of the Cumberland moved forward from its base at Murfreesboro, southeastward toward Chattanooga. In its path General Braxton Bragg's Army of Tennessee had its headquarters at Tullahoma, Tennessee, and its troops ranged along a chain of hills northwest of Tullahoma called the Highland Rim. An army could pass the Highland Rim only at one of several gaps, where defenders had a significant advantage. Rosecrans divided his army into several columns in order to confuse Bragg as to his intended route through the hills. Major General Thomas L. Crittenden's Twenty-first Corps swung far to the east, marching to pass Bragg's right flank. Major General Gordon Granger's Reserve Corps, along with the army's cavalry corps under Major General David Stanley, proceeded down the main highway toward Tullahoma and skirmished with Confederate forces in broad, easily passable Guy's Gap, in front of the town of Shelbyville.

Granger's and Crittenden's advances formed the flanks of Rosecrans's advance. In the center of his formation were two more columns that were his true hope of crossing the Highland Rim. Major General Alexander McCook's Twentieth Corps, on Rosecrans's right center, advanced toward Liberty Gap, while Major General George

H. Thomas's Fourteenth Corps, on the left center, advanced toward Hoover's Gap. Confederate cavalry picketed both gaps, and Confederate infantry was encamped just beyond the Highland Rim, ready to march into the gaps as soon as their cavalry gave the warning. Both Union columns were led by powerful formations of mounted infantry armed with the new Spencer seven-shot repeating rifle, which dramatically multiplied their combat power. In front of Thomas's corps was an especially strong and aggressive force, Colonel John T. Wilder's Lightning Brigade, composed of four regiments of mounted infantry armed with Spencer Repeating Rifles. The brigade drove all the way through Hoover's Gap and out the far exit, dispersing the Confederate cavalry and securing the gap before the Confederate infantry could respond. When the gray-clad foot soldiers did arrive, Wilder's men repulsed them handily.

Bragg's army did not react well to Rosecrans's challenge. Its two corps commanders, lieutenant generals Leonidas Polk and William J. Hardee, were scarcely on speaking terms with Bragg. They were convinced that he was completely incompetent and were determined that the army should retreat, by means of mutiny if necessary, rather than fight while under Bragg's command. They balked at his orders for an offensive counterstroke to Rosecrans's advance and clamored constantly for retreat. In the face of their recalcitrance, Bragg relented and the Army of Tennessee abandoned its positions along the Highland Rim and concentrated in entrenched lines around Tullahoma.

Rosecrans continued with his plan, pulling McCook's column out of Liberty Gap and sending it around to follow in the wake of Thomas's Fourteenth Corps, which advanced rapidly through Hoover's Gap and on to the town of Manchester. In these movements the Army of the Cumberland was greatly hindered by the almost incessant rain that fell during the campaign, reducing Tennessee's dirt roads to bottomless mud. This condition especially delayed Crittenden's long flank march to the northeast, and Rosecrans paused for several days until the Twenty-first Corps could join the rest of the

army, now concentrated at Manchester. While he waited, Rosecrans dispatched Wilder's Lightning Brigade on a brief raid against Bragg's railroad communications, without dramatic results.

By the time Rosecrans was ready to renew the offensive by advancing against Tullahoma itself, Bragg's generals had again persuaded him to retreat, abandoning the entrenchments at Tullahoma. Bragg briefly entertained ideas of making a stand behind the Elk River or at the foot of the rugged Cumberland Plateau, prospects that again brought his corps commanders to the verge of mutiny. So the Confederate retreat continued over the Cumberland Plateau and down the other side to the strategically located town of Chattanooga. Rosecrans's army halted its pursuit at the northwestern foot of the Cumberland Plateau, concluding the campaign.

1 June 24: Rosecrans opened his campaign against Tullahoma by sending the Army of the Cumberland cavalry under Major General David Stanley and the Reserve Corps under Major General Gordon Granger to threaten and advance through broad Guy's Gap in the Highland Rim against Lieutenant General Leonidas Polk's Confederate corps at Shelbyville.

2 June 24: Simultaneous with the feint toward Shelbyville, Rosecrans sent Major General Edward McCook's Twentieth Corps through Liberty Gap, threatening the Confederate center.

3 June 24: At the same time, Rosecrans's main thrust, Major General George H. Thomas's Fourteenth Corps, marched through Hoover's Gap, led by Colonel John T. Wilder's "Lightning Brigade."

4 June 24: Yet another prong of Rosecrans's complicated offensive, Major General Thomas L. Crittenden's Twenty-first Corps swung wide around the Confederate right flank, headed for McMinnville but was slowed by heavy rains and muddy roads.

5 June 27: Bragg's forces began a rapid retreat toward Tullahoma.

6 June 28: Thomas's Fourteenth corps occupied Manchester; the rest of the Army of the Cumberland followed rapidly.

7 June 28–29: Wilder's Lightning Brigade raided in rear of Bragg's army, doing minor damage to the railroad on the Cumberland Plateau.

8 June 30: Bragg abandoned Tullahoma and fell back across the Cumberland Plateau to Chattanooga.

9 August 16: Rosecrans launched his next offensive with an even more complicated scheme, sending his divisions through a number of different gaps in the rugged Cumberland Plateau.

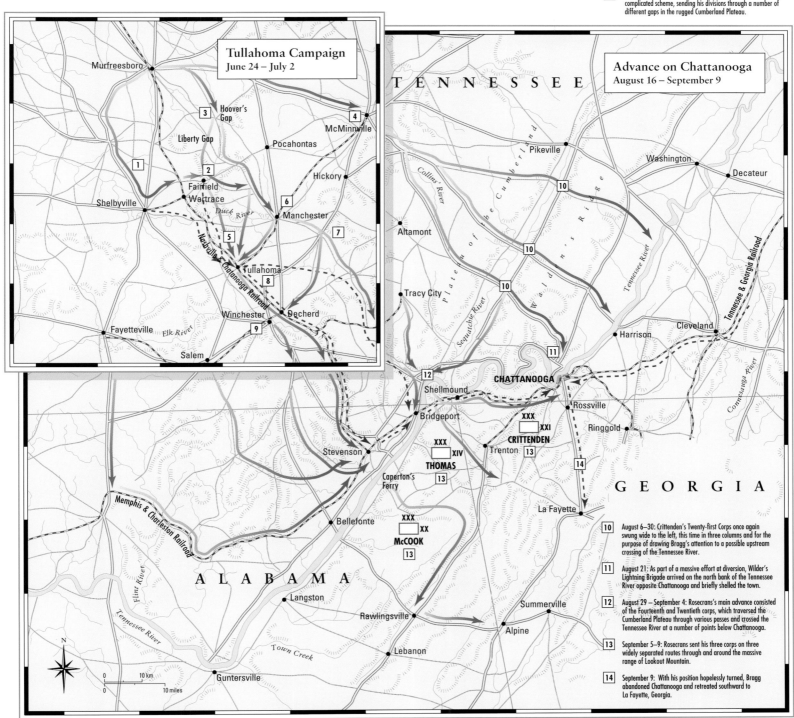

Tullahoma Campaign
June 24 – July 2

Advance on Chattanooga
August 16 – September 9

10 August 6–30: Crittenden's Twenty-first Corps once again swung wide to the left, this time in three columns and for the purpose of drawing Bragg's attention to a possible upstream crossing of the Tennessee River.

11 August 21: As part of a massive effort at diversion, Wilder's Lightning Brigade arrived on the north bank of the Tennessee River opposite Chattanooga and briefly shelled the town.

12 August 29 – September 4: Rosecrans's main advance consisted of the Fourteenth and Twentieth corps, which traversed the Cumberland Plateau through various passes and crossed the Tennessee River at a number of points below Chattanooga.

13 September 5–9: Rosecrans sent his three corps on three widely separated routes through and around the massive range of Lookout Mountain.

14 September 9: With his position hopelessly turned, Bragg abandoned Chattanooga and retreated southward to La Fayette, Georgia.

MORGAN AND QUANTRILL

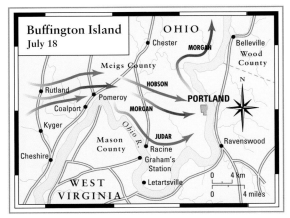

Buffington Island
July 18

O<small>N</small> J<small>ULY</small> 2, 1863, C<small>ONFEDERATE</small> Colonel John Hunt Morgan crossed the Cumberland River near Burksville, Kentucky, and rode north with 2,500 men. Two days later he reached Tebb's Bend on the Green River, but suffered a repulse at the hands of the small Union garrison there. Undeterred, Morgan headed further north and the following day took the towns of Lebanon and Bardstown, Kentucky. On July 8, Morgan and his men reached the Ohio River at Cummings' Ferry, Kentucky, west of Louisville. After minor skirmishing with Union militia and a small gunboat, Morgan succeeded in crossing his raiding party into Indiana. News of Morgan's incursion north of the Ohio River shocked the Midwest, which had not previously experienced a Rebel invasion. Many feared that disloyal residents of the lower Midwest, in cluding members of a nefarious organization called the "Knights of the Golden Circle," would stage a violent uprising in concert with Morgan's Confederate troops.

The next day Morgan and his raiders rode on, skirmishing intermittently with Indiana

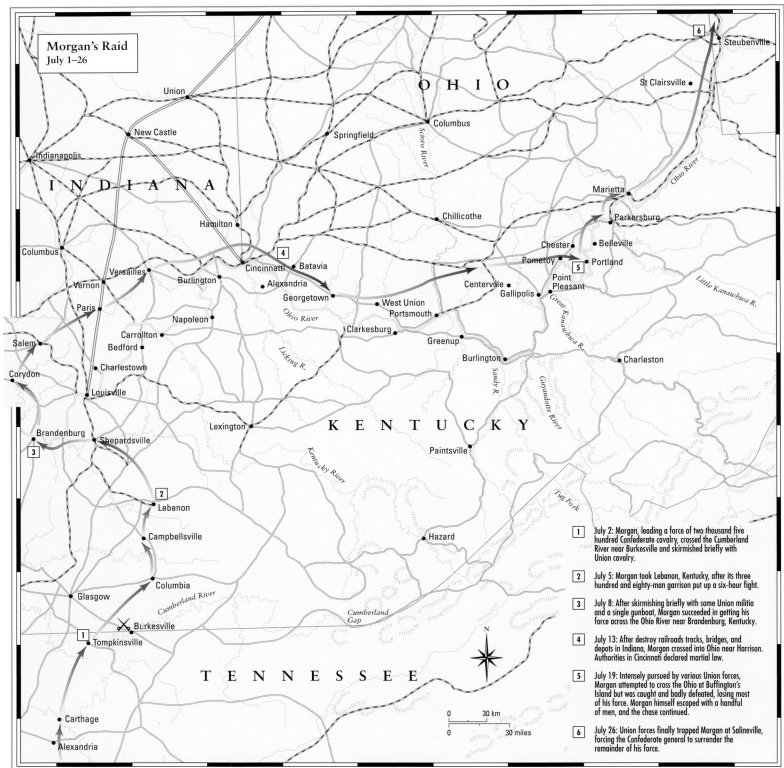

Morgan's Raid
July 1–26

1 July 2: Morgan, leading a force of two thousand five hundred Confederate cavalry, crossed the Cumberland River near Burkesville and skirmished briefly with Union cavalry.

2 July 5: Morgan took Lebanon, Kentucky, after its three hundred and eighty-man garrison put up a six-hour fight.

3 July 8: After skirmishing briefly with some Union militia and a single gunboat, Morgan succeeded in getting his force across the Ohio River near Brandenburg, Kentucky.

4 July 13: After destroy railroads tracks, bridges, and depots in Indiana, Morgan crossed into Ohio near Harrison. Authorities in Cincinnati declared martial law.

5 July 19: Intensely pursued by various Union forces, Morgan attempted to cross the Ohio at Buffington's Island but was caught and badly defeated, losing most of his force. Morgan himself escaped with a handful of men, and the chase continued.

6 July 26: Union forces finally trapped Morgan at Salineville, forcing the Confederate general to surrender the remainder of his force.

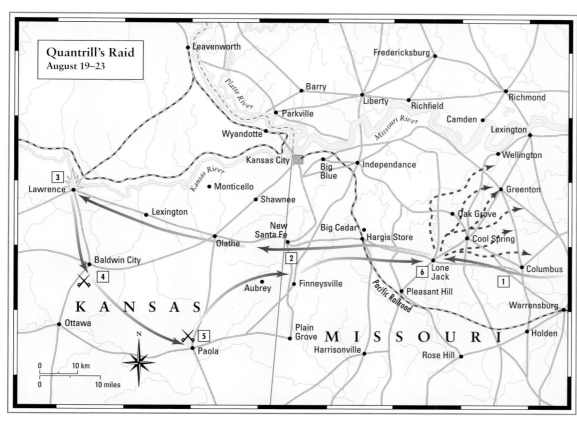

Quantrill's Raid
August 19–23

☐1 August 19: Quantrill leaves his camp and heads west with some three hundred men.

☐2 August 20: Quantrill crosses the state line and enters Kansas.

☐3 August 21, 5:00 p.m.: Raiders reach outskirts of Lawrence, attack immediately, looting and murdering for seven hours.

☐4 Noon: Quantrill leaves Lawrence. Finally alerted to events, Union forces converge on Lawrence. Quantrill routes some Unionists in bloodless skirmish south of Baldwin City.

☐5 c. 8:30 p.m.: Quantrill turns and attacks pursuers. Union forces flee, allowing raiders to escape into the growing darkness. They reenter Missouri on August 22nd.

☐6 August 23, noon: Three hundred Missouri militia attack raiders but fail to capture them. Although dispersed, raiders retreat safely with few casualties.

home guard units and taking the town of Corydon, where they plundered houses and stores. On July 10, Morgan's raiders struck Salem, Indiana, riding east toward Ohio. He crossed into Ohio three days later at Harrison. Union authorities in Cincinnati—which was directly in Morgan's path—declared martial law in the city. In fact, Morgan bypassed Cincinnati, riding between that city and the town of Hamilton, Ohio, to the north.

An increasing number of Union forces now dogged Morgan's steps, and the raiders continued eastward at a brisk pace because they had no choice. Meanwhile other Union forces maneuvered to block Morgan's advance. On July 17 he had a hard skirmish at Hamden, Ohio. With his force dwindling as his troopers' horses gave out, Morgan continued his flight southeastward, hoping to reach the Ohio River and cross into the relative safety of West Virginia. Desperately the raiders skirted the Ohio River town of Pomeroy and rode through nearby Chester, seeking a place where they could cross the river safely, undisturbed by the Union cavalry just behind them or by the gunboats that prowled the river.

On July 19, Morgan thought he saw his chance at Buffington, Ohio, but the attempt ended in disaster. Union cavalry and militia closed in from behind, and a gunboat blocked all hope of crossing the river. In the engagement that followed, Union casualties were light while approximately 120 of Morgan's men were killed and wounded and 700 captured. With all that was left of his force, some 364 men, Morgan fled northeastward, still paralleling the Ohio. Rebuffed at upstream crossings of the Ohio, Morgan had no choice but to turn northward. Finally, on July 26, Union forces cornered him at Salineville, Ohio, near the

Pennsylvania line. Morgan surrendered, and he and his officers, much to their chagrin, were confined in the Ohio State Penitentiary. Morgan's raid had been spectacular but foolhardy.

In a much different sort of raid in a different part of the country, Colonel William C. Quantrill led 450 Confederate raiders, including the brothers Frank and Jesse James, in an attack on the town of Lawrence, Kansas, on August 21, 1863. Lawrence had long been known as an antislavery town, and, when Kansas had rival pro- and antislavery governments in the 1850s, Lawrence was the free-state capital and was sacked, in May 1856, by proslavery forces. Quantrill planned to do much more. Recently, a building being used as a Union women's prison had collapsed in Kansas City, Missouri, killing several women who had been incarcerated for aiding Confederate guerrillas. Among those killed were several of Quantrill's female relatives. Seizing on this pretext, Quantrill determined not only to sack and loot Lawrence, but also to massacre all of its male inhabitants. In a three-hour orgy of slaughter, Quantrill and his men killed 150 men and boys and left most of the town in ashes.

General John Hunt Morgan (the Raider) of the Confederate Army around the time of his death.

KNOXVILLE CAMPAIGN

SINCE THE FIRST YEAR OF THE WAR, Lincoln had urged his generals to do something to reach the Union-loyal population of East Tennessee, which was suffering oppression from the Rebel authorities. Again and again he had been disappointed when his generals had told him that it was impossible. Rugged mountainous terrain, poor in supplies, intervened and made entering East Tennessee impractical for a Union force prior to the second half of 1863. Then, with major Confederate forces finally pushed out of Middle Tennessee and with the Confederate Army of Tennessee occupied with an offensive led by Major General William S. Rosecrans's Army of the Cumberland, it finally became feasible for a Union army to penetrate into East Tennessee.

On August 15, 1863, the Army of the Ohio, under the command of Major General Ambrose E. Burnside, marched out of Camp Nelson, Kentucky, near Lexington, bound for East Tennessee. After crossing the Cumberland Mountains, Burnside's troops reached Knoxville on September 2. Knoxville was not only the chief town of East Tennessee but also lay on the Virginia and Tennessee Railroad, the only direct rail link between Confederate forces in the two major theaters of the war. Jefferson Davis had been contemplating sending troops from Lee's army in Virginia to reinforce Braxton Bragg's Army of Tennessee at Chattanooga. With Burnside in Knoxville, those reinforcements would have to follow a long, roundabout route down the eastern seaboard and through Charleston, South Carolina, and Atlanta, Georgia, in order to reach Bragg. Furthermore, Burnside's presence in Knoxville presented a constant threat to Bragg's right flank, which seriously handicapped his maneuvers in the campaign he was even then waging against Rosecrans's advancing army.

Getting the Federals out of Knoxville and the rest of East Tennessee became a major goal of the Confederates. Attempting to achieve it, however, had to wait for the development of the contest between Bragg and Rosecrans. From September 18 to 20 Bragg's army, reinforced by troops from Virginia as well as elsewhere in the Confederacy, attacked Rosecrans at the Battle of Chickamauga. A costly Confederate victory, Chickamauga drove Rosecrans into Chattanooga, where Bragg was able to cut off his only practical supply lines. With the Army of the Cumberland starving in Chattanooga, the Union high command made major changes, sending reinforcements as well putting Ulysses S. Grant in command. Grant quickly succeeded in clearing Confederate troops out of the vital Tennessee River gorge and opening a viable supply line to the Union forces in Chattanooga.

With his plan of starving the Federals defeated, Bragg had to come up with a new scheme. A direct attack against Chattanooga would have been disastrous and a turning movement to the west almost equally so, taking Bragg directly into the path of approaching Union reinforcements. A turning movement to the northeast was the only alternative. To carry it out, Bragg would first have to clear Burnside out of East Tennessee, something Richmond had been urging on him for some time anyway. Bragg could further placate Davis and Lee by using the Army of Northern Virginia contingent under Lieutenant General James Longstreet for the task. Lee was eager to have Longstreet start on his way back to Virginia, and Knoxville lay on the shortest route between Chattanooga and Lee's camps. Finally, Longstreet had proven uncooperative under Bragg, who could not have been sorry to see him go.

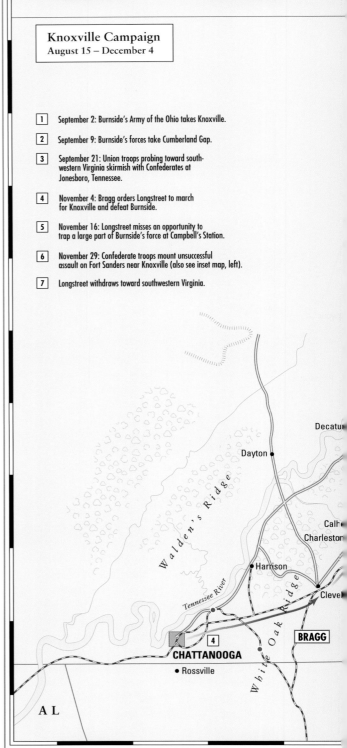

Knoxville Campaign
August 15 – December 4

1 September 2: Burnside's Army of the Ohio takes Knoxville.

2 September 9: Burnside's forces take Cumberland Gap.

3 September 21: Union troops probing toward southwestern Virginia skirmish with Confederates at Jonesboro, Tennessee.

4 November 4: Bragg orders Longstreet to march for Knoxville and defeat Burnside.

5 November 16: Longstreet misses an opportunity to trap a large part of Burnside's force at Campbell's Station.

6 November 29: Confederate troops mount unsuccessful assault on Fort Sanders near Knoxville (also see inset map, left).

7 Longstreet withdraws toward southwestern Virginia.

Knoxville
September 2

Bragg gave the order for Longstreet's movement into East Tennessee on November 4, but Longstreet moved very slowly, taking some thirteen days to cover the little more than one hundred miles to Knoxville. On November 16, at Campbell's Station, just south of Knoxville, Longstreet missed an opportunity to cut Burnside's line of retreat and allowed the Union commander instead to withdraw safely into the fortifications around the town. Longstreet laid siege to Knoxville, but Burnside possessed a prodigious stock of supplies and was receiving more, rafted in on the Holston River by Unionist East Tennesseeans. For the next twelve days, Longstreet's activities consisted of examining vari-

ous abortive schemes for an assault on Knoxville and pleading with Bragg for reinforcements.

After Bragg's defeat in the November 23–25 Battle of Chattanooga, it was apparent that no reinforcements would be forthcoming. So Longstreet proceeded with his plans for an assault. In the predawn hours of November 29, Confederate troops charged Fort Sanders, part of the Knoxville defenses. The attack was badly mismanaged and ended in failure. Confederate casualties totaled 813 and Union, 13. Upon learning that a Union relief force under Sherman was marching up from Chattanooga, Longstreet withdrew his force into southwestern Virginia.

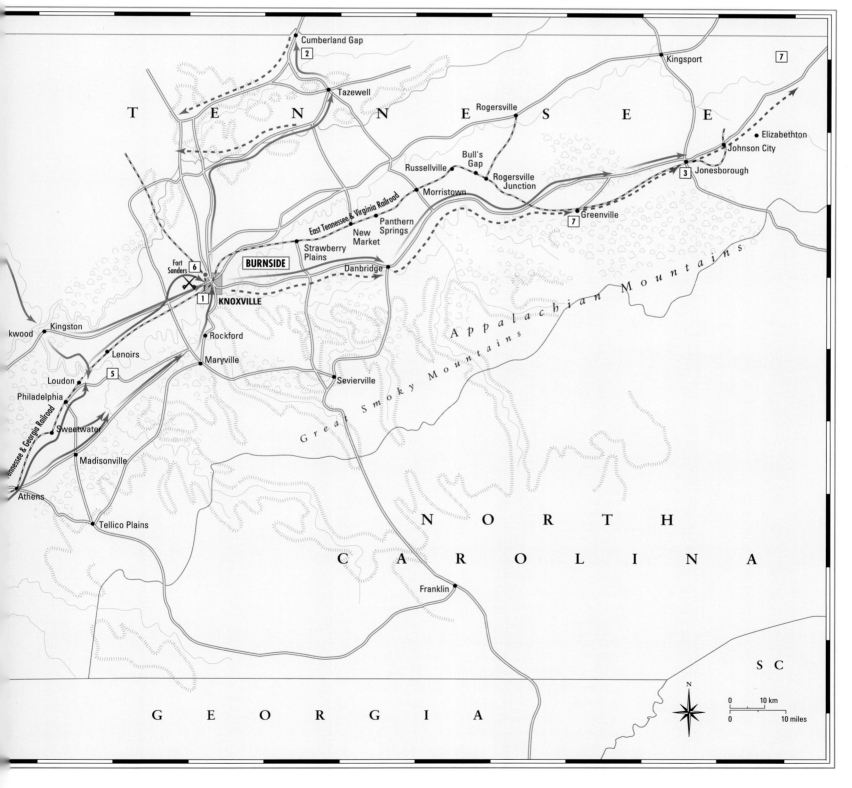

OPERATIONS IN VIRGINIA

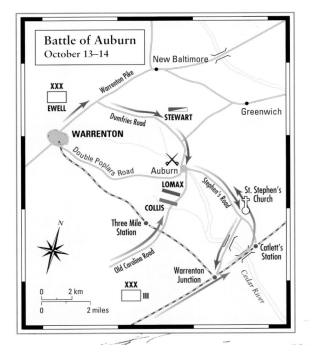

weakened condition of the Army of the Potomac and also to prevent Meade from detaching any more troops to the West. Lee took the offensive. In many ways his plan of campaign resembled the one he had used in the Second Bull Run campaign just over one year before.

The Army of Northern Virginia left its camps south of the Rapidan River on October 9. Moving around Meade's right flank, Lee marched his columns west, crossed the Rapidan, and continued northwest, past Culpeper Court House and Brandy Station. Once across the Rappahannock he turned northeast toward Manassas Junction, Virginia; Washington, D.C.; and a position astride Meade's supply lines.

Meade reacted quickly, marching his own army northward to block Lee's turning movement. On October 14, Lieutenant General Ambrose Powell Hill, commanding the Third Corps in the vanguard of Lee's army, encountered the rear guard of the Army of the Potomac, Major General Gouverneur

Union troops follow Lee's retreat along the destroyed railroad from Warrenton Junction.

AFTER THE CONCLUSION OF THE Gettysburg campaign both the Army of the Potomac and the Army of Northern Virginia spent several weeks resting and refitting while the Virginia front remained quiet. In September, Jefferson Davis transferred two divisions of Lee's army to join General Braxton Bragg near Chattanooga. With his force thus reduced, Lee was for a time content to rest on the defensive. Nor did Meade initiate any action.

Then, after William S. Rosecrans's defeat at the September 18–20, 1863, Battle of Chickamauga, the Lincoln administration decided to transfer the Eleventh and Twelfth corps from the Army of the Potomac to strengthen Federal forces at Chattanooga. Eager to take advantage of the

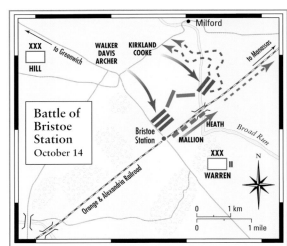

K. Warren's Second Corps. Hill attacked rashly, without making an adequate reconnaissance, and sent his troops into a deadly crossfire. They were repulsed with heavy casualties. By the following day, Meade had secured his supply lines and taken up a strong position, near the old Bull Run battlefield, squarely blocking Lee's further advance. The two armies confronted each other for the next two days before Lee gave up the campaign and turned back toward the Rappahannock. By October 20, his army was back on the south bank of the Rappahannock, and the campaign was over. Lee nevertheless determined to hold the south bank of the Rappahannock rather than retire all the way to the Rapidan, where the campaign had begun.

On November 7, Meade struck back, pushing his troops across the Rappahannock at Rappahannock Station and Kelly's Ford, forcing Lee to withdraw behind the Rapidan with only minor skirmishing. There matters rested for the

Union artillery concentrating northwest of Fredericksburg.

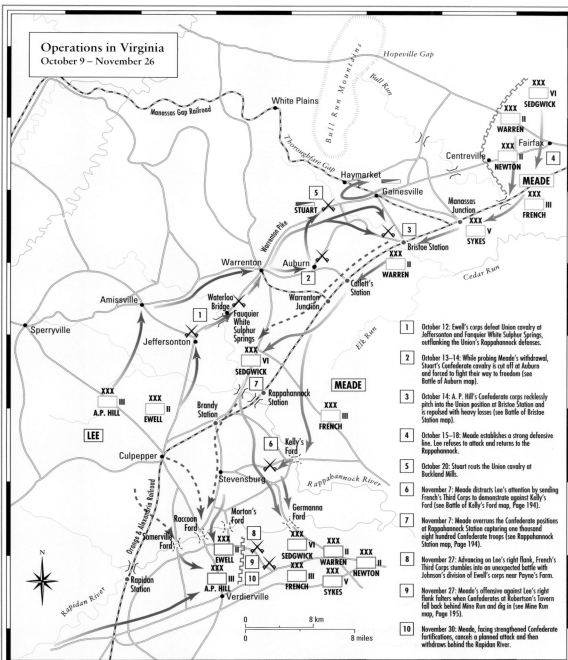

Operations in Virginia
October 9 – November 26

1. October 12: Ewell's corps defeat Union cavalry at Jeffersonton and Fanquier White Sulphur Springs, outflanking the Union's Rappahannock defenses.

2. October 13–14: While probing Meade's withdrawal, Stuart's Confederate cavalry is cut off at Auburn and forced to fight their way to freedom (see Battle of Auburn map).

3. October 14: A. P. Hill's Confederate corps recklessly pitch into the Union position at Bristoe Station and is repulsed with heavy losses (see Battle of Bristoe Station map).

4. October 15–18: Meade establishes a strong defensive line. Lee refuses to attack and returns to the Rappahannock.

5. October 20: Stuart routs the Union cavalry at Buckland Mills.

6. November 7: Meade distracts Lee's attention by sending French's Third Corps to demonstrate against Kelly's Ford (see Battle of Kelly's Ford map, Page 194).

7. November 7: Meade overruns the Confederate positions at Rappahannock Station capturing one thousand eight hundred Confederate troops (see Rappahannock Station map, Page 194).

8. November 27: Advancing on Lee's right flank, French's Third Corps stumbles into an unexpected battle with Johnson's division of Ewell's corps near Payne's Farm.

9. November 27: Meade's offensive against Lee's right flank falters when Confederates at Robertson's Tavern fall back behind Mine Run and dig in (see Mine Run map, Page 195).

10. November 30: Meade, facing strengthened Confederate fortifications, cancels a planned attack and then withdraws behind the Rapidan River.

next two weeks while Lincoln and U.S. Secretary of War Edwin M. Stanton continued to urge Meade to take the offensive. On November 26, America's first official national Thanksgiving Day, Meade finally did. The Army of the Potomac crossed the Rapidan in an effort to turn Lee's right flank. Lee moved with his accustomed swiftness to block Meade's effort. As the two armies maneuvered through the Wilderness—in which they had fought the Battle of Chancellorsville seven months before—Major General William H. French's corps took a wrong turn, became entangled with the Confederates, and failed to reach its assigned position in time for the attack Meade had ordered.

By the time the Army of the Potomac was ready to attack, Lee had taken up a strong position along a stream called "Mine Run." Meade spent the next three days fruitlessly looking for a weak point in Lee's defensive position and preparing for a grand assault that—fortunately for Meade's sol-

diers—never came off. Finally, on December 1, Meade faced the fact that Lee had outmaneuvered the Army of the Potomac again and turned back toward the Rapidan. By December 3 the Union and Confederate armies in Virginia once again faced each other, at a respectful distance, across the valley of the Rapidan, just where they had been two months before.

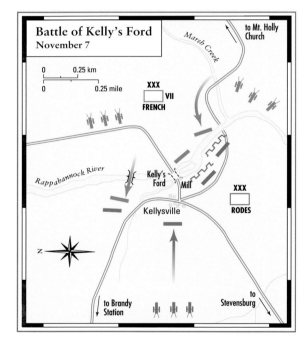

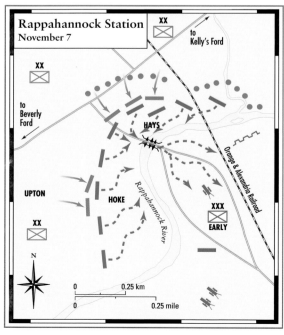

Union forces cross the Rapidan River at Germanna Ford. Now under the overall command of Grant, though with Meade still in charge, the 1864 Spring Offensive was under way.

Mine Run
November 27

CHICKAMAUGA CAMPAIGN

A T THE CONCLUSION OF THE TULLAHOMA campaign in early July, Rosecrans once again paused to make sure his supply arrangements were in order before crossing the dual obstacles of the Cumberland Plateau and the Tennessee River, much to the renewed frustration of the authorities in Washington. The Union leaders believed that additional heavy blows, coming on the heels of Vicksburg and Gettysburg, might bring the Confederacy to its knees. Finally, on August 16, Rosecrans advanced.

As had been the case in the Tullahoma campaign six weeks before, Rosecrans's plan of advance was elaborate, complicated, and skillfully conceived. The Army of the Cumberland again advanced in multiple columns. Several of these columns were intended to convince Bragg that the Federals planned to cross the Tennessee River upstream, to the northeast of Chattanooga. Such a move would have been particularly dangerous to the Confederates, as it would have

Temporary Union accommodations in downtown Chattanooga.

allowed the Army of the Cumberland to join Major General Ambrose Burnside's Army of the Ohio, near Knoxville, Tennessee. Bragg responded to this threat by shifting his cavalry to patrol the upstream crossings, but Rosecrans's main advance was in fact taking place west of Chattanooga. Undetected by Confederate patrols, the bulk of the Army of the Cumberland, moving in several columns, marched over the Cumberland Plateau, crossed the Tennessee River by September 4, and continued to move southeastward, threatening Bragg's communications south of Chattanooga.

In order to reach Bragg's possible lines of retreat, Rosecrans had to cross the 1,400-foot-high ridge of Lookout Mountain. This could be done either at the Tennessee River gorge near Chattanooga; or via Stevens Gap, twenty-four miles southwest of Chattanooga; or via Winston Gap, another eighteen miles to the southwest. Rosecrans decided to use all three crossings, sending Crittenden's Twenty-First Corps through the Tennessee River gorge, Thomas's Fourteenth Corps through Stevens Gap, and McCook's Twentieth Corps through Winston Gap. On September 8, Bragg responded to Rosecrans's successful turning maneuver by abandoning

Chattanooga and falling back. Believing Bragg was in headlong retreat toward Dalton, Georgia, to the southeast, Rosecrans ordered his three corps to push rapidly down the east slope of Lookout Mountain and cut Bragg's retreat.

Rosecrans was mistaken on several counts. Bragg had withdrawn toward La Fayette, due south of Chattanooga, rather than Dalton, and he was not in retreat but preparing to assume the offensive, having recently been reinforced to a strength of fifty-five thousand men, with another thirteen thousand on the way. Jefferson Davis had finally decided to shift troops from Lee's Army of Northern Virginia, and had sent Lieutenant General James Longstreet with two divisions. He sent additional reinforcements from various other points in the Confederacy. As Rosecrans's three widely separated columns emerged on the east side of Lookout Mountain, Bragg found himself closer to Thomas's center corps than any of the Union corps were to each other. The Confederates had an unparalleled opportunity to crush the isolated corps one by one.

On September 10, Bragg ordered an attack with overwhelming force on the front and flank of the leading divisions of Thomas's corps, which were in a position to be trapped in a valley called McLemore's Cove at the eastern foot of Lookout Mountain. His generals refused to move. This time the semi-mutiny was more widespread than it had been during the Tullahoma campaign. Generals Thomas C. Hindman, Simon B. Buckner, and Daniel H. Hill all refused to obey Bragg's orders to attack. The next day the Federals in McLemore's Cove recognized their danger and pulled back to safety atop Lookout Mountain. On September 12, Bragg had an opportunity to attack Crittenden's corps with most of his own army. He gave the order, and this time it was Leonidas Polk who refused to obey. Again the Federals escaped.

Rosecrans at first refused to believe his subordinates' reports that the Confederate army was taking the offensive. When he finally realized his danger he began frantic efforts to concentrate his army before Bragg could defeat it in detail. Over the next few days he maneuvered with that purpose in mind. Meanwhile, Bragg, dismayed with his generals' performance, awaited the arrival of additional reinforcements and maneuvered northward in hopes of getting between Rosecrans and Chattanooga, where Bragg would have a chance to trap and destroy the Army of the Cumberland. By the evening of September 17, Bragg, now reinforced to parity with Rosecrans at just over sixty thousand men, had almost achieved his purpose. He was northeast of the Army of the Cumberland and needed only to advance westward across the Chickamauga Creek to take up a blocking position between Rosecrans and Chattanooga. That evening Bragg gave the order to advance. Throughout the day on September 18, Confederate troops fought for the crossing of Chickamauga Creek against stubborn and resourceful Union cavalry and mounted infantry. By evening, Bragg's army had secured the crossing and was preparing to drive southward the next day onto the Army of the Cumberland's exposed northern flank.

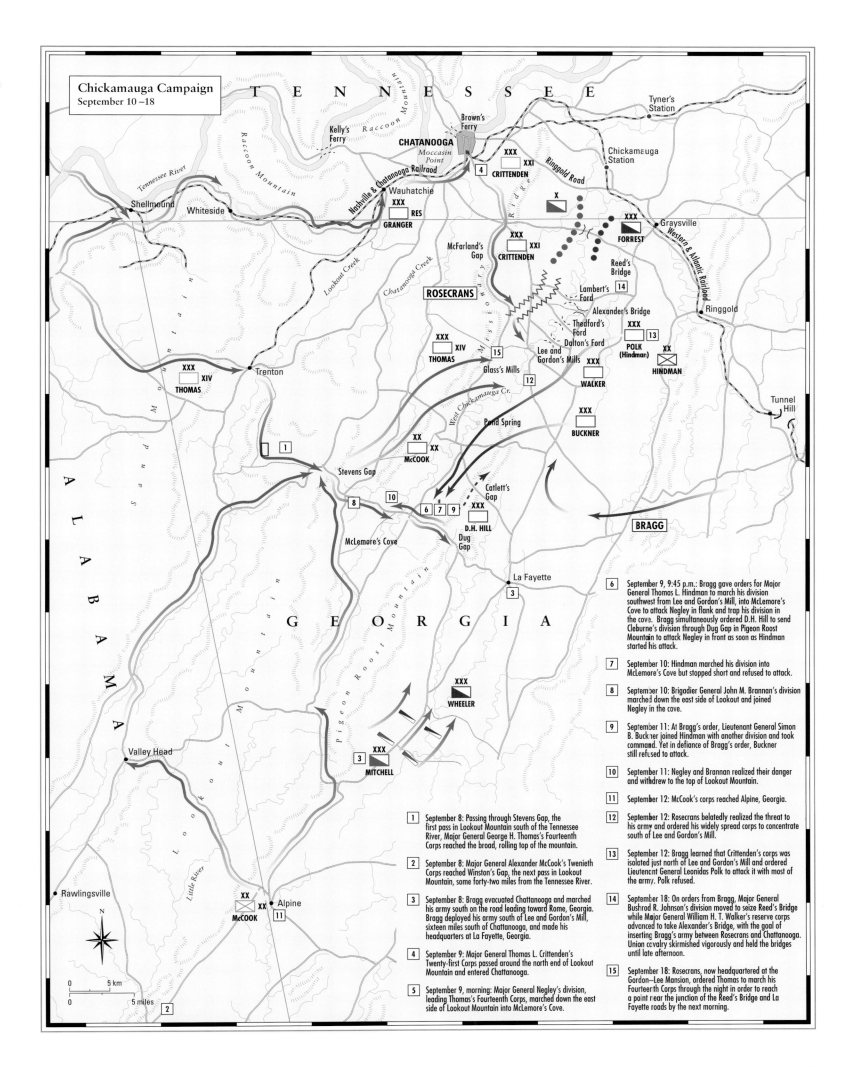

Chickamauga Campaign
September 10–18

TENNESSEE

ALABAMA

GEORGIA

Tyner's Station

Kelly's Ferry

Brown's Ferry

Chickamauga Station

Raccoon Mountain

Tennessee River

CHATANOOGA
Moccasin Point

XXX XXI
CRITTENDEN
4

X

Ringgold Road

XXX
FORREST
Graysville

Western & Atlantic Railroad

Shellmound

Whiteside

Nashville & Chattanooga Railraod

Wauhatchie

XXX RES
GRANGER

McFarland's Gap

XXX XXI
CRITTENDEN

Reed's Bridge
14

Ringgold

Lookout Creek

Chattanooga Creek

ROSECRANS

Lambert's Ford

Thedford's Ford

Dalton's Ford

Alexander's Bridge

XXX
POLK
(Hindman)
13

XX
HINDMAN

XXX XIV
THOMAS
15

Glass's Mills

Lee and Gordon's Mills

XXX
WALKER
12

Trenton

XXX XIV
THOMAS

Tunnel Hill

West Chickamauga Cr.

Pond Spring

XXX
BUCKNER

Stevens Gap

XX
McCOOK
XX

8

10

6 7 9

Catlett's Gap

XXX
D.H. HILL
Dug Gap

BRAGG

McLemore's Cove

La Fayette
3

XXX
WHEELER

Valley Head

XXX
MITCHELL
3

Rawlingsville

N

XX
McCOOK
XX
Alpine
11

0   5 km
0   5 miles
2

1

September 9, 9:45 p.m.: Bragg gave orders for Major General Thomas L. Hindman to march his division southwest from Lee and Gordon's Mill, into McLemore's Cove to attack Negley in flank and trap his division in the cove. Bragg simultaneously ordered D.H. Hill to send Cleburne's division through Dug Gap in Pigeon Roost Mountain to attack Negley in front as soon as Hindman started his attack.

7 **September 10:** Hindman marched his division into McLemore's Cove but stopped short and refused to attack.

8 **September 10:** Brigadier General John M. Brannan's division marched down the east side of Lookout and joined Negley in the cove.

9 **September 11:** At Bragg's order, Lieutenant General Simon B. Buckner joined Hindman with another division and took command. Yet in defiance of Bragg's order, Buckner still refused to attack.

10 **September 11:** Negley and Brannan realized their danger and withdrew to the top of Lookout Mountain.

11 **September 12:** McCook's corps reached Alpine, Georgia.

12 **September 12:** Rosecrans belatedly realized the threat to his army and ordered his widely spread corps to concentrate south of Lee and Gordon's Mill.

13 **September 12:** Bragg learned that Crittenden's corps was isolated just north of Lee and Gordon's Mill and ordered Lieutenant General Leonidas Polk to attack it with most of the army. Polk refused.

14 **September 18:** On orders from Bragg, Major General Bushrod R. Johnson's division moved to seize Reed's Bridge while Major General William H. T. Walker's reserve corps advanced to take Alexander's Bridge, with the goal of inserting Bragg's army between Rosecrans and Chattanooga. Union cavalry skirmished vigorously and held the bridges until late afternoon.

15 **September 18:** Rosecrans, now headquartered at the Gordon–Lee Mansion, ordered Thomas to march his Fourteenth Corps through the night in order to reach a point near the junction of the Reed's Bridge and La Fayette roads by the next morning.

1 **September 8:** Passing through Stevens Gap, the first pass in Lookout Mountain south of the Tennessee River, Major General George H. Thomas's Fourteenth Corps reached the broad, rolling top of the mountain.

2 **September 8:** Major General Alexander McCook's Twentieth Corps reached Winston's Gap, the next pass in Lookout Mountain, some forty-two miles from the Tennessee River.

3 **September 8:** Bragg evacuated Chattanooga and marched his army south on the road leading toward Rome, Georgia. Bragg deployed his army south of Lee and Gordon's Mill, sixteen miles south of Chattanooga, and made his headquarters at La Fayette, Georgia.

4 **September 9:** Major General Thomas L. Crittenden's Twenty-first Corps passed around the north end of Lookout Mountain and entered Chattanooga.

5 **September 9, morning:** Major General Negley's division, leading Thomas's Fourteenth Corps, marched down the east side of Lookout Mountain into McLemore's Cove.

CHICKAMAUGA

The country around Chickamauga Creek was mostly tangled woodland with few clearings. A Union officer who fought at Chickamauga, described the clash as "a mad, irregular battle, very much resembling guerrilla warfare on a vast scale, in which one army was bushwhacking the other."

ON THE EVENING OF SEPTEMBER 18, Rosecrans ordered Major General George H. Thomas to take his Fourteenth Corps on a night march six miles northward from its position near Crawfish Springs, Georgia, to the clearing of a farmer named Kelly. Unknown to either army, Thomas's corps that night marched directly across the front of Bragg's army. On the morning of September 19, instead of Bragg being well beyond Rosecrans's northern flank, in fact, Thomas's corps was sitting on Bragg's northern flank. Thus before the first shot was fired, the final arrangement of the forces made it very doubtful that Bragg would be able to trap Rosecrans and win a truly decisive victory.

Receiving vague reports of small numbers of Confederate troops in the woods between his position and Chickamauga Creek on the morning of September 19, Thomas probed eastward and collided with Brigadier General Nathan Bedford Forrest's Confederate cavalry, screening Bragg's right flank. The fight grew steadily throughout the day as each side fed more and more reinforcements into it. Bragg pulled units away from the attack formation that he had intended to launch to the south and instead sent them northeast toward the scene of the clash with Thomas, in the woods between the Kelly farm and Chickamauga Creek. Rosecrans hurried the rest of his army rapidly northward from Crawfish Springs to join Thomas. The fighting front spread southward along the La Fayette–Chattanooga Road. Fortunes changed repeatedly in the confused and ferocious fighting in the woods and clearings. By nightfall neither side had gained an advantage, but Rosecrans still held the La Fayette–Chattanooga Road.

That night Longstreet arrived at Bragg's headquarters, and Bragg reorganized his army so as to give the renowned eastern general a suitable command. Now Longstreet would command the left wing of the army, and Polk, who was next in rank, would command the right. Polk was to open the second day's fighting with a "day-dawn" assault on the Union left flank. Each of the army's divisions would then attack in succession from the Confederate right to the Confederate left, with the continued goal of driving Rosecrans south and cutting him off from Chattanooga.

Polk made no preparations at all for the attack ordered by Bragg; so on the morning of September 20 his assault was some three-and-a-half-hours late. Even then Bragg had to go in person to the front and order the troops forward. The assault by Polk's corps was awkward and uncoordinated because of the general's lack of preparation. During Polk's three-and-a-half-hour delay, the Union troops at which the attack was aimed—Thomas's heavily reinforced Fourteenth Corps around the Kelly farm—had built substantial log breastworks. The assault was a costly failure.

Meanwhile, as Longstreet prepared to begin his own phase of the Confederate assault, Rosecrans made a costly mistake. He had recently been exhibiting highly nervous behavior, eating and sleeping irregularly, and was attempting to shift his army northward, division by division, while much of it was engaged in front. In this situation he received a report that a gap existed in the left-center of his line. Without verifying the report, he had a staff officer write an order for the next division on the right to move left and close the gap. In fact, no gap had existed, and the division commander who received the vaguely worded order, Brigadier General Thomas J. Wood, not unreasonably interpreted it as requiring him to pull his division out of line and march it behind the division next on his left. He did so, creating exactly the sort of gap Rosecrans had thought to repair.

Just then, about 11:30 a.m., Longstreet launched his half of the Confederate attack, a superbly arranged attacking column of eight brigades in five lines. Longstreet's Confederates surged through the gap created by Wood, rolled up the Union left, reached the Army of the Cumberland's wagon trains, and made Rosecrans and his staff flee their temporary headquarters. Thomas, with about half of the Army of the Cumberland, stood his ground throughout the afternoon. Major General Gordon Granger, with most of the Reserve Corps, joined Thomas in his stand. Rosecrans had posted the Reserve Corps several miles to the north, but Granger marched to the sound of the guns on his own responsibility. As nightfall approached, a badly shaken Rosecrans, who had fled to Chattanooga himself, sent word for Thomas to withdraw.

Chickamauga was the only major Confederate victory west of the Appalachians. Yet, by the time the guns fell silent on the evening of September 20, there was no possibility for the Confederates to exploit the victory or make it decisive, as it had only served to push Rosecrans back toward his supply line at Chattanooga.

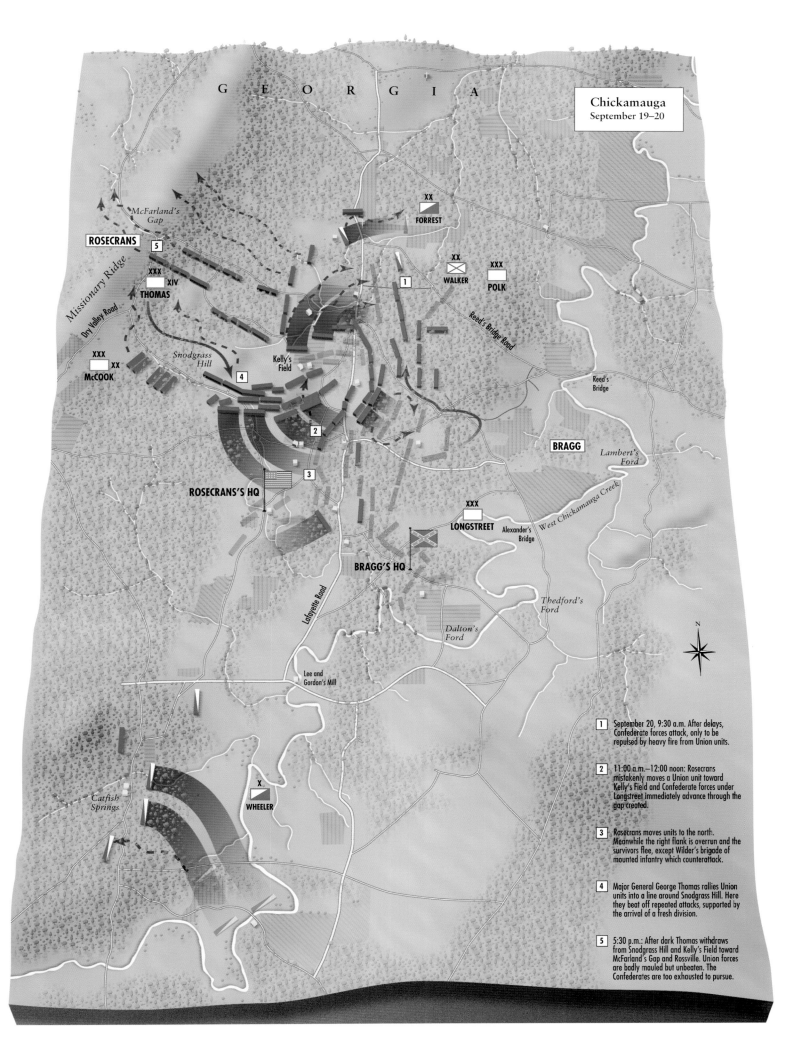

Chickamauga
September 19–20

GEORGIA

McFarland's
Gap

ROSECRANS

5

Missionary Ridge

XXX XIV
THOMAS

Dry Valley Road

XXX
XX
McCOOK

Snodgrass
Hill

4

Kelly's
Field

3

ROSECRANS'S HQ

XX
FORREST

XX
WALKER

XXX
POLK

Reed's Bridge Road

Reed's
Bridge

2

BRAGG

Lambert's
Ford

XXX
LONGSTREET

Alexander's
Bridge

West Chickamauga Creek

BRAGG'S HQ

Thedford's
Ford

Lafayette Road

Dalton's
Ford

N

Lee and
Gordon's Mill

Catfish
Springs

X
WHEELER

1 September 20, 9:30 a.m. After delays,
   Confederate forces attack, only to be
   repulsed by heavy fire from Union units.

2 11:00 a.m.–12:00 noon: Rosecrans
   mistakenly moves a Union unit toward
   Kelly's Field and Confederate forces under
   Longstreet immediately advance through the
   gap created.

3 Rosecrans moves units to the north.
   Meanwhile the right flank is overrun and the
   survivors flee, except Wilder's brigade of
   mounted infantry which counterattack.

4 Major General George Thomas rallies Union
   units into a line around Snodgrass Hill. Here
   they beat off repeated attacks, supported by
   the arrival of a fresh division.

5 5:30 p.m.: After dark Thomas withdraws
   from Snodgrass Hill and Kelly's Field toward
   McFarland's Gap and Rossville. Union forces
   are badly mauled but unbeaten. The
   Confederates are too exhausted to pursue.

CHATTANOOGA

AFTER THE CONFEDERATE VICTORY AT Chickamauga, Rosecrans ordered his army to fall back entirely within the Chattanooga defenses, giving Bragg the opportunity to cut Rosecrans's primary supply line, which ran west from Chattanooga through the Tennessee River gorge. With control of Lookout Mountain and neighboring Lookout Valley to the west, Bragg completely interdicted that route, leaving Rosecrans to supply his army via a sixty-mile wagon road over rugged Walden's Ridge. The Army of the Cumberland went on very short rations, and its draft animals died in droves.

Disgusted with Rosecrans's poor performance since Chickamauga, the Lincoln administration made a major command shake-up, consolidating the departments of the Ohio, Cumberland, and Tennessee into the single Military Division of the Mississippi to be commanded by Ulysses S. Grant. Grant's orders gave him the option of sacking Rosecrans, which he lost no time in doing. Grant repaired immediately to Chattanooga. He arrived there October 23, assessed the situation, and ordered the implementation of a plan to clear the Confederates out of Lookout Valley and to restore the supply line through the Tennessee River gorge. On the night of October 26 – 27 a surprise Union boat assault at Brown's Ferry in Lookout Valley was a complete success, opening the supply route for the first time in a month. The next day, elements of the Union Eleventh and Twelfth Corps, transferred by rail from Virginia, marched into Lookout Valley, and that night Confederate Lieutenant General James Longstreet failed in a half-hearted attempt to retake the valley.

Thereafter the Union "Cracker Line," as the supply line was known, was secure, and Bragg no longer had any hope of starving the Federals in Chattanooga into submission. Bragg's next move was to detach Longstreet's two divisions and send them into East Tennessee to destroy Ambrose Burnside's Army of the Ohio, possibly opening the way for a turning movement such as that which had brought him temporary success during the late summer of 1862. Burnside retreated into Knoxville before Longstreet's advance, but Longstreet moved slowly, achieving no decisive results.

Admonished by Washington to dispatch Bragg and aid Burnside, Grant was eager to comply, but the Army of the Cumberland was not ready for offensive operations beyond the immediate vicinity of its camps, as it had no draft animals to draw artillery or supply wagons. Grant also had doubts about the state of the army's morale after Chickamauga and several weeks of siege in Chattanooga. To open his offensive, he was eagerly awaiting the arrival of his old lieutenant Sherman with four divisions of the Army of the Tennessee. Days of rain, muddy roads, high water, and a weak pontoon bridge at Brown's Ferry delayed Sherman's approach, and he was not ready to begin the offensive until the night of November 23. That day Grant had Major General George H. Thomas, now commanding

the Army of the Cumberland, capture a hill called "Orchard Knob," between Chattanooga and the Confederate lines on Missionary Ridge.

On November 24, Sherman's troops successfully crossed the Tennessee River and seized some detached hills at the north end of Missionary Ridge. Meanwhile, Major General Joseph Hooker, commanding the Twelfth Corps and one division each from the armies of the Cumberland and the Tennessee, successfully drove the Confederates off of Lookout Mountain at the south end of the Bragg's position. The large mountain was in fact a deceptively weak defensive position.

Grant's plan for November 25 was for his two flank attacks to roll up the Confederate army, but difficulties arose. Retreating Confederates had

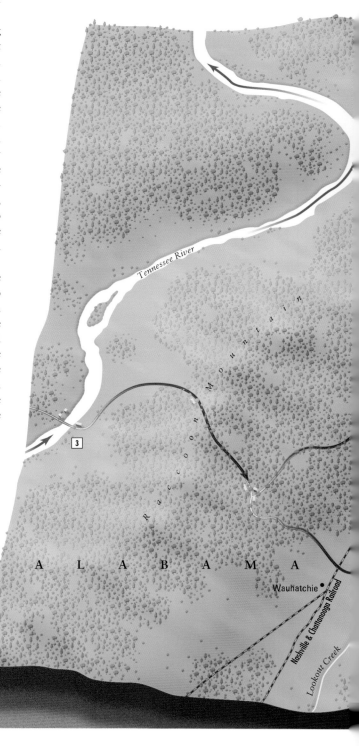

destroyed the bridge over the flooded Chattanooga Creek, so it took Hooker most of the day to get from Lookout Mountain to the southern end of the Confederate line on Missionary Ridge. At the other end of the ridge Sherman encountered deceptively difficult terrain, as well as the most skillful division commander in the Confederate army, Major General Patrick R. Cleburne. With both flank attacks stalled and only a few hours of daylight left, Grant ordered Thomas to advance his Army of the Cumberland to the line of Confederate rifle pits at the foot of Missionary Ridge, in preparation for an assault on the crest.

Reluctantly, Thomas ordered his men forward. Thanks to confusion of orders as well as the inspired improvisation of mid-ranking officers, the Union troops scarcely paused at the rifle pits

(which were untenable in any case) and plunged straight up the ridge. Once again the mountainous terrain proved deceptive. The ridge looked impregnable but in fact had many weaknesses as a defensive position. These factors, along with the exceptional determination of the Army of the Cumberland's troops to avenge their defeat at Chickamauga, produced one of the most dramatic victories of the war. Bragg's army broke and fled in disorder. Union casualties for the series of engagements that came to be known as the Battle of Chattanooga were 5,824 and Confederate, 6,667, including many men captured.

Chattanooga
September 21 – November 25

1 September 21: General Rosecrans abandons positions on Lookout Mountain and Missionary Ridge and establishes shorter defensive lines around Chattanooga.

2 September 21: Confederate forces under General Braxton Bragg move to occupy the abandoned positions.

3 September 25 – October 29: Union reinforcements arrive from the Army of the Potomac. October 23: General Grant arrives in Chattanooga. Grant holds overall command of the West.

4 October 26–27: General W. F. Smith sails down the Tennessee River with three thousand five hundred men, crosses Moccasin Point and builds a pontoon bridge across the river.

5 November 23–24: Sherman and Hooker are ordered to outflank the Confederate positions. Hooker captures Lookout Mountain and advances on Rossville, Sherman's attack is driven back.

6 November 25: Thomas's corps attacks the Confederate center followed by Hooker advancing on Rossville. The Confederate army is driven off Missionary Ridge. Defeated, it flees in disorder into Georgia briefly followed by the Union troops, who then return to their base in Chattanooga.

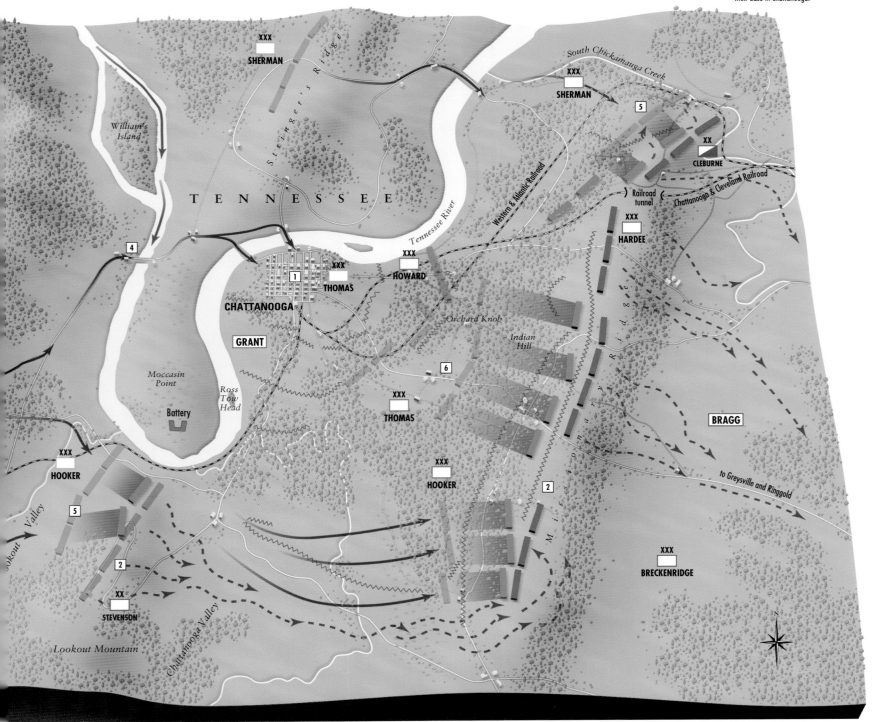

THE STATE OF THE CONFEDERACY, THE NATION, AND ITS ARMY

AFTER ACHIEVING IMPRESSIVE BATTLEFIELD victories and establishing an effective government during 1862, the Confederacy faced new challenges in the spring of 1863. The Confederate Army reached its peak enlistment at close to half a million but faced attacks on a broad range of fronts.

Along the Mississippi River, a Union army under General Ulysses S. Grant was about to take Vicksburg, win control of the Mississippi River, and cut the Confederacy in two. General William S. Rosecrans's army was penetrating East Tennessee and threatening Georgia. Assaults against coastal fortifications in North Carolina, South Carolina, and Louisiana were providing bases for the increasingly effective Union naval blockade. The Confederate secretary of war resigned when President Jefferson Davis overruled his attempts to shore up the beleaguered western theater. Lieutenant General James Longstreet and General Pierre G. T. Beauregard recommended shifting forces from the eastern theater and concentrating them in Tennessee. Instead, Davis and his new secretary of war, James Seddon, supported General Robert E. Lee's plan to defend Virginia by marching northward yet again across the Potomac.

The Confederate Congress addressed its perpetual manpower shortages by raising the age limit for draftees from thirty-five to forty-five and repealing the substitute clause. The draft proved more important and effective in the South than in the North, and by the end of the war one-fifth of Confederate soldiers were draftees. Desertion also ran higher in the Confederacy, where one-in-eight soldiers deserted. Desperate for revenue, the Confederate Congress enacted a new round of stringent taxes in April 1863, including an 8 percent sales tax, a 10 percent profits tax on merchants, and license taxes on most occupations. The new Confederate income tax ranged from 1 to 15 percent, triple the top northern rate, and the Congress even imposed a tax on slaves. The most resisted measure was the tax-in-kind that literally confiscated one-tenth of all agricultural products beyond a mere subsistence level. Recognizing the shortage of good money in the South, the tax-in-kind allowed Confederate armies to "live off the land" long before Sherman's army did. It also drove home the military's unrelenting demand for food.

With the Union Army occupying key food-producing regions in the Upper South, the Confederate Congress began limiting the acreage devoted to inedible crops, including cotton. The Union naval blockade was more effective than ever and cut southern imports by one-third. Even when the blockade runners got through, the South's credit was increasingly unreliable in Europe, and shortages plagued every industry.

In March, the Impressment Act allowed the military to confiscate raw materials and even impress slaves into military service. Confederate money, which totaled $700 million—as opposed to the North's $438 million in "greenbacks"—was increasingly worthless. Inflation exceeded 1800 percent at the beginning of 1863. Even the Confederate capital, Richmond, suffered food shortages, which were compounded by the military confiscations and a late snowstorm. In April, the infamous Richmond food riot broke out and drove home the Confederacy's desperate economic situation. One of Lee's motives for invading the North, in fact, was to procure food and materiel, including shoes, for his men.

The Confederate government had done all it could to mobilize men, food, and materiel for an increasingly precarious war effort. Somewhat ironically, in the face of food shortages, in August President Davis was reduced to proclaiming a day of "fasting, humiliation, and prayer" in hopes of turning the tide in favor of the Confederacy.

Right: *The third day of the Battle of Gettysburg—July 3—witnessed a disastrous Confederate repulse immortalized by "Pickett's Charge." In this scene painted by Edwin Forbes Confederate soldiers are closing on the Union center at about 3:00 p.m.*

Below: *The Confederate blockade runner Teaser at anchor off Fort Monroe. When such ships managed to penetrate the Union blockade they relied on the Confederacy's credit to fill their cargo holds; as the war progressed this became increasingly unreliable.*

THE STATE OF THE NORTH, THE NATION, AND ITS ARMY

THE UNION WAS REGROUPING IN the spring of 1863. A string of bloody battles and strategic missteps during the fall of 1862—Second Bull Run, Antietam, Fredericksburg—had prompted the adoption of the new policy of "hard war." Victory meant not simply winning battles and defending territory but attacking the South's very ability to fight, by freeing slaves, destroying enemy armies, and devastating the southern countryside.

On January 1, President Lincoln's Emancipation Proclamation transformed the war by elevating freedom into a paramount war aim and lending an imperative, moral dimension to the struggle. In March 1863, heightened mobilization cut more deeply into the Northern home front when Congress passed the Enrollment Act. Employing a lottery, this systematic draft targeted all able-bodied men aged twenty to forty-five, including immigrants who had applied for citizenship. The draft was never particularly effective as a recruitment tool, encouraging desertions at the rate of about ten percent over the course of the war. Another 160,000 draftees simply never reported for service.

Two features of this new draft provoked particular bitterness. Draftees could hire "substitutes" to take their place in the army or pay a "commutation" fee of three hundred dollars to escape service altogether. Combined with Lincoln's call for half a million more men, the draft led to the charge that this was a "a rich man's war but poor man's fight." Immigrants, in particular, resented the draft but they represented twenty-nine percent of white men of military age and were essential to the Union war effort. Overall, more than one-fourth of Union solders were immigrants.

Resistance to the draft culminated in the summer of 1863 in the New York City draft riots, which lasted five days and took one hundred and twenty lives. Amid the growing discontent, Peace Democrats, the reviled "Copperheads," found fertile ground, especially in the Midwest, where many southerners had settled. In April, General Ambrose Burnside issued an order prohibiting "treason" in the Department of the Ohio. When an Ohio Democrat, Clement Vallandigham, spoke out against the war, Burnside ordered his arrest. Imprisoned by a military court, Vallandigham received the Democratic nomination for governor of Ohio. Lincoln defused the situation by commuting Vallandigham's sentence and banishing him to the Confederacy. Despite draft resistance, the Union Army nearly doubled in size during 1863.

In the spring, the Bureau of Colored Troops began recruiting African Americans, filling one hundred and sixty-six regiments with fresh and highly motivated soldiers. Lincoln championed their enlistment and predicted that "The bare sight of fifty thousand armed and drilled black soldiers upon the banks of the Mississippi, would end the rebellion at once." When the Confederacy threatened to execute captured African American soldiers, Lincoln immediately cancelled all prisoner exchanges. African American troops soon served with distinction at Port Hudson and Milliken's

Bend in Louisiana and Fort Wagner in South Carolina, rewarding Lincoln's faith. As the army nearly doubled, so did the federal budget. The Union leaned less heavily on paper money than the Confederacy, with "greenbacks" providing only one-eighth of the revenue needed to win the war.

As a result, wartime inflation in the North reached just forty percent during 1863 while exceeding 1800 percent in the South. The expanded army and stepped-up war effort rested on a secure economic foundation. As General Robert E. Lee gathered all of his strength to head north yet again during the summer of 1863, the Union was poised to strike back.

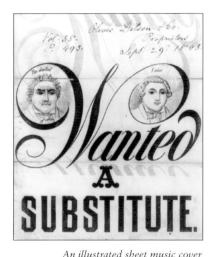

An illustrated sheet music cover protesting the inequities of the draft system enacted under the Enrollment Act of 1863. This Act allowed drafted men to purchase an exemption or to furnish a surrogate in lieu of their own service.

Left: *Company E of the Fourth U.S. Colored Infantry formed part of the defenses of Washington, D.C.*

Below: *Amid discontent with the progress of the war, the peace Democrats or "Copperheads" found support, especially in the midwest.*

TRADE AND BLOCKADE

The British-built Confederate ship Alabama raided across the world's oceans, in all taking some sixty-five prizes valued at over six million dollars. In June, 1864, her commander took the Alabama into Cherbourg, France, for a refit. Shortly after, the Federal steamer, U.S.S. Kearsarge, arrived and promptly challenged the Confederate ship to come out and fight. On June 19 the two ships confronted each other in the English Channel. The Alabama, outmatched by the Kearsarge's heavy guns, surrendered after one hour of fighting and finally went to the bottom.

UNION NAVAL POWER WAS CRUCIAL in winning the Civil War. The North began with a navy of only forty-two ships in 1861 but concluded the war with six hundred and seventy-one, representing the largest navy on Earth. The Confederate Navy comprised about one hundred and thirty ships at its peak. The Union Navy's primary role was blockading the three thousand five hundred miles of coastline in the Confederacy. One week after the attack on Fort Sumter, Lincoln proclaimed a blockade that was designed to deny European goods, including guns, to the Confederacy while preventing southern cotton from reaching lucrative European markets. The blockade became a crucial component of General-in-Chief Winfield Scott's "Anaconda Plan." Scott proposed surrounding the Confederacy like a snake encircling its prey, in hopes of forcing a surrender before a long and bloody war could erupt. Long after abandoning Scott's plan, the Union maintained the blockade as its chief naval strategy and economic weapon against the Confederacy. The Union Navy eventually relegated nearly five hundred ships to the task of blockading every southern port and countless inlets along the coast. Evading the blockade became a high priority. Smuggling generated huge profits and proved essential to the Confederate war effort.

The British officially recognized the blockade but traded with the Confederates when their ships broke through it. British shipyards also produced blockade-runners designed to evade and outrun the Union Navy. Built for speed with a shallow draft, the blockade-runners had a low profile, burned anthracite coal to minimize smoke, and were painted gray. During the first year of the war, nine-tenths of the blockade-runners evaded capture. The Confederate government began clamping down on the privately owned blockade-runners, requiring them to reserve one-third and later one-half of their cargo holds for guns and materiel. Eventually, state governments and the Confederacy itself commissioned blockade-runners of their own and banned the import of luxury items.

The Union was equally determined to enforce the blockade and captured strategic bases along the southern coast, including Port Royal, South Carolina, St. Augustine, Florida, and much of the North Carolina coastline. These footholds bottled up commerce and provided mainland bases for Union vessels to carry on the blockade. Southerners' desperation to break the blockade led to their decision to build thirty-seven armored ships, or "ironclads." The North built its own ironclads, and in March 1862 the Union's *Monitor* and the Confederacy's *Virginia* met in their decisive confrontation. Although a draw, the battle proved that the South's ironclads were useless in challenging the Union's naval superiority. By the end of the war, the Union Navy was capturing one-half of the ships that dared to test the blockade.

While the blockade suppressed oceanic trade, a lively overland traffic developed along the thousand-mile border that separated the two enemies.

The Union licensed trade with occupied areas in the South but prohibited trading with the Confederacy itself. Desperate to export cotton, however, the Confederacy condoned smuggling and welcomed the revenue that the illicit overland trade with the North provided. Defying military edicts, even Union soldiers defied the ban, and the rampant smuggling helped the Confederacy more than it helped the Union. Congress eventually abandoned the licensing system and declared all Confederate cotton "captured property." Overall, the coastal blockade reduced the Confederacy's imports and exports by about two-thirds, dealing a crippling blow to its economy and its ability to sustain the war.

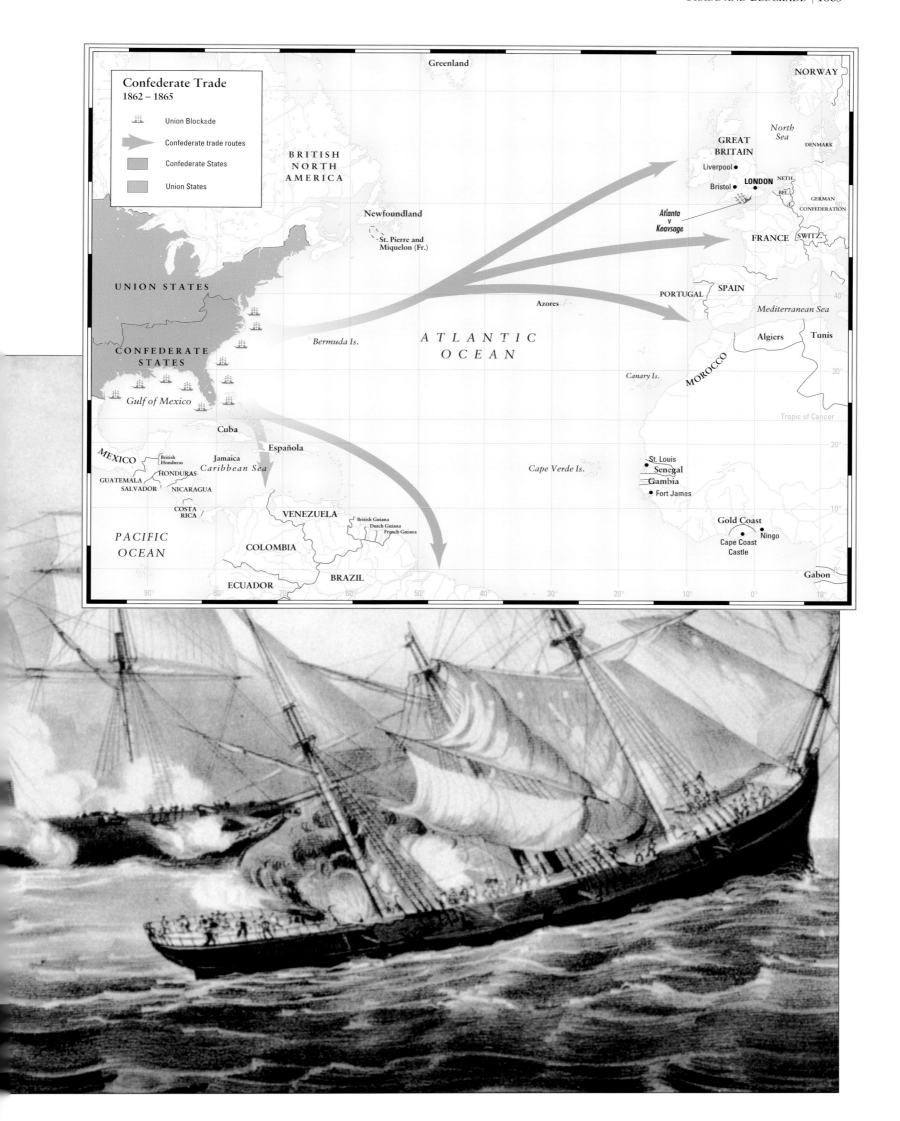

Confederate Trade
1862 – 1865

⚓	Union Blockade
➤	Confederate trade routes
▓	Confederate States
░	Union States

BRITISH NORTH AMERICA

Greenland

NORWAY

North Sea

GREAT BRITAIN

Liverpool

LONDON

Bristol

NETH

BEL

DENMARK

GERMAN CONFEDERATION

Newfoundland

St. Pierre and Miquelon (Fr.)

Atlanta v Keavsage

FRANCE

SWITZ.

UNION STATES

PORTUGAL

SPAIN

Azores

A T L A N T I C
O C E A N

Mediterranean Sea

CONFEDERATE STATES

Bermuda Is.

Algiers

Tunis

Canary Is.

MOROCCO

Tropic of Cancer

Gulf of Mexico

Cuba

Española

Cape Verde Is.

St. Louis

Senegal

Gambia

Fort James

MEXICO

British Honduras

Jamaica

Caribbean Sea

GUATEMALA

SALVADOR

HONDURAS

NICARAGUA

COSTA RICA

VENEZUELA

British Guiana

Dutch Guiana

French Guiana

Gold Coast

Ningo

Cape Coast Castle

Gabon

PACIFIC OCEAN

COLOMBIA

ECUADOR

BRAZIL

207

ENLISTMENT BY AFRICAN AMERICAN SOLDIERS

AFTER THE FIRING ON FORT SUMTER in April 1861, free African Americans across the North volunteered to fight for the Union and even raised their own regiments. President Lincoln, however, hoped to win the war without enrolling African American troops—or freeing any slaves—and turned them away. As the war dragged on, Union casualties mounted, and manpower shortages grew, several Union generals organized regiments of African Americans, enrolling fugitive slaves to fill support rather than combat roles. The logic and justice of organizing black regiments became clear, and in July 1862 Congress authorized the president to enlist free African Americans from the North and fugitive slaves from the South

fered double the average death rate from disease. Ironically, African Americans were kept in the army longer once the war ended so white soldiers could go home sooner. They also endured a major hazard not faced by whites: the Confederacy threatened to execute or enslave any black soldiers they captured. In response, President Lincoln promised to shoot one Confederate prisoner for each black soldier who was executed and sentence one to hard labor for each Union soldier who was enslaved. Lincoln's edict resulted in a Confederate policy of treating African American and white prisoners equally. Confederate soldiers, however, sometimes violated that policy, most infamously during the famed Fort Pillow Massacre in Tennessee. Reports of executions and enslavements at Fort Pillow in April 1864 tested Lincoln's policy. Without hard evidence, however, the Lincoln administration did not retaliate.

By the end of the war, the Union had organized 166 African American regiments, and 179,000 black soldiers served in the Union army, along with 10,000 black sailors. All told, 10 percent of the Union army and navy were African Americans. Victory would have been impossible without them. The participation of African Americans was both symbolically important

Slave "Contraband" Camps
1861–1863

- Union state/territory
- Confederate state/territory
- Under Union control, 1861–1863
- Contraband camp

but did not require him to do so. Lincoln resisted the idea, but by the time he issued the Final Emancipation Proclamation in January 1863, African American soldiers seemed like a godsend to the Union cause. Lincoln began enrolling African American troops into the Union army on January 1, 1863.

Most northerners agreed that African Americans should contribute to the military struggle against southern slavery, on both military and moral grounds. Still, black soldiers suffered discrimination in the Union army, whose initial policy established segregated units commanded by mostly white officers. In response to protests, the army eventually commissioned almost one hundred African American officers in the 166 black regiments, but none above the rank of captain. Black soldiers earned less than white soldiers—ten dollars versus thirteen dollars a month—until their pay was equalized in June 1864. Their nutrition and medical care was inferior, and they suf-

and crucial to the Union's military success. They demonstrated their value repeatedly in major engagements, such as Port Hudson, Milliken's Bend, and Fort Wagner, where the legendary tenacity and courage of the Fifty-fourth Massachusetts stunned the nation.

Overall, enlistment rates among African Americans were remarkable, especially among northern blacks, who were already free when the war began. Astoundingly, 82 percent of eligible African Americans in the North enlisted in the Union army. A majority (57 percent) of African Americans in the Border States enlisted. Encouraged by the prospect of winning their own freedom, 21 percent of military-age slaves fought for the Union. The enlistment of African American troops was indispensable to Union victory, denied crucial manpower to the Confederacy, and made an important symbolic statement that emancipation and equality was the true aim of a Union victory.

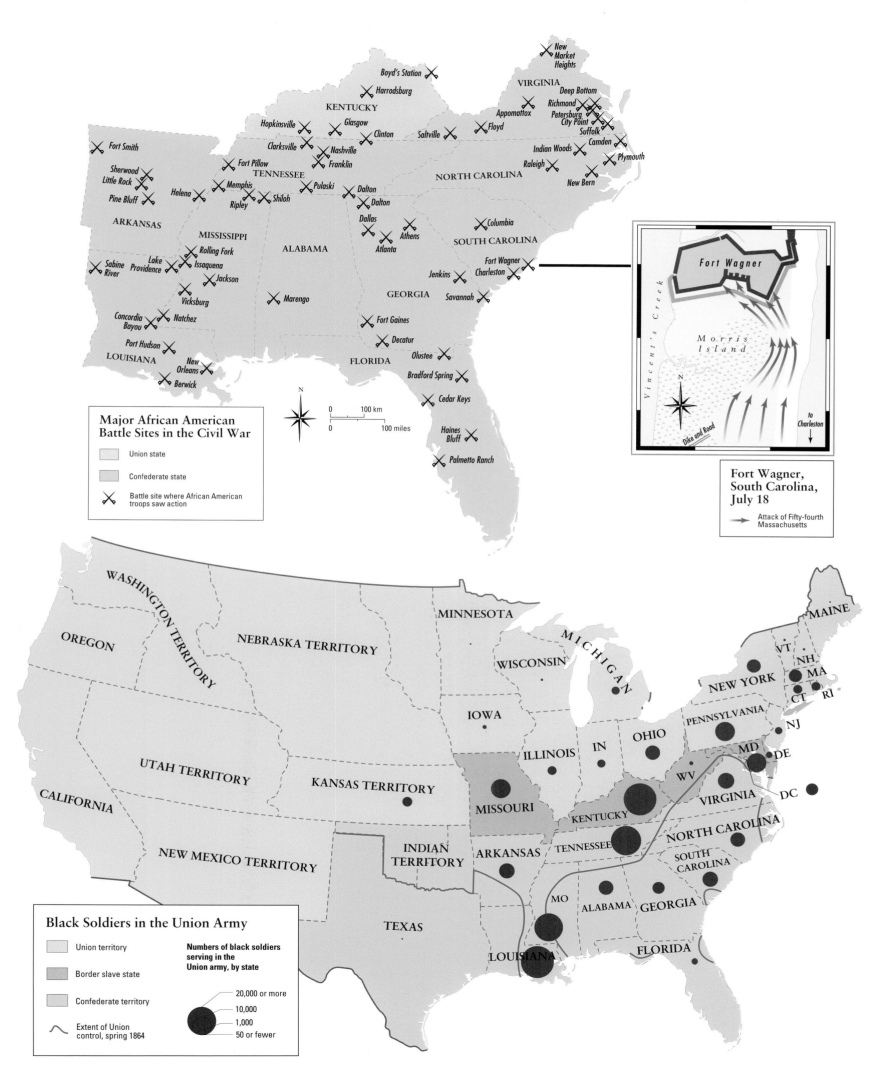

Major African American
Battle Sites in the Civil War

Union state

Confederate state

✗ Battle site where African American
troops saw action

Fort Wagner,
South Carolina,
July 18

→ Attack of Fifty-fourth
Massachusetts

Black Soldiers in the Union Army

Union territory

Border slave state

Confederate territory

⌒ Extent of Union
control, spring 1864

Numbers of black soldiers
serving in the
Union army, by state

20,000 or more
10,000
1,000
50 or fewer

THE COST OF WAR

THE UNION BEGAN FIGHTING A new kind of war in 1863. Despite the hideous casualties of 1862, the Civil War had been "limited" in the sense that most Northerners, and indeed President Lincoln himself, had hoped to bring the South back into the Union as quickly as possible without imposing any fundamental changes on the nation, above all freeing any slaves. General George McClellan's failure to take Richmond, followed by his army's demoralizing retreat and General Robert E. Lee's aggressive march northward to Antietam, forced the North to embrace a "hard war" designed to crush the Old South and rebuild a new one.

The year 1863 witnessed the Emancipation Proclamation, the enrollment of African American soldiers, a stepped-up draft, the suspension of prisoner exchanges, a doubling of military spending, and a war of attrition in both the East and the West. When Lincoln issued his Emancipation Proclamation on January 1, he called on African Americans to join the Union Army and Navy. All told, one hundred eighty-nine thousand of them enlisted, filling one hundred sixty-six segregated regiments and representing almost one-tenth of the North's men-at-arms. Their courageous actions at Port Hudson and Milliken's Bend in Louisiana and Fort Wagner in South Carolina proved their value.

As casualties mounted, however, Lincoln called for half a million more men. Congress passed the Enrollment Act in March, subjecting all men aged twenty to forty-five to the draft, including immigrants who had applied for citizenship. In May, Lincoln halted prisoner exchanges when the South threatened to execute African American prisoners, and Union and Confederate prisons began to proliferate and fill up. Just over one-fourth of the war's engagements, six hundred twenty-seven battles, took place during 1863. Continuing the pattern of previous years, most engagements occurred in the

Upper South. Tennessee led with one hundred twenty-four engagements, twenty percent of the total, as General William S. Rosecrans drove his army through East Tennessee into Georgia. The Union defeat at Chickamauga and its subsequent victory at Chattanooga cost both sides nearly fifty thousand in killed, missing, and wounded. Virginia followed closely behind Tennessee with one hundred sixteen engagements.

Lee's second major advance northward during the summer produced the bloody Union defeat at

On July 3 Grant and Pemberton met to discuss the surrender terms of Vicksburg under the oak tree shown in this sketch by Theodore R. Davis. Within a day of this meeting souvenir hunters moved in on the oak tree and trunk, root, and branch quickly disappeared.

Chancellorsville under General Joseph Hooker but also the climactic Union victory at Gettysburg in July. Lee lost one-third of his forces at Gettysburg, limped back across the Potomac, and never threatened to invade Union territory again.

The other major operation of the summer was the siege of Vicksburg, under General Ulysses S. Grant. On July 4, the day after Pickett's Charge, Vicksburg fell, surrendering command of the Mississippi River to the Union and dividing the Confederacy in half. Grant's army had killed or wounded ten thousand Confederates, captured another thirty-seven thousand, and dealt the most decisive single blow to the southern cause. Grant went on to orchestrate the victory at Chattanooga and develop a grand strategy for winning the war. Lincoln had found his general. "Grant is my man," he crowed, "and I am his the rest of the war." Overall, Confederate casualties continued to outpace Union losses during 1863. But, with the impending big push to end the war and the growing intensity of the Confederate defense around Richmond, that was about to change.

Logan's Division entering Vicksburg on July 4, 1863. General John Logan is the central figure in the group of horsemen; behind them Confederate soldiers are standing in lines with their arms stacked. Almost 30,000 Confederates laid down their arms at the surrender of Vicksburg. The Union had effectively split the South.

1864
TOTAL WAR

In March 1864 Lincoln promoted Grant to Lieutenant General (three stars) and appointed him General in Chief of all Union armies. Grant decided to make his headquarters with the Army of the Potomac in Virginia and he left Major General William T. Sherman in charge of an army group in Georgia. Grant immediately made plans for simultaneous advances by these two large armies and several smaller ones on their respective fronts. Coming off the victories in the second half of 1863, these campaigns inspired confidence among the Northern people that they would win the war by the Fourth of July. Confederate armies no longer had the strength to carry out offensive operations as they had in 1862 and 1863. But they were still strong enough to fight a war of attrition, as the Patriots had done in the war of 1775–1783 against Britain. If Southern forces could hold out long enough and inflict sufficient casualties on attacking Union armies, they might weaken the Northern will to continue fighting. In particular, if they could hold out until the Union presidential election in November, Northern voters might reject Lincoln and elect a Peace Democrat. "If we can break up the enemy's arrangements early and throw him back," wrote General James Longstreet, "he will not be able to recover his position or his morale until the Presidential election is over, and then we shall have a new President to deal with."

It almost happened that way. Even before Grant and Sherman began their offensives, Confederate victories in smaller campaigns in Florida, North Carolina, Louisiana, and Arkansas

General Sherman's army entering Savannah, Georgia, December 21, 1864.

from February to April pumped up Southern morale. From May to July, heavy fighting in Virginia and a war of maneuver in Georgia placed Richmond, Petersburg, and Atlanta under siege—but at great cost in casualties. In two months, Union armies on all fronts lost 100,000 men killed, wounded, and missing and Confederate armies experienced similar casualty rates though smaller in actual numbers—by far the worst carnage in any comparable period of the war. Most of the missing had been captured, and their fate was often worse than that of the wounded. The Confederacy refused to treat captured ex-slaves in a Union uniform as prisoners of war or to exchange them, and the Northerners refused to accept this unequal treatment of Union prisoners. As a result, the exchange cartel broke down and prison camps on both sides swelled to far beyond their capacity, resulting in horrendous death rates especially at Southern prison camps such as Andersonville in Georgia.

Northern civilian morale dropped to rock bottom by August 1864 because of the enormous number of casualties with no apparent progress toward winning the war. Peace Democrats called for an armistice and negotiations, which would have been tantamount to Confederate victory. The Democrats nominated George McClellan for president on a platform that called the war a failure. In August, Lincoln was certain he would be defeated for reelection "unless there is some great change" in the military situation.

Great change soon happened. On September 3 a telegram from

General Sherman arrived in Washington: "Atlanta is ours, and fairly won." During the next seven weeks a pieced-together Union Army of the Shenandoah won a series of spectacular victories in Virginia's Shenandoah Valley that virtually destroyed a Confederate army corps in that region. Once again morale in the North underwent a 180-degree turn and Lincoln was triumphantly reelected in November. In mid-December the Confederacy's second-largest army, the Army of Tennessee, was almost wiped out in the Battle of Nashville. Meanwhile, Sherman had departed from Atlanta on his famous March to the Sea, wrecking Confederate railroads, factories, and food supplies as he went. For the second year in succession, 1864 closed with a confident North and a demoralized South. This time it would stick. "The deep waters are closing over us," wrote the Southern diarist Mary Boykin Chesnut on December 19. "We are going to be wiped off the earth."

Below: *General Sherman's army occupying Atlanta, encamped in City Hall Square. Sherman then set about destroying Atlanta's usefulness to the Confederacy, blowing up factories, machine shops and wrecking railroads, while he simultaneously ordered the civilian population to leave the city. General Hood wrote to Sherman "The unprecedented measure you propose transcends in studied and ingenious cruelty all acts in the dark history of war. In the name of God and humanity, I protest." Sherman replied bluntly, "War is cruelty, and you cannot refine it, you might as well appeal against the thunder-storm as against these terrible hardships of war."*

THE CAMPAIGNS OF 1864

BY MAY 1864, WHEN THE YEAR'S major campaigns began, both sides were optimistic. The Union armies were now for the first time under the unified command of a competent, aggressive general, in the person of Ulysses S. Grant. The victor of Donelson, Vicksburg, and Chattanooga would accompany George Meade and the Army of the Potomac in Virginia in pursuit of the North's nemesis, Robert E. Lee. The northern public expected dramatic results.

Southerners likewise believed they had victory in sight. Minor victories that winter and early spring at Olustee, Florida, and Mansfield, Louisiana, helped convince them once again that their armies were superior to the North's, despite setbacks in the latter half of 1863. More important, the Lincoln administration faced a regular election in November of 1864. Many of the leaders of the opposing Democratic Party had declared the war a failure and called for a negotiated peace. If the Democrats won the election and carried through on their professed beliefs, it would guarantee the continuation of slavery and probably Confederate independence as well. Antiwar agitation in the North encouraged the Confederates' belief that their cause could succeed if the summer's military campaigns brought no dramatic Union successes.

The youthful enthusiasm of the new recruit is absent on the faces of these two Union soldiers, now experienced veterans of a well-equipped, professionally-led, battle-hardened Union army.

Major military operations opened in early May and were almost entirely focused in two states. In Virginia the Army of the Potomac, commanded by Meade under the immediate direction of Grant, was to attack Lee's Army of Northern Virginia with the goal of destroying it and taking Richmond. In Georgia Grant intended a precisely parallel campaign. A combination of armies under the command of Major General William T. Sherman would attack General Joseph E. Johnston's Army of Tennessee with the goal of destroying it and taking Atlanta. In each case, the Union had an approximate three-to-two superiority in numbers, a minimal advantage when assuming the burden of the offensive.

The two campaigns developed very differently. Grant and Lee were both daring and aggressive, closely matched in skill and style (though not in personality). Each time Grant moved around Lee's flank, the Confederate general responded by attacking savagely or deftly blocking the movement. If Lee did succeeded in blocking, Grant responded with powerful attacks of his own. The result was a series of bloody and inconclusive battles—the Wilderness, Spotsylvania, and Cold Harbor. Casualties were appalling, but, by early June, Grant was on the outskirts of Richmond.

When Lee succeeded in blocking him again at Cold Harbor, in a position completely impervious to attack, Grant responded by breaking contact and swinging his army across the James River and some miles to the south to threaten Petersburg, the nexus for railroads entering Richmond from the south and southwest. Without Petersburg, the Confederates could not hold Richmond, and Grant almost took Petersburg that June. The Army of the Potomac, however, a clumsy instrument at the best of times, had been staggered by recent losses. It performed poorly and failed to take the town from a small defensive force. Lee finally discovered Grant's move and again successfully countered. Grant then settled down to a quasi siege of Richmond and Petersburg that was to last almost ten months.

Several days earlier, Lee had set in motion a program for breaking such a siege, dispatching Lieutenant General Jubal Early with the Confederate Second Corps to move into the Shenandoah Valley and threaten to invade the North. Early got all the way to the outskirts of Washington that July, before troops detached from Grant's army stopped him. He then pulled back into the Shenandoah Valley and continued to be a nuisance. Grant sent Major General Philip H. Sheridan to command a reinforced Union Army of the Shenandoah with orders to eliminate the threat of Early's army and eliminate the valley as a source of supplies for the Confederates. Sheridan defeated Early at the Third Battle of Winchester as well as the battles of Fisher's Hill and Cedar Creek. His forces also extensively destroyed crops and livestock in the Shenandoah Valley.

The Georgia campaign took a different course. Sherman utilized his superb skills of maneuver to turn Johnston, forcing the unaggressive Confederate general to retreat again and again. Except for Kennesaw Mountain, where Johnston administered a brief check to Sherman's advance, no major battles had occurred by the time the armies reached the outskirts of Atlanta in July. Jefferson Davis, fearing with good reason that Johnston was about to give up Atlanta without a fight, replaced him with John B. Hood. As further retreat would surrender Atlanta, Hood had no choice but to fight when Sherman attempted another turning maneuver. At the battles of Peachtree Creek, Atlanta, and Ezra Church in late July, Hood suffered defeat but managed to hold Atlanta for another five weeks. When he finally had to evacuate the city in early September, the news brought rejoicing in the North and a substantial boost to Lincoln's previously flagging re-election hopes.

Subsequently Hood took his army west and then north in a disastrous campaign into Middle Tennessee, while Sherman skillfully marched his army through Georgia to Savannah, emphasizing the increasingly helpless state of the South.

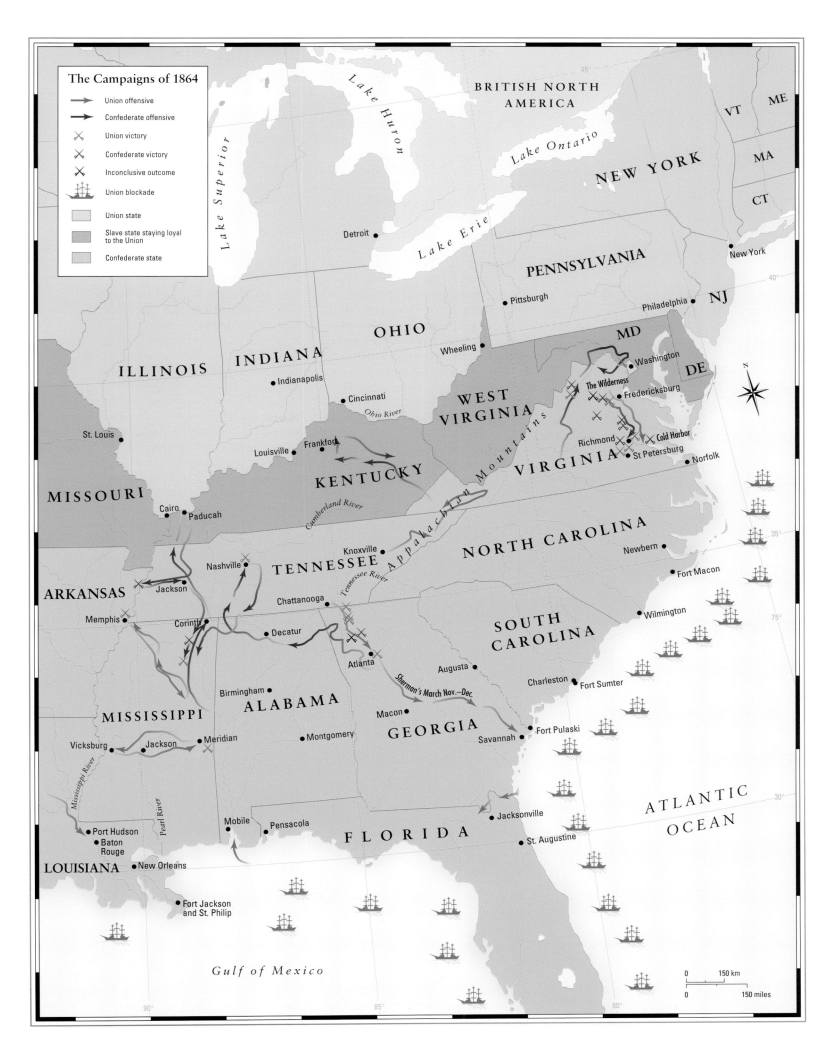

The Campaigns of 1864

- Union offensive
- Confederate offensive
- Union victory
- Confederate victory
- Inconclusive outcome
- Union blockade
- Union state
- Slave state staying loyal to the Union
- Confederate state

BRITISH NORTH AMERICA

Lake Superior

Lake Huron

Lake Ontario

Lake Erie

VT

ME

MA

CT

NEW YORK

PENNSYLVANIA

NJ

MD

DE

Detroit

Pittsburgh

Philadelphia

Washington

OHIO

INDIANA

ILLINOIS

WEST VIRGINIA

The Wilderness

Fredericksburg

Indianapolis

Cincinnati

Ohio River

Wheeling

Richmond

Cold Harbor

St Petersburg

Norfolk

St. Louis

Louisville

Frankfort

VIRGINIA

MISSOURI

KENTUCKY

Appalachian Mountains

Cumberland River

Cairo

Paducah

Knoxville

NORTH CAROLINA

Newbern

Fort Macon

Nashville

TENNESSEE

Tennessee River

ARKANSAS

Jackson

Chattanooga

Memphis

Corinth

Decatur

SOUTH CAROLINA

Wilmington

Atlanta

Augusta

Birmingham

Macon

Charleston

Fort Sumter

MISSISSIPPI

ALABAMA

GEORGIA

Sherman's March Nov.–Dec.

Vicksburg

Jackson

Meridian

Montgomery

Savannah

Fort Pulaski

Mississippi River

Pearl River

Mobile

Pensacola

FLORIDA

Jacksonville

Port Hudson

Baton Rouge

St. Augustine

ATLANTIC OCEAN

LOUISIANA

New Orleans

Fort Jackson and St. Philip

Gulf of Mexico

0   150 km

0   150 miles

THE OLUSTEE AND MERIDIAN CAMPAIGNS

Brigadier General Joseph Finegan's determined attack at the Battle of Ocean Pond effectively halted, and then drove back, the Union advance from the Atlantic coast.

URING THE WINTER OF 1863–1864, Major General William T. Sherman was contemplating taking most of the combat strength of the Army of the Tennessee eastward for the 1864 campaign. But first, he saw a need to neutralize central Mississippi by destroying much of the region's infrastructure and leaving it logistically incapable of supporting a major Confederate army that could potentially threaten Vicksburg and Union control of the Mississippi River. For this purpose he set out from Vicksburg on February 3 with twenty-six thousand troops of the Sixteenth and Seventeenth corps, bound for Meridian, Mississippi, one hundred and thirty miles to the east, near the Alabama state line. An additional force of seven thousand five hundred cavalrymen under Brigadier General William Sooy Smith was to move southeast out of Memphis and cooperate with Sherman. Opposing them, Lieutenant General Leonidas Polk had twenty thousand Confederate troops for the defense of Mississippi. As soon as the Union troops crossed the Big Black River, Confederate cavalry under Brigadier General Wirt Adams began to skirmish actively in Sherman's front. Fighting was almost constant, but Adams could neither stop Sherman nor slow him significantly.

On February 5, the Federals marched into Jackson. It was the third time that the Mississippi capital had fallen to troops under Sherman's immediate command. They quickly destroyed the remaining facilities of military importance and the next day continued their march to the east. Again, fighting was almost constant with the ever-present Confederate cavalry, but Polk made no serious effort to halt the expedition's advance. On February 9, Sherman's troops occupied Yazoo City, Mississippi, and on the 14th they entered Meridian. There they remained for

six days, destroying railroads, bridges, locomotives, arsenals, and storehouses. Then they turned and, in a leisurely manner, marched back to Vicksburg, still harassed by Confederate cavalry but having met with no significant opposition. In all, Sherman's troops destroyed some one hundred and fifteen miles of railroad track, sixty-one bridges, and twenty locomotives in the course of the Meridian expedition.

Meanwhile, William Sooy Smith's expedition left Memphis on February 5, several days later than planned. Smith proceeded slowly through Tennessee and northern Mississippi, skirmishing with Confederate cavalry under Colonel Nathan Bedford Forrest. On February 21, long after he should have rendezvoused with Sherman near Meridian, Smith lost his nerve and turned back toward Memphis. The next day Forrest attacked and defeated him at Okolona, Mississippi. Smith and what was left of his force fled to Memphis. Union casualties totaled three hundred and eighty-eight and Confederate, approximately 110.

Almost simultaneous with Sherman's Meridian expedition was another Union expedition into the interior of Florida. Believing that northern Florida contained a large number of Unionists whom he hoped to see form a loyal reconstruction government, Lincoln authorized Major General Quincy Gillmore, commanding the Department of the South, to send an expedition into Florida to liberate Unionists and slaves and to cut the Confederate supply line. On February 7, Brigadier General Truman Seymour's division of Gillmore's command occupied Jacksonville, Florida, with little opposition and prepared to march inland. Like Sherman's expedition, Seymour's encountered Confederate cavalry and skirmished frequently as it advanced westward through northern Florida.

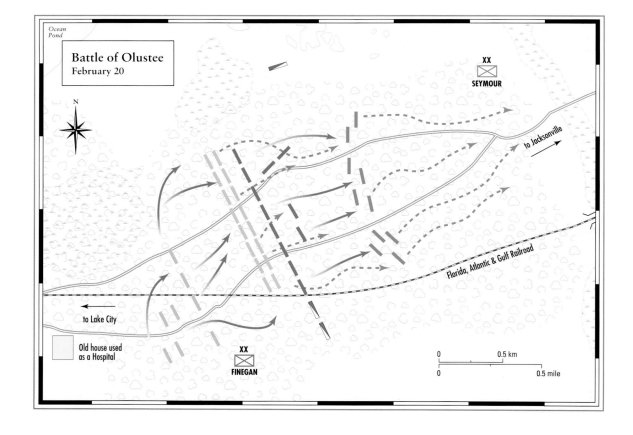

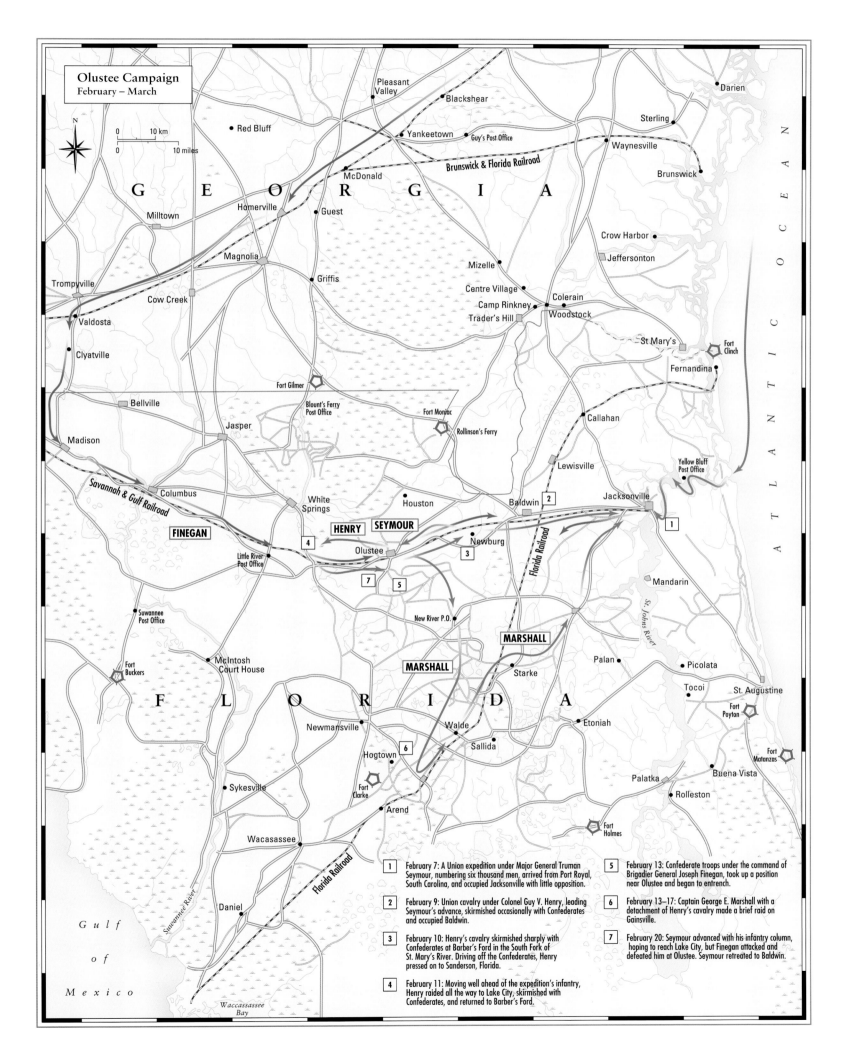

Olustee Campaign
February – March

N

0   10 km
0   10 miles

GEORGIA

Darien
Blackshear
Pleasant Valley
Sterling
Red Bluff
Yankeetown
Guy's Post Office
Waynesville
Brunswick & Florida Railroad
Brunswick
McDonald
Homerville
Guest
Milltown
Crow Harbor
Jeffersonton
Magnolia
Mizelle
Centre Village
Trompyville
Griffis
Colerain
Cow Creek
Camp Rinkney
Woodstock
Valdosta
Trader's Hill
Clyatville
St Mary's
Fort Clinch
Fernandina
Fort Gilmer
Bellville
Blount's Ferry Post Office
Fort Moniac
Callahan
Jasper
Rollinson's Ferry
Madison
Lewisville
Yellow Bluff Post Office
Savannah & Gulf Railroad
Columbus
White Springs
Houston
Baldwin [2]
Jacksonville [1]
FINEGAN
HENRY SEYMOUR
[4]
Olustee
[3] Newburg
Florida Railroad
Little River Post Office
[7] [5]
Mandarin
St Johns River
Suwannee Post Office
New River P.O.
MARSHALL
McIntosh Court House
MARSHALL
Palan
Picolata
Fort Buckers
Starke
Tocoi
St. Augustine
FLORIDA
Newmansville
Walde
Etoniah
Fort Poyton
Hogtown [6]
Sallida
Sykesville
Fort Clarke
Buena Vista
Fort Matanzas
Arend
Palatka
Rolleston
Wacasassee
Fort Holmes
Florida Railroad
Daniel
Suwannee River
Gulf
of
Mexico
Waccassassee Bay

ATLANTIC OCEAN

[1] February 7: A Union expedition under Major General Truman Seymour, numbering six thousand men, arrived from Port Royal, South Carolina, and occupied Jacksonville with little opposition.

[2] February 9: Union cavalry under Colonel Guy V. Henry, leading Seymour's advance, skirmished occasionally with Confederates and occupied Baldwin.

[3] February 10: Henry's cavalry skirmished sharply with Confederates at Barber's Ford in the South Fork of St. Mary's River. Driving off the Confederates, Henry pressed on to Sanderson, Florida.

[4] February 11: Moving well ahead of the expedition's infantry, Henry raided all the way to Lake City, skirmished with Confederates, and returned to Barber's Ford.

[5] February 13: Confederate troops under the command of Brigadier General Joseph Finegan, took up a position near Olustee and began to entrench.

[6] February 13–17: Captain George E. Marshall with a detachment of Henry's cavalry made a brief raid on Gainsville.

[7] February 20: Seymour advanced with his infantry column, hoping to reach Lake City, but Finegan attacked and defeated him at Olustee. Seymour retreated to Baldwin.

On February 20, however, at Olustee, Brigadier General Joseph Finegan and his five thousand Confederates attacked Seymour's five thousand five hundred Federals. In a hard-fought battle, also know as the Battle of Ocean Pond, Finegan was victorious and Seymour began a retreat back to the Atlantic coast. Total Union casualties were one thousand eight hundred and sixty-one and Confederate, nine hundred and thirty-four. The battles of Okolona and Olustee were minor, almost to the point of triviality, and had no impact at all on the outcome of the war. Nonetheless, many Southerners at the time considered them, along with the Meridian campaign—during which they feared Sherman intended to go all the way to Montgomery or Mobile—as great victories that portended the final success of Confederate arms.

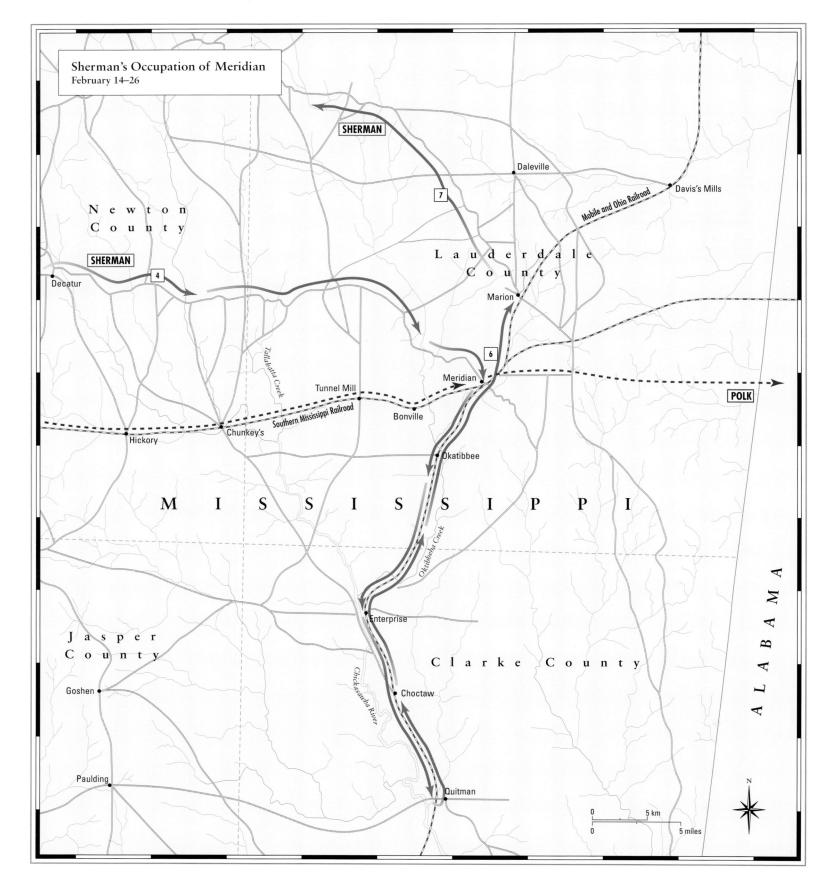

Sherman's Occupation of Meridian
February 14–26

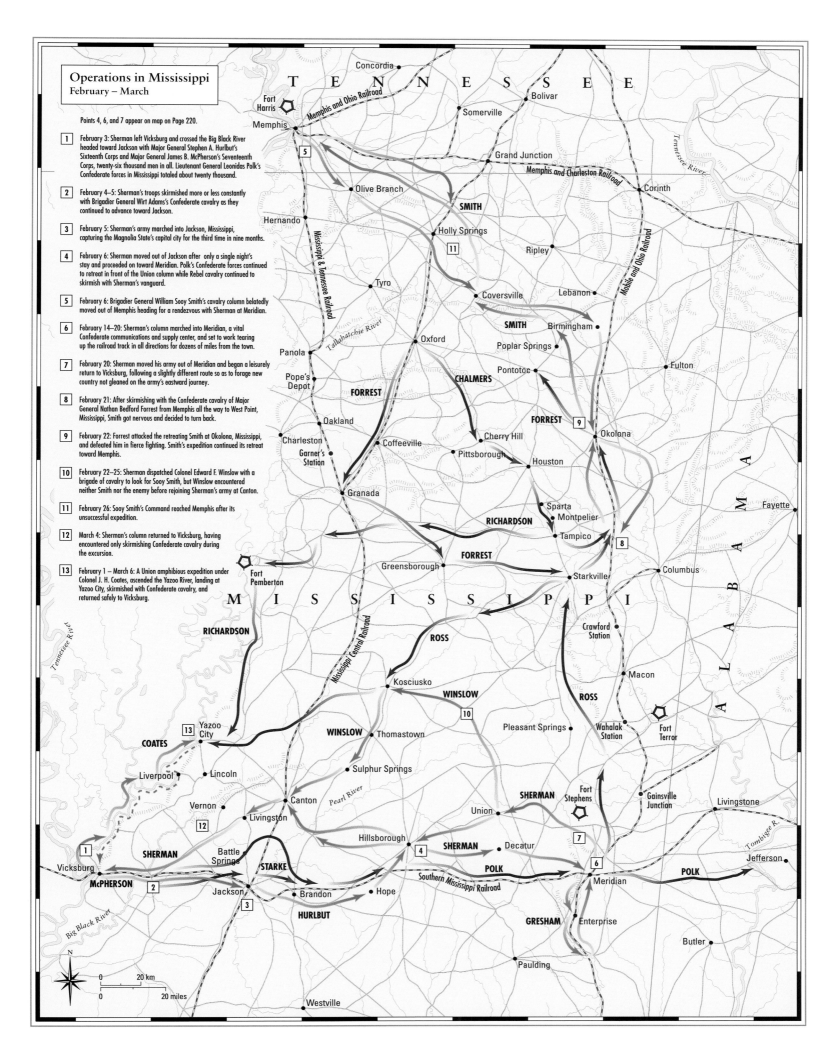

Operations in Mississippi
February – March

Points 4, 6, and 7 appear on map on Page 220.

1 February 3: Sherman left Vicksburg and crossed the Big Black River headed toward Jackson with Major General Stephen A. Hurlbut's Sixteenth Corps and Major General James B. McPherson's Seventeenth Corps, twenty-six thousand men in all. Lieutenant General Leonidas Polk's Confederate forces in Mississippi totaled about twenty thousand.

2 February 4–5: Sherman's troops skirmished more or less constantly with Brigadier General Wirt Adams's Confederate cavalry as they continued to advance toward Jackson.

3 February 5: Sherman's army marched into Jackson, Mississippi, capturing the Magnolia State's capital city for the third time in nine months.

4 February 6: Sherman moved out of Jackson after only a single night's stay and proceeded on toward Meridian. Polk's Confederate forces continued to retreat in front of the Union column while Rebel cavalry continued to skirmish with Sherman's vanguard.

5 February 6: Brigadier General William Sooy Smith's cavalry column belatedly moved out of Memphis heading for a rendezvous with Sherman at Meridian.

6 February 14–20: Sherman's column marched into Meridian, a vital Confederate communications and supply center, and set to work tearing up the railroad track in all directions for dozens of miles from the town.

7 February 20: Sherman moved his army out of Meridian and began a leisurely return to Vicksburg, following a slightly different route so as to forage new country not gleaned on the army's eastward journey.

8 February 21: After skirmishing with the Confederate cavalry of Major General Nathan Bedford Forrest from Memphis all the way to West Point, Mississippi, Smith got nervous and decided to turn back.

9 February 22: Forrest attacked the retreating Smith at Okolona, Mississippi, and defeated him in fierce fighting. Smith's expedition continued its retreat toward Memphis.

10 February 22–25: Sherman dispatched Colonel Edward F. Winslow with a brigade of cavalry to look for Sooy Smith, but Winslow encountered neither Smith nor the enemy before rejoining Sherman's army at Canton.

11 February 26: Sooy Smith's Command reached Memphis after its unsuccessful expedition.

12 March 4: Sherman's column returned to Vicksburg, having encountered only skirmishing Confederate cavalry during the excursion.

13 February 1 – March 6: A Union amphibious expedition under Colonel J. H. Coates, ascended the Yazoo River, landing at Yazoo City, skirmished with Confederate cavalry, and returned safely to Vicksburg.

THE RED RIVER CAMPAIGN

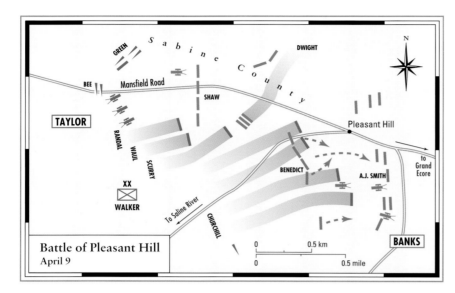

Battle of Pleasant Hill
April 9

By 1863, LINCOLN WAS EAGER to impress upon the French emperor Napoleon III the seriousness of U.S. disapproval of his puppet empire in Mexico. In order to do so, Lincoln strove to insert Union troops into Texas. Within the strategic context of the Civil War itself, sending troops to Texas made no sense at all, particularly after the fall of Vicksburg and Port Hudson in July 1863. Thereafter, with the Union controlling the Mississippi, nothing that could be accomplished west of that river would make any difference at all in the outcome or duration of the war—except by diverting Union resources that could have been used elsewhere. Nevertheless, Lincoln believed it was necessary.

Out of Lincoln's desire came the 1864 Red River campaign, to be commanded by Major General Nathaniel P. Banks of the Department of the Gulf. The Red River led into Texas, albeit northern Texas, six hundred miles from the Mexican border. Short of Texas, the river led past the Confederate Louisiana capital at Shreveport. It also led through

rich, cotton-producing areas of the state, where the expedition could, it was hoped, seize large enough amounts of the white fiber to help keep northeastern textile mills running and the operators and employees happy and voting. Banks was especially interested in their votes, as he hoped to win enough military glory in the expedition to boost his political career—possibly all the way to the presidency.

For the expedition Banks took not only the Eighth and Nineteenth corps of his own department but also three divisions—ten thousand men—from the Sixteenth and Seventeenth corps, borrowed from William T. Sherman's neighboring Department of the Tennessee. Major General Andrew J. Smith commanded the Army of the Tennessee contingent, which Banks promised to have back to Sherman in time to take part in his advance toward Atlanta. This gave Banks a force of some thirty thousand men, supported by Rear Admiral David D. Porter's gunboat fleet. The expedition got under way on March 12, as Smith's contingent and Porter's gunboats entered the Red River. On the 14th they combined to capture Fort De Russy, thirty miles up the Red, and two days later they occupied Alexandria, Louisiana. Meanwhile, Banks and his contingent left Berwick Bay, on the south coast of Louisiana, and marched north to Alexandria, arriving on March 25. Banks then delayed to supervise the holding of civilian elections for various offices in the loyal state government of Louisiana.

Orders from Grant to return Smith's contingent by April 25, whether he had taken Shreveport by then or not, prodded Banks on a bit. In early April the expedition proceeded up the river, reaching a river landing called Grand Ecore on April 3. There, following the directions of a disloyal local guide, Banks led the expedition away from the river road, where the gunboats could support him, and onto an inferior road that wound into the interior of Louisiana. Banks also adopt-

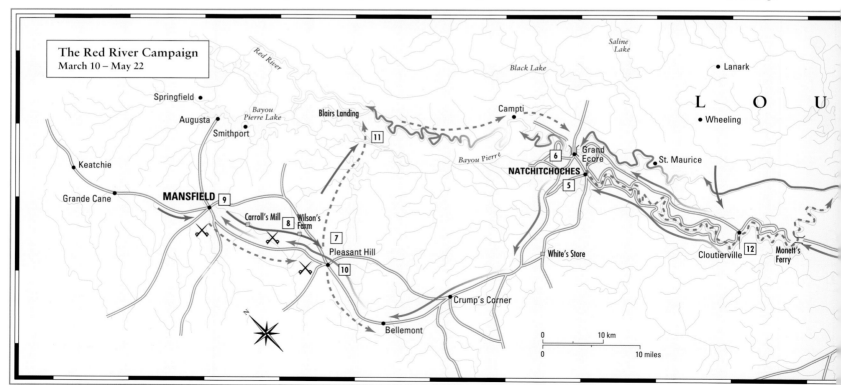

The Red River Campaign
March 10 – May 22

ed a clumsy arrangement for his march column, placing his vanguard in front of a cumbersome wagon train that separated it from the rest of his fighting strength. On April 8, just outside Mansfield, Louisiana, about thirty-five miles short of Shreveport, a Confederate army of eight thousand eight hundred men commanded by Major General Richard Taylor attacked Banks's vanguard, defeated it, and captured numerous wagons. Banks retreated, and Taylor pursued.

The next day Taylor's army, heavily reinforced, caught up with Banks at Pleasant Hill, Louisiana, and attacked again. This time the result was different. Smith's contingent, which had been at the rear of Banks's column the previous day, was present at Pleasant Hill. Smith's "Gorillas," as they had by this time been nicknamed for their combat prowess and their tendency to destroy civilian property, turned the tide and handed Taylor a defeat. To Smith's intense disgust, the thoroughly frightened Banks insisted on continuing the retreat, even abandoning his wounded.

Soon it was Taylor's turn to be outraged by an equally foolish mistake by his own superior, Lieutenant General Edmund Kirby Smith, who ordered him to detach much of his force to Arkansas to oppose Major General Frederick Steele's Camden expedition. Nevertheless, Taylor pursued and harassed the retreating Federals as best he could. Adding to the dry weather, the Confederates diverted the flow of the Red River, lowering the water level at the Alexandria shoals to the point that Porter's ironclads were nearly stranded. Only Lieutenant Colonel Joseph Bailey's inspired improvisation in building a series of wing dams, which extended from both banks part way across the river, provided enough depth of water for the fleet to escape. At Yellow Bayou, Smith's Gorillas again fended off Taylor's pursuit while Bailey built a pontoon bridge that enabled Banks's army to cross the Atchafalaya River and finally avoid a truly disastrous campaign.

David Porter's powerful squadron begins its advance up the Red River.

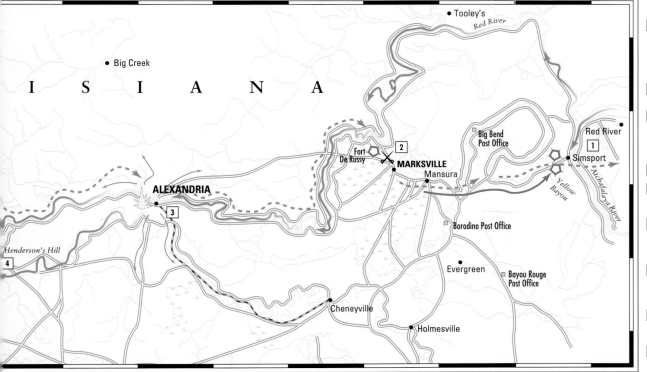

Battle of Mansfield
April 8

1. March 13: Major General A. J. Smith's three-division detachment of the Army of the Tennessee landed at Simsport.

2. March 14: Smith's veterans easily captured Fort De Russy.

3. March 15–16: Union gunboats under the commander of Rear Admiral David D. Porter arrived at Alexander on March 15 and occupied the town the following day.

4. March 21: Several skirmishes occurred as Banks's army continued to ascend the Red River Valley; one of the larger ones was at Henderson's Hill, where Brigadier General Joseph Mower's division of the Sixteenth Corps, along with a detachment of cavalry, captured four guns and two hundred and fifty prisoners.

5. April 2: Banks's troops occupied the old river town of Natchitoches.

6. April 3: A disloyal guide informed Banks that no road paralleled the river above Grand Ecore and he would therefore have to take his army well inland, far from the support of the gunboats. Banks believed him and led his army away from the river.

7. April 7: Banks arrived at Pleasant Hill.

8. April 7–8: Brigadier General Albert L. Lee's cavalry, leading Banks's advance, skirmished intensely with Confederates all along the advance from Pleasant Hill.

9. April 8: Major General Richard Taylor's army caught Banks's column strung out along the road as it approached Mansfield. In a fierce battle Taylor was victorious, and Banks retreated to Pleasant Hill.

10. April 9: Taylor pursued and attacked Banks again at Pleasant Hill. Banks, reinforced by A. J. Smith's troops, repulsed, but nevertheless determined to continue his retreat.

11. April 12: Confederate cavalry, led by Brigadier General Thomas Green, attacked the Union gunboats at Blair's Landing, but the attack was repulsed and Green killed.

12. April 13 – May 13: The Confederates continued to harass the expedition by constant skirmishing as it proceeded down the Red River.

FORREST'S OPERATIONS IN MISSISSIPPI AND TENNESSEE

Far-reaching cavalry raids led by Morgan and Forrest caused widespread consternation in the North.

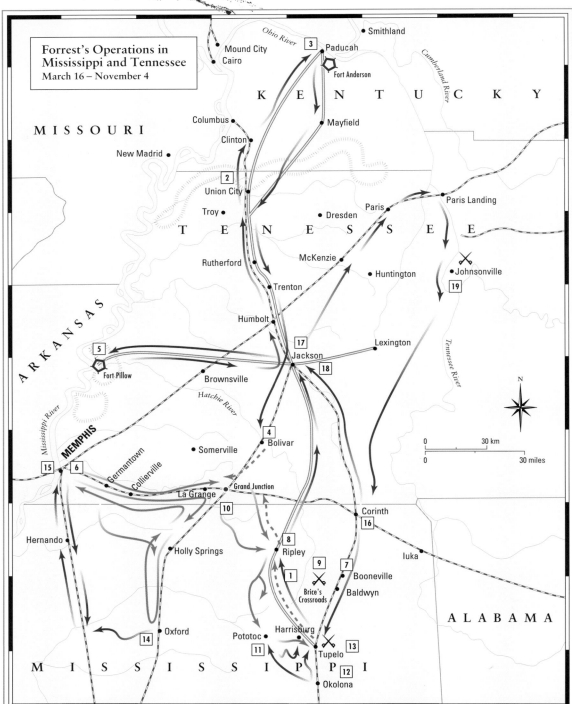

1. March 16: Forrest rode north for another raid into Tennessee and Kentucky.

2. March 24: Forrest captured at four hundred and fifty-man Union garrison at Union City, Tennessee.

3. March 25: Forrest reached Paducah and demanded the surrender of Fort Anderson. When the Unionists refused, he attacked but was repulsed and withdrew the next morning.

4. March 29: Moving rapidly, Forrest reached Bolivar, Tennessee, and drove off a small force of Union cavalry.

5. April 12: Forrest attacked and captured Fort Pillow, where his men slaughtered black troops attempting to surrender.

6. June 2: With orders from Sherman to hunt down Forrest, Major General Samuel D. Sturgis departed Memphis.

7. June 9: Learning of Sturgis's approach, Forrest met with his department commander, Major General Stephen D. Lee, at Booneville to plan a response.

8. June 9: Sturgis's expedition reached Ripley, Mississippi.

9. June 10: Forrest met and defeated Sturgis at Brice's Crossroads.

10. July 5: Sherman dispatched another expedition to hunt down Forrest, this time Major General A. J. Smith with two divisions of infantry and one of cavalry, all from the Sixteenth Corps, and totaling fourteen thousand men in all. They marched out of La Grange, Tennessee.

11. July 11: Smith's cavalry, commanded by Brigadier General Benjamin H. Grierson, met and drove off a force of Confederate cavalry.

12. July 13: The combined forces of Lee and Forrest, numbering nine thousand five hundred men, advanced from Okolona toward Pontotoc. Their advanced forces skirmished with Smith's cavalry.

13. July 13–14: Maneuvering to flank the Confederate position on the Okolona Road, Smith moved east to Harrisburg, near Tupelo. The next morning the Confederates attacked but were repulsed.

14. August 18: Forrest set out on yet another raid, bound this time for Memphis via Hernando, Mississippi.

15. August 21: Forrest and his raiders made an early-morning foray into Memphis before returning quickly the way they had come.

16. October 19: Once again Forrest went raiding, this time setting out from Corinth.

17. October 22: Forrest occupied Jackson, Tennessee.

18. October 29: Using his field artillery from the shore, Forrest captured one gunboat and two transports and began moving them southward, up the Tennessee River, while his troops kept pace on the bank.

19. November 4: Forrest again used his artillery to good advantage, damaging Union transports and supplies at Johnsonville, but he had to abandoned his captured vessels and march back to Corinth overland.

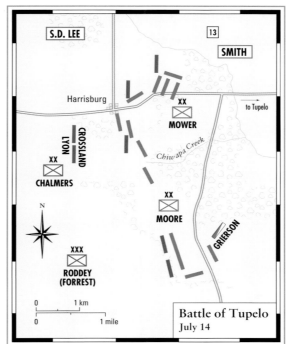

Colonel Nathan Bedford Forrest, one of the outstanding cavalry leaders of the Civil War. He exhibited military genious and a ferocity which earned him honors in the South and hatred in the North.

T HE MOST VULNERABLE ASPECT OF Sherman's campaign against Atlanta was his long railroad supply line. So he made plans to neutralize the Confederacy's most effective railroad breaker, Colonel Nathan Bedford Forrest. He dispatched Brigadier General Samuel D. Sturgis from Memphis on June 1 with eight thousand men to seek and destroy Forrest. Forrest, who had been at Tupelo, Mississippi, planning to attack Sherman's supply lines, chose instead to oppose Sturgis by concentrating his three thousand five hundred men at Brice's Crossroads, Mississippi. On the night of June 9 the Federals encamped nine miles northwest of Brice's Crossroads.

The next day Brigadier General Benjamin Grierson's cavalry led the march toward Brice's Crossroads, crossed Tishomingo Creek, and engaged Forrest's main body. Forrest attacked Grierson, who sent for help from the infantry. Sturgis's foot soldiers hurried forward at the double-quick on the muddy road through heat and humidity and reached the battlefield exhausted. Forrest, who had just received another brigade of cavalry as reinforcements, drove the Federals back to Tishomingo Creek, where a

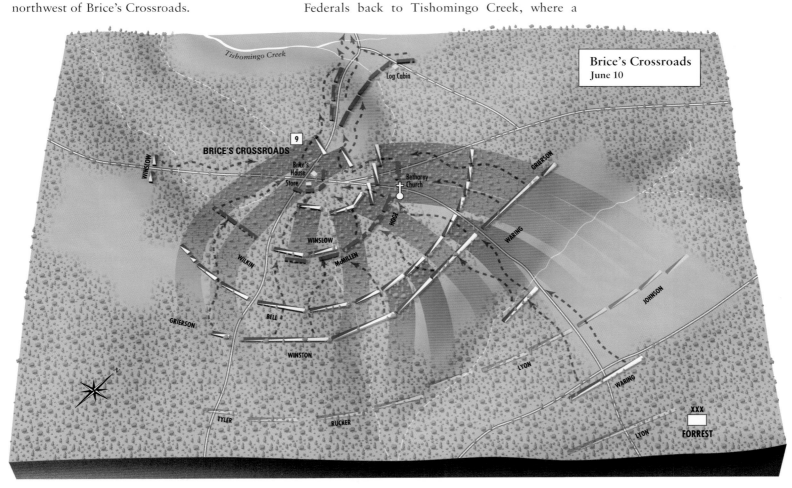

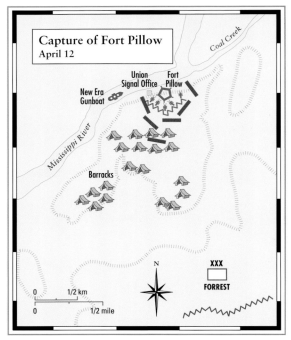

Capture of Fort Pillow
April 12

Far Right: A searing election year indictment of four prominent figures in the Democratic Party, among them, top right, is the Tennessee General Nathan Bedford Forrest. His fame—or infamy—followed him for years after the war, and he was widely held responsible for the Fort Pillow massacre.

tracks. That night Smith's main force encamped in a strong defensive position at Harrisburg, about one mile west of Tupelo.

Lee and Forrest both arrived in the vicinity at about the same time on the evening of July 13 and launched their first attack at 7:00 a.m. the next morning. They kept up their assaults through most of the morning. The attacks were poorly coordinated, however, and Smith's veterans easily repulsed them. When the Federals that night burned Harrisburg, Forrest attacked by the light of the fires and again suffered a repulse. The Battle of Tupelo was a stinging defeat for Forrest and Lee. The Union casualty total of six hundred and seventy-four was almost precisely half of the Confederate figure, one thousand three hundred and forty-seven.

On July 15, Smith's force remained on the field of battle until late afternoon in hopes that Forrest and Lee might attack again. Finally, with no sign of any further attacks by the Confederates and with his own supplies growing short, Smith started a leisurely march back toward Memphis. Forrest followed and struck at Smith's column at Old Town Creek. Once again the Wizard of the Saddle suffered defeat, as the Union rear guard swatted away his attack, and Forrest suffered a bullet wound in the right foot, putting him out of action for the next month.

In August, Forrest was back in the saddle but still not threatening Sherman's supply lines. Instead, on August 21, Forrest and two thousand men rode into Memphis in an early morning raid and came near to snatching major generals Stephen A. Hurlbut and Cadwalader C. Washburn before riding off as quickly as they had come.

Finally on September 16 Forrest with four thousand five hundred men left Verona, Mississippi, on an expedition aimed at attacking Sherman's supply lines in northern Alabama and Middle Tennessee. By that time, however, it was too late. Atlanta had fallen two weeks earlier. Forrest crossed the Tennessee River on September 21 and spent the next two weeks skirmishing with various Union forces and small garrisons between that river, on the south, and Columbia, Tennessee, on the north. He captured a few blockhouses but did no damage of consequence.

blocked bridge created panic in the Union ranks and began a rout that stretched most of the way back to Memphis. Union losses totaled two thousand two hundred and forty, including more than one thousand five hundred captured by Forrest, who also took some one hundred and ninety-two of Sturgis's supply wagons and sixteen cannons. Confederate casualties came to four hundred and ninety-two. The Battle of Brice's Crossroads is still studied by military students as an almost perfect example of how a smaller force may defeat a larger. All that was required was a Forrest on one side and a Sturgis on the other.

As the campaign for Atlanta continued, Sherman dispatched another expedition to find and fight Forrest and also to devastate the countryside, denying supplies to Confederate raiders. By this time the tough and capable Major General Andrew J. Smith was available along with two divisions of his Sixteenth Corps. Combined with Grierson's cavalry this gave Smith a total of fourteen thousand men. On July 5, Smith advanced from La Grange, Tennessee. After skirmishing with lurking Rebel cavalry for several days, he arrived at Pontotoc, Mississippi, on July 11. That same day Confederate department commander Lieutenant General Stephen D. Lee joined Forrest at Okolona, twenty-two miles southeast of Pontotoc. Their combined force totaled nine thousand five hundred men.

The armies remained in place for two days. Smith wanted to break the Mobile & Ohio Railroad; Lee and Forrest wanted to stop him. Rather than advance into the teeth of the Confederate concentration at Okolona, on July 13 Smith turned eastward instead and marched toward Tupelo, seventeen miles away. Like Okolona, Tupelo lay on the Mobile & Ohio. Grierson's cavalry reached the town around midday and began the hard work of tearing up the

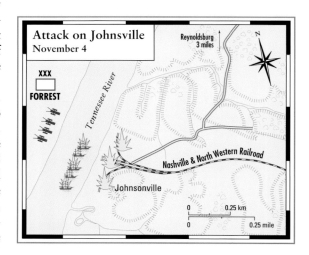

Attack on Johnsville
November 4

LEADERS
OF THE
DEMOCRATIC PARTY.

THE RIOTER SEYMOUR.

THE BUTCHER FORREST.

THE PIRATE SEMMES.

THE HANGMAN HAMPTON.

STEELE'S ARKANSAS CAMPAIGN

At Mark's Mill the Confederates under General Joseph O. Shelby attacked a Union supply train. They captured one thousand three hundred Union soldiers and several hundred supply wagons, but suffered some three hundred casualties in the action.

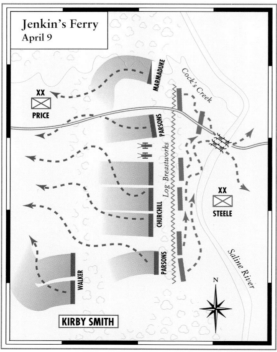

Jenkin's Ferry
April 9

MARMADUKE

Cock's Creek

XX
PRICE

PARSONS

CHURCHILL

Log Breastworks

XX
STEELE

Saline River

WALKER

PARSONS

N

KIRBY SMITH

Simultaneous with Banks's Red River campaign, Halleck ordered Major General Frederick Steele to cooperate by leading an expedition from Little Rock, Arkansas, toward Shreveport, Louisiana. Steele was reluctant to make the expedition because he believed that the lack of good roads and food for man and beast in southwestern Arkansas would render it very difficult. Though scheduled to depart in early March,

Steele's one division of infantry and two brigades of cavalry did not leave Little Rock until March 23. The three-week delay in beginning the expedition made its goal of cooperating with Banks almost impossible from the very outset.

Steele's column was hardly clear of Little Rock before its leading elements began skirmishing with Confederate cavalry. Such clashes became an almost daily occurrence as the expedition proceeded slowly southwestward. By March 29, Steele occupied Arkadelphia, Arkansas, seventy miles from Little Rock. There he was supposed to link up with another Union column, this one commanded by Brigadier General John M. Thayer, advancing southeastward from Fort Smith, Arkansas. With no sign of Thayer, Steele pressed on and finally met Thayer's column near Elkin's Ferry, Arkansas, on April 9. By that time Banks had already met defeat at the Battle of Mansfield, and Confederate forces were able to shift away from the Red River valley to confront Steele in Arkansas. By April 10, Confederate forces in front of Steele totaled some five thousand men, and the level of fighting heated up into a three-day-long running battle that began at Prairie D'Ane.

By this time Steele was seriously low on supplies. He turned to the southeast and headed for Camden, Arkansas, which he hoped to make into an advanced base of operations. Taking Camden on April 15, he found his supply situation rapidly growing worse. On April 17, Steele dispatched a large wagon train with a heavy escort to forage for much-needed supplies. As the train was returning to Camden the next day, Confederate cavalry commanded by Brigadier Generals John S. Marmaduke and Samuel B. Maxey attacked it at Poison Springs. The one thousand two hundred-man escort held off the attackers for a time, but the three thousand six hundred Rebels finally overwhelmed them, capturing or destroying some one hundred and ninety-eight wagons and perpetrating a massacre on wounded and surrendering black troops of the First Kansas Colored Volunteers. Most of the Union troops succeeded in returning to Camden, though without their wagons and four pieces of artillery.

One week later, Rebel horsemen under Brigadier General Joseph O. Shelby struck another Union supply train at Marks' Mills. After fierce fighting in which the commander of the Union escort, Colonel Francis M. Drake, was wounded, Shelby succeeded in capturing some one thousand three hundred out of the one thousand seven hundred-man escort along with all two hundred and forty wagons. Confederate casualties for the encounter totaled only two hundred and ninety-three.

For Steele, recent weeks had brought nothing but bad news. On top of the debacles at Poison Spring and Marks' Mills, he had also learned of Banks's defeat at the Battle of Mansfield and subsequent retreat. With his supply situation becoming desperate and a large Confederate force arriving from Louisiana, led by Confederate department commander General Edmund Kirby Smith, Steele decided he had no choice but to retreat to Little Rock. Frequent rain and muddy roads as well as almost constant heavy skirmishing with Confederate cavalry made the march difficult. On April 30, at Jenkins' Ferry on the Saline River, Steele had to fight a pitched battle to hold off Marmaduke's Confederate pursuers until his army could make its crossing via a pontoon bridge. Union casualties for the Battle of Jenkins' Ferry totaled five hundred and twenty-eight, while Confederate losses came to four hundred and forty-three.

Finally, on May 3, very hungry and much the worse for wear, Steele's column reached Little Rock. The six-week-long expedition cost the Union two thousand seven hundred and fifty men, nine cannons, and six hundred and fifty wagons. Confederate casualties totaled two thousand three hundred and fifty. The Camden expedition was another of the unsuccessful Union operations during the early spring of 1864 that helped raise Confederate morale, convincing Southerners that they could successfully stave off the major Union offensives that were certain to begin later in the season.

1 March 23: Steele's column moved out of Little Rock headed southwestward toward a planned junction with Banks's Red River expedition. They had to skirmish with Confederate cavalry almost immediately.

2 March 29: Skirmishing frequently with Confederate cavalry, Steele's vanguard reached Arkadelphia, where it again clashed with the Confederate horsemen.

3 April 4: Confederate Brigadier General John Sappington Marmaduke attacked Steele's column at Elkin's Ferry, on the Little Missouri River but was defeated and had to flee after five hours of hard fighting.

4 April 9: Brigadier General John M. Thayer's division, marching from Fort Smith and joined Steele's expedition.

5 April 15: Steele's troops entered Camden.

6 April 18: Confederates attacked a Union supply wagon train and captured it after a fierce fight with the escort. The victorious Confederates then massacred captured members of the First Kansas Coloured Cavalry.

7 April 26: Harassed by Confederate cavalry and having learned that Banks's campaign had ended in failure, Steele ordered a retreat to Little Rock.

8 May 3: Steele's column arrived back in Little Rock.

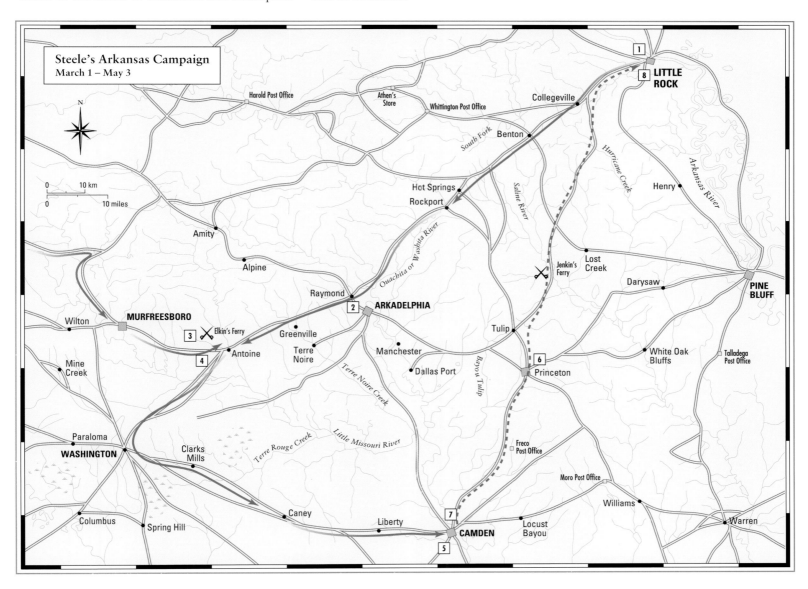

Steele's Arkansas Campaign
March 1 – May 3

SHERMAN'S ATLANTA CAMPAIGN, PHASE I

Confederate defenses at Etowah Bridge. As the Confederates withdrew they wrecked the railroads and as the Union advanced the railroad was quickly repaired.

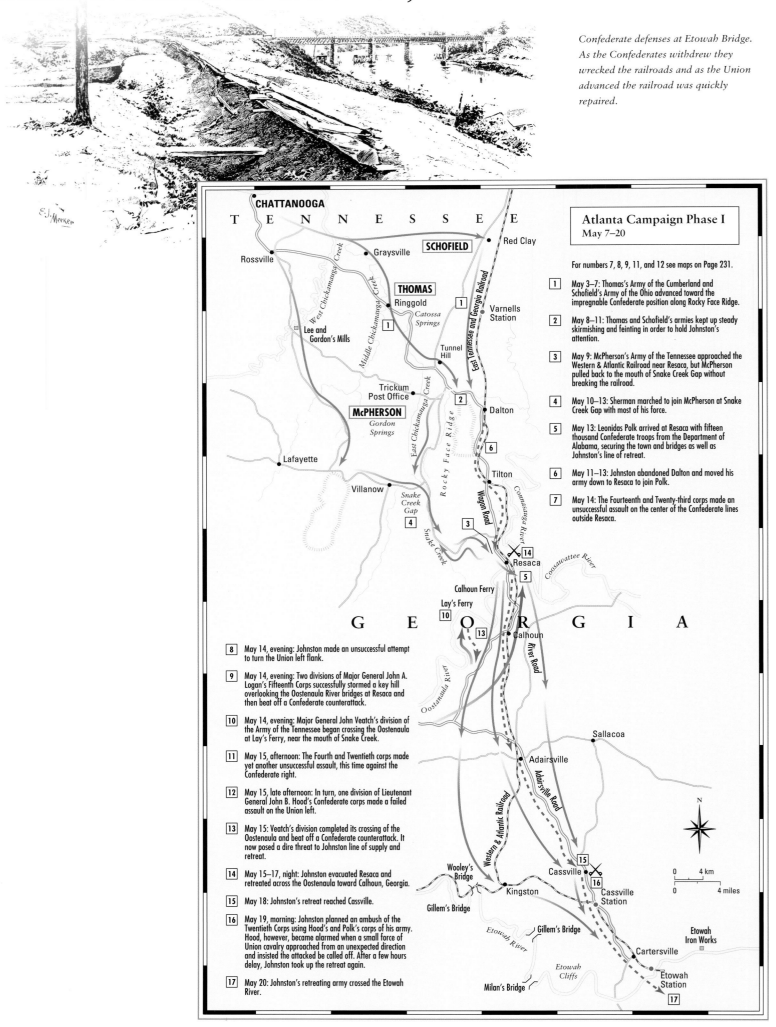

Atlanta Campaign Phase I
May 7–20

For numbers 7, 8, 9, 11, and 12 see maps on Page 231.

1 May 3–7: Thomas's Army of the Cumberland and Schofield's Army of the Ohio advanced toward the impregnable Confederate position along Rocky Face Ridge.

2 May 8–11: Thomas and Schofield's armies kept up steady skirmishing and feinting in order to hold Johnston's attention.

3 May 9: McPherson's Army of the Tennessee approached the Western & Atlantic Railroad near Resaca, but McPherson pulled back to the mouth of Snake Creek Gap without breaking the railroad.

4 May 10–13: Sherman marched to join McPherson at Snake Creek Gap with most of his force.

5 May 13: Leonidas Polk arrived at Resaca with fifteen thousand Confederate troops from the Department of Alabama, securing the town and bridges as well as Johnston's line of retreat.

6 May 11–13: Johnston abandoned Dalton and moved his army down to Resaca to join Polk.

7 May 14: The Fourteenth and Twenty-third corps made an unsuccessful assault on the center of the Confederate lines outside Resaca.

8 May 14, evening: Johnston made an unsuccessful attempt to turn the Union left flank.

9 May 14, evening: Two divisions of Major General John A. Logan's Fifteenth Corps successfully stormed a key hill overlooking the Oostenaula River bridges at Resaca and then beat off a Confederate counterattack.

10 May 14, evening: Major General John Veatch's division of the Army of the Tennessee began crossing the Oostenaula at Lay's Ferry, near the mouth of Snake Creek.

11 May 15, afternoon: The Fourth and Twentieth corps made yet another unsuccessful assault, this time against the Confederate right.

12 May 15, late afternoon: In turn, one division of Lieutenant General John B. Hood's Confederate corps made a failed assault on the Union left.

13 May 15: Veatch's division completed its crossing of the Oostenaula and beat off a Confederate counterattack. It now posed a dire threat to Johnston line of supply and retreat.

14 May 15–17, night: Johnston evacuated Resaca and retreated across the Oostenaula toward Calhoun, Georgia.

15 May 18: Johnston's retreat reached Cassville.

16 May 19, morning: Johnston planned an ambush of the Twentieth Corps using Hood's and Polk's corps of his army. Hood, however, became alarmed when a small force of Union cavalry approached from an unexpected direction and insisted the attacked be called off. After a few hours delay, Johnston took up the retreat again.

17 May 20: Johnston's retreating army crossed the Etowah River.

THE TWO MOST IMPORTANT PARTS of Grant's coordinated offensive for the spring of 1864 were his own pursuit of Lee in Virginia and William T. Sherman's drive toward Atlanta, Georgia. Sherman was not only to threaten Atlanta but also to keep Confederate General Joseph E. Johnston's army so occupied that he would be unable to detach troops to reinforce Lee. The axis of Sherman's advance would, of necessity, be the Western & Atlantic Railroad, a single line of track from Chattanooga to Atlanta that would serve as the Union supply line. Sherman's forces consisted of the Army of the Tennessee, the Army of the Cumberland, and the Army of the Ohio, numbering about 100,000 men in all. Johnston commanded the Army of Tennessee, which began the campaign numbering about forty-five thousand.

The campaign opened in early May with Johnston blocking Sherman's advance from an immensely powerful position on Rocky Face Ridge, just north of Dalton, Georgia. While the armies of the Cumberland and the Ohio feigned an attack on Rocky Face, Sherman sent the Army of the Tennessee, about twenty-three thousand strong, on a turning maneuver to his right. The troops moved through Snake Creek Gap, a long, winding passage through the mountains southwest of Dalton, to threaten Johnston's communications at Resaca, Georgia, where the tracks of the Western & Atlantic Railroad crossed the Oostenaula River. This movement had the potential to trap Johnston and his army at Dalton.

At first the plan worked better than expected, as the Army of the Tennessee, commanded by Major General James B. McPherson, reached the outskirts of Resaca on May 9 before Johnston realized what was happening. Then the Union plan began to unravel. Worried about the smallness of McPherson's force and about the threat from fifteen thousand Confederates under Major General Leonidas Polk in Alabama, Sherman had ordered McPherson merely to break the railroad and then withdraw into the mouth of Snake Creek Gap. There, Sherman wanted McPherson to take up a good defensive position until the rest of Sherman's forces could arrive. Instead McPherson approached to within a few hundred yards of the railroad, mistakenly decided it was too strongly defended, and withdrew into the gap leaving the tracks and bridges intact.

The Confederates finally reacted to the threat. From Richmond, Jefferson Davis ordered Polk to take his force to Resaca and secure Johnston's communications. At the same time, Johnston quickly pulled his army back to Resaca, escaping the trap. Sherman took the rest of his forces through Snake Creek Gap and confronted Johnston's now reinforced army of more than sixty thousand men around Resaca in mid-May. In two days of fighting, Johnston and Sherman each strove to turn the other's northeastern flank. Meanwhile, some of Sherman's troops successfully crossed the Etowah River west of Resaca. Once

again Johnston's position was turned, leaving him with the choice of fighting aggressively or retreating. As was to become habitual during the campaign, Johnston chose to retreat. This withdrawal took his army across the Oostenaula and all the way back to Cassville, Georgia, forty miles south-southeast of Dalton.

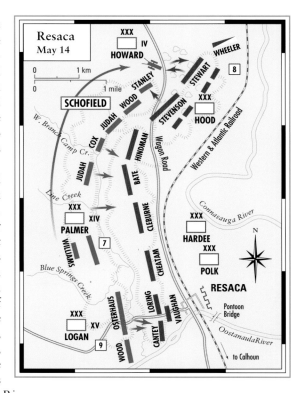

Sherman followed closely, and almost constant skirmishing took place between the opposing forces. Johnston hoped to strike a major counterblow against Sherman at Cassville, but one of his corps commanders, Major General John Bell Hood, became alarmed when he discovered a small force of Union cavalry in a quarter where he had not expected it. Needlessly, Hood aborted the planned attack, and Johnston saw no alternative but to continue the retreat, this time all the way across the Etowah River.

South of the Etowah, however, Johnston enjoyed one of the best defensive positions anywhere between Chattanooga and Atlanta. A twenty-mile-wide belt of mountains stretched across Sherman's path between the Etowah and the Chattahoochee rivers. The first strong position was at Allatoona Pass. Sherman decided not to attempt the pass head-on but instead to cast loose of the railroad temporarily, swing well to the west of Allatoona by way of the town of Dallas, Georgia, and then cut in behind Johnston. Sherman believed the move would at least get his forces past Allatoona Pass and hoped that it might allow him to reach Marietta, on the far side of the mountains almost to the Chattahoochee. Johnston proved too alert for that and met Sherman's forces just east of Dallas.

A week of fighting followed among steep hills and dense woods. Sherman launched attacks at New Hope Church—a sector his men dubbed "the Hell Hole" because of the intense fighting there—and also at Pickett's Mills, gaining nothing but a lengthening casualty list. Johnston launched an unsuccessful and costly attack of his own. By June 1 it had become apparent that the armies were deadlocked east of Dallas. The strong entrenchments that the troops built every time they halted during this campaign were all but impregnable to frontal assault. With his supplies beginning to run low, Sherman managed to disengage and slide back to the east, where he renewed his connection with the railroad at the town of Acworth, five miles southeast of Allatoona Pass. His movement on Dallas had succeeded in its primary goal of gaining the pass without assaulting it, but he was still twelve miles short of Marietta and only halfway through the mountains.

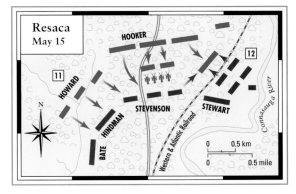

SHERMAN'S ATLANTA CAMPAIGN, PHASE II

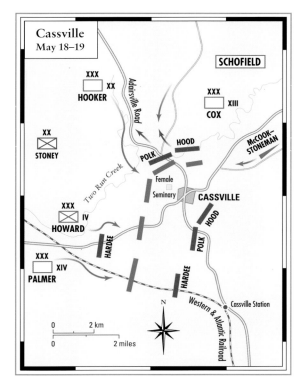

Cassville
May 18–19

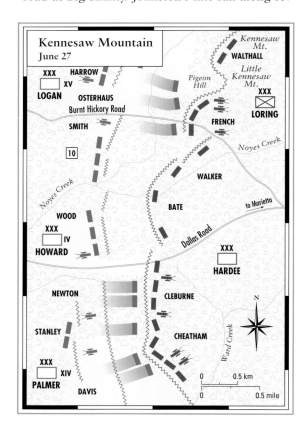

Kennesaw Mountain
June 27

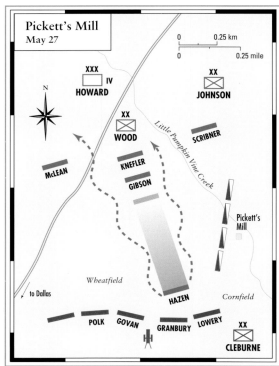

Pickett's Mill
May 27

eral of the mountains. By pressing forward as much as possible and applying pressure to the Confederate flanks, Sherman was sometimes able to attain positions from which his artillery could render one or another of the Confederate-held mountains untenable or his infantry could come near to enveloping it.

In the face of Sherman's maneuvers, Johnston abandoned Lost Mountain, Brush Mountain, and Pine Mountain. Just before the evacuation of Pine Mountain, on June 14, Johnston and two of his corps commanders, lieutenant generals Leonidas Polk and William J. Hardee, were making observations from the mountaintop when they were spotted but not recognized by Sherman. Knowing only that his positions were being observed by Confederate officers, Sherman ordered a battery to open fire and force the gray-clad generals to

O N JUNE 10, SHERMAN ADVANCED AGAIN, this time keeping close to the Western & Atlantic Railroad. The Federals easily occupied the town of Big Shanty (now Kennesaw, Georgia), but ran up against securely entrenched Confederates in appallingly strong positions in the Blue Ridge Mountains only a few miles beyond the town. For another two weeks Sherman strove to maneuver Johnston out of his mountain fastnesses. The Union commander stretched his army one way and another, threatening Johnston's flank while maintaining his own firm grip on the railroad at Big Shanty. Johnston's line ran along sev-

take cover. The second salvo instantly killed Polk, who, aside from being the second-ranking officer in Johnston's army, was also an Episcopal bishop and a close personal friend of Jefferson Davis. Polk was the second-highest-ranking Confederate general to be killed in action.

Despite these limited successes, Sherman was unable to maneuver Johnston off of Kennesaw Mountain, the strongest defensive position either side was to find during the entire campaign. On June 22 another of Sherman's flanking movements provoked a Confederate attack at Kolb's Farm, where the Federals administered a sharp and costly repulse. Still the Confederate position on Kennesaw remained unshakeable. Frustrated, Sherman reasoned that if he had stretched his own army as far as he thought he dared, then the smaller Confederate army must be near the breaking point somewhere. Remembering the improbable Union success at Missionary Ridge the previous November, Sherman decided to attempt an assault on Kennesaw Mountain. What he had not taken into his calculations was the degree to which both the mountain and the ubiquitous elaborate entrenchments multiplied the defenders' strength.

On a sweltering hot June 27, elements of the Army of the Tennessee and the Army of the Cumberland attacked the lower, southwest end of

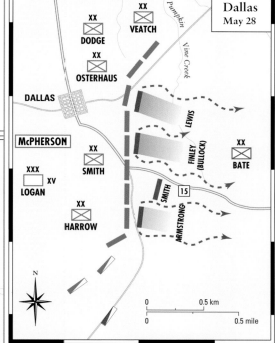

Dallas
May 28

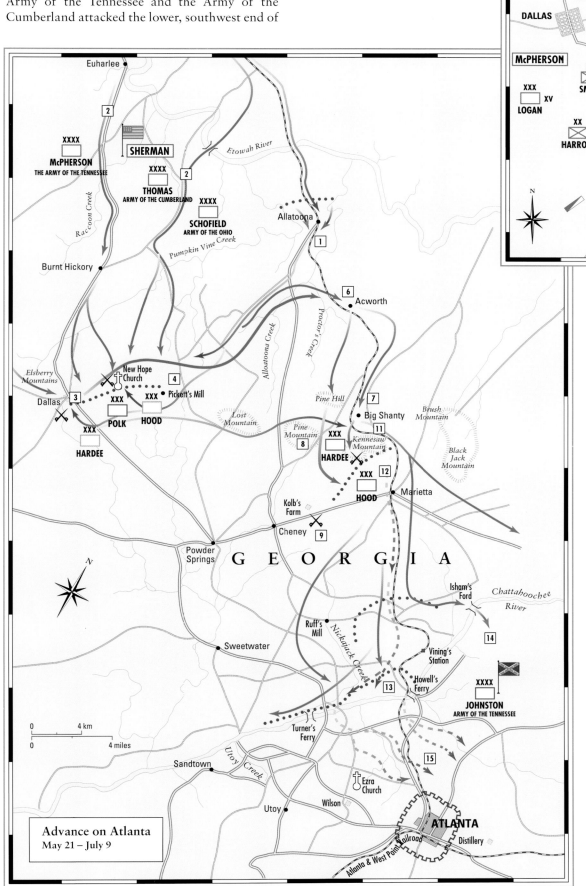

Advance on Atlanta
May 21 – July 9

GEORGIA

1 May 20–21: Johnston's army took up an impregnable position at Allatoona.

2 May 23–24: Rather than follow the railroad directly into the teeth of Johnston's defenses, Sherman struck out on roads leading due south, hoping to turn Johnston out of his powerful position.

3 May 25: Johnston responded alertly and blocked Sherman at Dallas and New Hope Church.

4 May 27: Howard's Fourth Corps attempted to turn Johnston's right flank at Pickett's Mill but met with repulse.

5 May 28: Acting on the basis of mistaken information, Hardee's corps assaulted the Fifteenth Corps just east of Dallas and suffered a bloody defeat.

6 May 31 – June 6: Sherman moved back to the east, reestablishing his railroad communications at Acworth.

7 June 10–19: Sherman advanced to Big Shanty, then worked his way forward slowly against strong Confederate positions on the surrounding hills.

8 June 14: Union artillery fire killed Leonidas Polk atop Pine Mountain.

9 June 22: Hood's corps attacked the Twenty-second and Twenty-third corps at Kolb's Farm and was repulsed with heavy loss.

10 June 27: Tiring of flanking maneuvers, Sherman hurled his troops at the system of Confederate works based on Kennesaw Mountain. Attacks aimed at the subsidiary summit known as Pigeon Hill and at Confederate works farther to the west ended in bloody failure.

11 June 27 – July 2: Schofield's Twenty-third Corps flanked Johnston out of the Kennesaw Mountain line.

12 July 3–4: Johnston took up a line in front of Smyrna but was flanked out of it the next day.

13 July 5: Johnston took up another line of entrenchments immediately in front of the Chattahoochee River.

14 July 8: The Twenty-third Corps and Sherman's cavalry crossed the Chattahoochee east of Johnston's position.

15 July 9: Johnston retreated across the Chattahoochee to the outskirts of Atlanta.

Edwin J. Meekers drawing of Confederate earthworks near New Hope Church, northwest of Atlanta. Both armies were now adept at creating such defensive positions, and General Sherman commented that "They are as dangerous to assault as a permanent fort." He complained that no sooner were the Confederates driven from one line of defenses than they had fallen back, created, and manned a new line of defense.

the mountain, known as Pigeon Hill, as well as entrenched Confederate lines on lower ridges farther to the southwest. Though the attackers advanced bravely, every assault met with bloody repulse in front of positions that turned out to be completely impregnable. Union casualties approached three thousand and included such valuable officers as Brigadier General Charles Harker and Colonel Daniel McCook, who were both killed. Confederate casualties were probably about one thousand.

Ironically, one of the diversionary operations Sherman had ordered to coincide with the assault actually revealed the possibility of flanking Johnston on the southwest. Once again Sherman cut loose of the railroad and swung his army around Johnston in a turning maneuver. In response, Johnston, on the night of July 2–3, evacuated Kennesaw Mountain and fell back to prepared entrenchments on the north bank of the Chattahoochee River at Smyrna Campground. Sherman's forces approached, made contact, and the almost constant skirmishing and sniping that characterized the campaign resumed all along the lines. Several days later, elements of Sherman's forces succeeded in crossing the Chattahoochee northeast of Johnston's lines. Once again, Johnston found his position turned and faced the choice of attacking aggressively so as to throw the Federals back across the river or else retreating. True to form, the Confederate general opted for retreat yet again, this time to the very outskirts of Atlanta.

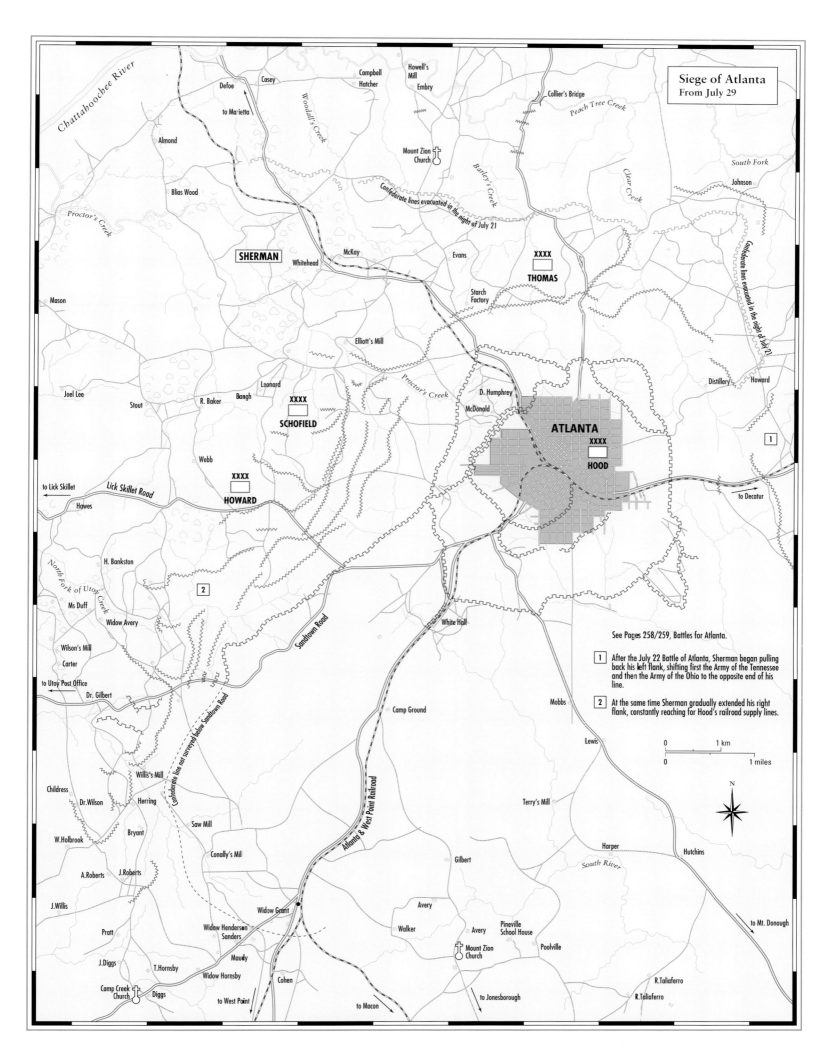

Chattahoochee River

Proctor's Creek

Defoe
Casey
Campbell Hatcher
Howell's Mill
Embry
Collier's Bridge
Peach Tree Creek
South Fork
Johnson

Almond

to Marietta

Woodall's Creek

Mount Zion Church

Barley's Creek

Clear Creek

Blias Wood

Confederate lines evacuated in the night of July 21

SHERMAN
McKay
Whitehead
Evans
XXXX
THOMAS

Confederate lines evacuated in the night of July 21

Mason

Starch Factory

Distillery
Howard

Joel Lee

Elliott's Mill

Proctor's Creek

D. Humphrey
McDonald

Leonard
R. Baker
Bangh
XXXX
SCHOFIELD

ATLANTA
XXXX
HOOD

1

Stout

Webb
XXXX
HOWARD

to Lick Skillet
Lick Skillet Road
Hawes

to Decatur

H. Bankston

North Fork of Utoy Creek

2

Ms Duff

Widow Avery

Sandtown Road

White Hall

See Pages 258/259, Battles for Atlanta.

Wilson's Mill
Carter

to Utoy Post Office
Dr. Gilbert

1 After the July 22 Battle of Atlanta, Sherman began pulling back his left flank, shifting first the Army of the Tennessee and then the Army of the Ohio to the opposite end of his line.

Mobbs

Lewis

2 At the same time Sherman gradually extended his right flank, constantly reaching for Hood's railroad supply lines.

Camp Ground

Confederate line not surveyed below Sandtown Road

Willis's Mill

0   1 km
0   1 miles

Childress
Dr. Wilson
Herring

Saw Mill

Terry's Mill

N

W. Holbrook
Bryant

Conally's Mil

A. Roberts
J. Roberts

Atlanta & West Point Railroad

Gilbert

Harper

Hutchins

South River

J. Willis

Widow Grant

Avery

to Mt. Donough

Pratt

Widow Henderson
Sanders

Walker
Avery
Pineville School House
Poolville

J. Diggs
T. Hornsby
Maudy
Widow Hornsby

Mount Zion Church

Camp Creek Church
Diggs
Cohen

to West Point
to Macon
to Jonesborough

R. Taliaferro
R. Taliaferro

Siege of Atlanta
From July 29

THE WILDERNESS, PHASE I

FOR THE SPRING OF 1864, GRANT planned a concerted offensive by both of the Union's major armies and three of its minor ones. At the heart of Grant's plan was the need to keep Lee's Army of Northern Virginia occupied, unable to seize the initiative or detach troops to help overwhelm one of the other Union armies. For this purpose the Army of the Potomac would have to operate much more aggressively than it had thus far in the war. In order to make sure that happened and to insulate the Army of the Potomac's high command from the political pressures that were bound to arise for an army operating in the vicinity of the national capital, Grant decided to accompany the Army of the Potomac personally, while leaving Meade in command. This proved to be an awkward arrangement, but it did accomplish the purposes for which Grant chose that course.

By the end of April 1864 the Army of the Potomac was in position and ready to begin its advance, only awaiting word that other Union armies were prepared to begin their simultaneous advances. When all were ready, Grant on May 3 gave orders to Meade to put the Army of the Potomac in motion the next morning. The army, numbering about 122,000 men, marched as ordered, crossing the Rapidan River into the Wilderness and moving southeastward to pass Lee's right flank. Lee had about sixty-six thousand men. Lee moved quickly to head off Grant's flanking movement, while the Army of the Potomac, ponderous and cumbersome as usual, did not move as rapidly as Grant intended. Lee was thus able to bring on battle within the confines of the dense second-growth forest of the Wilderness, at least partially negating Grant's superiority in numbers.

Only minor skirmishing occurred on the day the Army of the Potomac crossed the Rapidan, but on the following day, May 5, the armies clashed in force. In the dense foliage of the Wilderness, fighting followed the axes of roads, spreading into the thickets for some distance on either side. Lieutenant General Richard S. Ewell's Second Corps of the Army of Northern Virginia advanced on the Orange Turnpike and struck Major General Gouverneur K. Warren's Union Fifth Corps. Warren pushed back, and intense fighting raged. A similar encounter along the Orange Plank Road soon had Lieutenant General Ambrose Powell Hill's Confederate Third Corps fiercely engaged with Major General Winfield Scott Hancock's Union Second Corps.

This photograph, taken by James Gardner, shows wounded soldiers from the Battle of the Wilderness gathered near Fredericksburg, Virginia.

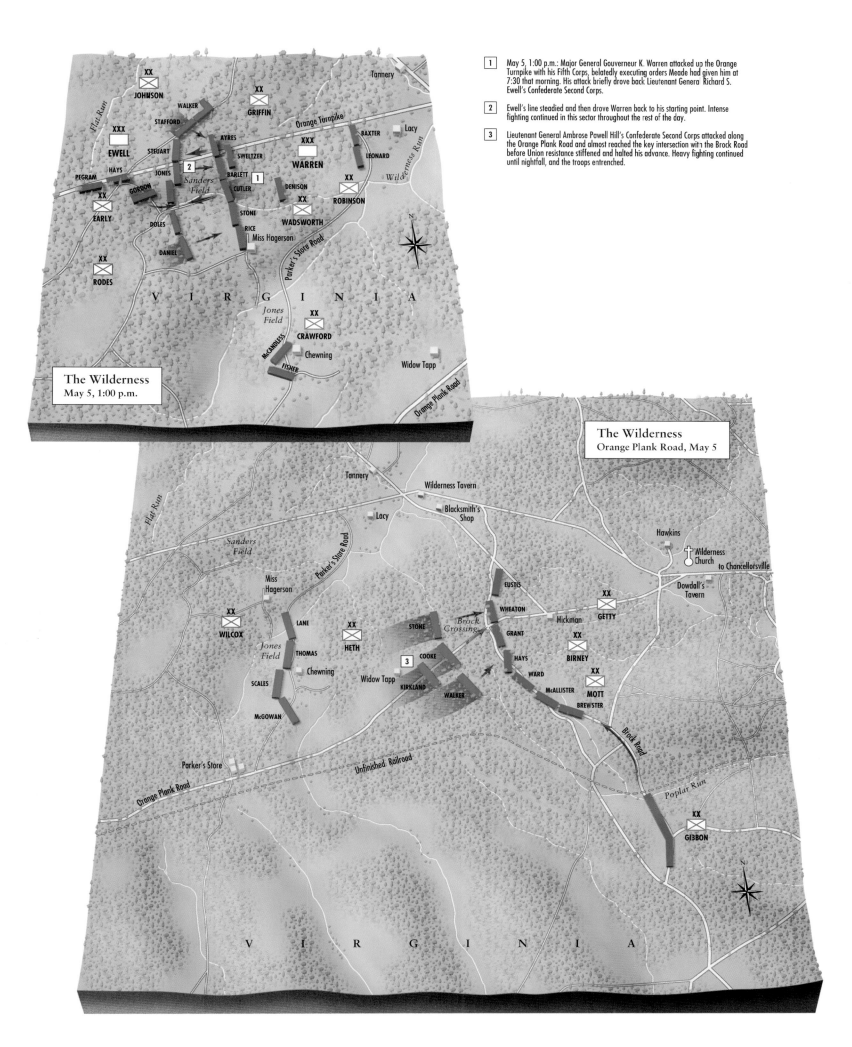

1 May 5, 1:00 p.m.: Major General Gouverneur K. Warren attacked up the Orange Turnpike with his Fifth Corps, belatedly executing orders Meade had given him at 7:30 that morning. His attack briefly drove back Lieutenant General Richard S. Ewell's Confederate Second Corps.

2 Ewell's line steadied and then drove Warren back to his starting point. Intense fighting continued in this sector throughout the rest of the day.

3 Lieutenant General Ambrose Powell Hill's Confederate Second Corps attacked along the Orange Plank Road and almost reached the key intersection wit the Brock Road before Union resistance stiffened and halted his advance. Heavy fighting continued until nightfall, and the troops entrenched.

The Wilderness
May 5, 1:00 p.m.

The Wilderness
Orange Plank Road, May 5

The fighting in dense underbrush had left the forces, especially Hill's, scattered and out of position. Lee decided not to try to straighten his troops out during the night because he expected Lieutenant General James Longstreet's First Corps to arrive from their camps some miles to the rear before morning. Early on the morning of May 6, however, Longstreet had not yet arrived when Hancock launched a powerful attack that drove Hill's corps back in disorder. With nothing but a battalion of artillery between the advancing Federals and his army's supply train, Lee spotted the Texas Brigade, the lead unit of Longstreet's corps, finally reaching the battlefield. Waving his hat, Lee shouted, "Hurrah for Texas! Texans always move them!" Then he directed the brigade into position and made as if to lead it personally in a charge. At that point the Texans began shouting "Lee to the rear," grabbing his horse's bridle, and urging him to fall back out of harm's way while they restored the broken line. Reluctantly, Lee did so, and the Texans, soon joined by the rest of Longstreet's corps, succeeded in stopping the Union attack.

Later that day, Longstreet made a flanking attack on the Union line. The attack enjoyed brief success, but Union forces quickly rallied, and again the situation stabilized. Shortly thereafter Longstreet was badly wounded in a friendly-fire incident eerily reminiscent of Jackson's fatal encounter in the same woods at the Battle of Chancellorsville just one year before. Late in the evening Brigadier General John B. Gordon's brigade made another briefly successful flank attack, but again the results were limited.

On May 7 the fighting in the Wilderness was less intense. That evening Grant put his army in motion again. He did not retreat back toward the fords of the Rapidan, as had been the case after every previous time when the Army of the Potomac had met Lee in Virginia. This time the army advanced, toward the crossroads hamlet of Spotsylvania Court House. If successful, the movement would turn Lee and force him either to retreat or to fight at a disadvantage. With that, the Battle of the Wilderness was over, though the armies remained in contact and the campaign went on unabated. Casualties for the two-day clash in the Wilderness totaled seventeen thousand six hundred and sixty-six for the Union. Confederate figures are very uncertain, but their losses would have been at least seven thousand five hundred.

This lithograph, published by Kurz & Allison, shows the desperate fight on the Orange Court House Plank Road, near Todd's Tavern, during the battle of The Wilderness on May 6.

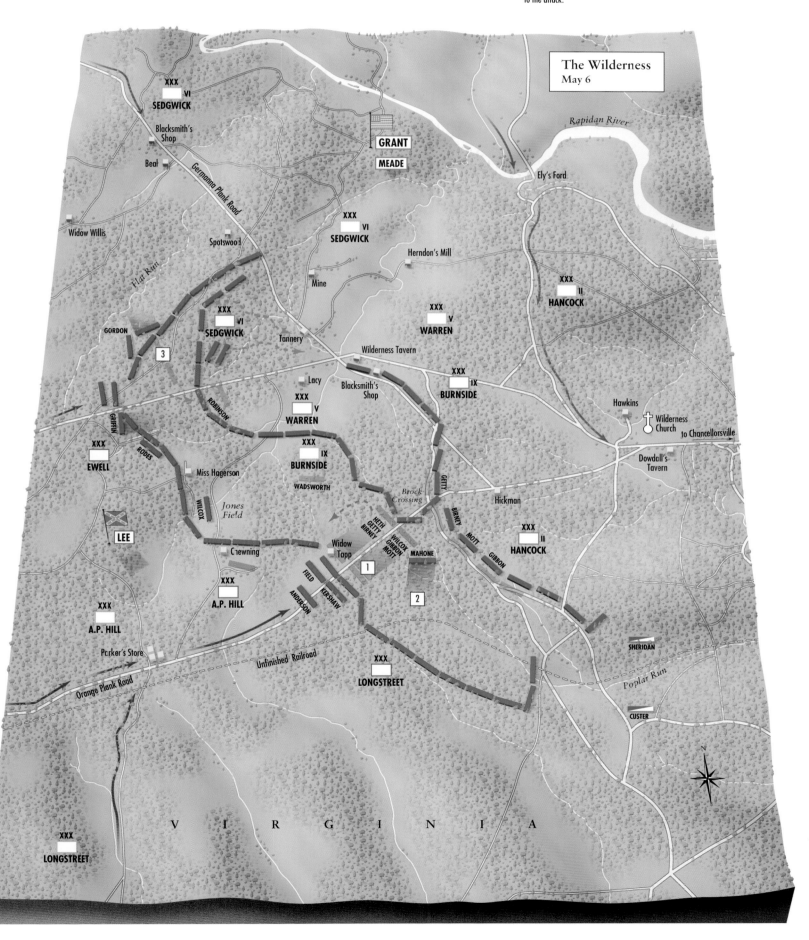

SHERIDAN'S RAIDS

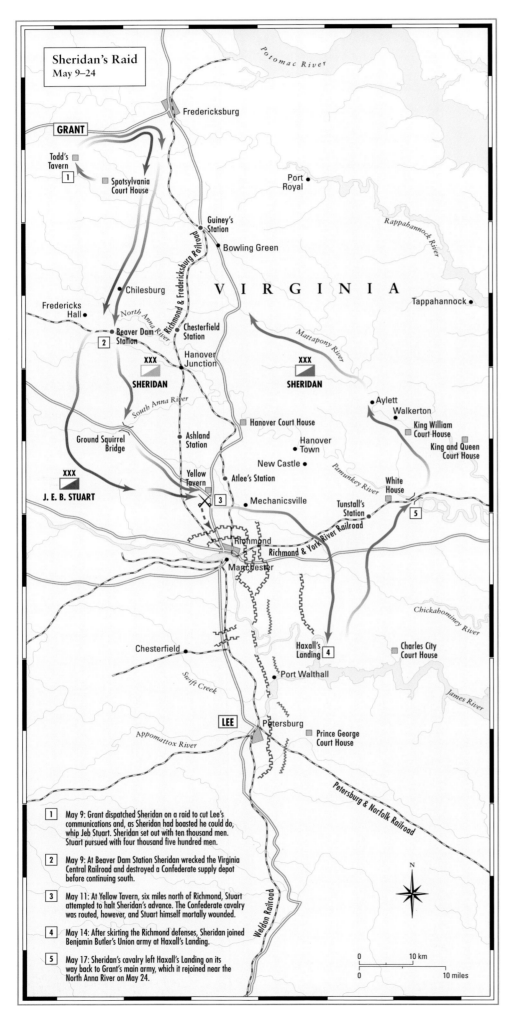

Sheridan's Raid
May 9–24

GRANT

Todd's Tavern

1

Spotsylvania Court House

Fredericksburg

Potomac River

Port Royal

Rappahannock River

Guiney's Station

Bowling Green

Chilesburg

V I R G I N I A

Tappahannock

Fredericks Hall

North Anna River

Beaver Dam Station

2

Chesterfield Station

Hanover Junction

Mattapony River

XXX

SHERIDAN

XXX

SHERIDAN

South Anna River

Hanover Court House

Aylett

Walkerton

King William Court House

King and Queen Court House

Ground Squirrel Bridge

Ashland Station

Hanover Town

XXX

J. E. B. STUART

Yellow Tavern

Atlee's Station

New Castle

Pamunkey River

White House

3

Mechanicsville

Tunstall's Station

5

Richmond

Manchester

Richmond & York River Railroad

Chickahominy River

Chesterfield

Haxall's Landing

4

Charles City Court House

Port Walthall

Swift Creek

James River

LEE

Petersburg

Prince George Court House

Appomattox River

Petersburg & Norfolk Railroad

Weldon Railroad

N

0   10 km
0   10 miles

1 May 9: Grant dispatched Sheridan on a raid to cut Lee's
communications and, as Sheridan had boasted he could do,
whip Jeb Stuart. Sheridan set out with ten thousand men.
Stuart pursued with four thousand five hundred men.

2 May 9: At Beaver Dam Station Sheridan wrecked the Virginia
Central Railroad and destroyed a Confederate supply depot
before continuing south.

3 May 11: At Yellow Tavern, six miles north of Richmond, Stuart
attempted to halt Sheridan's advance. The Confederate cavalry
was routed, however, and Stuart himself mortally wounded.

4 May 14: After skirting the Richmond defenses, Sheridan joined
Benjamin Butler's Union army at Haxall's Landing.

5 May 17: Sheridan's cavalry left Haxall's Landing on its
way back to Grant's main army, which it rejoined near the
North Anna River on May 24.

AFTER THE BATTLE OF THE WILDERNESS, Major General George G. Meade, commanding the Army of the Potomac, had a serious falling out with Major General Philip H. Sheridan, commanding the army's cavalry. The two had been destined to clash ever since Grant had brought Sheridan from the western theater of the war to serve in Virginia. Meade, competent but unspectacular, employed the slow, meticulous, by-the-book way of waging war that McClellan had taught so well to the officer corps of the Army of the Potomac. Sheridan was everything Meade was not—aggressive, energetic, and eager to take the fight to the enemy. Sheridan wanted to use his cavalry as a powerful mobile striking force. Meade believed cavalry should serve in a traditional role of scouting and screening. He further believed, with good reason, that Sheridan had not done particularly well in that role during the Wilderness campaign. When he reprimanded Sheridan, the two got into an unseemly shouting match. After Sheridan left headquarters, Meade remarked to Grant that Sheridan thought he could whip Confederate cavalry commander J. E. B. Stuart. Much to Meade's disgust Grant's reply was that Sheridan should be allowed to make the attempt.

Thus on May 9, as the Army of the Potomac and the Army of Northern Virginia were settling into their trenches around Spotsylvania Court House, Sheridan led two of the Army of the Potomac's three cavalry divisions, about twelve thousand men, away from the army, south toward Richmond. He moved at a slow, steady pace, not wishing to evade Stuart and the Confederate horses but rather to invite an encounter. Stuart led the five thousand horsemen of his command after Sheridan, and the outriders of the two cavalry forces skirmished along the way. On May 10 Sheridan's troopers, some of them tearing up the track of the Virginia Central Railroad, approached to within twenty miles of Richmond. Stuart succeeded that day in inserting his own command between Sheridan and Richmond.

The next day the two cavalry forces clashed head-on at Yellow Tavern, six miles north of Richmond. Sheridan was victorious. Stuart fell, mortally wounded, but his fight at Yellow Tavern did succeed in delaying Sheridan's advance while the Confederates strengthened the Richmond defenses. Union losses at Yellow Tavern totaled two hundred and fifty-nine men. Confederate reports did not enumerate their losses, but Fitzhugh reported his loss "very heavy," and Sheridan reported capturing between two hundred and three hundred prisoners during the course of the raid.

After the fight at Yellow Tavern, Sheridan approached the Richmond fortifications and found them impregnable to his force. He nearly found himself in serious difficulty inside the sharp angle formed by the Chickahominy River and the Richmond entrenchments but was able to extricate his command intact. After continued skirmishing with the Confederate cavalry, Sheridan reached Haxall's Landing on the James River and made contact with Major General Benjamin Butler's Army of the James. After several days of rest the Union cavalry returned to the Army of the Potomac, rejoining it on May 24.

On June 7, Grant dispatched Sheridan on another raid, this time to cover Grant's bold movement across the James River. Sheridan was to ride west, destroy the Virginia Central Railroad and the James River Canal, and then join Major General David Hunter's Union forces in the Shenandoah Valley. Sheridan took the divisions of David M. Gregg and Alfred T. A. Torbert, totaling about six thousand men. Lee countered the move with most of his own cavalry, the divisions of Wade Hampton and Fitzhugh Lee, numbering about five thousand. The two forces clashed on June 11 at Trevilian Station, fifty miles northwest of Richmond. Hampton's Confederate division clashed with Torbert's Union troopers, but Brigadier General George A. Custer's Union brigade got in rear of Hampton and captured his wagon train. Disengaging from Torbert, Hampton turned against Custer, who narrowly escaped being trapped between Hampton and Fitzhugh Lee. That night Hampton had his troopers dismount and dig in. Sheridan attacked the next day but the entrenched Confederates repulsed him. Deeming it impossible to join Hunter, Sheridan turned back toward the Army of the Potomac, which he rejoined on June 28. The raid had cost each side about one thousand men. Sheridan had torn up a few miles of the Virginia Central Railroad, and above all he had succeeded in the raid's chief purpose, drawing away Lee's cavalry so that they could not detect Grant's crossing of the James.

Brigadier General George Armstrong Custer led his union brigade into action at Trevilion Station, capturing a Confederate wagon train, but was almost himself trapped in the process.

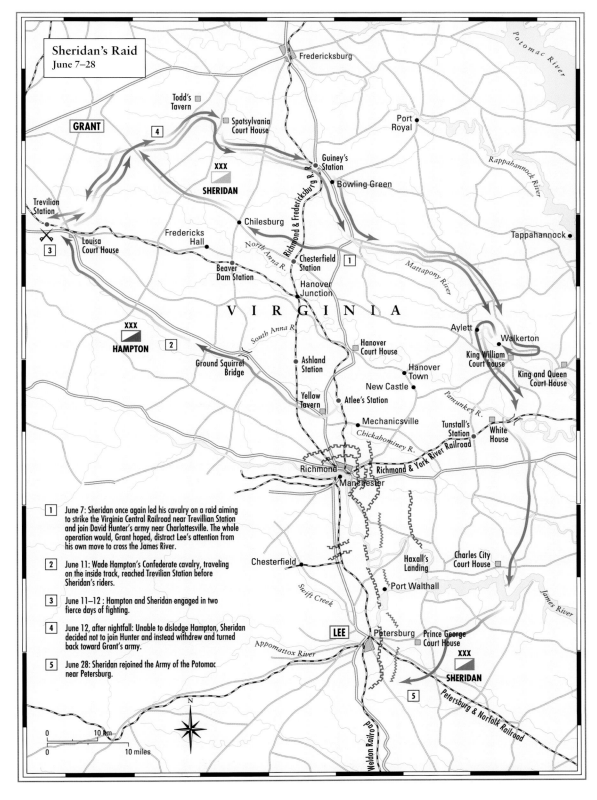

Sheridan's Raid
June 7–28

1 June 7: Sheridan once again led his cavalry on a raid aiming to strike the Virginia Central Railroad near Trevillian Station and join David Hunter's army near Charlottesville. The whole operation would, Grant hoped, distract Lee's attention from his own move to cross the James River.

2 June 11: Wade Hampton's Confederate cavalry, traveling on the inside track, reached Trevilian Station before Sheridan's riders.

3 June 11–12: Hampton and Sheridan engaged in two fierce days of fighting.

4 June 12, after nightfall: Unable to dislodge Hampton, Sheridan decided not to join Hunter and instead withdrew and turned back toward Grant's army.

5 June 28: Sheridan rejoined the Army of the Potomac near Petersburg.

THE DREWRY'S BLUFF CAMPAIGN

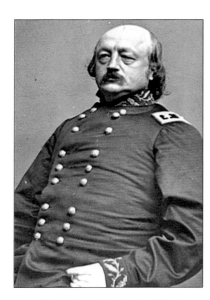

Major General Benjamin F. Butler, an influential and successful politician enjoyed less success in the field. He eventually resigned from his commission in November 1865.

O NE OF THE CAMPAIGNS GRANT planned as part of his nationwide offensive in the late spring of 1864 was an advance that would cut Richmond's vulnerable supply lines south of the city. Five different railroads, approaching from the south or southeast, all came together at Petersburg, twenty-five miles south of Richmond. From Petersburg a single line of tracks led north to Richmond. If a Union army could get astride that railroad either at Petersburg itself or anywhere along the twenty-five miles between there and Richmond, the Confederate capital would be untenable, and Lee's army itself would be in dire peril.

To lead this important component of his strategy, Grant unfortunately chose Major General Benjamin F. Butler. In Grant's defense, he knew that Butler was a very influential politician and that the Lincoln administration needed his support more than ever in this election year. As commander of the department in which the proposed operation was to take place, Butler would likely have been hard to avoid in any case, and being sidelined would certainly have outraged the touchy politician's grandiose delusions of military glory. After a conversation with Butler, Grant could at least persuade himself to hope that the one-time Massachusetts trial lawyer would not perform as incompetently as most professional soldiers feared. To hedge his bets, Grant assigned Butler two experienced officers as his corps commanders in this operation. Major General Quincy A. Gillmore would command the Tenth Corps, and Major General William F. Smith would command the Eighteenth. Both were highly respected military engineers.

On May 5, 1864, as Grant and Lee were begin-

ning their battle in the Wilderness, Butler landed his thirty thousand-man Army of the James south of Richmond. One division he placed at City Point, on the south bank of the James River just below the mouth of the Appomattox. The rest of his troops he put ashore at Bermuda Hundred Plantation, the peninsula formed by the convergence of the James and the Appomattox. Butler immediately proposed a rapid night march up the south bank of the James River toward Richmond but met the disapproval of his two corps commanders, who succeeded in talking him out of it. The following day opportunity still beckoned. Peters-burg was seven miles away, Richmond fourteen, and the Confederacy had scarcely ten thousand men in the entire area with which to oppose the Army of the James. Butler ordered Smith and Gillmore to advance their troops and seize the Richmond & Petersburg Railroad. The attempt was distinctly half-hearted, with Smith sending a single brigade and Gillmore sending no troops at all. George Pickett, commanding the Confederate defenders, succeeded in stopping the weak advance.

That action set the pattern for the next several days. Several times Butler made tentative advances with fractions of his force, seized small sections of the railroad, and then retreated when threatened by much smaller forces, having done only minimal damage. He and his corps commanders bickered more or less constantly before finally settling on the concept of an advance toward Richmond. By the time the movement began in earnest, however, the Confederates had had an additional week to make preparations. The capable Pierre G. T. Beauregard with a large force under this command superseded Pickett. Beauregard and his defenders confronted Butler at Drewry's Bluff, site of Fort Darling, on the south bank of the James River. During the 14th and 15th of May Butler's forces slowly approached the Drewry's Bluffs lines and began to position themselves, giving Beauregard even more time to prepare.

Using every last man the Richmond authorities could possibly borrow from other fronts, Beauregard attacked Butler on the morning of May 16 in a dense fog. The Confederates pushed back Butler's right wing, but the left and center held steady. Additional Confederate forces under the command of Major General W. H. C. Whiting were supposed to approach the battlefield from Petersburg and strike the Federals in rear, but for reasons that remain obscure, Whiting never came. Davis had warned Beauregard that a junction of forces on the battlefield was very difficult and should not be attempted, but Beauregard insisted on his elaborate plan. Without the arrival of Whiting, any chance of trapping and destroying Butler's army, and thus removing it as a threat to Richmond, vanished.

The Advance on Drewry's Bluff
May 12–14

Bermuda Neck

RICHMOND

Manchester

Seven Pines · Fair Oaks Station · Bottom's Bridge

V I R G I N I A

BEAUREGARD

HOKE
Drewry's Bluff

5

New Market

Malvern Hill

XXX
X

BUTLER
Wooldridge Hill

3

XXX
XVIII

OSBORN

Haxall

Chesterfield Court House

Chester Station

4

2
Cobb's Hill

Bermuda Hundred

1

Appomattox River

Port Walthall Junction

Richmond & Petersburg Railroad

City Pt.

James River

Spring Hill

Berkley Pt.

Fort Clifton

N

PETERSBURG

0   4 km

0   4 miles

1 May 5: After proceeding up the James River in transports, Major General Benjamin Butler landed his thirty-nine thousand Union soldiers at Bermuda Hundred, a peninsula formed by the James and Appomattox rivers.

2 May 6: On the advice of his two corps commanders, both of whom had been military engineers, Butler set his men to dig a strong line of entrenchments across the neck of Bermuda Hundred—while fewer then ten thousand Confederate stood between him and Richmond's vital southern rail connections.

3 May 11: By now heavily reinforced, Beauregard moved north to unite with additional Confederate troops moving south from Richmond and secure the fortifications at Drewry's Bluff on the James River.

4 May 12: Butler slowed advanced toward Richmond.

5 May 16: Beauregard attacked and defeated Butler, who withdrew to his fortified lines on Bermuda Hundred.

Still, events worked out much better than the Confederates had any cause to expect. Butler, seconded by Smith, decided his army needed to retreat all the way back to Bermuda Hundred. Beauregard followed and constructed defensive works across the neck of the peninsula, as Grant reported, containing Butler's army as effectively "as if it had been in a bottle strongly corked." Most of the Confederate troops that had been confronting Butler were then free for employment elsewhere.

Federal transports loaded with cargoes of artillery at anchor near Drewry's Bluff on the James River.

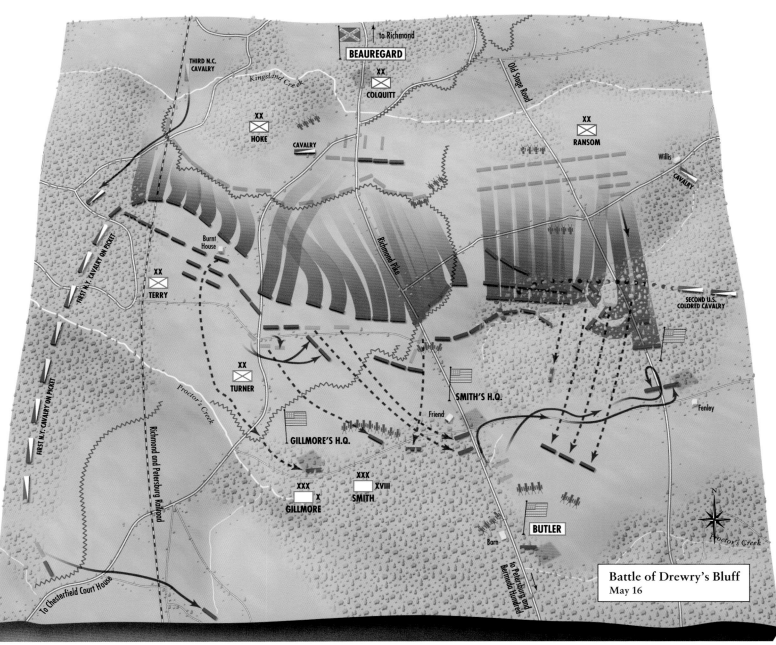

Battle of Drewry's Bluff
May 16

SPOTSYLVANIA, PHASE I

ON THE NIGHT OF MAY 7, Grant set the Army of the Potomac in motion southeast toward Spotsylvania Court House, possession of which would give him a significant advantage over Lee. Lee guessed what Grant was about to do and ordered Jeb Stuart with the Army of Northern Virginia's cavalry and Major General Richard H. Anderson with the First Corps to march quickly to Spotsylvania and hold the vital crossroads until the rest of the army could catch up. The Confederates had to build a new road in order to reach Spotsylvania, as no road led directly there from their position. The Army of the Potomac did have a good road available to it, but marched with its usual confusion and delay.

On the morning of May 8, Stuart's cavalry reached Spotsylvania before Major General Philip H. Sheridan's Union cavalry, and then Anderson's foot soldiers arrived before Major General Gouverneur K. Warren's Fifth Corps, leading the Union infantry column. Fighting flared at the point of contact and spread to either side, but the Confederates continued to hold Spotsylvania. Both sides began to entrench. More and more troops arrived over the next twenty-four hours, and clashes occurred at various points along the lines as the two armies established their positions. While inspecting his newly laid-out lines on the morning of May 9, Union

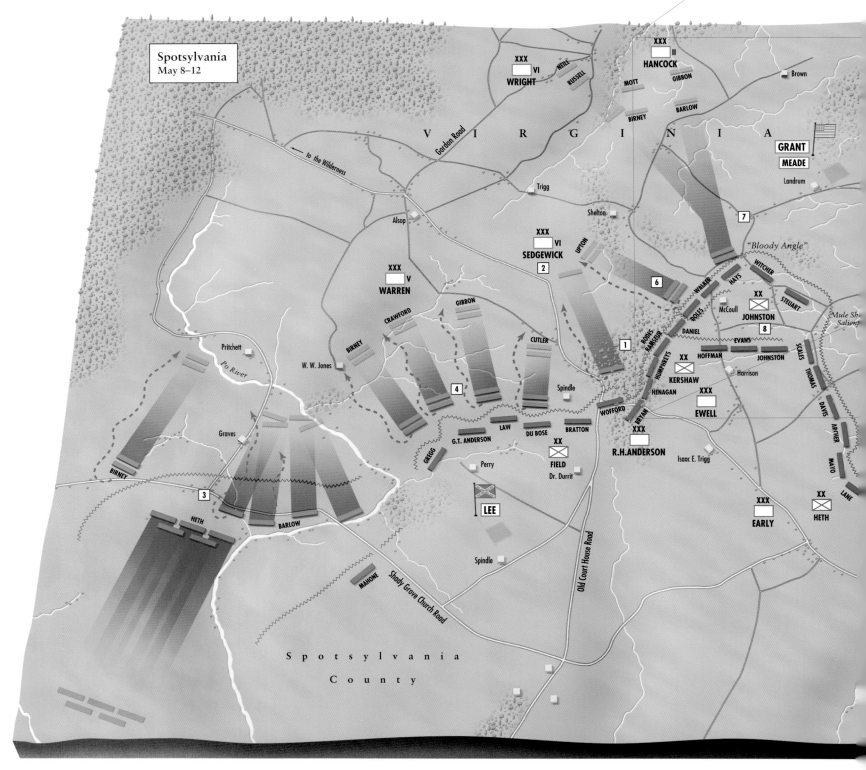

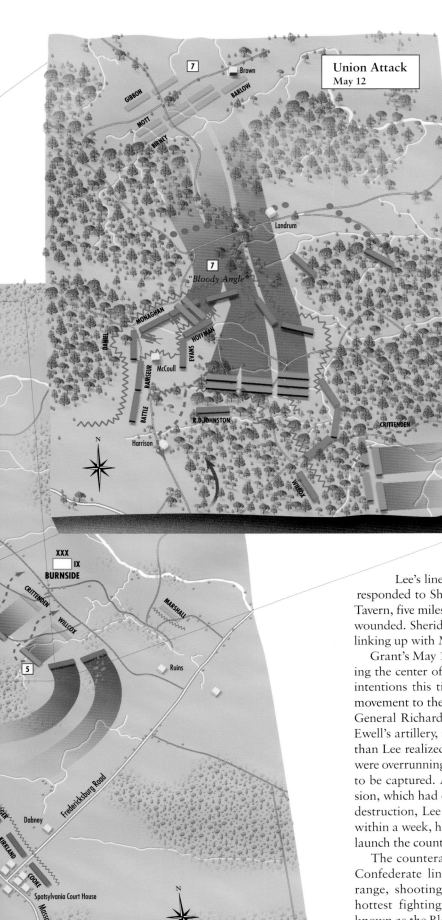

Union Attack
May 12

1   May 8, morning: Arriving near strategic Spotsylvania Court House after a night march from the Wilderness, Union cavalry found their way blocked by Confederate infantry and call for infantry support of their own. The division of Brigadier General John C. Robinson of the Fifth Corps came up and assaulted the Confederate lines but could not break through.

2   May 9: Major General John Sedgwick, commanding the Sixth Corps, was killed by a Confederate sharpshooter. His replacement was Major General Horatio Wright.

3   May 10: Barlow's and Birney's divisions of Hancock's Second Corps crossed the Po River with a view to flanking the strong Confederate position at Laurel Hill but were driven back by a strong counterattack from Major General Henry Heth's division.

4   May 10: Warren's Fifth Corps mounted poorly coordinated frontal assaults on the Laurel Hill lines but was repulsed.

5   May 10: At the other end of the line, Burnside's Ninth Corps launched an equally unsuccessful attack.

6   May 10, 6:00 pm.: The only success of the day came when Colonel Emory Upton led a carefully prepared attack by a dense column that briefly punched a hole in a section of the Confederate line known as the Mule Shoe. Upton's supports failed to come up, however, and Confederate reinforcements soon drove him off.

7   May 12, 4:30 a.m.: After a day's preparation, Grant sought to duplicate Upton's feets using the entire Third Corps. The attack broke the Confederate line, but Confederate reinforcements plugged the gap through twenty hours of hand-to-hand fighting near the Bloody Angle.

8   While the troops struggled at the Bloody Angle, other Confederates built another line of defenses across the base of the Mule Shoe.

Sixth Corps commander Major General John Sedgwick was killed by a Confederate sharpshooter's bullet.

Grant hoped he might break Lee's line and tried several attacks on May 10, all but one of which failed to score even temporary success. Arranged to take advantage of terrain features, the Confederate line was centered around a large, rounded salient, aptly named the Mule Shoe. The one brief Union success of the day was aimed at the western side of the Mule Shoe. In this initiative Colonel Emory Upton used an innovative tactic, arranging twelve picked regiments in a dense column and ordering his men not to stop and fire but to charge rapidly forward until they were actually inside the Confederate works. The daring scheme worked, and Upton's men broke through the line only to be driven back when Confederates counterattacked and supporting Union troops failed to come up. Impressed, Grant decided to try the same method on a much larger scale. Throughout May 11, planning went forward for a grand assault scheduled to take place before dawn on the 12th.

Meanwhile Grant had released Sheridan's cavalry to raid deep behind Lee's lines, all the way to the vicinity of Richmond. Stuart's Confederate horsemen responded to Sheridan's raid, as expected, and the two mounted forces clashed at Yellow Tavern, five miles north of Richmond, on May 11. In the fighting there Stuart was mortally wounded. Sheridan fought additional skirmishes in the Richmond area before temporarily linking up with Major General Benjamin Butler's Union forces at Bermuda Hundred.

Grant's May 12 assault occurred as scheduled with the entire Union Second Corps striking the center of the Mule Shoe well before dawn. Lee had guessed wrong about Grant's intentions this time. He had assumed that the Union commander would make another movement to the southeast. To be ready for a quick response, Lee had ordered Lieutenant General Richard S. Ewell's troops to prepare to evacuate the Mule Shoe. As a first step, Ewell's artillery, some twenty guns, pulled out. No sooner were the guns out of the salient than Lee realized his mistake and ordered them back. They arrived just as Grant's troops were overrunning the position, too late to deploy and open fire but in time for every last gun to be captured. Also captured was Major General Edward Johnson and most of his division, which had once been Stonewall Jackson's own. With his army in imminent danger of destruction, Lee was about to lead a counterattack in person when, for the second time within a week, his troops begged and finally forced him to go to the rear before they would launch the counterattack.

The counterattack proved successful in halting the Union advance and restoring the Confederate line. For the next twenty hours the opposing troops remained at close range, shooting, bayoneting, clubbing, and grabbling each other hand-to-hand. The hottest fighting centered on an angle in the Confederate earthworks, subsequently known as the Bloody Angle. On either side of the Bloody Angle, Grant ordered Warren's Fifth Corps and Major General Ambrose Burnside's Ninth Corps to attack the Confederate line along the Mule Shoe, but they could not break through. Finally in the predawn hours of May 13, Lee got a defensive line completed across the base of the Mule Shoe and ordered what was left of Ewell's Second Corps to fall back to the new position. Union casualties for May 12 alone totaled six thousand eight hundred men, while the Confederates lost some nine thousand, including four thousand prisoners.

SPOTSYLVANIA, PHASE II

HAVING FAILED TO PUNCH THROUGH the Confederate position by frontal assault, Grant returned to maneuver. On May 13 he began shifting his army to the left, and thus to the southeast. To do this he had Major General Gouverneur Warren's Fifth Corps pull out of line on the army's right, march all the way behind the army's front, and then take position on the left end of the line. Major General Horatio Wright's Sixth Corps was now on the right end of the line, and Grant had it repeat the same procedure. Then one corps after the other in the same manner, he gradually eased his army southeastward while maintaining contact and a strong front against Lee. Canny as usual, Lee matched Grant's movements. Little fighting occurred during the next several days, save for minor skirmishing generated as the armies jostled each other while maneuvering. On May 14, a planned Union assault was canceled due to heavy rain.

Hoping to catch Lee moving to the southeast a little too rapidly, or to induce him to move a little more slowly, Grant ordered an attack by his right wing against Lee's left. Instead of pulling out of line and marching to the left as had been the pattern in recent days, Major General Winfield Scott Hancock's Second Corps along with Wright's Sixth and Major General Ambrose Burnside's Ninth assaulted Lee's right at dawn on May 18. In front of them they found Lieutenant General Richard S. Ewell's Confederate Second Corps well entrenched. Several attacks achieved little, and the drive was called off. That night, the Army of the Potomac resumed its previous pattern of shifting to the left, extending its lines southeast and compelling Lee to match it move for move.

The next day, Lee needed to determine whether Grant was in fact moving southeast again and so ordered Ewell to probe his front—the Confederate left—and see if the Federals were still there. He quickly

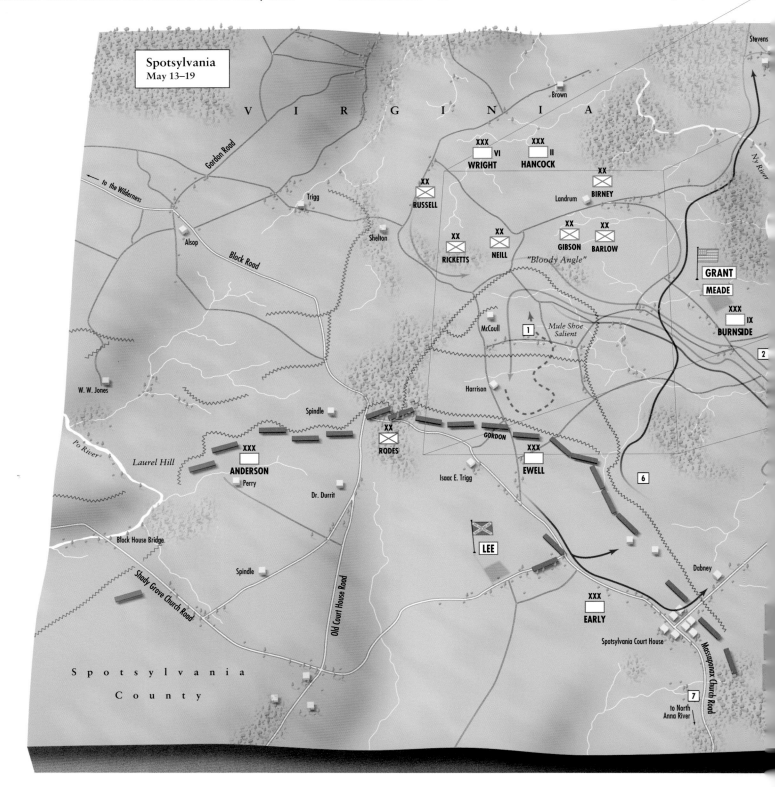

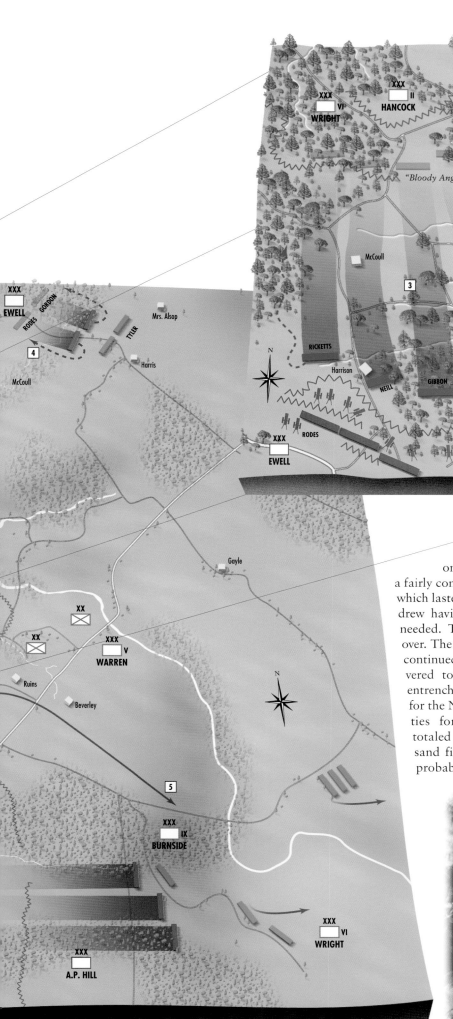

Union Assault
May 18

"Bloody Angle"

1 May 13: With a strong new line of breastworks completed across the base of the Mule Shoe, Lee abandoned the salient.

2 May 14: Planning another turning movement to the southeast, Grant concentrated his forces near the Fredericksburg Road.

3 May 18: Thinking that Lee might be weakening his left and center, Grant ordered another attack on the Mule Shoe by the Second and Sixth corps, but it ended in repulse.

4 May 19: Similarly, Lee dispatched Ewell's Confederate Second Corps to try the strength of the Union right. It proved adequate.

5 May 20: Grant pulled his troops out of their trenches and put them on the march to the southeast, toward the North Anna River.

6 May 21: Confederate troops advanced and discovered the Unions' absence.

7 May 21: Lee immediately put his army in motion to counter Grant's move.

found that enough of them were still present on that end of the line to give him a fairly considerable fight at Harris's Farm, which lasted until late evening. Ewell withdrew having gained the information Lee needed. The Battle of Spotsylvania was over. The movement to the southeast now continued more rapidly, as Grant maneuvered to try to draw Lee out of his entrenchments, and the armies headed for the North Anna River. Union casualties for the Battle of Spotsylvania totaled approximately seventeen thousand five hundred. Confederate losses probably totaled about ten thousand.

Confederate soldier of Ewell's corps killed in the attack on May 19.

NORTH ANNA

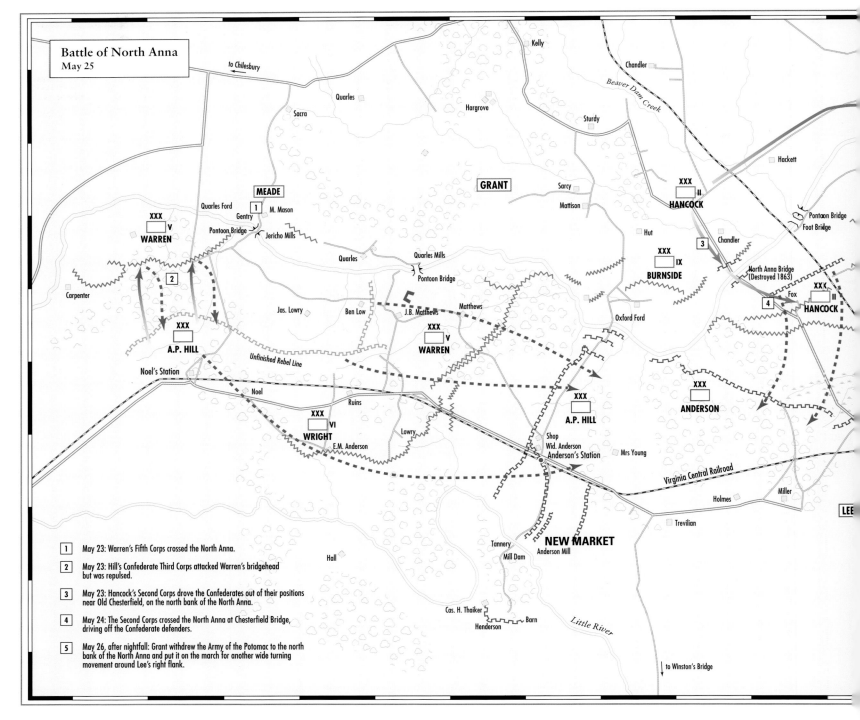

Battle of North Anna
May 25

1 May 23: Warren's Fifth Corps crossed the North Anna.

2 May 23: Hill's Confederate Third Corps attacked Warren's bridgehead but was repulsed.

3 May 23: Hancock's Second Corps drove the Confederates out of their positions near Old Chesterfield, on the north bank of the North Anna.

4 May 24: The Second Corps crossed the North Anna at Chesterfield Bridge, driving off the Confederate defenders.

5 May 26, after nightfall: Grant withdrew the Army of the Potomac to the north bank of the North Anna and put it on the march for another wide turning movement around Lee's right flank.

AFTER THE BLOODY STALEMATE AT Spotsylvania, Grant once again slid to his left. Beginning on the night of May 20, the Army of the Potomac marched southeastward, around Lee's right flank. The army's initial destination was the crossroads at Hanover Junction, about forty miles from Spotsylvania. Once again, Lee responded alertly to Grant's movement, and by the morning of May 22 had shifted his own army into a position to block Grant's march at the North Anna River.

Grant advanced aggressively on May 23, sending Major General Winfield Scott Hancock's Second Corps toward the bridge on the Telegraph Road and Major General Gouverneur K. Warren's Fifth Corps toward the ford at Jericho Mill, some distance upstream. Both movements were successful, as Hancock's troops

seized the bridge around 6:00 p.m. after skirmishing briefly with its Confederate defenders. Warren's men had no difficulty securing the crossing at Jericho Mill and then fought off a counterattack by Major General Ambrose Powell Hill's Confederate Third Corps.

That night Lee adopted a new plan and adjusted his army's position. He continued to hold Oxford Ford, between Jericho Mill and the Telegraph Road bridge, with Major General Richard H. Anderson's First Corps. On Anderson's left, however, facing Jericho Mill, Lee had Hill angle his Third Corps's line to the southwest, away from the river. Similarly, on his right Lee had Ewell angle his Second Corps's line to the southeast, also slanting away from the river. This arrangement placed Lee's army in an inverted V formation, with its somewhat flat-

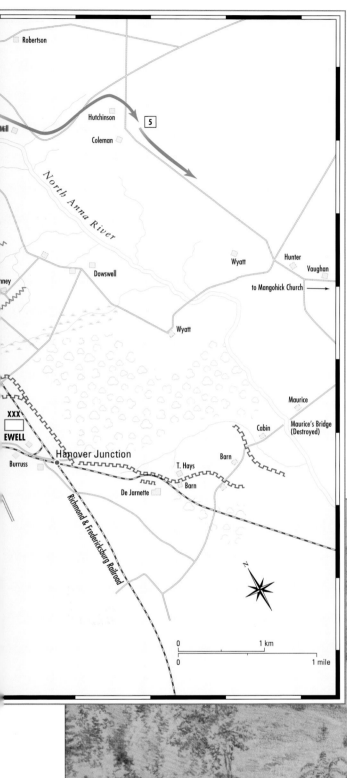

tened point on the North Anna River around Oxford Ford. Lee's army was now between the Union Second and Fifth corps. If Grant continued to push his army across the river at both crossings, as he undoubtedly would, Lee would have the opportunity of holding off one half of the Army of the Potomac with a small, entrenched force while concentrating most of his army to attack the other half.

As expected, Grant continued to drive forward on May 24, sending more troops across the river at the two crossings already held, but failing to budge the entrenched Confederates holding Oxford Ford. Late in the day, Grant discerned Lee's purpose and had his army entrench in anticipation of Lee's attack. The attack never came, however, as Lee fell ill that day and was confined to his cot, possibly with symptoms of the heart disease that would kill him six years later. After another day of skirmishing, Grant moved on, and the Battle of the North Anna was over. Union casualties totaled two thousand six hundred and twenty-three, and Confed-erate two thousand five hundred and seventeen.

The Battle of North Anna. In this pencil drawing by Edwin Forbes, the Fifth Corps of The Army of the Potomac is shown crossing the North Anna River at Jericho Ford.

COLD HARBOR

GRANT'S NEXT MOVEMENT WAS another march around Lee's right flank. It began on May 26 and by the last day of the month had reached the crossroads of Cold Harbor, almost on the outskirts of Richmond. Sheridan's Union cavalry got to the crossroads first and held it first against Major General Fitzhugh Lee's Confederate cavalry and then, on June 1, against an infantry attack by Anderson's First Corps. The rest of both armies began to arrive and dig in. Though Grant held the crossroads, Lee and the Army of Northern Virginia still lay across his path to Richmond.

That afternoon Grant hurled the Sixth Corps and Major General William F. Smith's newly arrived Eighteenth Corps at the Confederate entrenchments, but could not break through. With Richmond so close and Lee's army presumably depleted after almost a month of ferocious fighting, Grant reckoned that another and bigger assault might succeed where the first had failed. He hoped to deliver the attack on the morning of June 2, but Hancock's Second Corps, Grant's preferred striking force, was still on its way to the battlefield. Further delays postponed the attack until the morning of June 3, as the always-creaky command system of the Army of the Potomac functioned with its accustomed slowness,

cross-purposes, and confusion. Meanwhile, Lee strengthened his lines.

At 4:30 a.m. on June 3 the Second, Sixth, and Eighteenth corps attacked but achieved no significant gains. The main attack stalled within thirty minutes and the attackers suffered perhaps three thousand five hundred casualties. Further fighting during the day doubled the length of the casualty list but did not change the outcome. Lee's casualties for the day were about one thousand five hundred. Grant determined to find a different approach to Richmond.

The Battle of Cold Harbor, June 3. No clear plan was issued to the corps commanders for the forthcoming battle, Meade sent a circular postponing a late afternoon attack until dawn, allowing time for the individual commanders to "… perfect the arrangements for the assault." At headquarters there may have been a lofty confidence but among the troops it was different, many pinned notes to the back of their uniforms so that their bodies might be recognized and families informed. A bloodstained diary recovered from the battlefield had one final entry: "June 3. Cold Harbor, I was killed."

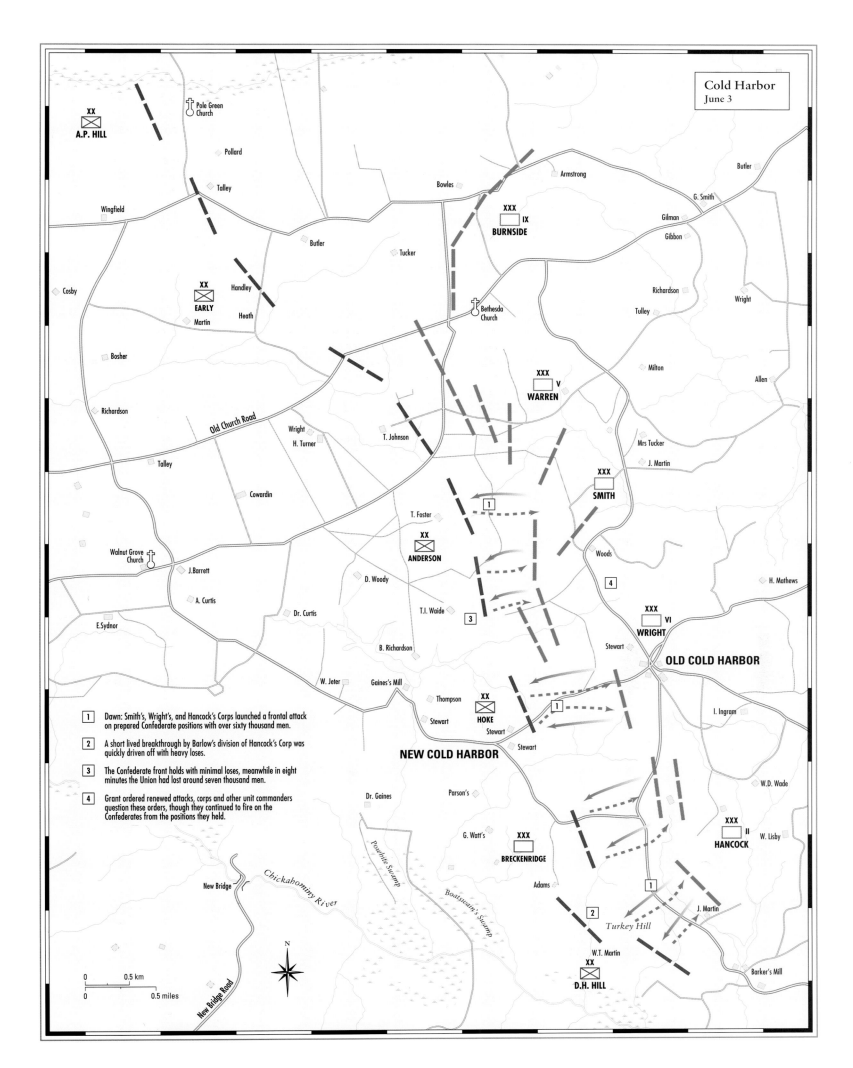

Cold Harbor
June 3

XX
A.P. HILL

Pole Green
Church

Pollard

Talley

Wingfield

Butler

Tucker

Bowles

Armstrong

Butler

G. Smith

Gilman

Gibbon

XXX
IX
BURNSIDE

Cosby

XX
EARLY

Handley

Heath

Martin

Bethesda
Church

Richardson

Tulley

Wright

Bosher

Milton

Allen

XXX
V
WARREN

Richardson

Old Church Road

Talley

Wright

H. Turner

T. Johnson

Mrs Tucker

J. Martin

XXX
SMITH

Cowardin

T. Foster

1

XX
ANDERSON

Woods

4

Walnut Grove
Church

J. Barrett

D. Woody

3

XXX
VI
WRIGHT

H. Mathews

A. Curtis

T.I. Waide

E. Sydnor

Dr. Curtis

B. Richardson

Stewart

OLD COLD HARBOR

W. Jeter

Gaines's Mill

Thompson

1

I. Ingram

Stewart

XX
HOKE

Stewart

Stewart

NEW COLD HARBOR

W.D. Wade

Dr. Gaines

Parson's

XXX
II
W. Lisby
HANCOCK

G. Watt's

XXX
BRECKENRIDGE

Powhite Swamp

Chickahominy River

Boatswain's Swamp

Adams

1

New Bridge

2

Turkey Hill

J. Martin

W.T. Martin

XX
D.H. HILL

Barker's Mill

New Bridge Road

1	Dawn: Smith's, Wright's, and Hancock's Corps launched a frontal attack on prepared Confederate positions with over sixty thousand men.
2	A short lived breakthrough by Barlow's division of Hancock's Corp was quickly driven off with heavy loses.
3	The Confederate front holds with minimal loses, meanwhile in eight minutes the Union had lost around seven thousand men.
4	Grant ordered renewed attacks, corps and other unit commanders question these orders, though they continued to fire on the Confederates from the positions they held.

0   0.5 km

0   0.5 miles

N

ADVANCE TO PETERSBURG

THE LINES AROUND COLD HARBOR remained quiet after the failure of the June 3 assaults. On the 5th Grant proposed to Lee a truce for the burying the dead and tending the wounded, who still lay between the lines. Negotiations became complicated as Lee insisted that Grant's request be worded in such a way as to give tacit acknowledgment that Lee had defeated Grant in battle. This Grant was reluctant to do, and so the truce did not take place until June 7.

Grant decided that nothing further could be gained by more attacks in the vicinity of Cold Harbor, so he decided to disengage from Lee's army, swing far to his left, cross the James River, and strike for Petersburg, directly south of Richmond. Petersburg was an important rail junction and the nexus of Confederate supply lines for both the city of Richmond and for Lee's army. If Grant could take Petersburg, Lee would be forced either to attack him at great disadvantage or to abandon Richmond and flee westward, vulnerable to the aggressive pursuit Grant would be sure to make.

The first step would be stealing a march on Lee to get across the James undetected. In order to distract Lee's attention from the coming operations on the Confederate left flank, Grant dispatched Sheridan with two divisions of cavalry to go around the Confederate right flank and join Major General David Hunter's Union army in the Shenandoah Valley. Sheridan's column left Grant's lines on June 7. Four days later they encountered the Confederate cavalry divisions of Major General Wade Hampton and Major General Fitzhugh Lee, dug in and blocking their path at Trevilian Station, a depot on the Virginia Central Railroad. In two days of fighting results were mixed, but Sheridan decided not to proceed with his plan of joining Hunter and instead rejoined Grant by the same way he had come. Union casualties at Trevilian Station totaled one thousand and seven. Confederate losses were not completely reported but were probably comparable.

Despite Sheridan's failure to get to Hunter, the Trevilian Station raid succeeded in achieving Grant's chief purpose of helping to distract Lee's attention. With Hampton's and Fitzhugh Lee's cavalry divisions occupied beyond the Army of Northern Virginia's left flank, they were not available for scouting beyond the army's right flank, where Grant had business. On the evening of June 12, the second day of the Battle of Trevilian Station, Grant began his movement across

the James River. For once the Army of the Potomac moved with the smoothness and efficiency to which Grant had been accustomed with the western armies. The movement began at nightfall, with four corps marching overland toward the James while Major General William F. Smith's Eighteenth Corps boarded ships for transport down the Pamunkey and York rivers and then up the James. The army got away cleanly, with Lee none the wiser.

Lee discovered the absence of the Army of the Potomac the next day but could not discern its destination. Thinking that Grant meant to make a direct lunge toward Richmond from the east, Lee moved the Army of Northern Virginia southward to block such an attempt. Meanwhile, unknown to him, Grant's troops, out of sight beyond the horizon, continued to march across his front toward the James River. The first of Grant's troops reached the river on the afternoon of June 13, at Wilcox's Landing, where engineers were at work building the longest pontoon bridge of the war. With the bridge still incomplete, Major General Winfield S. Hancock's Second Corps began crossing the river in boats on the morning of June 14, while the Eighteenth

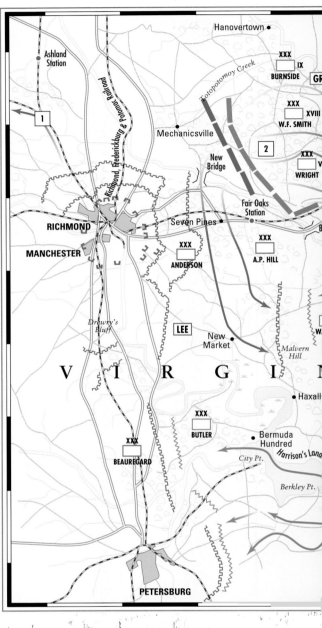

Union troops hastily dig in with bayonets and tin plates.

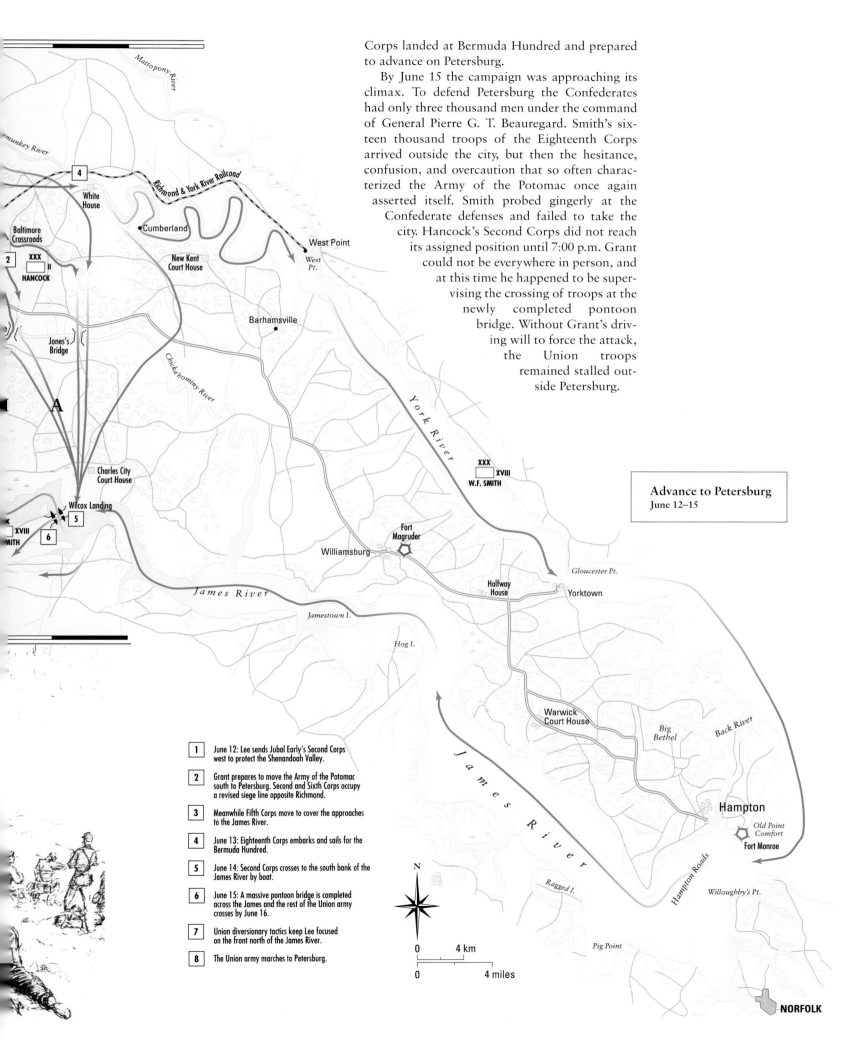

Corps landed at Bermuda Hundred and prepared to advance on Petersburg.

By June 15 the campaign was approaching its climax. To defend Petersburg the Confederates had only three thousand men under the command of General Pierre G. T. Beauregard. Smith's sixteen thousand troops of the Eighteenth Corps arrived outside the city, but then the hesitance, confusion, and overcaution that so often characterized the Army of the Potomac once again asserted itself. Smith probed gingerly at the Confederate defenses and failed to take the city. Hancock's Second Corps did not reach its assigned position until 7:00 p.m. Grant could not be everywhere in person, and at this time he happened to be supervising the crossing of troops at the newly completed pontoon bridge. Without Grant's driving will to force the attack, the Union troops remained stalled outside Petersburg.

Advance to Petersburg
June 12–15

1 June 12: Lee sends Jubal Early's Second Corps west to protect the Shenandoah Valley.

2 Grant prepares to move the Army of the Potomac south to Petersburg. Second and Sixth Corps occupy a revised siege line opposite Richmond.

3 Meanwhile Fifth Corps move to cover the approaches to the James River.

4 June 13: Eighteenth Corps embarks and sails for the Bermuda Hundred.

5 June 14: Second Corps crosses to the south bank of the James River by boat.

6 June 15: A massive pontoon bridge is completed across the James and the rest of the Union army crosses by June 16.

7 Union diversionary tactics keep Lee focused on the front north of the James River.

8 The Union army marches to Petersburg.

ASSAULTS ON PETERSBURG

On JUNE 16, LEE STILL REMAINED convinced that Grant's main force was north of the James River and likely to attack his lines east of Richmond. He therefore, did not send a large number of reinforcements to Beauregard, who was thus left to his own devices to defend Petersburg. To man the Petersburg lines, Beauregard pulled together some fourteen thousand men from the force with which he had been confronting Benjamin Butler's army at Bermuda Hundred, the peninsula between the James and Appomattox rivers. Threatening Petersburg by this time was almost the entire Army of the Potomac. In a series of assaults on June 16, Union troops captured a large section of the Petersburg entrenchments. Unable to retake the captured works, the Confederates had to begin frantically digging another line of works closer to town. Meanwhile, Butler's troops

A railroad gun and its crew, part of the increasing amount of firepower concentrated around Petersburg.

assaulted the thinly manned Confederate lines on Bermuda Hundred and drove them back. Reacting to that threat, Lee dispatched two divisions of his army to shore up the Bermuda Hundred position. Late in the day they succeeded in driving Butler's Federals back to the starting point and restoring the Confederate position.

On June 17, Grant's army renewed its assaults on the Confederate lines around Petersburg. The newly arrived Ninth Corps struck Confederate lines near the Shand House but could make little headway. Another day of assaults ended in frustration for the Army of the Potomac. After midnight that night, the Confederate defenders of Petersburg pulled back to another line of works, still closer to the city, but shorter and more defensible than the one they previously occupied. On the other side of the lines, Meade was planning yet another large assault. North of the James, Lee finally realized what was happening and ordered Richard H. Anderson's First Corps and Ambrose Powell Hill's Third Corps across the James and Appomattox rivers and join the Petersburg defenses.

On the morning of June 18 Lee was present in person, along with Anderson's and Hill's soldiers. Union troops once again assaulted the Petersburg lines, only to be driven off again. The process was repeated that afternoon, but, with the bulk of Lee's army in the trenches, the Federals had no hope of breaking through. Over the past four days the Army of the Potomac's assaults had progressively become more costly in casualties and less effective in taking ground. Union casualties during those assaults totaled about eight thousand one hundred and fifty, while Confederate losses, not precisely reported, were probably between three thousand and five thousand.

That evening, Grant decided that Petersburg could not be taken by storm and determined to besiege it instead. Union troops already bestrode two of the five railroads leading into the city. When Grant succeeded in getting the other three, Petersburg had to fall, and Richmond with it.

Though it had not been part of Grant's program at the outset of the Overland campaign (the name given to the campaign that began with the Battle of the Wilderness and continued through Spotsylvania, North

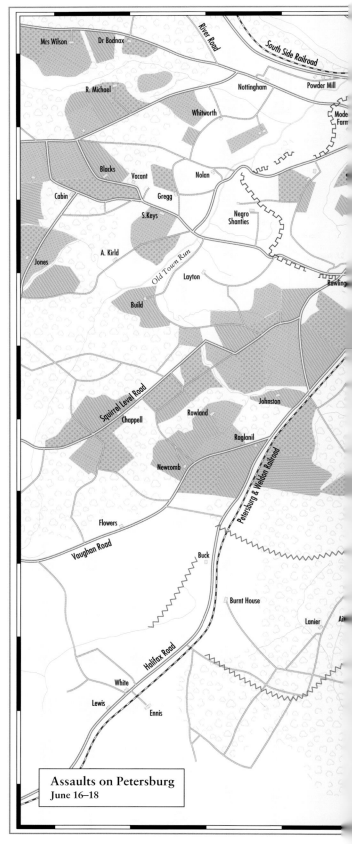

Assaults on Petersburg
June 16–18

Anna, and Cold Harbor) six weeks before, the movement to Petersburg had been the most promising of Grant's operations in the spring of 1864. Richmond's southern approaches had always been the Achilles' heel of the Confederate capital. Grant's lunge for the rail nexus at Petersburg was an inspired improvisation that had offered the best promise for the quick victory that the Northern populace expected. In the end, Grant's plans were foiled by the habitual slowness and hesi-

tance of the incurably McClellanized Army of the Potomac, further lamed by the debilitating effects of the hard campaign it had just suffered. For Beauregard these few days in June constituted his finest hours as a Confederate general, as he resourcefully defended Petersburg against what on paper at least appeared to be very long odds. For Lee, the Petersburg operations were proof that even the best of generals could sometimes be fooled by a cunning and resourceful adversary.

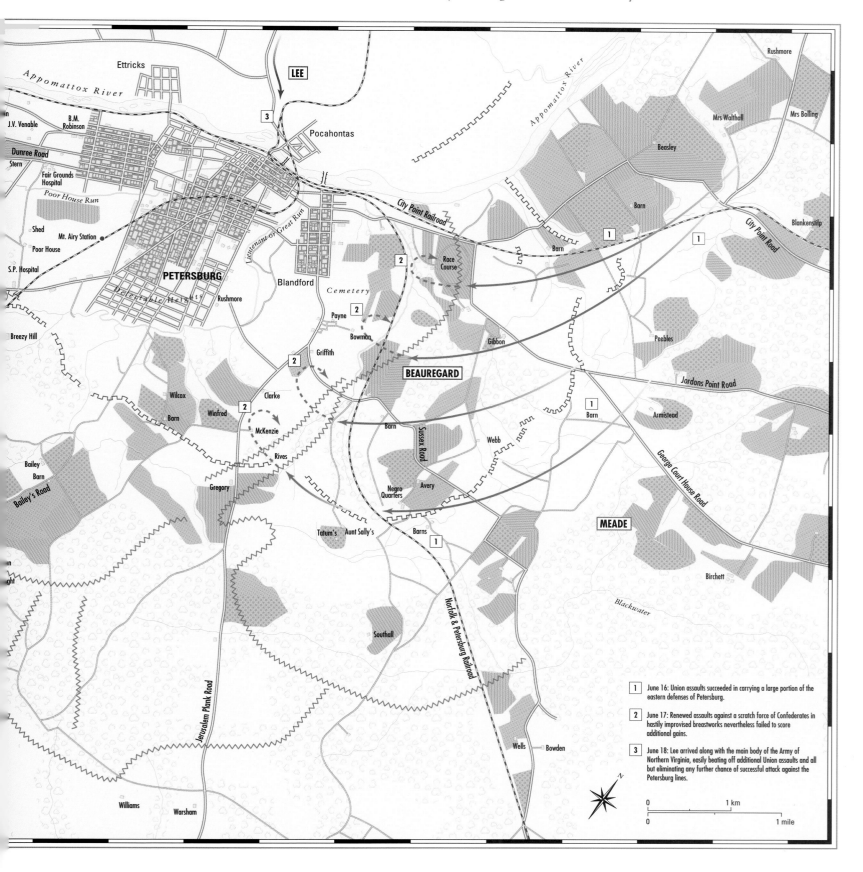

1 June 16: Union assaults succeeded in carrying a large portion of the eastern defenses of Petersburg.

2 June 17: Renewed assaults against a scratch force of Confederates in hastily improvised breastworks nevertheless failed to score additional gains.

3 June 18: Lee arrived along with the main body of the Army of Northern Virginia, easily beating off additional Union assaults and all but eliminating any further chance of successful attack against the Petersburg lines.

SIEGE OF PETERSBURG

AFTER A FINAL ROUND OF ASSAULTS failed to take or even significantly dent the fortified Confederate lines around Petersburg, Virginia, Ulysses S. Grant on June 18, 1864, decided that no alternative remained but to lay siege to that city and Richmond. Grant disliked the slow process of siege work, but with Lee's army having arrived at the Petersburg defenses, no prospect remained for

achieving anything by speedier methods. The Army of the Potomac began to dig elaborate trench systems facing those that Lee's army already occupied, and both armies continued to improve their fortifications.

Grant's goal in the siege was gradually to extend his line all the way around the southern side of Petersburg, cutting off all remaining railroads enter-

1 June 22: Grant sent the Second Corps, now under the command of Major General David Birney in place of the ailing Hancock, to secure the Jerusalem Plank Road and threaten the Weldon Railroad, but Lieutenant General Ambrose P. Hill's Confederate Third drove the Unions back administering a sharp defeat.

2 July 30: Grant's men detonated a large mine under a Confederate fort, but the subsequent infantry assault by Burnside's Ninth was incredibly bungled and resulted in failure and a Union bloodbath.

3 August 18–21: Warren's Fifth Corps seized a section of the Weldon Railroad around Globe Tavern and fought off subsequent Confederate counterattacks by A. P. Hill's corps.

4 September 29–30: Warren's Fifth Corps together with the Ninth Corps, now under the command of Major General John G. Parke, pushed farther west. In the Battle of Peeble's Farm, Hill's Confederate Third Corps drove them back some distance, but the Unions dug in and held at Squirrel Level Road, further stretching Lee's thin lines.

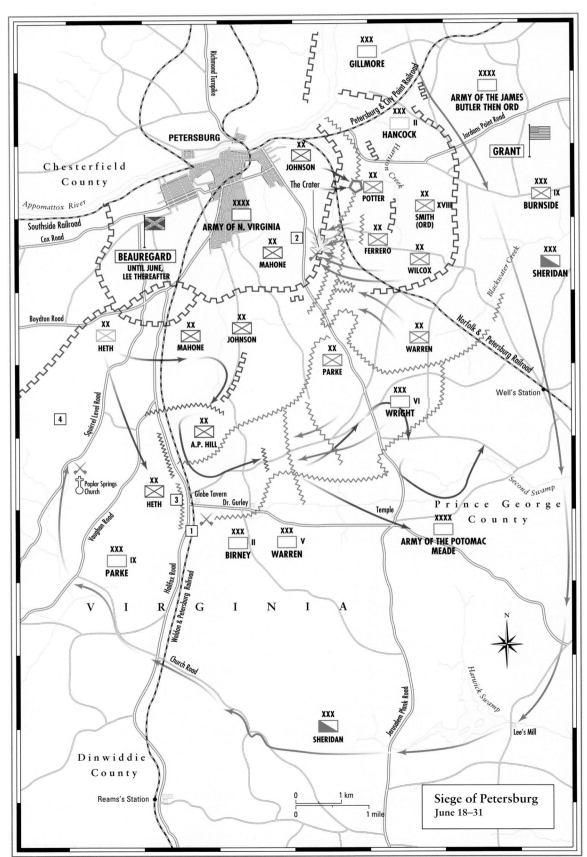

Siege of Petersburg
June 18–31

In the Battle of the Crater, a poorly-trained division led by an incompetent general resulted in a complete failure. The attacking troops shown in this illustration were driven back with heavy losses by a Confederate counterattack.

ing the city from the south. Grant's first operation toward that goal came only a few days into the siege and was aimed at the Weldon Railroad, easternmost of Petersburg's remaining railroad connections. Lee moved to counter Grant's bid for the Weldon, and the result was a June 22 clash at Jerusalem Plank Road, in which Lieutenant General Ambrose Powell Hill's Confederate Third Corps bested Major General David B. Birney's Union Second Corps, taking one thousand seven hundred prisoners.

Grant's next effort was of a different sort. If the Confederate army was stretched far enough to blunt his drive on the Weldon Railroad, he reasoned, perhaps it was thin in the center and could be broken. Some of Grant's subordinates approached him with an unusual plan for doing that. It involved digging a tunnel hundreds of feet long under the no-man's-land between the trenches in order to place a massive gunpowder mine beneath a Confederate strongpoint and blow it up. Mines placed under enemy fortifications by means of tunneling were not new in themselves; Grant's army had used two of them during the Vicksburg siege. Normally, however, besiegers used mines only after spending weeks digging zigzag trenches to within a few feet of the defenders' earthworks. The proposed plan for placing this mine involved a tunnel of unprecedented length, so long that army engineers said it was impossible. The men who had conceived the operation were ordinary infantrymen who had been coal miners in civilian life, and they had no doubt of their ability to carry it out.

With Grant's approval they began digging on June 25 and had completed a tunnel five hundred and eighty-six feet long by July 30. Early that morning the Federals detonated the mine, leaving a crater one hundred and seventy feet long by sixty feet wide and thirty feet deep where a Confederate fort had been. Then followed what was supposed to have been a carefully planned and executed infantry assault by Major General Ambrose Burnside's Ninth Corps in order to exploit the hole in the Confederate line. Abysmal leadership on the part of Burnside and his division commanders turned what should have been a splendid success into a dismal failure. Instead of charging around the crater to roll up the Confederate line on either side and penetrate deep into the defenders' position, most of the attacking Union troops rushed directly into the enormous hole.

Confederate reserves counterattacked and soon gained the rim of the crater, where they could fire down into the almost helpless mass of Union troops inside. One of the Union divisions participating in the attack was composed of black troops, and the Confederates responded by fighting with particular or acute ferocity and in many cases declining to take prisoners. Some black soldiers were killed after having surrendered. The surviving Federals withdrew from the crater that afternoon. Union casualties for what came to be known as the Battle of the Crater totaled about four thousand and Confederate, approximately one thousand five hundred. In his report to Washington the next day, Grant called the operation "the saddest affair I have witnessed in the war."

BATTLES FOR ATLANTA

B Y MID-JULY 1864, THE CONFEDERATE Army of Tennessee under the command of General Joseph E. Johnston had retreated more than ninety miles from Dalton all the way to the outskirts of Atlanta. Jefferson Davis had for several days been seriously weighing the possibility of relieving Johnston of his command and replacing him with a more aggressive general. When Johnston retreated across Peachtree Creek, just outside the city, and declined to provide Davis with any assurance that he would in fact fight to defend Atlanta, the Confederate president, on July 17, replaced him with John Bell Hood, whom he temporarily promoted to full general. A West Point roommate at different times of both Major General John Schofield, current command of the Army of the Ohio, and James B. McPherson, Hood had been an outstanding brigadier in Lee's Army of Northern Virginia. He rose to the rank of division commander before transferring to the Army of Tennessee that spring and taking over a corps. An aggressive leader, Hood lost a leg at Chickamauga and the use of an arm at Gettysburg. Hood would have to be aggressive now, as Johnston had left no more room to retreat without giving up Atlanta. He would now have to meet Sherman's every turning maneuver with an attack of his own.

In fact, Sherman already had a maneuver underway, swinging McPherson's Army of the Tennessee to the east side of the city in order to destroy the Georgia Railroad between Atlanta and Decatur. Hood decided to respond by striking Sherman's center, where Major General George H. Thomas's Army of the Cumberland was just in the process of crossing to the south bank of Peachtree Creek. Hood hoped to catch Thomas's Federals divided and unprepared. On July 20, Hood's troops attacked, but the Battle of Peachtree Creek did not go as Hood had planned. His infirmities prevented him from supervising the operation in person, and the general to whom he assigned that task, Lieutenant General William J. Hardee, was sulking because he had been passed over for command of the army. The movement was slow, late, and poorly coordinated. Thomas's troops were across the creek before the attack struck, and though not entrenched they fought stoutly and repulsed the Confederates. Union casualties totaled one thousand seven hundred and seventy-nine, and Confederate, four thousand seven hundred and ninety-six.

McPherson's Federals reached the Georgia Railroad and began tearing it up. Hood determined to strike again, this time directly at the Army of the Tennessee, between Atlanta and Decatur. Massing near-

ly forty thousand troops against McPherson's approximately twenty-five thousand, Hood sent Hardee's corps on an arduous night march in order to strike the Army of the Tennessee in the rear and on the left flank while other Confederates attacked in front. McPherson had anticipated such a move by his old roommate and had the Sixteenth Corps in position to block Hardee's attack. There was a gap, however, between the Sixteenth Corps and the Seventeenth, next on its right, and the Confederates poured through the gap, killing McPherson and attacking the Seventeenth Corps in rear.

The Federals fought with incredible tenacity, clambering over the breastworks to fight to the rear and as soon as that attack was over, climbing back behind them to beat off and assault from the front, then repeating the process again and again throughout the afternoon. Late in the day, the Confederates scored a breakthrough in the Fifteenth Corps sector, but Union troops rallied under the leadership of the charismatic Major General John A. Logan, who had succeeded McPherson, and hurled back the attackers. The Battle of Atlanta, as it was called, cost the Union three thousand seven hundred and twenty-two men, including the only Union army commander to fall in battle at any time during the war. Confederate losses have been variously estimated from five thousand five hundred to twn thousand, though the latter figure is undoubtedly too high.

After a pause of a few days, Sherman began another turning maneuver, moving the Army of the Tennessee—his "whip-lash" as he called it—around behind the other two Union armies to the west side of Atlanta, where it would be in a position to support Union cavalry striking at the Macon & Western Railroad southwest of Atlanta. Again Hood responded, this time dispatching the corps of lieutenant generals Stephen D. Lee and Alexander P. Stewart to counter the Army of the Tennessee, now commanded by Major General Oliver O. Howard. Once again Hood suffered from his inability to oversee the movement closely in person. The inexperienced Stephen Lee disregarded Hood's admonition not to launch frontal attacks and, on finding Howard's men already occupying a position he wanted, attacked recklessly. Howard's men had just arrived and had not had time to entrench, but in an afternoon of repeated Confederate charges, they won a lopsided defensive victory. Union casualties for this fight, known as the Battle of Ezra Church, totaled six hundred and thirty-two. Confederate losses were approximately three thousand. Hood still held Atlanta, but he had lost more than thirteen thousand men in nine days.

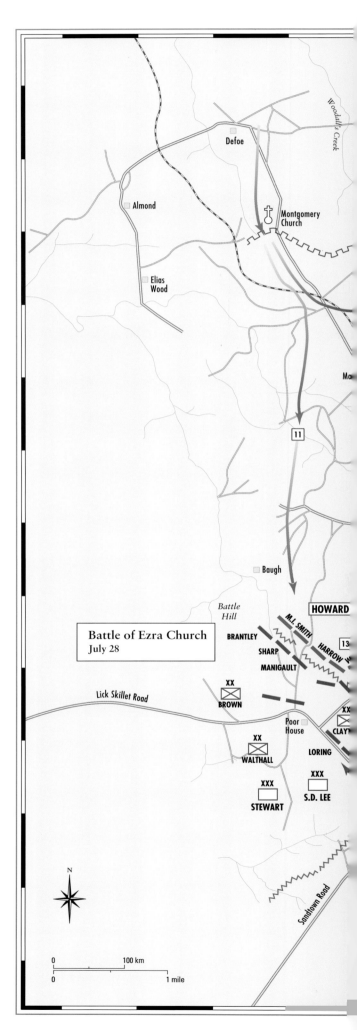

Battle of Ezra Church
July 28

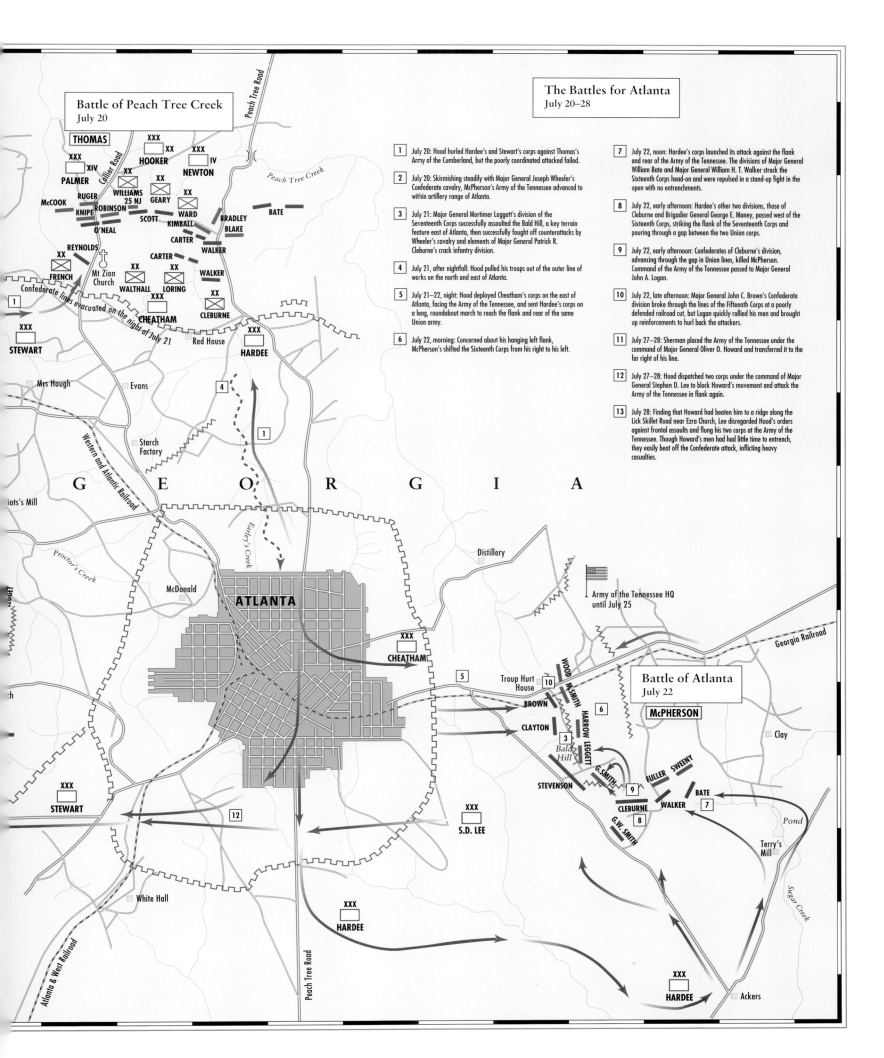

Battle of Peach Tree Creek
July 20

THOMAS

XXX XIV PALMER

XXX HOOKER

XX

XXX NEWTON

IV

Peach Tree Creek

McCOOK

RUGER KNIPE
ROBINSON
O'NEAL

XX WILLIAMS 25 NJ

XX GEARY

SCOTT

XX WARD

KIMBALL

CARTER

BRADLEY BLAKE

BATE

WALKER

REYNOLDS

XX

CARTER

WALKER

FRENCH

Mt Zion Church

XX WALTHALL

XX LORING

WALKER

Confederate lines evacuated on the night of July 21

XX

CHEATHAM

XX CLEBURNE

1

XXX
STEWART

Red House

XXX
HARDEE

Mrs Hough

Evans

4

Starch Factory

1

G   E   O   R   G   I   A

Western and Atlantic Railroad

Proctor's Creek

Early's Creek

iots's Mill

McDonald

ATLANTA

Distillery

Army of the Tennessee HQ until July 25

XXX
CHEATHAM

5

Troup Hurt House

10

WOOD

McSMITH

Georgia Railroad

Battle of Atlanta
July 22

McPHERSON

BROWN

HARROW

6

CLAYTON

3

Bald Hill

LEGGETT

Clay

FULLER

SWEENY

STEVENSON

G. SMITH

9

BATE

7

XXX
STEWART

12

CLEBURNE

8

WALKER

G. W. SMITH

Pond

XXX
S.D. LEE

Terry's Mill

White Hall

XXX
HARDEE

Sugar Creek

Atlanta & West Railroad

Peach Tree Road

XXX
HARDEE

Ackers

The Battles for Atlanta
July 20–28

1. July 20: Hood hurled Hardee's and Stewart's corps against Thomas's Army of the Cumberland, but the poorly coordinated attacked failed.

2. July 20: Skirmishing steadily with Major General Joseph Wheeler's Confederate cavalry, McPherson's Army of the Tennessee advanced to within artillery range of Atlanta.

3. July 21: Major General Mortimer Leggett's division of the Seventeenth Corps successfully assaulted the Bald Hill, a key terrain feature east of Atlanta, then successfully fought off counterattacks by Wheeler's cavalry and elements of Major General Patrick R. Cleburne's crack infantry division.

4. July 21, after nightfall: Hood pulled his troops out of the outer line of works on the north and east of Atlanta.

5. July 21–22, night: Hood deployed Cheatham's corps on the east of Atlanta, facing the Army of the Tennessee, and sent Hardee's corps on a long, roundabout march to reach the flank and rear of the same Union army.

6. July 22, morning: Concerned about his hanging left flank, McPherson's shifted the Sixteenth Corps from his right to his left.

7. July 22, noon: Hardee's corps launched its attack against the flank and rear of the Army of the Tennessee. The divisions of Major General William Bate and Major General William H. T. Walker struck the Sixteenth Corps head-on and were repulsed in a stand-up fight in the open with no entrenchments.

8. July 22, early afternoon: Hardee's other two divisions, those of Cleburne and Brigadier General George E. Maney, passed west of the Sixteenth Corps and poured through a gap between the two Union corps.

9. July 22, early afternoon: Confederates of Cleburne's division, advancing through the gap in Union lines, killed McPherson. Command of the Army of the Tennessee passed to Major General John A. Logan.

10. July 22, late afternoon: Major General John C. Brown's Confederate division broke through the lines of the Fifteenth Corps at a poorly defended railroad cut, but Logan quickly rallied his men and brought up reinforcements to hurl back the attackers.

11. July 27–28: Sherman placed the Army of the Tennessee under the command of Major General Oliver O. Howard and transferred it to the far right of his line.

12. July 27–28: Hood dispatched two corps under the command of Major General Stephen D. Lee to block Howard's movement and attack the Army of the Tennessee in flank again.

13. July 28: Finding that Howard had beaten him to a ridge along the Lick Skillet Road near Ezra Church, Lee disregarded Hood's orders against frontal assaults and flung his two corps at the Army of the Tennessee. Though Howard's men had had little time to entrench, they easily beat off the Confederate attack, inflicting heavy casualties.

EARLY'S WASHINGTON RAID

Lieutenant General Jubal A. Early, whose daring raid into Northern territory lasted from July 5 to August 3.

As Grant drove relentlessly toward Richmond, Lee came to realize by early June that the best result he could likely achieve in that campaign would be a siege of Richmond and that a siege would eventually end with the Federals capturing the city. Only by taking the initiative away from Grant, could Lee hope to disrupt the Union general's inexorable advance. In the past, most notably in the spring of 1862, the Shenandoah Valley had provided the ideal place for Confederate forces in Virginia to do just what Lee needed to do now. The rich farms of the valley could amply supply a Confederate army, and the valley itself, screened from the Virginia piedmont by the towering Blue Ridge, provided an ideal approach to politically sensitive targets north of the Potomac. Because the valley angled to the

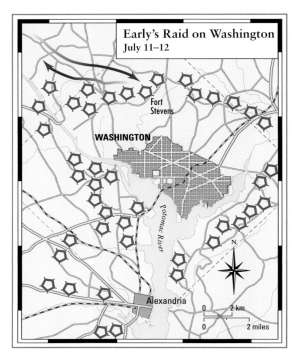

Early's Raid on Washington
July 11–12

northeast, every mile a Confederate army advanced down the valley brought it that much closer to cities such as Harrisburg, Baltimore, and most of all Washington, D.C.

Lee decided to play the valley card once more. On June 11 he detached Lieutenant General Jubal A. Early's fourteen thousand-man Second Corps from the Army of Northern Virginia and sent it to the Shenandoah Valley to defeat the Union army of Major General David Hunter, which was operating there. Then, if possible, Early was to proceed down the valley and threaten Washington. Early met and halted Hunter at Lynchburg, Virginia, on June 17, and then pursued Hunter down the valley. Hunter veered off into the mountains of West Virginia, leaving the valley almost open in front of Early, with only small Union forces to dispute his advance. He, and Lee, could have asked for nothing better.

Early's force marched down the valley, skirmishing occasionally. He threatened Harpers Ferry, found it too strong to take, and crossed the Potomac River on July 5 at Shepherdstown, West

Virginia. Proceeding into Maryland, Early's forces occupied Hagerstown on July 6, demanding twenty thousand dollars in cash and threatening to burn the town if they did not get it. The frightened townspeople paid the money. Still skirmishing occasionally with small Union forces, Early proceeded to take Frederick, Maryland, on July 8. Once again the Confederates held the town for ransom, this time demanding and getting the huge sum of $200,000.

Advancing southeastward from Frederick toward Washington, Early found his way blocked on July 9 at the Monocacy River by a force of six thousand hastily recruited and assembled, and mostly untrained, Union troops under the command of Major General Lew Wallace. Early attacked and, in a battle that lasted most of the day, succeeded in defeating Wallace's inexperienced and badly outnumbered force. Confederate casualties at the Battle of Monocacy totaled about seven hundred, while Union casualties were approximately two thousand, of whom one thousand two hundred were listed as missing. Still Wallace had accomplished exactly what he needed to do at Monocacy, delaying Early's approach to Washington by a full day.

On July 11, Early's force cautiously moved into the suburbs of Washington. His troops burned the house of U.S. Postmaster General Montgomery Blair at Silver Spring, Maryland. Advancing farther, Early's troops skirmished with the defenders of the Washington fortifications. Inside the city, Union authorities called up the District of Columbia militia, armed War Department clerks and invalids, and rushed forward units of the Sixth and Nineteenth corps that had recently arrived by water. President and Mrs. Lincoln visited Fort Stevens and witnessed a minor action between the defenders and Early's men, much to the dismay of Union officers worried about the president's safety.

Early had intended to attack the next day, but by that time there were obviously too many Union troops in the Washington defenses. Wisely Early opted to content himself with extensive skirmishing before beginning his retreat. The decision was wiser than Early knew, as most of the troops he now faced were no longer badly frightened militiamen but the battle-hardened veterans of the Sixth Corps, all of which was now up and in the trenches. Lincoln again came out to witness the proceedings and insisted on peering over the parapet, complete with stovepipe hat, until an exasperated captain in the Twentieth Massachusetts supposedly shouted, "Get down, you fool." The captain's name was Oliver Wendell Holmes, Jr.

Early went back the way he came, having accomplished very little. The raid had failed to break the Union grip on Richmond and Petersburg, where the siege Lee had feared was now almost a month old. Instead, Early's foray and depredations north of the Potomac set in motion Union operations that would eventually neutralize the Shenandoah Valley during the fall of 1864.

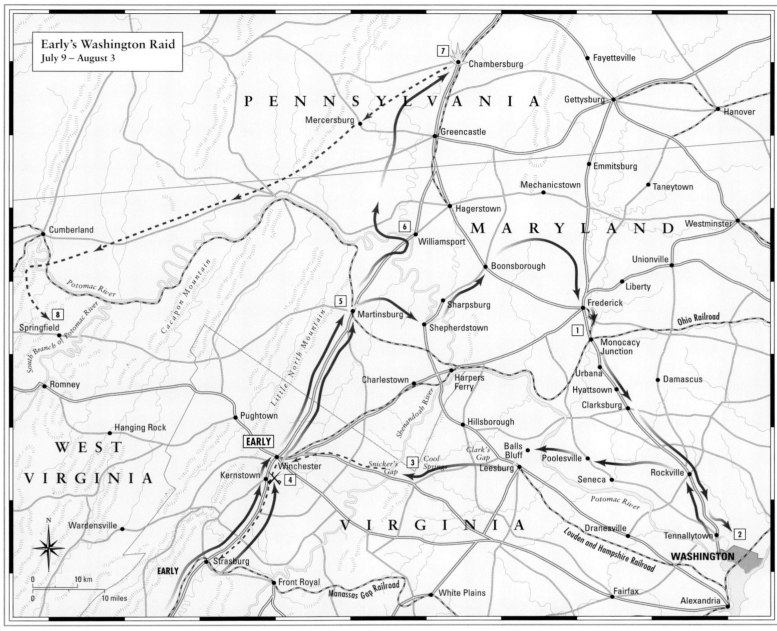

Early's Washington Raid
July 9 – August 3

The unfinished dome of the U.S. Capitol, which would have been just visible on the southwestern horizon to Early's raiding Confederates.

1 July 9: A scratch force of six thousand mostly inexperienced Unionists under the command of Major General Lew Wallace confronted Lieutenant General Jubal Early's eighteen thousand Confederates, barring their path to Washington. Early won the resulting Battle of Monocacy, but Wallace won his real objective, an extra day's delay in Early's march.

2 July 11–12: Early arrived in front of Washington on July 11 and skirmished with the occupants of the city's extensive fortifications. Around noon that day, two divisions of veterans from the Army of the Potomac arrived. The next day, Early began his retreat.

3 July 18: Pursuing Union cavalry under Colonel Joseph Thoburn clashed with Early's rear guard at Cool Spring. Early continued his retreat toward Strasburg.

4 July 24: Early attacked and defeated Major General George R. Crook's Seventh Corps in the Second Battle of Kernstown.

5 July 26: Early's men began wrecking the Baltimore & Ohio Railroad near Martinsburg, West Virginia.

6 July 29: Brigadier General John McCausland's Confederate cavalry detached from Early's command, crossed the Potomac, and headed north with orders from Early to demand $100,000 in gold from the residents of Chambersburg, Pennsylvania, and to burn the town if the ransom was not paid.

7 July 30: McCausland's troopers burned Chambersburg.

8 July 31 – August 3: McCausland made his get-away into West Virginia.

ATLANTA CAMPAIGN, FINAL PHASE

After the battles of Peachtree Creek, Atlanta, and Ezra Church, a lull ensued in the fighting around Atlanta. After the loss of more than thirteen thousand men in nine days, Hood's army was in no condition to undertake offensive operations. Jefferson Davis wrote to Hood to suggest that he refrain from further costly attacks, and Hood probably did not need that admonition. On the other hand, Sherman had problems of his own. Much to his disgust, his cavalry proved incapable of doing serious damage to a railroad. Accomplishing that would require infantry. Yet Sherman found that he could not extend his line far enough to get his infantry astride the Macon & Western Railroad without abandoning of his supply line, which he was loath to do deep in enemy territory. Consequently, for the next four weeks after the Battle of Ezra Church, the two armies faced each other in a sort of quasi-siege. Sherman's troops applied pressure on the Atlanta

defenses with snipers and artillery fire and by gradually advancing their lines.

Finally Sherman decided that bold action was necessary. On August 28 he marched southward, west of Atlanta, with the Army of the Tennessee, the Army of the Ohio, and two of the three corps of the Army of the Cumberland. He left only the Twentieth Corps, under Major General Henry W. Slocum, behind on the north side of Atlanta to provide at least minimal cover for the Union supply line. With the rest of his troops, Sherman marched toward Jonesboro, on the Macon & Western about seventeen miles due south of Atlanta. By August 30, Sherman's forces were approaching their goal. Hood realized his danger and reacted by sending two corps commanded by Lieutenant General Stephen D. Lee and Major General Patrick R. Cleburne, both under the command of Lieutenant General William J. Hardee, to Jonesboro to block Sherman's move.

The next day Hardee's Confederates attacked the Army of the Tennessee at Jonesboro. Major General Oliver O. Howard's troops were well entrenched and ready for them. The result was a dismal repulse for Hardee. Union casualties totaled about one hundred and seventy, while Hardee's force lost approximately one thousand seven hundred and twenty-five men. While Hardee was busy with Howard, Major General John M. Schofield's Army of the Ohio took up a position on the Macon & Western Railroad between Jonesboro and Atlanta, cutting Hood's last line of supply.

A courier brought Hood the bad news late that night, and the following afternoon, September 1, he began evacuating Atlanta. Because his men had no time to remove the large stocks of ammunition stored in the city, they set fire to them, along with a great deal of railroad equipment, instead. Exploding shells and spreading flames made that evening and night hideous for those still in the city of Atlanta. Meanwhile, during the course of September 1, Hardee's forces once again fought with Sherman's troops at Jonesboro but could not restore the rail line and suffered yet another defeat. Hardee withdrew and Sherman pursued as far as Lovejoy Station, on the railroad seven miles south of Jonesboro.

On the morning of September 2 Slocum's Twentieth Corps marched into Atlanta, and Slocum quickly sent word to Sherman that the city was now in Union hands. Sherman decided to content himself with this important capture, abandoned his pursuit of Hood, and pulled his army back to Atlanta to rest and refit. To the authorities in Washington he telegraphed jubilantly, "Atlanta is ours, and fairly won." The fall of Atlanta, more than any other single event, put to rest the Democrats' charge that the war was a failure and helped ensure Lincoln's re-election in November.

In this painting by Thure de Thulstrup, officers and soldiers of the Union army prepare for the final phase of the Atlanta campaign.

MOBILE BAY CAMPAIGN

By 1864, MOBILE, ALABAMA, WAS the most important Confederate port on the Gulf Coast, and an important haven for blockade-runners. Grant included a campaign against Mobile from New Orleans in his master plan for the spring of 1864, but Major General Nathaniel P. Banks's debacle in the Red River campaign prevented it from being carried out by keeping the necessary troops tied up elsewhere. In the summer of 1864 plans for the occupation or at least the neutralization of Mobile again were under way, this time as a combined army-navy operation, in which the navy would play the larger role.

Rear Admiral David G. Farragut led a fleet of eighteen warships from his Gulf Blockading Squadron in the expedition against Mobile. These included four powerful monitors, as well as fourteen conventional steam-powered wooden warships such as Farragut's flagship, U.S.S. *Hartford*. Accompanying Farragut's fleet on transports was a small army force under the command of Major General Gordon Granger.

Brigadier General Richard L. Page commanded the Confederate defenses of Mobile Bay, which were anchored on three forts. Fort Morgan, Page's headquarters, was located on Mobile Point and guarded the main channel into the bay. Fort Gaines lay northwest of Fort Morgan on Dauphin Island, covering the bay's western entrance. Fort Powell, the smallest of the three, was located still farther northwest on Grant Pass in Mississippi. Supporting the forts was a small Confederate naval flotilla under the command of Admiral Franklin Buchanan. Buchanan's squadron included the wooden gunboats

Morgan, *Gaines*, and *Selma*, and the powerful ironclad ram *Tennessee*, possibly the most formidable ironclad ever built by the Confederacy.

Confederate obstructions blocked every channel into Mobile Bay except the main passage, so Farragut determined to lead his fleet right past the guns of Fort Morgan. As he had when he ran the batteries of New Orleans and Port Hudson, Farragut had his fourteen wooden vessels lashed together in twos, side by side, with the stronger ships on the side facing the fort. The stronger ship in each pair thus protected the weaker from most enemy fire, and the weaker vessel could help to propel the stronger if its engines should be disabled. On August 5, 1864, Farragut took his fleet into the bay. At the head of his column, the monitor *Tecumseh* struck a submerged Confederate torpedo and quickly sank with most of its crew. The captain of the next ship in line, the wooden sloop-of-war *Brooklyn*, backed his engines to avoid a similar fate, throwing the column in disarray. From his vantage point in *Hartford*'s mizzen shrouds Farragut shouted, "Damn the torpedoes! Full speed ahead!" and took *Hartford* into the lead. The other Confederate torpedoes were apparently defective or had become so from their long submergence. Farragut's fleet successfully ran through the channel without further losses.

Once the fleet was inside the bay it encountered Buchanan's Confederate squadron. Farragut's ships quickly dealt with the three wooden Confederate gunboats: capturing *Selma*, disabling *Gaines*, and forcing *Morgan* to flee. *Tennessee* was another matter. In an hour-long melee, the Confederate ironclad took on the whole Union fleet. Despite her stout armor, *Tennessee* proved too slow and unwieldy to ram the Union ships and did not have enough firepower to destroy them. Farragut's ships repeatedly rammed *Tennessee* and poured hundreds of rounds into her until at last, with Buchanan wounded and *Tennessee*'s steering chains shot away, the ironclad surrendered.

The Confederate forts did not last long once Farragut's fleet controlled the bay. The Confederates evacuated Fort Powell on the night of August 5, and blew it up. Three days later, Fort Gaines surrendered. The next day Granger's troops began siege operations against Fort Morgan, and on August 23 General Page surrendered. Total Union casualties from the summer campaign at Mobile were three hundred and twenty-seven and Confederate, about one thousand five hundred.

While Farragut's operation closed Mobile Bay to blockade-runners, the city of Mobile itself, an important railroad center, remained defiant throughout the rest of 1864. The city was protected by two strong fortifications just to the northeast known as Spanish Fort and Fort Blakely. Finally, in March 1865, the Union could spare a force sufficient to take on the Mobile forts. Major General Edward R. S. Canby led forty-five thousand troops against the city and succeeded in capturing Spanish Fort on April 8 and Fort Blakely the following day. Occurring on the same day as Lee's surrender at Appomattox, the storming of Fort Blakely was the last major combat of the war.

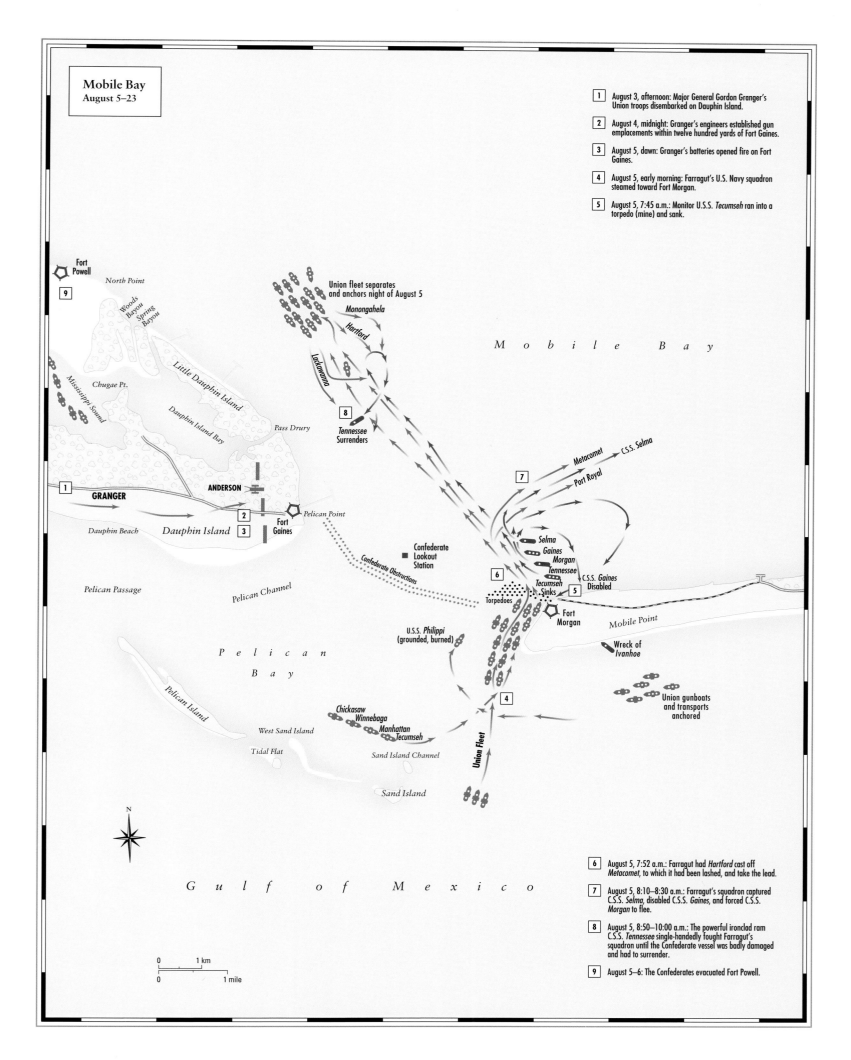

Mobile Bay
August 5–23

1 August 3, afternoon: Major General Gordon Granger's Union troops disembarked on Dauphin Island.

2 August 4, midnight: Granger's engineers established gun emplacements within twelve hundred yards of Fort Gaines.

3 August 5, dawn: Granger's batteries opened fire on Fort Gaines.

4 August 5, early morning: Farragut's U.S. Navy squadron steamed toward Fort Morgan.

5 August 5, 7:45 a.m.: Monitor U.S.S. *Tecumseh* ran into a torpedo (mine) and sank.

6 August 5, 7:52 a.m.: Farragut had *Hartford* cast off *Metacomet*, to which it had been lashed, and take the lead.

7 August 5, 8:10–8:30 a.m.: Farragut's squadron captured C.S.S. *Selma*, disabled C.S.S. *Gaines*, and forced C.S.S. *Morgan* to flee.

8 August 5, 8:50–10:00 a.m.: The powerful ironclad ram C.S.S. *Tennessee* single-handedly fought Farragut's squadron until the Confederate vessel was badly damaged and had to surrender.

9 August 5–6: The Confederates evacuated Fort Powell.

Labels on map:

Fort Powell
North Point
9
Woods Bayou
Spring Bayou
Little Dauphin Island
Chugae Pt.
Mississippi Sound
Dauphin Island Bay
Pass Drury
Union fleet separates and anchors night of August 5
Monongahela
Hartford
Lackawanna
8
Tennessee Surrenders
M o b i l e   B a y
Metacomet
C.S.S. *Selma*
Port Royal
7
Confederate Lookout Station
Selma
Gaines
Morgan
Tennessee
6
Tecumseh Sinks
5
C.S.S. *Gaines* Disabled
Torpedoes
Fort Morgan
Mobile Point
Wreck of *Ivanhoe*
Confederate Obstructions
1
GRANGER
ANDERSON
2
Fort Gaines
3
Pelican Point
Dauphin Beach
Dauphin Island
Pelican Passage
Pelican Channel
U.S.S. *Philippi* (grounded, burned)
P e l i c a n   B a y
Pelican Island
Chickasaw
Winnebaga
Manhattan
Tecumseh
West Sand Island
Tidal Flat
Sand Island Channel
Union Fleet
4
Union gunboats and transports anchored
Sand Island
N
G u l f   o f   M e x i c o

0   1 km
0   1 mile

SHERIDAN AND EARLY IN THE SHENANDOAH VALLEY, PHASE I

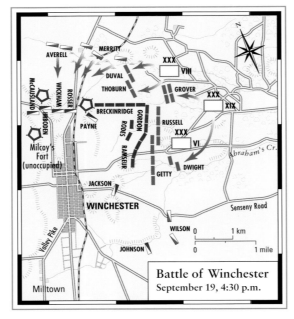

Battle of Winchester
September 19, 4:30 p.m.

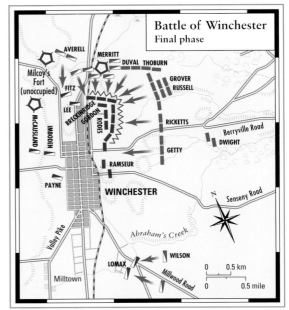

Battle of Winchester
Final phase

THE SHENANDOAH VALLEY HAD BEEN a boon to the Confederacy and a bane to the Union since the war first began. It contained some of the richest farmland on the eastern seaboard, and its farmers made good use of it. Year after year, bumper crops made the valley a rich source of supply for Confederate armies. Furthermore, the Blue Ridge that separated the valley from the rest of Virginia could screen an army there from observation by enemy cavalry to the east. And, because the valley angled from southwest to northeast, it provided an ideal covered approach for Confederate armies mov-

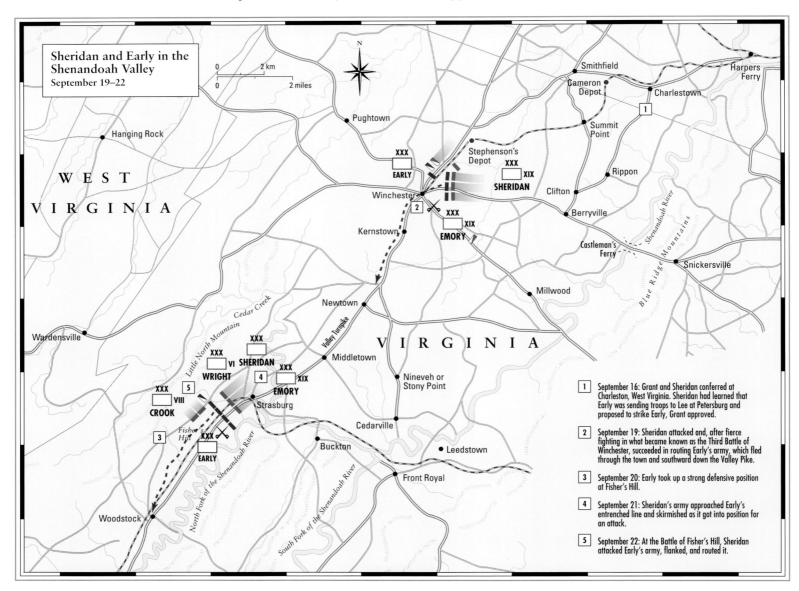

Sheridan and Early in the Shenandoah Valley
September 19–22

1 September 16: Grant and Sheridan conferred at Charleston, West Virginia. Sheridan had learned that Early was sending troops to Lee at Petersburg and proposed to strike Early. Grant approved.

2 September 19: Sheridan attacked and, after fierce fighting in what became known as the Third Battle of Winchester, succeeded in routing Early's army, which fled through the town and southward down the Valley Pike.

3 September 20: Early took up a strong defensive position at Fisher's Hill.

4 September 21: Sheridan's army approached Early's entrenched line and skirmished as it got into position for an attack.

5 September 22: At the Battle of Fisher's Hill, Sheridan attacked Early's army, flanked, and routed it.

ing north to threaten such sensitive Union targets as Washington, Baltimore, and Harrisburg.

The Confederates had used it for that purpose with good effect more than once. In 1862, Stonewall Jackson used the Shenandoah Valley to draw Union troops away from the struggle around Richmond, proceeding northward, down the valley, almost all the way to the Potomac River, giving the North a severe scare. In 1863, Lee had taken his entire army into the Shenandoah Valley for its march north across the Potomac, through Maryland, and into Pennsylvania. The year 1864 had already seen Lee attempt to use the valley as Jackson had in 1862, dispatching Jubal Early's corps to operate there, threaten the North, and distract Union forces. After Early's foray all the way to Washington in that year, Grant became convinced that forceful action was needed to secure the valley and end its usefulness to the Rebels.

During the summer of 1864, Grant dispatched Major General Philip H. Sheridan to the Shenandoah Valley along with most of the Army of the Potomac's cavalry. Sheridan was to take command of the various Federal units that had hitherto been ineffectually operating against Early—the Sixth, Eighth, and Nineteenth corps—and make them into an army that would settle once and for all who controlled the Shenandoah Valley. Sheridan, who had a reputation for extreme aggressiveness, proved fairly deliberate in making his preparations for offensive action in the valley. In mid-September, eager to have Sheridan attack, Grant left his siege lines around Petersburg, Virginia, to travel to Charleston, West Virginia, and confer with Sheridan about operations in the valley. Recent intelligence revealed that Early had begun to send some of his troops back to support Lee at Petersburg. This increased both the feasibility and the desirability of immediate action in the valley, and Grant and Sheridan agreed that the latter should advance at once.

Three days later, on September 19, 1864, Sheridan's forty-thousand-man Army of the Shenandoah struck Early's twelve-thousand-man force at Winchester, where they fought the war's third battle at that location. Early's Confederates, resisting stoutly and, finding a gap in the Union line, appeared briefly on the verge of overcoming the desperate numerical odds against them. Sheridan, however, refused to have victory snatched out of his grasp. Forcefully using his advantage in numbers, he overwhelmed Early's defenders and sent them fleeing through the town and southward up the Valley Pike. Union casualties in the Third Battle of Winchester totaled four thousand and eighteen and Confederate, three thousand nine hundred and twenty-one. Among the Confederate dead was Major General Robert E. Rhodes, one of the Army of Northern Virginia's best division commanders.

The next day, Early halted his retreat, regrouped his army, and took up a strong defensive position at Fisher's Hill, where he had previously built defensive works. Sheridan's army followed closely, skirmishing with the Confederate rear guard several times between Winchester and Fisher's Hill and then coming up in front of Early's position on September 21.

Forty thousand strong, the Union army under Major General Sheridan ravished the Shenandoah Valley denying its agricultural resources to the Confederacy.

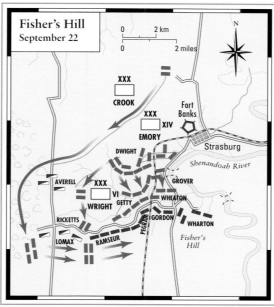

Fisher's Hill
September 22

With his advantage in numbers, Sheridan knew he could probably overwhelm Early's heavily entrenched defenders, though at a very heavy cost. To avoid that cost, Sheridan on September 22 dispatched Major General George Crook's Eighth Corps on a march that by 4:00 p.m. brought it into position for a crushing attack on the Confederate left flank. Early's line crumbled and fled. Union casualties totaled five hundred and twenty eight, while the entrenched Confederates lost one thousand two hundred and thirty-five. Among the Confederate dead this time was Early's chief of staff and one of the Army of Northern Virginia's premier staff officers, Lieutenant Colonel Alexander S. "Sandie" Pendleton. Early's much-weakened army continued its retreat southward, up the valley.

SHERIDAN AND EARLY IN THE SHENANDOAH VALLEY, PHASE II

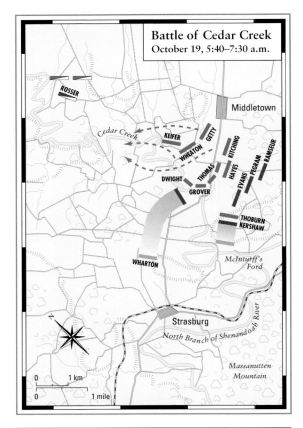

Battle of Cedar Creek
October 19, 5:40–7:30 a.m.

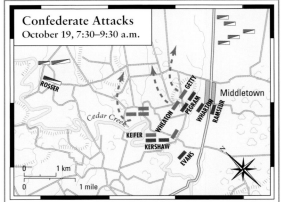

Confederate Attacks
October 19, 7:30–9:30 a.m.

AFTER HIS OVERWHELMING VIC-TORY AT Fisher's Hill, Sheridan pursued Early southward, up the Shenandoah Valley, as far as Staunton, Virginia. Convinced that Early was too badly whipped to undertake any offensive action, Sheridan turned his attention to the valley itself and went to work to carry out Grant's order to render it no longer useful to the Confederacy.

On October 6, he turned his army and set it marching back down the valley. For more than seventy miles, from Staunton to Strasburg, Sheridan's men burned barns, granaries, and mills, and killed or confiscated livestock. The Army of the Shenandoah used what it could and destroyed the rest. Few houses were burned except in the vicinity of an attack by Rebel guerrillas; Union soldiers usually retaliated for guerrilla actions by burning houses. The residents of the valley referred to this unpleasant passage as "the Burning." When it was over, Sheridan boasted that he had fulfilled Grant's instructions to devastate the valley so thoroughly that a crow flying over it would have to carry its own rations. This was not literally true, either for crows or for residents of the valley, but, for the first time in the war, it was true for an army.

Early made ineffectual efforts to hinder Sheridan, following him down the valley at a safe distance. He sent cavalry under Brigadier General Thomas L. Rosser to harass the Federals, but Union Brigadier General Alfred T. A. Torbert's cavalry easily defeated Rosser at Tom's Brook on October 9. Two days later Sheridan encamped his force in a strong defensive position behind Cedar Creek and straddling the Valley Pike not far from Middletown. On October 15, Sheridan turned over command of the army temporarily to Major General Horatio Wright and traveled to Washington to confer about future operations. He left the capital late on the 17th to return to his army, and by the evening of the 18th was at Winchester, Virginia, eleven miles from Middletown.

Early on the morning of October 19, Early, now reinforced to eighteen thousand men, launched a surprise attack that struck the flank and rear of the left wing of the Army of the Shenandoah, rolling it up and driving it back in disorder. The rest of the Union army fought stubbornly but had to fall back about three miles.

Early's triumphant Confederates captured dozens of cannons and about one thousand prisoners and overran the Federal camps. By then, however, the Confederate attack was losing momentum as troops fell out of ranks to plunder the captured camps. Early called a halt around mid-morning, despite the urging of his subordinate Major General John B. Gordon, who advised him to press on and destroy the Army of the Shenandoah.

Meanwhile, hearing the sounds of battle, Sheridan rode from Winchester to Middletown. Meeting disorganized Federals retreating from the morning's defeat, Sheridan called on them to rally and return to the battlefield, which most of them did. Rejoining the army, Sheridan found the Sixth Corps intact and presenting a solid front, while the rest of the army regrouped. At 4:00 p.m. Sheridan was ready to launch his counterattack. When he did, it was the Confederates' turn to be flanked and overwhelmed while fighting bravely. Early's army was crushed and fled back up the valley to Fisher's Hill. Sheridan's army recovered all that it had lost in guns, ground, and prisoners that morning. Conflicting figures abound for the casualties of the battle. Union losses were probably about 2,900 and Confederate losses about 5,700. The drain of high-quality leadership personnel continued in Early's army with the loss of Major General Stephen D. Ramseur, who was mortally wounded in the day's fighting.

The Battle of Cedar Creek concluded the year's campaigning in the Shenandoah Valley. In February 1865, however, Sheridan moved up the Valley again. On March 1 his cavalry skirmished with Early's at Mount Crawford, easily brushing aside the gray-clad horsemen. The following day, Sheridan's cavalry struck again, this time at the main body of Early's force, which was a poor shadow of what it had been the year before. The resulting clash was hardly more than a skirmish, as the Union horsemen rode roughshod over Early's pitiful remnant, capturing seventeen battle flags, two hundred supply wagons, and more than one thousand prisoners. Early himself escaped but his army had ceased to exist as a meaningful fighting force, and the war was over in the Shenandoah Valley.

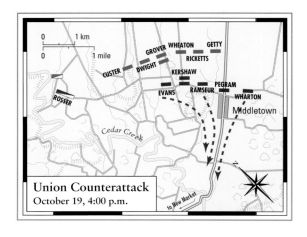

Union Counterattack
October 19, 4:00 p.m.

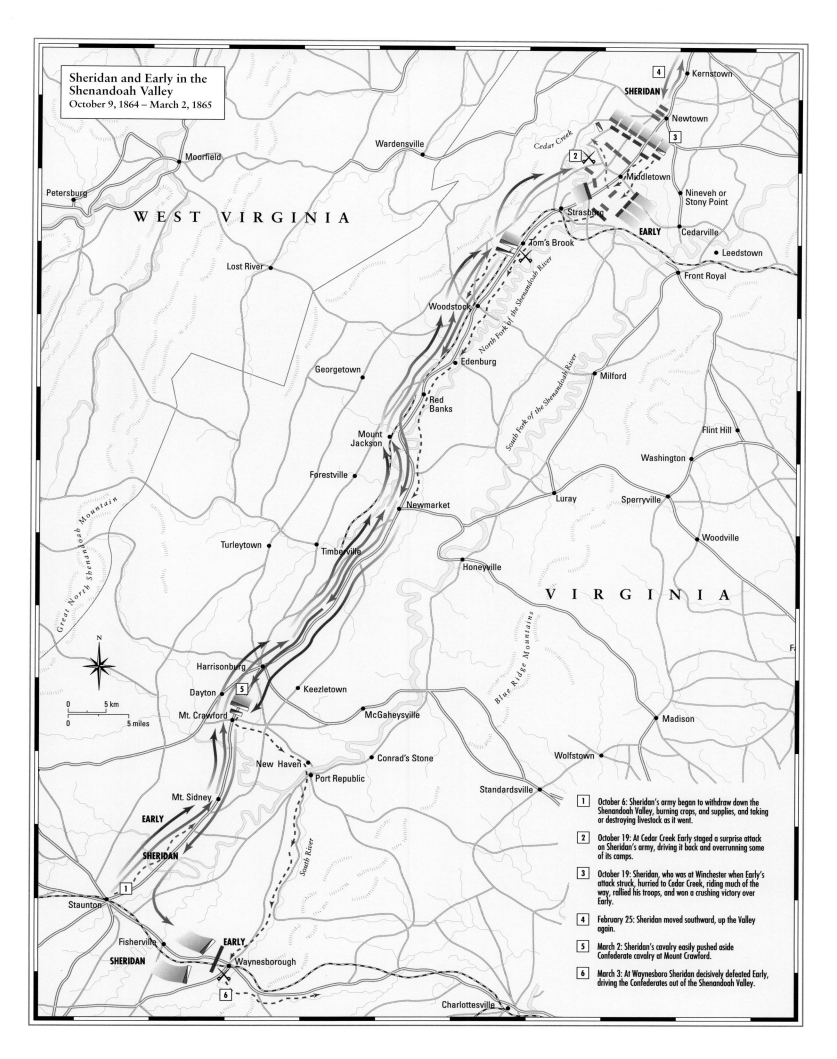

Sheridan and Early in the Shenandoah Valley
October 9, 1864 – March 2, 1865

WEST VIRGINIA

VIRGINIA

Great North Shenandoah Mountain

North Fork of the Shenandoah River

South Fork of the Shenandoah River

Blue Ridge Mountains

Cedar Creek

Moorfield

Petersburg

Lost River

Georgetown

Red Banks

Mount Jackson

Forestville

Turleytown

Timberville

Harrisonburg

Dayton

Mt. Crawford

New Haven

Mt. Sidney

Staunton

Fisherville

Waynesborough

Charlottesville

Wardensville

Woodstock

Edenburg

Newmarket

Keezletown

McGaheysville

Port Republic

Conrad's Stone

Standardsville

Honeyville

Luray

Milford

Flint Hill

Washington

Sperryville

Woodville

Madison

Wolfstown

Tom's Brook

Strasburg

Middletown

Nineveh or Stony Point

Cedarville

Leedstown

Front Royal

Newtown

Kernstown

SHERIDAN

EARLY

EARLY

SHERIDAN

EARLY

SHERIDAN

N

0   5 km
0   5 miles

1 October 6: Sheridan's army began to withdraw down the Shenandoah Valley, burning crops, and supplies, and taking or destroying livestock as it went.

2 October 19: At Cedar Creek Early staged a surprise attack on Sheridan's army, driving it back and overrunning some of its camps.

3 October 19: Sheridan, who was at Winchester when Early's attack struck, hurried to Cedar Creek, riding much of the way, rallied his troops, and won a crushing victory over Early.

4 February 25: Sheridan moved southward, up the Valley again.

5 March 2: Sheridan's cavalry easily pushed aside Confederate cavalry at Mount Crawford.

6 March 3: At Waynesboro Sheridan decisively defeated Early, driving the Confederates out of the Shenandoah Valley.

PRICE'S RAID IN MISSOURI

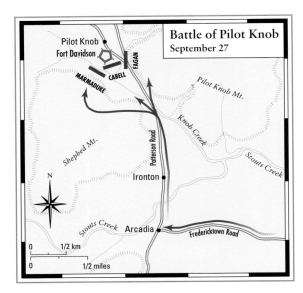

Battle of Pilot Knob
September 27

Fredericktown, ninety miles northeast of Doniphan, Price once again divided his force, sending Shelby's division to destroy the railroad at Mineral Springs. This action would prevent Major General Andrew J. Smith from transporting his Union corps at St. Louis to reinforce a small Union garrison at Ironton, which Price hoped to capture. Advancing toward Ironton with the rest of his force, Price attacked a Union garrison at the town of Pilot Knob, two miles northwest of Ironton, on September 26, but suffered a bloody repulse. The Union force withdrew during the night, and Price pursued briefly before learning that Union major general Alfred Pleasonton was advancing from St. Louis with four thousand five hundred cavalrymen.

Price now had to face the fact that he was not going to take St. Louis or enter Illinois. He continued to hope, however, that by extending his raid

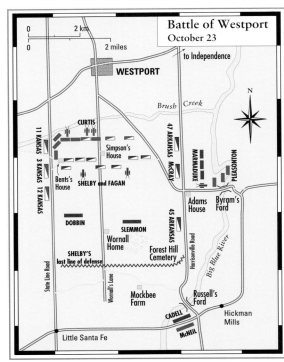

Battle of Westport
October 23

O N AUGUST 29, 1864, CONFEDERATE Major General Sterling Price assumed command of the Army of Missouri at Princeton, Arkansas, with a view to leading an expedition into Missouri and recovering the state for the Confederacy. Thomas C. Reynolds, Missouri's pro-Confederate governor in exile, had proposed such a move the previous July, and Price had recently secured the permission of Confederate Trans-Mississippi commander General Edmund Kirby Smith for an advance to capture St. Louis and then cross the Mississippi River and carry the war into Illinois. Price's army numbered twelve thousand men, all mounted but only about two thirds of them armed. He also had fourteen cannons.

Price began by dividing his force, sending Major General Joseph O. Shelby's division east of Little Rock to make a diversionary strike at DeVall's Bluff, on the Arkansas River, while the other two divisions proceeded west of the Arkansas capital. On September 13, Shelby rejoined the main body at Pocahontas, Arkansas, and the united column crossed into Missouri six days later, skirmishing with Union forces at Doniphan, Missouri. At

deeper into the interior of Missouri, he might draw large numbers of recruits and possibly hurt Northern morale on the eve of the 1864 presidential election. Price opened this phase of the campaign with another diversion, this time sending Shelby on a feint toward St. Louis while the rest of his force headed up the Missouri Valley toward Jefferson City. By the end of the first week in October, Price had reached the vicinity of Jefferson City, but, with Pleasonton in hot pursuit, he chose not to challenge the strong Union garrison in the Missouri capital. Instead, he detoured to the south of the city before turning northwest again and continuing up the Missouri Valley.

Reaching Boonville on October 9, Price dispatched two side expeditions to strike Sedalia and Glasgow. Although his forces captured both towns, they failed to acquire the supply of additional weapons that Price was seeking. By this time it was also clear that the expedition was not attracting recruits. Furthermore, in order to feed his troops, Price had to allow them to forage off

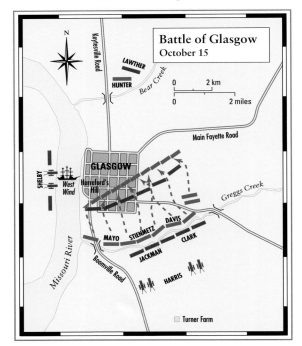

Battle of Glasgow
October 15

the civilian population, which did nothing to win the hearts and minds of the Missouri populace.

On October 18, Price's forces skirmished with advance elements of Major General James G. Blunt's Union column at Lexington, Missouri. At this point, Price became aware that Union troops were closing in on him from several directions. In fact, Blunt's two-thousand-man force was merely the advance guard of Major General Samuel R. Curtis's fifteen-thousand-man Army of the Border. In addition to Curtis, Pleasonton continued to pursue Price, and Smith's corps, after traveling to Sedalia by rail, had joined the pursuit as well. Price hoped to defeat the separate Union columns before they could come together, but the converging Union columns posed a serious threat to the survival of his command. On October 21 he pushed back Blunt's force at the Battle of the Little Blue River. The following day Price had two of his divisions, Shelby's and Major General James F. Fagan's, attack Curtis, while his third division, Brigadier General John S. Marmaduke's, held off Pleasonton. Shelby's and Fagan's men succeeded in opening a potential route of escape for Price's army by forcing a crossing of the Big Blue River

against spirited opposition by Curtis. However, Pleasonton drove Marmaduke's division across the Big Blue behind Shelby and Fagan, placing Price's command in a grave situation, nearly trapped between two converging Union forces.

October 23, Price made a desperate attempt to break out of the trap that was closing around him. Again Shelby attacked Curtis's force while Marmaduke tried to hold off Pleasonton. In what became known as the Battle of Westport (now part of Kansas City), both Confederate forces suffered defeat. Only a skillful rearguard action by Shelby prevented a complete rout. Each side lost about one thousand five hundred killed and wounded, but Price lost hundreds of prisoners and dozens of wagons. Union forces pursued and defeated Price again on October 25 at Mine Creek and the Marais des Cygnes River, on the Kansas side of the state line. The Federals took more wagons and prisoners and forced Price to burn a third of his wagons in order to escape. Union forces broke off the pursuit on October 28. Price returned to Confederate territory at Bonham, Texas, on November 23, with about eight thousand weary men.

[1] September 19: Price launched his raid from Pocahontas, Arkansas, crossing into Missouri the first day and skirmishing with Union troops at Doniphan, Missouri.

[2] September 27: Price attacked Fort Davidson, but the one thousand two hundred-man garrison under Brigadier General Thomas Ewing, Jr., repulsed him and then escaped quietly during the night.

[3] October 9: After several days of skirmishing, Price decided the fortifications of Jefferson City were too strong and by-passed it, still heading northwest.

[4] October 9–15: Within the space of a week Price's raiders hit Booneville, Sedaliam, and Glasgow, all against light to negligible Union opposition and with few casualties.

[5] October 23: Just outside Kansas City Price's eight thousand-man force was caught between the converging Union columns of Major General Samuel Curtis and Major General Alfred Pleasonton with a combined strength of twenty thousand men. Thoroughly defeated, Price turned tail for Arkansas.

[6] October 25: Pleasonton caught up with Price at the Marais des Cynges River and administered another stinging defeat to hurry the Confederate raiders on their way south.

[7] November 1: With Price safely back at Cane Hill, Arkansas, the ill-conceived raid was finally over.

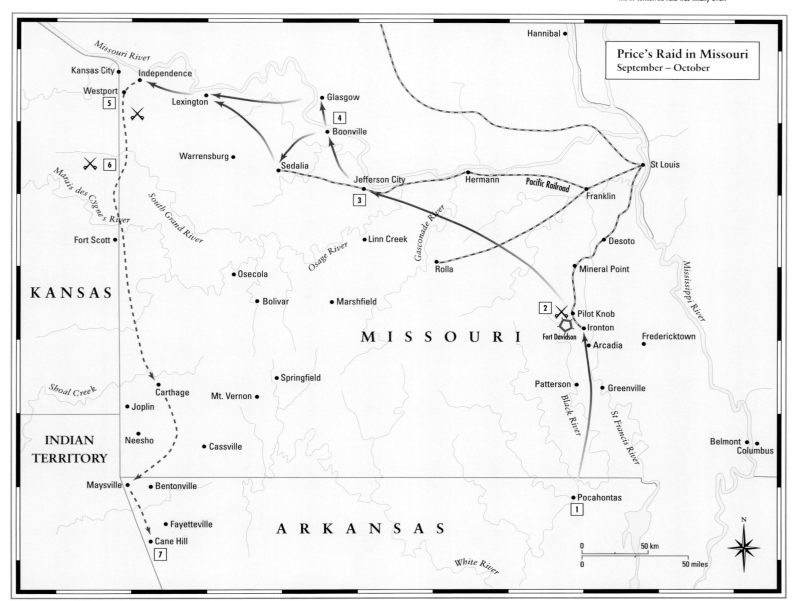

Price's Raid in Missouri
September – October

HOOD'S TENNESSEE CAMPAIGN

Part of Thomas's Army of the Cumberland—western armies were somewhat individualistic or less polished in appearance then their eastern counterparts.

AFTER THE FALL OF ATLANTA IN September 1864, Hood took his Confederate Army of Tennessee into northwestern Georgia to threaten Major General William T. Sherman's supply lines there. For several weeks the two armies maneuvered through the region, Hood never quite able to wreak decisive damage to Sherman's railroad and depots and Sherman never quite able to catch and destroy Hood's army. Ironically, both generals tired of the game at about the same time, each deciding on a bolder strategy. For Sherman, that bolder strategy was the March to the Sea, and for Hood, his Tennessee campaign, aimed at taking Nashville.

On October 17, Hood turned his army away from Sherman's railroad and marched west. Much depended on how fast Hood carried out his plan. Tennessee was defended by Major General George H. Thomas, with the Fourth and Twenty-third corps, plus the troops of various garrisons in the state that he would have to pull together to form his army. It would take him several weeks to complete that task, and those weeks would be Hood's opportunity. Hood's first problem was finding a suitable point to cross the Tennessee River. The search finally carried him as far west as Tuscumbia, Alabama. Hood also needed to wait for supplies, which further delayed the operation, and it was not until November 21 that his army marched north from the Tennessee River.

By that time, Thomas was almost ready to receive him. To gain the additional time he felt he still needed, Thomas posted Major General John M. Schofield with twenty-eight thousand men at Pulaski, Tennessee, to delay Hood's march into the state. Hood bypassed Pulaski on the west and tried to reach Columbia, Tennessee, ahead of Schofield. At Columbia the road from Pulaski to Nashville crossed the Duck River, and if Hood could get there first Schofield would be cut off. If Hood could destroy Schofield's army, he would be one very large step closer to fulfilling his plan for conquering Middle Tennessee, as Schofield's force represented a very

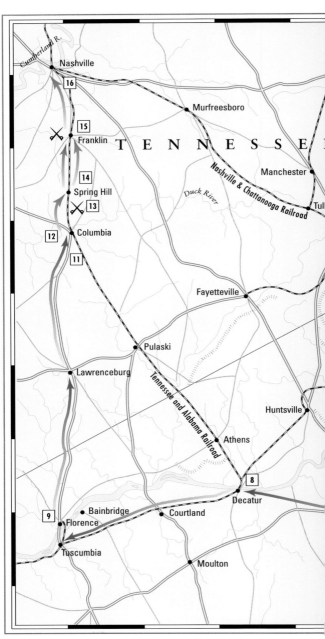

large portion of Thomas's overall strength.

On November 26, however, Hood reached Columbia to find Schofield's army already there. Hood planned another turning maneuver in hopes of getting around Schofield and trapping his army. Expecting such a movement, Schofield on the night of November 27–28 pulled his army back to the north bank of the Duck. Despite Schofield's preparations, Hood managed to pull off a surprise movement. Leaving one of his army's three corps to skirmish with the Federals in the vicinity of Columbia on November 29, Hood took the other two on a wide flanking march. The corps crossed the Duck River east of Columbia and raced northward for the town of Spring Hill, which lay astride the road to Nashville north of Schofield's position.

The plan worked to perfection--almost. By mid-afternoon Hood's troops began arriving at Spring Hill, while Schofield remained largely oblivious to his danger. Then as darkness gathered Hood's plan somehow went awry. Hood had ordered his generals to take Spring Hill, which was moderately well defended by a small garrison. Simply seizing the turnpike south of Spring Hill would have been relatively easy and just as effective at blocking Schofield's escape route. Instead, the Confederate generals became confused, skirmished ineffectually with the Union defenders of Spring Hill, and halted for the night a few hundred yards short of the turnpike. Hood, who was at the very least exhausted from his day's long ride strapped in the saddle (he had an artificial leg), went to bed without straightening out the situation. During the night, Schofield's entire army and wagon train marched across Hood's front within as little as two hundred yards of his men's campfires.

The next morning when Hood learned that the enemy had escaped he was furious and ordered an immediate pursuit. He caught up with Schofield at Franklin, thirteen miles north of Spring Hill, where Schofield had turned at bay with the Harpeth River at his back. Schofield needed a few hours for his engineers to repair the bridges over the Harpeth so that he could continue his retreat to Nashville. Hood determined to attack at once, without even waiting for his artillery and the corps he had left at Columbia to catch up. At about 4:00 p.m. he launched his entire force on hand—about twenty-five thousand men—in a frontal assault against Schofield's well-entrenched Federals, some of whom were armed with repeating rifles. The Confederates continued their attack until long after nightfall, without success. Union casualties totaled two thousand three hundred and twenty-six, while Hood's army lost six thousand two hundred and fifty-two, including six generals killed or mortally wounded. During the night Schofield's army crossed the Harpeth and continued to Nashville.

Hood's Tennessee Campaign
October 1 – November 30

1. September 29–30: Intent on a campaign against Sherman's lines of communication in North Georgia, Hood led his army across the Chattahoochee River and marched north.

2. October 2: Sherman left the Tenth Corps to hold Atlanta and pursued Hood with the rest of his force.

3. October 3–4: Hood's Confederates captured Big Shanty and broke the railroad.

4. October 5: The Confederates attacked the supply depot at Allatoona Pass, which was heroically defended by a small Union force under the command of Brigadier General John Corse.

5. October 13: Hood struck again, this time capturing the Union garrison at Dalton, Georgia.

6. October 14–15 : Hood retreated to Gadsden, Alabama.

7. October 14–15 : Sherman pursued Hood as far as Gaylesville and there halted.

8. October 26: Intent on his new plan of invading Tennessee, Hood reached Decatur, Alabama, hoping to cross the Tennessee River there, but found the north bank held by the Union force in too much force to allow a crossing.

9. October 30: Stephen D. Lee's Confederate corps, leading the advance of Hood's army, crossed the Tennessee River and occupied Florence, Alabama.

10. November 15: Having given up on chasing Hood and returned to Atlanta, Sherman this day began his March to the Sea.

11. November 27: Hood's army approached the Union army of Major General John M. Schofield near Columbia, Tennessee.

12. November 28: Concerned that Hood might cut him off from Nashville, Schofield retreated to the north bank of the Duck River.

13. November 29: Hood did indeed plan to trap Schofield and on this day led his army in a hard march around the Union army, beating Schofield to Spring Hill but, incredibly, failing to secure either the town on the pike that ran through it.

14. November 29–30 , night: Schofield's army escaped, marching along the pike in the darkness within a few hundred yards of Hood's camps. Hood had turned in early and slept through the entire episode.

15. November 30: Hood pursued Schofield to Franklin, where the Union troops waited in pre-existing entrenchments while their engineers re-built a bridge over the Harpeth River. Hood attacked but his troops were repulsed with disastrous slaughter.

16. November 30 – December 1, night: Schofield withdrew without difficulty and completed his planned march to Nashville.

SIEGE OF RICHMOND

Attack on Fort Harrison
September 28

THE SIEGE OF RICHMOND BEGAN more or less simultaneously with the siege of Petersburg. When Grant began his operations against the latter city, which was the nexus of Richmond's railroad supply lines, it was natural for him at the same time to mount siege operations against neighboring Richmond as well. Grant's primary focus continued to be on Petersburg, where his ultimate hope of breaking the Confederate hold on the capital city of Virginia lay in extending his lines far enough to the west to cut the last of the railroads leading into Richmond from the south. Operations directly in front of the Richmond fortifications during the ten months of the siege tended to be aimed at distracting Lee's attention from other operations south of the James River. However, Grant would have been perfectly content to accept a major breakthrough along the Richmond lines, and

Maryland. On September 29 troops of the Major General David Birney's Tenth Corps and Major General E. O. C. Ord's Eighteenth Corps crossed to the north bank of the James and launched very serious attacks against Fort Harrison and Fort Gilmer. The importance of the operation was underscored by the fact that both Lee and Grant were on hand personally to direct the activities of their troops in this sector. A Union division under Brigadier General George Stannard succeeded in capturing Fort Harrison and holding it against Confederate counterattacks the next day, but the Union attackers of Fort Gilmer were unsuccessful in their assault. Total Union casualties for the operation came to three thousand three hundred and twenty-seven. Confederate losses are unknown.

Lee was not content to let Grant retain the threatening position his troops had gained in the fighting around the end of September. One week later he launched an assault of his own along the Darbytown and New Market roads aimed at driving the Federals back from their important positions around Fort Harrison. Fighting raged around Johnston's Farm

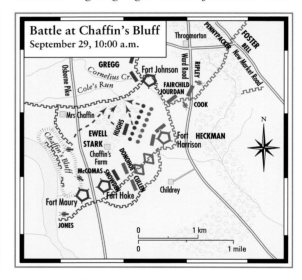

Battle at Chaffin's Bluff
September 29, 7:00 a.m.

Battle at Chaffin's Bluff
September 29, 10:00 a.m.

any of his feints north of the James were ready to become entirely earnest attacks of the Confederate defenders gave way.

The first such operation took place in late July 1864 and was aimed at drawing Lee's attention away from the impending Union operations that led to the July 30 Battle of the Crater on the Petersburg front. On July 27, Major General Winfield S. Hancock's Second Corps crossed to the north bank of the James River along with two divisions of cavalry under the command of Major General Philip Sheridan, and staged a feint against Confederate fortifications along the New Market Road in the vicinity of Deep Bottom. The relatively insignificant battle was also known as Darbytown and Strawberry Plains. On July 29, Hancock and Sheridan pulled their forces back to the south bank of the James.

Two months later Grant again ordered an operation north of the James, both to distract Lee from another grab at his southside rail connections and also to insure that the Confederate commander would not detach more of his troops to reinforce Lieutenant General Jubal A. Early's operations in

and Four-Mile Creek. Despite some initial successes, Lee's attacks failed, and the Federal continued to hold Fort Harrison and its environs, making Lee's task of holding Richmond more difficult. Still, the deadlock around the Virginia capital continued through the winter of 1864–1865 and was not broken until Confederate defeats south of the James River finally forced the evacuation of Richmond on April 2, 1865.

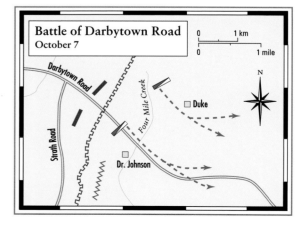

Battle of Darbytown Road
October 7

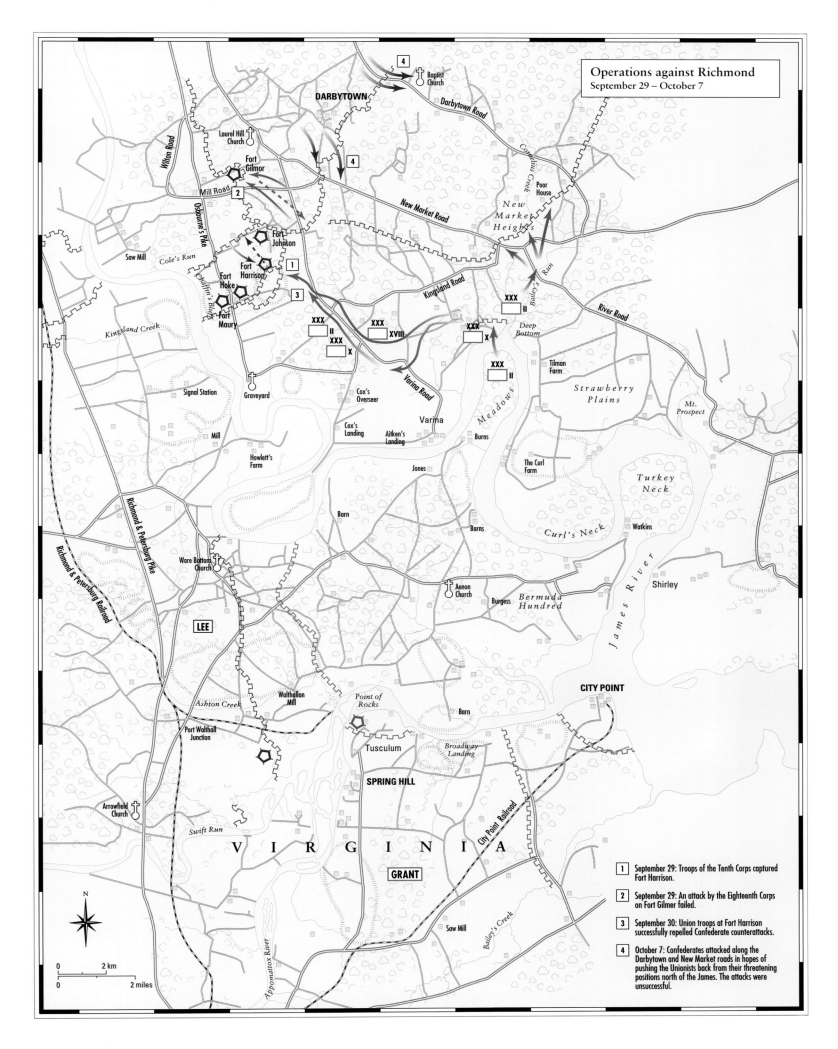

Operations against Richmond
September 29 – October 7

1 September 29: Troops of the Tenth Corps captured Fort Harrison.

2 September 29: An attack by the Eighteenth Corps on Fort Gilmer failed.

3 September 30: Union troops at Fort Harrison successfully repelled Confederate counterattacks.

4 October 7: Confederates attacked along the Darbytown and New Market roads in hopes of pushing the Unionists back from their threatening positions north of the James. The attacks were unsuccessful.

OPERATIONS IN THE SHENANDOAH VALLEY

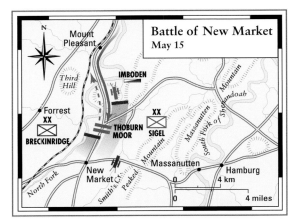

Battle of New Market
May 15

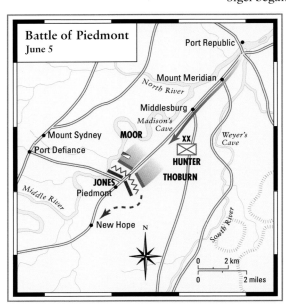

Battle of Piedmont
June 5

ONE OF THE FIVE PARTS OF GRANT'S coordinated 1864 offensive was to be an advance up the Shenandoah Valley. Unfortunately, command of the expedition went to Major General Franz Sigel. A graduate of a German military academy and veteran of service in the army of the Duke of Baden, Sigel had never shown the least spark of competence during the Civil War. Rather his repeated promotions had come because of his great popularity among his fellow ethnic Germans. Grant hoped he would prove adequate to the task of advancing through the lightly defended Shenandoah Valley.

Sigel began his advance in early May, simultaneous with the other components of Grant's great offensive. At first his army advanced easily, with only light opposition from Confederate cavalry commanded by Brigadier General John D. Imboden. By May 14, however, a skirmish at Rude's Hill betokened stiffening resistance produced by the arrival of an additional five thousand Confederate troops under the command of Major General John C. Breckinridge. The following day Breckinridge attacked Sigel at New Market. About five thousand five hundred Union troops faced some five thousand Confederates, including a contingent of two hundred and forty-seven cadets from the Virginia Military Institute. Breckinridge was victorious, and Sigel retreated to Strasburg, Virginia. Union casualties at the Battle of New Market totaled eight hundred and thirty-one and, Confederate five hundred and seventy-seven, including fifty-seven cadets.

After this debacle Union authorities sacked Sigel, replacing him on May 21 with Major General David Hunter. They also reinforced the Union army in the Shenandoah Valley to some sixteen thousand men. With this force Hunter advanced from Strasburg on May 26, marching toward Staunton, Virginia. Opposing him by this time was Breckinridge's replacement, Major General W. E. "Grumble" Jones, with eight thousand five hundred men. The two forces clashed at Covington, Virginia, on June 2, but Jones failed to halt Hunter's advance. Three days later Jones tried again at Piedmont, where a fierce battle developed. When it was over, Jones was dead, and his army had suffered defeat, with one thousand six hundred casualties, including about one thousand captured. Union casualties totaled seven hundred and eighty. Hunter followed up his victory by occupying Staunton.

On June 10, Hunter once again took up his advance and the next day entered Lexington,

Virginia, where his troops burned the buildings of the Virginia Military Institute. Virginians seethed with anger at Hunter for this act and because they believed that his soldiers had not been sufficiently respectful of civilian property during their advance. In fact, any Union commander making that campaign would have received the same opprobrium, for by that stage of the war the Union soldiery were finished with the concept of protecting the property of obviously hostile civilians who gave aid and comfort to the enemy.

By June 16, Hunter's forces were investing Lynchburg, which was defended by Breckinridge. On the following day, Breckinridge was joined by Lieutenant General Jubal Early and the Second Corps of the Army of Northern Virginia, which Lee had detached from his hard-pressed army near Richmond in order to take the offensive in the Shenandoah Valley and thus seize the initiative in the eastern theater of the war. Learning of Early's arrival, Hunter immediately put his own forces in retreat. Early pursued closely, and several skirmishes occurred as the armies proceeded down the valley.

Hunter opted not to continue his retreat all the way to the lower end of the valley but rather to turn to the northwest and withdraw into the mountains of West Virginia. That move was at least successful in getting his force out of Early's way, as the Confederate commander had more important business along the direct route to Washington. Hunter's turn into West Virginia left Early's path wide open for a dramatic raid across the Potomac. By June 26, Early and his fourteen thousand men had reached Staunton, and, after a day's rest there, they proceeded on their northward march. By the end of the month they were passing through New Market, scene of Sigel's discomfiture six weeks before, still marching rapidly toward the Potomac. In Washington, Early's advance became a matter of deep concern.

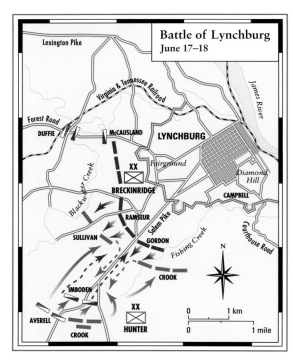

Battle of Lynchburg
June 17–18

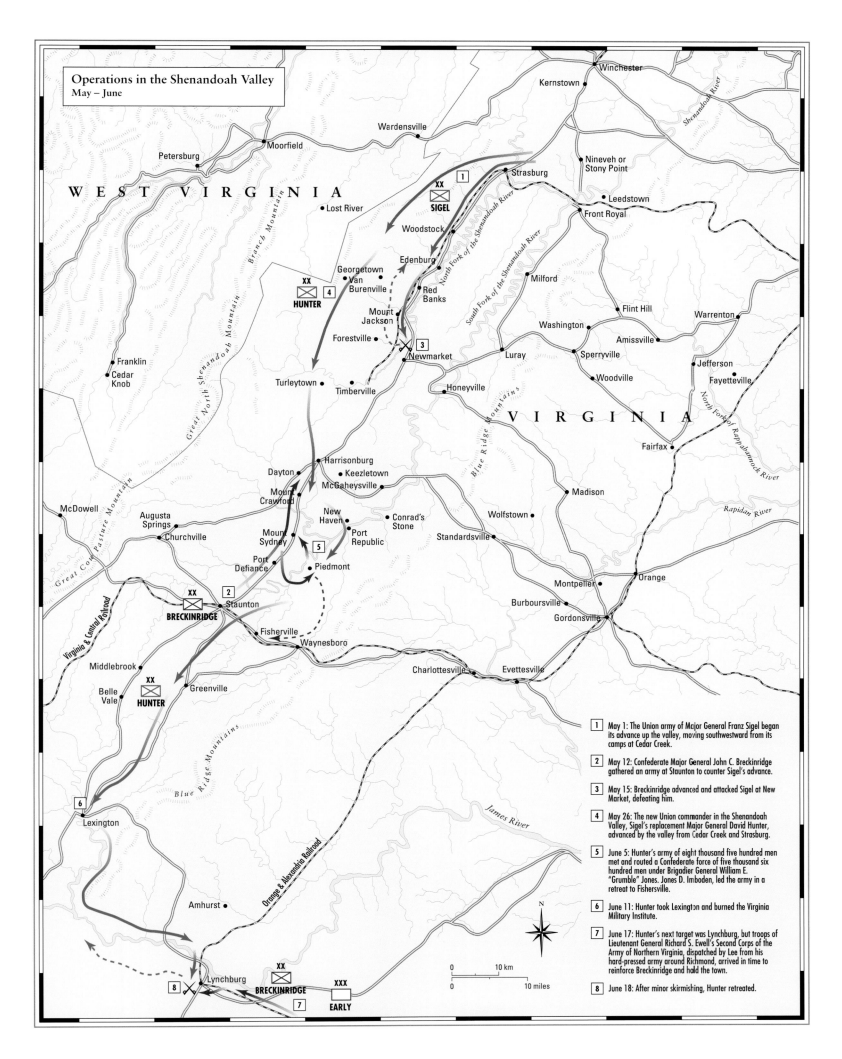

Operations in the Shenandoah Valley
May – June

WEST VIRGINIA

VIRGINIA

XX
SIGEL 1

XX
HUNTER 4

XX
BRECKINRIDGE 2

XX
HUNTER

6

8

XX
BRECKINRIDGE

XXX
EARLY

7

1 May 1: The Union army of Major General Franz Sigel began its advance up the valley, moving southwestward from its camps at Cedar Creek.

2 May 12: Confederate Major General John C. Breckinridge gathered an army at Staunton to counter Sigel's advance.

3 May 15: Breckinridge advanced and attacked Sigel at New Market, defeating him.

4 May 26: The new Union commander in the Shenandoah Valley, Sigel's replacement Major General David Hunter, advanced by the valley from Cedar Creek and Strasburg.

5 June 5: Hunter's army of eight thousand five hundred men met and routed a Confederate force of five thousand six hundred men under Brigadier General William E. "Grumble" Jones. Jones D. Imboden, led the army in a retreat to Fishersville.

6 June 11: Hunter took Lexington and burned the Virginia Military Institute.

7 June 17: Hunter's next target was Lynchburg, but troops of Lieutenant General Richard S. Ewell's Second Corps of the Army of Northern Virginia, dispatched by Lee from his hard-pressed army around Richmond, arrived in time to reinforce Breckinridge and hold the town.

8 June 18: After minor skirmishing, Hunter retreated.

Winchester

Kernstown

Nineveh or Stony Point

Wardensville

Strasburg

Leedstown

Front Royal

Moorfield

Petersburg

Lost River

Woodstock

Edenburg

Red Banks

Milford

Georgetown
Van Burenville

Mount Jackson

Forestville

Newmarket 3

Flint Hill

Washington

Warrenton

Amissville

Franklin

Cedar Knob

Turleytown

Timberville

Luray

Sperryville

Woodville

Jefferson

Fayetteville

Honeyville

Harrisonburg

Keezletown

Dayton

McGaheysville

Fairfax

Madison

Mount Crawford

New Haven

Conrad's Stone

Wolfstown

McDowell

Augusta Springs

Churchville

Mount Sydney

Port Republic 5

Standardsville

Port Defiance

Piedmont

Montpelier

Orange

Staunton

Burboursville

Gordonsville

Fisherville

Middlebrook

Waynesboro

Greenville

Charlottesville

Evettesville

Belle Vale

Lexington

Amhurst

Lynchburg

James River

Rapidan River

N

0   10 km
0   10 miles

Sherman's March from Atlanta to the Sea

After the fall of Atlanta, Sherman's army spent the next two months chasing Hood away from its lines of communication in northwestern Georgia. Sherman, among others, grew tired of that activity. He realized that his forces would probably never catch Hood's smaller army, that current operations were doing nothing to win the war, and that if his army continued attempting to guard its own supply lines, it would never be able to accomplish anything else as deep as it now was in Confederate territory. Rather than continue in the same manner, Sherman decided to do something radically different; he determined to cut loose of his supply lines and march across Georgia to either Savannah or Mobile. Along the way his army would, as in the Meridian campaign of the preceding February, destroy railroads, depots, factories, and other military or industrial targets, while foraging its food off the countryside. With some difficulty, Sherman persuaded Grant to allow him to undertake such an operation.

In preparation for the coming campaign Sherman reorganized his forces. He sent Thomas back up to Tennessee with the Fourth and Twenty-third corps to deal with Hood. The Fourteenth and Twentieth Corps, now comprising the Army of Georgia, he assigned to Major General Henry W. Slocum, who would command the left wing of the march through Georgia. Oliver O. Howard continued to command the Fifteenth and Seventeenth Corps, which comprised the Army of the Tennessee and formed the right wing of the march. The combined strength of Slocum's and Howard's corps totaled about sixty thousand men.

On November 14, before leaving Atlanta, Sherman's troops tore up the tracks and burned the roundhouse, machine shops, and other facilities of the Georgia Railroad as well as a Confederate ammunition depot. Some of the fires spread, and a number of other buildings were destroyed, though by no means the bulk of the city. The fires continued to smolder on November 15 and 16 as Sherman's troops marched out of Atlanta headed east and south, some of them singing, "John Brown's Body Lies a Mouldering in the Grave." The song commemorated the violent abolitionist who in 1859 staged a bloody raid on the Harpers Ferry arsenal in hopes of sparking a slave uprising. Brown went to the gallows convicted of insurrection, but within two years of Brown's execution, thousands of Union troops declared in song that they were singing, although the fiery abolitionist's body was "a mouldering in the grave," and that they were carrying on his fiery abolitionist's work by "marching on." As Sherman sat on his horse listening to the passing soldiers and looking back toward the pillars of smoke still rising over Atlanta, it occurred to him that he had never heard the John Brown song "done with more spirit, or in better harmony of time and place."

The two wings of Sherman's army traveled about sixty miles apart on parallel roads. Opposing Sherman was the cavalry of the Confederate Army of Tennessee under the command of Major General Richard Wheeler, as well as the Georgia militia. Sherman's army was much more powerful than these forces, but he could not afford prolonged fighting, as his troops had to keep moving in order to take in sufficient forage. In order to confuse the enemy, Sherman feinted toward Augusta on the east and Macon on the west but then took his forces between those towns, with Slocum's left wing passing through the state capital at Milledgeville. Sherman's cavalry under Major General Judson Kilpatrick helped to fend off Wheeler's horsemen.

Sherman's soldiers became adept at finding and

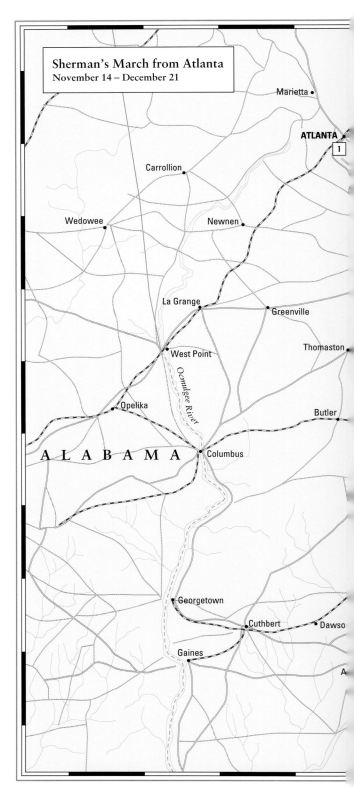

gathering up foodstuffs, even while the army continued to march ten or twelve miles per day. Each morning regimental commanders dispatched foraging parties that ranged far ahead and to either side of the column and then returned to the regiment toward evening, often bringing their large haul of victuals in commandeered farm wagons or buggies. All along the route, the troops destroyed military targets as planned. Occasionally other structures went up in flames, including the house and plantation buildings of Confederate cabinet member Howell Cobb. Throughout the march, Georgian citizens were completely secure. Murder,

rape, or other assaults were practically unknown. Untold tens of thousands of slaves fled their plantations on the approach of Sherman's troops and fell in behind the marching column.

At Griswoldville, Georgia, on November 21, a division of the Georgia militia attacked a brigade of the Army of the Tennessee. Howard's veterans easily repulsed the attack, and the march continued unabated. On December 10, Sherman's army arrived outside of Savannah. Three days later Sherman had one division assault the Confederate Fort McAllister, which fell in less than an hour. The capture of Fort McAllister opened the

1. November 16: Having destroyed military and industrial facilities in Atlanta, Sherman set out on his March to the Sea.

2. November 22: Slocum's wing of Sherman's force occupied the Georgia state capital at Milledgeville.

3. November 22: One brigade of Howard's wing defeated a division of Confederate militia at Griswoldville.

4. December 10: Sherman's forces invested the city of Savannah, closing off most of the escape routes for the Confederate garrison of Lieutenant General William J. Hardee.

5. December 13: Brigadier General William B. Hazen's division of Howard's Army of the Tennessee successfully stormed Fort McAllister, opening Ossabaw Sound and the Ogeechee River to Union navigation and the establishment of a sea-borne supply line for Sherman's armies.

6. December 21: Sherman's troops marched into Savannah after Hardee evacuated the night before.

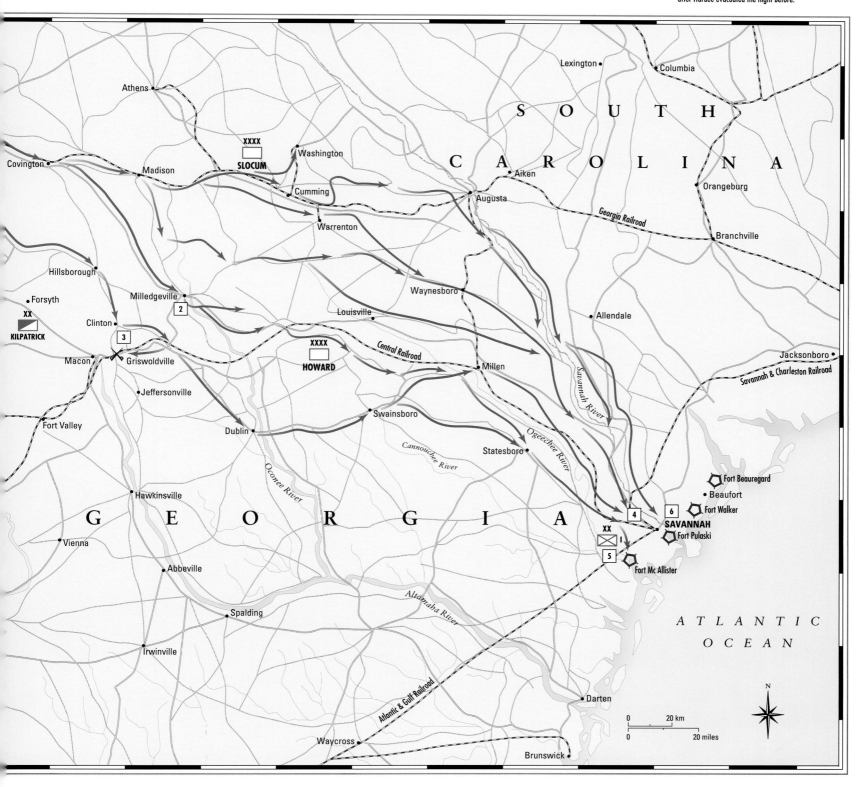

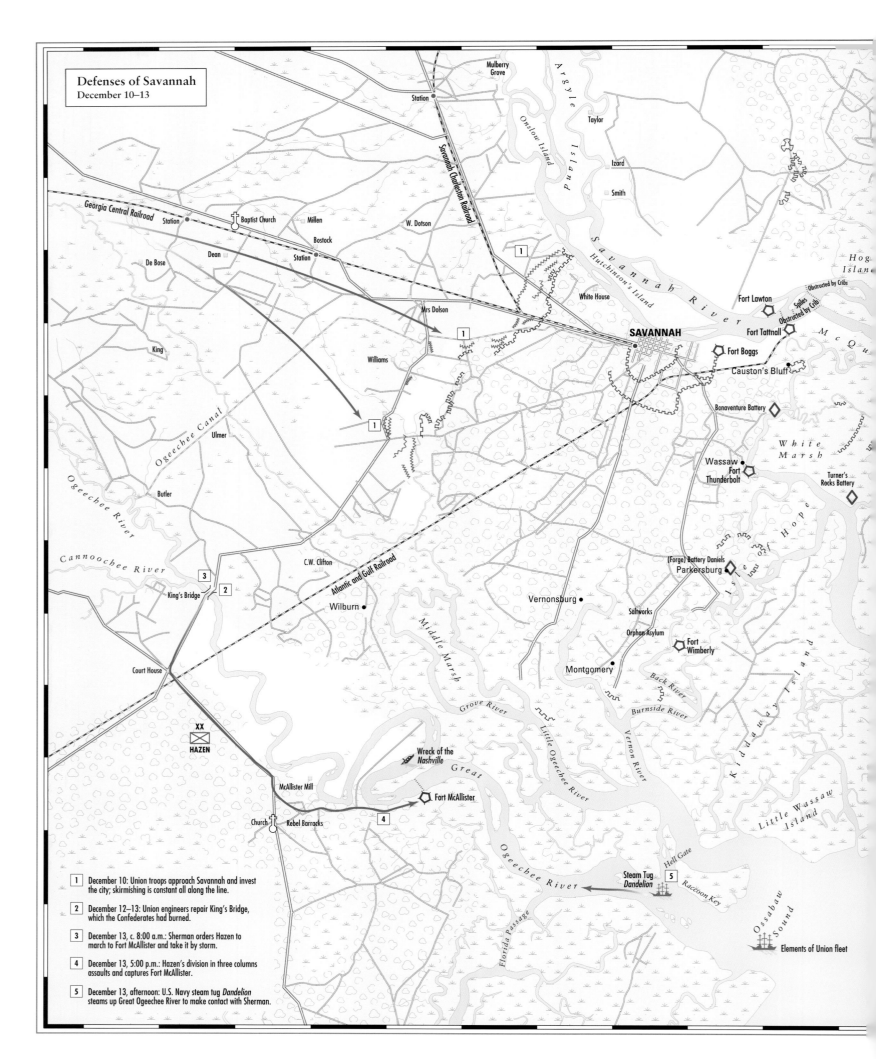

Defenses of Savannah
December 10–13

Station
Mulberry Grove
Argyle Island
Taylor
Izard
Onslow Island
Smith

Georgia Central Railroad
Station
Baptist Church
Millen
W. Dotson
Savannah Charleston Railroad
1
White House
Hutchinson's Island
Savannah River
Hog Island
Fort Lawton
Obstructed by Cribs
Spikes
Obstructed by Crib
Fort Tattnall
McQu...

Bostock
De Bose
Dean
Station
Mrs Dolson
1
SAVANNAH
Fort Boggs
Causton's Bluff

King
Williams
Bonaventure Battery

1
White Marsh

Ogeechee Canal
Ulmer
Wassaw
Fort Thunderbolt
Turner's Rocks Battery

Ogeechee River
Butler

Cannoochee River
C.W. Clifton
Atlantic and Gulf Railroad
(Forge) Battery Daniels
Parkersburg
Isle of Hope

3
2
King's Bridge
Wilburn
Vernonsburg
Saltworks
Orphan Asylum
Fort Wimberly

Court House
Montgomery
Back River
Burnside River
Vernon River
Kiddaway Island

XX
HAZEN
Middle Marsh
Grove River
Little Ogeechee River
Little Wassaw Island

McAllister Mill
Wreck of the *Nashville*
Great ... Ogeechee River

Church
Rebel Barracks
4
Fort McAllister

Hell Gate
Steam Tug *Dandelion*
5
Raccoon Key
Ossabaw Sound
Florida Passage
Elements of Union fleet

1   December 10: Union troops approach Savannah and invest the city; skirmishing is constant all along the line.

2   December 12–13: Union engineers repair King's Bridge, which the Confederates had burned.

3   December 13, c. 8:00 a.m.: Sherman orders Hazen to march to Fort McAllister and take it by storm.

4   December 13, 5:00 p.m.: Hazen's division in three columns assaults and captures Fort McAllister.

5   December 13, afternoon: U.S. Navy steam tug *Dandelion* steams up Great Ogeechee River to make contact with Sherman.

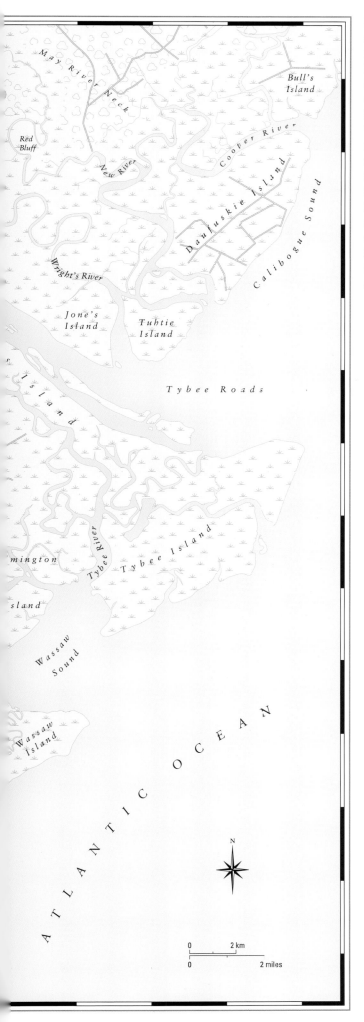

Ogeechee River to Union ships that had been standing by to meet Sherman. His army was soon receiving rations by sea; its supply line reestablished after nearly a month in the interior of Georgia. With a steady flow of supplies, Sherman was able to besiege the Confederate defenders of Savannah commanded by Lieutenant General William J. Hardee. On December 20, Hardee evacuated Savannah, and Sherman's troops occupied it the next day. In a dispatch to the president, Sherman wrote, "I beg to present you, as a Christmas gift, the city of Savannah, with 150 heavy guns and plenty of ammunition, and also about twenty-five thousand bales of cotton." More than any other single operation, the March to the Sea brought home to Southerners the fact that the Confederacy could no longer keep Union armies out of its interior and had in fact lost the war.

This sketch by Walton Taber shows a young cadet from the Virginia Military Institute as he appeared in 1865, less dashing than in former years, but more suitable for service in the field and in line with the Confederacy's supply capabilities.

BATTLE OF NASHVILLE

AFTER THE BATTLE OF FRANKLIN, Hood followed Schofield's retreating Union army and encamped his own badly battered army on a string of hills south of Nashville. There, with nothing else to do, he waited for something to turn up. He did not have anything like sufficient numbers to lay siege to Nashville, much less to assault it. All he could do was hope to win a defensive victory when Thomas delivered the inevitable attack. So he took the best defensive position he could find and waited.

It was not for nothing that Thomas had won the nickname "Old Slow Trot" in the old regular army. Though a thoroughly competent officer, he was never one to rush his preparations or do anything until he was completely ready. With an army of seventy thousand men giving him a better than two-to-one advantage over Hood, Thomas continued to make preparations despite an order from Grant to attack at once. When an ice storm further delayed the offensive, Grant's patience finally wore out, and he was on his way to Nashville to relieve Thomas when, on December 15, the latter's attack finally got underway.

When it came, Thomas's attack could hardly be other than devastating, given his overwhelming superiority. On the first day of the battle, a division of black troops under Major General James B. Steedman made a costly but valuable diversionary attack against the Confederate right while Schofield's troops pressured the left of Hood's line. Meanwhile, Major General Andrew Jackson Smith's superb Sixteenth Corps struck Hood's left flank and captured several key redoubts that anchored the Confederate position along the

Hillsboro Pike. Up to that point the battle had gone much to Hood's liking, but with his crucial left-flank redoubts gone his position was precarious. During the night, therefore, Hood withdrew his army several miles to the south and took up another defensive position. In the new position, Major General Benjamin Cheatham's corps held Shy's Hill, anchoring the Confederate line on the left, while Lieutenant General Stephen D. Lee's corps held Overton Hill on the right. In the center was Lieutenant General Alexander P. Stewart's corps, which had born the brunt of Smith's pounding.

On December 16, Thomas struck again. Once again Steedman's black troops attacked bravely and took fearful casualties fighting against the Confederate right on Overton Hill. To strengthen Lee's troops, Hood drew reinforcements from Cheatham's command on Shy's Hill. Then disaster struck. Major General John M. Schofield's Twenty-third Corps and Smith's unstoppable Sixteenth Corps attacked Cheatham's position and overran Shy's Hill. Hood's army collapsed and fled southward, hotly pursued by Union cavalry under the command of Major General James H. Wilson. Union casualties for the battle of Nashville totaled two thousand five hundred and sixty-two, and Confederate, probably about six thousand, of whom most were captured. The pursuit continued for days, until the Army of Tennessee managed to get across the Tennessee River in Alabama on December 27. When Hood finally halted his command in Tupelo, Mississippi, he had fewer than nineteen thousand men left of the forty thousand he had taken with him into Tennessee at the beginning of the campaign.

Battle of Nashville, First Day
December 15

1 December 15, 8:00 a.m.: Major General James B. Steedman's division of black troops attacked the Confederate right but suffered a bloody repulse.

2 2:00 p.m.: Schofield's corps attacked the Confederate left-center.

3 2:00 p.m.: A. J. Smith's corps decided the day's action by successfully assaulting a series of Confederate redoubts along the Hillsboro Pike, forcing Hood to retreat to a position farther to the rear.

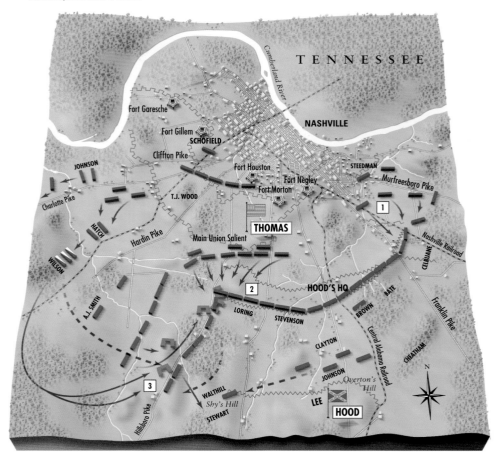

Brigadier General George H. Thomas, known to his troops as "Old Slow Trot," had a reputation as a methodical soldier and carefully planned his assault on Nashville.

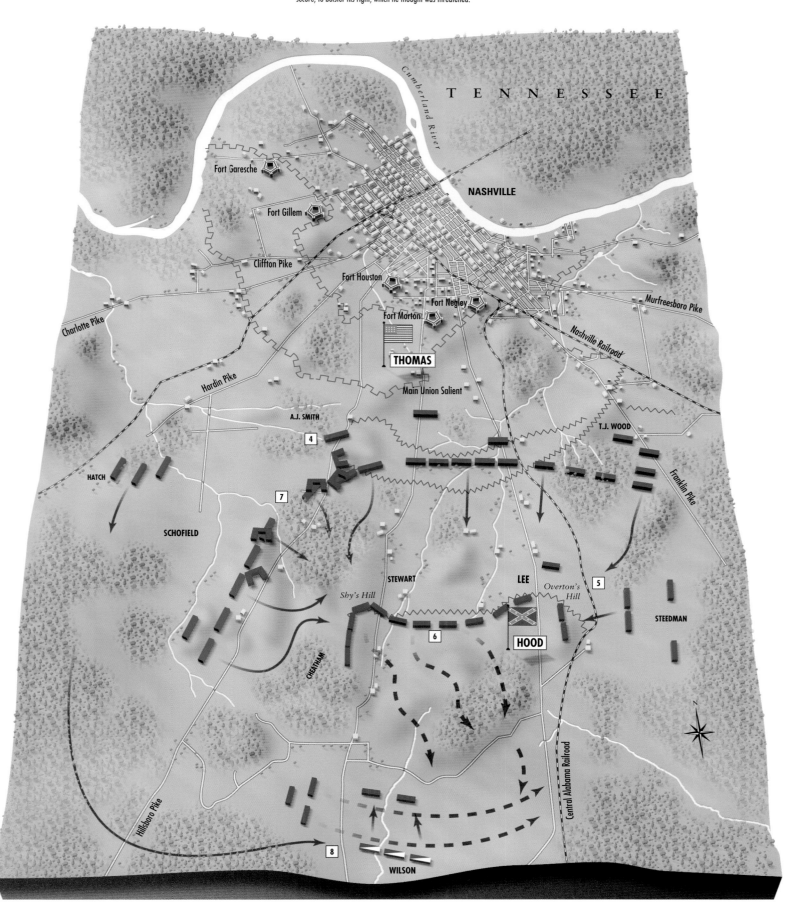

Battle of Nashville, Second Day
December 16

4 December 16, 8:00 a.m.: A. J. Smith's corps attacked the Confederate left on Shy's Hill but stalled in the face of stiff resistance.

5 c. 10:00 a.m.: Steedman's division of black troops attack the Confederate right on Overton's Hill but were repulsed with heavy loss.

6 Around midday: Hood transferred troops from his left, which seemed secure, to bolster his right, which he thought was threatened.

7 4:00 p.m.: Smith's corps renewed its attack and this time broke the Confederate line, sending Hood's army fleeing in disorder.

8 As the Confederate line began to break, Brigadier General James H. Wilson's Union cavalry rode deep into the Confederate rear, spreading confusion and cutting off the retreat of some of the Confederates.

NORTHERN INDUSTRY—THE FORCE OF PRODUCTION

In 1860, NORTHERN INDUSTRY WAS AN economic machine that was ready to be mobilized for war. America's industrial economy, which was the world's second largest (after Great Britain), was concentrated in the North. Unlike the agricultural South, the North had been industrializing for half a century, beginning with the New England textile industry that was fueled, ironically, by a growing supply of cheap southern cotton.

The North had such an insurmountable head start in textile manufacturing that a single mill town, Lowell, Massachusetts, boasted more cotton spindles than all the southern mills combined. The North jumped to similar leads in iron production, shoemaking, clockmaking, agricultural machinery, and—most importantly—small arms. The vast Springfield Armory and Colt Arms Works gave the North such an enormous advantage that one county in Connecticut produced more small arms than all of the southern armories put together. All told, at the outbreak of war, the North had 128,000 industrial firms, seven times as many as the South. New York and Pennsylvania each had more factories, mills, and shops than existed in the entire South. Three million immigrants came to America between 1845 and 1855 to man northern factories and work as skilled craftsmen. Overall, the North had ten times as many industrial workers as the South in 1860.

The North was equally dominant in transportation, building ninety percent of the nation's locomotives, two-thirds of all railroad track, and most ocean-going vessels. The Confederacy had to marshal every available resource, including raw materials, labor, transportation, and manufacturing, to support its meager war production. Instead of creating industries overnight or depending on imports, the Union simply had to mobilize its overwhelming industrial power and redirect it toward war. The Union allowed private control over industry to continue and used profit as motivation to boost production, rather than commandeering resources and industrial labor, as the Confederate government had to do.

Congress concentrated on creating a more efficient economic system and fostering opportunity by establishing national banks, subsidizing railroad construction, giving away land in the West, and instituting paper money. While imports into the Confederacy fell by one-third, the North could even afford to finance its war effort, in part, by taxing imports, increasing the tariff by forty-seven percent. An economic boom that began in 1862 provided revenues through excise taxes on manufactured goods, import duties, and the nation's first income tax. The profits from industrial production also generated a surplus of capital that could be reinvested in government bonds to support the war effort.

The North did suffer a labor shortage during the war, resulting from the mobilization of thirty-five percent of its draft-age men and a sharp decline in immigration. The labor shortage produced some benefits for workers, however, raising wages an average of fifty-five percent over the course of the war. It also stimulated even greater mechanization. In the shoe industry, the McKay stitcher, the first practical sewing machine, provided shoes for whole armies of Union soldiers and later revolutionized the garment industry. Despite the rise in wages, however, inflation totaled seventy-nine percent, so real wages actually declined, and workers' buying power fell to eighty-seven percent of its prewar level. Feeling the pinch, the workers created fifteen new labor unions during the war, which gave skilled workers a permanent organizational boost. Despite the North's temporary economic boom, however, the Civil War diverted resources away from long-term economic development. The war hastened mechanization, but when balanced against the economic devastation that the South suffered, total American economic growth actually slowed somewhat as a result of the war.

Only in defeat, with its slave labor force now free, did the South begin to mechanize and join the North as a region of mills, wage labor, and industrial cities.

Supported by the output of thousands of industrial companies, the North could ensure that hundreds of regiments, like this Pennsylvania Infantry unit on inspection parade at Brandy Station, were well equipped when the Union army reached its manpower peak in 1864.

THE STATE OF THE CONFEDERACY, THE NATION, AND ITS ARMY

AFTER THREE YEARS OF WAR, the Confederacy had been cut in half but renewed its commitment to defend Southern independence. President Lincoln began setting up loyal state governments in the four Confederate states—Tennessee, Arkansas, Louisiana, and Virginia—that were mostly under Union control. Popular dissent led to dramatic setbacks for President Davis in the Confederate congressional elections during the fall of 1863.

Still, Davis remained in command as the Confederate government stepped up its efforts to win the war by marshaling resources and controlling the southern economy. Davis wanted to defend both the eastern and western theaters simultaneously for the rest of the war, rather than sacrificing one or the other. He replaced Braxton Bragg with Joseph Johnston in command of the Army of Tennessee, because Johnston supported his strategy. Under this plan, however, the Confederacy had to provide men and materiel for two armies, General Robert E. Lee's Army of Northern Virginia and Johnston's Army of Tennessee. Congress met in February to plot a strategy for supplying both manpower and resources for the remainder of the war. A new conscription law expanded the draft age from eighteen to forty-five to seventeen to fifty and reduced the number of exempted occupations. This last-ditch effort at recruitment proved ineffective, and manpower actually declined during 1864.

The Confederate Army fell to 200,000, one-third of the Union total. For the rest of the war, Lee's and Johnston's armies were both outnumbered two-to-one, and the Confederate war effort was entirely defensive. During this period, the North suspended prisoner exchanges to deny troops to the South, reasoning that this would hurt the Confederacy worse than the Union, which it did. As a result, the South had to maintain a literal army of Union prisoners in addition to feeding its own men. Hunger, disease, and exposure killed thirteen thousand Union soldiers at Andersonville Prison in Georgia, which held thirty-three thousand men at its peak in 1864.

Meanwhile, Confederate soldiers languished in Northern prisons. To stifle swelling dissent and draft evasion, the Confederate Congress authorized Davis to suspend habeas corpus, in effect allowing arbitrary arrests for the duration of the war. Drastic economic measures wrung the last remaining resources from the Southern economy. Desperate for revenue from any source, the Confederate government confiscated cotton to export to Europe through the Union blockade. The Congress also commandeered half of all cargo space on blockade-runners to import essential war materiel. Confederate money was virtually worthless, and inflation jumped from eighteen thousand percent to twenty thousand percent during 1864.

Mobilizing labor, Congress allowed the Conscription Bureau to draft skilled workers and assign them to work in industry. In effect, the army took over key industries and ran the civilian economy for the sake of war production, giving the government near total control over the Southern economy. The army began employing slaves behind the front lines and even considered recruiting them into the military. The prospect of arming slaves led to two unthinkable possibilities—requiring African American slaves to fight in the defense of slavery or granting them their freedom. Increasingly desperate, the Confederacy would wait another year before choosing one of those drastic alternatives.

Right: Confederate prisoners photographed at Bell Plaine Landing on May 12, 1864. While the strength of the Confederate army steadily declined to around 200,000, compared to the Union's active total of more than 600,000, many experienced Confederate soldiers languished in the prisons of the North.

General Joseph E. Johnston, the newly appointed commander of the Army of Tennessee, was a keen supporter of President Davis's efforts to defend both eastern and western theaters of war simultaneously.

THE STATE OF THE NORTH, THE NATION, AND ITS ARMY

IN NOVEMBER 1863, PRESIDENT ABRAHAM Lincoln's Gettysburg Address gave the nation a new and more urgent war aim. Transcending the struggle to preserve the Union and to free the slaves, Lincoln saw the war as a test of democracy, a government "of the people, by the people, and for the people." In victory, Lincoln promised "a new birth of freedom," not just for slaves but for all Americans.

In March 1864, Lincoln solidified the North's military effort by appointing Lieutenant-General Ulysses S. Grant as his general in chief. Grant's vision of five Union armies coordinating simultaneous campaigns against the South and waging an unrelenting "hard war" seemed a formula for victory. With the Union in control of large parts of five Confederate states, Lincoln also began to think about how to reconstruct the Union.

In December 1863, he announced his reconstruction plan, allowing Southern states to re-enter the Union when ten percent of their voters pledged an oath of allegiance and accepted federal policies toward slavery. By the spring of 1864, Lincoln had a clear vision for Northern victory and national reunion. Even in the North, however, he still faced considerable opposition. Radical Republicans in Congress considered Lincoln too conciliatory and responded to his reconstruction plan with a harsher one of their own.

The Wade-Davis Bill required fifty percent of Southern voters to take a more stringent oath of loyalty while protecting the rights of former slaves. Radicals hoped to keep all of the Southern states out of the Union until the war ended, instead of readmitting them one-by-one, as Lincoln planned. Lincoln considered the Wade-Davis Bill too harsh and doomed it with a pocket veto. The war was also taking an economic toll.

The Northern standard of living was declining in the face of seventy percent inflation, higher taxes, and a national debt that was twenty-five times its prewar level. Casualties continued to

mount. This was the bloodiest year of the war, and the Northern public was impatient for victory. Calls for 700,000 men in March and July created more resistance. The notorious Copperhead Clement Vallandigham returned from exile, and even some Republicans put out peace feelers to the Confederacy. In June, Republicans renominated Lincoln, endorsing his war leadership, calling for unconditional Southern surrender, and reaffirming emancipation as a war aim. Hoping to attract Southern voters, they adopted the name National Union Party and nominated a War Democrat, Tennessee's Andrew Johnson, as vice president. The Democratic Party remained divided.

War Democrats supported the nomination of former general George McClellan, who pledged to win the war but also to negotiate and compromise with the South. Peace Democrats—the "Copperheads"—wrote the Democratic platform, calling for an immediate end to the war and restoration of the Union without freeing slaves. Many members of Lincoln's own party considered him too conciliatory and questioned his ability to win both the war and the election. Lincoln stood firm on his military strategy and his emancipation plans.

By mid-summer, however, his re-election was doubtful. Grant's army was besieging Petersburg, Sherman's was threatening Atlanta, and the public was impatient for a victory. Ever the statesman, Lincoln drafted a letter conceding defeat and pledging to cooperate with the incoming McClellan administration.

Lieutenant General Ulysses S. Grant (third from the left) and his staff encamped at City Point, Virginia, in the summer of 1864.

CONGRESSIONAL SUPPORT FOR THE THIRTEENTH, FOURTEENTH, AND FIFTEENTH AMENDMENTS

AT THE BEGINNING OF THE CIVIL WAr, President Abraham Lincoln feared that attacking slavery would drive the Border States out of the Union and help the Confederacy win the war. During the summer of 1862, however, Lincoln decided that emancipation was "an act of justice" and was vital to the Union war effort. In September, he issued his Emancipation Proclamation, freeing slaves in the rebellious South but not in the Border States. He emphasized that he considered emancipation a military measure justified by his powers as commander in chief, and he insisted that he had no presidential authority to free slaves in any loyal state. For this reason, Lincoln and most other Republicans supported a constitutional amendment that would free all the slaves permanently and throughout the nation by the time the war ended.

In January 1864, Senator Lyman Trumbull of Illinois introduced an amendment stating that "Neither slavery nor involuntary servitude, except as a punishment for crime whereof the party shall have been duly convicted, shall exist within the United States, or any place subject to their jurisdiction." The amendment needed a two-thirds vote to win passage in Congress before going to the states for ratification. The Senate approved it 38 to 6 in April 1864, but it failed in the House when only four Democrats gave theirsupport.

The Republicans included the amendment in their platform when they nominated Lincoln for re-election that summer. The elections in the fall of 1864 gave Republicans a three-fourths majority in Congress, which assured eventual passage of the amendment. Lincoln was impatient for ratification, however, and in December he asked the members of Congress who had already rejected the amendment to change their minds. He argued that emancipation would promote national unity and fulfill the will of the people, as well as correcting a horrific injustice. When the amendment came before Congress in January 1865, Lincoln appealed to Democrats to support it. Eventually, one-fifth of the Democrats in the House, sixteen of them, changed their votes and supported the amendment. Eight other Democrats abstained.

After adopting the amendment with seven votes more than the necessary two-thirds, the House adjourned for the day "in honor of this immortal and sublime event." Next, three-fourths of the states had to ratify the amendment. All three states that had voted for the Democratic presidential nominee, George B. McClellan, two Border States (Kentucky and Delaware) and one free state (New Jersey)—rejected the amendment. Every other free state and the loyalist legislatures in two Confederate states—Louisiana and Tennessee—approved it. Under Lincoln's plan of reconstruction, seceded states had to ratify the Thirteenth Amendment and accept emancipation as a condition for readmission into the Union. When Lincoln died, his successor, Andrew Johnson, continued this policy.

By December 1865, every former Confederate state had ratified the Thirteenth Amendment. Widely acknowledged as the cause of the Civil War, simultaneously the source of southern arrogance and economic backwardness and a grievous moral injustice, slavery was now illegal. The Thirteenth Amendment freed the slaves, but did not grant them citizenship, civil rights, or political rights. The struggle to guarantee those additional freedoms continued.

Black emigrants from the southern states waiting for a Mississippi River steamboat to ferry them on their way west. When the Thirteenth Amendment had been ratified, the majority of blacks still lived under difficult conditions encouraging many to consider life elsewhere. After Union troops pulled out the South and reconstruction collapsed, tens of thousands of blacks decided to leave the South and move westward, becoming known as "Exodusters," after the biblical exodus from Egypt.

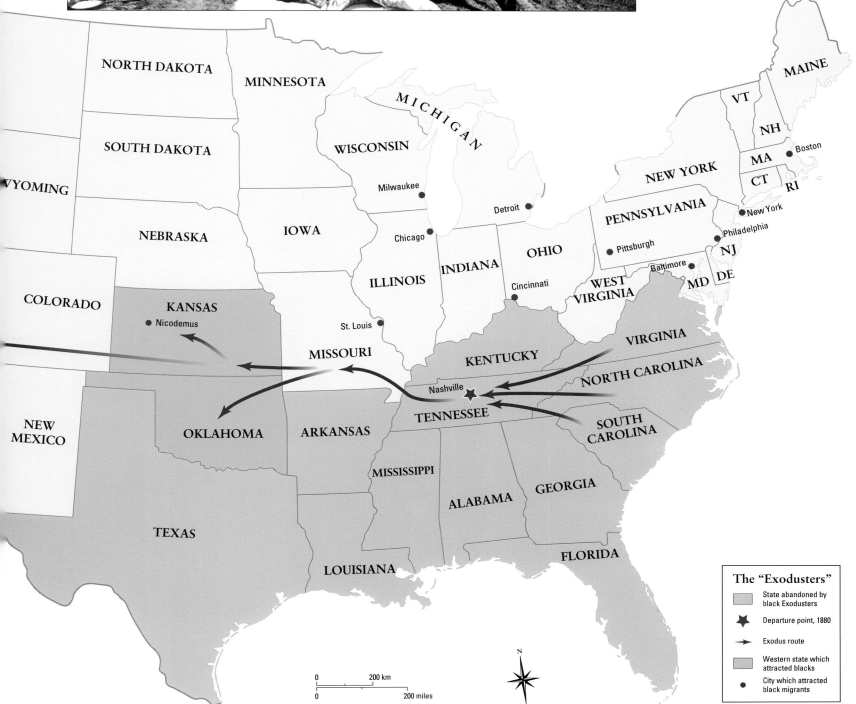

The "Exodusters"

State abandoned by black Exodusters

★ Departure point, 1880

→ Exodus route

Western state which attracted blacks

● City which attracted black migrants

UNION AND CONFEDERATE PRISON CAMPS

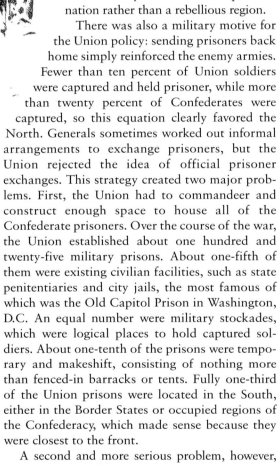

ONE OF THE MOST TROUBLING LOGISTICAL, political, and ethical problems to arise during the Civil War was the question of prisoners. About fifteen percent of Civil War soldiers were taken prisoner at some time during the war. All told, the Union held about 220,000 enemy prisoners, and the Confederacy held about 200,000. At the outset, the Lincoln administration refused to recognize Confederate captives as prisoners of war, which would have implied that the Confederacy was an independent nation rather than a rebellious region.

There was also a military motive for the Union policy: sending prisoners back home simply reinforced the enemy armies. Fewer than ten percent of Union soldiers were captured and held prisoner, while more than twenty percent of Confederates were captured, so this equation clearly favored the North. Generals sometimes worked out informal arrangements to exchange prisoners, but the Union rejected the idea of official prisoner exchanges. This strategy created two major problems. First, the Union had to commandeer and construct enough space to house all of the Confederate prisoners. Over the course of the war, the Union established about one hundred and twenty-five military prisons. About one-fifth of them were existing civilian facilities, such as state penitentiaries and city jails, the most famous of which was the Old Capitol Prison in Washington, D.C. An equal number were military stockades, which were logical places to hold captured soldiers. About one-tenth of the prisons were temporary and makeshift, consisting of nothing more than fenced-in barracks or tents. Fully one-third of the Union prisons were located in the South, either in the Border States or occupied regions of the Confederacy, which made sense because they were closest to the front.

A second and more serious problem, however, was the ethics of holding men prisoner in often squalid conditions as a political or even military strategy. The Confederacy had as many prisons as the Union but had fewer resources to maintain them. As a result, Union soldiers were twenty-eight percent more likely to die in Confederate prisons than vice versa, so Northerners demanded prisoner exchanges. In July 1862, Union General John Dix and Confederate General Daniel Harvey Hill set up an exchange cartel that allowed prisoners to rejoin their armies. Prisons on both sides nearly emptied.

In May 1863, however, the Confederacy refused to exchange African American troops and their officers and threatened to execute them instead. In response, the Lincoln administration halted the exchange cartel, in effect holding Confederate soldiers hostage to guarantee the safety of captured African American troops. Both President Lincoln

For the Confederate prisoners held at Johnson's Island, suviving Lake Erie's icy winters and sub-zero temperatures was a torment as this illustration by Walton Tabor suggests.

and General Ulysses S. Grant insisted that the Confederacy exchange African Americans on an equal footing with white soldiers. Soon, however, the incessant fighting of 1864 strained the capacity of both Union and Confederate prisons, some of which became death camps. The most infamous Confederate prison, Andersonville, in Georgia, was built to house ten thousand prisoners but held thirty-three thousand at its peak in 1864. Hunger, disease, and exposure were rampant, and at times one hundred of its Union prisoners died per day. A total of thirteen thousand died at this prison alone, representing one-third of its total population and

more than one-half of all deaths in Confederate prisons. Exchanges resumed in the winter of 1864 – 1865, and a thousand men were exchanged every day until the war ended.

As in most wars, Civil War prisoners became pawns in the grand strategic struggle. The harsh conditions on both sides resulted more from logistical problems and shortages than from premeditated policy. The Confederacy benefitted more from exchanges, however, so the Union could afford to set conditions. Insisting on the equality of African Americans halted the exchanges temporarily but seemed like a noble gesture at the time.

Issuing rations at Andersonville prison, Georgia. Originally intended to hold a maximum of ten thousand prisoners, by August 1864, the prison held forty-three thousand. The inmates' daily ration was three tablespoons of beans, half a pint of unsifted cornmeal, and a teaspoon of salt. A polluted stream called Sweet Water Branch provided drinking water and acted as a sewer. Approximately thirteen thousand men died at Andersonville and were buried in mass graves.

THE COST OF WAR

I N MARCH 1864, PRESIDENT ABRAHAM LINCOLN promoted Ulysses S. Grant to Lieutenant General and appointed him General in Chief of the Union armies. At last, the North had an overall plan and a grand military strategy for the entire Union war effort. Grant commanded five Union armies that would work together and coordinate their campaigns rather than attack the South piecemeal.

The Union onslaught would pin down the Confederates and prevent them from shifting troops between theaters. Each of the Union armies had its own role to play so that, as Lincoln put it, "Those not skinning can hold a leg." Grant brought to the eastern theater the kind of "hard war" that he had been waging in the West. In Virginia, his objective was not so much to capture Richmond as to destroy Lee's army.

The Army of the Potomac squared off with 115,000 men against the Army of Northern Virginia's sixty-four thousand. In the West, General William Tecumseh Sherman's army would penetrate Georgia with its 100,000 men against General Joseph Johnston's fifty thousand. Grant ordered Sherman "to move against Johnston's army, to break it up and to get into the interior of the enemy's country as far as you can, inflicting all the damage you can against their war resources." Concluding that "War is hell," Sherman set out to devastate the southern economy, defeat the Confederate will to resist, and "Make Georgia howl!" Then he would turn north toward Richmond.

Casualties reflected the effectiveness of this plan, and 1864 was the bloodiest year of the war. More than one-third of the entire war's engagements took place during this year alone. Virginia remained the focus of battle as Union forces closed in on Richmond, and one-fourth of the year's engagements occurred in Virginia. But the war finally reached the Deep South—Georgia, Alabama, and Mississippi—where another one-fourth of all engagements took place. The Union focused on major battles, each costing the Federals at least five hundred men, and the balance of casualties shifted ominously against them.

During 1864, the two sides fought fifty-two major battles, an average of one per week. One-half of them took place in Virginia, with the Wilderness, Spotsylvania Court House, and Cold Harbor heading the list. The Union onslaught was unrelenting, and the North suffered almost one-half of all its casualties in 1864 alone. For the first time in the war, the Union lost more men than the Confederacy. As manpower was depleted, the federal government issued three calls for men in 1864, in March, July, and December. As casualties mounted, desertion grew, exceeding seven thousand per month, but only about forty percent of deserters were ever arrested. Among those convicted, Lincoln commuted most death sentences, confirming his reputation for clemency. A total of one hundred and forty-seven deserters faced execution by firing squad, most of them

during 1864, when the Union was desperate for men. Still, most Union soldiers remained committed to the cause.

In 1864, three-year Union men who had enlisted in the first year of the war were free to go home. More than half of them re-enlisted. Meanwhile, the Confederacy amended its draft law to keep all its soldiers in the army for the duration. The burning of Atlanta and the March to the Sea symbolized the North's resolve to win at all costs by waging "hard war" against the South and accepting unprecedented casualties on both sides.

A makeshift field hospital at Savage's Station, Virginia. One of the war's chilling statistics is that approximately two out of every nine men that served in the Union and Confederate armies did not survive because of the quality of medical treatment.

1865
TRIUMPH, TRAGEDY, AND RECONSTRUCTION

By the beginning of 1865 only a few diehards in the South still believed in the possibility of a Confederate victory. In mid-January a Union army–navy task force captured Fort Fisher at the mouth of the Cape Fear River below Wilmington, North Carolina, closing off the last blockade-running port in the

Destroying everything of use to the Confederacy,
Sherman's troops dismantle a railroad.

Confederacy. At the end of the month, General Sherman's sixty
thousand-man wrecking crew began its destructive march north
from Savannah through South Carolina and into North
Carolina and they threatened to come up on the rear of General
Lee's Army of Northern Virginia even as it confronted
increasing pressure from Grant and the Army of the Potomac in
its front. President Lincoln and Secretary of State Seward met
with a Confederate delegation headed by Vice President
Alexander H. Stephens at Hampton Roads, Virginia on
February 3 to discuss possible terms of peace. Lincoln insisted
on unconditional surrender of Confederate forces and

"abandonment of slavery." The Confederates refused, and the war went on.

But not for long. On April 1–2 the Army of the Potomac finally broke through Confederate defenses southwest of Petersburg and cut the last rail lines into Petersburg and Richmond. Confederates abandoned their capital on the night of April 2–3, leaving Richmond ablaze for hours before entering Union troops could put out the fires. The Army of Northern Virginia fled westward toward Lynchburg, but never got there. General Sheridan's cavalry cut off their retreat at Appomattox Court House on April 9 as Union infantry closed in. Faced with a choice of surrender or guerrilla warfare that would leave the South a wasteland, Lee chose surrender. Grant's liberal terms

In this illustration by Alfred Waud, Union soldiers force a crossing of the Little Salkhatchie River as they push through the Carolinas.

paroled thirty thousand Confederate soldiers and officers, allowing them to go home and start their lives anew as civilians. One after another, other Confederate armies surrendered on the same terms during the next two months. On May 10 Union cavalry captured the fleeing Jefferson Davis in Georgia. The war was over, but the problem of reconstructing the Union and defining the freedom of four million slaves would take years. The task became vastly more difficult when John Wilkes Booth assassinated Lincoln, depriving the nation of his experienced and moderate leadership. Despite this tragedy, and despite the misguided opposition from Lincoln's successor Andrew Johnson, Congress forged ahead. From 1865 to 1870, three constitutional amendments (Thirteenth, Fourteenth, and

Fifteenth) mandated the abolition of slavery, the equal civil rights of freed slaves, and the prohibition of discrimination in voting rights. But declaring the principles of equality was one thing; enforcing those principles on the ground was quite another. During the postwar decade, Congress passed civil rights laws and enforcement legislation in an effort to accomplish this purpose. Federal marshals and troops patrolled the polls to protect black voters, arrested thousands of white paramilitary guerrillas and other violators of black civil rights, and even occupied state capitals to prevent the overthrow by illegal and violent means of legitimately elected Republican state governments in the South.

The end of the line—Appomattox Station. Lee hoped to reach the station where rations awaited his hungry soldiers, but Sheridan's cavalry troopers arrived at the station first and Lee's last hope evaporated.

THE CAMPAIGNS OF 1865

By THE BEGINNING OF 1865, little hope remained of Confederate victory. Yet thousands of Southerners continued to strive for the cause. Lee's army, though worn and battered, continued to hold tenaciously to its lines around Richmond and Petersburg, while most of the remaining troops of the all-but-defunct Army of Tennessee would soon be on their way to North Carolina to join Confederate forces there, set to resist further moves by Sherman. More fighting and dying and more destruction of property would be necessary before the war could end.

The year's campaigning opened with a second Union attack on Fort Fisher, near Wilmington, North Carolina. In December 1864 there was an almost farcical effort to take the fort, but the 1865 attempt included, in the person of Major General Alfred Terry, a competent commander for the landing force. Terry's troops landed on January 13, and after the heaviest naval bombardment in history up to that time, assaulted and captured the fort on January 16. The fall of Fort Fisher closed the last port available to Confederate blockade-runners.

On February 1, Sherman's army moved into South Carolina, beginning one of the most epic campaigns in mili-

On February 17 Union troops entered Columbia. On hand was Alfred Waud of Harper's Magazine *who sketched them raising the colors on the old State House.*

tary history. Once again Sherman cast loose of his supply line and had his army live entirely off the land. In contrast to his march through Georgia, however, this time significant Confederate military forces were on hand to impede his progress. This march was also made not in the relatively pleasant weather of late autumn, but rather in the heavy rains of a southern winter, crossing the myriad streams and swamps of the Carolina low country, sometimes wading for hours at a time. To the amazement of almost everyone outside his own army, Sherman and his men pulled it off, crossing the myriad streams and swamps of the Carolina low country and sometimes wading for hours at a time. They captured Columbia, South Carolina, on February 17, and their presence in the interior of the state forced Confederates to evacuate Charleston, South Carolina, the same day.

In an act of desperation, Jefferson Davis and the Confederate congress cooperated to make Robert E. Lee supreme commander of Confederate forces on February 6. Twelve days later, Lee appointed Joseph E. Johnston to command the Confederate forces attempting to resist Sherman's northward march through the Carolinas. Yet Johnston could do nothing to stop or even appreciably slow Sherman's advance. On March 11, Sherman's troops occupied Fayetteville, North Carolina. Four days later Johnston's forces ineffectually challenged Sherman's advance at Averasborough, but Sherman's troops brushed them aside. On March 19, Johnston made an all-out attack on one wing of Sherman's army at Bentonville, North Carolina, but after initial success suffered defeat in three days of fighting. On March 23, Sherman reached Goldsborough, North Carolina, and linked up with a smaller Union army under Major General John M. Schofield, which was moving inland from Wilmington on the coast. With a combined force of about 100,000, Sherman was poised to advance into Virginia.

Realizing that Sherman's arrival would spell his doom, Lee tried a final gambit. On March 25 his troops attacked Fort Stedman, on the eastern end of the Petersburg lines, in hopes that a Confederate breakthrough there would force Grant to contract his lines, opening a way for Lee's army to escape to the south and join Johnston in North Carolina. After a brief local success, the attack failed without even disturbing a routine morning for most of the troops in Grant's army. Four days later Grant launched his own effort to end the deadlock around Petersburg and Richmond, sending a powerful force of infantry and cavalry to threaten Petersburg's railroad connections southwest of the city. Lee countered and their forces clashed at Five Forks on April 1. The Federals were victorious. The next morning Grant's forces attacked all along the lines and broke through at dozens of places. Lee fought a desperate rearguard action to enable him to extricate his army to the west, and the Confederate government fled.

Union troops occupied Richmond and Petersburg on April 3, while Lee's desperate army fled westward with Grant's in hot pursuit. On April 6, the pursuers caught up with the rear elements of Lee's army and defeated them severely at the Battle of Sayler's Creek, taking eight thousand prisoners. Three days later, finally cornered near Appomattox Court House, Virginia, Lee surrendered the Army of Northern Virginia.

Meanwhile, other Union offenses mopped up what was left of the Confederacy. Union troops under Major General Edward R. S. Canby besieged Mobile on March 25 and took the city on April 12. A powerful Union cavalry force of some twelve thousand horsemen under the command of Major General James H. Wilson captured Selma, Alabama, on April 2. Sherman's army took up its pursuit of Johnston once again and entered Raleigh, North Carolina, on April 13. Five days later Johnston surrendered what was left of his army at Greensboro, North Carolina, although the surrender was not finalized until eight days later. This surrender marked the end of significant campaigning.

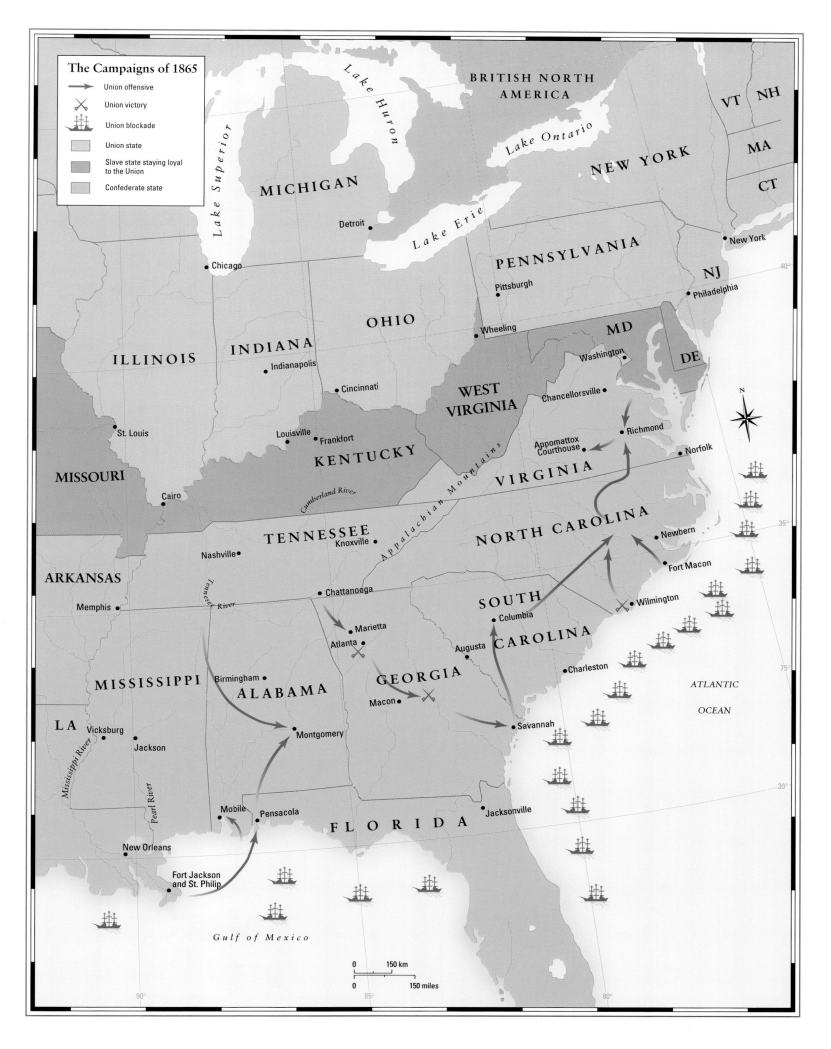

The Campaigns of 1865

- → Union offensive
- ⚔ Union victory
- ⛵ Union blockade
- Union state
- Slave state staying loyal to the Union
- Confederate state

NORTHERN AND SOUTHERN NEWSPAPERS

THE CIVIL WAR WAS NOT ONLY a military struggle but also a "war of words." The North's dense network of newspapers, connected by telegraph lines and supported by high literacy rates, gave the Union a distinct advantage in mobilizing support for the war, disseminating news, shaping public opinion, and controlling information.

When the war began, the Union boasted more than three thousand newspapers, while the Confederacy had just about one-fourth that number. Two northern states, New York and Pennsylvania, together had more newspapers than the entire Confederacy. New York alone had more newspapers than eight Confederate states combined. The press depended on an urban readership, widespread literacy, steam-powered presses, and cheap transportation, all of which favored the North. With the introduction of the telegraph in

1845, news traveled by wire, and newspapers began pooling their news stories to avoid high telegraph costs. The largest New York City newspapers formed the Associated Press in 1849, sharing their news and selling it by telegraph to other papers around the country. News traveled faster but fell under centralized control.

When the Civil War began, a veritable army of war correspondents—one hundred and fifty in all—followed the troops into battle. Some generals banned reporters from their armies to prevent the leakage of sensitive information. Others rewarded journalists who wrote favorable reports and thus were able to "slant" the news. Under Secretary of War Edwin Stanton, reporters needed press passes to visit the front, and unauthorized journalists faced arrest. Stanton also used the telegraphs to control the flow of news. He required all army dispatches to pass through his office so he could monitor and censor them. A telegraph line ran into the War Department, across the street from the White House. President

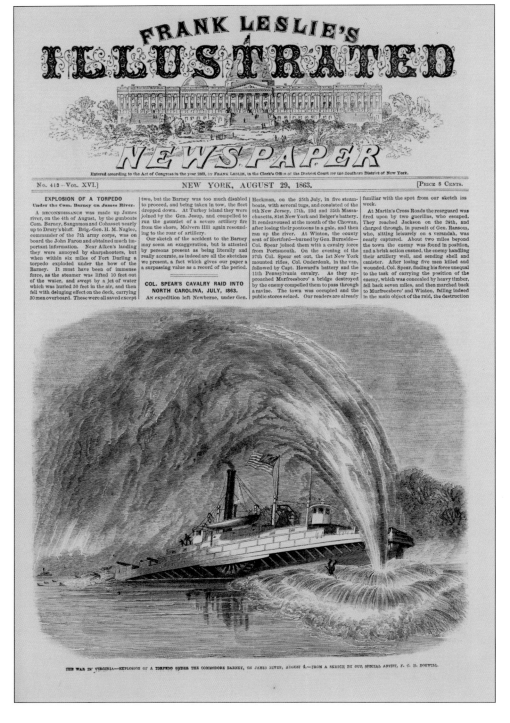

Edwin Stanton, Under Secretary of War, kept tight control of all news from the battle fronts. Every newspaper and magazine, like Frank Leslie's Illustrated Newspaper *(left) had access to the same information released by his office.*

Lincoln often sat next to the telegraph key for hours waiting for the latest war news. Stanton personally edited the reports and wrote a daily "War Diary" that he sent to the New York newspapers, which in turn distributed them through the Associated Press. In this way, the telegraph helped the War Department to control the war news.

In one sense, this system was democratic, because all newspapers had access to the same information. On the other hand, the government labeled its reports "official," which discouraged journalists from presenting opposing points of view. All telegraph lines leading out of Washington were monitored and censored, so reporters had to travel to New York City to file uncensored stories. Lincoln valued a free press as a cornerstone of democracy and often responded to editorial advice, such as Horace Greeley's calls for emancipation in the *New York Tribune*. He did not shut down newspapers who criticized his leadership, but he did sanction the arrest of editors who endangered the war effort by divulging secrets or printing false information.

Fewer in number to begin with, Southern newspapers suffered an entirely different array of prob-

lems. To gather and share their war news, southern editors created the Confederate Press Association, emulating the Associated Press. The Confederate government censored the news just as the Northern War Department did. But most problems were logistical. The South produced only five percent of America's paper, so the Confederate presses was always running short. Southern editors often smuggled paper in on blockade-runners. As Union troops advanced, they shut down or heavily censored Confederate newspapers. Other papers moved about, ahead of advancing troops. By the end of the war, editorial opinion turned against the Confederate cause, and the surviving Southern press sometimes undermined the war effort.

Northern newspapers were invaluable in supporting the Union and mobilizing public opinion. Their centralized organization allowed the government to control the flow of information and spread the official version of the war. Southern newspapers, however, never had enough resources to support the Confederacy effectively and may have, whether intentionally or not, undermined morale. A strength for the Union, the press proved a liability for the Confederacy.

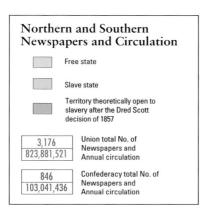

Northern and Southern Newspapers and Circulation

- Free state
- Slave state
- Territory theoretically open to slavery after the Dred Scott decision of 1857

| 3,176 | Union total No. of Newspapers and |
| 823,881,521 | Annual circulation |

| 846 | Confederacy total No. of Newspapers and |
| 103,041,436 | Annual circulation |

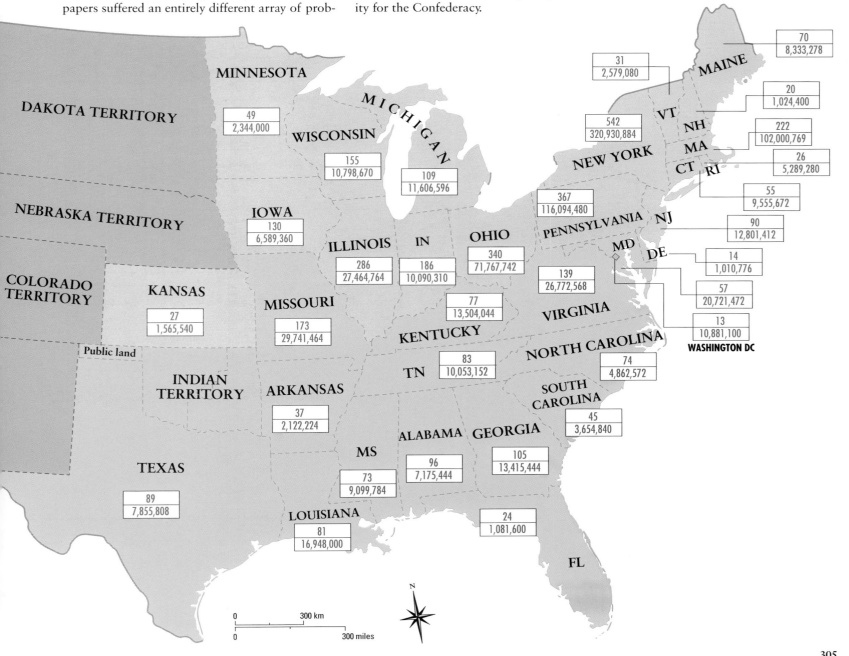

THE STATE OF THE CONFEDERACY, THE NATION, AND ITS ARMY

Above: The Reverend P. P. Cooney, Chaplain General, leads the Army of the Cumberland in a divine service in the field.

Right: This photograph, taken by George N. Barnard, shows the remains of Atlanta's freight depot which was blown up on the departure of Sherman's army.

Below: Atlanta photographed from the cupola of the Female Seminary shortly before it was damaged by fire.

WHILE MANY SOUTHERNERS DESPAIRED of victory and soldiers by the thousands deserted, Confederate leaders still hoped to regroup, survive, and achieve independence.

As General William Tecumseh Sherman's army drove into Georgia in July 1864, President Jefferson Davis removed General Joseph Johnston from his command of the Army of Tennessee for failing to counter-attack. When Johnston's successor, General John Bell Hood, did counter-attack, however, the results were disastrous. Davis had no choice but to suspend all counter-attacks and order a purely defensive strategy for the rest of the war.

After Sherman captured Atlanta in July 1864 and started his fabled March to the Sea, Hood led his men back into Tennessee, hoping to reinforce General Robert E. Lee's Army of Northern Virginia. After losing the battles of Franklin and Nashville, however, the Army of Tennessee disintegrated. As Sherman's army reached Savannah and turned northward through the Carolinas, the Confederate high command was in disarray. Secretary of War James Seddon resigned in January and Davis replaced him with John C. Breckinridge.

In February, Confederate vice president Alexander Stephens met with Abraham Lincoln at Hampton Roads to discuss peace. The Confederacy demanded independence, but Lincoln insisted on both national reunion and emancipation, and the conference ended in failure. On February 6, 1865, Lee at long last assumed command of all the Confederate armies as General in Chief. He put Johnston back in command of an army to try to stop Sherman's march through the Carolinas. Sherman's army burned Columbia, the capital of South Carolina, and pursued Johnston's army into North Carolina. Johnston planned to retreat northward in a vain attempt to unite with Lee. Desperate for troops, Lee asked the Confederate Congress to authorize the enlistment of African American soldiers, reasoning that "We must decide whether slavery shall be extinguished by our enemies and the slaves used against us, or use them ourselves."

Congress complied in March, one month before the war ended, but—defending slavery to the end—still refused to grant black soldiers their freedom. By the end of March, Petersburg, the southern gateway into Richmond, fell and the Confederate capital was doomed. In the early days of April, the Confederates evacuated their capital, setting fire to everything of military value. President Davis fled and was captured by Union troops a month later in Georgia. Lee marched his army of thirty-five thousand weary men two hundred miles westward, with Grant's eighty thousand in pursuit.

Rejecting the idea of a guerrilla war to preserve Southern honor and wear down the enemy, Lee concluded that "there is nothing left for me but to go and see General Grant, and I would rather die a thousand deaths." He surrendered his army at Appomattox Court House on April 10. Two weeks later, Johnston surrendered to Sherman at Greensboro, North Carolina. The war was over.

THE STATE OF THE NORTH, THE NATION, AND ITS ARMY

B Y THE END OF 1864, the North's grand strategy to defeat the South was nearing completion. General William Tecumseh Sherman had led three armies totaling 100,000 men through East Tennessee and into Georgia, driving General Joseph Johnston's Army of Tennessee ninety miles back toward Atlanta. In the eastern theater, General Ulysses S. Grant was hammering Petersburg, the southern gateway into Richmond.

Buoyed by the fall of Atlanta, President Abraham Lincoln was re-elected in November 1864 in a landslide. He won with fifty-five percent of the vote of the loyal states, and public confidence in his political and military leadership was

Conference, Lincoln met with Confederate vice president Alexander Stephens to discuss a peace settlement. The conference broke up when Lincoln insisted on both national reunion and emancipation as conditions for an armistice and refused to discuss Confederate independence or the continuation of slavery. Congress also created the Freedmen's Bureau, which was designed to help former slaves adjust to freedom by providing public education, dispensing justice, and overseeing the transition to wage labor.

Lincoln continued to hope for a quick and painless reconstruction, allowing Southern states to return to the Union as soon as ten percent of their voters declared their loyalty and accepted emanci-

Richmond, the once proud Confederate capital, by 1865 had paid a terrible price for its bid for independence. Washington, (far right) by comparison, remained undamaged and even had the time and money to complete the Capitol building.

reaffirmed. Nineteen states allowed their soldiers to vote in the field, and Lincoln received an overwhelming seventy-eight percent of their vote. The soaring morale of the Union Army belied the popularity of the "Little Napoleon," George B. McClellan, among his former troops. Sherman began his destructive March to the Sea in November and was able to offer Lincoln his famous "Christmas present" of Savannah in December. Sherman then turned his army north toward Virginia to join forces with Grant. January 1865 brought an all-out commitment to emancipation as a Union war aim.

With Lincoln's support, Congress adopted the Thirteenth Amendment, which was designed to make emancipation permanent and nationwide, freeing slaves everywhere, including the loyal Border States. Lincoln also resumed prisoner exchanges in January 1865 when the Confederacy agreed to release African American prisoners rather than return them to slavery or even execute them. During the Hampton Roads Peace

pation. In his Second Inaugural Address on March 4, Lincoln reached out to the South and pledged to oversee a reunion "With malice toward none; with charity for all." He rejected the idea of vengeance against the South and promised a healing process designed "to bind up the nation's wounds." Lincoln showed tremendous magnanimity by declaring that both sides had followed the course that they considered right and both had suffered an immeasurable loss. When at last Richmond fell in early April, Lincoln rode through the city to survey the damage and was hailed as the Great Emancipator.

In his last public speech, he took a huge step toward equal rights by endorsing the enfranchisement of African Americans who had served in the Union military or who were literate. His assassination on April 14, however, dashed all hopes for a peaceful reunion accompanied by expanded rights for former slaves. His successor, Andrew Johnson—a southerner, former slave owner, and former Democrat—would soon battle Radical Republicans in Congress to determine the nation's future.

THE WAR IN INDIAN TERRITORY

IN ITS WAR OF SECESSION, the Confederates sought help from foreign nations, and they also looked to the Indian nations of the West as potential allies. In particular, the Confederacy hoped that the "Five Civilized Tribes" of Indian Territory—modern Oklahoma—would come to their aid. These five tribes—Cherokees, Chickasaws, Choctaws, Creeks, and Seminoles—had long-standing grievances against the United States. They had been forcibly removed from the South during the 1830s and relegated to unfamiliar and relatively inferior land in Indian Territory. They were embittered by their treat-

Reservations in Indian Territory, 1833–1842

- Cherokee
- Chickasaw and Choctaw
- Creek and Seminole
- Delaware
- Miami
- Ottawa
- Peoria and Kaskaskia
- Potawatomi
- Quapaw
- Seneca
- Shawnee
- Wea and Piankasha
- Wyandot

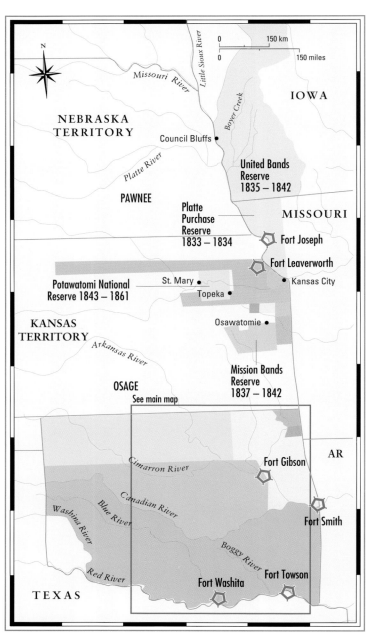

alliances with the Confederacy. But the Civil War divided the other three—the Creeks, the Seminoles, and especially the Cherokees. The Cherokee Nation made an official alliance with the Confederacy, and their military leader, Stand Watie, was eventually commissioned as a Confederate general. Many Cherokees, however, sided with the Union or strove to remain neutral.

In late 1861, Indian Territory erupted into civil war when Indian regiments, reinforced by Confederate troops, attacked the camps of Union sympathizers and neutrals and drove them out of Indian Territory into Kansas. In March 1862, Indian regiments marched into Arkansas to reinforce Confederate forces and fought at the Battle of Pea Ridge, where the Confederacy was decisively defeated. Soon, the Union army mounted a counterattack on Indian Territory, capturing the Cherokee capital, Tahlequah, and sending several Cherokee leaders to prison. After the Battle of Pea Ridge and the Union capture of New Orleans and Vicksburg knocked the Confederacy out of the western war, both sides abandoned the Indians. Still, they continued their own internal civil war—Confederate sympathizers against Union sympathizers and neutrals—for two more years. In fact, the Cherokees were the last combatants to stop fighting. Their general, Stand Watie, was the last Confederate general to surrender, in June 1865.

The Union punished the Indian tribes for supporting the Confederacy. They declared all their treaties void and required them to negotiate new ones. The Five Civilized Tribes eventually gave up one-half of their territory, the entire western half of Oklahoma. The United States carved this land into new Indian reservations for tribes removed from the North and then living in Kansas (Shawnees, Sacs and Foxes, Kickapoos, and Pottawatamies) and for Plains Indian tribes soon to be dispossessed from their own land (Pawnees, Comanches, and Kiowas). Overall, the Civil War

ment at the hands of the U.S. Army, especially during the long and deadly "Trail of Tears." They were southern in origin, and maintained economic ties with the South and even grew cotton. Finally, they recognized slavery, and many of them owned slaves.

Hoping for a military alliance, the Confederacy sent an Indian commissioner to Indian Territory, who promised to recognize and defend the independence of the five Indian republics. Two of the five tribes—the Chickasaws and the Choctaws—quickly made formal

intruded into Indian Territory and divided the tribes against themselves. The Confederacy and the Union both mobilized Indian troops to win an advantage in the West, and then abandoned them to their fate after they were no longer useful. The Union intensified the dispossession of the Indian tribes once the Civil War ended, sending generals William Tecumseh Sherman and Philip Sheridan, along with thousands of Civil War veterans, to unleash the new "total" warfare in the West.

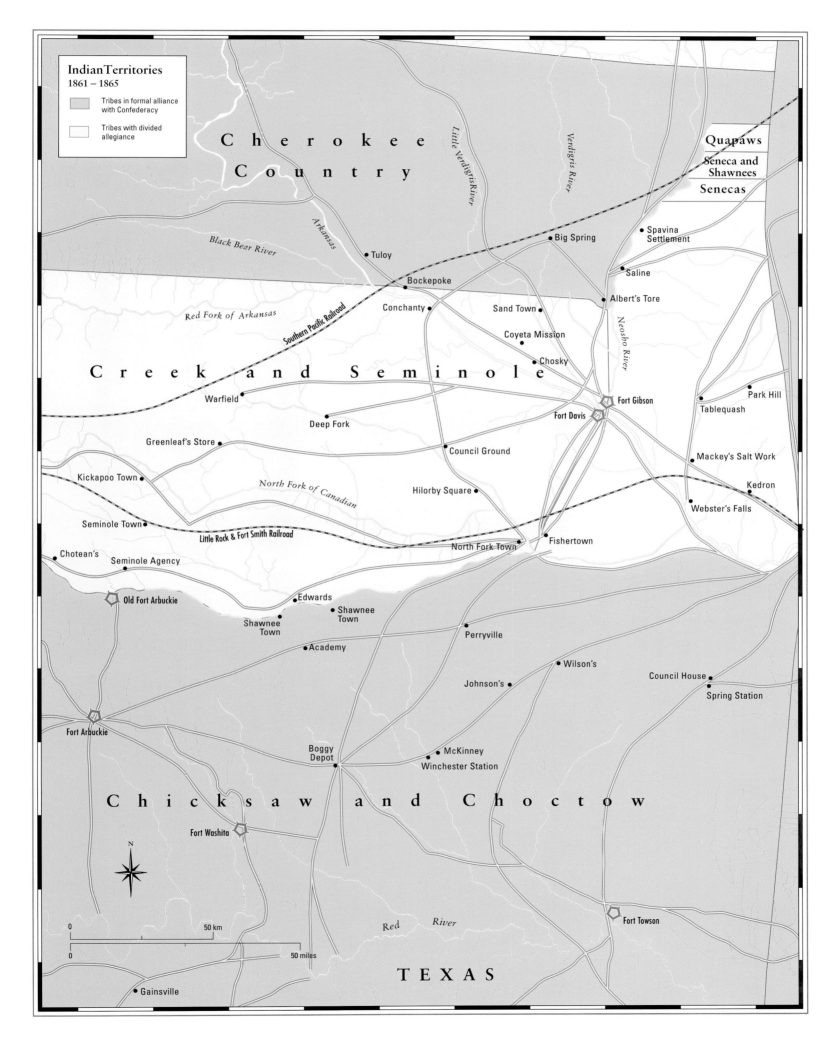

Indian Territories
1861 – 1865

Tribes in formal alliance with Confederacy

Tribes with divided allegiance

C h e r o k e e
C o u n t r y

Little Verdigris River

Verdigris River

Quapaws

Seneca and Shawnees

Senecas

Black Bear River

Arkansas

Tuloy

Big Spring

Spavina Settlement

Saline

Bockepoke

Red Fork of Arkansas

Conchanty

Sand Town

Albert's Tore

Coyeta Mission

Neosho River

Southern Pacific Railroad

C r e e k   a n d   S e m i n o l e

Chosky

Park Hill

Warfield

Fort Gibson

Tablequash

Deep Fork

Fort Davis

Greenleaf's Store

Council Ground

Mackey's Salt Work

Kickapoo Town

North Fork of Canadian

Hilorby Square

Kedron

Seminole Town

Little Rock & Fort Smith Railroad

Webster's Falls

North Fork Town

Fishertown

Chotean's

Seminole Agency

Old Fort Arbuckie

Edwards

Shawnee Town

Shawnee Town

Perryville

Academy

Wilson's

Council House

Johnson's

Spring Station

Fort Arbuckie

C h i c k s a w   a n d   C h o c t o w

Boggy Depot

McKinney

Winchester Station

Fort Washita

N

Red   River

Fort Towson

0   50 km

0   50 miles

T E X A S

Gainsville

THE WAR IN THE WEST

FEWER THAN ONE-FOURTH OF THE Civil War's engagements took place west of the Mississippi. But in a fundamental sense, the Civil War began in the West and forever transformed that region. Westward expansion continually reopened the sectional conflict as slavery threatened to move into new territories. In 1820, Congress passed the Missouri Compromise to head off a civil war by dividing the West into areas of slavery and freedom. That effort continued with the Compromise of the 1850 and the Kansas-Nebraska Act of 1854.

Postponing the ultimate conflict by dividing the West proved futile, however, when a civil war, pitting antislavery Jayhawkers against proslavery Bushwhackers, erupted in Kansas Territory in 1861. After Fort Sumter, guerrilla warfare intensified in Kansas, Missouri, and Arkansas. Almost one-half of all western engagements—mostly raids, ambushes, and skirmishes—took place in Missouri, where thirty thousand Southern sympathizers fought for the Confederacy. Another one-fourth took place in Arkansas. At the Battle of Pea Ridge in the spring of 1862, the Union established control of Missouri and northern Arkansas. However, three thousand guerrillas continued to operate in the area. William Quantrill, a Confederate Army captain, led a band of three hundred guerrillas that included Frank and Jesse James and Cole Younger. Midway through the war, Quantrill's rangers raided Lawrence, Kansas, burned the town, and killed one hundred and fifty civilians. Recriminations continued along the Kansas-Missouri border throughout the war and left a legacy of lawlessness for the succeeding generation.

The Confederacy also rallied support in Indian Territory among the "Five Civilized Tribes"—Cherokees, Choctaws, Chickasaws, Creeks, and Seminoles—who provided soldiers for both sides and fought their own civil war in modern-day Oklahoma. The most ambitious Confederate initiative in the West was a plan to drive Union troops out of New Mexico Territory and even to secure Colorado and California. In 1861, a band of Texans marched up the Rio Grande, defeated the Union at the Battle of Valverde, and captured Albuquerque and Santa Fe. In response, four hundred and eighteen Colorado miners, dubbed "Pike's Peakers," marched over the Rockies under Major John M. Chivington.

In March 1862, the miners fought the Texans at the Battle of Glorieta Pass, dubbed the "Gettysburg of the West," and forced them to retreat. The dream of a Confederate empire in the Southwest was over. The fall of New Orleans in April 1862 and Vicksburg in July 1863 gave the Union control of the Mississippi River, cut the Confederacy in half, and eliminated the West as a major factor in the war. President Abraham Lincoln could now dismiss the war in the West as "militarily unimportant," but it continued to rage for the Americans who lived there. The Plains Indian War that began in the 1850s continued and intensified.

Left: *This lithograph published by Courier and Ives shows the Battle of Pea Ridge, Arkansas.*

When the Civil War began, the United States withdrew troops from the West and stopped enforcing the Indians' treaty rights. In Minnesota, the government defaulted on its treaty obligations to the Santee Sioux, pushing them to the brink of starvation. In August 1862, the Sioux responded with a surprise attack that killed four hundred to eight hundred white settlers. After their experience in Indian Territory, the Lincoln administration assumed that the uprising was part of a Confederate plot and sent in an army under General John Pope. A military court sentenced three hundred and three Indians to death. Lincoln personally reviewed all the convictions, paring down the death sentences to thirty-eight. The Santee Sioux and Winnebagoes were forced onto reservations in the Dakota and Nebraska territories.

In November 1864, a militia under Major John M. Chivington attacked peaceful Cheyennes and Arapahos encamped at Sand Creek, Colorado. Almost five hundred Native American men, women, and children died during the Sand Creek Massacre. In retaliation, an Indian war erupted in early 1865. Sioux, Cheyenne, and Arapaho warriors swept through the Platte River valley killing every white man, woman, and child they could find. Facing a shortage of volunteers, the Union recruited Confederate prisoners-of-war and African American troops, the famous "Buffalo Soldiers," to man western armies.

Dubbed "Buffalo Soldiers" by the Cheyenne, African American troops, often former slaves, were recruited shortly after the Civil War and fought in Cuba and the Philippines as well as in campaigns against hostile Indians.

The war continued in the West until June 23, 1865, when the Cherokee chief Stand Watie became the last Confederate general to surrender. However, the bitterness and violence engendered by the war in the West continued for a generation to come.

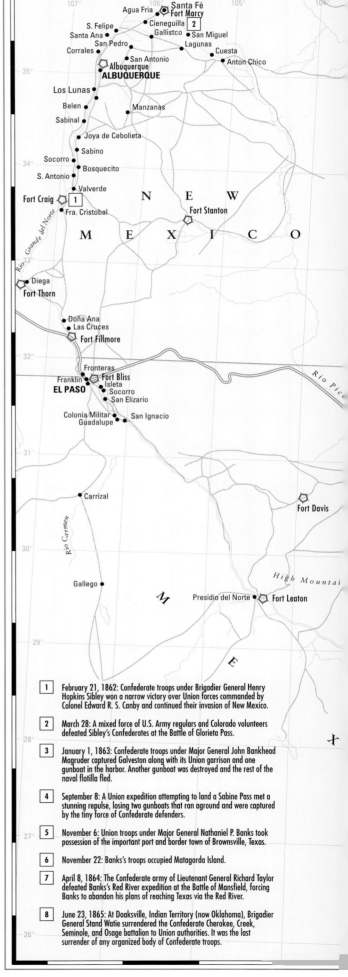

1. February 21, 1862: Confederate troops under Brigadier General Henry Hopkins Sibley won a narrow victory over Union forces commanded by Colonel Edward R. S. Canby and continued their invasion of New Mexico.

2. March 28: A mixed force of U.S. Army regulars and Colorado volunteers defeated Sibley's Confederates at the Battle of Glorieta Pass.

3. January 1, 1863: Confederate troops under Major General John Bankhead Magruder captured Galveston along with its Union garrison and one gunboat in the harbor. Another gunboat was destroyed and the rest of the naval flotilla fled.

4. September 8: A Union expedition attempting to land a Sabine Pass met a stunning repulse, losing two gunboats that ran aground and were captured by the tiny force of Confederate defenders.

5. November 6: Union troops under Major General Nathaniel P. Banks took possession of the important port and border town of Brownsville, Texas.

6. November 22: Banks's troops occupied Matagorda Island.

7. April 8, 1864: The Confederate army of Lieutenant General Richard Taylor defeated Banks's Red River expedition at the Battle of Mansfield, forcing Banks to abandon his plans of reaching Texas via the Red River.

8. June 23, 1865: At Doaksville, Indian Territory (now Oklahoma), Brigadier General Stand Watie surrendered the Confederate Cherokee, Creek, Seminole, and Osage battalion to Union authorities. It was the last surrender of any organized body of Confederate troops.

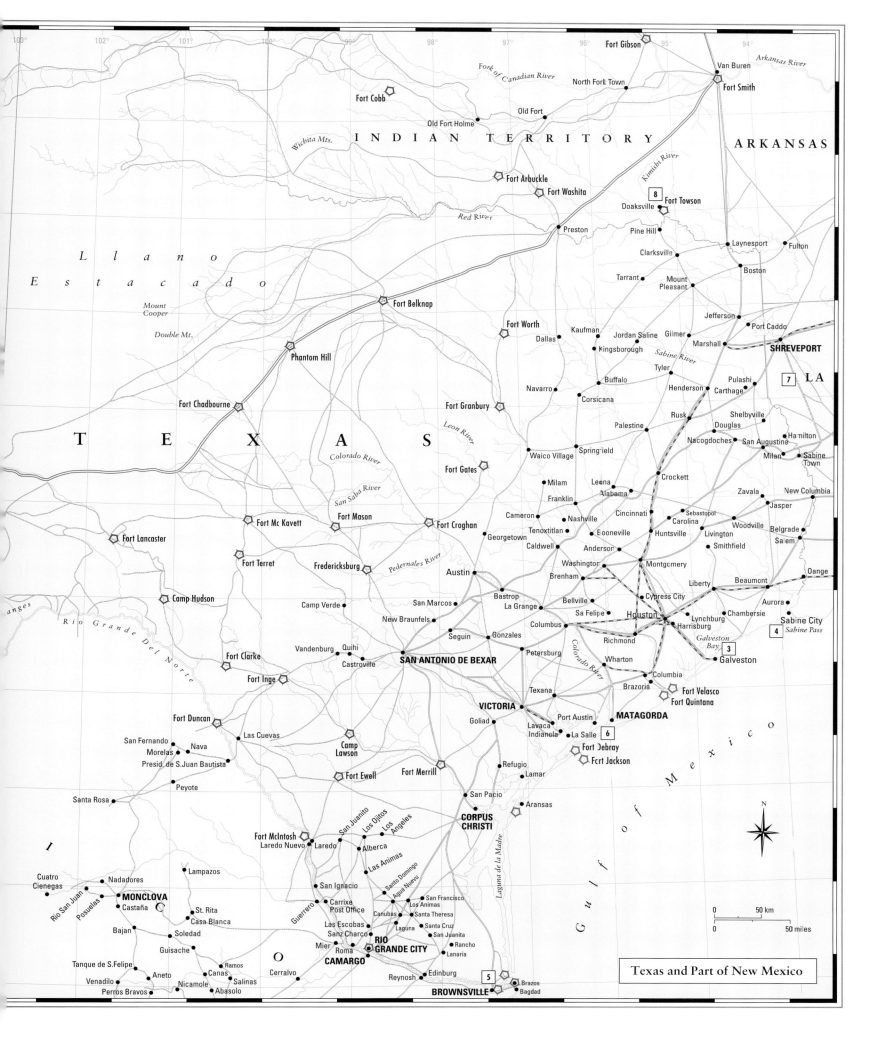

Texas and Part of New Mexico

FORT FISHER

FORT FISHER GUARDED THE APPROACHES TO Wilmington, North Carolina, which was, by late 1864, the only remaining Southern port open to blockade-runners. As early as October, Union authorities began discussing plans to capture the fort. On December 18 a large fleet under the command of Rear Admiral David D. Porter sailed from Fort Monroe, Virginia, for that purpose. Embarked on transports accompanying the fleet were six thousand five hundred soldiers under the command of Major General Benjamin F. Butler. On December 23, after a stormy passage, the fleet and transports arrived off Fort Fisher. Butler's plan for taking the fort involved an old hulk loaded with 215 tons of gunpowder, which he hoped to detonate close inshore and thereby seriously damage if not destroy the fort and its garrison. This could hardly have worked in any case, but, when it was attempted that night, the explosive hulk was detonated much too far off shore to produce even a slight effect on the fort, though it did lead members of the Confederate garrison to speculate that one of the ships of the Union fleet might have suffered a magazine explosion—well out to sea.

Admiral Porter, who from the beginning had contempt for the idea of the explosive hulk, began his naval bombardment the following morning. Though heavy and somewhat more effective than the hulk of the night before, the bombardment was not particularly destructive and fell far short of expectations. Butler's troops landed north of Fort Fisher on Christmas Day. When they approached the fort, however, the Confederate defenses looked more formidable than expected. The cost and probable outcome of an assault began to seem doubtful, and the Union generals became nervous about the approach of additional Confederate

troops from the north while they were engaging the fort to the south. Under the influence of these considerations, the decision was made to call off the expedition and return to Fort Monroe. The evacuation of troops was complete by December 27.

On January 12, 1865, the fleet returned, this time with eight thousand troops under the command of Major General Alfred H. Terry. On January 13 the fleet opened a three-day bombardment that was even heavier and much more effective than that of the previous month. On the first day of the bombardment, Terry's troops landed north of the fort and spent the next day building an entrenched line to guard against any approach of Confederate troops from the north. They also conducted reconnaissance for possible approaches to the fort. At last on January 16 all was in readiness and Terry launched a two-pronged assault against the fort. A brigade of two thousand sailors and marines stormed toward the fort along the open beach, but met disaster. The sailors were too inexperienced at this type of warfare, the marines were too few, and the fort was far too strong on this side. The sailors and marines took heavy casualties and were soon pinned down. They did, however, serve to divert Confederate attention from the second prong of Terry's attack, which was composed of Brigadier General Adelbert Ames's division, numbering three thousand three hundred men. Ames's troops stormed the northern face of Fisher and then in bloody fighting fought their way through the fort until all of it was in their hands. Union casualties totaled one thousand three hundred and forty-one, and Confederate only about five hundred. The capture of Fort Fisher, however, closed the Confederacy's last port, hastening its economic and military collapse.

The ruins of Fort Fisher. The three-day bombardment was far more effective than that made the previous month. The capture of Fort Fisher closed the South's last door to the outside world.

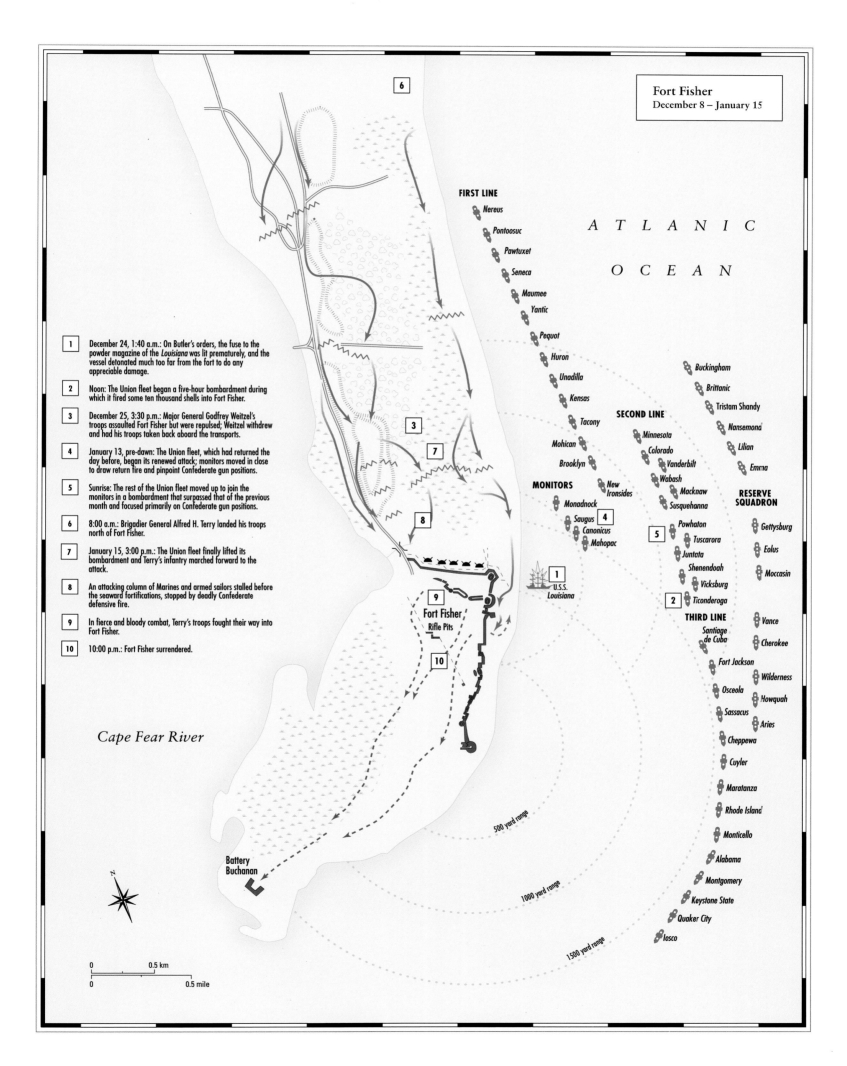

Fort Fisher
December 8 – January 15

FIRST LINE

Nereus
Pontoosuc
Pawtuxet
Seneca
Maumee
Yantic
Pequot
Huron
Unadilla
Kensas
Tacony
Mohican
Brooklyn

SECOND LINE

Minnesota
Colorado
Vanderbilt
Wabash
Macknaw
Susquehanna

New Ironsides

MONITORS

Monadnock
Saugus
Canonicus
Mahopac

[4]

[5]

Powhaton
Tuscarora
Juntata
Shenendoah
Vicksburg
Ticonderoga

[2]

THIRD LINE

Santiage
de Cuba
Fort Jackson
Osceola
Sassacus
Cheppewa
Cuyler
Maratanza
Rhode Island
Monticello
Alabama
Montgomery
Keystone State
Quaker City
Iosco

**RESERVE
SQUADRON**

Gettysburg
Eolus
Moccasin
Vance
Cherokee
Wilderness
Howquah
Aries

Buckingham
Brittanic
Tristam Shandy
Nansemona
Lilian
Emma

A T L A N T I C

O C E A N

[1] December 24, 1:40 a.m.: On Butler's orders, the fuse to the powder magazine of the *Louisiana* was lit prematurely, and the vessel detonated much too far from the fort to do any appreciable damage.

[2] Noon: The Union fleet began a five-hour bombardment during which it fired some ten thousand shells into Fort Fisher.

[3] December 25, 3:30 p.m.: Major General Godfrey Weitzel's troops assaulted Fort Fisher but were repulsed; Weitzel withdrew and had his troops taken back aboard the transports.

[4] January 13, pre-dawn: The Union fleet, which had returned the day before, began its renewed attack; monitors moved in close to draw return fire and pinpoint Confederate gun positions.

[5] Sunrise: The rest of the Union fleet moved up to join the monitors in a bombardment that surpassed that of the previous month and focused primarily on Confederate gun positions.

[6] 8:00 a.m.: Brigadier General Alfred H. Terry landed his troops north of Fort Fisher.

[7] January 15, 3:00 p.m.: The Union fleet finally lifted its bombardment and Terry's infantry marched forward to the attack.

[8] An attacking column of Marines and armed sailors stalled before the seaward fortifications, stopped by deadly Confederate defensive fire.

[9] In fierce and bloody combat, Terry's troops fought their way into Fort Fisher.

[10] 10:00 p.m.: Fort Fisher surrendered.

[6]

[3]

[7]

[8]

[9]

Fort Fisher

Rifle Pits

[10]

[1] U.S.S. *Louisiana*

Cape Fear River

Battery
Buchanan

N

500 yard range

1000 yard range

1500 yard range

0   0.5 km

0   0.5 mile

SHERMAN'S CAROLINAS' CAMPAIGN

HAVING TAKEN SAVANNAH IN DECEMBER 1864, Sherman turned his thoughts to future operations. Grant wanted him to transport most of his troops by sea to Virginia, accompanying them himself, and there join Grant in defeating Lee. The problem with that idea was that assembling the necessary shipping to transport Sherman's army would have taken considerable time. Sherman believed he could get to Virginia just as fast by marching, and he could damage the Confederacy, both materially and in morale, along the way. Sherman's soldiers were eager for such a march, as it would take them first through South Carolina, birthplace of secession, which they were eager to punish.

On February 1, Sherman's army moved north into South Carolina. To oppose them the Confederates had only the forces that had garrisoned Savannah, as well as a small cavalry force.

Still this was more than Sherman's troops had faced in Georgia, and the Confederates skirmished frequently with Sherman's lead troops. They also cut down trees across roadways and burned bridges, but the Federals restored the roads to working condition with amazingly speed. The Federals also proved adept at dealing with natural obstructions, such as swamps and flooded rivers in this rainy winter season. Such obstacles were generally much more of a hindrance than the Confederate troops. Nevertheless, with skill and vigor, Sherman's men built bridges, laid miles of corduroy road, and waded sometimes for hours up to their waists or deeper in ice-cold water, occasionally doing so while skirmishing with the enemy.

True to their intentions, Sherman's soldiers were more destructive in South Carolina than they had been in Georgia, burning a large num-

Union soldiers at Fort McAllister. The fort was stormed and fell on December 13, eight days prior to the capture of Savannah.

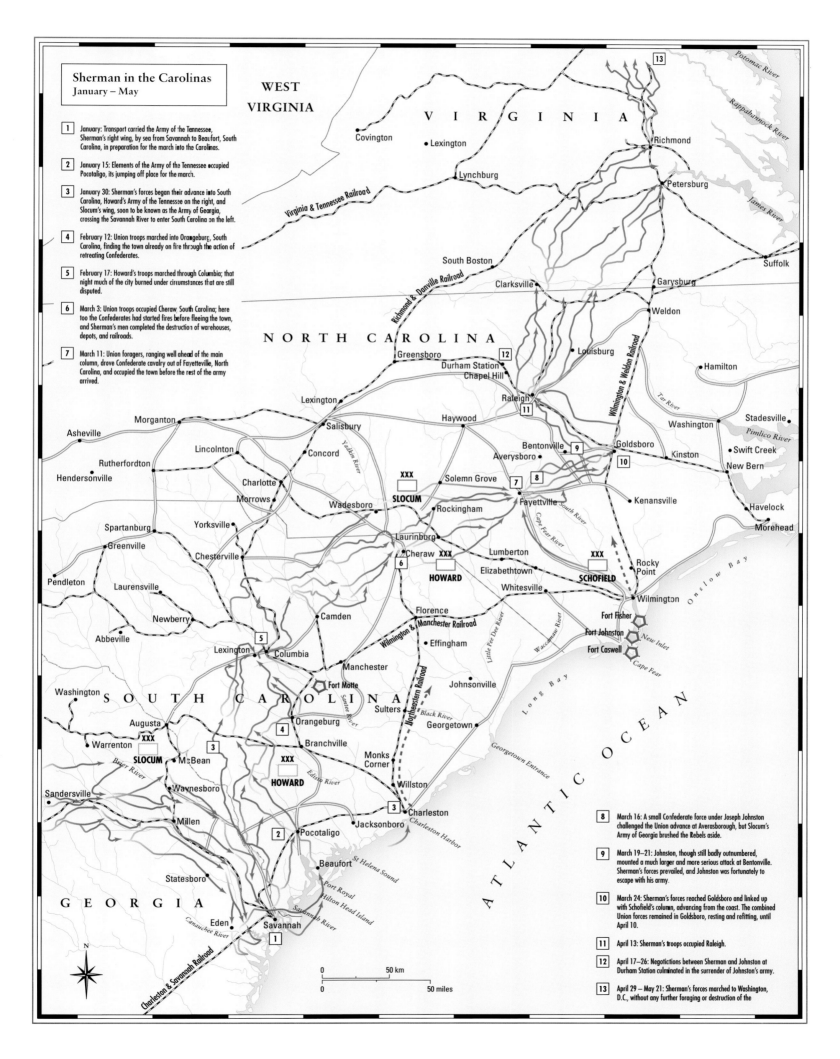

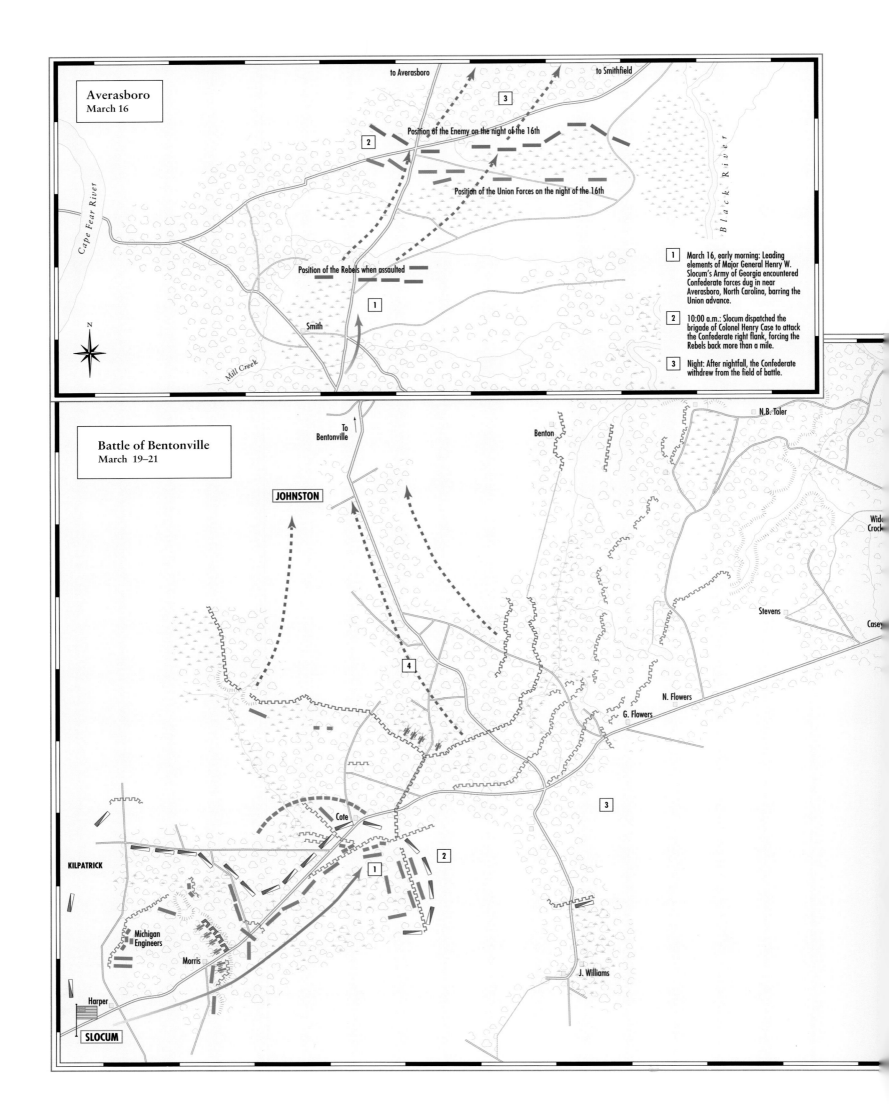

Averasboro
March 16

Position of the Enemy on the night of the 16th

Position of the Union Forces on the night of the 16th

Position of the Rebels when assaulted

Cape Fear River

Black River

to Averasboro

to Smithfield

3

2

2

1

Smith

N

Mill Creek

1   March 16, early morning: Leading elements of Major General Henry W. Slocum's Army of Georgia encountered Confederate forces dug in near Averasboro, North Carolina, barring the Union advance.

2   10:00 a.m.: Slocum dispatched the brigade of Colonel Henry Case to attack the Confederate right flank, forcing the Rebels back more than a mile.

3   Night: After nightfall, the Confederate withdrew from the field of battle.

Battle of Bentonville
March 19–21

To Bentonville

JOHNSTON

N.B. Toler

Benton

Widow Crock

Stevens

Casey

N. Flowers

G. Flowers

4

3

Cote

2

1

KILPATRICK

Michigan Engineers

Morris

Harper

SLOCUM

J. Williams

ber of dwellings as well as barns, cotton gins, and the like. Naturally, they continued to live off the land, helping themselves to any food they could find in the larders, smokehouses, or various ingenious hiding places where Southern white civilians attempted to conceal their victuals. Slaves often helped the soldiers to find food, livestock, and other possessions hidden by their masters.

Using the same method that had worked well for him in Georgia, Sherman contrived to keep the Confederates guessing about his true destination. On first entering South Carolina he created uncertainty as to whether he would be heading toward Charleston, South Carolina, or toward Augusta, Georgia. In fact he steered a course about halfway between those two cities and directly toward the South Carolina capital at Columbia. His army arrived outside of Columbia on February 16, opposed by a small force of Confederate cavalry under Major General Wade Hampton. Sherman's artillery fired a few shells into the city, and his troops forced their way across the Congaree River and into Columbia. Hampton and his troopers fled after setting fire to large stocks of cotton piled in the streets. The piles continued to smolder throughout the day. That night a strong wind came up, fanning fires that destroyed much of the city. The true origin of the conflagration is disputed, with the chief candidates being Hampton's burning cotton, Sherman's soldiers, recently released Union prisoners of war, or slaves. At any rate, many of Sherman's troops spent the night on fire fighting duty, trying to put out the blaze.

In much the same manner Sherman proceeded northeastward through Cheraw, South Carolina, and into North Carolina, where his soldiers greatly curtailed their destructiveness. They took Fayetteville, North Carolina, on March 11. By this time the Confederates had a somewhat larger force available to oppose Sherman's advance, as units from the Army of Tennessee arrived from Mississippi. General Joseph E. Johnston commanded the ragtag Confederate force. On March 16, Confederate and Union troops clashed at Averasboro, North Carolina, where the Federals were victorious. Three days later Johnston made a more serious attack at Bentonville, where fighting continued for three days. After some initial success, however, the Confederates again suffered defeat.

After the surrender of Lee's army at Appomattox, on April 9, Johnston opened surrender negotiations with Sherman. The agreement they reached on April 18 was so favorable to Johnston that the authorities in Washington, D.C., refused to ratify it. The generals negotiated a new agreement and the remaining Confederate forces in North Carolina surrendered to Sherman on April 26.

1 March 19, afternoon: Slocum's troops advanced up the road leading toward Goldsboro and drove in the Confederate cavalry of Major General Wade Hampton before encountering the main Confederate line.

2 Johnston's Confederates counterattacked and drove Slocum back.

3 March 20: The Army of the Tennessee arrived on the battlefield and took up a position on Slocum's right.

4 March 21: Major General Joseph Mower's division of the Army of the Tennessee attacked the Confederate left and scored a breakthrough that threatened to trap Johnston's army. Sherman, believing the Confederate army posed no further threat anyway, halted the fighting and allowed Johnston to escape.

THE FALL OF PETERSBURG AND RICHMOND

Far Right: The Dictator, an 8.5 ton 13-inch mortar, was the largest of the siege guns at Petersburg, firing a 200-pound missile.

THROUGHOUT THE WINTER MONTHS OF 1865 the siege of Petersburg and Richmond ground on. Both Lee and Grant knew that it could not continue this way through spring and summer. Grant made plans to break Lee's hold on Richmond and Petersburg and then trap Lee's army before it could escape to do more mischief. Lee hoped to escape the Richmond-Petersburg siege lines with his army intact, join Joseph E. Johnston's small Confederate army in North Carolina, and with him defeat Sherman and then Grant. Lee had to act quickly, however, because Sherman was approaching and his arrival would be the end of Lee's army.

On March 25, Lee launched an attack on Fort Stedman, a Union stronghold on the eastern end of the Petersburg lines. Lee knew that Grant could not afford to allow a Confederate breakthrough there. By threatening to achieve one, Lee's goal was to break Grant's lines and force the Union commander to draw in his extended left flank to reinforce the sector around Fort Stedman. If that occurred it would facilitate Lee's task of slipping his army around Grant's western flank and then southward to join Johnston. However, matters never proceeded nearly that far. The Confederates took the fort in a predawn assault but could neither roll up any substantial segment of the Union line nor take any of the neighboring forts. After a few hours, Union reinforcements crushed the small Confederate lodgment in their lines. Fort Stedman demonstrated that by early spring of 1865 the Army of Northern Virginia's hardest blow could scarcely attract the attention of the Army of the Potomac.

By contrast, Grant's own offensive program,

Below: A small section of the maze of trenches which surrounded Petersburg. The sharpened stakes facing to the right were intended to discourage direct assault.

when he put it into motion four days later, proved devastating. He dispatched his most aggressive subordinate, Major General Philip H. Sheridan, with most of the army's cavalry as well as the powerful Fifth Corps to strike at the vital crossroads of Five Forks, southwest of Petersburg. If Grant's troops took Five Forks, Lee's position in Petersburg and Richmond would quickly become impossible. To stop Sheridan, Lee dispatched a powerful force of his own under the command of Major General George E. Pickett, ordering him to "hold Five Forks at all hazards."

Pickett checked Sheridan on March 31, but the determined Union general struck again the next day and routed Pickett's force at the Battle of Five Forks. Learning of Sheridan's victory late that night, Grant ordered all of his artillery to begin a bombardment of the Confederate lines immediately and to keep it up through the night. A massive predawn infantry assault all along the Union lines was to follow the bombardment. When the Federals advanced, they broke through Lee's thin lines at numerous places. Confederate general Ambrose Powell Hill rode out to try to rally his men, and was killed. Lee and some of his force managed to fight a delaying action, allowing the Confederate army to evacuate Richmond and Petersburg and flee westward. Also evacuating Richmond that day was Confederate president Jefferson Davis and his cabinet, beginning a flight that, for Davis, would end a little more than a month later with his capture near Irwinville, Georgia. Meanwhile Union troops occupied Richmond and Petersburg on April 3 and the following day Lincoln toured the captured Confederate capital.

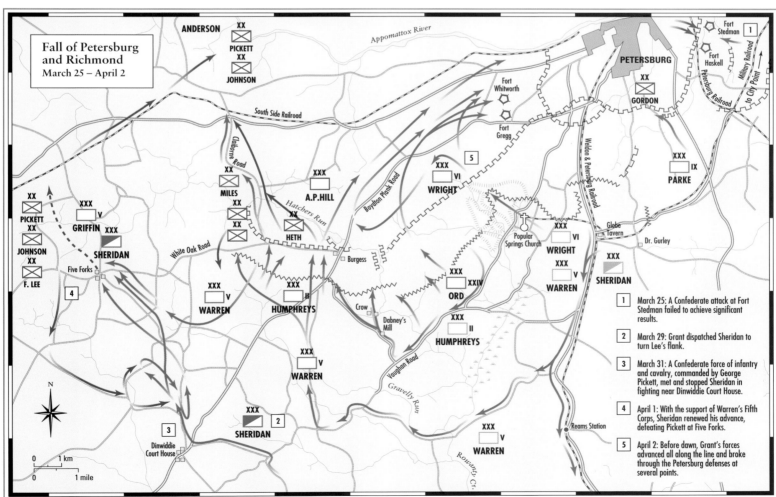

Fall of Petersburg
and Richmond
March 25 – April 2

1. March 25: A Confederate attack at Fort Stedman failed to achieve significant results.

2. March 29: Grant dispatched Sheridan to turn Lee's flank.

3. March 31: A Confederate force of infantry and cavalry, commanded by George Pickett, met and stopped Sheridan in fighting near Dinwiddie Court House.

4. April 1: With the support of Warren's Fifth Corps, Sheridan renewed his advance, defeating Pickett at Five Forks.

5. April 2: Before dawn, Grant's forces advanced all along the line and broke through the Petersburg defenses at several points.

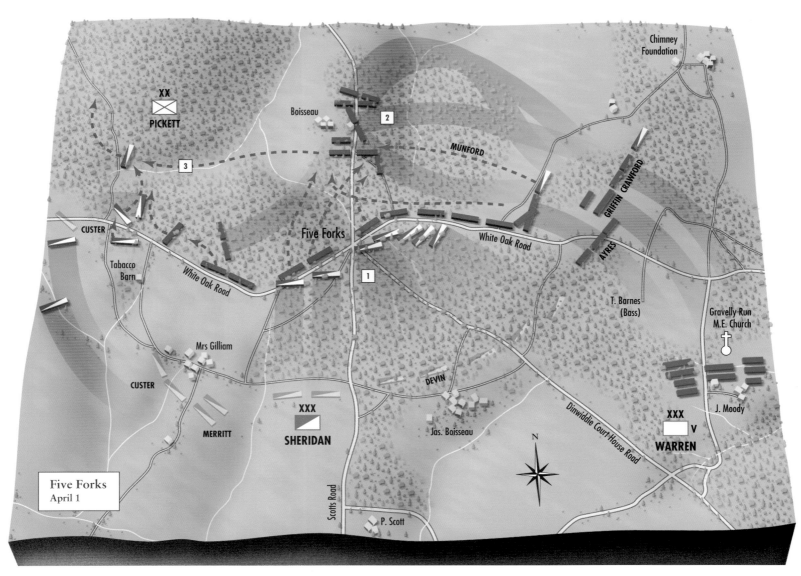

Five Forks
April 1

1. April 1, c. 3:00 p.m.: Sheridan launched the dismounted cavalry divisions of Brigadier General George A. Custer and Brigadier General Thomas C. Devin at Pickett's lines covering the road junction of Five Forks.

2. 4:00 p.m.: Major General. Gouverneur K. Warren's Fifth Corps struck the Confederate flank and rear.

3. Pickett's defeated Confederates fled, leaving five thousand prisoners and the vital road junction in Union hands.

Below left: *The Battle of Five Forks, April 1.*

The Union flag flies over the State House in Richmond.

APPOMATTOX

Robert E. Lee photographed in the uniform he had worn when surrendering the Army of Northern Virginia.

On April 1, 1865, Union troops under the immediate command of Major General Philip H. Sheridan defeated a portion of Lee's army under the direct command of Major General George E. Pickett at Five Forks, west of Petersburg. This made it impossible for Lee to continue holding Petersburg and Richmond and demonstrated that his army was weakening. Grant ordered an assault the next morning along the entire line. Union troops broke through the Confederate line in multiple locations. Lee notified Davis, and the Confederate government fled. After fighting a delaying action, Lee's army evacuated the Richmond and Petersburg lines later that day and marched westward.

Lee had two possibilities. He might be able to move west, get clear of Grant's pursuit, and then turn south to join a small Confederate army under Johnston that was making feeble efforts to slow Sherman's march through North Carolina. Or he might move westward to the Appalachian Mountains, and there hold off Grant while his army regrouped and recruited.

Both plans depended on escaping Grant's pursuit. In a war in which pursuits had rarely been fast or relentless, this one was both. Union cavalry under aggressive leaders such as the youthful Major General George A. Custer harried the rear of the Confederate column constantly, taking prisoners and forcing the Confederate infantry to deploy again and again to fend them off. By April 4, most of Lee's army had reached Amelia Court House, but to Lee's dismay the large shipment of rations he expected to find there was not on hand. This cost Lee twenty-four hours, as he had to keep his army at Amelia the following day to forage for supplies in the surrounding countryside. The delay gave Union forces time to reach Jetersville, blocking Lee's direct route southwestward, toward a possible link-up with Johnston.

The next day the Army of Northern Virginia marched westward, the only remaining direction that offered hope of escaping Grant. At Sayler's Creek a mistake in the march order opened a gap in the Confederate column, of which pursuing Union forces, the cavalry as well as infantry of the Second and Sixth Corps, were quick to take advantage. They struck and cut off a portion of Lee's army commanded by Lieutenant General Richard S. Ewell. A few miles away another segment of the Army of Northern Virginia under Major General John B. Gordon suffered heavy losses trying to cut its way out of an encirclement. In all, the Federals took some eight thousand Confederate prisoners, or nearly one-third of the army with which Lee had started the day.

The next day Grant sent Lee a note summoning him to surrender the Army of Northern Virginia. Lee declined but asked what terms Grant might be willing to give. Grant replied generously the next day that he would be willing to parole Lee's army, but Lee again declined. Lee proposed instead that he and Grant meet to discuss some sort of general armistice that might give the Confederacy the opportunity to win by negotiation at least some of

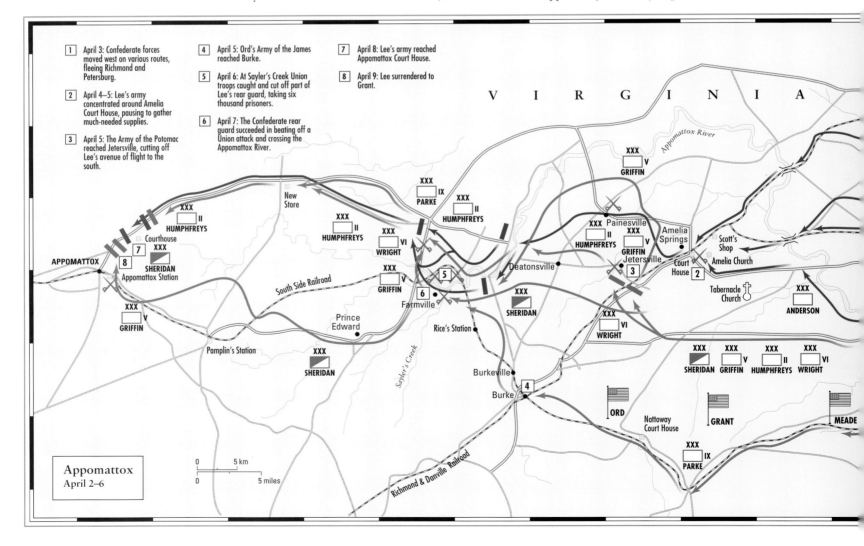

1. April 3: Confederate forces moved west on various routes, fleeing Richmond and Petersburg.

2. April 4–5: Lee's army concentrated around Amelia Court House, pausing to gather much-needed supplies.

3. April 5: The Army of the Potomac reached Jetersville, cutting off Lee's avenue of flight to the south.

4. April 5: Ord's Army of the James reached Burke.

5. April 6: At Sayler's Creek Union troops caught and cut off part of Lee's rear guard, taking six thousand prisoners.

6. April 7: The Confederate rear guard succeeded in beating off a Union attack and crossing the Appomattox River.

7. April 8: Lee's army reached Appomattox Court House.

8. April 9: Lee surrendered to Grant.

Appomattox
April 2–6

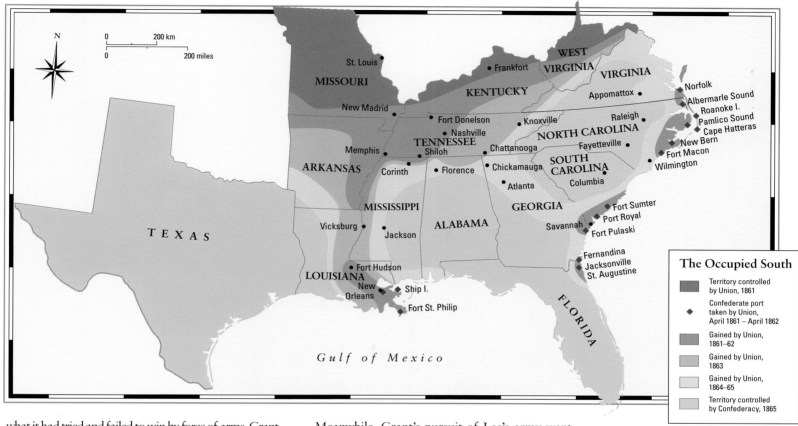

The Occupied South

▰ Territory controlled by Union, 1861

◆ Confederate port taken by Union, April 1861 – April 1862

▰ Gained by Union, 1861–62

▰ Gained by Union, 1863

▰ Gained by Union, 1864–65

▰ Territory controlled by Confederacy, 1865

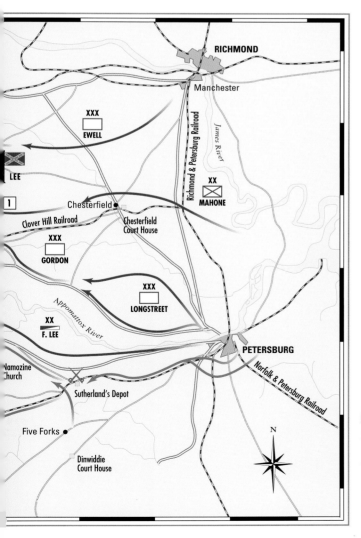

what it had tried and failed to win by force of arms. Grant declined, pointing out that he had no authority to negotiate for anything but the surrender of Lee's army.

Meanwhile, Grant's pursuit of Lee's army went on. By the evening of April 8, Union cavalry and infantry had moved in front of Lee, blocking all further escape to the west, and capturing and destroying supplies waiting for the Army of Northern Virginia at Appomattox Court House. The next morning, Palm Sunday, April 9, 1865, Lee made one final attempt to cut his way through. Finding the Union lines solid in his path, he sent a note to Grant asking for a meeting to discuss surrender. Lee had waited so late that it was only with considerable difficulty that his staff officers and couriers were able to convey notice of their impending surrender to the surrounding Union troops, who were about to launch a final offensive that would have crushed what remained of the Army of Northern Virginia.

Lee and Grant met in the parlor of the Wilmer McLean House, and there Grant gave terms even more generous than he had suggested. He allowed officers to keep their sidearms, horses, and baggage and each cavalryman and artilleryman to keep his horse for planting the next year's crops. Significantly, the terms provided that the paroled soldiers should return to their homes and not to be disturbed by U.S. authorities, as long as they kept the terms of their paroles and obeyed the laws in effect where they lived. This effectively blocked punishment for treason for Lee and others who had served in his army.

A pen and ink drawing of the village of Appomattox in Virginia. The McLean house is on the right.

RICHMOND DURING THE WAR

THE CONFEDERACY RECEIVED A TREMENDOUS boost when Virginia seceded after Fort Sumter. Virginia was the most populous state in the South, and its capital, Richmond, was an important center of transportation and industry. One hundred miles from Washington, D.C., Richmond was destined to become the strategic focus of the fighting. By moving its capital to Richmond, the Confederacy raised the stakes of the war even higher. Only the twenty-fifth largest city in America, Richmond became the symbol of Confederate defiance and the most coveted military target of the Union Army. Commanding the Army of Northern Virginia, General Robert E. Lee's primary task was to defend Richmond. Economically, Richmond had the South's leading foundry, the Tredegar Iron Works, and after Confederates plundered Harpers Ferry the city acquired a large armory, as well.

The war initially brought prosperity to the city. As the seat of the Confederate government, employment boomed in wartime Richmond, and there was a swirl of social opportunities. Soon, however, the realities of war intruded. Shortages brought inflation and scarcity, and the Union Army loomed as a constant threat on the horizon. Casualties poured in from throughout the eastern theater. Hospitals were limited, and the wounded crowded into private homes. The city had to set up makeshift prisons to house thousands of Union captives. In early 1862, the Army of the Potomac approached within six miles of the city, and Richmonders went on the defensive. After the enemy had been repelled, Richmond became a base for Lee's advances into Maryland (Antietam) in 1862 and Pennsylvania (Gettysburg) in 1863. But those campaigns destroyed Lee's offensive capacity, and the Confederates dug in around Richmond, spending the rest of the war defending their capital city

As casualties mounted, Richmond drained men and materiel from the western theater, leaving many Southerners resentful, wondering whether the city's defense was worthwhile. As shortages grew, the army commandeered supplies, and morale plummeted. In 1863, resentment boiled over into the famous "bread riot." After years of shortages, Richmond's women broke into shops and warehouses, seizing food and clothing for their families. President Jefferson Davis personally stopped the riot and ordered the crowd to disperse. The government suppressed news of the riot to prevent its repetition elsewhere and to maintain the reputation of the Confederate capital. The riot was soon followed by another blow to the city's morale, the death of General Stonewall Jackson. The entire city of Richmond mourned the beloved leader and symbol of Confederate defiance and watched his funeral procession as it trudged somberly to the Capitol. In 1864, the Army of the Potomac neared Richmond again, and General Ulysses S. Grant mounted a yearlong siege.

Staving off the inevitable, Richmonders threw up elaborate fortifications and trenchworks that made every attack on the city a virtual suicide mission. Union artillery shelled the city relentlessly, turning its buildings into burned-out symbols of Confederate defeat. Grant targeted the city of Petersburg, to the south of Richmond. When Petersburg fell, Richmond was cut off from the rest of the Confederacy and had to surrender. Jefferson Davis fled from the city, and Lee led his army westward toward the mountains. The day after its capture, President Abraham Lincoln toured Richmond by carriage. The once-proud Confederate capital lay in ruins.

Richmond, photographed by Alex Gardner in 1865, endured protracted Union artillery bombardment. This photograph shows the remains of the Confederate arsenal.

Defenses of Richmond

Totopotomoy Creek

Hungary
Yellow Tavern
Brook Turnpike
Atlee's Stn.
Central Railroad
Bridge Road
Mechanicsville
Richmond & Potomac Railroad
Deep Run Turnpike
Chickahominy River
Old Cold Harbor
New Cold Harbor
Plank Road
Mechanicsville Turnpike
James River
RICHMOND
Richmond & Danville Railroad
Fair Oaks Station
York River Railroad
Savage Station
Manchester
Williamsburg or Seven-Mile Road
Charles City Road
Central or Darbytown Road
Market or River Road
Drewry's Bluff
Cox's Landing
James River
Chesterfield
Richmond & Petersburg Railroad
Curl's Neck

N

0   2 km
0   2 miles

WASHINGTON, D.C., DURING THE WAR

LOCATED ONE HUNDRED MILES NORTH of Richmond, the nation's capital held tremendous strategic, political, and moral significance for both the Union and the Confederacy. Strategically, Washington was the greatest military target for Confederate armies, just as Richmond was the Union's primary military prize.

From First Bull Run onward, Confederate armies threatened Washington periodically as part of their strategy of taking the war to the enemy. General Robert E. Lee's summer offensives in 1862 and 1863, ending at Antietam and Gettysburg, were primarily designed to

The Chain Bridge across the Potomac River, one of Washington's most heavily guarded approaches.

threaten Washington. Stonewall Jackson's army could emerge from the Shenandoah Valley and advance on Washington whenever the Army of the Potomac neared Richmond. As a result, the Lincoln administration was careful to maintain an army of fifteen thousand to fifty thousand men around the capital, which denied needed manpower to the Union offensive.

During the winter of 1861–1862, after the First Bull Run scare, the Union built a thirty-seven-mile ring of fortifications around Washington. The defensive system included sixty-eight forts connected by twenty miles of trenches. Ninety-three artillery positions boasted eight hundred cannons. By the end of the war, Washington was the most heavily defended city on Earth. Within the fortified ring sat a city of sixty-three thousand people, America's twelfth largest in 1860. The city filled

with people and at times swelled to 200,000 during the war. Between 1860 and 1870, Washington doubled in size, experiencing the greatest growth in its entire history.

With the outbreak of war, the Union transferred its military headquarters to Washington from West Point, New York. The War Department, the Navy Department, the Union Army Headquarters, the Army of the Potomac Headquarters, and the Headquarters Defenses of Washington all sat within walking distance of the White House. Abraham Lincoln frequented them personally to oversee the war effort. Washington also housed the largest arsenal in the Union at what is now Fort McNair, as well as the U.S. Navy Yard and the Baltimore & Ohio Railroad depot, which moved thousands of troops into and through the city daily. Washington was also the main supply depot for the Army of the Potomac, which required ten thousand soldiers and civilians to supply and feed it.

South of the White House, the mall around the unfinished Washington Monument contained a cattle-grazing area and slaughterhouses. In addition to hosting Union soldiers, up to 140,000 at a time, Washington maintained prisons for captured Confederates and disloyal Northerners. The largest of which, the Old Capitol Prison, held more than two thousand seven hundred prisoners at its peak. Makeshift hospitals ministered to the wounded, more than fifty-six thousand at the end of 1862 alone. Midway through the war, new "pavilion" hospitals—about thirty of them—each with ten or twelve wards housing six hundred patients, dotted the city. Volunteers, including Clara Barton, Louisa May Alcott, and Walt Whitman, tended to the wounded, and President Lincoln and his wife Mary Todd visited. Later, the number of hospitals fell to nineteen when the wounded were shipped through Washington directly to hospitals in Philadelphia and New York. The gravely wounded who died were buried in pine coffins at a cost of $4.99. When Washington's Soldiers' Home Cemetery filled up in 1863, the government seized Lee's estate in Arlington. Coffins moved solemnly across the Long Bridge and over the Potomac to what became Arlington National Cemetery.

As a poignant reminder of the purpose of the war, fugitive slaves continually poured into the city. Forty thousand fugitives occupied shanty towns until the Emancipation Proclamation allowed them to join the Union Army. With its ebb and flow of armies, its sprawling defenses, and its overflowing hospitals, prisons, and cemeteries, Washington was a focal point of the war but also a microcosm of wartime America.

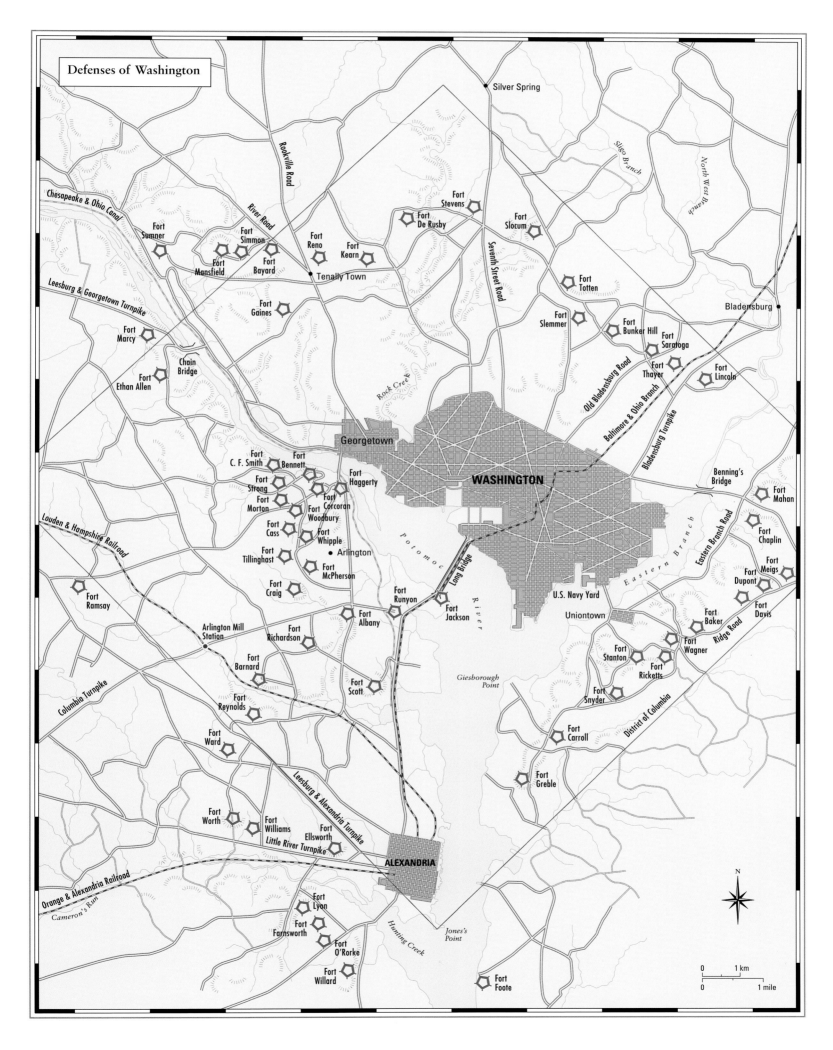

Defenses of Washington

Silver Spring

Chesapeake & Ohio Canal

River Road

Rookville Road

Fort Sumner

Fort Simmon

Fort Mansfield

Fort Bayard

Fort Reno

Fort Kearn

Fort De Rusby

Fort Stevens

Fort Slocum

Seventh Street Road

Fort Totten

Sligo Branch

North West Branch

Leesburg & Georgetown Turnpike

Fort Marcy

Fort Gaines

Tenally Town

Fort Slemmer

Fort Bunker Hill

Fort Saratoga

Old Bladensburg Road

Baltimore & Ohio Branch

Bladensburg Turnpike

Fort Thayer

Fort Lincoln

Bladensburg

Chain Bridge

Fort Ethan Allen

Rock Creek

Georgetown

WASHINGTON

Benning's Bridge

Fort C. F. Smith

Fort Bennett

Fort Strong

Fort Haggerty

Fort Morton

Fort Corcoran

Fort Woodbury

Fort Cass

Fort Whipple

Arlington

Fort Tillinghast

Fort McPherson

Eastern Branch

Eastern Branch Road

Fort Mahan

Fort Chaplin

Fort Meigs

Fort Dupont

Louden & Hampshire Railroad

Fort Ramsay

Fort Craig

Fort Runyon

Long Bridge

Potomac River

U.S. Navy Yard

Uniontown

Fort Baker

Fort Davis

Ridge Road

Arlington Mill Station

Fort Richardson

Fort Albany

Fort Jackson

Fort Wagner

Fort Barnard

Fort Scott

Fort Stanton

Fort Ricketts

Giesborough Point

Fort Reynolds

Columbia Turnpike

Fort Ward

Fort Snyder

District of Columbia

Fort Carroll

Fort Greble

Leesburg & Alexandria Turnpike

Fort Worth

Fort Williams

Fort Ellsworth

Little River Turnpike

ALEXANDRIA

Orange & Alexandria Railroad

Cameron's Run

Fort Lyon

Fort Farnsworth

Fort O'Rorke

Hunting Creek

Jones's Point

N

Fort Willard

Fort Foote

0   1 km

0   1 mile

EPILOGUE TO WAR

By 1875, many northerners had grown tired of, or alarmed by, the continued use of military power to intervene in the internal affairs of the states. Traditional fears of military power as a threat to individual liberties came to the fore again and the government withdrew the last of its troops from southern state capitals in 1877. "Reconstruction" came to an end. It had accomplished two of its goals: to reincorporate the former Confederate states into the Union; and to bring about a transition from slavery to freedom in the South. The third goal, the protection of equal rights promised in the Fourteenth and Fifteenth Amendments, awaited the "Second Reconstruction" accomplished by the civil rights movement nearly a century later as the Supreme Court stripped the federal government of much of its authority to enforce certain provisions of the Amendments.

"At this second appearing to take the oath of the presidential office there is less occasion for an extended address then there was at the first. Then a statement somewhat in detail of a course to be pursued seemed fitting and proper. Now, at the expiration of four years, during which public declarations have been constantly called forth on every point and phase of the great contrast which still absorbs the attention and engrosses the energies of the nation, little that is new could be presented. The progress of our arms, upon which all else chiefly depends,

is as well known to the public as to myself, and it is, I trust, reasonably satisfactory and encouraging to all. With high hope for the future, no prediction in regard to it is ventured.

On the occasion corresponding to this four years ago all thoughts were anxiously directed to an impending civil war. All dreaded it, all sought to avert it. While the inaugural address was being delivered from this place, devoted altogether to saving the Union without war, urgent agents were in the city seeking to destroy it without war—seeking to dissolve the Union and divide effects by negotiation. Both parties deprecated war, but one of them would make war rather than let the nation survive, and the other would accept war rather them let it perish, and the ware came.

One-eighth of the whole population were colored slaves, not distributed generally over the Union, but localized in the southern part of it. These slaves constituted a peculiar and powerful interest. All knew that this interest was somehow the cause of the war. To strengthen, perpetuate, and extend this interest was the object for which the insurgents would rend the Union even by war, while the Government claimed no right to do more than to restrict the territorial enlargement of it.

Neither party expected for the war the magnitude or the duration which it has already attained. Neither anticipated that the cause of the conflict might cease with or even before the conflict itself should cease. Each looked for an easier triumph, and a result less fundamental and astounding. Both read the same Bible and pray to the same God, and each invokes His aid against the other. It may seem strange that any men should dare to ask a just God's assistance in wringing their bread from the sweat of other men's faces, but let us judge not, that we be not judged. The prayers of both could not be answered. That of neither has been answered fully.

The Almighty has His own purposes. 'Woe unto the world because of offenses; for it must needs be that offenses come, but woe to that man by whom the offenses which, in the providence of God, must needs come, but which, having continued through His appointed time, He now wills to remove, and that He gives to both North and South this terrible war as the woe due to those by whom the offense came, shall we discern therein any departure from those divine attributes which the believers in a living God always ascribe to Him? Fondly do we hope, fervently do we pray, that this mighty scourge of war may speedily pass away. Yet, if God wills that it continue all the wealth piled by the bondsman's two hundred and fifty years of unrequited toil shall be sunk, and until every drop of blood drawn with the lash shall be paid by another drawn with the sword, as was said three thousand years ago, so still it must be said 'the judgements of the Lord are true and righteous altogether.'

With malice toward none, with charity for all, with firmness in the right as God gives us to see the right, let us strive on to finish the work we are in, to bind up the nation's wounds, to care for him who shall have borne the battle and for his widow and his orphan, to do all which may achieve and cherish a just and lasting peace among ourselves and with all nations."

Abraham Lincoln
Oath of Presidential Office,
March 4, 1865

The Cost of War—A Final Reckoning

In the years after the Civil War, visiting veterans, walking down a quiet country track at Antietam, sketched here by Walton Taber; would never forget its new name, Bloody Lane.

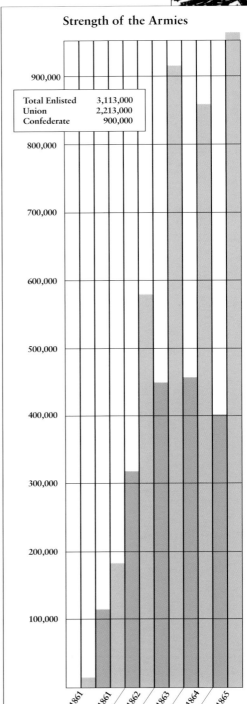

Strength of the Armies

Total Enlisted	3,113,000
Union	2,213,000
Confederate	900,000

(Chart: January 1, 1861; July 1, 1861; January 1, 1862; January 1, 1863; January 1, 1864; January 1, 1865)

THE CIVIL WAR ARMIES WERE IMMENSE, containing a total of nearly three million men, about one-tenth of all Americans. The North fielded two million white soldiers and 189,000 African-American men in the army and navy. The South recruited 900,000 white men. Overall, forty percent of white men of military age served in the Civil War.

Mobilization was much greater in the Confederacy—sixty-one percent of eligible men—simply because the South had fewer men to begin with. The North had at least three times as many men of military age and mobilized thirty-five percent of them. Both armies were manned mostly by volunteers. The Confederacy instituted a draft sooner, in April 1862, and twenty percent of Confederate soldiers were draftees or substitutes. The North instituted its draft in July 1862 and drafted only one-tenth of its men-at-arms.

The Civil War was by far the bloodiest war in American history. In absolute numbers, American casualties were fifty percent greater than during World War II. In relative terms, the Civil War produced the highest casualty rate in any American war, one hundred and eighty-two deaths per ten thousand people, six times the American casualty rate of World War II and sixteen times the rate of World War I. Overall, one in five soldiers died during the war, a total of 618,000, including 360,000 Union soldiers (one-tenth of them African-Americans) and 258,000 Confederate soldiers.

The casualty rate was much higher in the Confederate Army. One-fourth of Confederate soldiers died, as opposed to one-sixth of Union soldiers. With less manpower to mobilize, the Confederacy enrolled its men for the duration, so they had a greater chance of dying in battle. Also, disease took a higher toll in Confederate armies, accounting for one-half of all deaths. All told, eight percent of white men of military age died in the Civil War, six percent in the North and eighteen percent in the South.

The war also exacted a tremendous economic cost. The Union spent a total of $2.3 billion or $98 per capita fighting the war. The Confederacy spent $1.0 billion to fight the war or $111 per capita. But most of the war—ninety-eight percent of all engagements—was fought in the South. War damage actually cost the South more than all its military spending—$1.1 billion—and took decades to repair. Union armies that practiced "hard war" destroyed four-tenths of all the South's pre-war property.

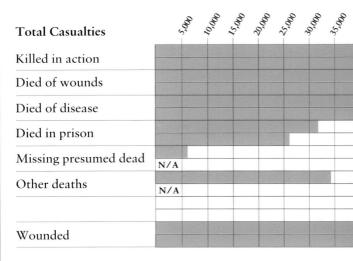

Total Casualties	5,000	10,000	15,000	20,000	25,000	30,000	35,000	4
Killed in action								
Died of wounds								
Died of disease								
Died in prison								
Missing presumed dead	N/A							
Other deaths	N/A							
Wounded								

Civil War Deaths Compared to Deaths of U.S. Soldiers in Other Wars

	Number	Rate per 10,000 population
American Revolution	25,324	117.9
War of 1812	6,780	8.3
Mexican War	13,271	6.2
Civil War	**665,850**	**181.7**
Spanish-American	5,807	0.8
World War I	116,516	11.1
World War II	405,399	29.6
Korean War	54,246	3.5
Vietnam War	57,777	2.8

Although the value of freeing four million slaves was immeasurable, economically emancipation cost slave owners another $1.6 billion. Agriculture—the South's economic foundation—was devastated. Union armies destroyed two-fifths of the South's livestock and one-half of its farm machinery. Because of its dependence on slave labor and overemphasis on cotton culture, agriculture was slow to recover and reached only seventy-five percent of its prewar levels by 1900, keeping most southern farmers mired in poverty until the twentieth century.

The South was a poor relative to the North before the Civil War, generating only seventy percent of the nation's per capita income. After the war, that figure was a mere fifty-one percent, and the average southerner was only half as wealthy as the average northerner. Meanwhile, the wealth of the North increased by fifty percent between 1860 and 1870. In the long run, of course, Americans considered the destruction of slavery as a legal, social, and economic status well worth any price.

Most of the soldiers buried at the Military Cemetery at City Point died of disease rather than as a result of combat. As Grant's supply base on the James River grew ever more crowded, disease and accidents took their toll.

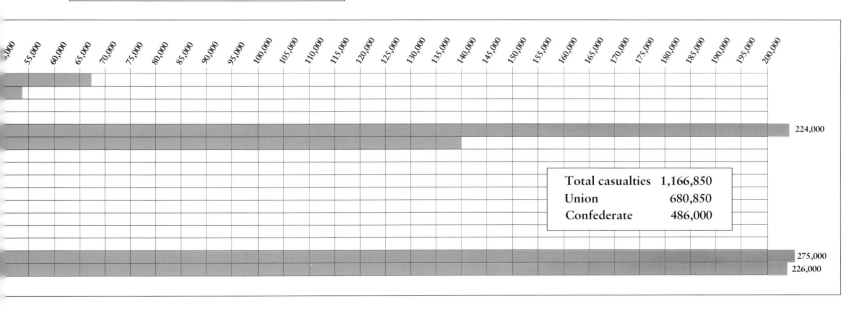

55,000	60,000	65,000	70,000	75,000	80,000	85,000	90,000	95,000	100,000	105,000	110,000	115,000	120,000	125,000	130,000	135,000	140,000	145,000	150,000	155,000	160,000	165,000	170,000	175,000	180,000	185,000	190,000	195,000	200,000

224,000

Total casualties 1,166,850
Union 680,850
Confederate 486,000

275,000

226,000

RECONSTRUCTION SOUTH

RADICAL REPUBLICANS HOPED TO reform the South before readmitting the former Confederate states into the Union. During Radical Reconstruction, which lasted from 1866 to 1877, Republicans controlled the South, created five military districts under an army of 200,000 occupation troops, required southern states to ratify the Thirteenth, Fourteenth, and Fifteenth Amendments, and supervised the adoption of new state constitutions. The Freedmen's Bureau put former slaves to work under a wage-labor system, opened three thousand schools, and dispensed equal justice for African Americans.

professional politicians provided leadership for the new Republican Party. Southern Republicans, called "Scalawags," predominated in cities and the hill country outside the plantation South—northern Georgia, Alabama, and Mississippi, eastern Tennessee, and northern Arkansas—where there had been few slaves and little support for secession. They hoped to put the war behind them and promoted economic progress. Almost one-third of the Republicans were former slaves, who gained the right to vote in 1870 under the Fifteenth Amendment.

Joining the Union League, a patriotic Republican

This engraving by J. L. Giles uses a a remarkable combination of patriotic and religious ideology to allegorize the reconciliation of the North and South through the Federal program of Reconstruction.

One of the first impulses of the newly freed slaves was to move away from the plantations where they had labored in bondage. Many searched for family members who had been "sold off." Others left white-dominated areas and gravitated toward the "Black Belt," where African Americans were the majority. Still others fled rural poverty and moved to cities. The African American population of the South's cities doubled in the decade after the Civil War. Launching the "Great Migration," nearly 100,000 former slaves left the South entirely and moved to northern cities or to homesteads on the Great Plains.

Churches were the foundation of the African American community, and Baptist and Methodist ministers emerged as social and political leaders. The Republican Party controlled government and politics in the Reconstruction South and consisted of three distinct groups. "Carpetbaggers" were northerners who moved to the South after the war to help reform the region or simply to take advantage of economic opportunities. These teachers, ministers, businessmen, retired army officers, and

club imported from the North, they voted at rates as high as ninety percent. Most southern whites, however, resented Reconstruction and the Republican Party that supported it. The political participation of African Americans and white northerners, in particular, engendered bitterness. Two of the main aims of the Ku Klux Klan, organized in Tennessee in 1866, were to drive African Americans out of the South's political system and to break up the Republican Party. Congress adopted military and legal measures that disabled the Klan. In response, Democrats launched a campaign to organize white voters peacefully, take control of southern politics and government, and create a "New South" that could compete with the North politically and economically.

A new generation of southern leaders strove to diversify their region's economy and accepted the need for cities, factories, and modern transportation systems. They borrowed northern strategies for economic development but wanted southerners to make their own political and economic decisions. These "Redeemers," as they called themselves, rebuilt the Democratic Party, took over the southern states one-by-one, and gradually ended Reconstruction by 1877. While the Redeemers recognized their continuing economic dependence on the labor of former slaves, their dream of a "New South" excluded African Americans from equal participation in social and political life. By voting heavily Democratic, this "Solid South" was eventually able to regain the national power that the region had lost by seceding and losing the Civil War.

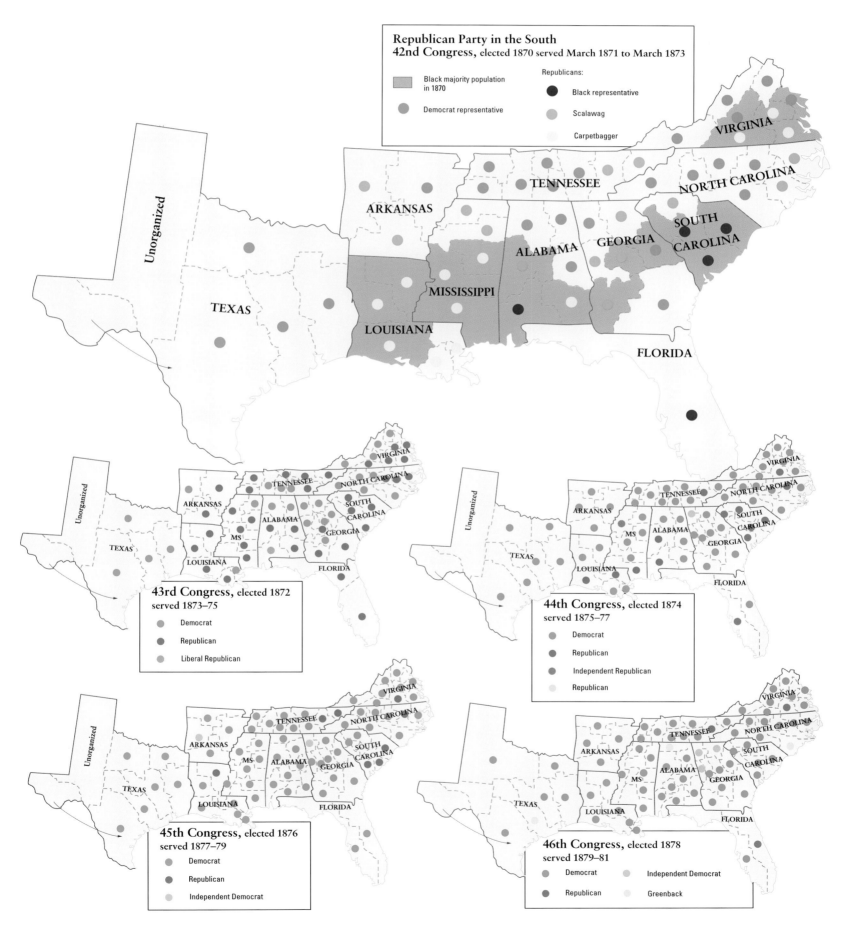

Republican Party in the South
42nd Congress, elected 1870 served March 1871 to March 1873

- Black majority population in 1870
- Democrat representative

Republicans:
- Black representative
- Scalawag
- Carpetbagger

43rd Congress, elected 1872 served 1873–75
- Democrat
- Republican
- Liberal Republican

44th Congress, elected 1874 served 1875–77
- Democrat
- Republican
- Independent Republican
- Republican

45th Congress, elected 1876 served 1877–79
- Democrat
- Republican
- Independent Democrat

46th Congress, elected 1878 served 1879–81
- Democrat
- Republican
- Independent Democrat
- Greenback

REDEMPTION OF FORMER CONFEDERATE STATES

This political cartoon attacks organizations such as the Ku Klux Klan and the White League for encouraging racial attacks on the freed slaves of the southern states and particularly for denying black voters access to the ballot box and education.

DURING RECONSTRUCTION, CONGRESS READMITTED southern states that satisfied stringent Republican demands. States had to ratify the Thirteenth, Fourteenth, and Fifteenth Amendments, provide free public education, repudiate secession and their Confederate war debts, and certify that a majority of their voters were loyal to the Union. When states were readmitted to the Union, or "reconstructed," the Republican Party was firmly in control. The Republicans were mostly transplanted northerners—"carpetbaggers"—and former slaves. Soon, however, white southerners wanted to reassume political control. They called that process "Redemption," and turned to the Democratic Party to achieve it.

Redeemers envisioned what they called "home rule," a natural majority of southern voters making their own decisions without interference from the North, from Congress, or from Republicans. The Redeemers organized the South aggressively, founding the Liberty League to motivate Democrats to re-enter politics. They championed a "New South" that would be economically independent and politically powerful, emulating the success of the North in building cities, factories, and railroads. The Redeemers' motto was "The South will rise again." Redemption had some positive dimensions, such as

modernizing education, expanding government, and attracting investment. Unfortunately, many of the tactics that the Redeemers adopted to regain power were far less positive.

The Ku Klux Klan arose in Tennessee in 1866 to intimidate African American voters and political leaders, undermine the Republican Party, and steal elections. Congress passed legislation suppressing the Klan, but political violence still spread across the South. Mississippi Democrats purged African Americans from political contests with a campaign of intimidation and violence dubbed the "Mississippi Plan." Voting laws, including the poll tax and literacy tests, disfranchised African Americans by targeting their poverty and their lack of education. Racist campaigns discouraged whites and blacks from cooperating with each other. In their pursuit of political power, Redeemers also depended on the complacency of northern whites, whose commitment to reforming the South and establishing racial justice gradually faded.

A depression that broke out in 1873 preoccupied northern voters, who blamed the Republican Party for the economic slowdown and increasingly supported Democrats. The U.S. Supreme Court weakened much of the legislation that underlay Reconstruction. Beginning in 1870, Democrats began regaining political control of southern states, one-by-one. This process of Redemption left African Americans at the mercy of white majorities who no longer respected the federal laws, and even the constitutional amendments, that guaranteed equal rights. By 1876, all but three southern states—Louisiana, South Carolina, and Florida—had been "redeemed." All of the others had Democratic majorities. The election of 1876 resulted in a virtual tie that provided southern Democrats with an opportunity to bring an end to Reconstruction and establish "home rule."

BLACK OFFICEHOLDERS DURING RECONSTRUCTION

| | STATE LEGISLATURE | | U.S. Congress | TOTAL OFFICEHOLDERS |
	Senate	House		(all offices)
ALABAMA	5	66	3	167
ARKANSAS	5	22	0	46
FLORIDA	12	36	1	58
GEORGIA	6	43	1	108
LOUISIANA	22	105	1	210
MISSISSIPPI	13	102	3	226
NORTH CAROLINA	10	48	1	180
SOUTH CAROLINA	29	210	6	314
TENNESSEE	0	0	0	20
TEXAS	2	15	0	46
VIRGINIA	8	36	0	85

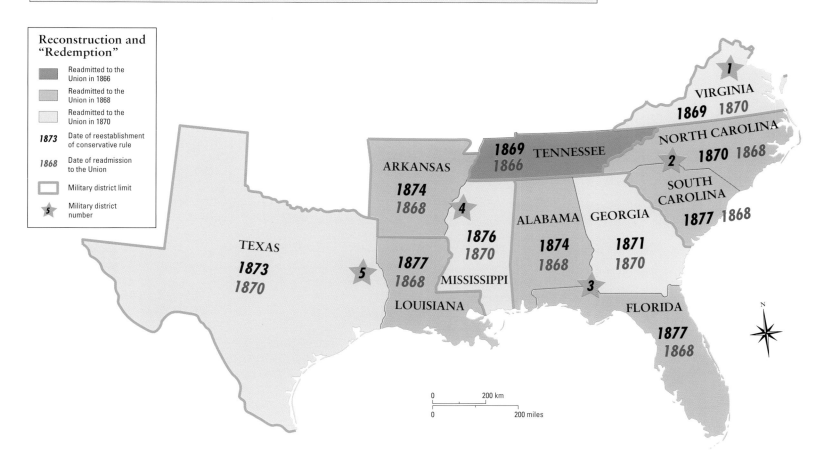

Reconstruction and "Redemption"

- Readmitted to the Union in 1866
- Readmitted to the Union in 1868
- Readmitted to the Union in 1870
- *1873* Date of reestablishment of conservative rule
- *1868* Date of readmission to the Union
- Military district limit
- ★ *5* Military district number

VIRGINIA
1869 *1870*

TENNESSEE
1869
1866

NORTH CAROLINA
1870 *1868*

ARKANSAS
1874
1868

SOUTH
CAROLINA
1877 *1868*

ALABAMA
1874
1868

GEORGIA
1871
1870

TEXAS
1873
1870

1876
1870

1877
1868

MISSISSIPPI

LOUISIANA

FLORIDA
1877
1868

0   200 km

0   200 miles

LAND GRANT COLLEGES (MORRILL ACT)

CIVIL WAR ERA REPUBLICANS WERE committed to using the federal government to promote reform in a wide variety of ways. In addition to abolishing slavery, they encouraged publicly supported education as a form of national improvement. Many reformers considered education the best way to disseminate enlightened ideals and promote progress but felt that private colleges were too expensive for most Americans. They also believed that private colleges overemphasized classical subjects, such as philosophy, languages, music, and art, that did not promote economic opportunity for working-class Americans. Most private colleges were also segregated along both racial and gender lines.

The Morrill Land Grant College Act of 1862 funded a system of state colleges devoted to teaching "agriculture and the mechanical arts," promoting economic opportunity and development, and putting a college education within the reach of more Americans. The Morrill Act, named for Republican senator Justin Morrill of Vermont, granted every loyal state thirty thousand acres of public land for each of its senators and representatives in Congress. Congress had already passed the Morrill Act in 1859, but President Buchanan vetoed it. Believing that public education was the responsibility of individual states, Buchanan feared that the Morrill Act would give too much power to the federal government. During the Civil War, Morrill reintroduced his proposal and added the requirement that the land-grant schools also teach military science. The Republican-controlled wartime Congress supported the bill overwhelmingly.

States were expected to use the income from the land grants to defray the cost of establishing and maintaining the colleges, thus providing less expensive public education for ordinary Americans. The first land-grant college, the University of Massachusetts, opened immediately. Over time, sixty-two land-grant institutions appeared, usually designated as "state universities" or agricultural and mechanical institutes—the "A&Ms." Some eastern states that already supported public education used their land grants to supplement universities that were already in operation. New York's Cornell University, New Jersey's Rutgers University, and Indiana's Purdue University, for example, were incorporated into the land-grant college system. In keeping with their emphasis on equality, the land-grant colleges were coeducational from the very beginning. Building on this foundation, Congress has continually enhanced and expanded the land-grant college system to meet new needs. In 1887, the Hatch Act funded an agricultural experiment station in association with each land-grant college. In 1914, the Smith-Lever Act initiated cooperative extension services to disseminate the latest agricultural techniques to farmers. County agents from the experiment stations criss-crossed the nation offering free advice for often-beleaguered farmers. The Second Morrill Act, passed in 1890, created a system of seventeen land-grant colleges for African

Right: A military review held in 1906, on the twenty-fifth anniversary of the founding of Tuskegee University, Alabama.

Americans throughout the South. These land-grant colleges promoted public education in the former Confederate states, which were reluctant to fund colleges and universities for former slaves. The 1890 land-grant colleges, which were segregated during most of their history, emphasized teacher training to lay the foundation for an even greater expansion of public school systems in the South during the twentieth century.

In 1994, twenty-nine Native American tribal colleges received land-grant status to support higher education on or near American Indian reservations. The same ideal of equal opportunity and national progress that led to the abolition of slavery also produced an accessible and egalitarian system of public universities that has expanded over time to reach more Americans than ever. Embodied in the Morrill Act of 1862, America's land-grant universities represent one of the most enduring legacies of the Civil War.

Land Grant Colleges

● 1862 Land Grant Program

○ 1890 Land Grant Program

Land Grant Colleges outside the 50 states

University of Guam

Community College of Micronesia

Northern Marianas Community College

University of Puerto Rico

University of the Virgin Islands

0   300 km

0   300 miles

N

ELECTIONS OF 1864, 1868, 1872, AND 1876

ABRAHAM LINCOLN WON THE PRESI-DENCY in 1860 with less than forty percent of the popular vote. Despite Lincoln's mythic stature in American history, his re-election was uncertain. He faced harsh criticism for the war's death toll, his decision to free the slaves, and his bold use of executive power. In 1864, his Democratic opponents nominated George B. McClellan, a popular Union general whom Lincoln had fired, to run against him. McClellan advocated ending the war by appeasing the South and welcoming back the seceded states without abolishing slavery. During the summer of 1864, the war was going so badly for the Union that Lincoln expected to lose the election and wrote a concession speech, which he never had to deliver. The fall of Atlanta in September boosted north-ern morale and ensured Lincoln's re-election. In November, Lincoln won a landslide victory with fifty-five percent of the popular vote, aided by the overwhelming support of Union soldiers, who voted in the field. McClellan's antiwar stance won him only two slave states, Kentucky and Delaware, as well as New Jersey.

Reiterating the themes of loyalty, sacrifice, and the Union, Republicans controlled the North for the next three-quarters of a centu-ry. Civil War general Ulysses S. Grant won two solid victories, in 1868 and 1872, largely because Republicans continued to control the Reconstruction South. When the former Confederate states rejoined the Union, however, southern Democrats regained power and the Republican majority gradually eroded. A major depression, the Panic of 1873, also damaged the Republicans' reputation. In the election of 1876,

Abraham Lincoln (1809–65). On January 1, 1863, President Lincoln made history by signing the Emancipation Proclamation freeing all slaves in the rebelling states, and giving the Union cause increased credibility.

all but three southern states—Louisiana, South Carolina, and Florida—were firmly under Democratic control. Republicans nominated Rutherford B. Hayes of Ohio, who ran on a plat-form of restoring "home rule" for the South. Democrats nominated Samuel Tilden of New York, who pledged to root out corruption from government.

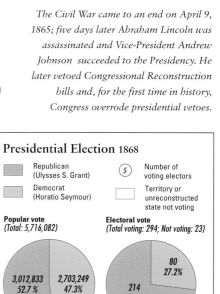

The Civil War came to an end on April 9, 1865; five days later Abraham Lincoln was assassinated and Vice-President Andrew Johnson succeeded to the Presidency. He later vetoed Congressional Reconstruction bills and, for the first time in history, Congress overrode presidential vetoes.

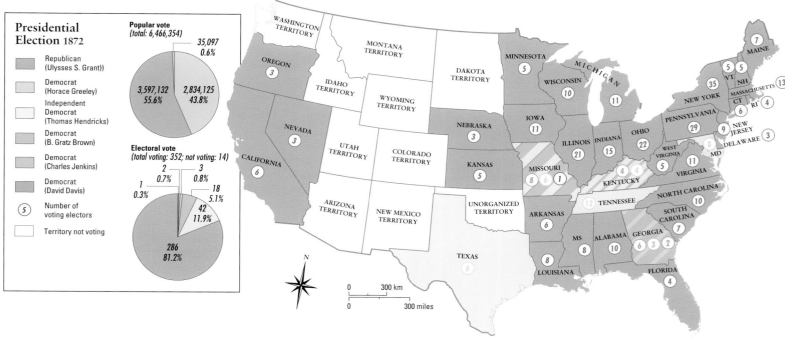

Presidential Election 1872

Popular vote (total: 6,466,354)

- Republican (Ulysses S. Grant))
- Democrat (Horace Greeley)
- Independent Democrat (Thomas Hendricks)
- Democrat (B. Gratz Brown)
- Democrat (Charles Jenkins)
- Democrat (David Davis)
- (5) Number of voting electors
- Territory not voting

Popular vote (total: 6,466,354)

35,097 0.6%
3,597,132 55.6%
2,834,125 43.8%

Electoral vote (total voting: 352; not voting: 14)

2 0.7%
3 0.8%
1 0.3%
18 5.1%
42 11.9%
286 81.2%

Of all the Northern heroes to emerge from the Civil War, the ex-slave-owning Ulysses S. Grant was the most popular. His popular vote benefited from the support of newly enfranchised ex-slaves.

Tilden won a majority of the popular vote, including most southern states. But Louisiana, South Carolina, and Florida, still occupied by federal troops, returned two sets of disputed returns. With no clear winner in the Electoral College, a deadlock ensued. In the resulting Compromise of 1877, Democrats agreed to support Hayes's election. In return, Hayes pledged to remove the last federal troops from the South and grant southerners "home rule." Between 1864 and 1876, the Republican Party slipped from a landslide majority of fifty-five percent to a minority position in the nation, largely because of the return of the seceded states to the Union. Republicans staved off defeat in 1876 only by granting crucial concessions, including political independence, to the defeated South. In seven presidential elections from 1876 to 1904, Republicans averaged forty-eight percent of the popular vote. Enjoying a balance of power with the Republicans, Democrats in the South felt free to undermine many of the reforms of the Civil War era, including civil rights. The southern Redeemers' prediction that "The South will rise again" had come true.

Rutherford B. Hayes 1822–93. The election of 1876 became one of the most drawn out in American history, and also one of only four elections in which the popular vote winner was not elected.

Presidential Election 1876

- Republican (Rutherford B. Hayes)
- Democrat (Samuel J. Tilden)
- Others
- (5) Number of voting electors
- Territory not voting

Popular vote (total: 8,430,783)

93,895 1.1%
4,036,298 47.9%
4,300,590 51.0%

Electoral vote (total: 369)

185 50.1%
184 49.9%

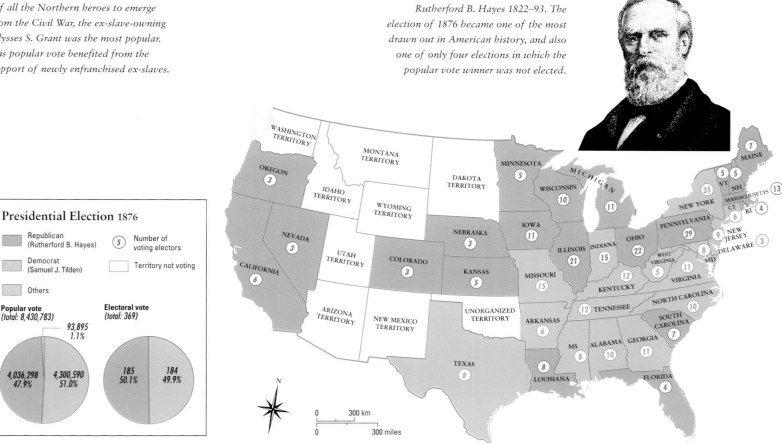

POSTWAR POLITICS

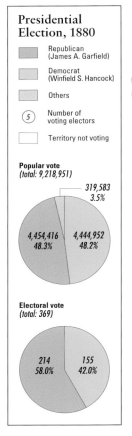

Presidential Election, 1880

- ■ Republican (James A. Garfield)
- ■ Democrat (Winfield S. Hancock)
- ■ Others
- ⑤ Number of voting electors
- □ Territory not voting

Popular vote
(total: 9,218,951)

319,583
3.5%

4,454,416
48.3%

4,444,952
48.2%

Electoral vote
(total: 369)

214
58.0%

155
42.0%

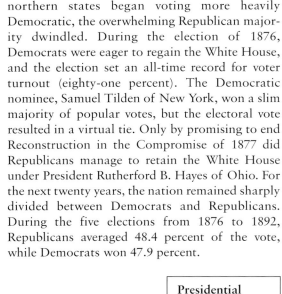

*James Abram Garfield (1851-1881)
A congressman for the state of Ohio for seventeen years, he was elected to the Senate in 1880
and elected to the presidency in the same year.*

THE SINGLE MOST IMPORTANT DEVELOPMENT in postwar politics was the gradual return to power of the Democratic Party in the South. During the Civil War, the northern Democratic Party was divided between War Democrats, who supported the war effort, and Peace Democrats, who sympathized with the South. As a result, Republicans were able to build an overwhelming majority in the North and re-elect President Abraham Lincoln in 1864 by a landslide.

When the war ended, Radical Reconstruction —which kept southern states out of the Union until they accepted emancipation and civil rights for former slaves and demonstrated their loyalty to the Union—further weakened the Democrats. Reconstruction gave Republicans an opportunity to gain a foothold in the South among African Americans and among whites in areas where slavery and secession had never been popular. In 1868 and 1872, Republicans won the presidency under Ulysses S. Grant, the most popular military hero to emerge from the war. Despite his personal popularity, however, Grant's administration was politically corrupt. A major depression that broke out in 1873 also hurt the Republicans and helped Democrats regain control of the House of Representatives. Meanwhile, Democrats began "redeeming" the southern states, beginning with Virginia in 1870.

As southern states re-entered the Union and northern states began voting more heavily Democratic, the overwhelming Republican majority dwindled. During the election of 1876, Democrats were eager to regain the White House, and the election set an all-time record for voter turnout (eighty-one percent). The Democratic nominee, Samuel Tilden of New York, won a slim majority of popular votes, but the electoral vote resulted in a virtual tie. Only by promising to end Reconstruction in the Compromise of 1877 did Republicans manage to retain the White House under President Rutherford B. Hayes of Ohio. For the next twenty years, the nation remained sharply divided between Democrats and Republicans. During the five elections from 1876 to 1892, Republicans averaged 48.4 percent of the vote, while Democrats won 47.9 percent.

Grover Cleveland (1837–1908). Despite the political and social liabilities of having fathered an illegitimate child and avoiding service in the Civil War, Cleveland beat his better-known opponent in 1884.

Presidential Election, 1884

- ■ Democrat (Grover Cleveland)
- ■ Republican (James G. Blaine)
- ■ Others
- ⑤ Number of voting electors
- □ Territory not voting

Popular vote
(total: 10,052,706)

325,739
3.2%

4,851,981
48.3%

4,874,986
48.5%

Electoral vote
(total: 401)

182
45.4%

219
54.6%

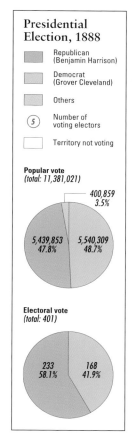

Presidential Election, 1888

- Republican (Benjamin Harrison)
- Democrat (Grover Cleveland)
- Others
- ⑤ Number of voting electors
- Territory not voting

Popular vote (total: 11,381,021)

400,859 3.5%
5,439,853 47.8%
5,540,309 48.7%

Electoral vote (total: 401)

233 58.1%
168 41.9%

This peculiar situation produced a distinctive political era known as the Gilded Age. Five presidents in a row—Hayes, Garfield, Cleveland, Harrison, and Cleveland—were elected without a majority of the popular vote. None of these presidents was particularly popular, so the power and prestige of the presidency eroded during this period. Parties were so desperate to win votes that they drilled their followers like a well-disciplined army to bring them out on Election Day. They rewarded their supporters with patronage and therefore elevated the "spoils system" to a new height of efficiency and corruption. (President Garfield, in fact, was assassinated by a political supporter who was disappointed at not receiving a patronage appointment.) The parties also bought votes by literally bribing members of the opposing party to switch sides. As a result, political corruption reached new lows during the Gilded Age. Because the parties were so evenly divided and neither Republicans nor Democrats had a majority, third parties exercised extraordinary power. They could swing their votes behind one of the major parties and decide the outcome of an election.

During this period, the most successful third parties in American history, including the Greenbackers, the Grangers, the Prohibitionists, and the Populists, flourished. Parties also appealed to voters' emotions to try to break the political deadlock. Republicans reiterated their record in fighting and winning the Civil War and portrayed Democrats as unpatriotic and even treasonous, a strategy known as "waving the bloody shirt." Both parties drew on religious prejudices to rally voters, with Republicans appealing to Protestants and Democrats to Catholics and Jews. The parties adopted popular emblems—the Republican elephant and the Democratic donkey—to personify their organizations and instill party loyalty. Eventually, the memory of the war—and the old party divisions—faded.

The election of 1896 broke the party deadlock, when William McKinley of Ohio defeated William Jennings Bryan of Nebraska with fifty-one percent of the vote. Republicans regained a solid national majority and dominated the White House from 1896 to 1928 with an average of fifty-three percent of the vote.

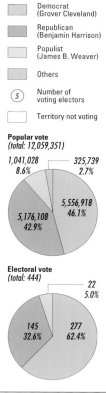

Presidential Election, 1892

- Democrat (Grover Cleveland)
- Republican (Benjamin Harrison)
- Populist (James B. Weaver)
- Others
- ⑤ Number of voting electors
- Territory not voting

Popular vote (total: 12,059,351)

1,041,028 8.6%
325,739 2.7%
5,556,918 46.1%
5,176,108 42.9%

Electoral vote (total: 444)

22 5.0%
145 32.6%
277 62.4%

Benjamin Harrison (1833–1901). His grandfather was the nation's ninth President; his supporters chanted "Grandfather's hat fits Ben."

HOMESTEAD CLAIMS (HOMESTEAD ACT)

BEYOND ITS CENTRAL MISSION TO stop the spread of slavery westward, the Republican Party advocated an economic policy of using the federal government to boost economic growth. One of their most important economic goals was accelerating the settlement of the West. Originally championed by Democrats, homesteading was designed to promote economic opportunity for landless Americans by giving free land to families who were willing go westward. Southerners feared that poor factory workers and immigrants would claim the free land, settle the West, and oppose the spread of slavery. So Congress did not have enough votes to enact a homestead program before the South seceded. With the Confederate states out of the Union, Congress was free to create a national banking system, award huge land grants to railroads, fund land-grant colleges, and pass the Homestead Act.

Republicans supported homesteading as a good way not only to promote economic opportunity and development but also to encourage northern farm families to move west, vote against slavery, and "redeem" the region as free territory. As enacted in May 1862, the Homestead Act provided one hundred and sixty acres—one-quarter of a square mile—of public land to any adult household head, male or female, who would live on the grant for at least five years, improve it by building a house and cultivating part of the land, and pay an eighteen dollar filing fee. The law's impact was immediate. When it became effective on January 1, 1863, Daniel Freeman filed the first homestead claim for 160 acres near the town of Beatrice, Nebraska. In 1866, Congress passed the Southern Homestead Act, designed to provide free land for former slaves. Forty-four million acres of public land were available for homesteading in five southern states—Alabama, Mississippi, Louisiana, Arkansas, and Florida. The program failed, however, because public lands in these states were unproductive and most African Americans could not afford to start up a farm, even on free land. Only seven thousand families claimed these eighty-acre grants, and only one-in-seven of those succeeded. Homesteading made its biggest impact in the West, especially on the Great Plains. There were relatively few claims east of the Mississippi River and west of the Rocky Mountains, and two-fifths of all homesteaders settled in five Plains states—Montana, the Dakotas, Nebraska, and Colorado.

A myriad of problems came along with the free land, however. A semiarid climate, frequent droughts and blizzards, and isolation made agriculture a hazardous proposition on the Great Plains. Three-fifths of homesteading families gave up farming and abandoned their claims before the five years were up. During the late nineteenth century, western farmers called for more government help, organizing the Grange, the Farmers Alliance, the Populist Party, and other agricultural protest movements. Still, the impact of the Homestead Act on American agriculture was enormous. All told, 1.6 million homesteaders claimed 270 mil-

lion acres— one-tenth of the land in the United States. Between 1860 and 1890, the total amount of American farmland doubled. Along with agricultural mechanization, homesteading helped to turn the vast American heartland into the proverbial "breadbasket of the world." Homesteading continued well into the twentieth century and, in fact, the peak years for homestead claims were from 1910 to 1915. Seventy percent of all successful homestead claims were made in the twentieth century, and the Homestead Act remained in effect until its repeal in 1976. One of the most important economic legacies of the Civil War, homesteading represented a major source of opportunity for farmers in the West for over a century.

After the Civil War, the military might of the United States turned westward in support of the millions of settlers moving to the new states and territories which offered 160 acres of free land to every farmer. Among the multitude moving west were thousands of ex-slaves answering the call made by Benjamin "Pap" Singleton, a minister from Tennessee, to abandon the racial prejudice of the south and go west.

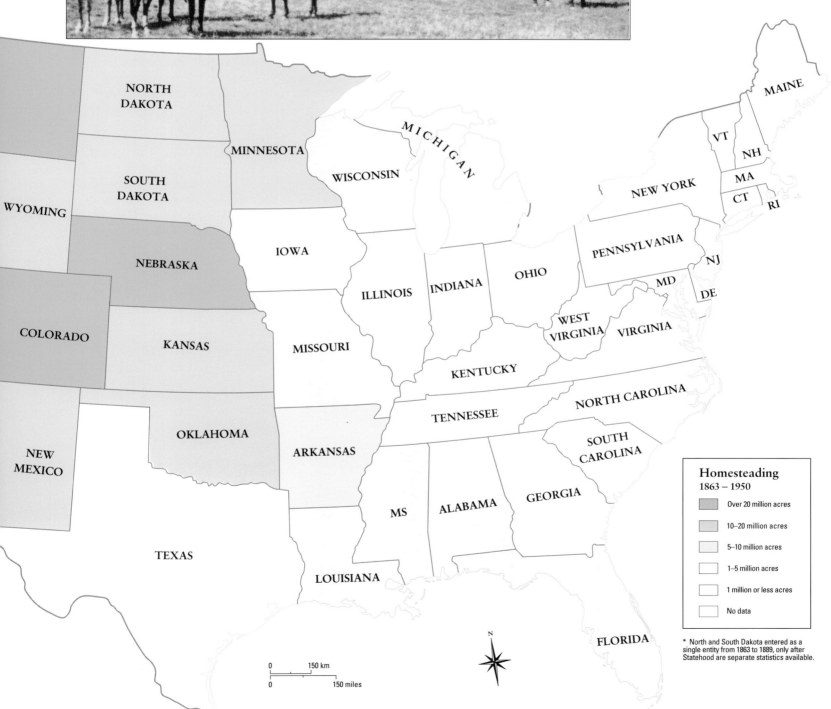

Homesteading
1863 – 1950

- Over 20 million acres
- 10–20 million acres
- 5–10 million acres
- 1–5 million acres
- 1 million or less acres
- No data

* North and South Dakota entered as a single entity from 1863 to 1889, only after Statehood are separate statistics available.

0   150 km

0   150 miles

READMISSION OF FORMER CONFEDERATE STATES

DURING RECONSTRUCTION (1866–1877), Radical Republicans in Congress attempted to reform the defeated South in the image of the industrial, urban North. They kept the former Confederate states out of the Union until they seemed committed to establishing free societies and modern governments. In a series of Reconstruction Acts (1867–1868), Congress divided the former Confederacy into five military districts, imposed martial law, and oversaw the writing of new state constitutions. To re-enter the Union, states had to accept emancipation, repudiate secession and war debts, adopt democratic political systems, provide free public education, and certify that a majority of their voters were loyal to the Union. To oversee these reforms, Congress's Joint Committee on Reconstruction surveyed conditions in the South, held hearings, and investigated charges of corruption and racial discrimination.

One-by-one, the former Confederate states met all the conditions, submitted new constitutions to Congress, and returned to the Union. The first state to be readmitted, Tennessee, was exempted from the most stringent Reconstruction requirements, including martial law, which encouraged other states to follow. The economic, strategic, and political heart of the Confederacy, Virginia, was the last state to be readmitted, in 1870. Congress took readmission very seriously, continued to monitor the southern state governments, and did not hesitate to throw a state out of the Union and require it to undergo readmission all over again. When Congress began readmitting the southern states, however, the North started to lose control over them. To ensure that former slaves received basic protection of their civil and political rights, Congress approved two new amendments to the Constitution that every state would need to obey.

The Fourteenth Amendment, ratified in 1868, protected civil rights. It granted citizenship to anyone born in America, guaranteed equal protection and due process under the law, and required states to treat all citizens—including African Americans—equally. The Fifteenth Amendment, ratified in 1870, granted all adult male citizens (with the exception of Native Americans) the right to vote. Republicans reasoned that after a state re-entered the Union, African Americans could help govern the reconstructed South, defend their rights by voting, and contribute to democratic government. African Americans, they believed, would also support the creation of new Republican Party organizations in southern states, as well. Many southerners resented the new amendments, so Congress required states to ratify them before they could re-enter the Union.

President Andrew Johnson opposed Radical Reconstruction, which was designed to empower African Americans and reform the South, especially the Fourteenth and Fifteenth Amendments. When he obstructed their enforcement, the House of Representatives impeached him. In 1868, the Senate came up one vote short of the two-thirds necessary for conviction and acquitted him of all charges. Republicans controlled the former Confederate states when they re-entered the Union. Gradually, however, Democrats regained power, re-established firm Democratic control under the label the "Solid South," and set out to undo much of the work of Reconstruction.

Right: This lithograph, published and printed by Thomas Kelly in 1870, shows a parade surrounded by portraits and vignettes of black life illustrating rights granted by the Fifteenth Amendment.

Black Americans constituted a majority population in South Carolina. In the state's first legislative session after readmission to the Union they held a 2:1 majority in the House.

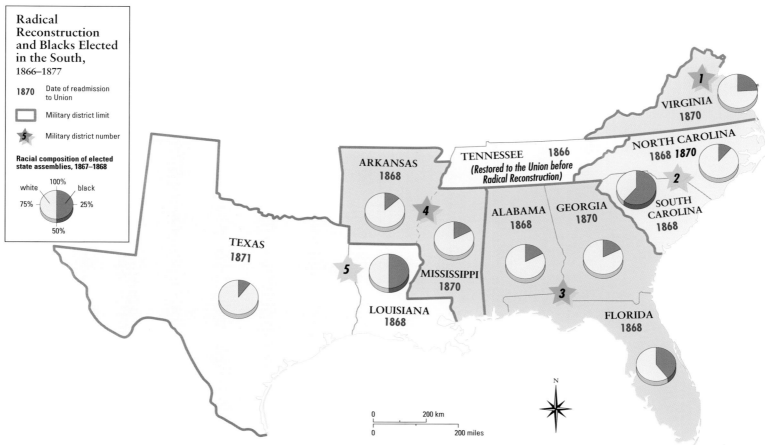

Radical Reconstruction and Blacks Elected in the South,
1866–1877

1870 — Date of readmission to Union

☐ — Military district limit

⭐ 5 — Military district number

Racial composition of elected state assemblies, 1867–1868

white — black
75% — 25%
50%

TEXAS 1871

ARKANSAS 1868

⭐ 4

⭐ 5

LOUISIANA 1868

MISSISSIPPI 1870

ALABAMA 1868

GEORGIA 1870

⭐ 3

FLORIDA 1868

TENNESSEE 1866
(Restored to the Union before Radical Reconstruction)

VIRGINIA 1870

⭐ 1

NORTH CAROLINA 1868 *1870*

⭐ 2

SOUTH CAROLINA 1868

0 — 200 km
0 — 200 miles

N

DISFRANCHISEMENT LAWS IN THE SOUTH

This photograph shows a white farm manager weighing cotton picked by black farm workers.

THE LAST OF THE THREE "Civil War amendments" to the Constitution was the Fifteenth. Ratified in 1870, it guaranteed all adult male citizens the right to vote. Supporters considered the right of suffrage a crucial foundation of the racial equality that had emerged as the leading aim of the Civil War. They also believed that granting suffrage to freedmen would give them, for the first time, a voice in running the South and in controlling their own destiny. Republicans in Congress hoped that African Americans would support the new Republican Party and help them challenge the overwhelming Democratic orientation of the postwar South.

When Reconstruction ended in 1877, however, southern Democrats began devising ways to undermine the Fifteenth Amendment by keeping former slaves from voting, a process called "disfranchisement." Democrats reasoned that two-fifths of southern Republicans were African Americans. If they lost the right to vote, the southern wing of the Republican Party would crumble. Southern states passed laws that did not target African Americans directly but made it difficult or even impossible for poor or illiterate voters to cast ballots. The most popular disfranchisement law—adopted by every former Confederate state—was the poll tax. Voters had to pay an annual tax of one to two dollars before they could vote. Representing one or two weeks' wages for the poorest southern voters, the poll tax turned voting into a luxury that few African Americans could afford.

In five states, property tests prevented the landless from voting under the assumption that only taxpayers should have a voice in raising and spending taxes. In reality, property tests were designed to disfranchise sharecroppers and tenant farmers, both blacks and whites, who might challenge the political dominance of the wealthy planter elite. Before the Civil War, teaching slaves to read and write was illegal in most southern states. After the war, the South severely limited African Americans' access to education, and many of them remained illiterate. Seven southern states adopted literacy tests that were designed to bar African Americans from the polls. Even when black voters were literate, they faced "understanding clauses" that required them to interpret legal documents to the satisfaction of election officials. A final form of disfranchisement was the notorious "grandfather clause" that required a voter to be descended from someone who had the right to vote or someone who had fought for the Confederacy. As a practical matter, the grandfather clause, adopted in four southern states, limited suffrage to white voters.

Although clearly discriminatory, the disfranchisement laws were ruled constitutional by the U.S. Supreme Court. They prevented most African Americans from voting, devastated the Republican Party, and gave Democrats a virtual monopoly on southern politics and government. By 1900, every southern state had a Democratic majority, supporting the nickname the "Solid South." The disfranchisement laws were overturned one-by-one during the twentieth century. Grandfather clauses were ruled unconstitutional in 1915, the Twenty-fourth Amendment banned poll taxes in 1964, and the Voting Rights Act outlawed literacy tests in 1965. For the ninety years following the end of Reconstruction, however, most African Americans were denied the right to vote, despite the Fifteenth Amendment, and the Democratic Party ruled the South with little opposition.

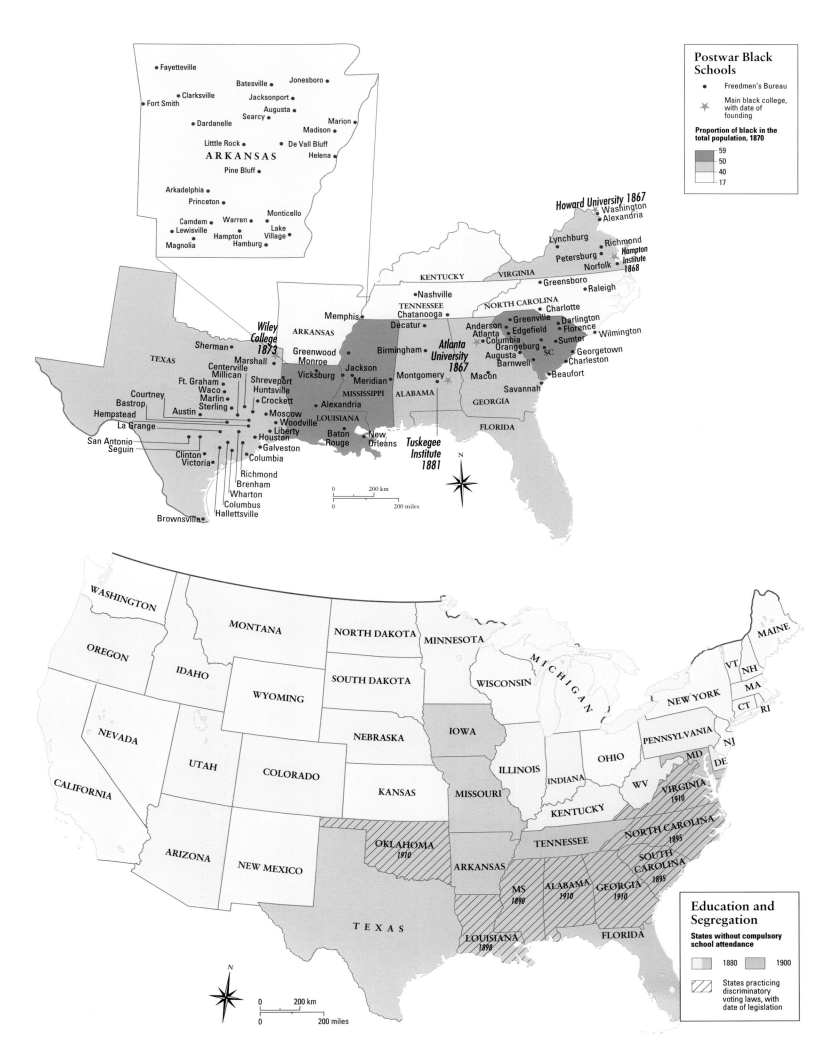

Postwar Black
Schools

•   Freedmen's Bureau

✦   Main black college,
with date of
founding

Proportion of black in the
total population, 1870

59
50
40
17

Howard University 1867
Washington
Alexandria
Lynchburg
Petersburg   Richmond
Norfolk   Hampton
    Institute
    1868
Greensboro
Raleigh
NORTH CAROLINA
Charlotte
Anderson   Greenville   Darlington
Atlanta   Edgefield   Florence
Columbia   Sumter   Wilmington
Augusta   Orangeburg
Barnwell   SC   Georgetown
    Charleston
Beaufort

KENTUCKY   VIRGINIA

Nashville
TENNESSEE
Chatanooga
Memphis
Decatur
ARKANSAS
Birmingham
Atlanta
University
1867
Macon
Savannah
GEORGIA
FLORIDA
Montgomery
ALABAMA
Tuskegee
Institute
1881

Wiley
College
1873
Sherman
TEXAS
Marshall
Centerville
Millican
Ft. Graham   Waco
Courtney   Marlin
Bastrop   Sterling
Hempstead   Austin
La Grange
San Antonio
Seguin   Clinton
    Victoria
Richmond
Brenham
Wharton
Columbus
Brownsville   Hallettsville

Greenwood
Monroe
Vicksburg   Jackson
Meridian
MISSISSIPPI
Shreveport
Huntsville
Crockett
Moscow
Woodville
Liberty
Baton
Rouge   New
    Orleans
LOUISIANA
Alexandria
Galveston
Columbia
Houston

ARKANSAS

Fayetteville
Batesville   Jonesboro
Clarksville   Jacksonport
Fort Smith   Augusta
Dardanelle   Searcy   Marion
    Madison
Litttle Rock   De Vall Bluff
    Helena
A R K A N S A S
Pine Bluff
Arkadelphia
Princeton
Camdem   Warren   Monticello
Lewisville   Lake
Magnolia   Hampton   Village
    Hamburg

200 km
0
0   200 miles

N

Education and
Segregation

States without compulsory
school attendance

1880   1900

States practicing
discriminatory
voting laws, with
date of legislation

WASHINGTON
OREGON
MONTANA
NORTH DAKOTA
MINNESOTA
IDAHO
SOUTH DAKOTA
WYOMING
WISCONSIN
M I C H I G A N
MAINE
VT   NH
NEW YORK   MA
CT   RI
IOWA
NEVADA
UTAH
COLORADO
NEBRASKA
ILLINOIS
INDIANA
OHIO
PENNSYLVANIA
NJ
CALIFORNIA
KANSAS
MISSOURI
WV   MD   DE
KENTUCKY
VIRGINIA
1910
ARIZONA
NEW MEXICO
OKLAHOMA
1910
ARKANSAS
TENNESSEE
NORTH CAROLINA
1895
SOUTH
CAROLINA
1895
MS
1890   ALABAMA   GEORGIA
    1910   1910
T E X A S
LOUISIANA
1898
FLORIDA

N

0   200 km
0   200 miles

353

SHARECROPPING

WHEN THE THIRTEENTH AMENDMENT FREED four million southern slaves at the end of the Civil War, freedmen enjoyed many new economic opportunities. They could farm for themselves, work for wages, earn an education and learn a trade or profession, or even leave the South entirely. They had little incentive to continue the menial work of cultivating cotton, so southern planters confronted a massive labor shortage. During the war, the Confederacy embargoed cotton and the Union blockaded the southern coastline, so European nations developed new sources of raw cotton in Egypt and India. When the war ended, southerners faced tremendous competition from these new sources, and the price of cotton fell dramatically. Instead of diversifying their crops or investing in industry, southerners tried boosting profits by growing even more cotton.

Between 1866 and 1890, southern cotton production quadrupled, from two million to eight million bales. Desperate to coerce former slaves into growing cotton, planters developed the system of sharecropping. Under sharecropping, an African American family rented a plot of land from a planter and paid the rent at the end of the growing season, not in cash, but in cotton. In theory, sharecropping allowed impoverished former slaves to rent their own farms, live independently, and enjoy some of the profits of their own labor for the first time. Typically, they signed an annual contract, which obliged the planter to provide the land and the necessary capital (tools, farm animals, and seed), while the sharecropping family provided all the labor. In exchange for the land and supplies, sharecroppers turned over two-thirds of the cotton they grew to the planter, keeping one-third for themselves.

In practice, sharecropping proved an exploitative and even coercive economic system. Planters required their "croppers" to grow cotton instead of food to feed themselves and assigned a production quota to all family members—men, women, and children. Sharecropping families were often required to buy food and other necessities, at unfair prices, at a store that the planter owned. Sharecroppers inevitably fell into debt, and laws required them to continue working for the same planter until they repaid their debts. An endless cycle of "debt peonage" emerged, in which African American families were tied to the land, sometimes for generations, growing cotton for planters who held them in virtual bondage.

Sharecropping dominated southern agriculture after the Civil War, accounting for almost one-third of all farms in nine cotton-growing states. While three-fourths of African American farmers practiced some form of sharecropping, many managed to escape the system. Eventually, one-third of African American farmers owned their own land, and one-fourth gained some independence by paying their rent in cash. Over time, however, sharecropping spread beyond the Cotton Belt of Georgia, Alabama, Mississippi, and Arkansas into the Upper South, where one-fourth of poor white farmers became entangled in the system. With the expansion of American agriculture, sharecropping spread to the West, where it was often called "crop-sharing." By 1900, this economic legacy of the Civil War and emancipation dominated agriculture in the South and much of the agrarian West.

A painting of sharecroppers in the Deep South by William Aiken Walker.

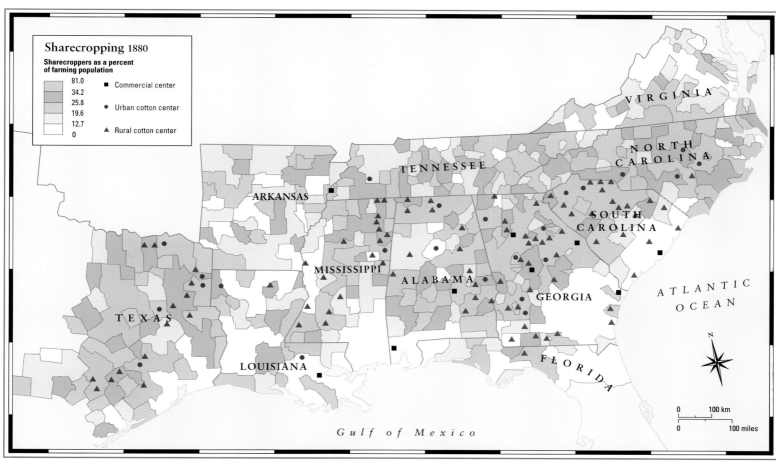

Sharecropping 1880

Sharecroppers as a percent of farming population

81.0
34.2
25.8
19.6
12.7
0

■ Commercial center

● Urban cotton center

▲ Rural cotton center

VIRGINIA

NORTH CAROLINA

TENNESSEE

ARKANSAS

SOUTH CAROLINA

MISSISSIPPI

ALABAMA

GEORGIA

TEXAS

LOUISIANA

FLORIDA

ATLANTIC OCEAN

Gulf of Mexico

0   100 km
0   100 miles

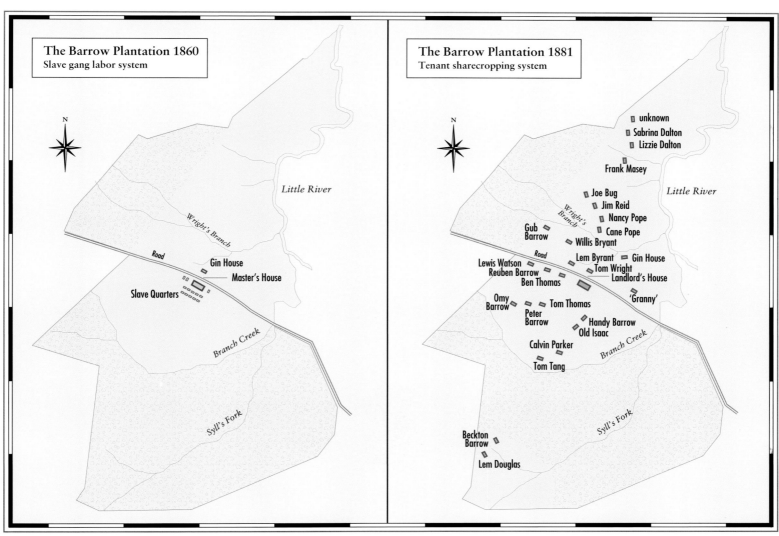

The Barrow Plantation 1860
Slave gang labor system

Little River

Wright's Branch

Road

Gin House

Master's House

Slave Quarters

Branch Creek

Syll's Fork

The Barrow Plantation 1881
Tenant sharecropping system

unknown

Sabrina Dalton

Lizzie Dalton

Frank Masey

Joe Bug

Jim Reid

Nancy Pope

Cane Pope

Gub Barrow

Willis Bryant

Lewis Watson

Reuben Barrow

Ben Thomas

Lem Byrant

Tom Wright

Gin House

Landlord's House

Little River

Wright's Branch

Road

'Granny'

Omy Barrow

Tom Thomas

Peter Barrow

Handy Barrow

Old Isaac

Calvin Parker

Branch Creek

Tom Tang

Beckton Barrow

Syll's Fork

Lem Douglas

LANDSCAPE AND MEMORY

THE CIVIL WAR CHANGED THE landscape of America forever, and the nation is dotted with monuments and historic sites commemorating the epic struggle, more than one thousand five hundred of which are open to the public. The first monuments to the Civil War were, of course, the military cemeteries. Fittingly, the first military cemetery was established in Washington, D.C., when the board of governors of the Soldiers' Home donated part of its land in 1861 for this solemn purpose.

In April 1862, the War Department issued a general order instructing generals to set aside plots near every battlefield to bury the fallen, mark their graves, and compile a registry of interments. In July 1862, the National Cemetery system began when Congress authorized the president to establish burial grounds to inter and honor the Union dead. Quartermaster General Montgomery Meigs oversaw the program, and fourteen national cemeteries were established by the end of 1862 alone. Most were located at troop assembly points, such as Alexandria, Virginia; Fort Leavenworth, Kansas; and Philadelphia.

Two battle sites received designation as national cemeteries—Antietam, Maryland, and Mill Springs, Kentucky. Another was established at Cypress Hills, New York, after a train carrying Confederate prisoners wrecked. Six national cemeteries were established in 1863, including the one at Gettysburg, which Lincoln "consecrated" through his Gettysburg Address on November 19. When the Soldiers' Home Cemetery filled up, the government created Arlington National Cemetery on the site of General Robert E. Lee's estate. General Meigs buried his only son, John, at Arlington. Most national cemeteries were designated after the war in former Confederate states, where well over one-half of the forty-nine sites are located. Virginia alone claims one-third of all the Civil War era national cemeteries. Most battlefield interments were not registered, so only about thirty percent of all buri-

als, those which occurred behind the front lines and generally in hospitals, were recorded. The federal government also maintains fifty national parks, monuments, and sites related to the Civil War. The eleven battlefields that the National Park Service maintains include Fort Sumter, Shiloh, Antietam, Gettysburg, Vicksburg, Chickamauga, Chattanooga, and Appomattox Court House.

Other Park Service sites include the armories at Springfield and Harpers Ferry; the Confederate prison at Andersonville, Georgia; and the homes of Frederick Douglass, Clara Barton, and Abraham Lincoln. Regrettably, three hundred battlefield sites remain neglected and unprotected. America abounds with a wide variety of less well known but equally revered and informative sites, including the gravesites of more than one hundred Union and Confederate generals and government officials. Abraham Lincoln in the North and Robert E. Lee in the South vie as the most popular historical subjects, with General Ulysses S. Grant coming in a distant third. As a result, Virginia, the home of Robert E, Lee, has the nation's most Civil War sites, almost one-sixth of the total, followed closely by Illinois, the home of Abraham Lincoln.

Statues and cannons dot town squares throughout both the North and the South to remind Americans of their Civil War heritage and to commemorate sacrifices for what each side considered a noble cause. Nearly every cemetery in America honors Civil War veterans buried there. Many communities support museums that highlight the history of this tumultuous era. A host of libraries and archives house documents, photographs, diaries, and memoirs detailing the experiences of officers and soldiers on both sides, former slaves and slaveowners, and the Northern and Southern families who endured the loss of loved ones. They truly live on, as does the war itself, in landscape and memory.

A thoughtful crowd gathers around the newly-erected monument to the Battle of Bull Run in 1866.

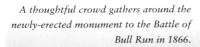

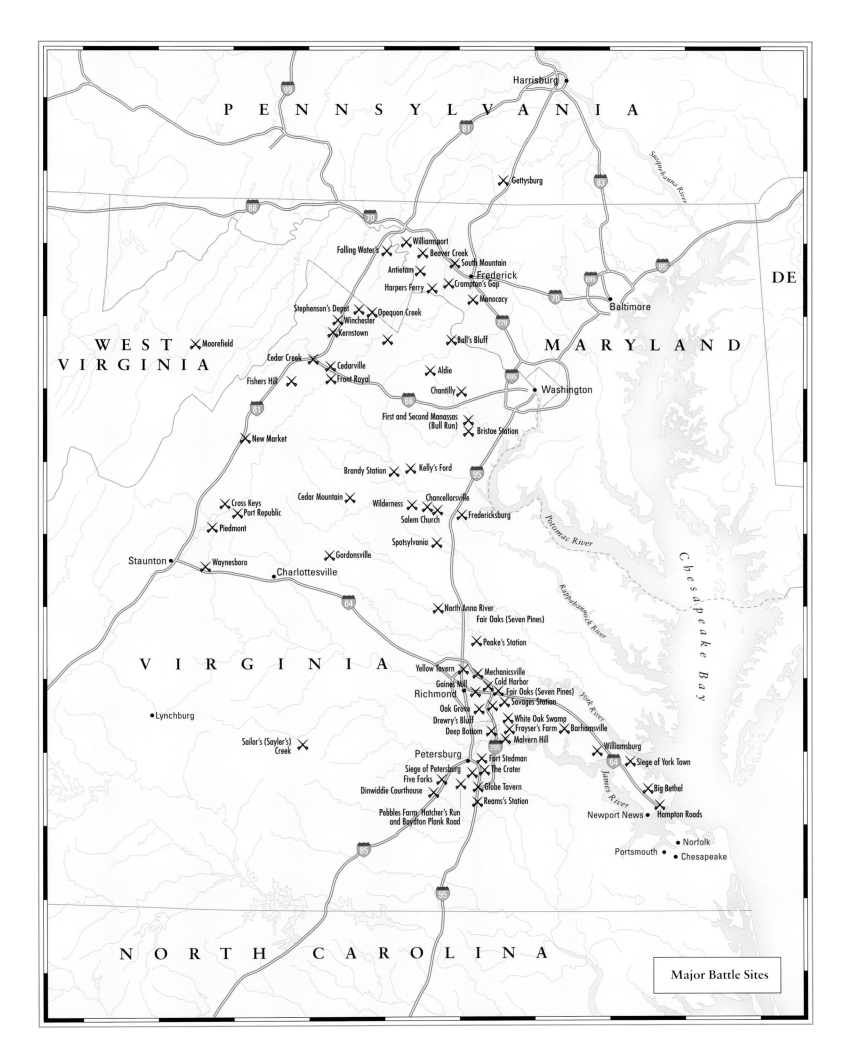

PENNSYLVANIA

Harrisburg

Gettysburg

WEST
VIRGINIA

Falling Waters
Williamsport
Beaver Creek
South Mountain
Antietam
Frederick
Harpers Ferry
Crampton's Gap
Monocacy
Stephenson's Depot
Opequon Creek
Winchester
Kernstown
Ball's Bluff
MARYLAND
Moorefield
Cedar Creek
Cedarville
Aldie
Fishers Hill
Front Royal
Chantilly
Washington
First and Second Manassas
(Bull Run)
Bristoe Station
New Market
Brandy Station
Kelly's Ford
Cross Keys
Port Republic
Cedar Mountain
Chancellorsville
Wilderness
Piedmont
Salem Church
Fredericksburg
Spotsylvania
Staunton
Gordonsville
Waynesboro
Charlottesville

VIRGINIA

North Anna River
Fair Oaks (Seven Pines)
Peake's Station
Yellow Tavern
Mechanicsville
Gaines Mill
Cold Harbor
Richmond
Fair Oaks (Seven Pines)
Savages Station
Oak Grove
White Oak Swamp
Lynchburg
Drewry's Bluff
Frayser's Farm
Barhamsville
Deep Bottom
Malvern Hill
Sailor's (Sayler's)
Creek
Williamsburg
Petersburg
Fort Stedman
Siege of York Town
Siege of Petersburg
The Crater
Five Forks
Big Bethel
Dinwiddie Courthouse
Globe Tavern
Reams's Station
Pebbles Farm, Hatcher's Run
and Boydton Plank Road
Newport News
Hampton Roads
Norfolk
Portsmouth
Chesapeake

Susquehanna River

DE

Baltimore

Potomac River

Rappahannock River

Chesapeake Bay

York River

James River

NORTH CAROLINA

Major Battle Sites

357

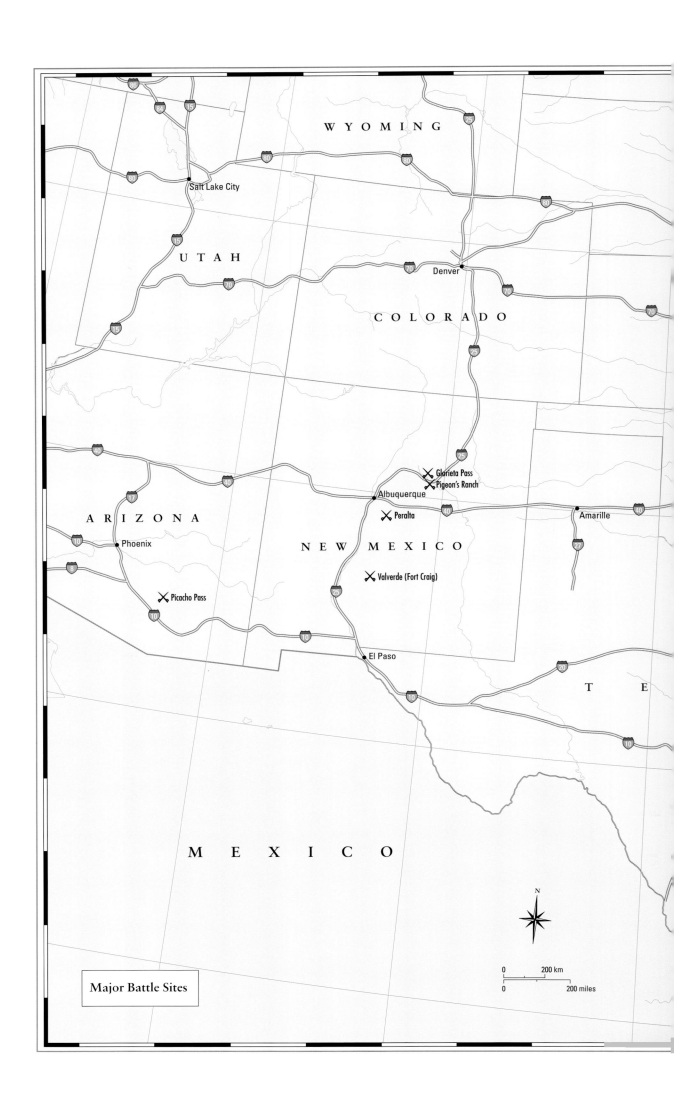

Major Battle Sites

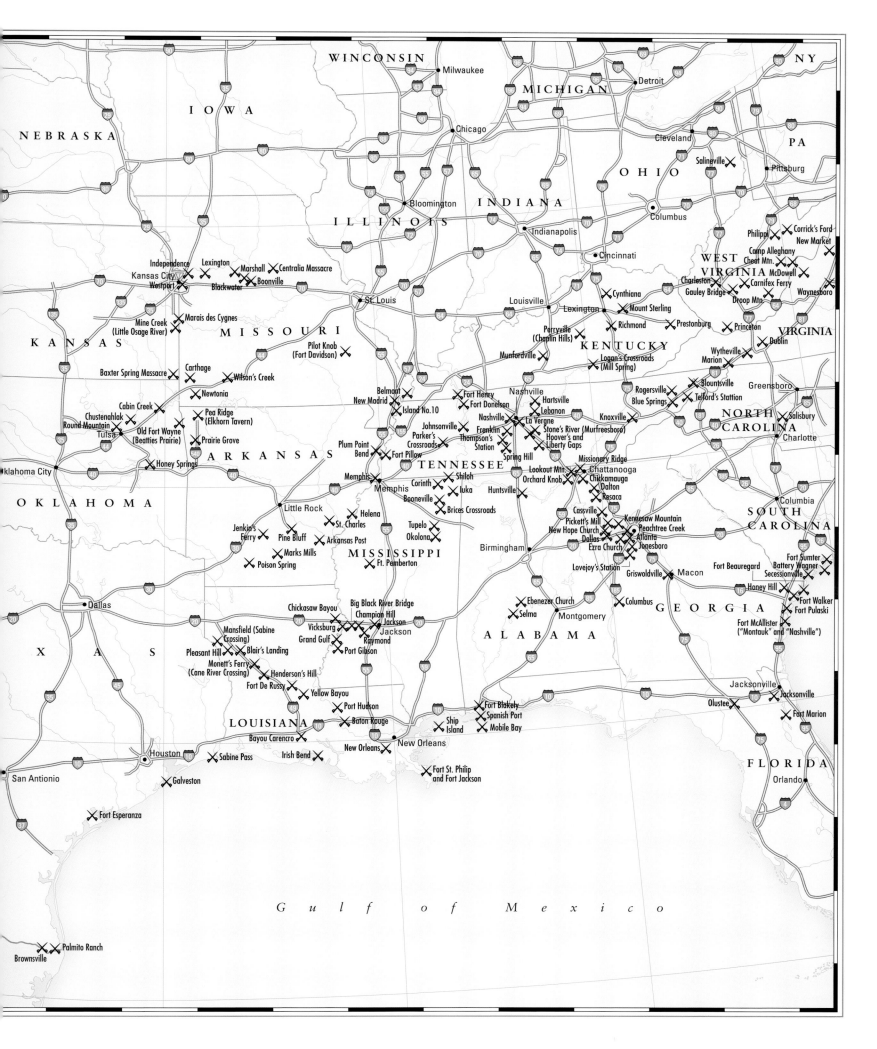

MAJOR BATTLE SITES

ANTIETAM

Date: September 17, 1862

Opposing Commanders:

Union: Major General George B. McClellan, Army
of the Potomac

Confederacy: General Robert E. Lee, Confederate
Army of North Virginia

Number of Combatants:

Union: 75,000

Confederacy: 38,000

Casualties:

Union: 12,401

Confederacy: 10,318

State and Location:

Maryland, Antietam (Sharpsburg)

Outcome:

Narrow victory for Lee but with heavy losses,
Antietam saw more casualties in a day than any
other battle before or since.

APPOMATTOX COURT HOUSE

Date: April 9, 1865

Opposing Commanders:

Union: General Ulysses S. Grant (U.S. Army
General in Chief) and Major General
George C. Meade of the Army of the
Potomac

Confederacy: General Robert E. Lee of the Army
of Northern Virginia

Number of Combatants:

Union: 63,285

Confederacy: 31,900

Casualties:

Union: 164

Confederacy: 500 killed and wounded, 28,231
surrendered and paroled

State and Location:

Virginia, 21 miles east of Lynchburg

Outcome:

Except for 2,400 cavalry, the Army of Northern
Virginia was unable to escape the trap. Lee met
Grant to discuss terms of surrender.

ATLANTA

Date: July 20 to August 31, 1864

Opposing Commanders:

Union: Major General William T. Sherman, Major
General George H. Thomas of the Army of
the Cumberland, Major General James B.
McPherson of the Army of the Tennessee
and Major General John M. Schofield of the
Army of the Ohio

Confederacy: General John B. Hood of the Army
of the Tennessee

Number of Combatants:

Union: Approx. 100,000

Confederacy: Approx. 60,000

Casualties:

Union: Approx. 8,000

Confederacy: Approx. 15,000

State and Location:

Georgia, Atlanta

Outcome:

Hood evacuated Atlanta in the night of August 31.

BRANDY STATION

Date: June 9, 1863

Opposing Commanders:

Union: Major General Alfred Pleasanton of the
Army of the Potomac

Confederacy: Major General J.E.B. Stuart of the
Army of Northern Virginia

Number of Combatants:

Union: 11,000

Confederacy: 9,500

Casualties:

Union: 868

Confederacy: 515

State and Location:

Virginia, near Culpeper

Outcome:

The Confederates had the advantage of the battle,
but Lee was spotted and Hooker followed him with
the Army of the Potomac.

BULL RUN, FIRST (FIRST MANASSAS)

Date: July 21, 1861

Opposing Commanders:

Union: Major General Irvin McDowell of the
Union Army

Confederacy: Major General Joseph E. Johnston
and Major-General Pierre Beauregard
of the Confederate Army

Number of Combatants:

Union: 39,000

Confederacy: 32,000

Casualties:

Union: 2,896 killed, wounded or missing

Confederacy: 1,982 killed, wounded or missing

State and Location:

Virginia, near Manassas 26 miles southwest of
Washington

Outcome:

Confederate victory.

BULL RUN, SECOND (SECOND MANASSAS)

Date: August 28–30, 1862

Opposing Commanders:

Union: Major General John Pope of the Army of
Virginia

Confederacy: Robert E. Lee of the Army of
Northern Virginia

Number of Combatants:

Union: 63,000

Confederacy: 55,000

Casualties:

Union: 13,826

Confederacy: 8,353

State and Location:

Virginia, near Manassas 26 miles southwest of
Washington

Outcome:

Pope's Army of Virginia was defeated and this
made possible the first invasion of the North.

CEDAR CREEK

Date: October 19, 1864

Opposing Commanders:

Union: Major General Phillip Sheridan of the Army
of the Shenandoah

Confederacy: Lieutenant General Jubal A. Early of
the Army of the Valley

Number of Combatants:

Union: 32,000

Confederacy: 21,000

Casualties:

Union: 5,672

Confederacy: 2,910

State and Location:

Virginia, north of Strasburg

Outcome:

After initial success Early had to retreat. This battle
signaled the end of the Confederate threat from the
Valley.

CEDAR MOUNTAIN

Date: August 9, 1862

Opposing Commanders:

Union: Major General Nathaniel P. Banks, of the
Union Army of Virginia

Confederacy: Major General Thomas J.
"Stonewall" Jackson of the
Confederate Army of Northern
Virginia

Number of Combatants:

Union: 12,000

Confederacy: 22,000

Casualties:

Union: 2,500

Confederacy: 1,400

State and Location:

Virginia, between Orange and Culpeper

Outcome:

Union defeat and retreat enabled the Confederated
to advance to the north.

CHANCELLORSVILLE

Date: May 1–5, 1863

Opposing Commanders:

Union: Major General Joseph "Fighting Joe"
Hooker of the Army of the Potomac

Confederacy: General Robert E. Lee of the Army
of Northern Virginia

Number of Combatants:

Union: 130,000

Confederacy: 60,000

Casualties:

Union: 16,792

Confederacy: 12,754

State and Location:

Virginia, west of Fredericksburg

Outcome:

The Army of the Potomac was defeated.
"Stonewall" Jackson was mortally wounded on
May 2.

CHATTANOOGA

Date: November 24–25, 1863

Opposing Commanders:

Union: Major General Ulysses S. Grant,
Commander in Chief of the Union forces
in the West.

Confederacy: General Braxton Bragg of the
Confederate Army of Tennessee
Number of Combatants:
Union: 70,000
Confederacy: 50,000
Casualties:
Union: 5,815 (752 killed, 4,713 wounded, and 350
missing)
Confederacy: 6,667 (361 killed, 2,160 wounded,
and 3,164 missing)
State and Location:
Tennessee, Chattanooga
Outcome:
Defeat of one of the Confederates major field army
and opened the way for a Union invasion of
Georgia.

CHICKAMAUGA
Date: September 18–20, 1863
Opposing Commanders:
Union: Major General William S. Rosecrans of the
Army of the Cumberland
Confederacy: General Braxton Bragg of the Army
of the Tennessee
Number of Combatants:
Union: 62,000
Confederacy: 65,000
Casualties:
Union: 16,170 (1,657 killed, 9,756 wounded, and
4,757 missing)
Confederacy: 18,472 (2,312 killed, 14,674
wounded, and 1,486 missing)
State and Location:
Georgia, south of Chattanooga and near Fort
Oglethorpe
Outcome:
Tactical Confederate victory and went on to
besiege Chattanooga.

COLD HARBOR
Date: May 31 to June 3, 1864
Opposing Commanders:
Union: Lieutenant General Ulysses S. Grant (US
Army General in Chief) and Major General
George G. Meade of the Army of the
Potomac
Confederacy: Robert E. Lee of the Army of
Northern Virginia
Number of Combatants:
Union: 114,000
Confederacy: 59,000
Casualties:
Union: approx. 10,000
Confederacy: 59,000
State and Location:
Virginia, 15 miles northeast of Richmond
Outcome:
The assault of the Army of the Potomac was
violently driven away by Lee's Army of Northern
Virginia blocking Grant's direct access to Richmond.

CORINTH
Date: October 3–4 ,1862
Opposing Commanders:

Union: Major General William S. Rosecrans of the
Union Army of the Mississippi
Confederacy: Major General Earl Van Dorn of the
Confederate Army of the West
Number of Combatants:
Union: 23,000
Confederacy: 22,000
Casualties:
Union: 2,350
Confederacy: 4,800
State and Location:
Mississippi, northwest of Corinth
Outcome:
Corinth stayed in Union hands after the
Confederated army was resolutely pushed from the
town's inner defenses. This outcome now enabled
the Unionists to advance on Vicksburg.

CRATER, THE
Date: July 30, 1864
Opposing Commanders:
Union: Major General George G. Meade of the
Army of the Potomac
Confederacy: General Robert E. Lee of the Army
of Northern Virginia
Number of Combatants:
Union: Major General Ambrose E. Burnside's
Ninth Corps
Confederacy: Uncertain
Casualties:
Union: 3,793
Confederacy: 1,182
State and Location:
Virginia, south of Petersburg
Outcome:
Burnside's incompetence failed to secure the town
leaving the Confederates to successfully
counterattack. Burnside was later dismissed.

FIVE FORKS
Date: April, 1 1865
Opposing Commanders:
Union: Lieutenant General Ulysses S. Grant
(General in Chief of the U.S. Army) and
Major General George C. Meade of the
Army of the Potomac
Confederacy: General Robert E. Lee of the Army
of Northern Virginia
Number of Combatants:
Union: 22,000
Confederacy: 10,600
Casualties:
Union: 820
Confederacy: 4,444
State and Location:
Virginia, southwest of Petersburg
Outcome:
Lee abandoned Petersburg and Richmond, and
retreated to Appomatox Court House.

FORT DONELSON
Date: February 6–16, 1862
Opposing Commanders:
Union: Brigadier General Ulysses S. Grant

Confederacy: Brigadier General John B. Floyd
Number of Combatants:
Union: 27,000
Confederacy: 21,000
Casualties:
Union: 2,832
Confederacy: Approx 2,000 killed and wounded,
plus 15,000 taken prisoner, and 48
artillery weapons captured
State and Location:
Tennessee, on the Cumberland River, 28 miles west
of Clarksville
Outcome:
First major Confederate defeat of the war.

FORT SUMTER
Date: April 12–14, 1861
Opposing Commanders:
Union: Major Robert Anderson of the Union
garrison
Confederacy: Brigadier General Pierre Beauregard
of the Confederate troops in
Charleston
Number of Combatants:
Union: 84
Confederacy: 5,000
Casualties:
Union: 11 (the majority from accidental causes)
Confederacy: 4
State and Location:
South Carolina, in Charleston Harbor
Outcome:
Anderson surrendered on April 14.

FREDERICKSBURG
Date: December 13, 1862
Opposing Commanders:
Union: Major General Ambrose E. Burnside of the
Army of the Potomac
Confederacy: General Robert E. Lee of the Army
of Northern Virginia
Number of Combatants:
Union: 120,000
Confederacy: 78,000
Casualties:
Union: 12,600
Confederacy: 5,300
State and Location:
Virginia, Fredericksburg, 45 miles south of
Washington, D.C.
Outcome:
A serious defeat for the Federals who had to put
their advance on Richmond on halt for several
months.

GETTYSBURG
Date: July 1–3, 1863
Opposing Commanders:
Union: Major General George C. Meade of the
Army of the Potomac
Confederacy: General Robert E. Lee of the Army
of Northern Virgina
Number of Combatants:
Union: 95,000

Confederacy: 75,000

Casualties:

Union: 23,049 (3,155 killed, 14,529 wounded, and
          5,365 missing)

Confederacy: 28,063 (3,903 killed, 18,735
          wounded, and 5,425 missing)

State and Location:

Pennsylvania, Gettysburg

Outcome:

Lee's Army of Northern Virginia was defeated and
sustained heavy losses which could not be made up
due to the South's limited resources in manpower.

HARPER'S FERRY

Date: September 13–15, 1862

Opposing Commanders:

Union: Colonel Dixon S. Miles of the Union
          garrison

Confederacy: Major General Thomas "Stonewall"
          Jackson

Number of Combatants:

Union: 14,000

Confederacy: 22,000

Casualties:

Union: 219 killed and wounded, 12,500 taken
          prisoner plus 73 guns, 11,000 small arms,
          and 200 wagons captured

Confederacy: 286 killed and wounded

State and Location:

West Virginia, Harpers Ferry (now National Park)

Outcome:

The largest Unionist capitulation of the war.

KENNESAW MOUNTAIN

Date: June 27, 1864

Opposing Commanders:

Union: Major General William T. Sherman aided by
          Major General George H. Thomas of the
          Army of the Cumberland, Major General
          James B. McPherson of the Army of the
          Tennessee and Major-General John M.
          Schofield of the Army of the Ohio.

Confederacy: General Joseph E. Johnston
          commanding the reinforced Army of
          Tennessee.

Number of Combatants:

Union: 110,000

Confederacy: 65,000

Casualties:

Union: 3,000

Confederacy: 1,000

State and Location:

Georgia, near Marietta, northwest of Atlanta

Outcome:

The Union frontal assaults were fended off.

MANSFIELD (SABINE CROSSROADS)

Date: April 8–9, 1864

Opposing Commanders:

Union: Major General Nathanial P. Banks of the
          Union Army

Confederacy: Major General Richard Taylor of the
          Confederate Army

Number of Combatants:

Union: 7,000

Confederacy: 8,800

Casualties:

Union: 2,235 (113 killed, 581 wounded and 1,541
          missing) plus 20 guns, 150 wagons and
          1,000 horses captured

Confederacy: Approx. 1,000 killed, wounded and
          missing

State and Location:

Louisiana, 4 miles south of Mansfield

Outcome:

The Union vanguard was engulfed and Banks
decided on a general withdrawal.

MONOCACY, THE

Date: July 9, 1864

Opposing Commanders:

Union: Major General Lewis Wallace

Confederacy: Lieutenant General Jubal A. Early

Number of Combatants:

Union: 5,800

Confederacy: 14,000

Casualties:

Union: 1,968

Confederacy: 900

State and Location:

Maryland, 3 miles south of Fredericksburg

Outcome:

Union Defeat.

NASHVILLE

Date: December 15–16, 1864

Opposing Commanders:

Union: Major General George H. Thomas of the
          Army of the Cumberland

Confederacy: General John B. Hood of the Army
          of Tennessee

Number of Combatants:

Union: 49,773

Confederacy: 31,000

Casualties:

Union: 3,061 (499 killed, 2,562 wounded)

Confederacy: 5,962 (1,500 killed or wounded,
          4,462 captured)

State and Location:

Tennessee, Nashville

Outcome:

Confederate defeat.

PERRYVILLE

Date: October 8, 1862

Opposing Commanders:

Union: Major General Don Carlos Buell of the
          Army of the Ohio

Confederacy: General Braxton Bragg of the Army
          of the Mississippi

Number of Combatants:

Union: 36,940

Confederacy: 16,000

Casualties:

Union: 3,696

Confederacy: 3,145

State and Location:

Kentucky, Perryville, 35 miles southwest of

Lexington

Outcome:

Bragg suffered very heavy casualties and withdrew
through the Cumberland Gap into Tennessee.
Lincoln replaced Buell with Major General William
S. Rosecrans as he did not pursue the Army of the
Mississippi.

PETERSBURG

Date: June 15–18, 1864

Opposing Commanders:

Union: Lieutenant General Ulysses S. Grant
          (General in Chief of the U.S. Army) with
          Major General George C. Meade of the
          Army of the Potomac and Major General
          Benjamin F. Butler of the Army of the
          James.

Confederacy: General Robert E. Lee of Northern
          Virginia aided by General Pierre
          Beauregard and his troops

Number of Combatants:

Union: 65,000 (14,000 on June 15)

Confederacy: 38,000 (2,500 on June 15)

Casualties:

Union: 8,150

Confederacy: 4,752

State and Location:

Virginia, Petersburg, 25 miles south of Richmond

Outcome:

Grant's attempt to capture Petersburg failed and
both stayed entrenched for the next $9^1/2$ months.

PORT REPUBLIC

Date: June 9, 1862

Opposing Commanders:

Union: Brigadier General Erastus B. Tyler

Confederacy: Major General Thomas "Stonewall"
          Jackson

Number of Combatants:

Union: 3,000

Confederacy: 6,000

Casualties:

Union: 500

Confederacy: 800

State and Location:

Virginia, 15 miles north of Waynesboro

Outcome:

Union retreat, Jackson joined Lee in the Seven
Days' Battle.

SAVANNAH (1864)

Date: December 9–21, 1864

Opposing Commanders:

Union: Major General William T. Sherman

Confederacy: Major General William J. Hardee

Number of Combatants:

Union: 68,000 available

Confederacy: 15,000

Casualties:

Union: Light

Confederacy: Light

State and Location:

Georgia, Savannah

Outcome:

Hardee evacuated the town. The eastern states of the Confederacy were now divided in half and the field armies were trapped between Grant in Petersburg and Sherman in Savannah.

SEVEN-DAYS BATTLE

Date: June 25 to July 1, 1862
Opposing Commanders:
Union: Major General George B. McClellan of the Army of the Potomac
Confederacy: General Robert E. Lee of the Army of Northern Virginia
Number of Combatants:
Union: 100,000
Confederacy: 72,000
Casualties:
Union: 15,849 (1,734 killed, 8,062 wounded, and 6,053 missing-mainly prisoners)
Confederacy: 20,614 (3,478 killed, 16,261 wounded, and 875 missing)
State and Location:
Virginia, east of Richmond between the York and James Rivers.
Outcome:
The Confederates suffered the heaviest losses but the Unionists were pushed back to Harrison's Landing on the James River where they were protected by the U.S. Navy's gunboats.

SEVEN PINES (FAIR OAKS)

Date: May 31 to June 1, 1862
Opposing Commanders:
Union: Major General George B. McClellan of the Army of the Potomac
Confederacy: General Joseph E. Johnston of the Confederate Army
Number of Combatants:
Union: Approx. 45,000
Confederacy: 60,000
Casualties:
Union: 5,000
Confederacy: 6,100
State and Location:
Virginia, 6 miles east of Richmond
Outcome:
Result was ambiguous, but McClellan stopped his advance on Richmond grossly overestimating the Confederates' puissance. Johnston was seriously wounded and Lee was appointed nominated commander of the Confederate Army which came to be the Army of Northern Virginia.

SHILOH (PITTSBURG LANDING)

Date: April 6–7, 1862
Opposing Commanders:
Union: Major General Ulysses S. Grant of the Army of the Tennessee and Brigadier-General Don Carlos Buell of the Army of the Ohio.
Confederacy: General Albert Sidney Johnston of the Army of the Mississippi, later replaced by Lieutenant General Pierre Beauregard.
Number of Combatants:

Union: 62,000
Confederacy: 44,000
Casualties:
Union: 13,047
Confederacy: 11,694
State and Location:
Mississippi, Shiloh on the Tennessee River, 25 miles north of Corinth
Outcome:
Beauregard replaced Johnston who got killed. Grant received 20,000 of Buell's men and made Beauregard disengage and withdraw.

SPOTSYLVANIA COURT HOUSE

Date: May 8–18, 1864
Opposing Commanders:
Union: Lieutenant General Ulysses S. Grant (General in Chief of U.S. Army) with Major General George G. Meade of the Army of the Potomac.
Confederacy: Robert E. Lee of the Army of the Army of Northern Virginia.
Number of Combatants:
Union: 111,000
Confederacy: 63,000
Casualties:
Union: 14,267
Confederacy: 10,000
State and Location:
Virginia, southwest of Fredericksburg
Outcome:
Both sides sustained substantial casualties at Bloody Angle. Lee was unable to hold Grant back.

STONES RIVER (MURFREESBORO)

Date: December 31, 1862 to January 2, 1863
Opposing Commanders:
Union: Major General William S. Rosecrans of the Army of the Cumberland
Confederacy: General Braxton Bragg of the Army of Tennessee
Number of Combatants:
Union: 44,000
Confederacy: 34,000
Casualties:
Union: 12,906
Confederacy: 11,740
State and Location:
Tennessee, Murfreesboro, 25 miles southeast of Nashville
Outcome:
On President Jefferson Davis's orders Bragg withdrew south to the Tennessee.

VICKSBURG, SIEGE OF

Date: May 19 to July 4, 1863
Opposing Commanders:
Union: Major General Ulysses S. Grant of the Army of the Tennessee
Confederacy: Lieutenant General John C. Pemberton of the Confederate garrison
Number of Combatants:
Union: Approx. 75,000

Confederacy: Approx. 30,000
Casualties:
Union: 9,362
Confederacy: Approx. 1,000 killed and wounded, 29,000 captured, and paroled and 172 guns captured.
State and Location:
Mississippi, Vicksburg
Outcome:
Confederate surrender destroyed any hope of a Southern outright victory.

WILDERNESS, THE

Date: May 5–6, 1864
Opposing Commanders:
Union: Lieutenant General Ulysses S. Grant (U.S. Army General in Chief) with Major General George G. Meade of the Army of the Potomac.
Confederacy: General Robert E. Lee of the Army of Northern Virginia
Number of Combatants:
Union: 118,769
Confederacy: 62,000
Casualties:
Union: 18,000
Confederacy: 10,800
State and Location:
Virginia, 10 miles west of Fredericksburg, overlapping the old Chancellorsville battlefield
Outcome:
Despite Grant's heavy losses, Lee was unable to stop the Army of the Potomac. The Wilderness being a densely wooded area was very difficult to survey by the commanders which made the battle a close-range one. The outbreak of fires claimed the lives of many wounded soldiers who were trapped in them.

YELLOW TAVERN

Date: May 11, 1864
Opposing Commanders:
Union: Major General Philip H. Sheridan of the cavalry corps of the Army of the Potomac.
Confederacy: Lieutenant General J.E.B. Stuart of the Confederate cavalry
Number of Combatants:
Union: 10,000
Confederacy: 4,500
Casualties:
Union: 400
Confederacy: 1,000
State and Location:
Virginia, 10 miles north of Richmond
Outcome:
The Union cavalry corps drove the Confederates off the field and Stuart was killed in the process.

SOLDIERS AND THEIR ORIGINS

MORE THAN THREE MILLION MEN served in the Civil War armies and navies, supporting Abraham Lincoln's characterization of the conflict as "a people's contest." Despite the necessity of a draft in both the Union and the Confederacy and rates of desertion that would be unacceptable in any modern army, the military effort on both sides was broadly based if not always popular. Ninety-two percent of Union soldiers and eighty percent of Confederate soldiers were volunteers, motivated primarily by patriotism but also by a commitment to liberty and a sense of obligation to their families and communities.

These motivations meant different things to the two armies, however. In the North, patriotism meant loyalty to the Constitution and the Union, while southerners fought for a specific state and the preservation of a traditional way of life under the Confederacy. In the North, liberty meant preservation of democratic self-government under the Constitution and later the end of African American slavery. In the South, liberty meant freedom from government overall or more specifically the right to own slaves. Soldiers on both sides felt the call of duty to defend their communities, preserving and enhancing their personal and family honor by marching off to battle. Once in the army, camaraderie and esprit de corps—a commitment to comrades and a call to duty—became primary motivating impulses on the battlefield.

As a result of this popular support for the war effort, both armies were broadly representative of the societies for which they fought. The Union drafted men upt to age forty-five, the Confederacy up to age fifty. But most soldiers were young, twenty-three and a half years old, on average, and about two-fifths of them were not yet twenty-one when they enlisted. Despite the ability of wealthier men to avoid the draft through substitution, commutation, and the "twenty slave law," there is no evidence that the poor served in either army at substantially higher rates than the rich. Given the agricultural and rural foundation of southern society, however, farmers and farm laborers represented a greater proportion of Confederate than Union soldiers. Reflecting the urban dimension of the northern economy, skilled and unskilled workers were more prevalent in the Union Army. The stereotype of southern soldiers responding to personal honor as a motivation to fight may explain the higher representation of middle-class and professional men in the Confederate Army. Reflecting their more heterogeneous society, Union soldiers were much more ethnically and racially diverse than the Confederates. Ninety percent of America's immigrants lived in the North, and the Union Army depended on them for about one-quarter of its fighting men. The northern draft, in fact, conscripted immigrants who had applied for but had not yet received their citizenship. Conscription therefore provoked bitterness among some immigrants, leading to higher rates of desertion and contributing to the New York City Draft Riots of 1863.

Overall, however, the half million immigrants who served in the Union Army, symbolized by the Irish 69th New York Regiment, were indispensable to victory. The South had many fewer immigrants—about seven and a half percent—but they were in fact over-represented in the Confederate Army. About one-in-ten Confederate soldiers were immigrants. The Union Army's heterogeneity was enhanced by the nine percent who were African American soldiers. Overall, two-thirds of Union soldiers were native-born whites, one-fourth were immigrants, and almost one-tenth were African Americans. More homogeneous in background, ninety percent of Confederate soldiers were native-born whites. Lacking a large pool of immigrant soldiers to mobilize and refusing to enlist African Americans—which meant freeing them—the Confederacy had to keep its men in the army for the duration of the war. As a result, the South suffered lower morale, heavier casualties, and higher rates of desertion than the North.

The Civil War armies exhibited unique strengths and weaknesses that reflected dramatic differences between the two societies for which they fought.

Social Origins of Soldiers	Union Soldiers (in percentages)	Confederate Soldiers (in percentages)
Farmers and Farm laborers	47.5	61.5
Skilled laborers	25.1	14.1
Unskilled laborers	15.9	8.5
White-collar and commercial	5.1	7.0
Professional	3.2	5.2
Miscellaneous and unknown	3.2	3.7
Native-born whites	67	90
Immigrants	24	10
African Americans	9	—

CHRONOLOGY

1860

December 20   A special South Carolina convention, meeting in Charleston, declared the state to be out of the Union.

December 26   Feeling threatened by the Charleston mob in his indefensible position at Fort Moultrie, Major Robert Anderson, commanding U.S. Army forces in Charleston, moved his eighty-five-man garrison to Fort Sumter, located on a man-made sandbar in the harbor.

1861

January 9   When the unarmed steamer *Star of the West* attempted to enter Charleston harbor carrying supplies and reinforcements for the garrison at Fort Sumter, Confederate guns around the harbor opened fire, driving her off. Anderson's Union garrison in Fort Sumter made no reply.

January 9   A state convention in Mississippi voted to secede, declaring that state to be no longer part of the Union.

January 10   Florida declared itself out of the Union.

January 11   Alabama seceded.

January 19   Georgia seceded.

January 26   Louisiana seceded.

February 1   Texas seceded.

February 4   Delegates from six of the seven seceded states (the Texans were still on the way) met in convention in Montgomery, Alabama, for the purpose of establishing a pro-slavery government of their own.

February 8   The Montgomery convention adopted a constitution for the "Confederate States of America."

February 9   The Montgomery convention elected Jefferson Davis of Mississippi president of the Confederate States and Alexander Stephens of Georgia vice-president.

February 18   Jefferson Davis was inaugurated.

March 4   Abraham Lincoln was inaugurated. In his inaugural address Lincoln promised not to be the initiator of hostilities but to hold the remaining federal installations in the states claiming to have seceded.

April 6   Lincoln notified the governor of South Carolina of his intent to re-supply Fort Sumter by sea but to make no attempt to insert reinforcements unless resistance was offered.

April 11   Brigadier General Pierre G. T. Beauregard, commanding Confederate forces in Charleston, demanded that Major Anderson surrender Fort Sumter.

April 12   When Anderson refused to surrender, Beauregard's forces opened fire on Fort Sumter at 4:30 a.m.

April 13   Fort Sumter surrendered.

April 15   Lincoln issued a proclamation that an insurrection existed and called on the states to provide seventy-five thousand militia, for the term of ninety-days, in order to put it down.

April 17   The Virginia convention voted for secession.

April 19   As the Sixth Massachusetts Militia marched through Baltimore on its way to Washington, D.C., in response to Lincoln's call for troops, a pro-secession mob attacked it. At least four soldiers and nine civilians perished in the resulting riot .

April 19   Lincoln declared a naval blockade of the rebellious states.

May 6   The legislatures of Arkansas and Tennessee passed ordinances of secession.

May 10   Captain Nathaniel Lyon, acting to forestall an anticipated secessionist grab for the St. Louis arsenal, led regular army troops and Unionist Missouri home guards in capturing a nearby encampment of secessionist Missouri militia. As Lyon's men marched their prisoners through St. Louis, pro-secession citizens rioted and attacked the troops. Before the violence was over, twenty-eight or twenty-nine persons were dead.

May 20   North Carolina seceded.

June 3   A Union troops easily routed and chased a small secessionist force in western Virginia in an affair that came to be known as the "Philippi Races."

June 10   A force of two thousand five hundred Federals under Major General Benjamin F. Butler advanced westward from Fort Monroe, on Virginia's Chesapeake coast but met defeat at the hands of one thousand two hundred Confederates under the command of Major

General John B. Magruder at Big Bethel. Union casualties totaled seventy-six; Confederate, eight.

June 17 Union forces under Nathaniel Lyon, now a Brigadier General, routed the Confederates in a skirmish at Boonville, Missouri, northwest of Jefferson City on the Missouri River.

July 4 The U.S. Congress convened for the first time during the war, a special session called by Lincoln.

July 11 Union troops under the overall command of Maor General George B. McClellan attacked and routed a Confederate force under Lieutenant Colonel John Pegram at Rich Mountain in western Virginia.

July 13 The pursuing Federals again defeated the Confederates in western Virginia, this time at Corrick's Ford.

July 16 A Union army of about thirty-five thousand men under the command of Major General Irvin McDowell marched away from the Potomac at the beginning of a movement that was supposed to take it to the Confederate capital at Richmond, Virginia.

July 17 Apprised of McDowell's movement, Jefferson Davis ordered General Joseph E. Johnston to take his force from the Shenandoah Valley and reinforce the twenty-two thousand-man Confederate army of Brigadier General Pierre G. T. Beauregard, standing in McDowell's path behind Bull Run, a creek just north of Manassas Junction, Virginia.

July 18 McDowell's and Beauregard's forces skirmished at Blackburn's Ford on Bull Run, and the Confederate got the better of the encounter.

July 2 McDowell attacked the combined forces of Beauregard and Johnston, about equal in numbers to his own, and after some initial success suffered defeat and ignominious rout.

July 27 Lincoln appointed Major General George B. McClellan, fresh from his victories in western Virginia, to command of the Union forces around Washington and in northern Virginia.

August 10 Nathaniel Lyon was defeated and killed at the Battle of Wilson's Creek by the combined forces of Confederate Ben McCulloch and Missouri rebel Sterling Price.

August 28 Confederate forts Hatteras and Clark surrendered to a Union combined land and naval force under Flag Officer Silas Stringham and Major General Benjamin F. Butler, giving the Union control of Hatteras Inlet.

August 30 Union commander in Missouri, Major General John C. Frémont, issued an unauthorized emancipation proclamation as well as a decree for shooting Rebels taken in arms behind Union lines and confiscating Rebel property. Lincoln revoked it.

September 3 Confederate troops under the command of Major General Leonidas Polk moved without authorization to occupy the town of Columbus, Kentucky, ending the state's neutrality and driving many of its undecided citizens to side with the Union.

September 10 Union troops under Rosecrans defeated Confederates under Brigadier General John B. Floyd at Carnifix Ferry in western Virginia.

September 11–15 Robert E. Lee's Confederate offensive in western Virginia failed in the Cheat Mountain Campaign.

September 12–20 Sterling Price's rebel Missourians besieged and captured the Union garrison at Lexington, Missouri.

October 21 Colonel Edward D. Baker led his Union brigade to defeat at Ball's Bluff, Virginia, on the Potomac River. Among the nine hundred and twenty-one casualties was Baker himself, killed. Confederate casualties numbered one hundred and fifty-five.

November 1 Lincoln promoted George McClellan to commanding general of all U.S. armies in place of the aged Winfield Scott. McClellan retained his duties as immediate commander of the Army of the Potomac.

November 2 Lincoln removed the inefficient John C. Frémont in Missouri, replacing him temporarily with Major General David Hunter.

November 7 Brigadier General Ulysses S. Grant led a Union force in attacking a Confederate encampment at Belmont, Missouri, with inconclusive results, before returning to his base at Cairo.

November 7 Combined Union forces under Flag Officer Samuel Du Pont and Brigadier General Thomas W. Sherman captured Port Royal, South Carolina.

November 8 Captain Charles Wilkes, commanding USS *San Jacinto*, stopped the British packet *Trent* in the Old Bahama Channel, and removed Confederate diplomats James M. Mason and John Slidell, who were traveling from Cuba to Europe aboard the British vessel.

December 26 Under threat of war by Great Britain, the United States released Mason and Slidell.

1862

January 19 Union troops under Brigadier General George H. Thomas defeated Confederates commanded by Felix Zollicoffer at the Battle of Mill Springs, Kentucky. Zollicoffer was killed in the fighting.

January 27 Lincoln issued General War Order Number 1, directing all the armies of the United States to advance on February 22.

February 6 A combined Union force under Flag Officer Andrew H. Foote and Brigadier General Ulysses S. Grant captured the Confederate bastion of Fort Henry, opening the Tennessee River to Union gunboats and transports all the way into northern Alabama.

February 8 Major General Ambrose E. Burnside's Federals took Roanoke Island, in the North Carolina sounds, away from Brigadier General Henry A. Wise's Confederates, forcing Wise and his two thousand men to surrender.

February 13 Grant's forces arrived at Fort Donelson, on the Cumberland River in Tennessee, and prepared to lay siege.

February 14 Foote's gunboats attacked Fort Donelson but were repulsed with heavy damage.

February 15 The garrison of Fort Donelson, commanded by Brigadier General John B. Floyd, made a surprise attack on Grant in an ultimately unsuccessful effort to cut its way out.

February 16 The garrison of Fort Donelson surrendered after the two ranking Confederate officers, Floyd and Brigadier General Gideon Pillow, made good their personal escapes.

February 25 Union forces occupied Nashville, Tennessee, without opposition.

March 6–8 Union forces under the command of Brigadier General Samuel Curtis defeated Confederates led by Major General Earl Van Dorn at the Battle of Pea Ridge in northwestern Arkansas.

March 8 The Confederate ironclad *Virginia* (ex-USS *Merrimac*) entered Hampton Roads and destroyed the frigates USS *Cumberland* and USS *Congress* before retiring for the night to its base at Norfolk.

March 9 *Virginia* returned to Hampton Roads with expectations of finishing off the U.S. Navy squadron there but was met by the newly arrived ironclad USS *Monitor*. *Virginia* returned to base after an inconclusive contest with the Union ironclad.

March 11 Lincoln relieved McClellan as general-in-chief but retained him in command of the Army of the Potomac.

March 14 Union troops under Major General John Pope captured New Madrid, Missouri, on the Mississippi River.

March 14 Burnside's Union troops took New Berne, North Carolina.

March 23 In the Shenandoah Valley, Major General Thomas J. "Stonewall" Jackson's Confederate attacked a Union force at Kernstown under Brigadier General James Shields. Jackson suffered a sharp repulse.

March 28 Union forces under the command of Colonel John P. Slough defeated Brigadier General H. H. Sibley's Confederates at the Battle of Glorieta Pass, in New Mexico Territory, ending the Confederate threat to the Far West.

April 5 Having landing the Army of the Potomac on the peninsula between the York and James rivers in eastern Virginia, McClellan laid siege to a much smaller Confederate force at Yorktown.

April 6–7 The Confederate army of General Albert Sidney Johnston launched a surprise attack against Grant's Union army at Pittsburg Landing, Tennessee. The ensuing battle brought unprecedented casualties, including Johnston, killed, but Grant held on and, reinforced by additional Union forces under Don Carlos Buell, took the offensive on the second day, driving off the Confederates.

April 7 The Confederate garrison at Island No. 10, on the Mississippi River, surrendered to Pope's Federals.

April 24 In a dramatic night action, a Union fleet commanded by Flag Officer David Farragut successfully ran past Confederate forts Jackson and St. Philip, guarding the Mississippi below New Orleans.

April 25 Farragut's fleet proceeded up the Mississippi and captured New Orleans.

May 3 General. Joseph E. Johnston withdrew his Confederate forces from the defensive works around Yorktown, Virginia, retreating toward Richmond.

May 5   McClellan's Union troops, pursuing Johnston, clashed with the Confederates at Williamsburg, Virginia, but results were inconclusive.

May 8   Stonewall Jackson fought the first battle of his Shenandoah Valley Campaign, standing off Union forces at McDowell, in the mountains west of the valley.

May 11   CSS *Virginia* was destroyed by its own crew after Confederate forces abandoned its base at Norfolk, Virginia.

May 15   A U.S. Navy squadron, including *Monitor*, proceeded up the James River toward Richmond but was stopped by Confederate batteries and channel obstructions at Drewry's Bluff.

May 23   Continuing his Shenandoah Valley Campaign, Jackson clashed successfully with Union forces at Front Royal, Virginia.

May 24   Jackson fought and won a pitched battle with the Union army of Major General Nathaniel P. Banks at Winchester, Virginia.

May 30   Facing the slow but inexorable advance of Union forces under Major General Henry W. Halleck, Confederate General Pierre G. T. Beauregard withdrew his troops from the key railroad junction at Corinth, Mississippi.

May 31   With McClellan's army on the outskirts of Richmond, Johnston, under pressure from Davis, finally gave battle. The resulting conflict, known as Fair Oaks in the North and Seven Pines in the South, was inconclusive save that Johnston suffered a serious wound and was replaced by Robert E. Lee.

June 6   Flag Officer Charles Davis's Union gunboat fleet defeated the Confederate River Defense Fleet of Captain James E. Montgomery in the naval battle of Memphis, compelling the surrender of the city.

June 8   With two Union columns closing in on him in the Shenandoah Valley, Jackson successfully fended off one of them, that of John C. Frémont, at the Battle of Cross Keys.

June 9   Jackson turned and defeated the other Union column, Shields's, in the Battle of Port Republic.

June 12–15   Flamboyant Confederate cavalry commander James Ewell Brown "Jeb" Stuart led his horsemen on a ride all the way around McClellan's army, bringing Lee important intelligence that McClellan's right flank was "in the air."

June 26   Lee launched a major offensive against McClellan with the Battle of Mechanicsville. Union troops handily repulsed the attack, but McClellan nevertheless decided to retreat and shift his base from the York to the James River.

June 27   Lee attacked again, this time at Gaines' Mill, and succeeded in driving the defenders back after bloody fighting.

June 28   On the Mississippi River, Farragut's fleet successfully passed the Confederate batteries at Vicksburg.

June 29   As McClellan's retreat continued, he and Lee clashed again at Savage's Station, another indecisive battle.

June 30   In the decisive day of the week of fighting, Lee made his bid to cut off and trap a large portion of McClellan's army by attacking at Frayser's Farm. In fierce fighting, Union forces held off the attackers long enough to secure the Federal army's retreat.

July 1   Unwilling to accept McClellan's escape, Lee attacked again, hurling his forces against Union troops in an excellent defensive position at Malvern Hill. The Confederates were slaughtered, but McClellan continued his retreat. Taken together with a small skirmish on June 25, the six days of intense fighting ending on this day were known as the Seven Days' Battles. About ninety-seven thousand Confederates had attacked some 103,000 Federals. Union casualties totaled fifteen thousand eight hundred and forty-nine; Confederate, twenty thousand one hundred and forty-one.

July 22   Lincoln presented his draft of the Preliminary Emancipation Proclamation to his cabinet.

August 5   Confederate under Major General John C. Breckinridge unsuccessfully attacked the Union garrison at Baton Rouge, Louisiana.

August 9   Stonewall Jackson defeated Nathaniel P. Banks again, this time at the Battle of Cedar Mountain, as Banks led advance forces of the Union Army of Virginia, commanded by John Pope, in an advance southward through the Virginia piedmont.

August 27   Jackson captured Pope's supply depot at Manassas Junction.

August 28   Jackson attacked a Union column at Groveton, near the old Bull Run battlefield. Fighting was intense but indecisive.

August 29–30 In what became known as the Second Battle of Bull Run in the North (Second Battle of Manassas in the South), Pope attacked Jackson, was repulsed, and then was driven from the battlefield when the other corps of Lee's army, commanded by Major General James Longstreet, counterattacked.

August 30 Confederate forces commanded by Major General Edmund Kirby Smith, leading a Southern invasion of Kentucky, defeated Union forces, mostly raw levies, under the commander of Brigadier General William Nelson at the Battle of Richmond, Kentucky.

September 1 At the Battle of Chantilly, Virginia, Pope's Union forces repulsed an attempt by Jackson's Confederates to cut off their retreat.

September 2 Lincoln ordered the Army of Virginia consolidated into the Army of the Potomac, which was now once again operating in northern Virginia. McClellan would command the combined force.

September 4 Lee's Army of Northern Virginia began crossing the Potomac into Maryland near Leesburg, Virginia.

September 13 Union troops at Frederick, Maryland, found a copy of Lee's Special Orders Number 191, detailing the Confederate general's plans for dividing his army in order to capture the Union garrison at Harpers Ferry.

September 14 McClellan's forces pushed westward after Lee's Confederates, defeating holding forces at Crampton's, Turner's, and Fox's gaps in the South Mountain range.

September 15 Colonel Dixon S. Miles surrendered the Union garrison at Harpers Ferry so precipitately as to arouse questions about his loyalty but ironically was killed by a final Confederate shot.

September 17 McClellan attacked Lee on the high ground between Antietam Creek and the Potomac River; in the bloodiest one-day battle of the war twelve thousand four hundred and sixty-nine Federals and thirteen thousand seven hundred and twenty-four Confederates fell. McClellan used scarcely three-fifths of his large army, and Lee escaped destruction by the narrowest of margins.

September 19 In Mississippi, Confederate general Sterling Price narrowly escaped Grant's plan to trap and destroy his army, collided with one of Grant's converging columns, and fought the short but intense Battle of Iuka.

September 22 Lincoln issued the Preliminary Emancipation Proclamation.

October 3–4 The combined forces of Price and Major General Earl Van Dorn, commanded by the latter, attacked the Union garrison of Corinth, Mississippi, commanded by Major General William S. Rosecrans under Grant's overall command. The Confederate suffered a bloody repulse.

October 8 Braxton Bragg's Confederate army attacked Don Carlos Buell's Federals at Perryville but had to retreat after some initial success.

October 24 Lincoln appointed Rosecrans to serve in place of Buell as commander of what would soon be called the Army of the Cumberland.

November 4 In the fall elections, Democrats made significant gains in Congress.

November 5 Lincoln issued the order for Major General Ambrose E. Burnside to replace McClellan as commander of the Army of the Potomac.

December 7 Union forces under Brigadier General James G. Blunt defeated Confederates under Major General Thomas C. Hindman at Prairie Grove, Arkansas.

December 13 Burnside's Army of the Potomac met lopsided defeat at the hands of Lee's Army of Northern Virginia at Fredericksburg, Virginia.

December 20 Earl Van Dorn led Confederate cavalry on a raid that destroyed Grant's supply depot at Holly Springs, Mississippi, forcing him to retreat from the interior of the state.

December 29 Unaware of Grant's retreat from the interior of Mississippi, Major General William T. Sherman attacked the Vicksburg defenses at Chickasaw Bayou but suffered a bloody repulse.

December 31 Rosecrans's Army of the Cumberland fought an intense battle with Bragg's Army of Tennessee along Stone's River, near the town of Murfreesboro, Tennessee. Rosecrans narrowly avoided defeat.

1863

January 1 Lincoln issued the final Emancipation Proclamation declaring free all slaves in areas still in rebellion against Union authority. He also stated that henceforth blacks would be recruited into the Union armies.

January 2   With the armies still facing each other along Stone's River in Tennessee, Bragg launched another attack, but this time Rosecrans repulsed the Confederates handily, concluding the Battle of Stone's River.

January 11   Union troops under Major General John A. McClernand captured Fort Hindman, at Arkansas Post, Arkansas, along with its five thousand-man garrison.

January 25   Lincoln appointed Major General Joseph Hooker to replace Burnside as commander of the Army of the Potomac.

March 3   Lincoln signed the conscription act, instituting the first effective national draft in U.S. history.

March 14   Farragut once again led his squadron past the now strengthened batteries of Port Hudson. Two vessels got through, two turned back, and one was destroyed.

April 2   In what became known as the Richmond Bread Riot, citizens of Richmond, especially women, went on an orgy of plundering, claiming that they needed to do so in order to avoid starvation.

April 7   A powerful Union fleet including seven ironclads under Flag Officer Samuel Du Pont attacked the Confederate defenses of Charleston, including Fort Sumter, but were driven off.

April 16   Rear Admiral David D. Porter's river gunboat fleet successfully ran past the Vicksburg batteries, reaching the key section of the river south of the city.

April 28   Hooker's Army of the Potomac began crossing the Rappahannock River on a new offensive against Lee.

April 30   Grant's Army of the Tennessee began crossing the Mississippi River in Grant's bold offensive against Vicksburg.

May 1   Grant's troops met and defeated a smaller Confederate force at Port Gibson, Mississippi.

May 1–4   Lee and Jackson combined for the greatest, and last, collaboration, defeating Hooker in the dramatic Battle of Chancellorville. Jackson was wounded by friendly-fire and died on May 10.

May 12   Grant's army defeated another Confederate force at the Battle of Raymond, Mississippi.

May 14   Again Grant was victorious, this time over the Confederate garrison of Jackson, Mississippi; his troops occupied the Mississippi capital and began destroying targets of military value.

May 16   Grant's Army of the Tennessee met and defeated the main Confederate army in Mississippi, underMajor General John C. Pemberton, at Champion's Hill.

May 17   Grant won his fifth victory in less than three weeks, defeating a Confederate force at Big Black Bridge, Mississippi, and sending what was left of Pemberton's army fleeing into the fortifications of Vicksburg.

May 18   Grant's siege of Vicksburg began.

May 19   Grant made his first unsuccessful general assault on Vicksburg.

May 21   Major General Nathaniel P. Banks's forces laid siege to the Confederate bastion of Port Hudson, Louisiana.

May 22   Grant launched a much large, and more costly, assault on Vicksburg but again was unsuccessful. The siege continued.

May 27   Banks's troops staged an unsuccessful assault on Port Hudson.

June 9   With Lee's army shifting westward toward the Blue Ridge, the Union cavalry corps under Major General Alfred Pleasanton probed south across the Rappahannock, surprised Confederate cavalry leader Jeb Stuart, and fought his forces with about even honors at the Battle of Brandy Station, the largest cavalry engagement of the war.

June 14   Banks's army again attacked Port Hudson but met with bloody repulse. There, as at Vicksburg, farther up the river, the siege went on.

June 14–15   In the Second Battle of Winchester, Lieutenant General Richard S. Ewell's corps, leading the advance of Lee's army northward through the Shenandoah Valley and toward a planned invasion of the North, scored an overwhelming victory of the Union garrison at Winchester, Virginia, commanded by Major General Robert Milroy.

June 16   Lee's troops began to cross to the north side of the Potomac River near Martinsburg, Virginia.

June 20   West Virginia was formally admitted to statehood.

June 24 – July 2   Rosecrans's Army of the Cumberland advanced against Bragg's Army of Tennessee. In the nine-day-long Tullahoma

Campaign Rosecrans maneuvered Bragg all the way back to Chattanooga.

June 27   Lincoln replaced Hooker with Major General George G. Meade as commander of the Army of the Potomac.

July 1–3   In one of the most celebrated encounters of the war, the Army of Northern Virginia and the Army of the Potomac met at Gettysburg. Meade emerged victorious after fending off three days of attacks by Lee.

July 4   Lee began his retreat back to Virginia.

July 4   Pemberton surrendered Vicksburg and thirty thousand men to Grant.

July 8   Confederate Major General Franklin Gardner surrendered Port Hudson and seven thousand men to Banks.

July 11   Union troops unsuccessfully assaulted Battery Wagner, outside Charleston, South Carolina.

July 13   After being trapped for several days between the Army of the Potomac and the rain-swollen river of that name, Lee and his army finally made good their escape into Virginia, much to Lincoln's dismay.

July 13–15   Major draft riots raged in New York City.

July 18   Some six thousand Union troops, including several hundred men of the 54th Massachusetts Colored Infantry, made another unsuccessful and bloody assault on Battery Wagner.

September 8   Confederate troops repulsed a small Union expedition at Sabine Pass, Texas.

September 9   Troops of Rosecrans's Army of the Cumberland occupied Chattanooga after maneuvering Bragg's Confederates out of the key southwest Tennessee rail junction town.

September 10   Union troops occupied Little Rock, Arkansas.

September 18–20   Bragg's Army of Tennessee, reinforced to sixty-eight thousand men attacked the Army of the Cumberland along Chickamauga Creek ten miles south of Chattanooga and drove it back to the town but failed to cut it off and destroy it.

October 14   As the Army of the Potomac and the Army of Northern Virginia maneuvered west of Washington, D.C., elements of the two armies met at Bristoe Station, where the Union was victorious in a sharp encounter.

October 16   Lincoln created a new Military Division of the Mississippi, encompassing the departments of the Tennessee, the Cumberland, and the Ohio, and appointed Ulysses S. Grant to take command of it.

October 18   Grant replaced Rosecrans with Maj. Gen. George H. Thomas as commander of the Army of the Cumberland.

October 23   Grant arrived at Army of the Cumberland headquarters in semi-besieged Chattanooga.

October 27   Grant successfully opened a supply line to the half-starved Army of the Cumberland in Chattanooga.

November 19   Lincoln attended the dedication of the new national cemetery at Gettysburg and delivered "a few appropriate words," subsequently known as the Gettysburg Address.

November 23   Under Grant's command, the Army of the Cumberland, now supported by large detachments from the Army of the Tennessee and the Army of the Potomac, opened the Battle of Chattanooga by capturing Orchard Knob.

November 24   In a phase of the Battle of Chattanooga known as "the Battle above the Clouds," Union troops captured Lookout Mountain.

November 25   On the climactic day of the Battle of Chattanooga Grant's troops stormed Missionary Ridge and routed Bragg's Army of Tennessee.

November 26   By proclamation of Abraham Lincoln, the country celebrated its first national Thanksgiving Day.

November 26 – December 1   Meade advanced against Lee in what became known as the Mine Run campaign, but Lee maneuvered Meade into a disadvantageous position and the Union army retreated without giving battle. The relative positions of the two armies remained as they had been before Meade advanced.

November 29   Confederate troops under Lieutenant General James Longstreet launched an unsuccessful assault on Fort Sanders, near Knoxville, Tennessee.

November 30   Jefferson Davis removed Braxton Bragg from command of the Army of Tennessee at his own request.

December 16 Davis appointed General Joseph E. Johnston to command the Army of Tennessee.

1864

February 17 The Confederate submarine Hunley sank the sloop-of-war USS *Housatonic* of Charleston.

February 20 Confederate troops under Brigadier General Joseph Finegan defeated a Union expedition under Brigadier General Truman Seymour at Olustee, Florida.

February 22 Confederate cavalry under Nathan Bedford Forrest defeated a Union cavalry expedition under Brigadier General William Sooy Smith at Okolona, Mississippi.

March 1 Lincoln nominated Grant for the newly created rank of Lieutenant General. He was officially commissioned March 9.

April 8 Confederate troops under the command of Lieutenant General Richard Taylor defeated the Union Red River expedition at Mansfield, Louisiana, near Shreveport. The Federals, commanded by Nathaniel P. Banks, retreated.

May 4 The Army of the Potomac, still commanded by Meade but with Grant accompanying to supervise directly, crossed the Rapidan River at the opening of another offensive against Lee.

May 5–6 The Army of the Potomac immediately collided in a major battle in an area of dense thickets known as the Wilderness. Casualties were high, results indecisive, and Grant kept moving on.

May 7 The armies of the Tennessee, Cumberland, and Ohio, all under the command of William T. Sherman, advanced toward Dalton, Georgia, on a campaign ultimately aimed at Atlanta and its defenders, the Confederate Army of Tennessee under Joseph E. Johnston.

May 8–21 Grant's and Lee's forces fought again in another inconclusive and bloody battle at Spotsylvania Court House.

May 11 Union cavalry under Major General Phillip Sheridan clashed with their Confederate counterparts under Jeb Stuart at Yellow Tavern, Virginia; Stuart was mortally wounded.

May 14–15 In Georgia, Sherman's forces met Johnston's in the Battle of Resaca; Johnston retreated.

May 15 A Confederate force under Major General John C. Breckinridge stopped Major General Franz Sigel's Union advance in the Shenandoah Valley by defeating Sigel at the Battle of New Market.

May 16 A Confederate force under General Pierre G. T. Beauregard stopped Major General Benjamin Butler's Union advance toward Richmond via the south bank of the James River by defeating Butler at the Battle of Drewry's Bluff.

May 23–26 Grant and Lee met again at the Battle of the North Anna.

June 1–3 On the outskirts of Richmond, Grant's and Lee's armies fought the Battle of Cold Harbor.

June 8 The Republican Party, now styling itself the "National Union Party," met in convention at Baltimore and nominated Lincoln for a second term.

June 10 A Confederate force under Nathan Bedford Forrest stopped Major General Samuel D. Sturgis's Union advance from Memphis into the interior of Mississippi by defeating and routing Sturgis at the Battle of Brice's Crossroads.

June 11 At Trevilian Station, Virginia, Sheridan's cavalry clashed again with its Rebel counterparts, the latter now commanded by Wade Hampton.

June 14 At Pine Mountain, Georgia, Union artillery fire killed Confederate Lieutenant General Leonidas Polk.

June 15–18 Having stolen a march on Lee, Grant attacked the vital Confederate rail nexus at Petersburg, Virginia, but was unable to take it. Lee's army arrived to defend Petersburg, and a siege began.

June 19 USS *Kearsarge* sank the Confederate commerce raider *Alabama* off Cherbourg, France.

June 27 Sherman launched a bloody and unsuccessful attack on Johnston's entrenched Confederates at Kennesaw Mountain, Georgia.

July 9 A scratch force of Union troops under Major General Lew Wallace met Lieutenant General Jubal Early's Confederate raiding force at the Battle of Monocacy, in Maryland; though defeated, Wallace succeeded in his purpose of delaying Early.

July 11 Early's Confederates reached the outskirts of Washington and skirmished with Union troops in the Washington fortifications.

July 14 In the Battle of Tupelo, Mississippi, Forrest suffered defeat at the hands of a Union expedition commanded by Major General A. J. Smith; however Smith returned to Memphis and Forrest returned to raiding.

July 17 Jefferson Davis relieved Joseph E. Johnston as commander of the Army of Tennessee, replacing him with John B. Hood.

July 20 At the Battle of Peachtree Creek, Georgia, Hood attacked one wing of Sherman's forces, George H. Thomas's Army of the Cumberland, but was repulsed.

July 22 At the Battle of Atlanta, Hood attacked another part of Sherman's force, James B. McPherson's Army of the Tennessee. McPherson was killed but the Army of the Tennessee handed Hood another defeat.

July 28 Again Hood attacked, this time at Ezra Church, also near Atlanta. Once again the Army of the Tennessee repulsed his forces.

July 30 Along the Petersburg lines Union forces exploded a mine under the Confederate trenches but then failed in their attempt to attack through the gap thus created. The Battle of the Crater was another bloody Union setback in Virginia.

July 30 Confederate raiders burned Chambersburg, Pennsylvania.

August 5 Rear Admiral David Farragut successfully led his Union fleet into Mobile Bay, defeating two Confederate forts and three vessels of war, including the powerful ironclad CSS *Tennessee*.

August 31 The Democratic Party met in convention in Chicago and nominated George B. McClellan for president on a platform that Lincoln was a tyrant, the war was a failure, and peace negotiations should be opened at once.

August 31 – September 1 Elements of Sherman's forces cut Hood's supply line at Jonesborough, Georgia. Hood counterattacked but was again repulsed by the Army of the Tennessee.

September 1 After setting fire to ammunition stocks at the railroad depot, Hood's Confederates evacuated Atlanta.

September 2 Union troops occupied Atlanta.

September 19 Sheridan, commanding the Army of the Shenandoah, defeated Early's corps at the Third Battle of Winchester.

September 22 Sheridan defeated early again at Fisher's Hill, Virginia.

October 4 In North Georgia, Hood struck at Sherman's supply lines but his forces were repulsed by the Union garrison at Allatoona.

October 19 Early attacked Sheridan's army, but after initial Confederate success, the Federals rallied and defeated Early more decisively than in previous battles.

November 8 The voters elected Lincoln to a second term.

November 16 Sherman departed Atlanta on his March to the Sea.

November 30 Having advanced into Tennessee, Hood launched his army in a series of suicidal attacks against entrenched Federals under the command of Major General John M. Schofield at Franklin, Tennessee.

December 13 Sherman's troops captured Fort McAllister, near Savannah, Georgia, opening communication with Union naval forces and completing the March to the Sea.

December 15–16 Union forces under the command of George H. Thomas routed Hood's army at the Battle of Nashville.

December 20 Confederate forces under William J. Hardee evacuated Savannah, Georgia. Federal occupied the city the next day.

1865

January 13–15 Union forces captured Fort Fisher, guarding the entrance to the Confederacy's last open port, Wilmington, North Carolina.

January 31 Jefferson Davis named Robert E. Lee general-in-chief of all Confederate armies.

February 3 Lincoln and Secretary of State William H. Seward met with Confederate Vice-President Alexander Stephens and two other Confederate representatives aboard the steamer River Queen at Hampton Roads, off Fort Monroe, Virginia, to see if it might be possible to negotiate a peaceful restoration of the Union. It was not.

February 17 Sherman's army captured Columbia, South Carolina.

February 22   Union forces from the coast occupied Wilmington, North Carolina.

March 2   Sheridan destroyed what was left of Early's force at Waynesborough, Virginia.

March 4   Lincoln was inaugurated for his second term.

March 5   Sherman's army occupied Cheraw, South Carolina.

March 11   Sherman's army occupied Fayetteville, North Carolina.

March 16   Confederate troops under William J. Hardee briefly attempted to block the route of Sherman's advance toward Goldsborough, North Carolina, resulting in the small battle of Aversaborough. The Confederates withdrew, and Sherman's march continued.

March 19–21   Confederate forces commanded by Joseph E. Johnston attacked one wing of Sherman's army at Bentonville, North Carolina. After some initial success, the Confederates were driven off, and Sherman's march continued.

March 25   The Army of Northern Virginia made an unsuccessful assault on Fort Stedman, part of the Petersburg siege lines.

April 1   Union forces under Sheridan defeated a detachment of the Army of Northern Virginia at Five Forks, west of Petersburg, rending Lee's position around Richmond and Petersburg completely untenable.

April 2   Grant launched an assault all the along the Petersburg lines, sweeping away the Confederate defenders. The Confederate government fled Richmond as Lee gave notice he could no longer hold the city.

April 3   Union troops occupied Richmond while the bulk of Grant's army pursued Lee's fleeing Confederates westward.

April 6   Union pursuers tore at the flanks and rear of Lee's column, defeating and capturing some eight thousand Confederates at Sayler's Creek, Virginia.

April 9   Cornered at last, Lee surrendered to Grant at Appomattox Court House, Virginia.

April 12   Mobile, Alabama, the Confederacy's last major city, surrendered to Union forces commanded by Major General Edward R. S. Canby.

April 13   Sherman's troops occupied Raleigh, North Carolina.

April 14   John Wilkes Booth assassinated Lincoln while the president was watching a play at Ford's Theater in Washington. Lincoln died shortly after 7:00 a.m. the next morning.

April 15   Andrew Johnson took the oath of office as seventeenth president of the United States.

April 18   Johnston and Sherman reached a surrender agreement at Durham Station, North Carolina. The agreement was subsequently rejected by the U.S. government.

April 26   Johnston and Sherman came to another, this time satisfactory, agreement at Durham Station.

April 26   Union cavalry surrounded John Wilkes Booth on a farm in Virginia. There he was mortally wounded, either by his own bullet or by that of a Federal cavalryman.

May 4   At Citronelle, Alabama, Confederate Lieutenant General Richard Taylor surrendered the remaining Confederate forces in Alabama, Mississippi and eastern Louisiana.

May 10   Union cavalry captured Jefferson Davis near Irwinville, Georgia, where the fugitive Confederate president had halted for the night on his flight toward the Mississippi River.

May 10   President Andrew Johnson proclaimed that armed resistance by rebel forces was at an end.

May 26   At New Orleans, Lieutenant General Simon B. Buckner surrendered Confederate forces in the trans-Mississippi to Union Major General Peter J. Osterhaus.

GLOSSARY

Abatis An abatis was an obstruction formed by felling trees so that their tops lay all in the direction from which the enemy was expected to approach and then sharpening the end of their branches. The interlocking branches formed an obstruction that could delay and disrupt an advancing line of Infantry. An abatis would be built in front of a defensive position.

Balks See "Pontoon Bridge."

Battalion A battalion was usually a unit consisting of anywhere from two to eight companies, although each regiment was also considered to be a single "battalion" for purposes of the tactics manuals.

Battery A battery was a unit of artillery. A field battery normally consisted of four or, more frequently, six cannons, and had a compliment of one hundred to one hundred and fifty men. The term could also refer to a fixed position mounting artillery, and then any number of guns might be present and referred to by the term "battery."

Bayonet A long blade that could be attached to the muzzle of a rifle or musket. Few Civil War wounds were causes by bayonets, but then bayonets were not intended to wound the enemy but rather to make him run away—when he saw a line of troops running toward him with fixed bayonets. Alternatively, detached from the rifle and with its blade stuck in the ground, the bayonet made a nice candle-holder.

Brigade A brigade was a unit consisting of two or more regiments; usually the number was four or five. Late in the war as the size of regiments decreased, the Union especially tended to increase the number of regiments in a brigade, sometimes to as many as eight or ten. Brigades were the basic maneuver units of the Civil War armies.

Butternut Butternut was a yellowish-brown color common in homespun cloth that had been dyed with the hulls of butternuts. The presence of such cloth in the clothing of Confederate troops became so common that butternut became almost a second official uniform color for the Rebels.

These 10-ton mortars, amongst one of the fifteen batteries located at Yorktown, were the largest available in the Union arsenal.

Caisson   A caisson was a wheeled vehicle used by artillery to carry a large ammunition chest.

Canister   Canister was the most deadly type of ammunition used by Civil War artillery. It came in a fixed cartridge that included a propellant charge of black powder and a cluster of iron or lead balls about the size of musket balls as the projectiles. A canister round for a 12-pounder gun, the most common field piece of the war, contained twenty-seven balls. The effective range of canister was only three to four hundred yards, the shortest of any type of artillery ammunition, but when used it was deadly, turning a half-ton cannon into a giant sawed-off shotgun. In desperate situations, double or even triple loads of canister could be fired. In such cases, the propellant charges were removed from the second and third rounds.

Cartridge box   Civil War soldiers carried their ammunition supply, composed of paper cartridges, in a leather cartridge box suspended by a strap over their shoulder. A cartridge box could normally carry forty rounds of .58 or .577 caliber ammunition.

Case shot   See "Spherical case."

Chesses   See "Pontoon Bridge."

Chevaux-de-Frises   Chevaux-de-Frises were another type of obstruction (along with abatis) that could be placed in front of a defensive position. They consisted of logs bored through with rows of holes into which rows of sharpened stakes were inserted, half of the stakes being at an angle of ninety degrees to the other half so that they formed an "X" in cross-section.

Close order   Close order was a formation in which each soldier stands with his elbows touching the elbows of the soldiers on either side of him. Usually a second rank, similarly arranged, stood immediately behind the first.

Colt Revolver   The most popular handgun of the Civil War, the six-shot Colt Revolver came in two sizes, the .36 caliber Colt "Navy" and the .44 caliber Colt "Army" revolvers. Either could be found in Civil War armies. They were cap-and-ball revolvers that took paper cartridges and were cumbersome and time-consuming to load. Therefore those who expected to do a

good deal of shooting with their Colts took spare cylinders, already loaded, that could be quickly changed out almost like spare magazines. The Colt, like other types of revolvers, was carried almost exclusively by cavalrymen and officers. Foot soldiers found them too heavy to lug around on long marches.

Colt Revolving Rifle   Lee successful than its hand-gun cousin, the Colt Revolving Rifle fired five shots from a revolving cylinder similar to those in Colt handguns. Its chief drawback, aside from its tendency to jam and its annoying way of venting gas into the face of the shooter, was its occasional problem with detonating all five charges at once. Still, the Colt Revolving Rifle was much sought after and occasionally did good service.

Columbiad   A Columbiad was a large smoothbore, muzzle-loading gun (the most common calibers were 8- and 10-inch) designed to throw a spherical shell at low velocity so that instead of breaking through the wooden side of a ship, the shell would imbed itself there just before exploding, thus creating more damage. Though a venerable design at the time of the war, Columbiads were used by both sides in any situation in which they were available and heavy cannon were needed.

Company   The company was the basic unit of recruitment in the Civil War armies. A company was in theory composed of one hundred men, but most were much smaller by the time they had been in service a year or more. Most companies were recruited entirely from a single community and maintained community ties among the men even as they became soldiers.

Conscription   Conscription is the practice of a government forcing citizens to enter the army.

Contraband   The term contraband had a special meaning in the Civil War thanks to Benjamin Butler, a lawyer and Union general who early in the war found a way to avoid the legal absurdity of having to return escaping slaves to their Rebel masters. He declared that the slaves had been used to help the Rebel war effort and were therefore "contraband of war"—liable to confiscation and forfeit to their masters. The term contraband came to apply to any slave who had left his master.

Corn Pone A small, elongated loaf of cornbread called a corn pone was often a prominent item in the rations of Confederate soldiers. When short on rations, Union soldiers were happy to get them too, usually by means of capture.

Corps A corps, sometimes known as a corps d'armée, consisted of two or more divisions.

Cracker Civil War soldiers commonly referred to their squares of hard tack as crackers.

Dahlgren Gun The Dahlgren Gun was a naval gun developed by Union Rear Admiral John A. Dahlgren when he worked as a lieutenant in the naval ordnance bureau before the war. It was a smoothbore and fired a spherical projectile. The gun was a favorite of the U.S. Navy, which used it in 9-, 11-, and eventually 15-inch calibers.

Desiccated vegetables One of the advantages of soldiering in the Union, rather than the Confederate, armies was the availability of desiccated vegetables in the rations. These were large cakes of processed, dried, vegetables, mostly green in color, which could be reconstituted, after a fashion, by boiling in water. Soldiers learned to break off small pieces of the cake for boiling in their mess kettles, since desiccated vegetables would expand to many times their size. Once they got used to them, most Union soldiers became quite fond of desiccated vegetables, although it is doubtful that any of them ever sought out the food after being discharged from the army.

Division A division was composed of two or more brigades, usually three in the Union armies, four in the Confederate.

Enfield The most common imported infantry weapon of the Civil War was the .577 caliber muzzle-loading Enfield rifle-musket, made in Britain and patterned after the Springfield. Like the American weapon, it had a rate of fire of two to three rounds per minute and an effective range of three hundred and fifty yards, though few soldiers could use it effectively at that range.

Fascine A fascine was a large bundle of sticks usually carried by assaulting infantrymen for the purpose of being thrown down into the outer ditch of the enemy's fortifications, enabling the attacking infantry to cross the ditch quickly and scale the enemy's earthworks.

Forage The word "forage" had very different meanings depending on whether it was used as a noun or a verb. As a noun, forage was food for horses and mules—oats, corn, hay, or fresh grass. As a verb, to forage was to appropriate foodstuffs from the populace, which soldiers of both armies did whenever they had the chance, if necessary in defiance of the orders of their superiors.

Forage cap The forage cap was one of the two most common types of uniform caps in Civil War armies of both sides (the other was the kepi). Like the kepi, the forage cap had a small visor in front. The body of the cap was made of soft cloth, and it was designed to slump down and forward when worn so that the round top of the hat was presented to the front. Many Civil War soldiers dispensed with both the forage cap and the kep—if their officers permitted—and instead equipped themselves with more comfortable and practical broad-brimmed hats of the slouch hat variety.

Frigate The frigate was the largest type of naval vessel actually employed in the Civil War. It was a three-masted, square-rigged, wooden sailing ship that carried its armament—usually between forty and sixty guns—on two decks. Older frigates, like USS *Cumberland* and USS *Congress*, destroyed by the Confederate ironclad *Virginia*, relied on sails alone for propulsion. More modern ones used both steam and sail. These included the four rivers-class frigates that were the pride of the U.S. Navy at the outbreak of the war, each carrying approximately fifty heavy guns, most of them 9-inch Dahlgrens. One of them, USS *Merrimac*, was drastically altered to become CSS *Virginia*. The most modern frigate of the war, USS *New Ironsides*, was an ironclad encased in four inches of iron plate and depending solely on steam power for propulsion.

Gabion A gabion was a cylindrical wicker basket, about six feet long and several feet in diameter, filled with earth or tightly packed cotton and used as a component in the building of fortifications, in much the same function that sandbags fulfilled in later wars and occasionally in this one. Unlike sandbags, gabions were usually used in an upright position.

Goober peas Southern soldiers, especially

Georgia troops, referred to peanuts as goober peas and ate them whenever they could.

Grape shot   Grape shot was a type of artillery ammunition consisting of a number of small iron balls held together around a bolt. When fired, grape shot came apart, spraying the small iron balls in shotgun fashion. Though often referred to in the Civil War— for example by officers claiming to have received fire of "canister and grape"—it was in fact very rarely used, having been replaced almost completely by canister.

Grayback   Occasionally Union soldiers used this term to refer to their gray-clad enemies in the Confederate army. More often, soldiers of both armies used it to refer to the lice that were an almost constant plague of army life in the field.

Greenbacks   Greenbacks were paper money issued as legal tender (fiat money) by the U.S. government after February 1862 and so called because of the color of ink used on them.

Hardtack   Hardtack was the staple of the Civil War soldier's diet, especially in the Union army. It was a flat unleavened bread made of refined wheat flour, water, and a little salt. The water all vanished in the baking, and what remained was very hard, though not unpalatable if one could get around the near impossibility of bighting or chewing it. The soldiers devised many ingenious ways of preparing it, many of them involving frying it with the grease of the bacon or salt pork.

Hardee Hat   The Hardee Hat, named after William J. Hardee, a former West Point commandant and author of the army's prewar tactics manual who became a Confederate general, was the standard dress-uniform headgear of the U.S. Army when the Civil War began. It was a stiff, broad-brimmed, high-crowned, tapering, flat-topped, black hat that was worn with one side of the brim pinned up. One soldier thought it made his comrades look like "the pilgrim fathers." The Hardee Hat was issued to many Union troops early in the war but soon was discarded in favor of more practical headgear. An exception to that practice was in the only all-western brigade to serve in the Army of the Potomac. Composed of three Wisconsin regiments, one Indiana, and, later, one Michigan, the "Black Hat Brigade" was at first known for its distinctive headgear but earned a well-deserved reputation as the best fighting brigade in the eastern armies and later came to be known as the Iron Brigade.

Havelock   A havelock was a cloth cover for a kepi with a cloth flap that cascaded down over the back of the wearer's neck and perhaps shoulders. It was frequently seen in artists' depictions of the French Foreign Legion serving in desert conditions. Many northern women sewed havelocks and presented them to the local troops as they prepared to depart for the torrid South. The havelock was meant to keep the hot rays of the sun off of the wearer's neck, but, at least in the humid climate of the South, cooling breezes were more sought after than protection from the sun, and havelocks were rarely if every used. A broad-brimmed hat was more practical.

Haversack   To a Civil War soldier the most important part of the equipment he carried on his person was probably his haversack. It was a leather bag, slung by a strap over the shoulder, in which a soldier carried his supply of hardtack, salt pork, corn pones, bacon, or whatever other food items he had been able to acquire—all jumbled together. It was a dirty, messy way to carry food.

Housewife   Probably the most useful and sought-after item—other than clothing— manufactured by local ladies and sent off to war with their troops was the "housewife." It was a small folding cloth pouch designed to carry needles, thread, spare buttons, and whatever else soldiers might need to repair their uniforms.

Howitzer   A howitzer was a relatively short-range, short-barreled, light-weight artillery piece designed to be fired either with a flat trajectory or with considerable elevation so as to lob its shells over fortress walls and the like. They were usually made of bronze. The army used 12- and 24-pounder howitzers, and the navy had a 12-pounder Dahlgren boat howitzer.

Impressment   In the Civil War the term "impressment" referred to the practice of agents of the Confederate government of taking their citizens' property whenever they found it convenient. Such property could range from hogs, to slaves, to wagons, to steamships. The practice of impressment was highly pernicious in its effects, removing productive resources from the Southern economy, imposing an unfair burden of taxation, discouraging production, and encouraging Confederate citizens to hide their resources rather than use them. Furthermore, by allowing the government to acquire assets without reference to their market value, it encouraged the government to use such assets wastefully—which any government is all too prone to do in the best of situations.

Ironclad   An ironclad was a wooden warship covered, at least over most of its above-waterline surface area, with an inch or more of iron plate.

Kepi   The kepi was one of the two most common types of uniform caps in Civil War armies of both sides (the other was the forage cap). Like the forage cap, the kepi had a small visor in front. Unlike the forage cap, however, the body of the cap was short and low and was made of cloth that was stiffened so that the kepi retained its crisp appearance—at least until thoroughly battered—and its round top remained slanting only slightly forward. Many Civil War soldiers dispensed with both the kepi and the forage cap—if their officers permitted—and instead equipped themselves with more comfortable and practical broad-brimmed hats of the slouch hat variety.

Limber   The limber was a two-wheeled vehicle that was hitched between the cannon and its team of horses when the gun was "limbered up" for transport. The limber also carried a limber chest filled with ammunition.

Lunette   A lunette was a two- or three-sided fortification that was open to the rear.

Minié Ball   The Minié Ball was a conical bullet with a hollow base and made of soft lead. It was developed by Captain Claude Minié of the French army during the 1850s. Its value was that it allowed a muzzle-loading rifle-musket to be loaded as rapidly and easily as a musket yet still have the advantages of range and accuracy offered by a rifle. This was because the Minié Ball could be small enough to drop easily down the barrel on loading but would expand on firing so as to fill the bore and engage the rifling grooves on the inside of the barrel. Most Civil War rifles, including the .58 caliber Springfield and the .577 caliber

Enfield, used Minié Balls. Their presence on the battlefield made infantry fire much more deadly at longer ranges.

Monitor   Monitor was originally the name of an individual warship, but it came to be a name for a type of vessel. Civil War monitors had one or two round turrets, each mounting two heavy guns, located on a low, flat deck. They had only a foot or two of freeboard and were not very seaworthy, but they presented very small targets. That along with their heavy armor—at least eight inches on the turret, more in later models—rendered them all but impervious to enemy gunfire.

Musket   A musket was a smoothbore, muzzle-loading infantry weapon that fired a spherical lead ball. It featured low velocity, atrocious accuracy, and an effective range of one hundred yards or less. Yet its rate of fire of two to three rounds per minute was faster than any rifle prior to the invention in the 1850s of the Minié rifle-musket. Many Civil War soldiers on both sides carried musket during the first year or two of the war.

Napoleon (Gun)   The 12-pounder Napoleon was so called because it was copied from a French design used by the army of the French emperor Napoleon III. It was made of bronze, weighed about one thousand five hundred pounds, fired either canister or a 4.62 inch spherical projectile weighing about twelve pounds (if solid shot was selected). Its maximum range was about one thousand six hundred yards, but it was most effective using canister at ranges of less than four hundred yards.

Open order   Open order was a formation in which individual soldiers are several yards apart in line.

Ordnance Rifle, 3-inch   The 3-inch Ordnance Rifle, sometimes erroneously called that Rodman Gun, was the best of the Civil War rifled field guns. Made of iron, its tube weighed less than one thousand pounds, yet it could fire a conical-cylindrical shell more than two thousand yards with good accuracy. It was more reliable than the Parrott Gun. Many Union batteries were equipped with the 3-inch Ordnance Rifle, but the Confederates had to rely on captures for such of the guns as it used.

Parrott Gun   The Parrott was the most

common of Civil War rifled cannon and appeared in a variety of forms. The 10-pounder Parrott, in 2.75 inch caliber, was a common light field gun. The 20-pound version accompanied the field armies in smaller numbers as a more heavy and effective field gun. Union army siege trains usually contained several 30-pounder Parrotts. Union naval vessels sometimes carried 100-pounders, and a 200-pounder, the famous Swamp Angel, was used in the siege of Charleston. Made of iron, the Parrotts were relatively light and had good range and accuracy. However, they had a tendency to burst, as did the Swamp Angel.

Picket   A picket was a guard posted outside an encampment to give warning of the approach of the enemy.

Pontoon bridge   A pontoon bridge was a portable, temporary bridge formed by mooring a line of specially constructed boats, called pontoons, side by side across a river. A framework of balks and chesses, as the bracing pieces were called, was then constructed across the pontoons and a deck laid on top. Pontoons were made of wood or occasionally canvas and were a heavy, bulky, but essential part of an army's baggage train.

Pumpkin slinger   Pumpkin slinger as a derisive nickname the soldiers gave to .69 caliber Belgian rifles issued to them early in the war when no better weapons could be obtained.

Redoubt   A redoubt was a fortified, enclosed earthwork, usually made of earth and logs. Redoubts functioned as parts of larger systems of defensive works.

Regiment   A regiment was a unit composed of ten companies in the infantry or twelve in the cavalry. Regiments were supposed to number one thousand men (one thousand two hundred in the cavalry) and most were at least close to that at the time of mustering in. However, few numbered more than five or six hundred by the time they finished their first campaign, the reduction coming mostly as a result of sickness. By the middle of the war, many regiments numbered less than three hundred men. For political reasons the states, which did most of the recruiting in both North and South, chose to recruit new regiments rather than provide replacements for existing ones.

Rifle-Musket   A rifle-musket was a weapon that loaded as quickly and easily as a musket but fired with the range and accuracy of a rifle. It was developed by Captain Claude Minié of the French army during the 1850s and fired a bullet called the Minié Ball. The most popular rifle-muskets of the Civil War were the .58 caliber Springfield and the .577 caliber Enfield.

Rodman Gun   See "Ordnance Rifle, 3-inch."

Sap   In the military parlance of the day, a sap was a trench, usually zigzag, by which a besieging force would approach fortifications of a besieged defender.

Sap Roller   A sap roller was a large cylinder made of wood and earth—or, occasionally, packed cotton—which soldiers slowly rolled in front of them as they advanced their siege trenches, or saps, toward the enemy's fortifications. The purpose of the sap roller was to provide cover from bullets until the sap could be dug deep enough to do so.

Secession   Secession was the act of on the part of a state by which it severed its relationship with the United States and became no longer a part of the United States. One of the questions at issue in the war was whether a state had the right to secede for any reason or for no reason. The Southern states reason for wishing to secede was the election of a president pledged to oppose the further spread of slavery.

Section   In the military parlance of the time, a section was a sub-unit of a battery and consisted of two guns. Normally, a field battery consisted of two or, more frequently, three sections.

Sharps Rifle/Carbine   The Sharps Rifle, designed by Christian Sharps, was an early breech-loading design. The soldier would open the breech, insert a single paper cartridge, and then close the breech. The action of closing the breech caused a knife to cut through the cartridge, exposing the gunpowder inside ready for ignition. The Sharps was also produced in a carbine version that was issued to cavalry. Both versions were used chiefly by Union troops, with the Confederates depending on captures for their supply.

Shebang   A shebang was a make-shift shack built by the soldiers, especially in winter quarters.

Shell   Shell was a type of long-range artillery ammunition used against personnel or opposing artillery. It consisted of an iron sphere or cylinder filled with black powder and fused to explode a certain amount of time after being fired. Ideally, shell was meant to explode just above and in front of the enemy. In practice it was difficult to achieve this result, especially for Confederate gunners who were usually supplied with defective ammunition and unreliable fuses.

Shelter Tent   The most common type of tent in the second half of the war was the shelter tent. Made of cotton duck and composed of two shelter halves that buttoned together at one edge, the shelter tent was held up by two sticks obtained locally. It was just large enough for two men to sleep side by side, and each man carried one shelter half for pairing up with that of another soldier. The shelter tent was so low that the men had to get down on hands and knees to crawl into it. The soldiers despised the shelter tent, calling it the dog tent or pup tent.

Sibley Tent   The tent that the soldier much preferred to the shelter tent was the Sibley Tent. Designed by pre-war U.S. Army officer Henry Hopkins Sibley and patterned after the teepees of the plains Indians, the Sibley tent was conical, twelve feet tall and eighteen and a half in diameter. It had two door flaps and a vent flap at the top. A specially designed portable stove could be placed in the center, with its pipe protruding from the vent. It accommodated twelve soldiers. The men loved it, but it weighed seventy-three pounds and had to be hauled in a wagon; so the army phase out its use in favor of the hated but far more portable shelter tent.

Skirmisher   A skirmisher was a soldier who advance along with other skirmishers in open order—that is, in a line with five to ten yards between men—several hundred yards in front of the main body of the army as it advanced or when it was in close proximity to the enemy. The skirmishers' job was to engage the enemy with long-range fire so as to give the main body warning of the presence of the enemy as well as information on the enemy's strength and numbers.

Sloop-of-War   A sloop-of-war was a three-masted, square-rigged, wooden warship that carried all of its guns on a single deck, except perhaps for two or three at the bow and stern. Almost all Civil War era sloops were powered by both steam and sails. The largest type of sloops, which included Admiral Farragut's flagship, USS *Hartford*, were second only to frigates as the most powerful vessels in the U.S. Navy at the outbreak of the war. Sloops also included smaller vessels such as USS *Kearsarge*, which sank the Confederate commerce raider Alabama.

Solid shot   The type of artillery ammunition offering the longest range was solid shot. As the name implies, it was solid iron. Its lack of an explosive charge made it less lethal than shell in most cases, and of course both were much less lethal than canister. Aside from achieving maximum range, however, there were other reasons for using solid shot. When firing over the heads of friendly troops, artillerists often chose solid shot because Civil War era shell fuses were often unreliable and might explode prematurely, creating casualties among the friendly infantry. Solid shot was safer. In naval settings, solid shot offered the greatest penetrating power and thus was the ammunition of choice for use against ironclads. On a land battlefield, spherical solid shot from such guns as the common 12-pounder Napoleon could bounce, skip, and roll across the battlefield, completely visible yet still lethal, in a way that tended to demoralize the troops on the receiving end.

Spencer Rifle/Carbine   The best infantry and cavalry weapons of the war were the Spencer repeating rifle and carbine, respectively. Patented by Christopher M. Spencer in 1860, the Spencer repeating rifle took seven metallic cartridges in a detachable tubular magazine that was inserted into the butt stock. The trigger guard served as a lever. When pulled downward, it opened the breech and ejected the spent cartridge case. Returning it to position chambered another round and closed the breech. Some claimed the Spencer could achieve a rate of fire of up to twenty rounds per minutes, or six to ten times that which could be achieved with an ordinary Springfield or Enfield. The rifle version had about the same ballistic performance as the conventional rifles. The carbine was used in much larger numbers and issued to Union cavalry late in the war. Troops with Spencers were typically equal to several times their numbers in battle.

Spherical Case   Spherical case shot was a type

of long-range anti-personnel artillery ammunition developed by British General Henry Shrapnel during the Napoleonic Wars. It consisted of a hollow iron ball containing numerous small lead or iron balls and a bursting charge of black powder in the center. It was a popular type of ammunition for 12-pounder Napoleon guns and other smoothbore cannon when firing at infantry beyond the range of canister.

Springfield   The most commonly used infantry weapon of the Civil War was the .58 caliber muzzle-loading Springfield rifle-musket. It had a rate of fire of two to three rounds per minute and an effective range of three hundred and fifty yards, though few soldiers could use it effectively at that range.

Squadron   The term "squadron" had two meanings in the Civil War. In the navy it was a unit of two or more warships. In the army it was a unit of two or more companies of cavalry.

Timberclad   A timberclad was a river gunboat that depended on thick wooden bulwarks for its protection from enemy fire. It was, of course, less robust than an ironclad but also much less expensive and time-consuming to build. Timberclads were simply existing riverboats, buttressed with thick wooden walls above the waterline. The Union built three timberclads on the western rivers early in the war, Tyler, Lexington, and Conestoga, and they did good service in a number of actions, most notably the Battle of Shiloh, or Pittsburg Landing, where Tyler's and Lexington's shelling helped Grant hold his last line of defense. When engaging the enemy's heavy guns, timberclad had to maintain extremely long range or else risk rapid destruction.

Tinclad   A tinclad was a light-weight, shallow-draft river gunboat protected by less than one inch of iron plate over its wooden sides and armed with light guns. It was used for operations on small secondary streams.

Torpedo   Unlike its modern namesake, the torpedo of the Civil War did not travel anywhere on its own. The term was used to refer to any explosive charge, such as a mine. The Confederates used underwater torpedoes, detonated by remote control, as anti-ship weapons and succeeded in sinking such powerful vessels as the ironclad USS *Cairo* in the Yazoo River and the monitor

USS *Tecumseh* at Mobile Bay. Land mines might also be called torpedoes, or subterra shells. Though used by the Confederacy on a number of occasions, they were considered a violation of the rules of civilized warfare when used anywhere except in front of fortified lines. Another type of Civil War torpedo was an explosive charge on the end of a long spar, or pole, such as the one with which the Confederate submarine *Hunley* sank the Union sloop-of-war *Housatonic*.

Videttes   Videttes were mounted cavalry outposts who patrolled the front and flanks of an army. They were the equivalent of pickets in the infantry.

Vivandiere   A vivandiere was a women who accompanied troops on campaign in order to wash clothes, prepare meals, and tend sick or wounded soldiers. They often wore uniforms and were distinct from common camp followers and prostitutes.

Zouaves   Originally, Zouaves were Algerian colonial troops in the French army. The performance of Zouave units during the European wars of the 1850s caught the attention of Americans. Elmer Ellsworth helped popularize the concept in the United States during the years before the war by taking his demonstration Zouave drill team on tour to various cities. When the Civil War broke out, many new units of volunteers styled themselves as Zouaves and adopted the gaudy Zouave uniform—a short, close-fitting jacket, very baggy red or striped pants, white gaiters, and a turban or tasseled fez. Among them were Ellsworth's 11th New York (New York Fire Zouaves), Rush Hawkins's 9th New York, Morgan L. Smith's 8th Missouri, Roberdeau Wheat's 1st Louisiana Battalion (Louisiana Tigers), and many others. Zouave service was equally popular on both sides of the Mason-Dixon line. Some of the many Zouave units, such as Lew Wallace's 11th Indiana, adopted somewhat more staid versions of the garb. Zouaves boasted special tactics emphasizing rapid movement, open order, and fighting when possible from a prone position. Before the war was very old, other troops had informally adopted all that was useful of the Zouave tactics, and some, though by no means all, of the Zouave units had adopted more conventional uniforms.

BIBLIOGRAPHY

According to the historian James M. McPherson, there are some fifty thousand volumes on the Civil War, and more books about Abraham Lincoln alone than there are about any other historial figure, except for Jesus of Nazareth and William Shakespeare.

Beringer, Richard E.; Hattaway, Herman; Jones, Archer; and Still, William N. Jr., *Why the South Lost the Civil War* (University of Georgia Press, 1986).

Berlin, Ira, ed., *Freedom: A Documentary History of Emancipation 1861–1867*, 2 vols. (Cambridge, 1982).

Bicheno, Hugh, *Gettysburg* (Cassell & Co., London, 2001).

Boatner, Mark, *The Civil War Dictionary*, 2nd ed. (New York, 1991).

Bowman, John S., ed., *The Civil War Almanac* (New York, 1983).

Cadwallader, Sylvanus, (edited by Benjamin P. Thomas) *Three Years With Grant* (New York, 1955).

Coddington, E., *The Gettysburg Campaign: A Study in Command* (Touchstone, New York, 1997).

Cunliffe, Marcus, *Soldiers and Civilians: The Martial Spirit in America, 1775–1865*, 3rd ed. (Gregg Revivals, 1993).

Davis, William C., *Jefferson Davis: The Man and His Hour* (New York, 1991).

Dowdey, Clifford, *Death of a Nation* (New York, 1958).

Dowdey, Clifford, *Lee's Last Campaign* (Boston, 1960).

Fehrenbacher, Don E., *The Dred Scott Case: Its Significance in Law and Politics* (New York, 1978).

Foote, Shelby, *The Civil War: A Narrative*, 3 vols. (New York, 1958, 1963, 1974).

Griffith, Paddy, *Battle Tactics of the American Civil War* (Yale University Press, 1990).

Grimsley, Mark, *The Hard Hand of War* (Cambridge University Press, 1995).

Hagerman, Edward, *The American Civil War and the Origins of Modern Warfare* (Indiana University Press, 1988).

Hattaway, Herman and Jones, Archer, *How the North Won: A Military History of the Civil War* (University of Illinois Press, 1984).

Hay, Thomas Robson, *Hood's Tennessee Campaign* (New York, 1929).

Henry, Robert Selph, *As They Saw Forrest* (Jackson, Tennessee, 1965).

Howes, Philip, *The Catalytic Wars: A Study of the Development of Warfare, 1860–1870* (Minerva Press, 1998).

Jones, Virgil Carrington, *The Civil War at Sea*, 3 vols. (New York, 1960–1962).

Kay, William, *The Battle of Atlanta and the Georgia Campaign* (New York, 1958).

Linderman, Gerald F., *Embattled Courage: The Experience of Combat in the American Civil War* (The Free Press, New York, 1987).

Long, E. B., *The Civil War Day by Day: An Almanac, 1861–1865* (Garden City, New York, 1971).

Luvaas, Jay, *The Military Legacy of the Civil War* (University of Kansas Press, 1959 and 1989).

McPherson, James M., *Battle Cry of Freedom: The Civil War Era* (Oxford University Press, New York, 1988).

McPherson, James M., *Ordeal by Fire: The Civil War and Recontruction* (Alfred A. Knopf, New York, 1982).

McPherson, James M., and Cooper, W. Jr., (eds.) *Writing the Civil War: The Quest to Understand* (Columbia: University of South Carolina Press, 1998).

Nevins, Allan, *The War for the Union*, 4 vols. (New York, 1959–1971).

Parish, Peter J., ed., *The Reader's Guide to American History* (Fitzroy Dearbon, 1997).

Patrick, Rembert W., *The Fall of Richmond* (Baton Rouge, 1960).

Reed, Rowena, *Combined Operations in the Civil War* (University of Nebraska, 1978, Bison Books, 1993).

Sifakis, S., *Who Was Who in the Civil War* (Facts on File, New York, 1988).

Steere, Edward, *The Wilderness Campaign* (Harrisburg, Pennsylvania, 1960).

Stockesbury, James L., *A Short History of the Civil War* (Morrow, 1995).

Vandiver, Frank, *Jubal's Raid* (New York, 1960).

Woodworth, Steven E., ed., *The American Civil War: A Handbook of Literature and Research* (Greenwood Press, 1996).

Woodworth, Steven E., *Jefferson Davis and His Generals* (Lawrence, Kansas, 1990).

INDEX

Note: For clarification—page references in *italic* typeface denote photographs or illustrations. Pages containing maps are shown in **bold** typeface.
The ranks of officers are the highest achieved by the end of the war, as far as is known.

N

ACKNOWLEDGMENTS

Every effort has been made to contact the copyright holders of the images reproduced in this book. The publishers would welcome any errors or omissions being brought to their attention.

The publishers wish to thank the following picture libraries for their kind permission to use their pictures and illustrations:

National Museum of American History   p. 10
Library of Congress   p. 19, 21, 26, 29, 31, 33, 34, 36, 37, 39, 40, 46, 52, 52/53, 65, 68, 69, 70, 71, 72, 73, 74, 75, 81, 82, 86, 88, 91, 93, 96, 110, 117, 124, 139, 141, 153, 155, 157, 158/159, 160/161, 162, 170 (top), 174, 176 (right), 184, 189, 193, 203, 204, 205, 206/207, 213, 216, 218, 236, 238, 241, 242, 243, 247, 249, 254, 260, 261, 262/263, 267, 273, 282, 284/285, 286/287, 287, 288/289, 291, 304, 306, 306/307, 307, 308, 312/313, 314, 318, 322, 323, 324, 325, 326, 328, 330, 332, 338, 340, 343, 349, 350, 351, 352, 356, 363
Stowe Day Foundation   p. 25
Museum of the City of New York   p. 42
Peter Newark's Pictures   p. 44
British Library   p. 47 (top)
Collection of Christiane Harzig   p. 47 (bottom)
Addison Wesley Longman   p. 49
New York State Historical Association   p. 50
U.S. Army Military Historical Institute   p. 54, 144, 225
Yale University Art Gallery   p. 57
John F. Stover   p. 58
Private Collection   p. 62, 227, 228
Walton Taber   p. 76, 79, 94, 122, 136, 151 (bottom), 169, 198, 214/215, 224, 281, 292, 293, 296/297, 300/301, 316, 336,
Allan C. Redwood   p. 86
Xanthus Smith   p. 98 (top)
Thomas Hogan   p. 89 (bottom)
Edwin J. Meeker   p. 101, 114, 120, 148, 180, 230, 234, 337
Fred B. Schell   p. 102
Chicago Historical Society   p. 105,
Henry A. Ogden   p. 109, 118
Alfred R. Waud   p. 126 (top), 151 (top), 250, 252, 257, 298/299, 302,
Harry C. Edwards   p. 126 (bottom)
Harry Fenn   p. 133, 146
Edwin Forbes   p. 135, 170, 171, 194/195,
J. O. Davidson   p. 164,
Robert Sneden   p. 173
Harry Fenn   p. 176 (left),
Charles A. Vanderhoof   p. 192,
Minnesota Historical Society   p. 196,
Theodore R. Davis   p. 210, 210/211,
Frank H. Schell and Thomas Hogan   p. 223
Frank H. Schell   p. 265
Behringer-Crawford Museum   p. 272
Thure de Thulstrup   p. 295
Hughson Hawley   p. 327
National Archives   p., 354

For Cartographica Limited:

Design and Cartography: Malcolm A. Swanston

Cartography: Francesca Bridges, Peter Gamble, Isabelle Lewis, Jeanne Radford and Jonathan Young

Typesetting: Jeanne Radford

Picture Research: Francesca Bridges

Illustrations: Peter A. B. Smith

Text Editor: Brigit Dermott